Fifth Edition

Marketing Research: The Impact of the Internet

Carl McDaniel, Jr.
*University of Texas
at Arlington*

Roger Gates
DSS Research

SOUTH-WESTERN
*
THOMSON LEARNING

Australia · Canada · Mexico · Singapore · Spain · United Kingdom · United States

Marketing Research: The Impact of the Internet, Fifth Edition
By Carl McDaniel and Roger Gates

Publisher: Dave Shaut
Acquisitions Editor: Pamela Person
Developmental Editor: Rebecca von Gillern
Production Editor: Tamborah Moore
Media Development Editor: Christine Wittmer
Media Production Editor: Robin Browning
Cover Design: Liz Harasymczuk, Liz Harasymczuk Design
Cover Illustration: Kevin N. Ghiglione, Studio Ghiglione
Internal Designer: Liz Harasymczuk, Liz Harasymczuk Design
Design Manager: Rick Moore
Marketing Manager: Marc Callahan
Manufacturing Coordinator: Sandee Milewski
Photo Researcher: Fred M. Middendorf, Script Pict Ltd.
Photo Manager: Cary Benbow
Production House: Lifland et al., Bookmakers
Printer: Quebecor World—Taunton, MA

Printed in the United States of America
1 2 3 4 5 04 03 02 01

For more information, contact South-Western, 5101 Madison Road, Cincinnati, Ohio, 45227 or find us on the Internet at http://www.swcollege.com

For permission to use material from this text or product, contact us by
• **telephone: 1-800-730-2214**
• **fax: 1-800-730-2215**
• **web: http://www.thomsonrights.com**

ISBN: 0-324-06797-6   (core text with student CD and InfoTrac)
      0-324-13166-6   (core text with student CD)
      0-324-12968-8   (core text only)
      0-324-12581-X   (student CD only)

Library of Congress Cataloging-in-Publication Data
McDaniel, Carl D.
    Marketing research : the impact of the Internet / Carl McDaniel, Jr., Roger Gates.—5th ed.
      p. cm
    Rev. ed. of: Contemporary marketing research. 4th. c1999.
    Includes bibliographical references and index.
    ISBN 0-324-06797-6
    1. Marketing research. I. Gates, Roger H., 1942-II. McDaniel, Carl D. Contemporary marketing research. III. Title

HF5415.2 .M382 2001
658.8'3–dc21

                                        2001020090

To Our Children

Chelley, Mark, Raphaël, Michèle, and Sèbastien
CARL MCDANIEL

Stephanie, Lara, and Jordan
ROGER GATES

Contents in Brief

Contents

2 The Marketing Research Industry 28

3 Problem Definition and the Research Process 52

Part Two

Creating a Research Design   85

4   Secondary Data and Databases   86

The Nature of Secondary Data   88

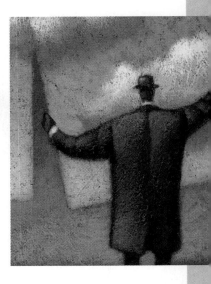

5

Qualitative Research   120

6 Survey Research: The Profound Impact of the Internet   162

7 Primary Data Collection: Observation   206

8 Primary Data Collection: Experimentation   240

Part Three

Data Acquisitions   283

10 Using Measurement Scales to Build Marketing Effectiveness 312

12 Basic Sampling Issues 394

13 Sample Size Determination 428

Part Four

Data Analysis 459

14 Data Processing and Fundamental Data Analysis 460

15 Statistical Testing of Differences   504

19 Managing Marketing Research and Research Ethics   648

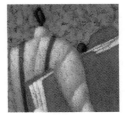

What Do Clients Want?   650

Communication   651

Managing the Research Process   651

Data Quality Management   651
- IN PRACTICE: MAKING A GOOD FIRST IMPRESSION IS CRITICAL   652
Time Management   653
- IN PRACTICE: DOING HIGH-QUALITY WORK—ON TIME   654
Cost Management   655
Client Profitability Management   656
Staff Management and Development   658
- GLOBAL ISSUES: GLOBAL VERSUS U.S. RESEARCH MANAGEMENT   658

Marketing Research Ethics   660

Supplier Ethics   660
- IN PRACTICE: THE MARKETING RESEARCH INDUSTRY MUST IMPROVE RESPONDENT SATISFACTION   663
Client Ethics   665
Field Service Ethics   666
Data Collection Code of Ethics   667
Respondents' Rights   668
Ethics and Professionalism   670
- GLOBAL ISSUES: MARKETING RESEARCH ETHICS ARE A WORLDWIDE CONCERN   671
- IN PRACTICE: RAISING PROFESSIONALISM IN THE MARKETING RESEARCH INDUSTRY   673

Summary   674

Marketing Research across the Organization   680

Ethical Dilemma   680

Preface

A REVISION SO THOROUGH, WE EVEN CHANGED THE NAME OF THE TEXT!

The 5th edition of *Marketing Research* is brand new from top to bottom, reflecting the accelerating pace of change in the world of marketing research. The profound impact of the Internet has put a new face on the marketing research industry. We have incorporated the changes, which reflect how every facet of marketing research has been affected by the World Wide Web. However, this revision is not just about the effect of the Internet. You will find new marketing research concepts and fresh examples throughout the text. We went through every chapter line by line in order to add the latest developments in the field of marketing research.

McDANIEL AND GATES ARE WIRED TO THE MARKETING RESEARCH INDUSTRY.

Every marketing research author talks about having the latest material available. Yet, there is only one author team that is not simply looking at marketing research as an outsider, and that team is Carl McDaniel and Roger Gates. It's like sitting in the stands versus being on the playing field. When you are on the field, you see changes as they occur—up close and personal. We can tell you that marketing research is much more than computing sample size or conducting a focus group. It is also about getting managers to use your findings, managing people, controlling costs, and a host of other things. Sure, like other texts, *Marketing Research* covers research design, data acquisition, and data analysis, but it does so with a dose of reality unmatched by our competitors.

"GET REAL" IS NOT AN EMPTY PHRASE TO McDANIEL AND GATES.

Our "real world" view of marketing research comes from being on the firing line. The 5th edition is written from the unique perspective of two authors with over 40 years of marketing research experience. Roger Gates is president of a marketing research firm with over 100 full-time employees. His company offers cutting-edge technology to hundreds of large clients throughout North America. Carl McDaniel, a former partner in a successful marketing research company, is chairman of the marketing department at The University of Texas at Arlington.

As chairman, he has ultimate responsibility for the department's Master of Science in Marketing Research program. A unique aspect of the program is its internationally renowned advisory board, which consists of leaders and top executives from the field of marketing research. Carl's ongoing interaction with the leaders in the field enables him to keep his finger on the pulse of change in marketing research. You can view the membership list of this extraordinary advisory board at http://www2.uta.edu/msmr.

THE INTERNET HAS PERMANENTLY CHANGED MARKETING RESEARCH.

It may not be an exaggeration to say that the Internet has turned the world of marketing research upside down. By 2005, Internet marketing research is expected to account for half of all marketing research revenue in the United States. This statistic alone illustrates the new world of marketing research. More than simply offering a new way to conduct research, the Internet changes the speed, flow, and usage of information. For example, the Internet enables managers to use research information to make decisions faster than ever before. And it allows decision makers across the globe to view and comment on research findings instantaneously. The Internet also makes follow-up studies and longitudinal research easier to conduct. It slashes the costs associated with labor- and time-intensive research activities. You will find all of these topics, and much more about the Internet, discussed in every chapter.

WE HAVE TEAMED WITH web**SURVEYOR**™ TO ENABLE YOUR STUDENTS TO LEARN ALL FACETS OF INTERNET MARKETING RESEARCH.

When you need to know. Now.

Each professor will have the capability of assigning multiple class projects using real-world Internet marketing research surveys. WebSurveyor makes the tasks of survey research a breeze, allowing students to format questions, use the questionnaire library, and download survey data quickly and efficiently.

Exercises at the end of the chapter will help students become familiar with WebSurveyor before they conduct a survey. Students will learn about Internet marketing research by using the same tool that marketing research professionals do.

EACH TEXT COMES WITH A CD-ROM TO MAKE THE WORLD OF MARKETING RESEARCH COME ALIVE FOR THE STUDENT.

All the information your students will need to use WebSurveyor is provided on the CD-ROM that accompanies this text. This CD allows your students access to cutting-edge Internet marketing research technology. Not only will you be able to assign problems and exercises provided in the text and on our Web site; you'll also be able to ask your students to perform original work assignments, such as creating minisurveys, marketing research projects, graphs, charts, and Web pages.

As an added bonus, with your adoption of the McDaniel/Gates text, you will be given access, for the life of your adoption, to the full WebSurveyor product for classroom, personal, or consulting purposes—a value to you of several hundred dollars. We're opening the door to a whole new way of doing research!

WE ALWAYS FOCUS ON THE RESEARCH USER.

Your feedback from previous editions instructed us to maintain the "user of research" focus of the text. You said that most of your students, at some point in their careers, will have to use marketing research to make critical decisions, but few students will become marketing researchers. Accordingly, we continue to present marketing research through the eyes of a manager using, and perhaps purchasing, marketing research information. For talented students who might wish to pursue a career in marketing research, we suggest considering a specialized master's degree in the field.

Our research user focus begins in Chapter 1, where the exciting and ever-changing world of marketing research is introduced. We offer students insight into when managers should and should not fund or use marketing research. Chapter 2 helps future managers understand the players in the research industry. Chapter 3 discusses not only the research process but also where and how managers get involved—that is, through the research request. Chapter 18 tells the reader what to look for in a marketing research report and how to get managers to use marketing research data. Chapter 19 discusses management of the marketing research function and concludes with another important topic for future managers—research ethics.

OUR MOST THOROUGH REVISION EVER HAS RESULTED IN A NEW STREAMLINED TEXT.

Every chapter has been examined, word for word, to make certain that we give students the very latest in marketing research methodology, tools, and theory. We reread every paragraph to make certain it is as clear, interesting, and easy-to-understand as possible. We have also added fresh new examples, concepts, and tools. You told us that covering 21 chapters in a semester was very difficult. We listened to your suggestions and moved the material on competitive intelligence (formerly Chapter 20) and marketing research in practice (formerly Chapter 21) to our Web site. For those professors who wish to cover these subjects, they may be found in their entirety at http://mcdaniel.swcollege.com.

WHAT ELSE IS NEW IN THE 5TH EDITION?

New and rewritten material abounds in the 5th edition.

- *All new Internet emphasis.* As mentioned above, an in-depth discussion of how the Internet is affecting marketing research is introduced in Chapter 1 and continues throughout the text. Our Internet coverage is thorough, yet balanced with traditional material.

- *New ethical dilemmas.* A real-life ethical dilemma can be found at the end of each part. Part Two, for example, presents the results of a new *Business Week*/Harris Poll on how Americans view ethics and social responsibility. The poll raises a number of ethical issues for student discussion. Part Three describes how Liberty Financial Companies was reprimanded by the FTC for failing to protect the anonymity of children on its kids' Web site. Part Five discusses how an elementary school has been allowing researchers to interview children in exchange for cash.

- *All new opening vignettes.* Every chapter-opening vignette has been either updated or replaced. The companies/products featured include The National Cattleman's Beef Association, Wal-Mart, Federal Migratory Bird Hunting and Conservation stamps, *Fast Company* magazine, Bose Corporation, and LaQuinta Inns.

- *All new Internet addresses for opening vignettes.* Want to know more about the company or issue discussed in the opening case? In every chapter, students can follow up by going to the Web site suggested at the end of the opening vignette. We all know that Internet addresses frequently change; to solve this problem, we maintain a continual list of updates at our Web site at http://mcdaniel.swcollege.com.

- *New marketing research War Stories.* Students readily recall material that is unusual or funny. In selected chapters, we have added short, amusing anecdotes about the trials and tribulations of conducting marketing research. This feature is designed not only to entertain, but also to help students recall important concepts in the text.

- *All new end-of-chapter Internet exercises.* In the 5th edition, we have added new exercises entitled *Working the Net.* These exercises are designed to help students learn how researchers use the Internet to solve real problems. This is "hands on" experience at its best. For your convenience, links to the URLs mentioned are available on our Web site at http://mcdaniel.swcollege.com.

- *A fully revised feature to help students integrate marketing research activities with the rest of the organization. Marketing Research across the Organization* presents a series of questions and scenarios that require students to consider the impact of marketing research on basic business activities related to finance, production, human resources, and so forth. Students are asked to determine a course of action for the given company based on the information provided. Marketing research does not exist in a vacuum. We have created scenarios that call for students to think both specifically and generally about the issues involved in conducting marketing research and the implementation of action plans based on its results.

■ *Two new comprehensive cases with data.* We have added two new cases with data sets. The first is a survey of Lufthansa Airlines' business travelers. Our second new case is a satisfaction survey for Discover Card. The cases have been classroom-tested for student comprehension and interest. We also retained the Rockingham National Bank case with data set, based on instructor feedback.

EACH CHAPTER HAS BEEN THOROUGHLY REVISED.

Here's what's new on a chapter-by-chapter basis:

Chapter 1—The Role of Marketing Research in Management Decision Making. New in-depth discussion of applied research; new comprehensive introduction to how the Internet has affected marketing research.

Chapter 2—The Marketing Research Industry. New material on the structure of the marketing research industry and large marketing research companies; new section on cybermarketing research companies and Internet marketing research support firms; new section on how support firms (e.g., Survey Sampling) deliver their products via the Internet; new material on global marketing research.

Chapter 3—Problem Definition and the Research Process. New major section on correctly defining the problem; new material on exploratory research; new section on using the Internet to conduct exploratory research; new section on translating a management problem into a marketing research problem; new material on judging the quality of a research report; new section on using the Internet to disseminate reports; new section on requests for proposals (RFPs); new section on what decision makers want from marketing research; new section on the importance of good communication.

Chapter 4—Secondary Data and Databases. New section on creating an internal database from conversations; new section on creating a database from Web site visitors; major new section on data mining; new section on privacy issues with databases; new material on search engines and databases; new section on finding federal government data on the Internet; new material on geographic information systems.

Chapter 5—Qualitative Research. New material on recruiting focus group participants; major new section on online focus groups; new section on viewing focus groups on the Internet.

Chapter 6—Survey Research: The Profound Impact of the Internet. New material on refusal rates; new material on mall-intercept interviews; major new section on how the Internet has changed survey research; new material on the advantages and disadvantages of online survey research; new section on using Internet bulletin boards for research; new section on downloadable surveys; new major section on recruiting sources for online surveys; new section on creating online questionnaires; new section on the Interactive Marketing Research Organization (IMRO).

Chapter 7—Primary Data Collection: Observation. New section on ethnographic research; new material on mystery shoppers; new material on shopping patterns;

new section on radio listenership tracking; new material on the people meter; new material on scanner-based research from Information Resources Incorporated; major new section on observation research on the Internet.

Chapter 8—Primary Data Collection: Experimentation. New material on test marketing.

Chapter 9—The Concept of Measurement. New discussion about anonymous responses.

Chapter 10—Using Measurement Scales to Build Marketing Effectiveness. New examples of measurement scales throughout the chapter.

Chapter 11—Questionnaire Design. New examples of screener questionnaires; new section on Internet self-service questionnaire builders; new section on software for questionnaire development.

Chapter 12—Basic Sampling Issues. New introduction to sampling concepts; new section on sampling over the Internet.

Chapter 13—Sample Size Determination. New material on estimating the number of phone numbers needed for a sample.

Chapter 14—Data Processing and Fundamental Data Analysis. New section on electronic data capture and coding; new material on setting up frequencies and crosstabulations in Excel.

Chapter 15—Statistical Testing of Differences. New material on statistical software sites on the Internet.

Chapter 16—Bivariate Correlation and Regression. New material on spurious relationships.

Chapter 17—Multivariate Data Analysis. New material on using multivariate modeling to score direct mail prospects on their probability of responding.

Chapter 18—Communicating the Research Results. New material on speaking more confidently; new material on publishing presentations on the Internet.

Chapter 19—Managing Marketing Research and Research Ethics. New material on time management in marketing research; new section on client profitability management; new section on research staff management and development; new material on managing a global marketing research project; updated material on CASRO.

CLASSROOM-TESTED PEDAGOGY PUTS STUDENTS IN THE KNOW

The pedagogy for the 5th edition has been developed in response to what you told us delivers the most value to you and your students. The following learning tools have been refined to help strengthen student learning while making the book more enjoyable and easier to read.

Learning Objectives
These objectives challenge the student to explain, discuss, understand, and clarify the concepts presented.

Opening Vignettes
Each chapter opens with a case-type synopsis of a marketing research situation. Your students will recognize many of the companies profiled, such as NASCAR and Wal-Mart, and may be surprised by some of the successes, failures, and challenges described.

In-Chapter Boxed Features

Typically, boxed items interrupt the flow of a text and impede student understanding by creating a disjointed reading experience. For that reason, we have been conscientious not only in the placement of boxed material, but also in the design elements used to differentiate them from the body of the text. Two types of boxed features are included in this edition: *In Practice* and *Global Issues*.

War Stories

Interesting and often amusing anecdotes of marketing research gone awry demonstrate to students that designing questionnaires, selecting respondents, gathering data, and producing results are not always cut-and-dried tasks. These short extracts come from *Quirk's Marketing Research Review.*

Clear, Concise Chapter Summaries

Concise summaries present the core concepts that underpin each chapter. Although the summary is located at the end of the chapter, students can read it along with the opening vignette as a pre-reading exercise before diving into the chapter.

Key Terms and Definitions

Key terms appear in boldface in the text, with definitions in the margins, making it easy for students to check their understanding of marketing research terminology. A complete list of key terms and definitions appears at the end of each chapter as a study checklist. Students will find a full glossary of all key terms at the end of the text.

Questions for Review and Critical Thinking

Our society's ability to use data to make good decisions has lagged behind its enormous capacity for generating data. In the hope of better preparing the next generation of business leaders, many educators are beginning to place greater emphasis on developing critical-thinking skills. Accordingly, we have added a number of critical-thinking questions at the end of each chapter. Review questions also direct students' attention to the core concepts of the chapter.

Working the Net

Working the Net exercises send students to Web sites containing materials that amplify and update concepts discussed within the text. These exercises help students use the Internet as an actual marketing researcher would. Links to the URLs are available on our Web site at http://mcdaniel.swcollege.com.

Real-Life Marketing Research Minicases

Over half of the real-life situations presented in the minicases are new to this edition. These cases help students to synthesize chapter concepts by focusing on real marketing research problems.

In Practice

Global Issues

AN INTEGRATED TEACHING AND LEARNING SYSTEM FOR YOU AND YOUR STUDENTS

Each component of our comprehensive support package has been developed to help you prepare lectures and tests as quickly and easily as possible. We provide a wealth of information and activities beyond the text to supplement your lectures, as well as teaching aids in a variety of formats to fit your own teaching style. Careful attention has been given to all text supplements, to ensure that they work together to make teaching and learning as effortless as possible. Adopting *Marketing Research: The Impact of the Internet*, **5th edition**, will lighten your teaching load while giving your students the tools they need to master the fascinating subject of marketing research.

INNOVATIVE TEACHING SUPPLEMENTS FOR YOU

Instructor's Manual with Video Guide

The Instructor's Manual for this edition has been designed to facilitate convenient lesson planning. Each chapter includes the following:

- *Suggested Lesson Plans.* Suggestions are given on dividing up the chapter material, based on the frequency and duration of your class period.
- *Chapter Scan.* A quick synopsis highlights the core material in each chapter.
- *Learning Objectives.* The list of learning objectives found in the text is repeated here.
- *General Chapter Outline.* The main headers provide a quick snapshot of all the content areas within the chapter.
- *List of Key Terms.* The key terms introduced to the students in the text are repeated here.
- *Detailed Chapter Outline.* This outline fleshes out the general outline given previously. It also indicates where ancillary materials fit into the discussion: PowerPoint slides, exhibits from the text, learning objectives, and review questions. Opening vignettes and boxed features are also included in this outline.
- *Summary Explaining Learning Objectives.* An explanation of how the learning objectives are satisfied by chapter material is the basis of the IM summary.
- *Answers to Pedagogy.* Suggested answers and approaches to the critical-thinking questions, the Internet activities, the cases, the cross-functional questions, and the ethical dilemmas are offered at the end of each chapter or part.

The video guide includes a full entry for each of the segments on the cassette. A list of appropriate chapters is followed by a brief summary of the video segment. Detailed previewing, viewing, and follow-up activities are suggested to help you use the video effectively, so that you don't have to compromise valuable lecture time. Exercises are designed to aid you in presenting content through the video in such a way as to encourage student engagement.

Test Bank

This test bank is unlike any other. Based on cognitive learning theory, the tests are designed to assess students on six levels: knowledge, comprehension, application, analysis, synthesis, and evaluation. This test bank also features an introduction on test writing. It addresses the critical areas of recognizing and writing good test questions, how to create a balanced test, how to ensure accurate evaluation of student performance, and other assessment issues that are normally absent from traditional test banks. Tests will not all be the same length and configuration but are designed to appropriately test the material in the given chapter.

PowerPoint Slides

For this edition, we have created a comprehensive, fully integrated PowerPoint presentation, consisting of 18 to 20 slides per chapter. With roughly 400 slides in the package, you can tailor your visual presentation to the material you choose to cover in class. This PowerPoint presentation gives you the ability to completely integrate your classroom lecture with a powerful visual statement of chapter material. The entire collection of slides will be available for downloading from our Web site at http://mcdaniel.swcollege.com.

Video

A mix of familiar and fresh material, the videos not only address standard research issues in real-world companies, but also show how marketing research influences advertising campaigns and promotional pieces. The exercises found in the video guide will help you incorporate these videos into your class without compromising the time you need to present the core concepts.

INNOVATIVE SUPPLEMENTS TO ENHANCE STUDENT LEARNING

Marketing Research and Alternate Media:
A Workbook of Internet and Database Activities

Written by Bernard and Diane Jackaki, this supplement can help you expand your incorporation of the Internet into the classroom. This product features beginning, intermediate, and advanced activities. Students can further their knowledge of marketing research and database applications on the Internet by doing these detailed, guided exercises.

STATISTICA *by StatSoft*

This highly rated software package is an integrated statistical analysis, graphics, and database management system. The student edition features a wide array of basic and advanced analytical procedures, such as regression analysis, factor analysis, discriminant function analysis, and cluster analysis. This user-friendly package is available to accompany the text at a substantially discounted price.

SPSS—Student Version

We are happy to be able to give you the option of packaging the latest SPSS—Student Version with the text for a nominal additional charge. Please contact your local sales representative for a complete list of packaging options.

INNOVATIVE INTERNET SUPPLEMENTS FOR YOU AND YOUR STUDENTS

http://mcdaniel.swcollege.com

New Internet coverage is not limited to the features within the textbook. *Marketing Research: The Impact of the Internet,* **5th Edition,** also has its own Web site. Links are provided for all URLs mentioned in the text and are organized by chapter and feature. The URLs will be updated throughout the life of the text. Complete materials on competitive intelligence and marketing research in practice are now available on the Web site for your teaching convenience. The full PowerPoint presentation is also available on our site for you to download as lecture support for yourself and as a study aid for your students. Our site includes interactive quizzes and additional WebSurveyor exercises for your students, and additional comprehensive cases and solutions as well as teaching strategies for you! This material expands on the core coverage in the textbook and is easily accessible. Regular updates make this a dynamic site.

ACKNOWLEDGMENTS

Producing a major text with many supplements, such as this one, is always a team effort. We have no doubt that we are working with the finest people in both academia and publishing. We would like to thank our developmental editor, Rebecca von Gillern, whose support and encouragement made this text possible. We thank Pamela Person, our acquisitions editor, and Marc Callahan, our marketing manager, for their dedication and commitment to making this project the best in the market. We thank Tamborah Moore, our production editor, for her work in getting the text produced and into the hands of our adopters. We also thank Charles Pflanz for producing the PowerPoint presentation, Kenneth Lawrence for preparing the Test Bank, and Barbara Oates and Craig Hollingshead for preparing the Instructor's Manual. We thank the conscientious reviewers of this fifth edition who helped guide many of the important changes in this text. Our appreciation goes to

Brett Boyle	St. Louis University
Forrest Carter	Michigan State University
Dena Cox	Indiana University
David Gilliland	Colorado State University
Ronald Goldsmith	Florida State University
Charles Hofacker	Florida State University
Michael R. Hyman	New Mexico State University
Johny Johanssen	Georgetown University
Robert Mackoy	Butler University
Sanjay S. Mehta	Sam Houston State University
Pallab Paul	University of Denver
James A. Roberts	Baylor University
Steve Strombeck	Union University
Michael Tsiros	University of Miami

Part One

An Introduction to Marketing Research

1

The Role of Marketing Research in Management Decision Making

2

The Marketing Research Industry

3

Problem Definition and the Research Process

Check it out!

Remember to visit <u>http://mcdaniel.swcollege.com</u> for information to help you with the new material in Part I. Study hints and resources here and at <u>http://marketing.swcollege.com</u> can also help you review for your final exam!

Chapter One

The Role of Marketing Research in Management Decision Making

Learning Objectives

To review the marketing concept and the marketing mix.

To comprehend the marketing environment within which managers must make decisions.

To define marketing research.

To understand the importance of marketing research in shaping marketing decisions.

To learn when marketing research should and should not be conducted.

To learn how the Internet is changing marketing research.

To understand the history of marketing research.

ONLINE SHOPPING REVENUES ARE PROJECTED TO REACH MORE THAN $78 billion by 2003, according to New York City–based Jupiter Communications, an e-commerce research firm. But while some consumers may be spending e-bucks, many others are not. "Sixty percent or more of shopping carts are abandoned on the Web," says Jens Schlueter, vice president of marketing research for San Francisco–based Informative, Inc., an online information services company. Finding out what drives customer loyalty on the Web—and what drives customers away—can mean the difference between profits and closing a store's virtual doors.

ONLINE QUESTIONNAIRES CAN help retail Web sites gauge customer satisfaction, profile visitors, and provide a way to measure traffic for advertisers beyond banner click-throughs. Pittsburgh-based PNC Bank, which offers an online banking product called Account Link by Web, conducted a customer satisfaction survey, designed by Informative. A random sample of Account Link customers were invited to fill out a questionnaire after they finished their banking sessions. Almost 39 percent of the 1,300 invited customers agreed to take the survey, says Joseph Pullella, marketing project manager.

"SATISFACTION WITH THE SERVICE WAS VERY HIGH—MUCH HIGHER THAN WE'D anticipated," says Pullella. Almost 80 percent of participants rated Account Link "good" to "excellent." There were other surprises as well: 82 percent of users turned out to be male, rather than the expected 50/50 split, and more than 70 percent visited the site either a few times a week or daily. Although the survey was mainly designed as a satisfaction tracking tool, discovering such patterns has prompted PNC to consider using space on the Web site to pitch special services, such as its loan auction program, to this high-frequency group. Customers' preferences were integrated back into the site as well. For example, electronic bill payment—the top feature customers said they wanted on the site—was added.[1] ■

PNC Bank used marketing research to determine the level of customer satisfaction with its online banking product, Account Link.

Find out more about PNC Bank's commitment to customer satisfaction by clicking on "Account Link" at

http://www. pncbank.com

PNC Bank is using marketing research to measure customer satisfaction and desires. But what exactly is marketing research? And how important is it to shaping marketing decisions? How has the Internet affected marketing research? When should marketing research be conducted? These are some of the questions we will address in this chapter.

The Nature of Marketing

marketing
The process of planning and executing the conception, pricing, promotion, and distribution of ideas, goods, and services to create exchanges that satisfy individual and organizational objectives.

Marketing is the process of planning and executing the conception, pricing, promotion, and distribution of ideas, goods, and services to create exchanges that satisfy individual and organizational objectives. The potential for exchange exists when there are at least two parties and each has something of potential value to the other. When the two parties can communicate and deliver the desired goods or services, exchange can take place. How do marketing managers attempt to stimulate exchange? They follow the "right" principle. They attempt to get the right goods or services to the right people at the right place at the right time at the right price, using the right promotion techniques. The "right" principle describes how marketing managers control the many factors that ultimately determine marketing success. To make the "right" decisions, management must have timely decision-making information. Marketing research is a primary channel for providing that information.

The Marketing Concept

marketing concept
A business philosophy based on consumer orientation, goal orientation, and systems orientation.

consumer orientation
The identification of and focus on the people or firms most likely to buy a product and the production of a good or service that will meet their needs most effectively.

goal orientation
A focus on the accomplishment of corporate goals; a limit set on consumer orientation.

systems orientation
The creation of systems to monitor the external environment and deliver the marketing mix to the target market.

To efficiently accomplish their goals, firms today have adopted the **marketing concept,** which requires (1) a consumer orientation, (2) a goal orientation, and (3) a systems orientation. A **consumer orientation** means that firms strive to identify the people (or firms) most likely to buy their product (the target market) and to produce a good or offer a service that will meet the needs of target customers most effectively in the face of competition. The second tenet of the marketing concept is **goal orientation;** that is, a firm must be consumer oriented only to the extent that it also accomplishes corporate goals. The goals of profit-making firms usually center on financial criteria, such as a 15 percent return on investment.

The third component of the marketing concept is a **systems orientation.** A system is an organized whole—or a group of diverse units that form an integrated whole—functioning or operating in unison. It is one thing for a firm to say it is consumer-oriented and another actually to *be* consumer-oriented. First, systems must be established to find out what consumers want and to identify market opportunities. As you will see later, identifying target market needs and finding market opportunities are the tasks of marketing research. Next, this information must be fed back to the firm. Without feedback from the marketplace, a firm is not truly consumer-oriented.

The Opportunistic Nature of Marketing Research

Marriott's marketing research uncovered an opportunity to create a new hotel chain that would serve business travelers, offering homey surroundings at moderate prices. That is, Marriott used marketing research to identify marketing opportunities. The Courtyard concept was aimed at a new target market for Marriott.

After the target market was identified, a marketing mix had to be created. A **marketing mix** is the unique blend of product/service, pricing, promotion, and distribution strategies designed to reach a specific target market. Marriott spent two years creating the marketing mix for Courtyard. Research identified the best sites for courtyard units (distribution), prices to be charged in various markets, how to position the product in the marketplace, and what features to promote. Marriott also used research to determine the size of the rooms and the features and amenities most desired by business travelers (product/service offering). Marketing research identified an opportunity, which then enabled Marriott to further use the research to create a very successful addition to its product line: Courtyard by Marriott.

marketing mix
The unique blend of product/service, pricing, promotion, and distribution strategies designed to meet the needs of a specific group of consumers.

The External Marketing Environment

Over time, the marketing mix must be altered because of changes in the environment in which consumers and businesses exist, work, compete, and make purchasing decisions. Some new consumers and businesses will become part of the target market, while others will drop out of the market; those who remain may have different tastes, needs, incomes, lifestyles, and purchase habits than the original target consumers.

Although managers can control the marketing mix, they cannot control elements in the external environment that continually mold and reshape the target market. Unless management understands the external environment, the firm cannot intelligently plan its future, and organizations are often unaware of the forces that influence their future.

Marketing research is a key means for understanding the environment. Knowledge of the environment helps a firm not only to alter its present marketing mix, but also to identify new opportunities. For example, through marketing research devoted to environmental scanning (looking for threats and opportunities in the marketplace), Goodyear found that drivers were becoming more and more concerned about safety. Part of this concern involved driving in bad weather. Needs analysis research determined that consumers desired a tire that would be stable on wet roads. Goodyear took the data to its engineers, who created a design system that removed water from the tire as it rolled down the road. The Goodyear Aquatread was born. Target consumers for this product are 10 times as likely to mention Aquatread as any other brand.[2]

The Goodyear Aquatread tire is a direct result of marketing research efforts. Go to http://www.goodyear.com to learn more about the Aquatread tire.

Marketing Research and Decision Making

Marketing research plays two key roles in the marketing system. First, as part of the marketing intelligence feedback process, marketing research provides decision makers with data on the effectiveness of the current marketing mix and offers insights into necessary changes. Second, marketing research is the primary tool for exploring new opportunities in the marketplace. Segmentation research and new product research help identify the most lucrative opportunities for a firm.

Marketing Research Defined

Now that you have an understanding of how marketing research fits into the overall marketing system, we can proceed with a formal definition of the term, as stated by the American Marketing Association:

Marketing research is the function which links the consumer, customer, and public to the marketer through information—information used to identify and define marketing opportunities and problems; generate, refine, and evaluate marketing actions; monitor marketing performance; and improve understanding of marketing as a process. Marketing research specifies the information required to address these issues; designs the method for collecting information; manages and implements the data collection process; analyzes the results; and communicates the findings and their implications.[3]

We prefer a shorter definition: **Marketing research** is the planning, collection, and analysis of data relevant to marketing decision making and the communication of the results of this analysis to management.

The Importance of Marketing Research to Management

Marketing research can be viewed as playing three functional roles: descriptive, diagnostic, and predictive. Its **descriptive function** includes gathering and presenting statements of fact. For example, what is the historic sales trend in the industry? What are consumers' attitudes toward a product and its advertising? The second role of research is the **diagnostic function,** wherein data and/or actions are explained. For example, what was the impact on sales when the package design was changed? How can product/service offerings be altered to better serve customers and potential customers? The final role of research is the **predictive function.** How can the firm best take advantage of opportunities as they arise in the ever-changing marketplace?

The Unrelenting Drive for Quality and Customer Satisfaction Quality and customer satisfaction have become the key competitive weapons of the early 2000s. Few organizations can prosper in today's environment without a focus on quality, continual improvement, and customer satisfaction. Corporations across the globe have implemented quality improvement and satisfaction programs in an effort to reduce costs, retain customers, increase market share, and, last but not least, improve the bottom line.

marketing research
The planning, collection, and analysis of data relevant to marketing decision making and the communication of the results of this analysis to management.

descriptive function
The gathering and presentation of statements of fact.

diagnostic function
The explanation of data or actions.

predictive function
Specification of how to use descriptive and diagnostic research to predict the results of a planned marketing decision.

When the concept of total quality management swept through corporate America in the late 1980s, the emphasis was strictly on product improvement. But product improvement alone wasn't the answer. Consider the case of Varian Associates Incorporated, a manufacturer of scientific equipment. The company put 1,000 of its managers through a four-day course on quality. The company's Silicon Valley headquarters buzzed with quality-speak. Talk of work teams and cycle times replaced discussions of electrons and X-rays. Varian went about virtually reinventing the way it did business—with what seemed to be stunning results. A unit that makes vacuum systems for computer clean rooms boosted on-time delivery from 42 percent to 92 percent. The semiconductor unit cut the time it took to put out new designs by 14 days. However, producing quality products wasn't enough. Obsessed with meeting production schedules, the staff didn't return customers' phone calls, and the operation ended up losing market share. Repair people were so rushed to meet deadlines that they left before explaining their work to customers.

"All of the quality-based charts went up and to the right, but everything else went down," says Richard M. Levy, executive vice president for quality.[4] The company actually lost money for several years.

return on quality
Management objective based on the principles that (1) the quality being delivered is at a level desired by the target market and (2) that level of quality must have a positive impact on profitability.

The drive for quality, as demonstrated by Varian, was often a production-oriented, mechanistic exercise that proved meaningless to customers. And quality that means little to customers usually doesn't produce a payoff in improved sales, profits, or market share; it represents wasted effort and expense. Today, the new mantra is **return on quality,** which means that (1) the quality being delivered is the quality desired by the target market and (2) the added quality must have a positive impact on profitability. For example, banking giant NationsBank Corporation measures every improvement in service quality, from adding more tellers to offering new mortgage products, in terms of added profitability.

Asking the right questions in marketing research can be as important as getting good answers. UPS found that customers wanted more interaction with their UPS driver. Go to http://www.ups.com to find out how UPS uses marketing research to better serve its customers.

The key to making return on quality work is marketing research. Marketing research is the mechanism that enables organizations to determine what types and forms of quality are important to the target market. And it can sometimes force companies to abandon long-held beliefs. United Parcel Service Inc., for example, had always assumed that on-time delivery was the paramount concern of its customers. Everything else came second. Before long, UPS's definition of quality centered almost exclusively on the results of time-and-motion studies. Knowing the average time elevator doors took to open on a certain city block and figuring how long people took to answer their doorbells were critical parts of the quality equation. So was pushing drivers to meet exacting schedules. The problem was that UPS's marketing research survey was asking the wrong questions. It asked customers if they were pleased with delivery time and whether they thought delivery could be even faster.

When UPS began asking broader questions about how it could improve service, it discovered that its customers weren't as obsessed with on-time delivery as the company had previously thought. The biggest surprise to UPS management was that customers wanted more interaction with drivers, who provided the only face-to-face contact customers had with the company. Drivers who were less harried and more willing to chat, could offer customers some practical advice on shipping. "We've discovered that the highest-rated element we have is our drivers," says Lawrence E. Farrel, UPS's service-quality manager.[5]

In a sharp departure from the tradition, the company has encouraged its 62,000 delivery drivers to get out of their trucks and go along with salespeople to visit customers. It also allows drivers an additional 30 minutes a week to spend at their discretion to strengthen ties with customers and perhaps bring in new sales.

The Paramount Importance of Keeping Existing Customers   An inextricable link exists between customer satisfaction and customer loyalty. Long-term relationships don't just happen; they are grounded in the delivery of service and value. Customer retention pays big dividends for firms. Powered by repeat sales and referrals, revenues and market share grow. Costs fall because firms spend less funds and energy attempting to replace defectors. Steady customers are easy to serve because they understand the modus operandi and make fewer demands on employees' time. A firm's ability to retain customers also drives job satisfaction and pride, which leads to higher employee retention. In turn, long-term employees acquire additional knowledge that increases productivity. A Bain & Company study estimates that a 5 percent decrease in the customer defection rate can boost profits by 25 to 95 percent.[6]

The ability to retain customers is based on an intimate understanding of their needs. This knowledge comes primarily from marketing research. For example, British Airways recast its first-class transatlantic service based on detailed marketing research. Most airlines stress top-of-the-line service in their transatlantic first-class cabins. However, British Air research found that most first-class passengers simply want to sleep. British Air now gives premium flyers the option of dinner on the ground, before takeoff, in the first-class lounge. Then, once on board, they can slip into British Air pajamas, put their heads on real pillows, slip under blankets, and enjoy an interruption-free flight. On arrival at their destination, first-class passengers can have breakfast, use comfortable dressing rooms and showers, and even have their clothes pressed before they set off. These changes in British Air's first-class service were driven strictly by marketing research.[7]

Understanding the Ever-Changing Marketplace   Marketing research also helps managers to understand trends in the marketplace and to take advantage of opportunities. Marketing research has been practiced for as long as marketing has existed. The early Phoenicians carried out market demand studies as they traded in the various ports on the Mediterranean Sea. Marco Polo's diary indicates he was performing a marketing research function as he traveled to China. There is evidence that the Spanish systematically conducted marketing surveys as they explored the New World, and examples exist of marketing research conducted during the Renaissance.

Today, Internet marketing research can help companies to quickly and efficiently understand what is happening in the marketplace. For example, Women.com, an online community site that offers editorial content and e-commerce services, has surveyed visitors for several years but recently boosted its research efforts. Its current surveys are designed to determine visitors' demographic and psychographic profiles for internal use, as well as to share with advertisers.

Along with collecting basic demographic data, the site asks visitors about their e-commerce habits (for example, whether they've shopped for or purchased anything online recently), their feelings about privacy on the Internet, and their personal values and attitudes (for example, whether they agree or disagree with statements like "I'm usually the first in my peer group to try something new"). Such information allows them to provide a more complete picture of the person on the other side of the computer—one that goes beyond average age and income. According to Regina Lewis, director of research for Women.com, understanding whether visitors are more risk-oriented, family-focused, or career-minded helps Women.com set the right tone when communicating with visitors and has resulted in page redesigns.[8]

The necessity of understanding the marketplace is not restricted to the United States or other industrialized markets. It is important for managers all over the world to understand the ever-changing marketplace and their customers. The following Global Issues feature illustrates this point.

The Proactive Role of Marketing Research

Understanding the nature of the marketing system is a necessity for a successful marketing orientation. By having a thorough knowledge of factors that have an impact on the target market and the marketing mix, management can be proactive rather than reactive. Proactive management alters the marketing mix to fit newly emerging patterns in economic, social, and competitive environments, whereas reactive management waits for change to have a major impact on the firm before deciding to take action. It is the difference between viewing the turbulent marketing environment as a threat (a reactive stance) and as an opportunity (a proactive stance). America's large department store chains, such as, Sears and JCPenney, have largely been reactive to Internet retailing. A proactive position would have been to become cutting-edge Internet marketers. Marketing research plays a key role in proactive management by allowing managers to anticipate changes in the market and customer desires and then design goods and services to meet those changes and needs.

A proactive manager not only examines emerging markets but also seeks, through strategic planning, to develop a long-run **marketing strategy** for the firm. A marketing strategy guides the long-term use of the firm's resources based on the firm's existing and projected internal capabilities and on projected

marketing strategy
A plan to guide the long-term use of a firm's resources based on its existing and projected internal capabilities and on projected changes in the external environment.

Japanese High-School Girls Are Trendsetters

FOREIGN COMPANIES HAVE DISCOVERED JAPAN'S BEST MARKETING BELLWETHER: the teenage girl. As Japanese companies have long known, the nation's high-school girls have an uncanny ability to predict which products will be hits with consumers of all age groups. What's more, a select pool of these teens can create a buzz that turns a new product into a nationwide smash.

"A fad that catches on among teenage girls often becomes a big trend throughout the country and among consumers in general," says Etsuko Katsube, a Coca-Cola Co. marketing executive who used teenage girls to market a now-popular soft drink made with fermented milk.

Girl guides are taken very seriously in Japan. Food makers like Calbee Foods Co. and Meiji Seika Kaisha Ltd. frequently round up school girls from Tokyo's streets to sample potato-chip recipes or chocolate bars. Asahi Broadcasting Corp. surveys high-school girls to fine-tune story lines for higher ratings on the television network's prime-time dramas. Other companies pay girls to keep diaries of what they buy.

Boom, one of a group of Tokyo research firms that specialize in teen surveys, offers a portfolio of several thousand Tokyo-area high-school girls that includes, it says, 500 girls deemed to be "trend setters." Boom's clients include giants such as 7-Eleven Japan Co. and Shiseido Co.

On a recent afternoon, a trio of Tokyo high-school girls sat in a Boom interview room, poking at blobs of fruit gelatin. They were helping Meiji Milk Products Co. narrow down a list of six flavors to four that Meiji Milk will sell in 7,300 Japanese convenience stores. Swallowing a spoonful of apple gelatin, 15-year-old Kanako Yonemura cocked her head and proclaimed, "This is too sweet." The interviewer listened intently. The girl added: "And I'd like to know how many calories it has per serving."

And Shiseido says that by tapping teen insights it unexpectedly hit on a broad market for a low-priced line of nail polishes. The cosmetics maker had named the line Chopi; the girls preferred another name, Neuve. They also persuaded Shiseido to change the container's color from the usual black, white or silver to beige.

"Just about all the basic ideas for Neuve came from high-school girls," says Masaru Miyagawa, a Shiseido marketing director. The company credits the girls with the fact that a product originally aimed at teens proved appealing to women of all ages. Over the past year, Neuve sales totaled 20 million units. Annual sales of one million units is considered a marketing success in Japan.[9] ■

changes in the external environment. A good strategic plan is based on good marketing research. It helps the firm meet long-term profit and market share goals.

Ford Motor Company has used marketing research to create an aggressive e-commerce marketing strategy. Ford set up the BuyerConnection Web site and joined the MSN CarPoint site, where consumers can order custom-assembled cars, track their progress, and apply for financing. Ford's OwnerConnection site lets owners get online help, manage their warranty service, and check on financing. The company has also teamed up with Yahoo!, TeleTech, iVillage, and bolt.com to conduct research on consumer auto interests and the buying patterns of Web-surfing customers.[10] Ford's management views the Internet as an opportunity, not a threat.

Applied Research versus Basic Research

Virtually all marketing research is conducted to better understand the market, to find out why a strategy failed, or to reduce uncertainty in management decision making. All research conducted for these purposes is called **applied research.** For example, should the price of frozen dinners be raised 40 cents? What name should Ford select for a new sedan? Which commercial has a higher level of recall: A or B? On the other hand, **basic,** or **pure, research** attempts to expand the frontiers of knowledge; it is not aimed at a specific pragmatic problem. Basic research is conducted to validate an existing theory or learn more about a concept or phenomenon. For example, basic marketing research might test a hypothesis about high-involvement decision making or consumer information processing. In the long run, basic research helps us understand more about the world in which we live. The findings of basic research usually cannot be implemented by managers in the short run. Most basic marketing research is now conducted in universities; the findings are reported in such publications as *The Journal of Marketing Research* and *The Journal of Marketing*. In contrast, most research undertaken by businesses is applied research because it must be cost-effective and of demonstrable value to the decision maker.

applied research
Research aimed at solving a specific, pragmatic problem—better understanding of the marketplace, determination of why a strategy or tactic failed, or reduction of uncertainty in management decision making.

basic, or **pure, research**
Research aimed at expanding the frontiers of knowledge rather than solving a specific, pragmatic problem.

The Nature of Applied Research

Marketing research studies can be classified into three broad categories: programmatic, selective, and evaluative. **Programmatic research** is conducted to develop marketing options through market segmentation, market opportunity analysis, or consumer attitude and product usage studies. **Selective research** is used to test decision alternatives. Some examples are testing concepts for new products, advertising copy testing, and test marketing. **Evaluative research** is done to assess program performance; it includes tracking advertising recall, doing organizational image studies, and examining customer attitudes on a firm's quality of service.

Programmatic research arises from management's need to obtain a market overview periodically. For example, product management may be concerned that the existing market information base is inadequate or outdated for present decision making, or marketing plans may call for the introduction of new products, ad campaigns, or packaging. Whatever the specific situation, current information is needed to develop viable marketing options. Typical programmatic research questions include the following.

programmatic research
Research conducted to develop marketing options through market segmentation, market opportunity analyses, or consumer attitude and product usage studies.

selective research
Research used to test decision alternatives.

evaluative research
Research done to assess program performance.

- Does the market exhibit any segmentation opportunities?
- If so, what are the profiles of the various segments?
- Do some segments appear to be more likely candidates than others for the firm's marketing efforts?
- What new product opportunities lie in the various segments?
- What marketing program options should be considered in light of the segmentation analysis?

The marketing research department's role is to suggest a research program that will answer these questions within the firm's budgetary constraints.

Selective research typically is conducted after several viable options have been identified by programmatic research. If no one alternative is clearly superior, product management usually will wish to test several alternatives. However, selective research may be required at any stage of the marketing process, such as when advertising copy is being developed, various product formulations are being evaluated, or an entire marketing program is being assessed, as in test marketing.

The need for evaluative research arises when the effectiveness and efficiency of marketing programs must be evaluated. Evaluative research may be integrated into programmatic research when program changes or entirely new options are demanded because of present performance. The response of the marketing research department to the need for evaluative information is often to conduct tracking studies.

The Decision to Conduct Marketing Research

A manager who is faced with several alternative solutions to a particular problem should not instinctively call for applied marketing research. In fact, the first decision to be made is whether to conduct marketing research at all. In a number of situations, it is best not to conduct research.

- *Resources are lacking.* There are two situations in which a lack of resources should preclude marketing research. First, an organization may lack the funds to do the research properly. If a project calls for a sample of 800 respondents but the budget allows for only 50 interviews, the quality of the information would be highly suspect. Second, funds may be available to do the research properly but insufficient to implement any decisions resulting from the research. Small organizations in particular sometimes lack the resources to create an effective marketing mix. In one case, for example, the director of a performing arts guild was in complete agreement with the recommendations that resulted from a marketing research project. However, two years after the project was completed, nothing had been done because the money was not available.
- *Research results would not be useful.* Some types of marketing research studies measure lifestyle and personality factors of steady and potential customers. Assume that a study finds that introverted men with a poor self-concept yet a high need for achievement are most likely to patronize a discount brokerage service. The management of Charles Schwab discount brokerage service might be hard-pressed to use this information.

- *The opportunity has passed.* Marketing research should not be undertaken if the opportunity for successful entry into a market has already passed. If the product is in the late maturity or decline stage of the product life cycle (such as record turntables or black-and-white television sets), it would be foolish to do research on new product entry. The same is true for markets rapidly approaching saturation, such as super-premium ice cream (Häagen-Dazs, Ben and Jerry's). For products already in the market, however, research is needed to modify the products as consumer tastes, competition, and other factors change.

- *The decision already has been made.* In the real world of management decision making and company politics, marketing research has sometimes been used improperly. Several years ago, a large marketing research study was conducted for a bank with over $300 million in deposits. The purpose of the research project was to guide top management in mapping a strategic direction for the bank during the next five years. After reading the research report, the president said, "I fully agree with your recommendations because that was what I was going to do anyway! I'm going to use your study tomorrow when I present my strategic plan to the board of directors." The researcher then asked, "What if my recommendations had been counter to your decision?" The bank president laughed and said, "They would have never known that I had conducted a marketing research study!" Not only was the project a waste of money; it also raised a number of ethical questions in the researcher's mind.

The super-premium ice cream market is reaching saturation. At this point, marketing research would not be required for a new product entry, although it is necessary to keep products already in the market ahead of the competition.

- *Managers cannot agree on what they need to know to make a decision.* Although it may seem obvious that research should not be undertaken until objectives are specified, it sometimes happens. Although preliminary or exploratory studies are commonly done to better understand the nature of the problem, a large, major research project should not be. It is faulty logic to say "Well, let's just go ahead and do the study and then we will better understand the problem and know what steps to take." The wrong phenomena might be studied or key elements needed for management decision making may not be included.
- *Decision-making information already exists.* Some companies have been conducting research in certain markets for many years. They understand the characteristics of their target customers and what they like and dislike about existing products. Under these circumstances, further research would be redundant and a waste of money. Procter & Gamble, for example, has extensive knowledge of the coffee market. After it conducted initial taste tests, P&G went into national distribution with Folger's Instant Coffee without further research. The Sara Lee Corporation did the same thing with its frozen croissants, as did

Quaker Oats with Chewy Granola Bars. This tactic, however, does not always work. P&G thought it understood the pain reliever market thoroughly, so it bypassed marketing research for Encaprin, encapsulated aspirin. The product failed because it lacked a distinct competitive advantage over existing products and was withdrawn from the market.

■ *The costs of conducting research outweigh the benefits.* There are rarely situations in which a manager has such tremendous confidence in her or his judgment that additional information relative to a pending decision would not be accepted if it were available and free. However, the manager might have sufficient confidence to be unwilling to pay very much for it or wait long to receive it. Willingness to acquire additional decision-making information depends on a manager's perception of its quality, price, and timing. The manager would be willing to pay more for perfect information (that is, data that leave no doubt as to which alternative to follow) than for information that leaves uncertainty as to what to do. Therefore, research should be undertaken only when the expected value of the information is greater than the cost of obtaining it.

Two important determinants of potential benefits are profit margins and market size. Generally speaking, new products with large profit margins are going to have greater potential benefit than products with smaller profit margins, assuming that both items have the same sales potential. Also, new product opportunities in large markets are going to offer greater potential benefits than those in smaller markets if competitive intensity is the same in both markets (see Table 1.1).

Table 1.1

Deciding Whether to Conduct Marketing Research

Market Size	Small Profit Margin	Large Profit Margin
Small	Costs likely to be greater than benefits (e.g., eye-glass replacement screw, tire valve extension). DON'T CONDUCT MARKETING RESEARCH.	Benefits possibly greater than cost (e.g., ultra-expensive Lamborghini-type sportswear, larger specialized industrial equipment like computer-aided metal stamping machines). PERHAPS CONDUCT MARKETING RESEARCH. LEARN ALL YOU CAN FROM EXISTING INFORMATION PRIOR TO MAKING DECISION TO CONDUCT RESEARCH.
Large	Benefits likely to be greater than costs (e.g., Stouffers frozen entrees, Crest's tartar control toothpastes). PERHAPS CONDUCT MARKETING RESEARCH. LEARN ALL YOU CAN FROM EXISTING INFORMATION PRIOR TO MAKING DECISION TO CONDUCT RESEARCH.	Benefits most likely to be greater than costs (e.g., medical equipment like cat scanners, Toshiba's high-definition television). CONDUCT MARKETING RESEARCH.

The Profound Impact of the Internet on Marketing Research

The Internet has turned the world of marketing research upside-down. Current methods of conducting some types of research soon may seem as quaint as a steam-engine train. New techniques and strategies for conducting traditional marketing research are appearing online in increasing numbers every day. By 2005, Internet marketing research will account for about 50 percent of all marketing research revenue in the United States.[11] Following are some growth drivers of such research:

- The Internet provides more rapid access to business intelligence and thus allows for better and faster decision making.
- The Internet improves a firm's ability to respond quickly to customer needs and market shifts.
- The Internet facilitates conducting follow-up studies and longitudinal research.
- The Internet slashes labor- and time-intensive research activities (and associated costs), including mailing, telephone solicitation, data entry, data tabulation, and reporting.[12]

Internet surveys have several specific advantages:

- *Rapid development, real-time reporting.* Internet surveys can be broadcast to thousands of potential respondents simultaneously. The results can be tabulated and posted for corporate clients to view as the returns arrive. Thus, Internet surveys results can be in a client's hands in significantly less time than traditional survey results.
- *Dramatically reduced costs.* The Internet can cut costs by 25 to 40 percent while providing results in half the time it takes to do a traditional telephone survey. Data-collection costs account for a large proportion of any traditional market research budget. Telephone surveys are labor-intensive efforts incurring training, telecommunications, and management costs. Using the Internet eliminates these costs completely. While costs for traditional survey techniques rise proportionally with the number of interviews desired, electronic solicitations can grow in volume with little increase in project costs.
- *Personalization.* Internet surveys can be highly personalized for greater relevance to each respondent's own situation, thus speeding the response process. Respondents enjoy answering only pertinent questions, being able to pause and resume the survey as their schedule allows, and having the ability to see previous responses and correct inconsistencies.
- *Higher response rates.* Busy respondents are growing increasingly intolerant of "snail mail" or telephone-based surveys. Internet surveys take half the time to complete that phone interviews do, can be accomplished at the respondent's convenience (after work hours), and are much more stimulating and engaging. Graphics, interactivity, links to incentive sites, and real-time summary reports make Internet surveys more enjoyable. The result: much higher response rates.

- *Ability to contact the hard-to-reach.* Certain of the most surveyed groups are als the most difficult to reach—doctors, high-income professionals, and to management in Global 2000 firms. Many of these groups are well repr sented online. Internet surveys provide convenient anytime/anywhei access that makes it easy for busy professionals to participate.[13]

With the mushrooming number (currently around 50 percent) Americans online, researchers are finding that online research and offlir research yield the same results. America Online's (AOL) Digital Marketir Services (DMS), an online research organization, has done a number of surve with both online and offline samples for clients such as IBM, Eastman Koda and Procter & Gamble. Side-by-side comparison of over 100 online and offlir studies showed that both techniques led clients to the same business decisions. That is, the guidance provided by both sets of data was the same.

Conducting surveys is not the sum total of the Internet revolution in ma keting research. Management of the research process and dissemination information also have been greatly enhanced by the Internet. Several key are have been greatly affected by the Internet:

- *Libraries and various printed materials,* which may be virtually replaced sources of information. On its Web site, the Bureau of Census (http:/ www.census.gov) indicates that it plans to gradually make the Internet tl major means of distributing census data. The same is true for a number other government agencies. Information from countless databases (bo governmental and nongovernmental) can be called up almost instant neously on the user's desktop or notebook PC.
- *The distribution of requests for proposals (RFPs) and the proposals themselv* Companies can now quickly and efficiently send RFPs to a select email list research suppliers. In turn, the suppliers can develop proposals and em; them back to clients. A process that used to take days now occurs in a m; ter of hours.
- *Collaboration between the client and the research supplier* in the management of research project. Both the researcher and the client might look at a pr posal, RFP, report, or some type of statistical analysis at the same time their computer screens while discussing it over the telephone. This is ve effective and efficient, as changes in sample size, quotas, and other aspec of the research plan can be discussed and made immediately.
- *Data management and online analysis.* Clients can access their survey via tl research supplier's secure Web site and monitor the data gathering in re time. The client can use sophisticated tools to actually carry out data analy as the survey develops. This real-time analysis may result in changes in t questionnaire, sample size, or types of respondents interviewed. The resear supplier and the client become partners in "just-in-time" marketing researc
- *Publishing and distribution of reports.* Reports can be published directly to t Web from such programs as PowerPoint and all the latest versions of leadir word processing, spreadsheet, and presentation software packages. Tl means that results are available to appropriate managers worldwide on almost instantaneous basis. Reports can be searched for content of speci interest, with the same Web browser used to view the report.

- *Oral presentations of marketing research surveys,* which now can be viewed by widely scattered audiences. Managers throughout the world can see and hear the actual client presentation on password-protected Web sites. This saves firms both time and money, as managers no longer need to travel to a central meeting site.

As we pointed out earlier, the Internet represents the present and the future of a significant portion of the world of marketing research. Its impact is limited only by the researcher's imagination.

The Development of Marketing Research

The many benefits that accrue to management from using marketing research served as the initial impetus to begin conducting marketing research in the United States. In light of the competitive advantage a company can gain from engaging in marketing research, it is surprising that the industry did not move out of its embryonic stage until 1900.

Inception: Pre-1900

The first recorded marketing research survey was taken in July 1824 by the *Harrisburg Pennsylvanian.* It was an election poll in which Andrew Jackson received 335 votes; John Quincy Adams, 169; Henry Clay, 29; and William H. Crawford, 9. Later the same year, another newspaper, the *Raleigh Star,* canvassed political meetings held in North Carolina, "at which the sense of the people was taken." Perhaps the first marketing researcher was John Jacob Astor, who in the 1790s employed an artist to sketch the hats worn by fashionable New York women so that he could keep abreast of fashion trends.[15]

The first documented use of research to make informed marketing decisions was carried out by the advertising agency N. W. Ayer in 1879. That systematic effort was a simple survey of state and local officials to determine expected levels of grain production. The purpose of the research was to develop the scheduling of advertising for a producer of farm equipment. The second documented instance of marketing research appears to have been at E. I. duPont de Nemours & Company toward the end of the 19th century. It involved the systematic compilation of salespersons' reports on a variety of customer characteristics. The response to this second research effort was a harbinger of things to come. The salespersons who were responsible for obtaining and reporting the data were outraged because they didn't like the extra paperwork.

Academic researchers entered into marketing research about 1895, when Harlow Gale, a professor of psychology at the

Marketing research is a serious business. Information flowing from marketing research guides billions of dollars of decisions in American and other businesses throughout the world each year. Because marketing research is inherently a people-driven process, it is susceptible to the foibles and whimsical occurrences of everyday life. Throughout the text, you will find these little "war stories" that show the comic and human side of marketing research.

We want to begin by offering you a couple of examples that happened to us (your authors). In a test of two different prototype dryer sheet fabric softeners, consumers were supposed to use product A for one load of clothes and then product B for the second. A telephone callback was used to get respondent feedback . . . and did we get feedback! Test product B had been formulated

(continued)

incorrectly at the lab. When the clothes came from the dryer, they all had a distinct shade of pink. One woman asked how in the world we could expect her husband to wear pink blue jeans!

Another time we were testing two versions of dog food (canned and semi-moist) especially formulated for older, less active dogs. Respondents were supposed to feed their dogs semi-moist food for five days and then canned food for five days to see which type the dogs preferred. On the first day of the test, a dog owner called, her tone alternating between hysteria and extreme anger. She had fed her registered boxer the semi-moist dog food, whereupon the dog had died. She assured us that a lawsuit would be forthcoming very soon. When our client was informed of the situation, its management immediately offered to pay for an autopsy. Fortunately, it revealed that poor Rover had had a heart attack, which had nothing to do with the food.

Source: "War Stories: True Life Tales in Marketing Research," by Art Shulman, *Quirk's Marketing Research Review*. Reprinted with permission of Art Shulman.

University of Minnesota, introduced the use of mail surveys to study advertising. He mailed 200 questionnaires and received 20 completed questionnaires, a 10 percent response rate. Gale's work was quickly followed by the pioneering work of Walter Dill Scott at Northwestern University. Scott introduced the use of experimentation and psychological measurement to the fledgling practice of advertising.

Early Growth: 1900–1920

It was not until after the turn of the century that consumer demand surged; the growth of mass production meant larger and more distant markets. No longer was America characterized by cottage industries where the craftsman-seller was in daily contact with the marketplace. The need arose to understand consumers' buying habits and attitudes toward manufacturers' wares. In response to this need, the first formal marketing research department was established by the Curtis Publishing Company in 1911. The research focused primarily on the automobile industry, as manufacturers had decided that everyone who had the money and inclination to buy a car had done so. The manufacturers were seeking a new group of consumers to which to target their promotions. A few years later, Daniel Starch pioneered recognition measures of advertising response, and E. K. Strong introduced recall measures and scaling to marketing research.

The Adolescent Years: 1920–1950

Percival White developed the first application of scientific research to commercial problems. White's words express his realization of the need for systematic and continual marketing research:

Perhaps the greatest advantage of the company's having its own market analysis department is that the work then becomes a continuous process, or at least a process which is carried forward at periodic intervals, so that altered conditions in the market and in the industry at large are always kept in view. The necessity for regarding markets as constantly changing and not as fixed phenomena should not be lost sight of.[16]

White's book bore scant resemblance to this text. For example, the book avoided the use of statistics and mathematics, only briefly mentioning the U.S. Census.

The 1930s saw widespread use of survey research. A. C. Nielsen entered the research business in 1922. He expanded on White's earlier work by developing the "share of market" concept plus many other services that became the foundation for one of America's largest marketing research organizations. It was not until the late 1930s that formal courses in marketing research became common on college campuses; a substantial body of knowledge developed within both the practice and academic communities. Two events—the spread of broadcast media and World War II—helped the fledgling discipline coalesce into a well-defined profession. Social scientists found that broadcast media created interesting new phenomena and increased the variability of human behavior.

By the end of the 1930s, simple examinations of respondents' replies were becoming categorized and compared across groups classified by differences in income, gender, or family status. Simple correlation analysis came into use but was not widespread; those who would use it had to be able to go directly to the statistical sources for such techniques, using texts by some of the pioneers in the field at this time, including G. Udney Yule, Mordecai Ezekiel, and Horace Sechrist.

The requirements of World War II pressed social scientists into service on a number of fronts. Tools and methods that had been novelties before the war were adopted and adapted to study the consumer behavior of soldiers and of their families on the home front. Among those tools were experimental design, opinion polling, human factors research, and operations research techniques.

In the 1940s, focus groups developed under the leadership of Robert Merton. During the late 1940s, the importance of random selection in sampling became widely recognized, and major advances were made in sampling techniques and polling procedures. A small number of psychologists who had been assigned to work in the Army Quartermaster Corps found their way into industry, where they introduced techniques for consumer tests of products.[17]

The Mature Years: 1950–Present

The change from a seller's market to a buyer's market (resulting from post–World War II pent-up demand) necessitated better marketing intelligence. No longer could producers sell all of anything they made. The rising costs of production "tooling up," advertising, inventories, and other factors made the price of failure much higher than it had been in the past. Now, marketing research first determines what the market wants and then goods are crafted to meet those needs.

The mid-1950s brought the concept of market segmentation, based largely on easily identifiable demographic characteristics of customers. The same period gave rise to motivation research, with its emphasis on why consumers behave as they do. The underlying concepts of segmentation and motivation analysis, combined with the power of survey techniques, led to such innovations as psychographics and benefit segmentation. In the 1960s, mathematical models were developed for description and prediction—stochastic models, Markovian models, linear learning models. Even more significant was the development of the computer during the early 1960s, greatly enhancing the researcher's ability to quickly analyze, store, and retrieve large amounts of data.

A Preview of the Text

Now that you understand the role of marketing research in the management decision-making process, situations in which research should be undertaken, the impact and potential of the Internet, and how the field has evolved, you are prepared to venture ahead in the book. You will find that every chapter in this text is written from the perspective of a research user (a manager) rather than that of a technical marketing researcher. This approach is deliberate, because most readers will never be researchers but will need to apply the results of marketing research in decision making. For those interested in pursuing a career in marketing research, an appendix to this chapter provides a description of various types of jobs available in the field; it can be found at **http://mcdaniel. swcollege.com.** Chapter 2 describes the marketing research industry and marketing research suppliers and takes a detailed look at who uses marketing research and how it is used. Chapter 3 discusses problem definition and the steps involved in conducting marketing research.

Part Two of the book focuses on creating a marketing research design. Chapter 4 provides a description of the sources and uses of published secondary data, computerized databases, secondary data on the Internet, and information management. Chapter 5 explains the differences between quantitative and qualitative research and elaborates on various qualitative techniques. Chapter 6 looks at the nature of survey research, which is the most popular means of gathering primary data. Chapter 7 examines collecting data through observation techniques. Part Two concludes with an explanation of experimentation in marketing research in Chapter 8.

Part Three describes primary data acquisition tactics. Measurement concepts are set forth in Chapter 9. Chapter 10 describes attitude scaling techniques and the nature of attitudes. Data collection forms and questionnaire design are illustrated in Chapter 11. Chapters 12 and 13 detail basic sampling concepts and sample size determination.

Part Four of the text demonstrates various techniques for data analysis. Chapter 14 focuses on data processing and basic statistical analysis. Chapter 15 discusses statistical testing of differences, while Chapter 16 discusses bivariate correlation and regression. Chapter 17 concludes Part Four with a discussion of multivariate analysis methodologies.

The fifth part of the text is devoted to other topics in marketing research. Communicating the results of marketing research is summarized in Chapter 18. Chapter 19 describes the key elements of managing the marketing research function and ethical issues in marketing research.

Summary

Marketing is a process of planning and executing the conception, pricing, promotion, and distribution of ideas, goods, and services to create exchanges that satisfy individual and organizational objectives. Marketing managers attempt to get the right goods or services to the right people at the right place at the right time at the right price, using the right promotion technique. This may be accomplished by following the marketing concept, which is based on consumer orientation, goal orientation, and systems orientation.

The marketing manager must work within an internal environment of the organization and understand the external environment over which he or she has little, if any, control. The primary variables over which the marketing manager has control are distribution, price, promotion, and product/service decisions. The unique combination of these four variables is called the *marketing mix.*

Marketing research plays a key part in providing the information for managers to shape the marketing mix. Marketing research has grown in importance because of management's focus on customer satisfaction and retention. It also is a key tool in proactive management. Marketing research should be undertaken only when the perceived benefits are greater than the costs.

A marketing research study can be described as programmatic, selective, or evaluative. Programmatic research is done to develop marketing options through market segmentation, market opportunity analysis, or consumer attitude and product usage studies. Selective research is used to test decisional alternatives. Evaluative research is done to assess program performance.

The Internet has had a major impact on the marketing research industry. The use of Internet surveys has increased dramatically because they can be quickly deployed, cost significantly less, are readily personalized, have high response rates, and provide the ability to contact the hard-to-reach respondent. Most importantly, as Internet participation by households has increased, identical online and offline surveys have been shown to produce the same business decisions.

Marketing research has also found other uses for the Internet. It serves as a major information source, aids in the distribution of RFPs and proposals, facilitates collaboration between the client and the research supplier in the management of a research project, provides data management and online analysis, and allows for the publication and distribution of reports and the viewing of oral presentations by a widely scattered audience. The Internet represents the present and the future of marketing research.

Marketing research in the United States traces its roots back to 1824, when the first public poll was taken. Its early growth period, from 1900 to 1920, was characterized by the establishment of the first formal marketing research department. Its adolescent years, from 1920 until 1950, saw the widespread use of marketing research. The maturing of marketing research began in 1950 and continues today, with growth in use of the Internet and in the number and sophistication of both quantitative and qualitative marketing research techniques.

Key Terms and Definitions

marketing The process of planning and executing the conception, pricing, promotion, and distribution of ideas, goods, and services to create exchanges that satisfy individual and organizational objectives.

marketing concept A business philosophy based on consumer orientation, goal orientation, and systems orientation.

consumer orientation The identification of and focus on the people or firms most likely to buy a product and the production of a good or service that will meet their needs most effectively.

goal orientation   A focus on the accomplishment of corporate goals; a limit set on consumer orientation.

systems orientation   The creation of systems to monitor the external environment and deliver the marketing mix to the target market.

marketing mix   The unique blend of product/service, pricing, promotion, and distribution strategies designed to meet the needs of a specific group of consumers.

marketing research   The planning, collection, and analysis of data relevant to marketing decision making and the communication of the results of this analysis to management.

descriptive function   The gathering and presentation of statements of fact.

diagnostic function   The explanation of data or actions.

predictive function   Specification of how to use descriptive and diagnostic research to predict the results of a planned marketing decision.

return on quality   Management objective based on the principles that (1) the quality being deliv-

ered is at a level desired by the target market and (2) that level of quality must have a positive impact on profitability.

marketing strategy   A plan to guide the long-term use of a firm's resources based on its existing and projected internal capabilities and on projected changes in the external environment.

applied research   Research aimed at solving a specific, pragmatic problem—better understanding of the marketplace, determination of why a strategy or tactic failed, or reduction of uncertainty in management decision making.

basic, or **pure, research**   Research aimed at expanding the frontiers of knowledge rather than solving a specific, pragmatic problem.

programmatic research Research conducted to develop marketing options through market segmentation, market opportunity analyses, or consumer attitude and product usage studies.

selective research   Research used to test decision alternatives.

evaluative research   Research done to assess program performance.

Questions for Review & Critical Thinking

1. The role of marketing is to create exchanges. What role might marketing research play in facilitating the exchange process?
2. Marketing research traditionally has been associated with manufacturers of consumer goods. Today, an increasing number of organizations, both profit

PART 1:
An Introduction to Marketing Research

and nonprofit, are using marketing research. Why do you think this trend exists? Give some examples.

3. Explain the relationship between marketing research and the marketing concept.

4. Comment on the following statement by the owner of a restaurant in a downtown area: "I see customers every day whom I know on a first-name basis. I understand their likes and dislikes. If I put something on the menu and it doesn't sell, I know that they didn't like it. I also read the magazine *Modern Restaurants* to keep up with industry trends. This is all the marketing research I need to do."

5. Why is marketing research important to marketing executives? Give several reasons.

6. What differences might you note among marketing research conducted for (a) a retailer, (b) a consumer goods manufacturer, (c) an industrial goods manufacturer, and (d) a charitable organization?

7. Comment on the following: Ralph Moran is planning to invest $1.5 million in a new restaurant in Saint Louis. When he applied for a construction financing loan, the bank officer asked whether he had conducted any research. Ralph replied, "I checked on research, and a marketing research company wanted $20,000 to do the work. I decided that with all the other expenses of opening a new business, research was a luxury that I could do without."

8. What is meant by "return on quality"? Why do you think that the concept evolved? Give an example.

9. Describe three situations in which marketing research should not be undertaken. Explain why this is true.

10. Give an example of (a) the descriptive role of marketing research, (b) the diagnostic role of marketing research, and (c) the predictive function of marketing research.

11. Using the Internet and a Web browser, visit a search engine such as Lycos or Yahoo! and type, "marketing research." From the thousands of options you are offered, pick a Web site that you find interesting and report on its content to the class.

12. Divide the class into groups of four. Each team should visit a large organization (profit or nonprofit) and conduct an interview with a top marketing executive to discover how this firm is using marketing research. Each team then should report its findings in class.

Real-Life Research • 1.1

Maxwell and Dawn's Dream

Maxwell and Dawn are products of the Internet age. After rising rapidly at Dell Computer and Microsoft, both decided at the ripe old age of 36 to cash out and begin anew. They longed for a simpler life and a more relaxed pace. Owning a bed-and-breakfast in the country had always been their dream. The couple returned to their native Texas to begin exploring the idea of a bed-and-breakfast, the location of which would most likely be Texas hill country.

Never inclined to follow the leader, Maxwell and Dawn wanted their bed-and-breakfast to be different—perhaps more activities or a unique theme might be in order. They read everything they could get their hands on. One piece of information came from Roper Starch Worldwide, one of America's most respected marketing research firms.

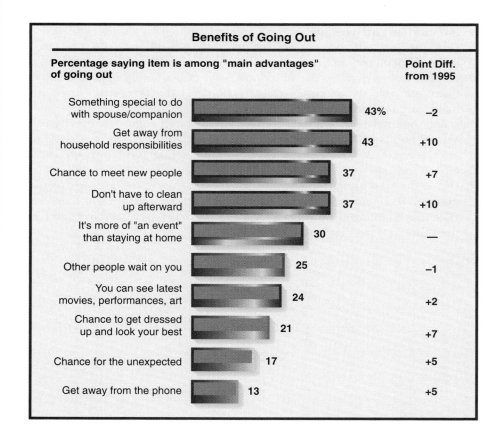

Benefits of Going Out

Percentage saying item is among "main advantages" of going out		Point Diff. from 1995
Something special to do with spouse/companion	43%	−2
Get away from household responsibilities	43	+10
Chance to meet new people	37	+7
Don't have to clean up afterward	37	+10
It's more of "an event" than staying at home	30	—
Other people wait on you	25	−1
You can see latest movies, performances, art	24	+2
Chance to get dressed up and look your best	21	+7
Chance for the unexpected	17	+5
Get away from the phone	13	+5

Why Go Out? To Get Away

Connecting with that special someone is still important. However, escaping the responsibilities of home, letting someone else clean up the dirty dishes, and just getting more zing out of life are becoming more of a factor in Americans' decisions to go out. Being able to "get away from household responsibilities" (43%, up 10 from 1995) is now tied with doing "something special" with a spouse or companion (43%, down slightly) as the leading advantage of going out rather than staying home. Meeting new people (37%, up 7) and not having to clean up afterward (37%, up 10) are the next most cited reasons. Being able to "get dressed up and look your best" (21%, up 7), "the chance for the unexpected" (17%, up 5), and being able to "get away from the phone" (13%, up 5) have also had notable increases.[18]

Questions

1. How might Maxwell and Dawn use this information?
2. Is this research basic or applied? Why?
3. What other marketing research might Maxwell and Dawn want to gather?
4. Go to the Roper Starch Worldwide Web site at http://www.roper.com. Describe their clients, offerings, and "what's new" at the marketing research company.

Real-Life Research • 1.2

Courtyard by Marriott

Forget American Express. Some businesspeople don't leave home without their teddy bears. That was one of the surprising facts Courtyard by Marriott found when it commissioned research on its customer base. At Courtyard, market research is "very important to us to understand the wants and needs of our customers. We can't find out if we don't ask," said Geary Campbell, director of national public relations at Marriott.

The survey also serves as a marketing tool "to tell the media and customers what our customer base does while they are on the road," Campbell said, "and to get greater recognition for the Courtyard brand."

The Courtyard by Marriott Business Traveler Profile of 300 business travelers who had taken at least six work-related trips in the previous twelve months was conducted by D. K. Shifflet & Associates of McLean, Va. The 30-question telephone survey focused on how travelers communicated with their homes and offices, as well as what they do or what they bring with them to make life on the road feel more like home. "We also wanted to find out quirky things," Campbell said, "such as their travel behaviors."

Marriott predicted some of the results ahead of time. For example, the survey found that 58 percent of business travelers bring along a laptop computer. Other findings came as a surprise: 70 percent of those with laptops said they have games on their computer, and seven percent of business travelers said they travel with a teddy bear or other type of stuffed animal.

Survey results confirmed that business travelers want "more than a friendly face" greeting them at the front desk, Campbell said. Business travelers who are on the road want the opportunity to purchase breakfast in advance and efficient check-ins and check-outs.

Marriott launched its Courtyard brand after two years of research conducted on guests of their full-service hotels, asking what features they would want in a moderately priced hotel. Courtyard's main customer base is the business traveler, Campbell said.[19]

Questions

1. How might Courtyard use these research findings?
2. Based on this study, do you think more research is needed? If so, what types of information would you look for?
3. Do you think all hotel/motel chains should conduct marketing research? Why?

Real-Life Research • 1.3

"Got Milk?" and More

Researchers are always striving to uncover consumer purchase motivations. Striving to better understand consumer psyches has led to some rather offbeat techniques. The success of the "Got Milk?" advertising campaign has been attributed to an "outside-the-box" technique. The ads were inspired by an exercise in consumer deprivation. Goodby, Silverstein & Partners, a unit of Omnicom Group, asked dozens of people to skip milk for a week and record their feelings in a diary. By the fifth day, one man said he was so desperate he was looking in his cat's bowl. The San Francisco agency recreated the scene in a TV spot, complete with a cat meowing fiercely in the background.

Another unusual technique is called naked behavior, or unguarded reactions. Researchers from Greenfield Consulting Group in Westport, Connecticut, for example, regularly sidle up to shoppers in stores, mumbling, "Gosh, I don't understand, there are so many brands." Ideally, unsuspecting consumers will offer to share their impressions of products far more candidly than they would tell a survey taker.

Then there's the early morning ambush. Leo Burnett, the Chicago agency that creates Kellogg ads, has sent researchers out to knock on test subjects' doors at sunrise, to discover "what drives a dynamic choice at 7:30 A.M.," says Catherine DeThorne, Burnett's director of planning.[20]

Questions

1. Does the type of research discussed here qualify as marketing research?
2. Do you think that the elements of a firm's marketing mix should be modified after receiving results from these methods?
3. Could these techniques be used to evaluate service quality?

Chapter Two

The Marketing Research Industry

Learning Objectives

To appreciate the structure of the marketing research industry.

To comprehend the nature of corporate marketing research departments.

To learn about the various types of firms and their functions in the marketing research industry.

To understand the impact of the Internet on the marketing research industry.

To learn who uses marketing research.

To understand the growing importance of strategic partnering.

To appreciate trends in global marketing research.

THE BLUE AND WHITE CAR BANKING THE DAYTONA INTERNATIONAL Speedway track at 165 miles per hour on February 13 was not sponsored by one of the circuit's usual suspects. Alltel—the cellular, Internet, and local phone-service provider—was the name fans saw emblazoned across the roof and side of the car each time it pulled into the lead position in the season's first NASCAR Busch Series Grand National race. Though the driver wiped out in the 65th lap, Alltel is still elated with its choice to back the team, and the following week sponsored an entire race, the Alltel 200.

ALLTEL IS NO ANOMALY AMONG NASCAR sponsors. It is just one of several high-tech companies, including Lycos, Philips, 3M, and Bell-South, that have woken up to the power of NASCAR, particularly to the attractive demographics of its fans.

FAN DEMOGRAPHICS HAVE CHANGED DRA-MATICALLY SINCE THE MID-90S, AS new race tracks have opened outside of the sport's traditional stronghold in the Southeast, television networks have expanded their race coverage, and drivers like Jeff Gordon—who are slicker, less down-home, and more media-savvy—have joined the NASCAR ranks. And car-racing fans are more educated than in the past: those with at least a college degree comprised 22 percent of the pool in 1998, an increase of 18 percent from 1995. Female fans have grown 5 percent since 1995, currently comprising almost 40 percent of NASCAR enthusiasts, a greater percentage of women than in any other sport.

Fan demographics for NASCAR changed dramatically in the 1990s. Many high-tech companies now sponsor NASCAR teams.

AS THE DEMOGRAPHICS HAVE GROWN, SO TOO HAS THE SPONSOR LIST, ALLTEL got in on the car two years ago when it learned that 71 percent of the households in its wireless service areas are also fans of the sport. Half of NASCAR devotees now use a cell phone, according to Performance Research in Newport, Rhode Island. That's 10 percent higher than all phone use by the average U.S. citizen, according to a study by NFO Worldwide Research. Lycos, too, is sponsoring a team for the second season in a row. "It allows for a tremendous amount of pure brand exposure on television," says Jim Hoenscheid, Lycos' director of brand marketing and promotions. And, he adds, "NASCAR fans are an extremely loyal and wired audience."[1] ∎

Find out more about NASCAR's commitment to its fans at

 www.nascar. com/fans

Alltel and Lycos are marketing research users, while Performance Research and NFO Worldwide Research are research suppliers. What are the various types of marketing research suppliers and users? What are the basic characteristics of the marketing research industry today? We will examine these questions in this chapter.

The Evolving Structure of the Marketing Research Industry

Today, over $11 billion a year is spent on marketing/advertising/public opinion research services around the world.[2] Spending on marketing research is $6.4 billion in the United States alone.[3] During the past two decades, the research market has become highly concentrated, with about 54 percent of the market being held by the 50 largest worldwide organizations. The other half of the market is shared by a thousand or more small research firms. The concentration is even more pronounced in the United States, where the 10 largest firms account for 77 percent of total U.S. spending for marketing research.[4]

The various types of organizations encountered in the marketing research industry are summarized in Table 2.1. Figure 2.1 (on page 32) summarizes the structure of the marketing research industry and shows the process for survey-based research operating at four levels. Companies at Levels 1 and 2 are the ultimate consumers of marketing research data: the information users. The information they need originates with individual consumers and those who make business purchase decisions: the respondents. Companies at Level 3 are the research designers and providers, and those at Level 4 are the data collectors. Let's take a closer look at each level.

Level 1: Primary Information Users (Corporate Marketing Departments)

Corporate marketing departments (Level 1 organizations) are the ultimate users of the research data provided by their marketing research departments. Their primary business is the sale of products and services. They use marketing research data on an ongoing basis in a variety of ways to support the marketing decision-making process:

1. To determine how various target groups will react to alternative marketing mixes.
2. To evaluate the ongoing success of operational marketing strategies.
3. To assess changes in the external, or uncontrollable, environment and the implications of those changes for their product or service strategy.
4. To identify new target markets.
5. To create new marketing mixes for new target markets.

We will discuss corporate users of marketing research in greater detail later in the chapter.

As Figure 2.1 shows, Level 1 organizations and their marketing research departments may work with both custom and syndicated research firms, go directly to ad agencies, or use some combination of these alternatives to satisfy their many marketing research needs.

Table 2.1

General Categories of Organizations Involved in Marketing Research

Organization	Activities, Functions, and Services
Level 1. Corporate marketing departments	Marketing departments in firms such as Kraft General Foods and Procter & Gamble
Level 2. Ad agencies	Advertising agencies such as J. Walter Thompson, Young & Rubicam, and Foote, Cone & Belding
Level 3. Research suppliers (a) Syndicated service firms	Marketing research data gathering and reporting firms like ACNielsen, Arbitron, and Information Resources Incorporated, which collect data of general interest to many firms but for no one firm in particular (that is, anyone can buy the data they collect); prominent in the media audience field and retail sales data
(b) Custom, or ad hoc, research firms	Marketing research consulting firms such as Market Facts, Data Development, and MARC, which do customized marketing research projects that address specific problems for individual clients
Level 4. Field service firms	Firms that collect data only, on a subcontract basis for corporate marketing research departments, ad agency research departments, custom research firms, or syndicated research firms
Specialized service firms*	Firms that provide specialized support services to the marketing research industry, such as SDR in Atlanta, which provides sophisticated quantitative analysis
Others*	Government agencies, university research bureaus, individual university professors, database providers, etc.

*These organizations typically operate at Level 1, 2, or 3.

Level 2: Information Users (Ad Agencies)

Although ad agencies (Level 2 organizations) also are in the position of serving corporate clients, these organizations may be ultimate consumers of marketing research data. Their main business is the development and execution of advertising campaigns. To properly fulfill this role, they often need marketing research data. They may obtain such data from custom and syndicated research firms or from field service firms, or they may use some combination of these alternatives.

Level 3: Research Suppliers

Custom and syndicated marketing research firms (Level 3 organizations) represent the front line of the research industry. They sell research services, design research studies, analyze the results, and make recommendations to their clients. They may also buy data collection and other services from field service firms.

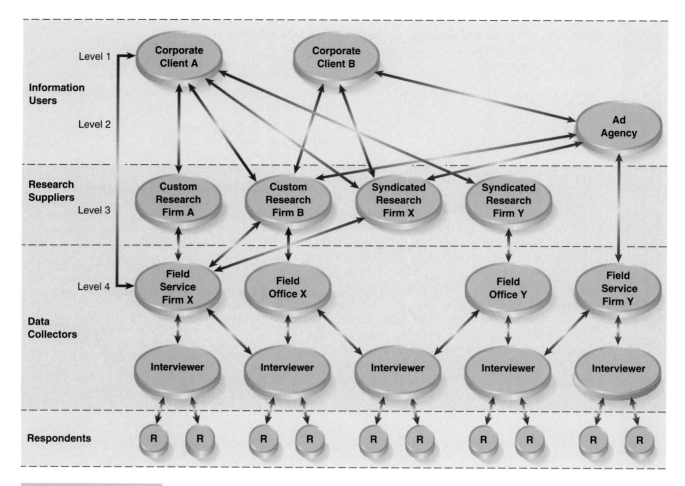

Figure 2.1

**The Structure of the
Marketing Research
Industry**

Level 4: Data Collectors (Field Service Firms)

Field service firms (Level 4 organizations) collect data for syndicated research firms, custom research firms, ad agencies, and corporate marketing departments. In the past, many were run by custom or syndicated research firms; however, this is rare today.

At Level 4 are the interviewers who actually collect the data. They typically work on a part-time, as-needed basis and may work for several different field service firms.

Measurement of the opinions, intentions, and behaviors (as well as many other characterizing factors) of respondents or potential buyers is the goal of the research process. What potential buyers feel, think, do, and intend to do is the focus of the entire marketing research industry.

Corporate Marketing Research Departments

Because corporations are the final consumers and the initiators of most marketing research, they are the logical starting point in developing an understanding of how the industry operates. Most large corporations (and virtually all consumer package goods manufactures of any size) have marketing research departments. Currently, some are melding marketing research and strategic planning whereas others are combining marketing research and customer satisfaction departments.

The average size of marketing research departments is quite small. One recent study found that only 15 percent of service companies such as Federal Express and Delta Airlines had marketing research departments with more than 10 employees. Only 23 percent of manufacturers' research departments had more than 10 employees. The size of marketing research departments has been experiencing a downward trend because of mergers and reengineering. On an encouraging note, few research managers expect the staff reduction to continue, and about 50 percent expect corporate research budgets to continue to grow.[5] The implication of smaller internal research staffs and growing budgets is clear: Companies are conducting less research internally and are outsourcing more to research suppliers. Often, persons in small corporate marketing research departments act as intermediaries between internal research users and outside suppliers.

Because we cannot cover all types of marketing research departments in this text, we will focus our attention on those found in larger, more sophisticated companies, where marketing research is a staff department and the director of the department generally reports to the top marketing executive. Most of the work of the department is with product or brand managers, new product development managers, and other front-line managers. With the possible exception of various recurring studies that may be programmed into a firm's marketing information system, the marketing research department typically does not initiate studies. In fact, the research manager may control little or no actual budget. Instead, line managers have funds in their budgets earmarked for research.

When brand managers perceive that they have a problem that requires research, they go to the marketing research department for help. Working with the marketing research manager or a senior analyst, they go through a series of steps that may lead to the design and execution of a marketing research project.

Research Suppliers

Although the marketing research industry is characterized by hundreds of small firms, there are some giants in the industry. Table 2.2 shows total revenues for the 30 largest marketing research firms. The four largest firms in the industry—ACNielsen Corp., IMS Health Inc., Information Resources Inc., and Nielsen Media Research, Inc.—are largely syndicated service firms. The remaining 26 firms are either primarily custom research firms or combination firms offering some syndicated service along with custom research services.

Table 2.2 The 30 Largest Marketing Research Firms

Rank	Organization	Headquarters	Total Research Revenues (millions)
1	ACNielsen Corp.	Stamford, Conn.	$1,525.4
2	IMS Health Inc.	Westport, Conn.	1,275.7
3	Information Resources Inc.	Chicago	546.3
4	NFO Worldwide Inc.	Greenwich, Conn.	457.2
5	Nielsen Media Research Inc.	New York	453.3
6	The Kantar Group Ltd.	Fairfield, Conn.	250.2
	Diagnostic Research Int'l Inc.	Los Angeles	39.3
	IntelliQuest Info. Group Inc.	Austin, Texas	26.9
	Remaining Kantar	Fairfield, Conn.	184.0
7	Westat Inc.	Rockville, Md.	242.0
8	The Arbitron Co.	New York	215.4
9	Maritz Marketing Research Inc.	St. Louis	174.3
10	Market Facts Inc.	Arlington Heights, Ill.	160.0
11	The NPD Group Inc.	Port Washington, N.Y.	143.4
12	United Information Group USA	New York	130.0
13	Opinion Research Corp.	Princeton, N.J.	109.4
	Opinion Research Corp.	Princeton, N.J.	56.7
	Macro International Inc.	Calverton, Md.	52.7
14	Taylor Nelson Sofres Intersearch	Horsham, Pa.	83.6
15	J.D Power and Associates	Agoura Hills, Calif.	75.4
16	Roper Starch Worldwide Inc.	Harrison, N.Y.	65.7
17	Ipsos-ASI Inc.	Norwalk, Conn.	64.1
18	Abt Associates Inc.	Cambridge, Mass.	50.8
19	Burke Inc.	Cincinnati	48.8
20	Total Research Corp.	Princeton, N.J.	47.8
21	MORPACE International Inc.	Farmington, Mich.	44.4
22	M/A/R/C Research	Irving, Texas	38.8
23	C&R Research Services Inc.	Chicago	38.3
24	Harris Interactive Inc.	Rochester, N.Y.	37.3
25	Market Strategies Inc.	Livonia, Mich.	34.3
26	Wirthlin Worldwide	McLean, Va.	33.5
27	Lieberman Research Worldwide	Los Angeles	31.2
28	Walker Information	Indianapolis	29.1
29	Custom Research Inc.	Minneapolis	28.2
30	Yankelovich Partners Inc.	Norwalk, Conn.	27.9

Source: Jack Honomichl, reprinted with permission from *Marketing News*, published by the American Marketing Association, "Top 50 U.S. Research Organizations" (June 5, 2000), p. H4.

ACNielsen (ACN) Corporation has about 20,700 full-time employees in offices in 80 countries and customers in more than 100 countries. ACN's Retail Measurement Services provides continuous tracking of consumer purchases at the point of sale via scanning and in-store audits in food, drug, and other retail outlets in more than 80 countries. Information includes actual purchases, market shares, distribution, pricing, merchandising, and promotional activities. For the motion picture industry, ACN provides continuous tracking of box-office receipts from more than 45,000 movie screens in 11 countries. ACN's Consumer

PART 1:

An Introduction to Marketing Research

Panel Services tracks the buying behavior and demographics of more than 126,000 households through purchase panels in 18 countries. In the United States, a panel of 52,000 households uses in-home scanners to record buying behavior and shopping patterns from a variety of outlets, including warehouse clubs, convenience stores, supermarkets, independent drugstores, mass merchandisers, and bookstores.

IMS Health Incorporated, the number two research firm, has about 8,000 employees providing services in 94 countries from offices in 74 countries. IMS's marketing research services include pharmacy and hospital audits plus the measurement of disease and treatment patterns. Information Resources Incorporated (IRI) has about 4,100 employees. Its two main offerings are InfoScan and BehaviorScan. InfoScan is a syndicated market tracking service that provides weekly sales, price, and store condition information on products sold in a sample of food, drug, and mass merchandise stores. BehaviorScan, an electronic test marketing service, enables marketers to test new products or new marketing programs by targeting TV commercials to specific households and tracking the effectiveness of those ads in six smaller markets.

Nielsen Media Research (NMR) Incorporated, the fourth largest research firm, has 2,500 full-time employees. NMR's core business is providing TV audience measurement information for broadcast and cable networks and station providers, program developers and distributors, and advertisers and their agencies in the United States and Canada. Nielsen TV ratings are the currency for transactions between buyers and sellers of television time—more than $43 billion per year in the United States and Canada.

ACNielsen, one of the four largest marketing research firms, continuously tracks movie theater box office receipts. Find out more about ACNielsen at http://www.acnielsen.com.

Custom, or Ad Hoc, Research Firms

Custom, or **ad hoc, research firms,** as noted earlier, are primarily in the business of executing custom, one-of-a-kind marketing research projects for corporate clients. If a corporation has a new product or service idea, a packaging idea, an ad concept, a new pricing strategy, a product reformulation, or a related marketing problem or opportunity, it typically will go to a custom research firm for research help.

There are thousands of custom marketing research firms in the United States. Examples of large custom research firms include Market Facts, Inc.; the MARC Group; Opinion Research Corp. International; Elrick and Lavidge Marketing Research; Burke, Inc.; and Wirthlin Worldwide. However, the overwhelming majority of custom marketing research firms are small, with billings of less than $1 million and fewer than 10 employees. They may limit their client base to their local area and may or may not specialize by type of industry or type of research.

Syndicated Service Firms

In sharp contrast to custom research firms, **syndicated service research firms** collect and sell the same marketing research data to many firms. Anyone willing

custom, or **ad hoc, research firms**
Companies that carry out customized marketing research to address specific projects for corporate clients.

syndicated service research firms
Companies that collect, package, and sell the same general market research data to many firms.

Table 2.3

Syndicated Service Research Firms

Firm	Syndicated Services
AC Nielsen Corp. Schaumberg, Illinois	Television ratings Scanner-based data Wholesale/retail audits
Audits and Surveys Worldwide Inc. New York, New York	Retail sales Product/service distribution data
Connect Consultants International Minneapolis, Minnesota	Web-based surveys
FIND/SVP New York, New York	Large variety of industry/product studies
Kadence Ltd. London, England	European market studies
Maritz Marketing Research Inc. Fenton, Missouri	Customer satisfaction studies
Roper Starch Worldwide Inc. New York, New York	Public opinion surveys Lifestyle data Media/advertising effectiveness data
Information Resources Incorporated Chicago, Illinois	Scanner-based data

to pay the price can buy the data these firms collect, package, and sell. Syndicated service firms are relatively few and, compared to customer research firms, relatively large. They deal primarily with media audience and product movement data and are based on serving information needs common to many companies. For example, companies that advertise on network television want to select shows that reach their target customers most efficiently. They need information on the size and demographic composition of the audiences for various TV programs. It would be extremely inefficient for each company to collect these data itself.

Approximately 31 percent of all research monies are spent on syndicated research; the remainder is spent for custom research. Custom quantitative studies account for 50 percent of all research dollars and custom qualitative research, 19 percent.[6] Table 2.3 shows a list of syndicated service firms and the specific type of marketing research they offer.

Field Service Firms

field service firms
Companies that only collect survey data for corporate clients or research firms.

A true **field service firm** does nothing but collect survey data—no research design, no analysis. Field service firms are data collection specialists, collecting data on a subcontract basis for corporate marketing research departments, custom research firms, and ad agency research departments.

The following description of the sequence of activities under-taken by a typical field service company provides a good idea of how these firms operate:

1. *Client contact.* Custom or syndicated research firm or corporate or ad agency research department alerts field service firm, usually by email, that it wants to conduct a particular type of study (telephone interview, mall interview, etc.).
2. *Interviewer training.* The day the job is to begin, a briefing or training session is held to acquaint interviewers with the requirements of the particular job or questionnaire.
3. *Interviewing status reports.* Daily progress reports are made via email to the client regarding number of interviews completed and costs incurred. These reports permit the client to determine whether the job is on schedule and within budget and allow the field service to advise the client of any problems.
4. *Quality control.* The interviews are edited; that is, specially designed software is used to verify that they were completed correctly.
5. *Ship to client.* Finally, the completed, edited interviews are shipped (typically electronically) to the client.

Most custom research firms rely on field services because it is not cost-effective for them to handle the work themselves. There are too many geographic areas to cover, and it is hard to know which areas will be needed over time. On the other hand, field service firms in particular areas maintain a steady work flow by having numerous research firms and corporate and ad agency research departments as their clients.

Until about 25 years ago, most field service firms were operated as home businesses. Their major asset typically was a pool of a dozen or so interviewers readily available for assignment. Although field service firms of this type still exist, the trend is toward larger, more professional, and better equipped organizations.

The major field service firm of today has a permanent office. It probably has one or more permanent mall test centers, focus group facilities, a central telephone interviewing facility, as well as other specialized facilities and equipment. A recent trend among field service firms is the establishment of satellite offices in multiple cities.

WAR Stories

Consultant Alan Fine reports that when he worked for a supplier earlier in his career, clients occasionally called and asked if his firm could complete a study and provide a report within a very unreasonable time period. Fine would tell them, "Listen, I have a report on tuna fish, and if you want I'll just replace 'tuna fish' with [the client's product type]. And that's the only way I can get you the report in the time you want it."

Fine indicates that once in a while a client tried to take him up on his offer, with one of them saying, "Okay, but I want a 25 percent discount."

Source: "War Stories: True Life Tales in Marketing Research," by Art Shulman, *Quirk's Marketing Research Review* (April 1998). Reprinted by permission of Art Shulman.

Other Organizations and Individuals

Various organizations and individuals, although not truly a part of the marketing research industry, make a special contribution to it. Included in this group are government agencies at the federal, state, and local levels; university centers of business and economic research; university professors; and research units associated with various industry groups and others. These organizations (with the exception of university professors) serve primarily as sources of extremely valuable and useful data for the marketing research industry. Professors—particularly those who also are marketing research consultants—provide a pool of sophisticated talent that is tapped on an as-needed basis by corporate marketing research departments, companies with no internal marketing research capabilities, custom research firms, and others.

The role of various government agencies is important, though they serve primarily as providers of secondary data. Specific examples of such agencies and the types of data they provide are presented and discussed in Chapter 4.

The Impact of the Internet on the Marketing Research Industry

The Internet has been responsible for the emergence of new cybermarketing research and service firms. The Web also has changed the way some old-line marketing research service firms deliver their products.

Cybermarketing Research Firms

Many new marketing research firms conduct research only via the Internet. A pioneer in this area is Greenfield Online, http://www.greenfieldonline.com, which conducts both quantitative research and qualitative research (research not subject to quantitative analysis). Greenfield claims to have the world's largest Internet-based marketing research panel. A **research panel** consists of a group of individuals who agree to participate in a series of research studies over time. Often, participants receive cash or gifts.

research panel
A group of individuals who agree to participate in a series of research studies over time.

Another Internet-bred marketing research firm is Vividence, http://www.vividence.com, which specializes in providing comprehensive customer insight, via its products and services, for evaluating the effectiveness of Web sites (see Figure 2.2). The firm has customers go to target Web sites; then, using its proprietary software, it evaluates the customers' success at performing tasks at the site and overall customer experience at the site. The site may be the client's own live site, a beta site, or a competitor's site. For example, Drugstore.com had been debating adding a new feature to its site when suddenly a competitor added the proposed feature. Drugstore.com wanted to know the effectiveness of the feature before it added its own version. Vividence conducted marketing research to determine the effectiveness of the competitor's feature and also developed feedback from Drugstore.com's target customers on how the feature could be improved.

Some cyberresearch firms focus on tracking the popularity of Web sites. Media Metrix, the pioneer in this area, now is being challenged by two newcomers—Relevant Knowledge and Net Ratings, Incorporated. Nielsen Media Research, which has been rating television programs for decades, also has joined the battle.

Cybersupport Firms

A number of cyberfirms have been created to support the marketing research function; most provide support in conducting Internet surveys. Perhaps the most popular is WebSurveyor, http://www.websurveyor.com, access to which we make available to you, our readers, via the CD that accompanies this text.

WebSurveyor enables users to create a questionnaire, using either the site's standardized questions or questions they develop to meet their specific needs. Responses to the questionnaire are collected by WebSurveyor. The researcher then is offered a variety of statistical tools that can be used to analyze the data. Designing questionnaires and analyzing data have never been easier!

Cyberdata

Survey Sampling, Incorporated (SSI), founded in 1997, is the most cost-effective and reliable source of samples of all types. With SSI-SNAP software, a marketing research company can order a very specific type of sample online—for example, males, 25–35 years of age, living in Florida, with a college degree. Their names and addresses are then delivered electronically to the research firm over the Internet.

Claritas, one of the world's largest providers of segmentation research information, also maintains one of the largest databases on American consumers and businesses. The company now offers Internet user–oriented software, which enables clients to access and analyze Claritas's databases and then apply that information to business decisions.

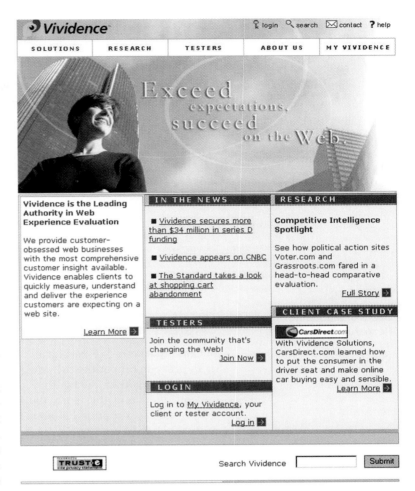

Users of Marketing Research

Now that you are familiar with providers of marketing research, let's look at the other side of the coin: research users. There is a very good possibility that any future encounters that you, as a businessperson, have with marketing research will be as a research user. Figure 2.3 shows the various types of marketing research clients. Despite the importance of nonmarketing, *internal* clients to the success of an organization, some firms' research departments have paid little attention to their specific marketing information needs. As you might expect, these poorly served clients have demonstrated little interest in marketing research information. It has been our experience that the most successful marketing research departments and firms are those committed to the complete satisfaction of all their clients. Let's take a closer look at the types of information these various clients need and use.

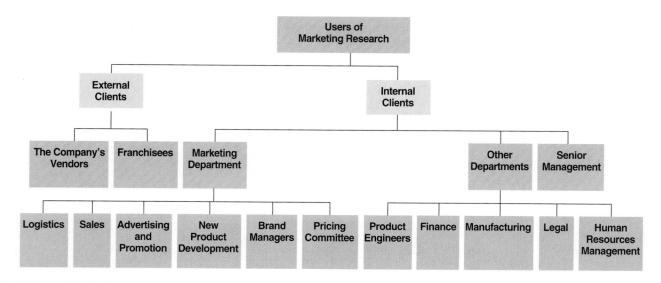

Figure 2.3

Users of Marketing Research

External Clients

Because marketing research can be a valuable source of information about new or improved competitive advantages and because such information is often very expensive to gather, data gathered by a firm's research department is rarely circulated outside of the firm. Many firms don't provide any information to outsiders, such as suppliers. However, those that do usually find that it is to their mutual benefit.

strategic partnership
An alliance formed by two or more firms with unique skills and resources to offer a new service for clients, provide strategic support for each firm, or in some other manner create mutual benefits.

Vendors   Manufacturers are moving into **strategic partnerships** with their vendors in order to implement just-in-time manufacturing. These alliances are based on fully integrated manufacturer–supplier logistics systems that get the component to the assembly line just when it is needed. The result is little or no raw materials inventory and significantly reduced carrying costs. The backbone of this system is shared information. Large retailers, such as Wal-Mart, have such relationships with their major vendors.

Within the framework of strategic partnering, marketing research information is fed back to a manufacturer's suppliers when consumers voice opinions about a component on the manufacturer's customer satisfaction surveys. For example, if Pioneer was supplying radios for Honda automobiles and customers were complaining about how difficult a certain model was to program, this research information would be shared with Pioneer. In one case, a major retail chain commissioned a study on changes in customer preferences for Christmas-related items such as gift wrap, cards, artificial trees, and ornaments, to help its suppliers of production materials understand the importance of making specific product changes and to provide guidance in making those changes.

Franchisees   Most major franchisors of consumer goods and services provide marketing research data to their franchisees. Perhaps the most common way of gathering data is from *mystery shoppers.* A mystery shopper, posing as a customer, observes how long it takes to be waited on and/or make a purchase, the courtesy of the clerks, the cleanliness of the operation, and whether his or her purchase or order was properly prepared. Mystery shopping is discussed in detail in Chapter 7.

Franchisors also share marketing research information with their franchisees to support certain recommendations or actions. When McDonald's suggests to a franchisee that a restaurant be remodeled in a particular style, it

A major retail chain commissioned a study on changes in customer preferences for Christmas-related items in order to help suppliers understand the need for product change and what product changes to make.

will show research data indicating that the building is perceived as out-of-date or old-fashioned. Other data might reveal which theme or style is preferred by current customers. When Burger King launches a major new promotional campaign, it may share with franchisees research data showing that the selected campaign theme was preferred by customers and noncustomers over alternative themes.

Internal Clients

Marketing Managers   Virtually every manager within an organization will, at some point, be a user of marketing research information. However, marketing managers use research data more than any other group. Recall that the marketing mix consists of decisions regarding products or services, promotion, distribution, and pricing. Marketing research helps decision makers in each of these areas make better decisions. Product managers, for example, begin by using research to define their target market. In some cases, managers use research to determine the heavy users of their product within the target market. Marketing research revealed that heavy users of Miracle Whip consume 550 servings, or 17 pounds, of the product a year. These data were used to target a $30 million promotional campaign to core users, telling them not to "skip the zip." As a result, Miracle Whip's market share went up 2.1 percent, to $305 million annual sales.[7] The ad campaign also was thoroughly tested for effectiveness by marketing research before it was launched.

New product development managers are among the heaviest users of marketing research. From qualitative research techniques that generate product ideas to concept testing, product prototype testing, and then test marketing, marketing research is the key to creating a new product. For example, Post's research on cereals had always shown that bananas are America's favorite cereal fruit. Therefore, why not a banana-flavored cereal? Post's new product manager concocted cereals with dried banana pieces, but they failed marketing research taste tests. Further research, conducted to explain why this happened, uncovered the fact that consumers saw no reason to buy a cereal with preserved bananas, as the fresh fruit is quite cheap year-round. If consumers wanted a banana-flavored cereal, they'd peel a banana and make one on the spot. One day, the new product manager had an inspiration: Consumers had said that they liked banana nut bread; it conjured up thoughts of something delicious that grandma used to make. The manager had Post's labs create a new cereal for test marketing in consumers' homes, where it received very high consumer test scores. Thus, Banana Nut Crunch, Post's hottest new cereal, was born.[8] It is solely a product of marketing research, created from the initial concept of a new product manager.

Marketing research also plays an important role in the distribution function. It is used to choose locations for new stores and to test consumer reactions to internal store design fixtures and features. Banana Republic, for example, has relied on marketing research to create the right atmosphere in its stores.

Within larger organizations, pricing decisions are usually made by committees composed of representatives from marketing, finance, production, and perhaps other departments. A recent marketing research study conducted by Ford Motor Company took a look at some of the new ideas generated by its engineers in order to determine first whether target customers were interested in a particular feature and then, if the concept had appeal, whether consumers would pay the suggested retail price. The research was conducted in both the United States and the United Kingdom. Twenty-eight new technology features were evaluated using computer-aided multimedia personal interviewing on desktop computers (see Table 2.4). Video descriptions were integrated with a computerized quantitative questionnaire for all feature evaluations. Qualitative research (see Chapter 5) was conducted to clarify customer likes and dislikes of specific features.

Some concepts were perceived as a bit "gimmicky" or just "something else to break." For example, Fingerprint Passive Entry was not perceived as a benefit over current remote keyless entry systems. On the other hand, features that are inexpensive but offer high utility appeared to be desirable. Examples include the Sun Tracking Visor and the Infinite Door Check. As might be expected, consumers overestimated the manufacturer's target retail price for some items and underestimated it for others. Correspondingly, consumers were willing to pay the manufacturer's suggested retail price for some features but not for others.[9]

Top Management   Senior management uses strategic marketing research to help plan the strategic vision, mission, and long-term allocation of resources for the organization. Sears steadily lost market share and profits during the 1980s through the late-1990s. "We didn't know who we wanted to serve," concedes CEO Arthur C. Martinez. "That was a huge hole in our strategy. It was not clear on what basis we thought we could win against the competition."

A major strategy overhaul led to the disposal of nonretail assets and a renewed focus on Sears's core business. Under Martinez, Sears renovated dowdy stores, upgraded women's apparel, and launched a new ad campaign designed to engineer a major turnaround at the department store giant. But Martinez had to prove he could make the business grow—a tough assignment, since Sears was essentially locked into relatively cramped, mall-based stores. Martinez enlisted Slywotsky's Corporate Decisions to help Sears create a new future. "What I liked most about them is that they came at it from a customer perspective," says Martinez.

Table 2.4

Ford's Marketing Research on Sample New Technology Features

Fingerprint Passive Entry
(US $980, reg. power locks—$350
UK £504, central locks—£280)

Fingerprint Passive Entry allows the driver to gain access to vehicles equipped with power locks, without the use of a key. The driver's own fingerprint is used as a unique identification to lock and unlock the vehicle. The vehicle recognizes the driver's fingerprint through the use of a touch pad. To lock the driver's door or all the vehicle's doors, simply touch the pad for half a second. (UK VERSION) Fingerprint Passive Entry is also available for easy trunk or liftgate access. The vehicle can still be locked or unlocked with a key.

Night Vision System
(US $2,100/UK £1,400)

The Night Vision System enhances driver visibility at night without causing glare to oncoming drivers. The system uses infrared headlamps to illuminate the road ahead. Sensors form an image of the road on a transparent display which lowers into the driver's view. An enhanced image of the road ahead is displayed on the screen, improving visibility.

Sun Tracking Visor
(US $42/UK £35)

The Sun Tracking Visor slides along a track from the inside rearview mirror to the edge of both front side doors, providing more accurate coverage. This feature is easy to use and provides a wide range of coverage.

Front Impact Warning
Indicator Light and Tone (US $420, UK £210)
Indicator Light and Voice (US $420/UK £210)
Indicator Light and Brake Tap (US $490/UK £252)

The Front Impact Warning System alerts drivers when approaching another vehicle or object. Sensors located in the bumper detect obstacles in front of the vehicle. The Front Impact Warning System combines an indicator light and audible tone to alert the driver: a combined indicator light and voice warning, or a combined indicator light and automatic brake tap.

Infinite Door Check
(US $35/UK £14)

The Infinite Door Check holds the door at any open position selected. When in a cramped parking space or on an inclined surface, the door can be stopped at any position without bumping the vehicle next to you.

Skin Temperature Sensor
(US $28, reg. ATC—$245
UK £14, reg. ATC—£420)

The Skin Temperature Sensor can be added to vehicles equipped with automatic temperature control to automatically cool the temperature inside the vehicle. The Skin Temperature Sensor uses an interior infrared sensor to measure a face's skin temperature. The sensor adjusts the fan and air conditioning to cool the vehicle's interior, until the skin temperature is within a normal range.

Source: Courtesy of Ford Motor Company. (Prices are not actual.)

"Strategy can sometimes be this inside-out, self-absorbed self-examination process. But they have an outside-in view of strategy. I was mightily taken with that, because one of the things that got the company in trouble was its lack of focus on the customer."

Extensive customer research discovered high levels of brand loyalty to Sears's hardware lines. The research also suggested that by segmenting the do-it-

Marketing research helped Gatorade position its product toward those who use it most often—men between the ages of 19 and 44. Go to http://www.gatorade.com to see if the company positions its Web site for this demographic.

yourself market and focusing on home projects with a low degree of complexity—say, papering a bathroom or installing a dimmer switch—Sears could avoid a major competitive collision with Home Depot and other home improvement giants. Marketing research showed that Sears customers desire convenience more than the depth of product line offered by such stores.

After successfully testing the concept of hardware outlets, Martinez now is making a billion-dollar capital bet that Sears can grow in this new market. He hopes to have 1,000 freestanding, 20,000-square-foot hardware stores built in five years.[10] To date, market penetration has been slow because of heavy competition.

Other Internal Users From time to time, other individuals besides marketing managers and senior management find a need for marketing research. As discussed earlier, Ford's engineers sometimes invent new items for which demand must be assessed. Ford's marketing research, however, feeds engineering management a steady stream of consumer desires and dislikes. Manufacturing also receives continual feedback, from customer satisfaction surveys, about loose-fitting door panels, balky sunroof openers, and the like.

Finance departments use test market data to forecast revenue streams for one to three years. Similarly, repositioning research helps financial managers forecast revenue spurts from older products. Originally, Gatorade was promoted as a drink for competitive athletes. Marketing research found that its main users were men, aged 19–44, who understood the product, had a good perception of what it did, and knew when to drink it. The product was repositioned toward physical activity enthusiasts as a drink that would quench their thirst and replenish the minerals lost during exercise better than other beverages did. The new positioning dramatically increased sales.

Human resource managers may call on marketing research to survey employees about a variety of topics. Quality customer service requires that employees have a positive image of the company, an attitude that they then convey to customers. Firms like Southwest Airlines and NationsBank monitor employee attitudes through survey research.

Legal departments increasingly are relying on marketing research to win over juries. Recently, a San Francisco jury ruled against Kendall-Jackson Winery in its case against E. & J. Gallo Winery. Kendall-Jackson claimed that Gallo copied the design of its Vintner's Reserve label, which features a grape leaf with fall colors, by using a similarly styled logo on the Gallo Turning Leaf line of varietal wines (see Figure 2.4). After a two-week trial and several days of deliberation, the jury found that Gallo had not infringed on Kendall-Jackson's bottle design or trade dress. It also ruled that Gallo had not tried to "palm off" its wine as a Kendall-Jackson product. Kendall-Jackson was asking for $30 million in damages, but the jury awarded none.[11] For more detailed information about the case, visit http://www. ipmag.com/moskin.html.

Marketing research plays a major role in such trials by supporting or disproving consumer confusion between brands. When customer attitudes and impressions are important in deciding a court case, lawyers are turning to marketing research to prove their positions.

The Growing Role of Strategic Partnering

Marketing research is becoming a team effort between supplier and client/user. Under pressure from clients and the cost of increasingly sophisticated technology, research companies are forming strategic alliances; that is, they are sharing data or capabilities as a cost-effective way to grow. The trend toward strategic partnering—even with competitors—will continue, industry executives says.

"The '90s were the decade of the strategic alliance agreement" said Tom Daley, president of Spectra Marketing, Chicago. "The technology is so expensive and leadership positions so vulnerable that it's the way business has to go. It used to be that when you introduced a new [research] product or service, it was two or three years before everyone matched it. Now Nielsen can have it in the marketplace next week. So everyone's asking 'How can I get smarter faster?' And strategic alliances are the answer."[12]

Spectra, a geodemographic research company founded in 1988, has developed its customer base through a series of strategic alliances. It has deals with several major companies, including Information Resources Incorporated (IRI), Claritas Corporation, Market Facts, and Donnelly Marketing's Carol Wright unit. IRI has been particularly active in forming alliances, having made deals with Arbitron Company, Citicorp. VideOCart, and Simmons Marketing Research. The latter partnership combines IRI's data on who buys what in the United States with *Simmons Magazine* readership data, enabling the partnership to develop indices about what products appeal to magazine readers. "In 1979, we introduced BehaviorScan on an investment of a few million dollars. You couldn't even begin to think of duplicating that system for anywhere near that cost," said

Figure 2.4

A Case in Which Marketing Research Did Not Support the Claim of Consumer Confusion

Source: (left) Reproduced with permission of Kendall-Jackson Winery, Ltd., all rights reserved. (right) © E. & J. Gallo Winery, Modesto, California. TURNING LEAF and the leaf label design are registered trademarks of E. & J. Gallo Winery. All rights reserved. Reprinted by permission.

Global ISSUES

The Expanding Universe of Marketing Research

MOST MAJOR BUYERS AND USERS OF RESEARCH HAVE AN INternational dimension to their business. This often involves regional or global brands, and much of the supply-side has evolved to provide not only multi-country coordination but also a more consistent research offer country-by-country.

The marketing research industry has been showing annual real growth of 5–10% in market economies; much higher in emerging markets. The current position is a world research market of around $11 billion in which Europe has become the biggest player and, together with the U.S., still accounts for more than 80% of global expenditures [see figure].

Relative to the size of the main national economies, Japan has a small research market and the U.K. a very large one.

Who's doing the spending? Packaged goods remain, by far, the largest sector (approximately 40%) and the remainder divides largely between healthcare; media; consumer durables/automotive; consumer services; business to business and government-regulated industries.

Globalization and Entwining

I don't think that global consolidation has yet run its course. Also, as more global research businesses emerge so they will face transnational management challenges already addressed by our clients through various forms of matrix management. This will also involve an increasing demand for truly multi-cultural people (not necessarily great linguists) who can live with a high level of ambiguity in their professional lives.

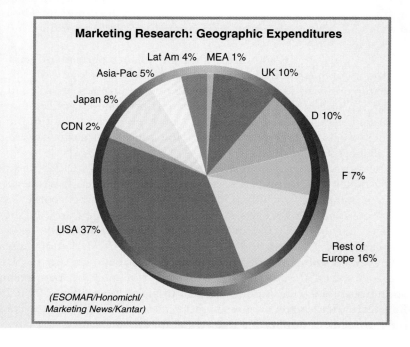

Marketing Research: Geographic Expenditures

Lat Am 4% MEA 1% UK 10%
Asia-Pac 5%
Japan 8%
CDN 2%
D 10%
F 7%
USA 37%
Rest of Europe 16%

(ESOMAR/Honomichl/ Marketing News/Kantar)

Some geographic specialization and division of labor is to be expected too. For example, some of the world's best software developers are in India; and they are cheap and speak English.

By entwining, I mean we will see more cooperation between competitors, as in many other industries. This can take the form of joint ventures; franchising; licensing; project collaboration; strategic alliances . . . So, we'll be kissing and punching at the same time!

Contacts

Associated with some of the other trends I've mentioned is the growing number of major contracts which are often multi-country and span several years. Industry contracts, especially in the market and media measurement area, are not new but I'm referring here to proprietary studies for a client who may put out to competitive tender all its consumer services or brand tracking work across, say, 20 countries for the next three years.

Such multi-million dollar research programs provide major revenue and morale boosts to research companies when won but can have a drastic effect if cancelled or not renewed. The staffing and organizational impacts are much closer to an advertising agency's winning and losing accounts.[13] ■

former IRI Chairman-CEO Gian Fulgoni. "The cost of dong business and the complexity of the business are driving the trend to strategic alliances."[14]

In a strategic partnership, the client and the research firm work together on a forward-looking and ongoing basis. A partnering relationship establishes a defined set of activities for which a research firm provides services, without bidding project by project. Services provided may include data collection, product- or customer-tracking systems, or any research activity in which the firm may have special expertise or productive capability.

About half of all large marketing research departments engage in strategic partnering with research suppliers.[15] Strategic partnerships are most common among service companies and consumer package goods manufacturers. The advantages of this type of partnering include better coordination of effort and increased productivity as the supplier develops intimate knowledge of the research's needs and its customers. The research user, in turn, can concentrate its resources on a client's projects rather than on selling and making proposals.

Global Marketing Research Trends

Strategic partnering is not just an American phenomenon; it is occurring worldwide. The predominant buyers of global marketing research are the world's big multinational companies. As these organizations grow and their strategies become more comprehensive, they require an ongoing strategic counseling relationship rather than one characterized by a string of individual projects. Research suppliers that hope to capitalize on global strategic partnerships will have to have offices in a number of countries (or at least a local presence). The suppliers also must have the personnel and expertise to conduct global research studies, combined with a high level of technical expertise in the home office. Finally, a global marketing research supplier must possess a knowledge of international marketing. Philip Barnard, former chairman of Kantar, one of the largest marketing research firms in the world (with offices in over 40 countries), discusses several trends he foresees in the preceding Global Issues feature.

Summary

This chapter focuses on the types of firms that form the marketing research industry and the functions each performs. The marketing research industry is structured as follows:

1. Corporate marketing research departments, found in major firms such as Kraft General Foods and Ralston Purina
2. Advertising agencies, such as J. Walter Thompson and Grey Advertising
3. Research suppliers
    a. Custom, or ad hoc, research firms, which handle customized marketing research projects that address specific problems for individual clients
    b. Syndicated service firms, which collect and offer for sale data of general interest; these companies are prominent in the media audience and scanner data research fields
4. Field service firms, which collect data

Government agencies, university business centers, university professors, and industry research groups also serve as suppliers of research data.

Users of marketing research can be further categorized as external or internal to the firm. External users include company vendors and franchisees. The primary internal user of marketing research is the marketing department, which seeks data for decision making in such areas as logistics, sales, promotions, new product development, brand management, and pricing. Other internal groups and departments using marketing research are senior management, product engineers, finance, manufacturing, human resources management, and legal.

The Internet has had a profound impact on the marketing research industry. New cyberresearch firms have been created, including support firms that aid researchers in creating questionnaires online. Many old-line marketing research support organizations also deliver their product via the Internet.

A key trend in today's marketing research industry is strategic partnering, in which two or more firms form an alliance for their mutual benefit and the benefit of their clients.

Key Terms & Definitions

custom, or **ad hoc, research firms**
Companies that carry out customized marketing research to address specific projects for corporate clients.

syndicated service research firms
Companies that collect, package, and sell the same general market research data to many firms.

field service firms   Companies that only collect survey data for corporate clients or research firms.

research panel   A group of individuals who agree to participate in a series of research studies over time.

strategic partnership   An alliance formed by two or more firms with unique skills and resources to offer a new service for clients, provide strategic support for each firm, or in some other manner create mutual benefits.

Questions for Review & Critical Thinking

1. Compare and contrast custom and syndicated marketing research firms.
2. What is the role of field service firms in marketing research?
3. Describe the levels of the marketing research industry.
4. List several key characteristics of corporate marketing research departments.
5. Discuss the various project offerings of syndicated service firms.
6. Define strategic partnering. Why has it become so prominent in the marketing research industry?
7. Divide the class into groups of five. Each group should select one section of the city in which the course is being taught (or the closest large city) and determine the zip codes for this section of the city. Next, go to http://www.claritas.com and follow the instructions for getting Prizm profiles by zip code. Each group should then discuss the marketing profile for its section of the city.

Working the Net

1. Compare the offerings of two marketing research firms, DSS Research and Burke Incorporated, by visiting their Web sites at http://dssresearch.com and http://www.burke.com.
2. Research International, which is part of the Kantar group, is a major international marketing research firm, with offices in 54 countries. Go to its Web site at http://www.research-int.com and report on its global research capabilities.

Real-Life Research • 2.1

ACNielsen Corporation

ACNielsen Corporation (ACN) in Stamford, Connecticut was founded in 1923. Its annual revenues are over $1.5 billion.

ACN, with about 20,700 full-time employees in offices in 80 countries and customers in more than 100 countries, provides market information, research and analysis to the consumer products and service industries in four areas:

- *Retail Measurement Services* provides continuous tracking of consumer purchases at POs via scanning and in-store audits in food, drug and other retail outlets in more than 80 countries. In the United States and other countries, ACN's Scantrack services provide information on actual purchases, market shares, distribution, pricing, merchandising and promotional activities on a weekly basis. ACNielsen EDI provides motion-picture industry clients with continuous tracking of box-office receipts, gathering them from over 45,000 movie screens in 11 countries.
- *Consumer Panel Services* tracks the buying behavior and demographics of over 126,000 households through purchase panels in 18 countries. In the United States, a panel of 52,000 households uses in-home scanners to record buying behavior and shopping patterns from a variety of outlets including warehouse clubs, convenience stores, supermarkets, independent drugstores, mass merchandisers and bookstores. Other methods of data collection, which vary by country, include diaries, cash register receipts and in-home interviewing.
- *Customized Research Services* is available in more than 60 countries (primarily in Asia Pacific, Western Europe and emerging markets) and includes quantitative and qualitative studies delivering information and insights into consumer attitudes and purchasing behavior. Other studies measure customer satisfaction, brand awareness and advertising effectiveness. Simulated test marketing services are used to launch new products or reposition existing brands.
- *Media Measurement Services* provides information on international television and radio audiences as well as advertising expenditure and print readership measurement. This information serves as the principal currency for negotiating advertising placement and rates. TV ratings are available in 18 countries outside the United States and Canada, radio ratings in 12 markets and advertising expenditure measurement in 31 markets.[16]

Questions

1. Who are the primary customers for each area served by ACN?
2. Would you like to work for ACN? If so, in which area? Why?
3. What other areas of research do you think ACN might enter in the future?

Real-Life Research • 2.2

Maritz Marketing Research Goes Global

Maritz Marketing Research Inc., Fenton, Mo., recently announced partnerships with six European research firms. Going global is a "defensive strategy at this point," said Ron Lipovsky, company president. Bigger research companies, and Maritz is one of them, know that if they can't provide their clients with data from around the world that's comparable to what they're getting in the U.S., those clients will find a company that can.

In the past, Maritz had lined up partners on a project-by-project basis, said Lipovsky. "The benefit [of the new partnerships] for clients is that we've established good, strong working relationships with these companies. That should reduce the number of communication problems" and ensure that "common practices are followed all the way through."

All of the partners are expected to adhere to a common code of ethics and protocols. In many areas, for example, single entry of data is acceptable, but because Maritz believes the error rate is too high, companies will be required to employ a double-entry system. Maritz is reviewing research companies in Latin America and Asia-Pacific area and hopes to have partnerships established soon.[17]

Questions

1. Do you think that strategic partnering is the best way for U.S. research firms to go global?
2. What problems can arise from strategic partnering?
3. Do you think that it is important for a U.S. firm to be the dominant partner in a strategic relationship? Why or why not?

Chapter Three

Problem Definition and the Research Process

Learning Objectives

To understand the problem definition process.

To learn the steps involved in the marketing research process.

To understand the components of the research request.

To learn the advantages and disadvantages of survey, observation, and experiment research techniques.

To become familiar with how the marketing research process is initiated.

THE NATIONAL CATTLEMAN'S BEEF ASSOCIATION AND THE NATIONAL Pork Producers Council are very concerned about what we eat. For these groups, the fewer the number of vegetarians, the better. Both groups, in fact, try very hard to get you to eat more of their type of meat. Remember, for example, that pork is "the other white meat" and "beef is what's for dinner." Both organizations use marketing research to measure their success. Recently, both have been quite pleased with their efforts.

A SMALL CORE OF THE PUBLIC REMAINS TRUE TO VEGETARIANISM: 1% describe themselves as "strict vegetarians" and 4% as "pretty much vegetarians," about the same as in the past. But, in another sign of relaxing/rethinking diets, there's been a decline in Americans saying they're "careful about how much" meat they eat (20%, down 5 since 1992). In turn, more say they eat meat "quite often and regularly" (73%, up 5). The results suggest that the predicted shift to quasi-vegetarianism as the population ages has been put on hold; apparently, Americans plan to eat meat as long as they can.

VEGETARIANS LOOSEN UP. THOSE WHO ARE CAREFUL ABOUT meat eating or are vegetarians have relaxed their diets: Most still avoid red meat (61%, down marginally from 1994). But far smaller percentages avoid eggs (22%, down 18) and dairy products (13%, down 6).

FOR HEALTH, NOT BUDGET. WHY EAT A VEGETARIAN DIET? Increasingly, the response is that it's "better for your health" (72%, up 7 from 1992 and up 28 from 1978), rather than that it's "a lot more economical" (10%, down 9 from 1992 and down 12 from 1978), say vegetarians and those who watch how much meat they eat. Relatively few cite animal welfare (14%) or world hunger (12%).[1] ■

Many people who restrict their meat eating or are vegetarians have relaxed their diets in recent years. Groups like NCBA and NPPC use such marketing research information to help focus their marketing efforts.

Find out more about NCBA's and NPPC's efforts to promote beef and the "other white meat" at

 http://www.beef.org
http://www.nppc.org

Gathering data about meat eaters versus vegetarians (or any other subject) requires marketing research. Conducting marketing research involves a series of logical steps, beginning with problem definition. What are the steps in the marketing research process? How is the research process initiated? These are the issues we will address in this chapter.

The Critical Importance of Correctly Defining the Problem

Correctly defining the problem is the crucial first step in the marketing research process. If the research problem is defined incorrectly, the research objectives will also be wrong and the entire marketing research process will be a waste of time and money. For example, suppose a new product manager asks a marketing researcher to determine which recipe for a new peppermint and honey salad dressing consumers prefer, and the researcher correctly tells the manager that recipe A is strongly preferred over recipe B. If, in fact, target customers do not like peppermint and honey salad dressing at all, the real problem was never addressed.

The process for defining the problem is shown in Figure 3.1. Note that the ultimate goal is to develop clear, concise, and meaningful marketing research objectives. Such objectives will yield precise decision-making information for managers.

Recognize the Problem or Opportunity

The marketing research process begins with the recognition of a marketing problem or opportunity. As changes occur in the firm's external environment, marketing managers are faced with the questions "Should we change the existing marketing mix?" and, if so, "How?" Marketing research may be used to evaluate products and services, promotion, distribution, and pricing alternatives. In addition, it may be used to find and evaluate new opportunities, in a process called **opportunity identification.**

Let's look at an example of opportunity identification. There have been over 30 million babies born in the United States since 1990. They represent the largest generation since the baby boomers. More impressive than their numbers, though, is their wealth. Because of the increase in single-parent and dual-earner households, kids are making shopping decisions once left to Mom. With their allowance, earnings, and gifts, children 14 and under will spend an estimated $20 billion this year, and they will influence another $200 billion in purchases.[2]

For savvy marketers, these statistics represent an opportunity. Marketing research can hone in and clarify where the best opportunities lie. Walt Disney, for example, is launching a 24-hour kids' radio network based on its marketing research. Sometimes research leads to unexpected results, requiring creative uses

Recognize the problem or opportunity

↓

Find out why the information is being sought

↓

Understand the decision-making environment
(the industry, company, products, and target market)

↓

Use the symptoms to help clarify the problem

↓

Translate the management problem
into a marketing research problem

↓

Determine whether the information already exists

↓

Determine whether the question really can be answered

↓

State the research objectives

Figure 3.1

The Problem Definition Process

of the marketing mix. General Motors recently completed an analysis of "backseat consumers"—that is, children between 5 and 15 years of age. Marketing research discovered that parents often let their children play a tie-breaking role in deciding what car to purchase. Marketing managers, armed with this information, launched several programs. GM purchased the inside cover of *Sports Illustrated for Kids,* a magazine targeted to boys from 8 to 14 years old, for a brightly colored, two-page spread on the Chevy Venture minivan, a vehicle targeted toward young families. GM also sent the minivan into malls and showed Disney movies on a VCR inside the van.

Children 14 and under spend an estimated $20 billion a year. Marketing research can help clarify where the best opportunities lie for marketing to this group.

Of course, marketing research doesn't always deal with opportunities. Managers may want to know, for example, "Why are we losing marketing share?" or "What should we do about Ajax Manufacturing lowering its prices by 10 percent?" In these instances, marketing researchers can help managers solve problems.

Find Out Why the Information Is Being Sought

Large amounts of money, effort, and time are wasted because requests for marketing information are poorly formulated or misunderstood. For example, managers may not have a clear idea of what they want or may not phrase their questions properly. Therefore, marketing researchers often find the following activities helpful:

- Discuss what the information will be used for and what decisions might be made as a result of the research. Work through detailed examples to help clarify the issue.
- Try to get the client or manager to prioritize their questions. This helps sort out central questions from those of incidental interest.
- Rephrase the questions in several slightly different forms, and discuss the differences.
- Create sample data, and ask if such data would help answer the questions. Simulate the decision process.
- Remember that the more clear-cut you think the questions are and the more quickly you come to feel that the questions are straightforward, the more you should doubt that you have understood the real need.

In the In Practice feature, Paul Conner, president of Application, a St. Louis–based marketing research firm, discusses the steps that must be taken to define marketing research objectives that will be management-oriented.

opportunity identification
Using marketing research to find and evaluate new opportunities.

Management-Oriented Applications of Marketing Research

APPLICATIONS REPRESENT THE DECISIONS THAT WILL BE MADE on the basis of the research. Objectives, or information objectives, represent the data that will be needed to support the applications. The key is developing information objectives that relate to the applications. The steps in the applications and objectives process are as follows:

1. *Applications.* Clearly list the decisions you want to make or actions you want to take on the basis of the research.
2. *Application options.* For each decision or action, delineate all clearly existing decision or action options (for some decisions the options may not clearly exist).
3. *Application criteria.* For each decision or decision option, make a statement of the criteria upon which the decision will be based. Don't forget to include whom you need the information from to direct the sampling procedures.
4. *Information objectives.* The decision criteria will directly or indirectly contain the information needed to support the decisions to be made or actions to be taken. Extract and list needed information from the decision criteria.

An example: A product manager for a bank needed to decide whether to use a humorous or serious ad approach for a new product targeting senior citizens. Here's how he proceeded.

Application: Decide what type of ad approach to use for the new product.

Application options: Use humor, or use a serious approach.

Application criteria: Use the approach that, among senior citizens, generates the highest amount of interest in using the new bank product while communicating the name of the bank to at least 75 percent of the target.

Information objectives: To support the applications through their criteria, the research will need to collect the following information from senior citizens about their reactions to the two ad approaches: how interested they are in using the product on the basis of each ad approach, and whether they recall the name of the bank in each approach.[3] ∎

Understand the Decision-Making Environment

Once researchers understand the motivation for conducting the research, often they need additional background information to fully comprehend the problem. This may mean simply talking to brand managers or new product managers, reading company reports, visiting production facilities and retail stores, and perhaps talking with suppliers. If the industry has a trade association, researchers might peruse its Web site for information published by the association. The better the marketing researcher understands the decision-making environment, including the industry, the firm, its products or services, and the target market, the more likely it is that the problem will be defined correctly. This step may be referred to as conducting a **situation analysis.**

Sometimes informed discussions with managers and suppliers and on-site visits aren't enough. **Exploratory research** may be conducted to obtain greater understanding of a concept or to help crystallize the definition of a problem. It is also used to identify important variables to be studied. Exploratory research is preliminary research, not the definitive research used to determine a course of action.

Exploratory research can take several forms: pilot studies, experience surveys, secondary data analysis, and case analysis. (Other techniques used in exploratory research are discussed in Chapter 5.) **Pilot studies** are surveys using a limited number of respondents and often employing less rigorous sampling techniques than are employed in large, quantitative studies.

Nickelodeon, for example, was well aware of the new baby boom and wanted to know what it meant for the network. Exploratory research uncovered that a long-held assumption about kids' attitudes was not accurate: the belief that female images in TV programming generally work with girls but alienate boys. The exploratory research consisted of a small-scale pilot study on the Internet and focus groups in which children were brought together to discuss their attitudes toward television. Like Nickelodeon's research, much exploratory research is highly flexible, with researchers following ideas, clues, and hunches as long as time and money constraints permit. Often ideas are obtained from so-called experts in the field. Nickelodeon, for example, could have spoken with child psychologists.

As the researcher moves through the exploratory research process, a list of marketing research problems and subproblems should be developed. The investigator should identify all factors that seem to be related to the problem area, as these are probable research topics. This stage of problem definition requires a brainstorming-type approach, but one guided by the previous stage's findings. All possibilities should be listed without regard to the feasibility of addressing them via research. Nickelodeon ultimately decided to define the marketing research problem as determining whether a live-action show with girls as the protagonists would appeal to both sexes. Quantitative marketing research results showed that such a program would have dual appeal. Managerial action taken as a result yielded "The Secret World of Alex Mack." The star was female, but the audience was 53 percent male.[4]

A second form of exploratory research is experience surveys. **Experience surveys** involve talking with knowledgeable individuals, both inside and outside the organization, who may provide insights into the problem. Rarely do experience surveys include a formal questionnaire. Instead, the researcher may simply have a list of topics to be discussed. The survey, then, is much like an informal discussion.

Secondary data analysis is another form of exploratory research. Because secondary data analysis is covered extensively in Chapter 4, we will touch on it only lightly here. *Secondary data* are data that have been gathered for some

situation analysis
Studying the decision-making environment within which the marketing research will take place.

exploratory research
Preliminary research conducted to increase understanding of a concept, to clarify the exact nature of the problem to be solved, or to identify important variables to be studied.

pilot studies
Surveys using a limited number of respondents and often employing less rigorous sampling techniques than are employed in large, quantitative studies.

experience surveys
Discussions with knowledgeable individuals, both inside and outside the organization, who may provide insights into the problem.

purpose other than the one at hand. Today, marketing researchers can use the Internet to access countless sources of secondary data quickly and at minimal expense. There are few subjects that have not been analyzed at one time or another. With a bit of luck, the marketing researcher can use secondary data to help precisely define the problem.

Case analysis represents the fourth form of exploratory research. The purpose of **case analysis** is to review information from a few other situations that are similar to the present research problem. For example, electric utilities across America are scrambling to adopt a marketing concept and to become customer-oriented; these utilities are conducting market segmentation research, customer satisfaction studies, and customer loyalty surveys. To better understand the deregulation of the electric utility industry, marketing researchers are examining case studies on the deregulation of the airline industry. Researchers, however, must always take care to determine the relevancy of any case study to the present research problem.

The computer can be a very powerful tool for doing exploratory research. In very large organizations with intranets, the researcher has the capability of determining whether needed or relevant information is available somewhere inside the organization. The corporate marketing research department at Texas Instruments, for example, has developed a powerful intranet application that permits TI managers worldwide to search for past research studies and those currently in progress on the basis of key words. They have immediate online access to a brief description of each study and can send email seeking permission to view the full text of reports on old projects. Permission can be granted electronically via email by the owner of the report (the person who paid for it), and the full text can be accessed online.

More and more organizations are developing similar systems to permit much more effective managerial use of information resources. In large organizations, it is not uncommon for a group in one part of the organization to conduct a research project that might have great value to managers in another part of the organization. Too often, there is no way for one group to find out what another group has already done. Intranet systems like the one at Texas Instruments will help organizations get the most mileage out of their research dollars.

While intranets provide easy access to internal data, the Internet is an invaluable resource for searching tens of millions of external sources for the information needed. At the exploratory stage, a researcher might use any one or several of the online search engines to find information needed. (Names and URLs of popular search engines are provided in Chapter 4.) This type of search not only is much faster than a traditional library search but also provides access to an incredible array of information that is not available in any library. The researcher can perform an Internet search and point out or download the desired information in a matter of hours rather than the days or weeks a standard library search might require. Finally, the researcher can identify a range of discussion or special-interest groups on the Internet that may be relevant to a research project.

Use the Symptoms to Clarify the Problem

Marketing researchers must be careful to distinguish between symptoms and the real problem. A symptom is a phenomenon that occurs because of the existence of something else. For example, managers often talk about the problem of poor sales, declining profits, increased customer complaints, or defecting customers. Each of these is a symptom of a deeper problem. That is, something is causing a company's customers to leave. Is it lower prices offered by the competition? Or is it better service? Focusing on the symptoms and not the true problem is often referred to as the *iceberg principle*. Approximately 10 percent of an iceberg rises out of the ocean; the remaining 90 percent is below the surface. Preoccupied with the obstacle they can see, managers may fail to comprehend and confront the deeper problem, which remains submerged.

Ensuring that the true problem has been defined is not always easy. Managers and marketing researchers must use creativity and good judgment. Cutting through to the heart of a problem is a bit like peeling an onion—you must take off one layer at a time. One approach to eliminating symptoms is to ask "What caused this to occur?" When the researcher can no longer answer this question, the real problem is at hand. For example, when a St. Louis manufacturer of pumps faced a 7 percent decline in sales from the previous year, managers asked, "What caused this?" A look at sales across the product line showed that sales were up or about the same on all items except large, heavy-duty submersible pumps, whose sales were down almost 60 percent. They then asked, "What caused this?" Sales of the pump in the eastern and central divisions were about the same as in the previous year. However, in the western region, sales were zero! Once again they asked, "What caused this?" Further investigation revealed that a Japanese manufacturer was dumping a similar submersible pump in western markets at about 50 percent of the St. Louis manufacturer's wholesale price. This was the true problem. The manufacturer lobbied the Justice Department to fine the Japanese company and to issue a cease and desist order.

Translate the Management Problem into a Marketing Research Problem

Once the true management decision problem has been identified, it must be converted into a marketing research problem. The **marketing research problem** specifies what information is needed to solve the problem and how that information can be obtained efficiently and effectively. The **marketing research objective,** then, is the goal statement, defining the specific information needed to solve the marketing research problem. Managers must combine this information with their own experience and other related information to make a proper decision. Recall that GM's marketing research objective was to determine what role, if any, backseat consumers played in a family's decision to purchase an automobile.

In contrast to the marketing research problem, the **management decision problem** is action-oriented. Management decision problems tend to be much broader in scope and far more general than marketing research problems, which must be narrowly defined and specific if the research effort is to be successful. Sometimes several research studies must be conducted to solve a broad management decision problem. Once GM had determined that children within the target market played a tie-breaker role, the question became "What can be done to influence the tie-breakers?" GM used marketing research to determine that direct advertising to children in the target market and mall promotions would be the best forms of promotional activity.

marketing research problem
A statement specifying the type of information needed by the decision maker to help solve the management decision problem and how that information can be obtained efficiently and effectively.

marketing research objective
A goal statement, defining the specific information needed to solve the marketing research problem.

management decision problem
A statement specifying the type of managerial action required to solve the problem.

In the In Practice feature, Diane Schmalensee and Dawn Lesh warn researchers to make certain that the management problem is clearly defined by the most senior management decision maker.

Determine Whether the Information Already Exists

It often seems easier and more interesting to develop new information than to delve through old reports and data files to see whether the required information already exists. There is a tendency to assume that current data are superior to data collected in the past, as current data appear to be a "fix on today's situation." And because researchers have more control over the format and comprehensiveness of fresh data, they promise to be easier to work with. Yet, using existing data can save managers time and money if such data can answer the research question.

Determine Whether the Question Can Be Answered

When marketing researchers promise more than they can deliver, they hurt the credibility of marketing research. It is extremely important for researchers to

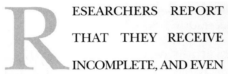

The Importance of Top Management's Definition of the Management Problem

In PRACTICE

RESEARCHERS REPORT THAT THEY RECEIVE INCOMPLETE, AND EVEN incorrect, answers if the person who commissions the study is not the ultimate decision maker. In one case, the commissioning agent (a mid-level manager) said the research was being conducted to learn about the market. In reality, the senior decision maker wanted to know whether version A or B would gain a bigger share of the market. The research did a great job of exploring the boundaries of the market, defining customer segments and their needs, and identifying likely competitors. But the senior decision maker found the research largely irrelevant, because it did not tell him whether to go with version A or B.

While senior decision makers may say they are too busy to talk or insist on delegating the task to someone junior, researchers who have stood firm and insisted on talking to the senior person report the effort is worth it. "First, I asked to meet the [CEO] to discuss the firm's mission and strategy and how the research would help him make better decisions. When that wasn't an option, I wrote up a one-page description of the situation and the research objectives and asked to have the CEO approve it before I designed the research. When he didn't have time to look at it, I said I couldn't waste the firm's resources by starting without clear goals. *Then* I got his full attention. We met and, believe me, the CEO's needs were quite different from what I had been told. I was really glad I had insisted. If I'd waited until the research was done, I'd never have gotten his attention, and the research would have been largely irrelevant."[5] ■

avoid being impelled—either by overeagerness to please or by managerial macho—into an effort that they know has a limited probability of success. In most cases, you can discern in advance the likelihood of success by identifying the following:

- Instances in which you know for certain that information of the type required exists or can be readily obtained.
- Situations in which you are fairly sure, based on similar prior experiences, that the information can be gathered.
- Cases in which you know that you are trying something quite new and there is a real risk of drawing a complete blank.

State the Research Objectives

The culmination of the problem definition process is a statement of the research objectives. These objectives are stated in terms of the precise information necessary to address the marketing research problem/opportunity. Well-formulated objectives serve as a roadmap in pursuing the research project. They also serve as a standard that later will enable managers to evaluate the quality and value of the work by asking "Were the objectives met?" and "Do the recommendations flow logically from the objectives and the research findings?"

Research objectives must be as specific and unambiguous as possible. Remember that the entire research effort (in terms of time and money) is geared toward achieving the objectives. When the marketing researcher meets with a committee to learn the goals of a particular project, committee members may not fully agree on what is needed. We have learned from experience to go back to a committee (or the individual in charge) with a written list of research objectives. The researcher should then ask the manager, "If we accomplish the objectives on this list, will you have enough information to make informed decisions about the problem?" If the reply is yes, the manager should be asked to sign off on the objectives. The researcher should then give the manager a copy and keep a copy for the research files. Putting the agreed-on objectives in writing prevents the manager from saying later, "Hey, this is not the information I wanted." In a busy and hectic corporate environment, such misunderstandings happen more frequently than one might imagine.

Avoiding the Nice-to-Know Syndrome   Even after conducting exploratory research, managers often tend to discuss research objectives in terms of broad areas of ignorance. They say, in effect, "Here are some things I don't know." When General Motors managers say, "I wonder whether the target consumers are thinking about having larger families," they might implicitly be thinking, "When the research results come in, it will be nice to know more about the target market's trend in family size. Once I have more knowledge, then I can make some decisions." Unfortunately, this scenario usually leads to disappointment. There is nothing wrong with interesting findings, but they must also be *actionable*. That is, the findings must provide decision-making information. Accomplishment of a research objective has to do more than reduce management's level of ignorance. Unless all the research is exploratory, it should lead to a decision. Perhaps the

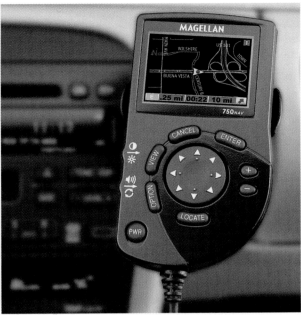

GM marketing research revealed that many middle-class families would be interested in a global positioning system in their cars, like the systems widely available in rental cars today.

best way to assure that research is actionable is to determine how the research results will be implemented. In the case of General Motors, suppose that exploratory research uncovered a number of reports on middle-class families with children (the primary target market). One report described a satellite global positioning system now available on some cars. The system essentially guides the driver from point A to point B by means of video maps, offering an alternative to crumpled road maps, sticky with peanut butter. Other reports noted that families taking a vacation by car tend to bring "a lot of stuff" for over-the-road entertainment and consumption. This could have implications for food storage space, vehicle electronics and plug-ins, and so forth.

Management Decisions and Research Objectives The research objectives for the General Motors case basically would be a restatement, in research terms, of what management needs to know to make a decision. In this study, the research objectives might be as follows:

1. To determine the percentage of families who get lost at least once on a family driving vacation.
2. To determine the receptiveness of minivan owners to a satellite video mapping system at alternative price levels.
3. To determine the demand for a food warmer in the minivan.
4. To determine the demand for a refrigerator in the minivan.
5. To determine the demand for a built-in VCR player in the minivan.
6. To determine the need for additional food/drink holders throughout the vehicle.

Research Objectives as Hypotheses Often researchers state a research objective in the form of a hypothesis. A **hypothesis** is a conjectural statement about a relationship between two or more variables that can be tested with empirical data; it is considered to be plausible, given the available information. A good hypothesis will contain clear implications for testing stated relationships. For example, based on exploratory research, a researcher might hypothesize that the addition of a satellite video mapping system as an exclusive General Motors Venture minivan option at a price of $2,000 will increase GM's share of the minivan market by 4 percent. A second hypothesis might be that customers for the new Venture minivan will be predominately families with adult heads of household between 28 and 45 years of age, two children living at home, and a total family income of $55,000 to $90,000 annually. The development of research hypotheses sets the stage for creating the research design.

hypothesis
A conjectural statement about a relationship between two or more variables that can be tested with empirical data.

The Marketing Research Process

We have just discussed the first step in the marketing research process: identifying the problem/opportunity and stating the marketing research objectives. The other steps in the process are creating the research design, choosing the method of research, selecting the sampling procedure, collecting the data, analyzing the data, writing and presenting the report, and following up on any recommendations that were made as a result of the report (see Figure 3.2). The overview of the process in this section forms the foundation for the remainder of the text. Following chapters examine specific aspects of the marketing research process.

Creating the Research Design

The **research design** is a plan for addressing the research objectives or hypotheses. In essence, the researcher develops a structure or framework to answer a specific research problem/opportunity. There is no single best research design. Instead, different designs offer an array of choices, each with certain advantages and disadvantages. Ultimately, tradeoffs are typically involved. A common tradeoff is between research costs and the quality of the decision-making information provided. Generally speaking, the more precise and error-free the information obtained, the higher the cost. Another common tradeoff is between time constraints and the type of research design selected. Overall, the researcher must attempt to provide management with the best information possible, subject to the various constraints under which he or she must operate. The researcher's first task is to decide whether the research will be descriptive or causal.

research design
The plan to be followed to answer the marketing research objectives.

Descriptive Studies **Descriptive studies** are conducted to answer who, what, when, where, and how questions. Implicit in descriptive research is the fact that management already knows or understands the underlying relationships among

descriptive studies
Research studies that answer the questions who, what, when, where, and how.

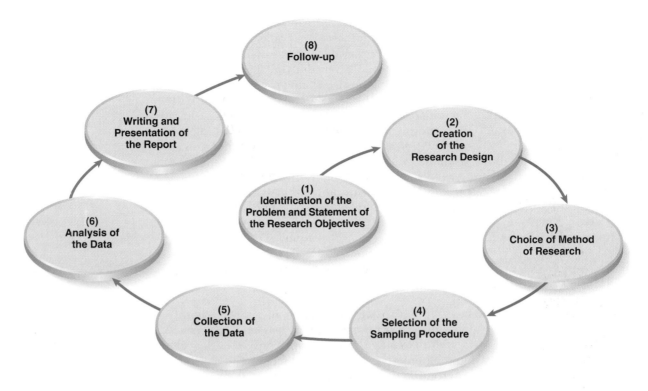

Figure 3.2

The Marketing Research Process

variable
A symbol or concept that can assume any one of a set of values.

causal studies
Research studies that examine whether the value of one variable causes or determines the value of another variable.

dependent variable
A symbol or concept expected to be explained or influenced by the independent variable.

independent variable
A symbol or concept over which the researcher has some control and that is hypothesized to cause or influence the dependent variable.

the variables in the problem. A **variable** is simply a symbol or concept that can assume any one of a set of values.

In the General Motors example, it is assumed, based on the exploratory research, that if Americans on road trips are getting lost with some degree of regularity or would like to know where hotels, motels, and restaurants are located, they will be interested in a satellite video mapping system. Without knowledge of underlying relationships, descriptive research would have little value for decision makers. For example, it would make no sense to perform a research study in the northeastern United States that provided age, income, family size, and educational data on various geographic segments if GM had no idea what effects, if any, these variables might have on the demand for a Venture minivan.

Descriptive research can tell us that two variables, such as advertising and sales, seem to be somehow associated, but it cannot provide convincing evidence that high levels of advertising cause high sales. Because descriptive research can shed light on associations or relationships, it helps the researcher select variables for a causal study.

Causal Studies   In **causal studies,** the researcher investigates whether the value of one variable causes or determines the value of another variable, in an attempt to establish linkage between them. Experiments (see Chapter 8) often are used to measure causality. A **dependent variable** is a symbol or concept expected to be explained or affected by an independent variable. In contrast, an **independent variable** is a variable that the market researcher can, to some extent, manipulate, change, or alter. An independent variable in a research project is a presumed cause of or influence on the dependent variable, the presumed effect. For example, General Motors would like to know whether the level of advertising (independent variable) determines the level of sales (dependent variable).

A causal study for General Motors might involve changing one independent variable (for example, the number of direct mailings over a six-month period to target customers) and then observing the effect on minivan sales. Here, there is an appropriate causal order of events, or **temporal sequence;** the effect follows closely the hypothesized cause. Temporal sequence is one criterion that must be met for causality.

A second criterion for causality is **concomitant variation**—the degree to which a presumed cause (direct-mail promotion) and a presumed effect (minivan sales) occur together or vary together. If direct-mail promotions are a cause of increased minivan sales, then when the number of direct-mail promotions is increased, minivan sales should go up, and when the number of promotions is decreased, sales should fall. If, however, an increase in direct-mail promotions does not result in an increase in minivan sales, the researcher must conclude that the hypothesis about the relationship between direct-mail promotions and minivan sales is not supported.

An ideal situation would be one in which sales of minivans increased markedly every time General Motors increased its direct-mail promotions (up to a saturation level). But, alas, we live in a world where such perfection is rarely achieved. One additional bulk mailing might bring a small increase in sales and the next mailing a larger increment, or vice versa. And, during the next six-month period, an increase in direct-mail promotions might produce no increase or even a decline in sales.

Remember, even perfect concomitant variation would not prove that A causes B. All the researcher could say is that the association makes the hypothesis more likely.

An important issue in studying causality is recognizing the possibility of **spurious association,** in which other variables are actually causing changes in the dependent variable. In an ideal situation, the researcher would demonstrate a total absence of other causal factors. However, in the real world of marketing research, it is very difficult to identify and control all other potential causal factors. Think for a moment of all the variables that could cause sales of GM minivans to increase or decrease—for example, prices, newspaper and television advertising, coupons, discounts, and dealer inventory levels. The researcher may be able to lower spurious associations by trying to hold constant these other factors. Alternatively, the researcher may look at changes in sales in similar socio-economic areas.

temporal sequence
An appropriate causal order of events.

concomitant variation
The degree to which a presumed cause and a presumed effect occur or vary together.

spurious association
A relationship between a presumed cause and a presumed effect that occurs as a result of an unexamined variable or set of variables.

Choosing a Basic Method of Research

A research design, either descriptive or causal, is chosen based on a project's objectives. The next step is to select a means of gathering data. There are three basic research methods: (1) survey, (2) observation, and (3) experiment. Survey research is often descriptive in nature but can be causal. Observation research is typically descriptive, and experiment research is almost always causal.

Scanning bar code information is a means of observation research that is widely used today.

survey research
Research in which an interviewer interacts with respondents to obtain facts, opinions, and attitudes.

observation research
Typically, descriptive research that monitors respondents' actions without direct interaction.

experiments
Research to measure causality, in which the researcher changes one or more variables and observes the effect of the changes on another variable.

Surveys **Survey research** involves an interviewer (except in mail and Internet surveys) who interacts with respondents to obtain facts, opinions, and attitudes. A questionnaire is used to ensure an orderly and structured approach to data gathering. Face-to-face interviews may take place in the respondent's home, a shopping mall, or a place of business.

Observations **Observation research** monitors respondents' actions without direct interaction. The fastest growing form of observation research involves the use of checkout terminals with scanners, which read bar codes to identify the items being purchased and/or the consumer. The potential of observation research is mind-boggling. For example, for years ACNielsen has been using black boxes on television sets to silently siphon off information on a family's viewing habits. But what if the TV is on and no one is in the room? To overcome that problem, ACN is introducing infrared passive "people meters," which identify the faces of family members watching the television program. Thus, if the set is on and no one is watching, that fact will be duly recorded.

Experiments **Experiments** are the third method researchers use to gather data. Experiment research is distinguished by the researcher's changing one or more independent variables—price, package, design, shelf space, advertising theme, or advertising expenditures—and observing the effects of those changes on a dependent variable (usually sales). The objective of experiments is to measure causality. The best experiments are those in which all factors other than the ones being manipulated are held constant. This enables the researcher to infer with confidence that changes in sales, for example, are caused by changes in the amount of money spent on advertising.

Holding all other factors constant in the external environment is a monumental and costly, if not impossible, task. Factors such as competitors' actions, weather, and economic conditions in various markets are beyond the control of the researcher. One way researchers attempt to control factors that might influence the dependent variable is to use a laboratory experiment—that is, an experiment conducted in a test facility rather than in the natural environment. Researchers sometimes create simulated supermarket environments, give consumers scrip (play money), and then ask them to shop as they normally would for groceries. By varying package design or color over several time periods, for example, the researcher can determine which package is most likely to stimulate sales. Although laboratory techniques can provide valuable information, it is important to recognize that the consumer is not in a natural environment; how people act in a test facility may differ from how they act in an actual shopping situation. Experiments are discussed in detail in Chapter 8.

Selecting the Sampling Procedure

A sample is a subset from a larger population. Although the basic nature of the sample is specified in the research design, selecting the sampling procedure is a separate step in the research process. Several questions must be answered before a sampling procedure is selected. First, the population or universe of interest must be defined. This is the group from which the sample will be drawn. It should include all the people whose opinions, behaviors, preferences, attitudes, and so on will yield information needed to answer the research problem—for example, all persons who eat Mexican food at least once every 60 days.

After the population has been defined, the next question is whether to use a probability sample or a nonprobability sample. A **probability sample** is a sample for which every element in the population has a known nonzero probability of being selected. Such samples allow the researcher to estimate how much sampling error is present in a given study. All samples that cannot be considered probability samples are nonprobability samples. **Nonprobability samples** are those in which the chances of selection for the various elements in the population are unknown. Researchers cannot statistically calculate the reliability of a nonprobability sample; that is, they cannot determine the degree of sampling error that can be expected. Sampling is the topic of Chapters 12 and 13.

Collecting the Data

Most data collection is done by marketing research field services. Field service firms, found throughout the country, specialize in collecting data through personal and telephone interviewing on a subcontract basis. A typical research study involves data collection in several cities and requires working with a comparable number of field service firms. To ensure that all subcontractors do everything exactly the same way, detailed field instructions should be developed for every job. Nothing should be left to chance; in particular, no interpretations of procedures should be left to the subcontractors.

In addition to doing interviewing, field service firms often provide group research facilities, mall intercept locations, test product storage, and kitchen facilities for preparing test food products. They may also conduct retail audits (counting the amount of product sold from retail shelves).

Analyzing the Data

After the data have been collected, the next step in the research process is data analysis. The purpose of this analysis is to interpret and draw conclusions from the mass of collected data. The marketing researcher may use a variety of techniques, beginning with simple frequency analysis and culminating in complex multivariate techniques. Data analysis will be discussed in Part Four.

Writing and Presenting the Report

After data analysis is completed, the researcher must prepare the report and communicate the conclusions and recommendations to management. This is a key step in the process because a marketing researcher who wants project conclusions acted on must convince the manager that the results are credible and justified by the data collected.

probability sample
A subset of a population that can be assumed to be a representative cross-section because every element in the population has a known nonzero chance of being selected.

nonprobability sample
A subset of a population in which the chances of selection for the various elements in the population are unknown.

The researcher usually will be required to present both written and oral reports on a project. The nature of the audience must be kept in mind when these reports are being prepared and presented. The oral report should begin with a clear statement of the research objectives, followed by an outline of the methodology. A summary of major findings should come next. The report should end with a presentation of conclusions and recommendations for management. In today's fast-paced world of marketing research, long, elaborately written reports are virtually a thing of the past. Decision makers today typically want only a copy of the PowerPoint presentation.

Judging the Quality of a Report   Because most people who enter marketing become research users rather than research suppliers, it is important to know what to look for in a research report. The ability to evaluate a research report is crucial. As with many other items we purchase, the quality of a research report is not always readily apparent. Nor does paying a high price for a project necessarily guarantee superior quality. The basis for measuring a report's quality lies in the research proposal. Does the report meet the objectives established in the proposal? Has the methodology outlined in the proposal been followed? Are the conclusions based on logical deductions from the data analysis? Do the recommendations seem prudent, given the conclusions?

Using the Internet to Disseminate Reports   It is becoming increasingly commonplace for research suppliers and clients to publish reports directly to the Web. All of the latest versions of major word-processing, spreadsheet, and presentation packages have the capability to produce Web-ready material, which simplifies the process of putting reports on the Web. Most companies, such as Texas Instruments, locate this material not in public areas on the Web, but on corporate intranets or in password-protected locations on Web sites. Publishing reports on the Web has a number of advantages:

1. The reports become immediately accessible to managers and other authorized and interested parties worldwide.
2. The reports can incorporate full multimedia presentation, including text, graphs, various types of animation, audio comments, and video clips.
3. The reports are fully searchable. Suppose a manager is interested in any material relating to advertising. Instead of manually scanning a long and detailed report for such mentions, he or she can search the report for comments relating to advertising.

Following Up

After a company has spent a considerable amount of effort and money on marketing research and the preparation of a report, it is important that the findings be used. Management should determine whether the recommendations were followed and, if not, why not. As you will learn in the next section, one way to increase the likelihood that research conducted by a corporate marketing department will be used is to minimize conflict between that department and other departments within the company.

Managing the Research Process

The Research Request

Before conducting a research project, a company like General Motors might require approval of a formal research request. Moderate- and large-size retailers, manufacturers, and nonprofit organizations often use the **research request** as a basis for determining which projects will be funded. Typically, in larger organizations there are far more requests by managers for marketing research information than monies available to conduct such research. Requiring a research request is a formalized approach to allocating scarce research dollars.

It is very important for the brand manager, new product specialist, or whoever is in need of research information to clearly state in the formal research request why the desired information is critical to the organization. Otherwise, the person with approval authority may fail to see why the expenditure is necessary.

In smaller organizations, the communication link between brand managers and marketing researchers is much closer. Their day-to-day contact often removes the need for a formal research request. Instead, decisions to fund research are made on an ad hoc basis by the marketing manager or the director of marketing research.

Completion and approval of the request represent a disciplined approach to identifying research problems and obtaining funding to solve them. The degree of effort expended at this step in the research process will be reflected in the quality of the information provided to the decision maker, because a well-conceived research request will guide the design, data gathering, analysis, and reporting processes toward a highly focused objective. The sections of a formal research request are as follows:

research request
An internal document used by large organizations that describes a potential research project, its benefits to the organization, and estimated costs; it must be formally approved before a research project can begin.

1. *Action.* The decision maker should describe the action to be taken on the basis of the research. This will help the decision maker focus on what information should be obtained and guide the researcher in creating the research design and in analyzing the results.
2. *Origin.* The decision maker should state the events that led to a need for a decision. This will help the researcher understand more deeply the nature of the management decision problem.
3. *Information.* The decision maker should list the questions that she or he needs to have answered to take action. Carefully considering the questions will improve the efficiency of the research.
4. *Use.* This section should explain how each piece of information will be used to help make the actual decision. By giving logical reasons for each part of the research, it will ensure that the questions make sense in light of the action to be taken.
5. *Target groups and subgroups.* By describing those from whom information must be gathered to address the research problem, this section will help the researcher design the sample procedure for the research project.
6. *Logistics.* Time and budget constraints always affect the research technique chosen for a project. For this reason, approximations of the amount of

money available and the amount of time left before results are needed must be included as a part of the research request.

7. *Comments.* Any other comments relevant to the research project must be stated so that, once again, the researcher can fully understand the nature of the problem.

The Request for Proposal

request for proposal (RFP)
A solicitation sent to marketing research suppliers inviting them to submit a formal proposal, including a bid.

The research request is an internal document used by management to determine which projects to fund. A **request for proposal (RFP)** is a solicitation sent to marketing research suppliers inviting them to submit a formal proposal, including a bid. An actual RFP, adapted slightly for the purposes of this text, is shown in Figure 3.3. The RFP is the lifeblood of a research supplier. Receiving it is the initial step in getting new business and, therefore, revenue

A typical RFP provides background data on why a study is to be conducted, outlines the research objectives, describes a methodology, and suggests a time frame. In some RFPs, the supplier is asked to recommend a methodology or even help develop the research objectives. Most RFPs also ask for (1) a detailed cost breakdown, (2) the supplier's experience in relevant areas, and (3) references. Usually, a due date for the proposal will be specified.

Suppliers must exercise care in preparing their proposals in response to the RFP. More than one client has said, "We find the quality of the proposals indicative of the quality of work produced by the firm." Thus, a research supplier that doesn't have the necessary time to adequately prepare a proposal should simply not submit a bid.

What to Look For in a Marketing Research Supplier

Market Directions, a Kansas City marketing research firm, asked marketing research clients around the United States to rate the importance of several statements about research companies and research departments. Replies were received from a wide range of industries, resulting in the following top 10 list of desirable qualities in marketing researchers:

1. Maintains client confidentiality.
2. Is honest.
3. Is punctual.
4. Is flexible.
5. Delivers against project specifications.
6. Provides high-quality output.
7. Is responsive to the client's needs.
8. Has high quality-control standards.
9. Is customer-oriented in interactions with client.
10. Keeps the client informed throughout a project.[6]

The two most important qualities, confidentiality and honesty, are ethical issues; the remaining factors relate to managing the research function and maintaining good communications.

Background

Mega Health has been tracking consumers' awareness and image of our plan on an annual as well as monthly basis for many years. These studies have been conducted for the purpose of understanding our brand awareness, brand image, and brand benchmarking vs. the competition. As we plan for advertising and public communication, we first need to determine how Mega Health is perceived in the marketplace. The annual Brand Image Benchmarking study allows Mega Health to assess its brand image in a competitive context.

Issue

Assess overall Mega Health brand strength by surveying individuals (in MD/DC/VA regions) in the 3rd–4th quarter of 2002, using a version of the current survey instrument.

Objectives

- Assess brand awareness and image of Mega Health in the MD/DC/VA regions.
- Benchmark Mega Health awareness and image vs. competitors in all regions.
- Determine importance of health insurance company/HMO attributes.
- Assess rating of Mega Health and competitor performance on health insurance company/HMO attributes.
- Assess reaction to attributes of Mega Health.
- Profile insured population.
- Create comprehensive brand image analysis.

Methodology

Quantitative telephone survey with the general public and business decision-makers.*

Sample:
- Total interviews: 1,950.
  General public: approx. 1,250 interviews (may need as many as 300 over sample—1,550 total—to improve representation in harder-to-recruit areas). RDD methodology.
  Business decision-makers: approx. 400 interviews.
- List sources and detailed sampling methodology: TBD.
- Quota for the study should be representative of 5 mid-Atlantic regions: Baltimore Metro, DC Metro, Eastern Shore MD, Southern MD, and Western MD (Southern and Western MD may be combined after study completion). Mega Health will provide zip codes in order to delineate regions.

Questionnaire: This study is being conducted for benchmarking and tracking purposes. Thus, the questionnaire that has previously been used to conduct this research has been included (see attachment). Some modifications to this questionnaire may be necessary for improved analysis.

Proposed Timing

Develop RFP for research	8/11/02
Select vendor	8/17/02
Sample and survey adjusted/finalized	8/30/02
Initiate interviews (including recruiting)	9/1/02
Complete interviews	10/4/02
Topline analysis	10/15/02
Final analysis**	11/1/02

We would like to begin the preparation for this study, so please expedite the return of proposals as soon as possible. Thank you for your consideration. Please contact Joe Bedlow at 999-998-7513 (fax: 999-998-7660; email: joebedlow@megahealth.com) with any questions or proposals.

*Sample of general public and decision-makers subject to change. Note: The population from which to sample business decision-makers is typically not very large and can be more difficult to to recruit, especially larger businesses (1000+ employees).

**It is most important that the "general public" sample be completed within this time frame. Business decision-makers' results may be afforded a later date, if needed.

Note: The real company name, contract name, and phone numbers have been disguised.

Figure 3.3

An RFP to Conduct an Image Benchmark Study

Good communications are a necessity. Four of the qualities on the top 10 list—flexibility, responsiveness to clients' needs, customer orientation, and keeping the client informed—are about good communications. A successful marketing research organization requires good communications both within the research company and with clients.

How important is communication? Consider this: Managers spend at least 80 percent of every working day in direct communication with others. In other words, 48 minutes of every hour is spent in meetings, on the telephone, or talking informally. The other 20 percent of a typical manager's time is spent doing desk work, most of which is communication in the form of reading and writing.[7] Communications permeate every aspect of managing the marketing research function.

What Motivates Decision Makers to Use Research Information?

When research managers communicate effectively, generate quality data, control costs, and deliver information on time, they increase the probability that decision makers will use the research information they provide. Yet academic research shows that political factors and preconceptions can also influence whether research information is used. Specifically, the determinants of whether or not a manager uses research data are (1) conformity to prior expectations, (2) clarity of presentation, (3) research quality, (4) political acceptability within the firm, and (5) lack of challenge to the status quo.[8] Managers and researchers both agree that technical quality is the most important determinant of research use. However, managers are less likely to use research that does not conform to preconceived notions or is not politically acceptable.[9] This does not mean, of course, that researchers should alter their findings to meet management's preconceived notions.

Marketing managers in industrial firms tend to use research findings more than do their counterparts in consumer goods organizations.[10] This tendency among industrial managers is attributed to a greater exploratory objective in information collection, a greater degree of formalization of organizational structure, and a lesser degree of surprise in the information collected.

Summary

The process for correctly defining the research problem consists of a series of steps: (1) recognize the problem or opportunity, (2) find out why the information is being sought, (3) understand the decision-making environment, (4) use the symptoms to help clarify the problem, (5) translate the management problem into a marketing research problem, (6) determine whether the information already exists, (7) determine whether the question can really be answered, and (8) state the research objectives. If the problem is not defined correctly, the remainder of the research project will be a waste of time and money.

The steps in the market research process are as follows:

1. Identification of the problem/opportunity and statement of the marketing research objectives
2. Creation of the research design
3. Choice of the method of research
4. Selection of the sampling procedure
5. Collection of data
6. Analysis of data
7. Preparation and presentation of the research report
8. Follow-up

In specifying a research design, the researcher must determine whether the research will be descriptive or causal. Descriptive studies are conducted to answer who, what, when, where, and how questions. Causal studies are those in which the researcher investigates whether one variable (independent) causes or influences another variable (dependent). The next step in creating a research design is to select a research method: survey, observation, or experiment. Survey research involves an interviewer interacting with a respondent to obtain facts, opinions, and attitudes. Observation research, in contrast, monitors respondents' actions and does not rely on direct interaction with people. An experiment is distinguished by the fact that the researcher changes one or more variables and observes the effects of those changes on another variable (usually sales). The objective of most experiments is to measure causality.

A sample is a subset of a larger population. A probability sample is one for which every element in the population has a known nonzero probability of being selected. All samples that cannot be considered probability samples are nonprobability samples. Any sample in which the chances of selection for the various elements in the population are unknown can be considered a nonprobability sample.

In larger organizations, it is common to have a research request prepared after the statement of research objectives. The research request generally describes the action to be taken on the basis of the research, the reason for the need for the information, the questions management wants to have answered, how the information will be used, the target groups from whom information must be gathered, the amount of time and money available to complete the project, and any other information pertinent to the request. The request for proposal (RFP) is the document used by clients to solicit proposals from marketing research suppliers.

Good communications are the foundation of research management and the basis for getting decision makers to use research information. The information communicated to a decision maker depends on the type of research being conducted.

Key Terms & Definitions

opportunity identification Using marketing research to find and evaluate new opportunities.

situation analysis Studying the decision-making environment within which the marketing research will take place.

exploratory research Preliminary research conducted to increase understanding of a concept, to clarify the exact nature of the problem to be solved, or to identify important variables to be studied.

pilot studies Surveys using a limited number of respondents and often employing less rigorous sampling techniques than are employed in large, quantitative studies.

experience surveys Discussions with knowledgeable individuals, both inside and outside the organization, who may provide insights into the problem.

case analysis Reviewing information from situations that are similar to the current one.

marketing research problem A statement specifying the type of information needed by the decision maker to help solve the management decision problem and how that information can be obtained efficiently and effectively.

marketing research objective A goal statement, defining the specific information needed to solve the marketing research problem.

management decision problem A statement specifying the type of managerial action required to solve the problem.

hypothesis A conjectural statement about a relationship between two or more variables that can be tested with empirical data.

research design The plan to be followed to answer the marketing research objectives.

descriptive studies Research studies that answer the questions who, what, when, where, and how.

variable A symbol or concept that can assume any one of a set of values.

causal studies Research studies that examine whether the value of one variable causes or determines the value of another variable.

dependent variable A symbol or concept expected to be explained or influenced by the independent variable.

independent variable A symbol or concept over which the researcher has some control and that is hypothesized to cause or influence the dependent variable.

temporal sequence An appropriate causal order of events.

concomitant variation The degree to which a presumed cause and a presumed effect occur or vary together.

spurious association A relationship between a presumed cause and a presumed effect that occurs as a result of an unexamined variable or set of variables.

survey research Research in which an interviewer interacts with respondents to obtain facts, opinions, and attitudes.

observation research Typically, descriptive research that monitors respondents' actions without direct interaction.

experiments Research to measure causality, in which the researcher changes one or more variables and observes the effect of the changes on another variable.

probability sample A subset of a population that can be assumed to be a representative cross-section because every element in the population has a known nonzero chance of being selected.

nonprobability sample A subset of a population in which the chances of selection for the various elements in the population are unknown.

research request An internal document used by large organizations that describes a potential research project, its benefits to the organization, and estimated costs; it must be formally approved before a research project can begin.

request for proposal (RFP) A solicitation sent to marketing research suppliers inviting them to submit a formal proposal, including a bid.

Questions for Review & Critical Thinking

1. The definition of the research problem is one of the critical steps in the research process. Why? Who should be involved in this process?
2. What role does exploratory research play in the marketing research process? How does exploratory research differ from other forms of marketing research?
3. Give some examples of symptoms of problems and then suggest some underlying real problems.
4. Give several examples of situations in which it would be better to take a census of the population than a sample.

5. Critique the following methodologies and suggest more appropriate alternatives:
   a. A supermarket is interested in determining its image. Cashiers drop a short questionnaire into the grocery bag of each customer prior to bagging the groceries.
   b. To assess the extent of its trade area, a shopping mall stations interviewers in the parking lot every Monday and Friday evening. After people park their cars, interviewers walk up to them and ask them for their zip codes.
   c. To assess the potential for new horror movies starring alien robots, a major studio invites people to call a 900 number and vote yes if they would like to see such movies or no if they would not. Each caller is billed a $2 charge.
6. You have been charged with determining how to attract more business majors to your school. Outline the steps you would take, including sampling procedures, to accomplish this task.
7. What are some sources of conflict between marketing researchers and other managers? How can these be minimized?
8. What are the conditions for causality? Discuss the criteria.
9. Do you think marketing researchers should always use probability samples? Why or why not?
10. What can researchers do to increase the chances that decision makers will use the marketing research information they generate?

Working the Net

1. Go to the Internet and search on "intranet + future." Report your findings to the class.
2. Describe how putting research reports on the Web can benefit managers.

PART 1:
An Introduction to Marketing Research

Real-Life Research • 3.1

The Pursuit of Happiness

Americans want more time to pursue leisure activities. They have higher expectations of their leisure time. They're trying to do more in their leisure time, from surfing the Internet, to going out on the town, to spending money in the consumer marketplace, as shown throughout this issue. And they appear to be attempting to expand their scope of activities while not letting go of traditional pastimes like family and friends. With so much to do and so little time, there appears to be growing demand for products and services that create time in today's high-pace lifestyle—or better yet, make time stand still.

Time Squeeze. Americans want more leisure time. A record 54% of Americans say they don't have "quite as much" or "nearly as much" leisure time as they would like. The percentage saying they don't have enough time is up 8

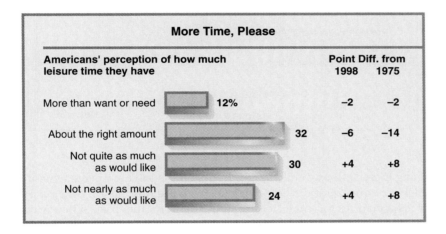

More Time, Please		
Americans' perception of how much leisure time they have	Point Diff. from 1998	1975
More than want or need — 12%	–2	–2
About the right amount — 32	–6	–14
Not quite as much as would like — 30	+4	+8
Not nearly as much as would like — 24	+4	+8

points from 1998, is 7 points higher than the average for the 1990s, and is a whopping 16 points higher than 1975 (which seems to be a bucolic time compared to today's high-paced lifestyle of two-income households, 24-7 business, e-mail, and voice mail). The shift has reduced the ranks of those who are satisfied with the amount of leisure time they have to 44%, down 8 from 1998, down 8 from the 1990s' average, and 16 lower than 1975. Among such leisure-strapped groups as dual-income couples, working women, executives and professionals, and parents, about 70% say they don't have enough leisure time. However, almost every segment is feeling more leisure-deprived than in previous years.

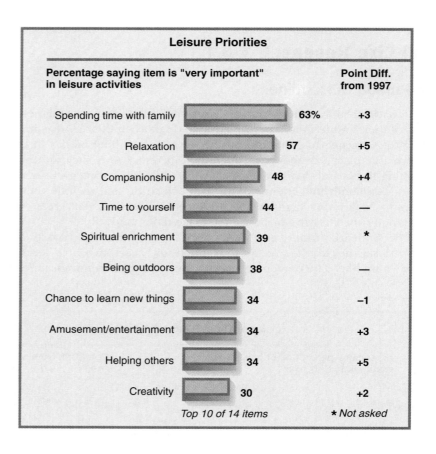

Leisure Priorities		
Percentage saying item is "very important" in leisure activities		**Point Diff. from 1997**
Spending time with family	63%	+3
Relaxation	57	+5
Companionship	48	+4
Time to yourself	44	—
Spiritual enrichment	39	*
Being outdoors	38	—
Chance to learn new things	34	−1
Amusement/entertainment	34	+3
Helping others	34	+5
Creativity	30	+2
Top 10 of 14 items		** Not asked*

Rising Expectations. While longer hours on the job have been a major force in the leisure squeeze of the 1990s, it's far from the only factor. Americans have higher expectations of their leisure time than in the past. They are more inclined to describe various leisure-time priorities as "very important." Spending time with family (63%, up slightly from 1997) remains the number-one leisure-time priority.

The results suggest that consumers are looking more for these features—relaxation, companionship, meaning, excitement—in their leisure-time activities. With the economy good, Americans are back in an expansive mood. Marketers who respond in their products and services will likely be rewarded.[11]

Questions

1. Is this information from an exploratory study? If not, what are the research questions?
2. Do you think this research is causal or descriptive? Defend your answer.
3. How might this information be of value to managers at (a) General Motors, (b) Copper Mountain Ski Resort, (c) Carnival Cruise Lines, and (d) Coleman Products, Inc.? Give examples to reinforce your answers.

Real-Life Research • 3.2

Cessna Aircraft

Cessna Aircraft is one of the largest manufacturers of small, private-business airplanes in the United States. It is always looking for new market opportunities, which may involve cultivating existing segments or developing and exploiting new ones. Recent research by Cessna uncovered that although a very small percentage of the total adult population enrolls in private pilot-training programs, about half of the individuals who enter a training program complete it. And the number of people with pilot's licenses is increasing. Eventually, about one out of five people with a private pilot's license buys a private airplane. Thus, pilot training is an important part of the total market for Cessna and its competitors.

A small percentage of pilots are women. Similarly, a small percentage of the students in training programs are women; this figure has shown only a slight increase in recent years. Moreover, there are very few women instructors in pilot-training programs. A substantial number of women have the necessary skills, time, and income to enroll in and complete the basic training program. Cessna is interested in learning why more women don't enter the program and how the program and/or promotional materials could appeal to and motivate more women to consider or inquire about such programs.

There may be several specific market segments worthy of examination. These include wives of pilots, businesswomen, women who have the income and desire to travel for pleasure, and young women who seek future employment as corporate aircraft pilots. Cessna realizes that the limiting factor may be low levels of interest or motivation and perhaps attitudes toward the desirability of women pilots. But opportunities for women are increasing in many different fields. Cessna therefore believes that a vital market may exist that is not being fully exploited.

Questions

1. What is the management decision problem?
2. Define the marketing research problem(s).
3. Develop the marketing research objectives.
4. Explain how a marketing researcher should use the problem definition process to answer the above questions.

Marketing Research across the Organization

1. How can top management formally integrate marketing research throughout the organization?
2. Strategic planning requires input from all areas of business—production, finance, engineering, etc. What do you see as the role of marketing research in the strategic planning process?
3. Ford Motor wants to make "Quality Job One." Is this just a problem for the production department? If not, what role should marketing research play?

Ethical Dilemma

PowerBase's Search for Respondents

ONE OF THE AUTHORS OF THIS BOOK RECEIVED THE FOLLOWING letter. Only the name of the sender has been changed.

Dear Valued Consumer,

I need your help! And I am willing to pay you handsomely for it. Let me explain . . . .

My name is Joyce Smith and I am the Vice President of Consumer Research for PowerBase, a national company that specializes in market research.

What is market research? That's just a fancy way of saying that people pay us to find out what people like you think about their products.

Which brings me back to you. I would like to pay you to test new products as well as to give me your comments and opinions on a variety of consumer goods and services. I am willing to compensate you greatly for your time.

Here are a couple of quick examples that will explain in greater detail the type of work that we do and how you would fit into the picture . . . .

When Sony, the world's largest manufacturer of electronic goods, is considering launching a new stereo system into the marketplace they first need to be sure that they have done a good job in designing not only the machine, but the packaging and the user's manual as well. So to get consumer feedback Sony would ship my company one thousand of these new stereo systems and we would distribute them to people across the country, like you, that fit various demographic groups.

You would try the stereo system for 30 days, then fill out a simple questionnaire. Based on the results of this questionnaire Sony gains valuable information that helps them improve the packaging and the user's manual as well as valuable insights that help them fine-tune the design of subsequent models.

And what happens to that new stereo system? You would keep it, absolutely free, your payment for providing Sony with valuable marketing information.

This is just one example of the type of market research that you could participate in. Here's another example . . . .

The country's largest airline, Delta Airlines, regularly does market research to see how they're doing servicing their customers. From the time that a reservation is made until the trip is completed, they want to know how well they did in providing good customer service. So they would send us several thousand airline vouchers good for free airline travel. We would distribute these vouchers, along with a detailed questionnaire, to people like you across the country. You would be given your choice of travel; you might want to travel alone, or with your family. You might choose to travel for pleasure or perhaps on business. When the trip was completed you would simply fill out the questionnaire and mail it back to us.

And the cost of the airline ticket? They are free, compliments of the airline in exchange for your valuable feedback about the customer service you received.

Here's one more example of the type of market research that you could participate in . . . .

General Mills, one of the world's largest manufacturers of breakfast cereals, might want to evaluate their advertising. So they would send us five thousand video tapes. Each ten minute tape would contain television ads for breakfast cereals. You would watch the tape, then fill out a questionnaire and mail it back to us.

Then we would send you a $50 check for providing General Mills with valuable marketing information with which they can then fine-tune their breakfast cereal advertising.

That's all there is to it! You can get cash and free products just for giving your opinions. Seem too good to be true? Not really, these companies make millions, and they are happy to spend hundreds of thousands of dollars with companies like ours in order to learn how to make millions more.

In the first example you could get a free stereo system, in the second example you could get free airline tickets, and in the third example you could get fifty bucks! Not bad for just telling someone what you think of their product!

So why do I need your help? Because business is booming and I don't have enough people in my consumer database to service all the requests that I will get from my clients over the next twelve months.

That's why I am inviting you to become one of my "Market Research Analysts," an "MRA" for short! That's a fancy term that was coined by the *National Association of Market Research Analysts* to describe people who regularly provide consumer information to market research organizations. Being an MRA is fun and profitable!

You might think that we would be inundated with requests from people that want to be MRA's. And actually, we are, but we have to turn most of them down. The problem is that we need to recruit people that fit specific criteria or that match up with specific demographic groups. You see, when our clients want consumer information, they typically specify particular groups of people that they want information from. We punch that criteria into our database of MRA's to find people that match up.

Which brings me to how I chose to invite you to become a PowerBase MRA. I purchased your name from a list broker, and boy were you expensive! I told the Broker that I needed people from across the country that were health conscious or who enjoy traveling. They punched those criteria into a computer and generated a list for me. Somehow you made it onto this list, perhaps because of products you purchased in the past or magazines that you subscribe to. I hope they hit their mark with you!

People in these demographic groups are the most requested MRA's that I have. I have national companies right now that are willing to pay people in this group one hundred dollars just for completing a survey!

As one of the oldest market research organizations in the country, we are privileged to have worked for hundreds of major corporations across the country. Over the next twelve months we'll pay out over one million dollars to our MRA's for completed surveys. We'll send out over ten million dollars worth of free merchandise to our MRA's to evaluate. Over the next twelve months our MRA's will go on free cruises, test drive brand new cars free for six months, test and keep new kitchen appliances, and consume over one hundred thousand free meals at restaurants across the country. And this is just a tiny fraction of the types of opportunities that await our MRA's. Like I said, it's fun and profitable to be an MRA!

I hope you will accept my invitation to become a PowerBase MRA! If you decide you want to become an MRA today, then as early as a week from now I can be sending you your first consumer survey to fill out. All you have to do is return the completed survey to PowerBase and we will mail you a check for $100 compliments of our clients!

So how do you become an MRA? It's simple! Just fill out the form on the address panel of this letter, then mail the entire panel back to us. When we receive it one of our database managers will input you into our national MRA database, then he or she will contact you for the purpose of asking you about a dozen questions.

The way that you answer these questions will determine which demographic subgroups you will be listed under in the database. As an example, you will be asked if you have any children living at home with you; If you don't, you wouldn't receive offers from manufacturer's of children's products. You can also choose to not answer any of the demographic questions in which case you will simply be listed under the subgroup heading of "General."

Our clients are interested only in high quality market research. That is why our clients specify in their contracts with us that we are to use only members of the *National Association of Market Research Analysts* (NAMRA) to provide us with consumer information. The association has a code of ethics that encourages its members to be professional, prompt, and honest while being a Market Research Analyst. Through newsletters the Association trains its members on how to objectively evaluate consumer products, thereby raising the skill levels of their members.

The Association has a $25 membership fee that is good for twelve calendar months. Besides receiving the free informative newsletter, being a member of NAMRA will allow you access to dozens of other Market Research firms, besides PowerBase, that may offer you other opportunities to make money and to receive products. And don't worry, it's fine with us if you choose to work for other Market Research companies besides PowerBase! In fact we encourage you to develop your skills as an MRA. Top MRA's are sought after by many companies and some earn as much as $25,000 thousand dollars a year doing market research in their spare time from the comfort of their home.

Please include the $25 NAMRA membership fee when you return the completed form containing your name, address, and telephone number. We'll even send you a special certificate good for a free dinner at a national restaurant chain when you fill in your birth date on the form!

You can expect to be contacted by one of our database managers within 72 hours after we receive your information. And your first survey will be mailed to you within 24 hours after we have input your demographic information into the computer. Simply complete that survey and return it to us and we will send you $100!

I apologize for the long-winded nature of this letter. But I find that the more information I give to people up front, the less work my secretary has in taking all of your calls for more information. As soon as you are in our database we will mail you a confirmation letter that confirms your status as a PowerBase MRA. This letter will also contain a membership card (you'll need to show this card at restaurants that you have tested to receive your meal for free), and the letter will also contain complete details, rules and regulations that govern the PowerBase/MRA relationship.

One more thing, PowerBase will personally refund your $25.00 membership to NAMRA anytime within your first year as a member should we fail to make the experience of being a Market Research Analyst enjoyable or profitable for you. This guarantee and its details are in writing in the confirmation letter that you will receive.

NAMRA accepts cash, checks or money orders. Please make your check or money order payable to either the *National Association of Market Research Analysts* or to *NAMRA*.

If you have made it this far, thanks! I look forward to doing business with you; we won't disappoint you!

Remember, you have nothing to lose! You can receive cash and/or free products, goods or services just for giving us your opinions on them! And if you decide that you no longer wish to be an MRA anytime within your first twelve months with us, we'll refund your $25 NAMRA membership fee!

Thank you for taking the time to carefully read this letter. If you have additional questions you can leave a detailed message for me at the PowerBase Electronic Message Center. That number is on the address panel of this letter. Because I travel extensively, it may take a week or two for me to return your call.

Thanks and good luck to you on reaching the dreams and goals that you have set for yourself and your family. . . .

Sincerely,

Joyce Smith
Vice President
Consumer Research

P.S. This offer to become a PowerBase MRA is limited to the first 500 respondents. If you are not one of the first 500, sorry, but this particular demographic group has an initial enrollment cap of 500. If you are not one of the first 500 we will return your check and place your name on a waiting list. As this group expands, we will notify you and allow you an opportunity to rejoin. If you have additional questions about being an MRA, we recommend you mail the MRA sign-up form with your check right away to assure that you are among the first 500 to apply. Then if you decide later that you do not wish to be an MRA, simply let us know and we will refund your $25 NAMRA membership fee. Being an MRA is fun and profitable; you're going to love being an MRA!

Questions

1. Would you like to be a PowerBase MRA? Why?
2. Does this company sound like a legitimate marketing research firm? Why?
3. This letter violates one of the key ethical principles of the marketing research industry. What is it?
4. Go to your Web browser and search for PowerBase and the National Association of Marketing Research Analysts. Report the results of your search to the class.
5. What impact do activities such as those performed by PowerBase have on the marketing research industry?

Check it out!

At the end of each chapter, you'll find Working the Net exercises that include Web addresses. Use these sources and the Internet to find out more information about the topics and to help you apply what you learn in Part Two.

Chapter Four

Secondary Data and Databases

Learning Objectives

To understand how firms create an internal database.

To learn about building a database from a Web site.

To become familiar with data mining.

To understand the advantages and disadvantages of using secondary data.

To understand the role of the Internet in obtaining secondary data.

To become familiar with the types of databases available on CD-ROM.

To learn about types of information management systems.

To UNDERSTAND HOW WAL-MART STORES INC. MAKES SENSE OF THE ZIL-lions of pieces of information it has on the thousands of purchases it rings up, think about bananas. Bananas, according to Wal-Mart's research, are the most common item in America's grocery carts—more common even than milk or bread. So even though Wal-Mart Supercenters sell bananas in the produce section, they also crop up in the cereal aisle to help sell a few more corn flakes.

WAL-MART'S BANANA-PLACEMENT SKILLS were put to the test when it opened its first Wal-Mart Neighborhood Market, near the retailer's headquarters in Bentonville, Ark. The suburban-style supermarket is the first. If Wal-Mart expands the concept—nicknamed "Small Mart"—on a large scale, it will put the giant retailer in head-to-head competition with Kroger Co., Safeway Inc. and other seasoned grocery rivals.

MANY RETAILERS TALK A GOOD GAME when it comes to mining data collected at cash registers as a way to build sales. Wal-Mart, the nation's largest retailer, has been doing it since about 1990. Now, it is sitting on an information trove so vast and detailed that it far exceeds what many manufacturers know about their own products.

WAL-MART'S DATABASE IS SECOND IN SIZE ONLY TO THAT OF THE U.S. GOVERN-ment. Along with raw sales, profit margin, and inventory numbers, Wal-Mart also collects "market-basket data" from customer receipts at all its stores, so it knows what products are likely to be purchased together. Wal-Mart, for example, found that people who buy suitcases often purchase other travel items. Now stores display travel irons and alarm clocks next to the luggage.

AT 192,000 SQUARE FEET, WAL-MART SUPERCENTERS ARE ABOUT THE SIZE OF four football fields. Wal-Mart quickly found customers have trouble navigating them. To address customers' frustrations, Wal-Mart dug through heaps of purchase data from its supercenters and unearthed lots of ways to help people find things they didn't even know they needed. Kleenex tissues are in the paper-goods aisle and also mixed in with the cold medicine. Measuring spoons are in housewares and also hanging next to Crisco shortening.

ANOTHER INTERESTING TACTIC IS THE WAY TRANSACTION DATA HELPS WAL-MART lead shoppers out of low-margin merchandise and into more profitable sections. At the supercenters, mops and brooms—two "hard goods" used in the kitchen—

Wal-Mart, the nation's largest retailer, has a database of information second only to that of the U.S. government. Wal-Mart uses this information in its choice and placement of products and in its marketing efforts.

Find out more about Wal-Mart's efforts to ensure customer satisfaction at

http://www.walmart.com/cservice

turn out to be a good segue between low-margin food and higher-margin household items, like gardening tools. Then, it is on to electronics and clothes. Wal-Mart also sprinkles high-margin products in with the staples: Wal-Mart's baby aisle now often features baby food, formula and diapers along with infant clothes and children's medicine.[1] ∎

Wal-Mart's huge database has been created from secondary data. What are secondary data? What are the pros and cons of using secondary data? How is the Internet enabling firms to build valuable and effective databases? What types of secondary data are available on the Internet? These are some of the questions we will answer in this chapter.

The Nature of Secondary Data

secondary data
Data that have been previously gathered.

primary data
New data gathered to help solve the problem under investigation.

Secondary data consist of information that has already been gathered and *might* be relevant to the problem at hand. **Primary data,** in contrast, are survey, observation, and experiment data collected to solve the particular problem under investigation. It is highly unlikely that any marketing research problem is entirely unique or has never occurred before. It also is probable that someone else has investigated the problem or one similar to it in the past. Therefore, secondary data can be a cost-effective and efficient means of obtaining information for marketing research. There are two basic sources of secondary data: the company itself (internal databases) and other organizations or persons (external databases).

Secondary information originating within the company includes annual reports, reports to stockholders, product testing results (perhaps made available to the news media), and house periodicals composed by company personnel for communication to employees, customers, or others. Often all this information is incorporated into a company's internal database.

Outside sources of secondary information include innumerable government (federal, state, and local) departments and agencies that compile and publish summaries of business data, as well as trade and industry associations, business periodicals, and other news media that regularly publish studies and articles on the economy, specific industries, and even individual companies. When economic considerations or priorities within the organization preclude publication of summaries of the information from these sources, unpublished summaries may be found in internal reports, memos, or special-purpose analyses with limited circulation. Most of these sources can be found on the Internet.

Advantages of Secondary Data

Marketing researchers use secondary information because it can be obtained at a fraction of the cost, time, and inconvenience associated with primary data collection. Additional advantages of using secondary information include the following:

PART 2:
Creating a Research Design

- *Secondary data may help to clarify or redefine the problem during the exploratory research process* (see Chapter 3). Consider the experience of a local YMCA. Concerned about a stagnant level of membership and a lack of participation in traditional YMCA programs, it decided to survey members and nonmembers. Secondary data revealed that there had been a tremendous influx of young single persons into the target market, while the number of "traditional families" had remained constant. The problem was redefined to examine how the YMCA could attract a significant share of the young single adult market while maintaining its traditional family base.

- *Secondary data may actually provide a solution to the problem.* It is highly unlikely that the problem is unique; there is always the possibility that someone else has addressed the identical problem or a very similar one. Thus, the precise information desired may have been collected, but not for the same purpose.

  Many states publish a directory of manufacturers (typically available online) that contains information on companies: location, markets, product lines, number of plants, names of key personnel, number of employees, and sales levels. When a consulting company specializing in long-range strategic planning for members of the semiconductor industry needed a regional profile of its potential clients, it used individual state directories to compile the profile; no primary data collection was necessary.

- *Secondary data may provide primary data research method alternatives.* Each primary data research endeavor is custom-designed for the situation at hand; consequently, the marketing researcher should always be open to sources that suggest research alternatives. For example, when we (the authors) started work on a research project for a large southwestern city's convention and visitor's bureau, we obtained a research report prepared by *Meeting and Convention Planners* magazine. In designing our questionnaire, we used a series of scales from the magazine's questionnaire. Not only were the scales well designed, but results from our study could be compared with the magazine's data.

- *Secondary data may alert the marketing researcher to potential problems and/or difficulties.* In addition to alternatives, secondary information may divulge potential dangers. Unpopular collection methods, sample selection difficulties, or respondent hostility may be uncovered. For example, examination of a study of anesthesiologists by a researcher planning to conduct a study of their satisfaction with certain drugs discovered a high refusal rate in a telephone survey. The researcher had planned to use a telephone study but instead switched to a mail questionnaire with a response incentive.

- *Secondary data may provide necessary background information and build credibility for the research report.* Secondary information often yields a wealth of background data for planning a research project. It may offer a profile of potential buyers versus nonbuyers, industry data, desirable new product features, language used by purchasers to describe the industry, and the advantages and disadvantages of existing products. Language used by target consumers can aid in phrasing questions that will be meaningful to respondents. Sometimes background data can satisfy some of the research objectives, eliminating the need to ask certain questions; shorter questionnaires typically have higher completion rates. And secondary data can enrich research findings by providing additional insights into what the data mean or by corroborating current findings. Finally, secondary data can serve as a reference base for subsequent research projects.

Limitations of Secondary Data

Despite the many advantages of secondary data, they also pose some dangers. The main disadvantages of secondary information are lack of availability, lack of relevance, inaccuracy, and insufficiency.[2]

Lack of Availability   For some research questions, there are simply no available data. Suppose Kraft General Foods wants to evaluate the taste, texture, and color of three new gourmet brownie mixes. No secondary data exist that can answer these questions; consumers must try each mix and then evaluate it. If McDonald's wants to evaluate its image in Phoenix, Arizona, it must gather primary data. If Ford wants to know the reaction of college students to a new two-seater sports car design, it must show prototypes to the students and evaluate their opinions. Of course, secondary data may have played a major role in the engineer's design plan for the car.

Lack of Relevance   It is not uncommon for secondary data to be expressed in units or measures that cannot be used by the researcher. For example, Joan Dermott, a retailer of oriental rugs, determined that the primary customers for her rugs were families with a total household income of $40,000 to $80,000. Higher-income consumers tended to purchase pricier rugs than those Dermott carried. When she was trying to decide whether to open a store in another Florida city, she could not find useful income data. One source offered class breakdowns of $30,000 to $50,000, $50,000 to $70,000, $70,000 to $90,000, and so forth. Another secondary source broke down incomes into less than $15,000, $15,000 to $30,000, and more than $30,000. Even if the given income brackets had met Joan's needs, she would have faced another problem: outdated information. One study had been conducted in 1990 and the other in 1992. In Florida's dynamic markets, the percentages probably were no longer relevant. This is often the case with U.S. census data, which are nearly a year old before they become available.

Inaccuracy   Users of secondary data should always assess the accuracy of the data. There are a number of potential sources of error when a researcher gathers, codes, analyzes, and presents data. Any report that does not mention possible sources and ranges of error should be suspect.

Using secondary data does not relieve the researcher from attempting to assess their accuracy. A few guidelines for determining the accuracy of secondary data are as follows:

1. *Who gathered the data?* The source of the secondary data is a key to their accuracy. Federal agencies, most state agencies, and large commercial marketing research firms generally can be counted on to have conducted their research as professionally as possible. Marketing researchers should always be on guard when examining data in which a hidden agenda might be

reflected. A chamber of commerce, for instance, is always going to put its best foot forward. Similarly, trade associations often advocate one position over another.

2. *What was the purpose of the study?* Data are always collected for some reason. Understanding the motivation for the research can provide clues to the quality of the data. A chamber of commerce study conducted to provide data that could be used to attract new industry to the area should be scrutinized with a great deal of caution. There have been situations in which advertising agencies have been hired by clients to assess the impact of their own advertising programs. In other words, they have been asked to evaluate the quality of the job they were doing for their clients!

3. *What information was collected?* A researcher should always identify exactly what information was gathered and from whom. For example, in a dog food study, were purchasers of canned, dry, and semimoist food interviewed, or were just one or two types of dog food purchasers surveyed? In a voters' survey, were only Democrats or only Republicans interviewed? Were the respondents registered voters? Was any attempt made to ascertain a respondent's likelihood of voting in the next election? Were self-reported data used to infer actual behavior?

4. *When was the information collected?* A shopping mall study that surveyed shoppers only on weekends would not reflect the opinions of "typical" mall patrons. A telephone survey conducted from 9:00 A.M. to 5:00 P.M. would vastly underrepresent working persons. A survey of Florida visitors conducted during the summer probably would reveal motivations and interests different from those of winter visitors.

5. *How was the information collected?* Were the data collected by mail, telephone, Internet, or personal interview? Each of these techniques offers advantages and disadvantages. What was the refusal rate? Were decision makers interviewed or representatives of decision makers? In short, the researcher must attempt to discern the amount of bias injected into the data by the information-gathering process. A mail survey with a 1 percent response rate (that is, only 1 percent of those who received the survey mailed it back) probably contains a lot of self-selection bias.

6. *Is the information consistent with other information?* A lack of consistency between secondary data sets should dictate caution. The researcher should delve into possible causes of the discrepancy. Differences in the sample, time frame, sampling methodology, questionnaire structure, and other factors can lead to variations in studies. If possible, the researcher should assess the reliability of the different studies as a basis for determining which, if any, study should be used for decision making.

Insufficiency   A researcher may determine that available data are relevant and accurate but still not sufficient to make a decision or bring closure to a problem. For example, a manager for Wal-Mart may have sufficient secondary data on incomes, family sizes, number of competitors, and growth potential to determine in which of five Iowa towns Wal-Mart wishes to locate its next store. But if no traffic counts exist for the selected town, primary data will have to be gathered to select a specific site for the store.

Internal Databases

internal database
A collection of related information developed from data within the organization.

For many companies, a computerized database containing information about customers and prospects has become an essential marketing tool. An **internal database** is simply a collection of related information developed from data within the organization.

Creating an Internal Database

A firm's Web site can be an excellent source of information for creating an internal database. A traditional starting point has been the firm's sales or inquiry processing and tracking system. Typically, such a system is built on salespersons' "call reports." A call report provides a blueprint of a salesperson's daily activities. It details the number of calls made, characteristics of each firm visited, sales activity resulting from the call, and any information picked up from the client regarding competitors, such as price changes, new products or services, credit term modifications, and new product or service features.

An internal marketing database built on sales results and customer preferences can be a powerful marketing tool. While large companies build mammoth internal databases (Yahoo! collects 400 billion bytes of information every day—the equivalent of a library of 800,000 books),[3] small businesses can profit from internal databases as well. Lucy Hirleman, owner of Berkshire Travel in Newfoundland, New Jersey, describes her success in the In Practice feature.

Even Small Businesses Can Profit from Databases

In PRACTICE

IN HER DATABASE, LUCY HIRLEMAN NOTES WHICH CLIENTS HAVE EXPRESSED an interest in last-minute trips, who likes to ski, who's a budget traveler, and other relevant bits of information. Every day, she boots up her database to retrieve the names of customers who may be interested in timely or targeted promotions. "If I get a fax about something special for kids, I call up the list of families in my database and let them know about it," she says.

It pays to pass on relevant information. This winter, Hirleman received a last-minute promotional offer for a Caribbean vacation and passed it on to eight clients she had tagged as last-minute travelers interested in the islands. She quickly sold two trips. "Anyone who values their time—whether they're a waitress or a Wall Street guy—still uses a travel agent," she says.[4] ■

The Growing Importance of Internal Database Marketing

Perhaps the fastest-growing use of internal databases is database marketing. **Database marketing** is marketing that relies on the creation of a large computerized file of customers' and potential customers' profiles and purchase patterns.

In the 1950s, network television enabled advertisers to "get the same message to everyone simultaneously." Database marketing can get a customized, individual message to everyone simultaneously through direct mail. This is why database marketing is sometimes called *micro marketing*. Database marketing can create a computerized form of the old-fashioned relationship that people used to have with the corner grocer, butcher, or baker. "A database is sort of a collective memory," says Richard G. Barlow, president of Frequency Marketing, Inc., a Cincinnati-based consulting firm. "It deals with you in the same personalized way as a mom-and-pop grocery store, where they knew customers by name and stocked what they wanted."[5]

The size of some databases is impressive: Ford Motor Company's is about 50 million names; Kraft General Foods, 30 million; Citicorp, 30 million; and Kimberly Clark, maker of Huggies diapers, 10 million new mothers. American Express, can pull from its database all cardholders who made purchases at golf pro shops in the past six months, who attended symphony concerts, or who traveled to Europe more than once in the past year, as well as the very few people who did all three.

Vons Company, the largest supermarket chain in Southern California and the ninth-largest in America, has upgraded its check-approval card into a VonsClub card. The card is the foundation for creating a database that gives automatic discounts on items selected for promotion. Vons's objective is to build a comprehensive database of exactly what's in shoppers' baskets each time they leave the store. Using that data, Vons can better understand consumer behavior and send a monthly mailing of individualized laser-printed discount coupons to each VonsClub member. Even food processors and manufacturers benefit from Vons's database. Beech-Nut, a maker of baby foods, has used the VonsClub mailer to identify every household that has purchased a baby product for the first time in the preceding eight weeks. Says Susan Widham, vice president of marketing at Beech-Nut, "This program enables me to target an offer specifically to a consumer based on the type and quantity of a product they buy, the frequency [with which] they buy it, and whether they buy my product or my competitor's."[6] Under consideration,

Beech-Nut uses the Vons Supermarket Club Card database to find out who is buying baby food and then targets offers specifically to those shoppers.

she says, is a 50-cents-off coupon for Beech-Nut customers—to hold on to them—and a $1-off coupon for Gerber Products customers—to get them to switch brands.

Creating an Internal Database from Conversations

"Your call may be monitored to ensure quality." This disclaimer crops up all the time these days. People are especially likely to hear it when they call various help desks to ask about product warranties, software problems, travel arrangements, medical services, and dozens of other issues. At many companies, the monitoring is done not by supervisors but by digital recorders. As a result, companies are accumulating mammoth databases of audio files.

Dragon Systems, Inc., in Newton, Massachusetts, offers computer-based tools to analyze conversations for insights into customer satisfaction, shifts in buying patterns, and other trends. Using the same speech-recognition technology that is employed in Dragon's NaturallySpeaking dictation software, the new program can create word indexes from reams of recorded speech. The indexes allow managers to move quickly to the locations on the tape where the keywords occur. Users can also query the database about the frequency with which a certain word is used in phone conversations. Managers can find out, for example, how many calls on a given day made reference to a particular glitch in the software.[7]

Database Design and Implementation

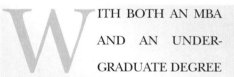

WITH BOTH AN MBA AND AN UNDERGRADUATE DEGREE in computer science, Mike Foytik, senior vice president for information science for DSS Research, exemplifies the new breed of marketing service managers with a strong background in computers. He is a proponent of the use of *relational databases*. He has designed dozens for DSS clients in direct marketing and retailing.

He notes that there are many advantages to using a relational database instead of the *traditional database approach,* sometimes referred to as the *flat-file method.* In a relational database, data are stored in several small structures, or files, rather than in a single large one. Each of the small files in a relational database contains key information that allows individual records in the database to be linked to associated data in other individual files that make up the entire database structure.

For example, a customer database might contain one file that includes customer information such as name, mailing address, and Social Security number. This information is updated occasionally. Products purchased by each customer would go into another file that is updated frequently (every time the customer buys something). The two files might be linked by the customer's Social Security number.

With each new order, a record is created that includes the product purchased, the price, other relevant information concerning the purchase, and the buyer's Social Security number. Under the traditional, flat-file approach, all this information (the product purchase information and the buyer's personal information) would have to be entered with each product purchase. Relational databases have a number of distinct advantages:

- *Less data storage space is required.* There is very little redundant information in a relational database. Data such as addresses are stored only once for each customer rather than being stored with every new purchase that is added. Foytik notes that "we have achieved 75 percent storage space reductions for some of our clients."
- *The database is more flexible.* Relational databases offer much greater flexibility and efficiency with respect to changes in the way data are stored and used. With flat-file databases, every time a new data field is added to the database, the database must be re-created in order to add the new data field to every record in the database. With a relational database, new information is stored in a new file and, therefore, has no effect on existing data in other files in the database.
- *Restricting access to sensitive information is easier.* Relational databases can be easily designed to restrict user access to certain areas of the database via the use of special passwords or codes while still allowing more general access to less sensitive areas. In flat-file databases, this sort of restricted access to some parts of the database is all but impossible. Users must have either total access or no access.
- *The database can easily be designed to accommodate many users.* Foytik notes that "most of our clients have a number of different departments with very different informational needs accessing customer data." With flat files, separate copies of the database must be created and modified to meet the needs of different users. With relational databases, the physical data remain unchanged while the data or reports seen by the different user groups (sometimes called the logical data) can be varied.

Finally, he notes, all these advantages come at some cost. First, relational databases require much more sophisticated software and more sophisticated people to program them. Second, relational databases require much more up-front planning if the company is to reap the full benefits of this type of data. Finally, relational databases tend to require more processor horsepower. This is becoming less of an issue with the price/performance ratio of computers constantly improving.[8] ■

Creating a Database from a Web Site—A Marketer's Dream[9]

If a person today were opening, say, a wine shop, which of the following would give the owner the best opportunity to build a database—a traditional store or a Web retailer like Virtual Vineyards, Incorporated?

WAR Stories

A Web merchant like Virtual Vineyards has access to data about its clients that would make its physical-world counterparts very envious. A customer's conduit to an online store is a two-way electronic link, allowing the online merchant to gather all sorts of information, particularly if that customer has shopped with that merchant before.

Getting the customer's name, address, and purchasing history is only the beginning. A Web merchant can record the customer's actions as he or she moves through the merchant's site, taking note not only of purchases but also of window shopping. The end result is a file that allows the merchant to determine what that customer is most likely to purchase next—and then offer inducements to make it happen.

Meanwhile, back in the physical world, the wine store owner sits behind the register, eyeing the anonymous customer who just went out empty-handed. Had the customer visited the site before? If so, what did he or she buy? Did the customer even see the new Chardonnay that just came in? Unfortunately, the owner was too busy to ask those questions (and the customer would have been offended if the owner had). Maybe the customer will come back—maybe not.

Preview Travel Inc., an online travel agency based in San Francisco, determined that Las Vegas, Orlando, and Cancun were the top three vacation spots among its customers. The firm quickly purchased keywords for the three destinations on several Internet-directory sites; when a Web surfer performs a search for any of the three vacation spots, a Preview Travel advertising banner accompanies the list of results. Karen Askey, senior vice president of consumer marketing at Preview Travel, says traditional travel agencies could employ the same promotional tactics, but she doubts they could spot top destinations as quickly. "When you're online, the speed at which you can get that data is basically instantaneous," she says.

Once Web surfers start clicking around the virtual aisles of an online store, merchants can monitor their every move. The best known method of doing so involves a **cookie,** a text file that sits on a user's computer and identifies that user when she or he revisits a Web site.

Even some privacy advocates admit that cookies have beneficial uses. For instance, they can store passwords, sparing users the hassle of having to identify themselves every time they go to a Web site, and they allow online shopping carts to work. Despite what some Net users believe, a site can read only the cookie that site put on the user's system, not any other cookies the user has collected from other Web sites.

Cookies are a powerful device for monitoring a user's behavior within a site, one that can tell a merchant whether the user lingers in lingerie or lawn chairs. "What it's like," says Nick Donatiello, president of Odyssey, a marketing research firm based in San Francisco, "is every time you walk into Macy's, they put a little tracker on you that follows you everywhere you go, how long you look at perfume and blue jeans."[10]

Cookies give Web merchants an advantage over their competitors in traditional retailing. Web merchants can follow window shoppers and then use the

cookie
A text file placed on a user's computer in order to identify the user when she or he revisits the Web site.

information they obtain to target promotions to them on return visits. And, unlike traditional counterparts, an online merchant can rearrange the entire layout of a store in real time, sticking an advertisement for, say, parkas on the front door when an avid skier comes calling.

Data Mining

American Express uses a neural network to examine the hundreds of millions of entries in its database that tell how and where individual cardholders transact business. A **neural network** is a computer program that mimics the processes of the human brain and thus is capable of learning from examples to find patterns in data. The result is a set of *purchase propensity scores* for each cardholder. Based on these scores, AmEx matches offers from affiliated merchants to the purchase histories of individual cardholders and encloses these offers with their monthly statements. The benefits are reduced expenses for AmEx and information of higher value for its cardholders; American Express is engaged in data mining.

Data mining is the use of statistical and other advanced software to discover nonobvious patterns hidden in a database. The objective is to identify patterns that marketers can use in creating new strategies and tactics to increase a firm's profitability. Camelot Music Holdings used data mining to identify a group of high-spending, 65-plus customers (members of its frequent shopper club) who were buying lots of classical and jazz music and movies. Further data mining revealed that a large percentage were also buying rap and alternative music; these were grandparents buying for the grandkids. Now, Camelot tells the senior citizens what's hot in rap and alternative music, as well as in traditional music.[11]

Data mining involves searching for interesting patterns and following the data trail wherever it leads. The discovery process often requires sifting through massive quantities of data; electronic point-of-sale transactions, inventory records, and online customer orders matched with demographics can easily use up hundreds of gigabytes of data storage space. Probability sampling, descriptive statistics, and multivariate statistics are all tools of data mining that make the task manageable. (Probability sampling was discussed in Chapter 3; descriptive statistics programs and multivariate statistics will be covered in Part Four.) Other more advanced data mining tools, such as genetic algorithms and case-based reasoning systems, must be left for an advanced text.

Data mining has many potential uses in marketing. Those with widest application include the following:

- *Customer acquisition.* In the first stage of a two-stage process, direct marketers apply data mining methods to discover customer attributes that predict their responses to special offers and communications such as catalogs. In the second stage, attributes that the model indicates make customers most likely to respond are matched to the attributes appended to rented lists of noncustomers in order to select noncustomer households most likely to respond to a new offer or communication.
- *Customer retention.* In a typical marketing application, data mining identifies those customers who contribute to the company's bottom line but who are likely to leave and go to a competitor. With this information, the company

neural network
A computer program that mimics the processes of the human brain and thus is capable of learning from examples to find patterns in data.

data mining
The use of statistical and other advanced software to discover nonobvious patterns hidden in a database.

can target the vulnerable customers for special offers and other inducements not available to less vulnerable customers.

■ *Customer abandonment.* Some customers cost more than they contribute and should be encouraged to take their business elsewhere. At Federal Express, customers who spend a lot with little service and marketing investment get different treatment from, say, those who spend just as much but cost more to keep. If their shipping volume falters, "good" clients can expect a phone call, which can head off defections before they occur. As for the "bad" clients—those who spend but are expensive to the company—FedEx is turning them into profitable customers, in many cases, by charging higher shipping prices. And the "ugly" clients, those customers who spend little and show few signs of spending more in the future? They can catch the TV ads. "We just don't market to them anymore," says Sharanjit Singh, managing director for marketing analysis at FedEx. "That automatically brings our costs down."[12]

■ *Market basket analysis.* By identifying the associations among product purchases in point-of-sale transactions, retailers and direct marketers can spot product affinities and develop focused promotion strategies that work more effectively than traditional one-size-fits-all approaches.[13] The American Express strategy of selectively stuffing offers in monthly statements is an example of how market basket analysis can be employed to increase marketing efficiency.

Farmers Group Insurance used data mining to find out that, as long as a sports car wasn't the only vehicle in a household, the accident rate for sports cars wasn't much greater than that for regular cars. This information led to lower insurance rates for sports cars in this category.

The Farmers Group has used data mining to better understand its customers. A few years ago, owning a Porsche or a Corvette almost guaranteed that you would pay more for car insurance. Conventional wisdom and decades of data collected by insurers suggested that drivers of high-performance sports cars were more likely to have accidents than were other motorists. But, by using data mining, the Farmers Group discovered something interesting: As long as the sports car wasn't the only vehicle in a household, the accident rate actually wasn't much greater than that for a regular car. Based on that information, Farmers changed its policy that had excluded sports cars from its lowest-priced insurance rates. By eliminating that rule, "we figured out that we could almost double our sports-car market," says Melissa McBratney, vice president of personal lines at the Los Angeles insurer.[14] Farmers estimates that just letting Corvettes and Porsches into its "preferred premium" plan could bring in an additional $4.5 million in premium revenue over the next two years, without a significant rise in claims. The pattern Farmers discovered isn't intuitive—it had eluded most insurance veterans.

Data mining and building databases is a worldwide phenomenon. The Nestlé story in the Global Issues feature discusses building databases in Asia.

Nestlé Builds a Database in Asia

Global ISSUES

MALAYSIANS, UNACCUSTOMED TO HAVING BIG COMPANIES reach out to them by mail, are inundating the local headquarters of Nestlé with phone calls. But they're not calling to complain about unwanted special offers, dietary tips or recipes; they want to create a dialogue with the Swiss food giant.

"As soon as we send out a mailing, people phone because they're so excited and want to call to say hello and thank you. It's an incredible way of finding out how people really feel," said Caroline Lim, a consultant with Ogilvy One, Ogilvy & Mather Worldwide's direct marketing arm, who is working solely on Nestlé business across Southeast Asia.

Such enthusiasm for direct contact plays neatly into Nestlé's global strategy, making Malaysia a suitable pilot for an Asian rollout of the serious database-building and one-to-one communication programs the Vevey, Switzerland–based company has embarked on elsewhere in the world. Detailed questionnaires on consumption patterns, lifestyle, race, religion and feelings about specific brands have been answered by 100,000 Malaysians, who were lured by the chance to win a new car. The idea is to learn about the buying population in a country of 19.5 million people who speak one or more of three languages (Bahasa Melayu, Chinese and English), vary in their religion (60% are Muslim) and traditionally eat out only on special occasions.

Nestlé's five-year plan forecasts a doubling in database numbers each year, building a sample which it will manipulate to suit its various brands. The database seeks to serve a country Nestlé has been present in since the early 1960s and where Nestlé has all of its product categories represented. By building up its knowledge, the company hopes not only to target its marketing but also to adapt its products accordingly. For example, some Malaysian products are gelatin-free to respect Muslim sensitivities.

Some of Nestlé's first targets in Malaysia are busy people who want combined products. Nestrum 3-in-1, for example, is a cereal with milk powder, sugar and oats provided in a packet, while a Nescafé variant provides coffee, milk powder and sugar. Other targets are those who want to cook traditional meals but don't have the skills or the time. Mailings include recipes for a Malay breakfast, typically *nasi lemak* (coconut rice with a hard-boiled egg and chili sauce) with meat or fish, that makes use of Nestlé's Maggi sauces and mixes. ∎

Source: Suzanne Bidlake, "Nestlé Builds Database in Asia with Direct Mail." Reprinted with permission from the January 1998 issue, p. 34, of *Advertising Age International.* Copyright, Crain Communications Inc. 1998.

The Battle over Privacy

The growth of databases both on and off the Internet is causing increasing concern about privacy issues. Recently, the U.S. Congress restricted states' sales of databases filled with personal information from drivers' licenses. And the Federal Trade Commission has investigated whether Yahoo! is complying with consumer-protection regulations in its use of users' information.

The Internet has received significant criticism from privacy advocates. The concept of privacy is changing radically as a result of our new computer-based lives. Privacy used to be achieved through the sheer friction of everyday life: distance, time, and lack of records. Information didn't travel well, and most people who wanted to escape their past could simply move to a new location. Now the picture has changed. People can escape their surroundings through the Internet, but their actions can easily catch up with them. And it's not just the Internet; it's electronic toll roads (exactly *when* did you leave that party?), credit card transactions (we know what hotel you went to), vendor databases (and what book you bought), cell-phone records (and whom you called), and more. At work, employee arrival and departure times may be recorded, along with their Web searches, email messages, and sick days.

What makes all this troubling to privacy advocates is the growing ability of technology to combine information: the products you bought from a variety of different merchants; your sick days plus someone else's hotel bills. It's not the routine use of this information for marketing purposes that people find troubling; it's the way someone with an agenda might put the pieces together.

The lightning rod for Internet privacy criticism has been Double Click, a database marketer. Double Click drew fire over its plans to connect people's names, addresses, and other personal information with data it collects on the Web about where people are surfing. Concerns were also raised about Double Click's plan to acquire Abacus Direct Corporation, a company that markets consumer purchase data on 90 million households to catalog firms. Privacy advocates were worried that the planned merger of the two companies' consumer databases would lead to privacy abuses. After an FTC investigation, Double Click announced a new privacy initiative, with its own internal privacy officer and a contract with PricewaterhouseCoopers to perform privacy audits.[15]

At some point, the federal government will probably pass privacy legislation for the Internet, which most likely will be administered by the Federal Trade Commission. The legislation is expected to have four key points:

1. Privacy polices, easy to find and written in easy-to-understand English, will be mandatory on Web sites.
2. The Web user will have a clear opportunity to "opt in" or "opt out" of data collection at each site.
3. Consumers will be given the ability to look at and correct sensitive information.
4. There will be penalties for noncompliance.

Finding Secondary Data on the Internet

Gathering secondary data from external sources, a necessity in almost any research project, has traditionally been a tedious and boring job. The researcher often had to write to government agencies, trade associations, or other secondary data providers and then wait days or weeks for a reply that might never come. Frequently, one or more trips to the library were required, and there the researcher might find that needed reports were checked out or missing. The rapid development of the Internet and World Wide Web in recent years promises to eliminate the drudgery associated with the collection of secondary data.

Finding the information that you need on the Web can be very easy, or it can require trial and error. Your Web connection provides access to over 100 million Web sites throughout the world, containing more information than any library can offer. No matter where you are on the globe, as long as you have an Internet connection you have access to all this information. There are basically two ways to find the information you need: entering a URL and using a search engine.

URLs

If you know the address of the Web site that you are searching for, you can type it directly into your Web browser. (Netscape Navigator and Microsoft Internet Explorer are the dominant browsers.) A Web address, or URL (Uniform Reference Locator), is similar to a street address in that it identifies a particular location (server and file on that server) on the Web.

Search Engines

Sites such as AltaVista, Excite, and Google have become popular among computer users looking for information on the Web. These organizations offer *search engines* that crawl the Web looking for sites that contain the information you are seeking. Each search engine has its own indexing system to help you locate information. All of them allow you to enter one or more keywords and search the databases of Web sites for all occurrences of those words. They then return listings of sites that you can go to immediately by clicking on the name.

Remember that the Internet is a self-publishing medium. Visits to search engines will yield files of diverse quality from a variety of sources. Be sure to try out multiple sites when you are investigating a topic.

Directories

In addition to search engines, you can use subject directories on the Web to explore a subject. There are two basic types of directories: *academic and professional directories* and *commercial portals*.

- *Academic and professional directories* are created by librarians or subject experts and tend to be associated with libraries and academic institutions. These directories are designed to enhance the research process and help users find high-quality sites of interest. A careful selection process is applied, and links to the selected resources are usually annotated. These collections are often created to serve an institution's constituency but may be useful to other researchers. As a rule, these sites do not generate income or carry advertising. INFOMINE, from the University of California, is an example of an academic directory.
- *Commercial portals* are created to generate income and serve the general public. These services provide links to a wide range of topics and often empha-

size entertainment, commerce, hobbies, sports, travel, and other interests not necessarily covered by academic directories. These sites seek to draw traffic in order to support advertising. To further this goal, the directory is offered in conjunction with a number of additional customer services. Yahoo! is an example of a commercial portal.

The lines between directories and search engines are blurring. Directories are present at some search engine sites, and sometimes their content is searched along with content from the general Web. For example, AltaVista offers the LookSmart directory, Infoseek shares the screen with the directory at the Go Network, Excite has its own directory, and Lycos offers the contents of Netscape's Open Directory. Directory results are sometimes placed before search results in order to steer users to the directory's content. Consulting a directory can be a useful way of getting at substantive content relating to your query. Most subject directories offer a search engine mechanism for querying the database. Table 4.1 lists popular search engines and directories.

<table>
<tr><td rowspan="20" style="writing-mode: vertical-lr;">Table 4.1</td><td colspan="2">**Popular Search Engines and Directories**</td></tr>
<tr><td>**AltaVista**
http://www.altavista.com</td><td>AltaVista is one of the largest search engines on the Web in terms of pages indexed. Its comprehensive coverage and wide range of power searching commands make it a particular favorite among researchers. It also offers a number of features designed to appeal to basic users (such as Ask AltaVista results, which come from Ask Jeeves) and directory listings (primarily from the Open Directory Project).</td></tr>
<tr><td>**AOL Search**
http://www.search.aol.com</td><td>AOL Search allows its members to search the Web and AOL's own content from a single starting point. The "external" version does not list AOL content. The main listings for categories and Web sites come from the Open Directory Project. Inktomi also provides crawler-based results, as backup to the directory information.</td></tr>
<tr><td>**Ask Jeeves**
http://www.askjeeves.com</td><td>Ask Jeeves is a human-powered search service that aims to direct users to the exact page that answers their question. If it fails to find a match within its own database, it will provide matching Web pages from various search engines.</td></tr>
<tr><td>**Direct Hit**
http://www.directhit.com</td><td>Direct Hit is a company that works with other search engines to refine their results. It does this by monitoring what users click on from the results they see. Sites that get clicked on more than others rise higher in Direct Hit's rankings. Thus, the service dubs itself a "popularity engine." Direct Hit's technology is currently best seen at HotBot. It also refines results at Lycos and is available as an option at LookSmart and MSN Search. The company also crawls the Web and refines its database, which can be viewed via the address given here.</td></tr>
<tr><td>**Excite**
http://www.excite.com</td><td>Excite is one of the most popular search services on the Web. it offers a medium-size index and integrates non-Web material such as company information and sports scores into its results, when appropriate.</td></tr>
<tr><td>**FAST Search**
http://www.alltheweb.com</td><td>Formerly called All the Web, FAST Search aims to index the entire Web. It was the first search engine to break the 200 million Web page index milestone.</td></tr>
</table>

PART 2:
Creating a Research Design

Table 4.1

Popular Search Engines and Directories (continued)

Go
http://www.go.com

Go is a portal site produced by Infoseek and Disney. It offers portal features such as personalization and free email, plus the search capabilities of the Infoseek search service, which has now been folded into Go. Searchers will find that Go consistently provides quality results in response to many general and broad searches. It also has an impressive human-compiled directory of Web sites.

Google
http://www.google.com

Google is a search engine that makes heavy use of link popularity as a way to rank Web sites. This can be especially helpful in finding good sites in response to general searches on keywords such as "cars" and "travel," because users across the Web have, in essence, voted for good sites by linking to them.

GoTo
http://www.goto.com

Unlike the other major search engines, GoTo sells its main listings. Companies can pay money to be placed higher in the search results, which GoTo believes improves relevancy. Free search results on GoTo come from Inktomi.

HotBot
http://hotbot.lycos.com

Like AltaVista, HotBot is another favorite among researchers, in large part because of its comprehensive index of the Web and many power searching features. In most cases, HotBot's first page of results comes from the Direct Hit service; secondary results come from the Inktomi search engine, which is also used by other services. It gets its directory information from the Open Directory Project.

Inktomi
http://www.inktomi.com

The Inktomi search engine originally was developed at the University of California at Berkeley. Its creators then formed their own company with the same name and created a new Inktomi index, which was first used to power HotBot. Now the Inktomi index also powers several other services. All of them tap into the same index, though each service's results may be slightly different. This is because Inktomi provides ways for its partners to use a common index, yet distinguish themselves. There is no way to query the Inktomi index directly, as it is made available only through Inktomi's partners with whatever filters and ranking tweaks they may apply.

iWon
http://www.iwon.com

Backed by U.S. television network CBS, iWon has a directory of Web sites generated automatically by Inktomi, which also provides its more traditional crawler-based results. iWon gives away daily, weekly, and monthly prizes in a marketing model unique among the major services.

LookSmart
http://www.looksmart.com

LookSmart is a human-compiled directory of Web sites. In addition to being a stand-alone service, LookSmart provides directory results to MSN Search, Excite, and many other partners. AltaVista provides LookSmart with search results when a search fails to find a match from among LookSmart's reviews.

Lycos
http://www.lycos.com

Lycos started out as a search engine, depending on listings that came from spidering the Web. In April 1999, it shifted to a directory model similar to that of Yahoo!. Its main listings come from the Open Directory Project, and then secondary results come from either Direct Hit or Lycos' own spidering of the Web.

MSN Search
http://search.msn.com

Microsoft's MSN Search service is a LookSmart-powered directory of Web sites, with secondary results that come from AltaVista. RealNames and Direct Hit data are also made available. MSN Search also offers a unique way for Internet Explorer 5.5 users to save past searches.

(continued)

Table 4.1

Popular Search Engines and Directories (continued)

Netscape Search
http://search.netscape.com

Netscape Search's results come primarily from the Open Directory Project and Netscape's own Smart Browsing database, which does an excellent job of listing "official" Web sites. Secondary results come from Google. At the Netscape Netcenter portal site, other search engines are also featured.

Northern Light
http://www.northernlight.com

Northern Light is another favorite search engine among researchers. It features one of the largest Web indexes, along with the ability to cluster documents by topic. Northern Light also has a set of "special collection" documents that are not readily accessible to search engine spiders. There are documents from thousands of sources, including news wires, magazines, and databases. Searching these documents is free, as is viewing those on the public Web, but there is a charge of up to $4 to view those within the special collection.

Open Directory Project
http://dmoz.org

The Open Directory Project uses volunteer editors to catalog the Web. It was acquired by Netscape in November 1998, and the company pledged that anyone would be able to use information from the directory through an open license arrangement. Netscape itself was the first licensee. Lycos and AOL Search also make heavy use of Open Directory data, while AltaVista and HotBot prominently feature Open Directory categories within their results pages.

RealNames
http://web.realnames.com

The RealNames system is meant to be an easier-to-use alternative to the current Web site addressing system. Those with RealNames-enabled browsers can enter a word like "Nike" to reach the Nike Web site. To date, RealNames has had its biggest success through search engine partnerships. In particular, it is strongly featured in results at AltaVista, Go, and MSN Search.

WebCrawler
http://www.webcrawler.com

WebCrawler has the smallest index of any major search engine on the Web—think of it as Excite Lite. The small index means WebCrawler is not the place to go when seeking obscure or unusual material. However, some people believe that, because it has indexed fewer pages, WebCrawler provides less overwhelming results in response to general searches.

Yahoo!
http://www.yahoo.com

Yahoo! is the Web's most popular search service and has a well-deserved reputation for helping people find information easily. The secret to Yahoo!'s success is human beings. It is the largest human-compiled guide to the Web, employing about 150 editors. Yahoo! has over 1 million sites listed and supplements its results with those from Inktomi. If a search fails to find a match within Yahoo!'s own listings, matches from Inktomi are displayed. Inktomi matches also appear after all Yahoo! matches have been shown. Yahoo! is the oldest major Web site directory, having been launched in late 1994.

Source: searchenginewatch.com

Sites of Interest to Marketing Researchers

A number of Web sites are accessed daily by marketing researchers in search of information. The most frequently used of these sites, which offer an incredible variety of information, are listed in Table 4.2.

PART 2:
Creating a Research Design

Table 4.2

Some Sources of Secondary Data for Marketing Researchers on the Web

Organization	URL	Description
American Demographics/ Marketing Tools	http://www.marketingtools.com	Allows users to search the full text of American Demographics and Marketing Tools publications.
American Marketing Association	http://www.ama.org	Enables users to search all of the AMA's publications by using keywords.
BLS Consumer Expenditure Surveys	http://stats.bls.gov/csxprod.htm	Provides information on the buying habits of consumers, including data on their expenditures, income, and credit ratings.
Bureau of Economic Analysis	http://www.bea.doc.gov	Offers a wide range of economic statistics.
Bureau of Transportation Statistics	http://www.bts.gov	Is a comprehensive source for a wide range of statistics on transportation.
CACI Marketing Systems	http://www.demographics.caci.com	Offers users a snapshot of the dominant profile type in their town when they type in their zip codes. Population figures are available for the zip codes, as are percentages for race and sex. Median household income, average home value, and average rent are also presented.
Center for International Earth Science Network	http://www.ciesin.org	Is an excellent source of demographic information concerning the United States.
Centers for Disease Control/ National Center for Health Statistics	http://www.cdc.gov/nchs	Maintains data on vital events, health status, lifestyle, exposure to unhealthy influences, onset and diagnosis of illness and disability, and use of health care, through the National Center for Health Statistics. The NCHS, a subdivision of the Centers for Disease Control and Prevention, is the federal government's principal agency for vital and health statistics.
Claritas International	http://www.claritas.com	Provides access to a wide range of secondary data on many topics. Most must be purchased.
Cyberatlas	http://cyberatlas.internet.com	Offers viewers the latest research compiled from several reputable firms, including Media Metrix, Greenfield Online, Intelliquest, and Inteco. The geography page provides information on surveys of online populations around the world. There's also a generous section on e-commerce that breaks down research into different areas, like advertising, finance, and retail. Peek into the Stats Toolbox for a mother lode of lists on everything from weekly usage data to the top 10 banner ads.

(continued)

CHAPTER 4:
Secondary Data and Databases

Table 4.2

Some Sources of Secondary Data for Marketing Researchers on the Web (continued)

Organization	URL	Description
The Dismal Scientist	http://www.dismal.com	Provides timely economic information, with comprehensive data and analyses at the metro, state, and national levels. This authoritative site also has data and analyses of global issues, including situations facing Asia, South America, and Europe. Visitors can rank states and metro areas on more than 100 economic, socioeconomic, and demographic categories.
Easy Analytic Software, Inc./The Right Site	http://www.easidemographics.com	Offers demographic site reports, or three-ring studies, including current estimates for population and households. Each three-ring study has census estimates for race, ethnicity, age distribution, and income distribution, as well as weather data. The New York City–based developer and marketer of demographic data also offers one million pages of demographic reports for zip codes, counties, metropolitan areas, cities, states, sectional centers, television markets, and other geographic areas.
EconData.Net	http://www.econdata.net	Enables users to access a tremendous number of links to government, private, and academic data sources. Check out the list of top 10 data sources at this premier site for researchers interested in economics and demographics.
Encyclopedia Britannica	http://www.britannica.com	Provides free online access to the entire 32-volume encyclopedia.
FIND/SVP	http://www.findsvp.com	Offers consulting and research services. The site claims to offer access to the largest private information center in the United States.
Harris InfoSource	http://www.harrisinfo.com	Provides business-to-business data on American manufacturers and key decision makers.
Marketing Research Association	http://www.mra-net.org	Offers causes and solutions of "declining respondent cooperation" and links to research suppliers.
Mediamark Research/ Top-Line Reports	http://www.mediamark.com/mri/ docs/toplinereports.html	Allows marketers and researchers to access demographic data on magazines, cable TV, and 53 different product or service categories. Top-Line Reports breaks down cable TV networks' viewers according to age, sex, and income. Magazines are listed by total audience, circulation, readers per copy, median age, and income.

	Some Sources of Secondary Data for Marketing Researchers on the Web (continued)		
	Organization	**URL**	**Description**
	Nielsen//NetRatings	http://www.nielsen-netratings.com	Is a source of Internet audience information. Researchers can find data on Internet growth and user patterns.
	Population Reference Bureau	http://www.prb.org	Is a source of demographic information on population issues.
	Service Intelligence	http://www.serviceintelligence.com	Has an area devoted to customer stories of unpleasant experiences with airlines, banks, restaurants, and other service businesses. However, "hero" stories are also included.
	Social Security Administration	http://www.ssa.gov/statistics/supplement/2000	Provides a range of government statistics.
	Tetrad Computer Applications, Inc./Pcensus	http://www.tetrad.com	Provides detailed information about the population of metropolitan areas.
	U.S. Census Bureau	http://www.census.gov	Is a very useful source of virtually all census data.
	U.S. Department of Agriculture/Economic Research Service	http://www.ers.usda.gov	Offers a wide range of agricultural statistics.
	USAData	http://www.usadata.com	Provides access to consumer lifestyle data on a local, regional, and national basis.
	WorldOpinion	http://www.worldopinion.com	Offers thousands of marketing research reports. This is perhaps the premier site for the marketing research industry.

Table 4.2

Periodical, Newspaper, and Book Databases   Several excellent periodical, newspaper, and book databases are available to researchers (see Table 4.3). Some can be directly accessed via the Internet and others through your local library's Web site.

Newsgroups

A primary means of communicating with other professionals and special interest groups on the Internet is through newsgroups. With an Internet connection and newsreader software, you can visit any newsgroup supported by your service provider. If your service provider does not offer newsgroups or does not carry the group in which you are interested, you can find one of the publicly available newsgroup servers that does carry the group you'd like to read.

Newsgroups function much like bulletin boards for a particular topic or interest. A newsgroup is established to focus on a particular topic. Readers stop

newsgroup
An internet site where people can read and post messages devoted to a specific topic.

Table 4.3

Full-Text Periodical, Newspaper, and Book Databases Used by Marketing Researchers

ABI/Inform Global	Provides bibliographic information and abstracts for approximately 1,000 journals in business and management. Has full-text entries for approximately 520 journals, including *Journal of Marketing, JMR: Journal of Marketing Research,* and *Journal of the Academy of Marketing Science.* Updated monthly.
Dow Jones Interactive	Has full-text news articles from over 3,400 sources, including newspapers from around the world, as well as information on companies, industries, stocks, bonds, mutual funds, and foreign exchange rates. Updated daily.
Electric Library	Contains over 5 million full-text documents in all subject areas and an archive of up to 12 years. Covers six separate media types: newspapers and newswires, periodicals, TV & radio program transcripts, literature and reference books, photos, and maps. Updated daily.
LEXIS-NEXIS	Contains 2.5 billion searchable documents and adds 14.7 million new documents each week. Includes 18,871 news and business sources. Is the largest business information service, offering access to thousands of newspapers, magazines, trade journals, and industry newsletters worldwide; tax and accounting information; financial data; public records; legislative data; and company information.
Periodical Abstracts Research II (PAR)	Covers current affairs, business, industry news, cultural events, editorial material, and general-interest topics from more than 1,800 general and academic periodicals. Includes full-text articles from more than 600 journals. Began full-text coverage in 1992. Does not heavily index marketing journals, but does include, in full text, *Direct Marketing, Journal of Consumer Affairs,* and *Sales and Marketing Management.* Updated monthly.

by that newsgroup to read messages left by other people, post responses to others' questions, and send rebuttals to comments with which they disagree. Generally, there is some management of the messages to keep discussions within the topic area and to remove offensive material. However, readers of a newsgroup are free to discuss any issue and communicate with anyone in the world who visits that newsgroup. Images and data files can be exchanged in newsgroups, just as they can be exchanged via email.

With over 250,000 newsgroups currently in existence and more being added every day, there is a newsgroup for nearly every hobby, profession, and lifestyle. Both Netscape Navigator and Microsoft Internet Explorer, as well as other browsers, come with newsgroup readers. If you do not already have a newsgroup reader, you can go to one of the search engines and search for a freeware or shareware newsgroup reader. These newsgroup readers function much like email programs. To find a particular newsgroup, follow these steps:

1. Connect to the Internet in your usual way.
2. Open your newsreader program.
3. Search for the topic of interest. Most newsreaders allow you to search the names of the newsgroups for keywords or topics. Some newsreaders, like

Microsoft Internet Explorer, also allow you to search the brief descriptions that accompany most newsgroups.

4. Select the newsgroup of interest.
5. Begin scanning messages. The title of each message generally gives an indication of its subject matter.

Newsgroup messages look like email messages. They contain a subject title, author, and message body. Unlike normal email messages, however, newsgroup messages are threaded discussions. This means that any reply to a previous message will appear linked to that message. Therefore, you can follow a discussion between two or more people by starting at the original message and following the links (or threads) to each successive reply. Images, sound files, and video clips can be attached to messages for anyone to download and examine.

Federal Government Data

Some 70 federal agencies regularly publish data, and diligent searchers are hard-pressed to wade through all the results. In the past two years, federal agencies have posted a rich array of current information on the Internet, from their latest press releases to a wide range of historical results. The issue for the user is zeroing in on the information needed.

Several new hubs have been created to help solve this problem. Statistical Universe, developed by the Congressional Information Service, Inc. (CIS), is available either as a Web-based service (http://www.cispubs.com) or through the LEXIS-NEXIS STATIS library.[16] Statistical Universe builds on the CIS *American Statistics Index* (ASI), which researchers have used for decades. But unlike the ASI, which is a catalog of materials, Statistical Universe displays actual results from about 60 percent of the reports available. Material dating back to the 1970s is included, but only about 2,000 of the early reports can be accessed directly. Using the Statistical Universe is like having a huge library card catalog that delves inside the books, taking users to the precise page or table they are looking for. Once they find what they want, users can display the specific material or download the entire report. Statistical Universe is the most comprehensive and fully indexed source of federal statistics online.

Users who are looking for a particular recent report or who know which agency issued the data they are looking for might be better served by first checking with the free government Web sites. A good place to start is FEDSTATS (http://www.fedstats.gov), which has links to the 70 federal agencies recognized by the office of Management and Budget as issuing statistical data. This site's search engine covers reports from the 14 major statistical agencies, including the U.S. Census Bureau, Department of Commerce, and Bureau of Labor Statistics, and provides links to all the other agencies.

Users looking for information related to subjects in the news should try the White House Briefing Room (http://www.whitehouse.gov/WH/html/briefroom.html). The Federal Statistics page offers data on both economic issues (http://www.whitehouse.gov/fsbr/esbr.html) and social issues (http://www.whitehouse.gov/fsbr/ssbr.html). These pages provide an overview of the most newsworthy trends.

Databases on CD-ROM

A number of companies offer database packages on CD-ROM for personal computers. For example, Claritas International has packages called Compass/ Agency (for advertising agencies) and Compass/Newspaper (for newspapers) to do segmentation and demographic studies and mapping. To Compass/Agency, Claritas recently added Arbitron ratings and data from Simmons Marketing Research Bureau and Mediamark on product usage. The Compass/Newspaper system contains more than 200 preformatted reports and maps. Users can also import data on subscribers, readership, and advertisers and display them as reports or maps, or they can export data into other standard software packages, such as spreadsheet, word processing, and graphics applications.[17]

InfoUSA, a large secondary information provider, offers the databases listed in Table 4.4.

Information Management

Computerized databases, secondary data published or posted on the Internet, and internal databases are important parts of an organization's information system. Intelligent decision making is always predicated on having good information. The problem today is how to manage all the information available.

Table 4.4 Databases Offered on CD-ROM by InfoUSA

BusinessUSA	Covers 10 million businesses in the U.S. Search by Company, SIC Code, Major Industries, Employee Size, Sales Volume, Headquarters/Branch and much more! Package includes CD-ROM and printed directory.
HouseholdsUSA	When your business relies on home consumers, this CD-ROM provides key information on 100 million U.S. households: names, addresses, estimated home value, length of residence, homeowner vs. apartment dweller, estimated household income.
Physicians & Surgeons	Search by Name of Physician, Specialty or even Computer Use. Listings include over 575,000 physicians in 105 specialties. Package includes CD-ROM and printed directory.
Big Businesses	Printed directory and CD-ROM include information on 177,000 top firms and 581,000 key executives. You can even search by Executive Name. Plus, you'll find fax numbers.
Manufacturers	All 612,000 manufacturers broken down by 6-digit SIC Code. Printed directory lists all manufacturers with 25 or more employees.
Small Business Owners	Over 4.5 million businesses with fewer than 100 employees are listed on this CD-ROM, and the compatible directory lists over 1 million successful entrepreneurs. Search by owner's or company's name, business size or geographic area.

Source: Information from an undated brochure from InfoUSA, 5711 South 86th Circle, Omaha, Nebraska 68127.

According to Max Hopper, it was sometime after the middle of the 20th century that—for the first time in human history—we began to produce information faster than we could process it. He notes that various innovations—computers, microwave transmissions, television, satellites, and the like—have pushed us from a state of information scarcity to a state of information surplus in a very short time.[18]

The need to make better decisions requires that emphasis move from the problems of data acquisition to the problems of effectively managing and utilizing the vast sea of data available. Everyone who has been faced with a decision recognizes that information is the single most important input influencing the quality of that decision. Information is necessary to define the problem, to determine its scope and magnitude, and to generate and evaluate alternatives. Poor decisions are usually the result of using incorrect information, making invalid assumptions, or inappropriately analyzing of the information available.

Today, most managers in large- and medium-size organizations and progressive smaller ones are bombarded with information. The concern at firms such as American Airlines, Parke-Davis Pharmaceuticals, and Citicorp has shifted from the generation of information to the shaping and evaluation of information to make it useful to decision makers.

Information management is the development of a system for capturing, processing, and storing data so that it can be readily found and retrieved when needed for management decision making. American Airlines foresees in the near future information systems that

will drive the transition from corporate hierarchies to networks. Companies will become collections of experts who form teams to solve specific business problems and then disband. Information technology will blur distinctions between centralization and decentralization; senior managers will be able to contribute expertise without exercising authority.

[Our information system] will allow senior executives to make their presence felt more deeply without requiring more day-to-day control. Eventually, executives should be able to practice selective intervention. The information system, by virtue of its comprehensiveness, will alert senior managers to pockets of excellence or trouble and allow them to take appropriate action more quickly. Over time, the role of management will change from overseeing and control to resolving important problems and transferring the best practices throughout the organization.[19]

information management
The development of a system for capturing, processing, and storing data so that they can be readily retrieved when needed for management decision making.

Geographic Information Systems

A **geographic information system (GIS)** typically includes a demographic database, digitized maps, and software that enables the user to add corporate data to the mix. Utilities, oil companies, large retailers, and government agencies have long used these systems to display and analyze various types of data geographically. Today the technology accounts for several billion dollars a year in hardware, software, and consulting sales. The big change is that the cost of a GIS has fallen so dramatically in recent years that it is now one of the hottest business information tools. Companies as diverse as Cigna, Sears, Super Valu, The Gap, and Isuzu have embraced mapping as an easier and more powerful way to interpret data than mind-numbing printouts, spreadsheets, and charts. Maps offer researchers, managers, and clients an intuitive way to organize data and to see relationships and patterns.

geographic information system (GIS)
Computer-based system that uses secondary and/or primary data to generate maps that visually display various types of data geographically.

Meineke uses geographic information systems to map its stores and competitors in relation to its customer base. Go to http://www.meineke.com to find out how it positions its Web site based on customer information.

After 113 years of direct selling, Avon Products decided to enter the mall. Avon turned to mapping software from Tactician Corporation, based in Andover, Massachusetts, to figure out where the kiosks should go. The software allows the company to manipulate more than 1.5 gigabytes of data. Analysts can overlay representative territories and sales information with population data from the U.S. Census Bureau to find out where Avon is and isn't selling. The mapping program with its Selling Machine add-ons can also help identify population shifts and determine which strategy works best among a given demographic. For example, the software helped Avon pinpoint a growing Asian-American population in the Southeast. To boost sales in this market, the company is showing local reps which products Asian-American women might prefer, such as lighter cremes and foundations. Selling Machine is Tactician's most popular specialty product, used by companies such as Hallmark, Ralston Purina, and Staples.[20]

Geographers talk about lines, points, and areas, while marketing researchers talk about roads, stores, and sales territories. But thinking in terms of lines, points, and areas is a good way to sort out the business uses of geovisual databases. Applications involving lines include finding the quickest truck routes for long-haul freight companies and the shortest routes for local delivery trucks. Applications involving points include finding the best potential sites for retail bank branches and devising the best strategy for a network of miniwarehouses. Applications involving areas range from finding the best markets for hardware sales to identifying the best location for a new Taco Bell. A GIS can also answer more detailed marketing questions. If a marketing researcher for Target wanted to know how many of the company's high performance stores have trading areas that overlap by at least 50 percent with trading areas for Wal-Mart, a geovisual system could perform a function geographers call *spatial querying* to address the question.

Aftermarket auto repair is a highly competitive $90 billion-a-year business in which dealerships have improved their services and marketshare. To stay ahead of the competition, Meineke Discount Muffler Shops have turned to GIS. Each week, Meineke's 900 franchisees send detailed customer and service records back to Meineke headquarters in Charlotte, North Carolina. Records include the customer's name and home address; vehicle make, model, and year; work performed; and payment method. They also explain how the customer learned about Meineke, such as through the Yellow Pages, a friend, or a TV commercial featuring George Foreman.

PART 2:

Creating a Research Design

Meineke processes 5,000 records a week through MapMarker, from MapInfo Corporation of Troy, New York. MapMarker cleanses the data, eliminating post office boxes and assigning "north" or "south" to appropriate addresses, and pinpoints each location on a map. Meineke can then map its stores, competitors, and other retail outlets in relation to its customer base. Using MapMarker, Meineke can gauge the effectiveness of an advertising campaign by mapping all of the households in a particular market that visited an outlet because of a local radio or TV commercial. The geocoding tool can also detect potential sites for new Meineke outlets (see Figure 4.1).

Meineke can customize trade areas as it sees fit. If marketing research shows that some customers won't cross a river or a state boundary to get to the nearest outlet but will drive two miles farther to another Meineke franchise in a different zip code, the company can use MapMarker to create a map that reflects those shopping patterns. Then it can overlay demographic data onto the map to determine the region's overall sales potential. "We can see what our share of the market is instantly," says Stacey Monroe, an analyst at Meineke.[21]

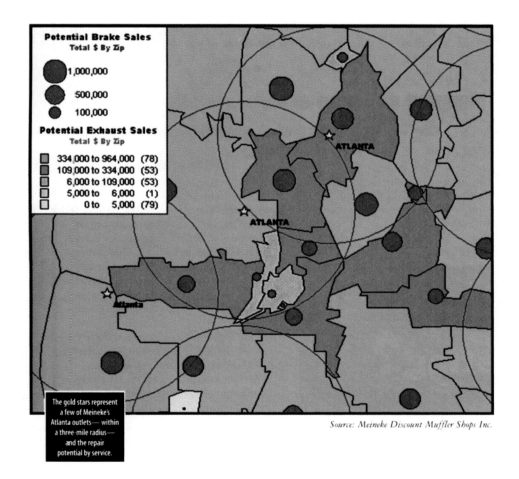

Source: Meineke Discount Muffler Shops Inc.

Figure 4.1

A GIS Map Created for Meineke Discount Muffler Shops in Atlanta, Georgia

Decision Support Systems

decision support system (DSS)

An interactive, personalized information management system, designed to be initiated and controlled by individual decision makers.

A **decision support system (DSS)** is designed to support the needs and styles of individual decision makers. In theory, a DSS represents something close to the ultimate in data management. We say "in theory" because, for the most part, the ideal has not been realized in practice. However, there have been some notable exceptions that have provided a glimpse of how a DSS can truly support the decision-making process. Characteristics of a true DSS are as follows:

- *Interactive.* The manager gives simple instructions and sees results generated on the spot. The process is under the manager's direct control; no computer programmer is needed and there is no need to wait for scheduled reports.
- *Flexible.* It can sort, regroup, total, average, and manipulate data in a variety of ways. It will shift gears as the user changes topics, matching information to the problem at hand. For example, the chief executive can see highly aggregated figures, while the marketing analyst can view detailed breakouts.
- *Discovery-oriented.* It helps managers probe for trends, isolate problems, and ask new questions.
- *Easy to learn and use.* Managers need not be particularly knowledgeable about computers. Novice users can elect a standard, or default, method of using the system, bypassing optional features to work with the basic system immediately. The opportunity to gradually learn about the system's possibilities minimizes the frustration that frequently accompanies use of new computer software.

Managers use a DSS to conduct sales analyses, forecast sales, evaluate advertising, analyze product lines, and keep tabs on market trends and competitors' actions. A DSS not only allows managers to ask "what if" questions but enables them to view any given slice of the data.

Here's a hypothetical example of using a DSS provided by a manager of new products:

To evaluate sales of a recently introduced new product, we can "call up" sales by the week, then by the month, breaking them out at [the vice president's] option by, say, customer segments. As he works at his terminal, his inquiries could go in several directions depending on the decision at hand. If his train of thought raises questions about monthly sales last quarter compared to forecasts, he wants his decision support system to follow along and give him answers immediately.

He might see that his new product's sales were significantly below forecast. Forecasts too optimistic? He compares other products' sales to his forecasts and finds that the targets were very accurate. Something wrong with the product? Maybe his sales department is getting insufficient leads, or is not putting leads to good use? Thinking a minute about how to examine that question, he checks ratios of leads converted to sales, product by product. The results disturb him. Only 5 percent of the new product's leads generate orders compared to the company's 12 percent all-product average. Why? He guesses that the sales force is not supporting the new product vigorously enough. Quantitative information from the DSS perhaps could provide more evidence to back that suspicion. But already having enough quantitative knowledge to satisfy himself, the VP acts on his intuition and experience and decides to have a chat with his sales manager.

PART 2:
Creating a Research Design

Summary

Secondary data are previously gathered information that *might* be relevant to the problem at hand. They can come from sources internal to the organization or external to it. Primary data are survey, observation, or experiment data collected to solve the particular problem under investigation.

A database is a collection of related data. A traditional type of internal marketing database is founded on customer information. For example, a customer database may have demographic and perhaps psychographic information about existing customers and purchase data such as when the goods and services were bought, the types of merchandise procured, the dollar amount of sales, and any promotional information associated with sales. A database can even be created from recorded conversations. An internal database also may contain competitive intelligence, such as new products offered by competitors and changes in competitors' service policies and prices.

Web site databases can produce important insights. A Web merchant can track a person as he or she clicks through a site. The merchant can examine what was looked at and what was bought. The screen the customer will see first on the next visit to the site can be tailored to the customer's past purchase and browsing behavior. Cookies are an important tool for monitoring a user's behavior within a site.

Data mining has dramatically increased users' ability to get insightful information out of databases. It can be used to acquire new customers, retain existing customers, abandon accounts that are not cost effective, and engage in market-based analyses.

The proliferation of databases on and off the Internet has raised consumer and government concerns over privacy. Most likely, the federal government will pass Internet privacy legislation that will protect consumer rights and place privacy responsibilities on database builders.

Using secondary data has several advantages. Secondary data may (1) help to clarify or redefine the problem during the exploratory research process, (2) actually provide a solution to the problem, (3) provide primary data research method alternatives, (4) alert the marketing researcher to potential problems and difficulties, and (5) provide necessary background data and build credibility for the research report. The disadvantages of using secondary data include lack of availability, lack of relevance, inaccuracy, and insufficient data.

The Internet has, in many ways, revolutionized the gathering of secondary data. Now, rather than wait for replies from government agencies or other sources, users can find millions of pieces of information on the Internet. Trips to the library may become a thing of the past for many researchers. Search engines and directories contain links to millions of documents throughout the world. Special-interest discussion groups on the Internet can also be valuable sources of secondary data.

CD-ROM database packages from firms like Claritas International and InfoUSA can leverage the value of primary data by marrying the data with secondary information found in the database packages. One application, for example, is using demographic data from a primary study to ascertain lifestyle information from secondary databases owned by Claritas or Equifax. Geographic information systems, which consist of a demographic database, digitized maps, and software, enable users to add primary data from a current study (or secondary corporate data) to the mix. The result is computer-generated maps that can reveal a variety of strategic findings to marketing managers; for example, a map may indicate an optimal location for a new retail store.

Decision support systems are designed from the individual decision maker's perspective. DSS systems are interactive, flexible, discovery-oriented, and easy to learn; they can offer many benefits to small and large firms alike.

Key Terms & Definitions

secondary data   Data that have been previously gathered.

primary data   New data gathered to help solve the problem under investigation.

internal database   A collection of related information developed from data within the organization.

database marketing   Marketing that relies on the creation of a large computerized file of customers' and potential customers' profiles and purchase patterns.

cookie   A text file placed on a user's computer in order to identify the user when she or he revisits the Web site.

neural network   A computer program that mimics the processes of the human brain and thus is capable of learning from examples to find patterns in data.

data mining   The use of statistical and other advanced software to discover nonobvious patterns hidden in a database.

newsgroup   An internet site where people can read and post messages devoted to a specific topic.

information management   The development of a system for capturing, processing, and storing data so that they can be readily retrieved when needed for management decision making.

geographic information system (GIS)   Computer-based system that uses secondary and/or primary data to generate maps that visually display various types of data geographically.

decision support system (DSS)   An interactive, personalized information management system, designed to be initiated and controlled by individual decision makers.

Questions for Review & Critical Thinking

1. Why should companies consider creating an internal marketing database? Name some types of information that might be found in this database and the sources of this information.
2. Why has data mining become so popular with firms like United Airlines, American Express, and Ford Motor Company?
3. What are some of the keys to ensuring the success of an internal database?
4. Why are secondary data often preferred to primary data?
5. What pitfalls might a researcher encounter in using secondary data?
6. In the absence of company problems, is there any need to conduct marketing research or develop a decision support system?

Working the Net

1. What makes vendors' Web sites a desirable tool for creating an internal database?
2. Why has the Internet been of such great value to researchers seeking secondary data?
3. Go to http://www.yankelovich.com. Explain to the class the nature and scope of the Yankelovich MONITOR. How can marketing researchers use the data from this research?
4. Go to http://www.icpsr.umich.edu/gss. What is the General Social Survey? Compare and contrast its usefulness to marketing researchers with that of the Yankelovich MONITOR.
5. You are interested in home-building trends in the United States, as your company, Whirlpool, is a major supplier of kitchen appliances. Go to http://www.nahb.com and describe what types of information at this site might be of interest to Whirlpool.
6. Go to http://www.claritas.com. Describe types of secondary data available at this site.

Real-Life Research • 4.1

U.S. Sports Car Market

Jack Marquardt recently received his MSMR (Master of Science in Marketing Research) from the University of Texas at Arlington. He accepted a position with Nissan USA as a marketing researcher and has been assigned to work with a product management group. The product management group is in the midst of a crash program to evaluate Nissan's current product portfolio for the U.S. market and make recommendations to senior management regarding auto product requirements for this market for the next 10 years.

Phase I of the process is to do background research on various broad segments of the market (e.g., sports utility vehicles, sports cars, economy cars, luxury cars, etc.). Different members of the marketing research team have been assigned to do the background research on individual market segments. Jack has been assigned to analyze the sports car segment. He needs to have his preliminary work completed by morning in order to present his analysis and preliminary conclusions regarding the future potential and trends in this segment.

Given the short time frame available, Jack knows his only hope is to use the Internet to find the information he needs in order to assemble his report.

Questions

Use the Internet sites recommended in this chapter to write a two-page report covering the following points:

1. Current size of the U.S. sports car market
2. Market growth trends
3. Leading brands in the market today
4. Demographic trends that will affect the market over the next 10 years
5. Other points you think are relevant to the questions above
6. Whether this is a good time or a bad time for Jack's company to establish a larger presence in this market

Real-Life Research • 4.2

Building a Hotel in Colorado

Bill and Mary Osborn hit it lucky with dot.com stocks. At the age of 39, they have amassed $5.2 million, and now they are ready to pursue their dream.

Bill and Mary have always wanted to live in Colorado and have dreamed of owning a small hotel. They've decided to do both—that is, build a hotel in Colorado that they can manage. Initial research has uncovered the following information.

When asked to name two or three things that are most important in choosing a hotel for a vacation, Americans put nonsmoking rooms first (40%), followed by 24-hour access to food (36%), quality in-room amenities such as coffee makers and hair dryers (34%), athletic facilities (31%), and "good evening facilities" (26%). They rank supervised activities for children much higher than do business travelers (10% versus 3%).

In contrast, overnight business travelers who traveled in the past year focus on things that will make their trip more productive. Like vacationers, they rate nonsmoking rooms top (46%). But they put quality in-room amenities (39%) and transportation to the airport (32%) next. And they put a much higher priority than do vacationers on in-room connections for computer, fax, and online access (21%, 17 points higher than vacationers), being able to earn airline miles (15%, up 8), and frequent guest programs (14%, up 5).[22]

Questions

Use the Internet to help answer the following questions:
1. In what price range should rooms be offered?
2. Where in Colorado should the hotel be built?
3. Should the hotel cater primarily to business or vacation travelers?
4. What amenities and features should the hotel offer?
5. Should the Osborns consider becoming franchisees?

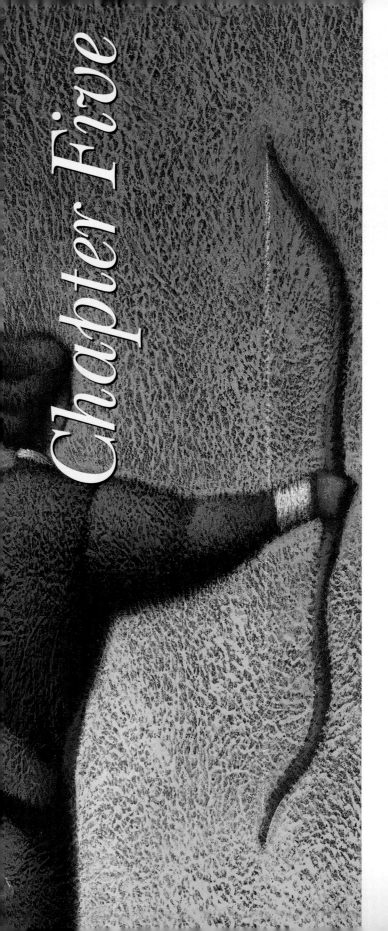

Chapter Five

Qualitative Research

Learning Objectives

To define qualitative research.

To explore the popularity of qualitative research.

To understand why qualitative research is not held in high esteem by some practitioners and academicians.

To learn about focus groups and their tremendous popularity.

To gain insight into conducting and analyzing a focus group.

To understand the controversy regarding online focus groups.

To understand the growing popularity of Internet focus groups.

To learn about other forms of qualitative research.

I N MANY WAYS, IT'S A COMMON MARKETING SITUATION: A MANUFACTURER faces dwindling sales of a venerable product due to a shrinking core market; an ancillary market holds some promise but its growth potential is hindered by pricing issues. In other ways, it's almost unique: most of the people who buy the product do so because they have to, not because they want to; and most of them have no idea what the product is used for.

THEN THERE'S THE PRODUCT ITSELF: DUCK STAMPS. KNOWN IN OFFICIAL PARL-

ance as Migratory Bird Hunting and Conservation Stamps, duck stamps are a required annual purchase for duck hunters. (Most hunters say they have little idea of what duck stamp fees are used for. They just know that you have to buy a stamp if you want to hunt ducks.) But the number of hunters is decreasing, and though the stamps are sought after by collectors, their hefty price (last year's stamp was $15) makes accumulating them an expensive proposition for the garden-variety philatelist. "We needed to find a way to reach a new audience, to broaden our market, as with any product," says Margaret Wendy, manager of sales and marketing, Federal Duck Stamp Office, Department of the Interior, U.S. Fish and Wildlife Service, Washington, D.C.

INITIALLY, THE IDEA WAS TO FOCUS THE marketing campaign on the stamps themselves, their beauty and the value of collecting them. But in focus groups conducted during the development of the campaign by The Ball Group, a Lancaster, Pennsylvania–based research and advertising firm, the stamps themselves weren't enough to make the sale. "The collecting aspect was of minimal interest," says Wes Ball, the firm's president.

The Federal Duck Stamp Office used focus groups to find out how to reach a new audience and broaden its marketing efforts.

FOCUS GROUPS WERE HELD IN CITIES AROUND THE COUNTRY, TWO GROUPS PER city, one with environmentally active people and the other with people who were not environmentally active but who were not predisposed against environmental issues. (In addition, a telephone survey with a random national sample was conducted to determine awareness of the Duck Stamp program and to gauge interest and participation in environmental issues.)

Find out more about the Duck Stamp program at

http:// duckstamps. fws.gov

THANKS TO NEW STRATEGIES BASED UPON THE MARKETING RESEARCH, HUNTERS and stamp collectors won't be the only ones making an annual duck stamp purchase. "We discovered a huge contingent who are concerned about the environment, especially air and water quality, and they believed that wetlands are a primary water filter for us, and felt that [up to] a $30 contribution was not only attractive but one that they would actively support again and again. We had people say, 'Now that I know about this I'll contribute money every year,' " Ball says.[1] ■

Focus groups—a form of a qualitative research—were used to better understand the potential buyers of duck stamps. What is qualitative research? How is it conducted? Is one form of qualitative research more popular than others? What makes qualitative research, and particularly online focus groups, so controversial? These are some of the issues we will explore in this chapter.

The Nature of Qualitative Research

qualitative research
Research whose findings are not subject to quantification or quantitative analysis.
quantitative research
Research that uses mathematical analysis.

Qualitative research is a term used loosely to refer to research whose findings are not subject to quantification or quantitative analysis. A quantitative study may determine that a heavy user of a particular brand of tequila is 21 to 35 years of age and has an annual income of $18,000 to $25,000. While **quantitative research** might be used to find statistically significant differences between heavy and light users, qualitative research could be used to examine the attitudes, feelings, and motivations of the heavy user. Advertising agencies planning a campaign for tequila might employ qualitative techniques to learn how heavy users express themselves and what language they use—essentially, how to communicate with them.

The qualitative approach was derived from the work of the mid-18th-century historian Giambattista Vico. Vico wrote that only people can understand people and that they do so through a faculty called *intuitive understanding*. In sociology and other social sciences, the concept of *Verstehen,* or the intuitive experiment, and the use of empathy have been associated with major discoveries (and disputes).

Qualitative Research versus Quantitative Research

Table 5.1 compares qualitative and quantitative research on several levels. Perhaps most significant to managers is the fact that qualitative research typically is characterized by small samples—a trait that has been a focal point for criticism of all qualitative techniques. In essence, many managers are reluctant to base important strategy decisions on small-sample research because it relies so greatly on the subjectivity and interpretation of the researcher. They strongly prefer a large sample, with results analyzed on a computer and summarized into tables. These managers feel comfortable with marketing research based on large samples and high levels of statistical significance, because the data are generated in a rigorous and scientific manner.

The Popularity of Qualitative Research

Why does the popularity of qualitative research continue to grow? First, qualitative research is usually much cheaper than quantitative research. Second, there is no better way to understand the in-depth motivations and feelings of consumers. When, in a popular form of qualitative research, product managers unobtrusively observe from behind a one-way mirror, they obtain first-hand experiences with flesh-and-blood consumers. Instead of plodding through a computer printout or consultant's report that requires them to digest reams of numbers, the product manager and other marketing personnel observe con-

PART 2:
Creating a Research Design

Table 5.1

Qualitative versus Quantitative Research

	Qualitative Research	Quantitative Research
Types of questions	Probing	Limited probing
Sample size	Small	Large
Amount of information from each respondent	Substantial	Varies
Requirements for administration	Interviewer with special skills	Interviewer with fewer special skills
Type of analysis	Subjective, interpretive	Statistical, summation
Hardware	Tape recorders, projection devices, video recorders, pictures, discussion guides	Questionnaires, computers, printouts
Degree of replicability	Low	High
Researcher training	Psychology, sociology, social psychology, consumer behavior, marketing, marketing research	Statistics, decision models, decision support systems, computer programming, marketing, marketing research
Type of research	Exploratory	Descriptive or causal

sumers' reactions to concepts and hear consumers discuss their and their competitors' products at length, in their own language. Sitting behind a one-way mirror can be a humbling experience for a new product development manager when the consumer begins to tear apart product concepts that were months in development in the sterile laboratory environment.

A third reason for the popularity of qualitative research is that it can improve the efficiency of quantitative research. Volvo Cars of North America was concerned that the U.S. automotive market was undergoing vast changes that could affect its market share. Volvo decided to embark on a major research study to gain an appreciation of the changing marketplace. The project involved both a quantitative and a qualitative phase. Because the qualitative initial phase of the

Volvo used both qualitative and quantitative research to gain an appreciation of the vast changes in the U.S. automotive market. Go to http://www.volvo.com to see Volvo's newest car models, such as the S-60 pictured here.

project enabled researchers to use a shorter questionnaire in the second phase, the quantitative study was both more informative and less expensive. Among the insights gained in the qualitative phase were the following:

1. The ways potential buyers considered Volvo fell into a number of different categories. Some very seriously considered purchasing a Volvo and narrowed the choice of cars to Volvo and one other make. Others seriously considered buying a Volvo, but it was not among the cars involved in the final decision.
2. Some people seriously considered buying a Volvo without ever visiting a showroom.
3. There are several important subsegments within Volvo's share of the U.S. market, despite its small size.

It is becoming more common for marketing researchers to combine qualitative and quantitative research into a single study or a series of studies. The Volvo example showed how qualitative research can be used prior to quantitative research; in other research designs, the two types of research are conducted in the reverse order. For instance, the patterns displayed in quantitative research can be enriched with the addition of qualitative information on the reasons and motivations of consumers. One major insurance company conducted a quantitative study in which respondents were asked to rank the importance of 50 service characteristics. Later, focus groups were conducted in which participants were asked to define and expound on the top 10 characteristics. Most of these characteristics dealt with client–insurance agent interactions. From these focus groups the researchers found that "agent responds quickly" may mean either a virtually instantaneous response or a response within a reasonable time; that is, it means "as soon as is humanly possible for emergencies" and "about 24 hours for routine matters." The researchers noted that, had they not conducted focus groups after the quantitative study, they could only have theorized about what "responds quickly" means to customers.[2]

In the final analysis, all marketing research is undertaken to increase the effectiveness of decision making. Qualitative research blends with quantitative measures to provide a more thorough understanding of consumer demand. Qualitative techniques involve open-ended questioning and probing. The resulting data are rich, human, subtle, and often very revealing.[3]

Limitations of Qualitative Research

Qualitative research can and does produce helpful and useful information—yet it is held in disdain by many researchers. One drawback relates to the fact that marketing successes and failures many times are based on small differences in attitudes or opinions about a marketing mix, and qualitative research does not distinguish those small differences as well as large-scale quantitative research does. However, qualitative research is sometimes able to detect problems that escape notice in a quantitative study. For example, a major manufacturer of household cleaners conducted a large quantitative study in an effort to learn why its bathroom cleanser had lackluster sales when in fact its chemical compound was more effective than those used by leading competitors. The quantitative study provided no clear-cut answer. The frustrated product manager then turned to qualitative research, which quickly uncovered that the muted pastel colors on

PART 2:
Creating a Research Design

the package did not connote "cleansing strength" to the shopper. In light of this finding and the finding that a number of people were using old toothbrushes to clean between their bathroom tiles, the package was redesigned with brighter, bolder colors and with a brush built into the top.

A second limitation of qualitative studies is that they are not necessarily representative of the population of interest to the researcher. One would be hard-pressed to say that a group of 10 college students was representative of all college students, of college students at a particular university, of business majors at that university, or even of marketing majors! Small sample size and free-flowing discussion can lead qualitative research projects down many paths. Because the subjects of qualitative research are free to talk about what interests them, a dominant individual in a group discussion can lead the group into areas of only tangential interest to the researcher. It takes a highly skilled researcher to get the discussion back on track without stifling the group's interest, enthusiasm, and willingness to speak out.

A final concern about qualitative research is the multitude of individuals who, without formal training, profess to be experts in the field. Because marketing research has no certification body, anyone can call himself or herself a qualitative expert. Unfortunately, it is often difficult for the client to discern the researcher's qualifications or the quality of the research. Given the extensive training required to conduct a sophisticated quantitative study, it is extremely difficult, if not impossible, to bluff one's way through this type of project.

The Growing Role of Focus Groups

Focus groups had their beginnings in group therapy used by psychiatrists. Today, a **focus group** consists of 8 to 12 participants who are led by a moderator in an in-depth discussion on one particular topic or concept. The goal of focus group research is to learn and understand what people have to say and why. The emphasis is on getting people to talk at length and in detail about the subject at hand. The intent is to find out how they feel about a product, concept, idea, or organization; how it fits into their lives; and their emotional involvement with it.

Focus groups are much more than merely question-and-answer interviews. A distinction is made between *group dynamics* and *group interviewing*. The interaction associated with **group dynamics** is essential to the success of focus group research; this interaction is the reason for conducting research with a group rather than with individuals. One of the ideas behind focus groups is that a response from one person will become a stimulus for another person, thereby generating an interplay of responses that will yield more information than if the same number of people had contributed independently.

The idea for group dynamics research in marketing came from the field of social psychology, where studies indicated that, unknown to themselves, people of all walks of life and in all occupations would talk more about a topic and do so in greater depth if they were encouraged to act spontaneously instead of reacting to questions. Normally, in group dynamics, direct questions are avoided. In their place are indirect inquiries that stimulate free and spontaneous discussions. The result is a much richer base of information, of a kind impossible to obtain by direct questioning.

focus group
A group of 8 to 12 participants who are led by a moderator in an in-depth discussion on one particular topic or concept.

group dynamics
The interaction among people in a group.

The Popularity of Focus Groups

The terms *qualitative research* and *focus groups* are often used as synonyms by marketing research practitioners. Popular writing abounds with examples of researchers referring to qualitative research in one breath and focus groups in the next. Though focus groups are but one aspect of qualitative research, the overwhelming popularity of the technique has virtually overshadowed the use of other qualitative tools.

How popular are focus groups? Most marketing research firms, advertising agencies, and consumer goods manufacturers use them. Today, about 25 percent of all marketing research expenditures go to qualitative research, and a vast majority of this money is spent on focus groups (approximately a billion dollars per year, worldwide). Leo Burnett Company, for example, conducts more than 350 focus groups each year for clients.[4] Focus groups tend to be used more extensively by consumer goods companies than by industrial goods organizations, as forming industrial groups poses a host of problems not found in consumer research. For example, it is usually quite easy to assemble a group of 12 homemakers; however, putting together a group of 10 engineers, sales managers, or financial analysts is far more costly and time-consuming.

Lewis Stone, former manager of Colgate-Palmolive's Research and Development Division, says the following about focus groups:

If it weren't for focus groups, Colgate-Palmolive Co. might never know that some women squeeze their bottles of dishwashing soap, others squeeeeeze them, and still others squeeeeeeeeze out the desired amount. Then there are the ones who use the soap "neat." That is, they put the product directly on a sponge or washcloth and wash the dishes under running water until the suds run out. Then they apply more detergent.

Stone was explaining how body language, exhibited during focus groups, provides insights into a product that are not apparent from reading questionnaires on habits and practices. Focus groups represent a most efficient way of learning how one's products are actually used in the home. By drawing out the panelists to describe in detail how they do certain tasks . . . you can learn a great deal about possible need-gaps that could be filled by new or improved products, and also how a new product might be received.[5]

Thus, an "experiencing" approach represents an opportunity to learn from a flesh-and-blood consumer. Reality in the kitchen or supermarket differs drastically from that in most corporate offices. Focus groups allow the researcher to experience the emotional framework in which the product is being used. In a sense, the researcher can go into a person's life and relive with him or her all the satisfactions, dissatisfactions, rewards, and frustrations experienced when the product is taken home.

Conducting Focus Groups

On the following pages, we will consider the process of conducting focus groups, illustrated in Figure 5.1. The space devoted to this topic is considerable because there is much potential for researcher error in conducting focus groups.

The Setting Focus groups are usually held in a **focus group facility.** The setting is often a conference room, with a large one-way mirror built into one wall.

focus group facility
Research facility consisting of a conference room or living room setting and a separate observation room with a one-way mirror or live audio-visual feed.

PART 2:
Creating a Research Design

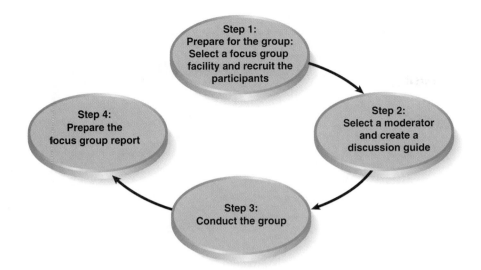

Figure 5.1

Steps in Conducting a Focus Group

Microphones are placed in an unobtrusive location (usually the ceiling) to record the discussion. Behind the mirror is the viewing room, which holds chairs and note-taking benches or tables for the clients. The viewing room also houses the recording or videotaping equipment. The photo in Figure 5.2 of a focus group facility illustrates how clients may view a focus group from behind a one-way mirror.

Some research firms offer a living-room setting as an alternative to the conference room. It is presumed that the informality of a living room (a typical home-like setting) will make the participants more at ease. Another variation is to televise the proceedings to a remote viewing room rather than use a one-way mirror. This approach offers clients the advantage of being able to move around and speak in a normal tone of voice without being heard through the wall. On more than one occasion, focus groups have been distracted by a flash seen through the mirror when a client lit a cigarette or moved too suddenly while watching the group.

The Participants   Participants for focus groups are recruited from a variety of sources. Two common procedures are *mall-intercept interviewing* and *random telephone screening*. (Both methods are described in detail in Chapter 6.) Researchers normally establish criteria for the group participants. For example, if Quaker Oats is researching a new cereal, it might request as participants mothers who have children between 7 and 12 years old and who have served cold cereal, perhaps of a specific brand, in the past three weeks.

Usually, researchers strive to avoid repeat, or "professional," respondents in focus groups. Professional respondents are viewed by many researchers as actors or, at the very least, less than candid participants. Questions also may be raised regarding the motives of the person who would continually come to group sessions. Is she or he lonely? Does she or he really need the respondent fee that badly? It is highly unlikely that professional respondents are representative of many, if any, target markets. Unfortunately, field services find it much easier to use repeat respondents than to recruit a new group of individuals each time. Sample screening questions to identify repeat respondents are shown in Figure 5.3.

Figure 5.2

A Focus Group Room with a One-Way Mirror

Focus groups most often evaluate new ideas, concepts, and products. Some individuals are more receptive to new things than others are. Also, certain people have a flair for coming up with new ideas. When focus groups call for "creative thinkers," screening questions can help identify those individuals. Figure 5.4 offers an example of a scaling question designed to uncover creative persons.

Although there is no ideal number of participants, a typical group will contain 8 participants. If the group contains more than 8 people, group members will have little time to express their opinions. Rarely will a group last more than two hours; an hour and a half is more common. The first 10 minutes is spent on introductions and an explanation of procedures. This leaves about 80 useful minutes in the session, and up to 25 percent of that time may be taken by the moderator. With 10 people in the group, an average of only six minutes per individual is left for actual discussion. If the topic is quite interesting or of a technical nature, fewer than 8 respondents may be needed. The type of group will also affect the number recruited.

Why do people agree to participate in focus groups? Research shows that the number one reason is money.[6] Other motivations, in rank order, are (2) the topic was interesting, (3) it was a convenient time, (4) focus groups are fun, (5) respondent knew a lot about the product, (6) curiosity, and (7) focus groups offer an opportunity to express opinions. The study also found that participants who came only for the money were less committed to research and tended to fulfill their roles in a more perfunctory way.

focus group moderator
A person hired by the client to lead the focus group; this person should have a background in psychology or sociology or, at least, marketing.

The Moderator   Having qualified respondents and a good focus group moderator are the keys to a successful focus group. A **focus group moderator** needs two sets of skills. First, the moderator must be able to conduct a group properly. Second, he or she must have good business skills in order to effectively interact with the client. Key attributes for conducting a focus group include the following:

PART 2:
Creating a Research Design

1. Past Participation Series

Sometimes it is important to talk with people who have participated in previous research because they have experience talking about certain topics. At other times, it is important to talk with people who have never participated in an opinion study. Often we are looking for a mix of different experiences. What type of opinion studies, if any, have you ever participated in? (DO NOT READ LIST.)

	CIRCLE ALL MENTIONS
One-on-one in-person depth interview	1
Group interview with two or more participants	2
Mock jury or trial	3
Product placement test with a follow-up interview	4
Mall interview	5
Taste test	6
Phone survey	7
Other (SPECIFY)	8
None	9

1A. When was the last time you participated in a

_____ Group interview with two or more participants

_____ (LIST ANOTHER TYPE OF RESEARCH YOU MIGHT CONSIDER INAPPROPRIATE.)

IF WITHIN THE LAST SIX MONTHS, THANK AND TERMINATE.

1B. What were the topics of all of the group interviews in which you have participated?

_____

_____

IF ONE OF THE TOPICS LISTED BELOW IS MENTIONED, THANK AND TERMINATE.

(   ) Banking

(   ) Telephone service: local and/or long distance

1C. Are you currently scheduled to participate in any type of market research study?

	CIRCLE	
Yes	1	➜ (THANK AND TERMINATE)
No	2	➜ (CONTINUE)

Source: Merrill Shugoll and Nancy Kolkebeck, "You Get What You Ask For," *Quirk's Marketing Research Review* (December 1999), pp. 61–65. Reprinted by permission.

1. Genuine interest in people, their behavior, emotions, lifestyles, passions, and opinions.
2. Acceptance and appreciation for the differences in people, especially those whose lives vary greatly from your own.

WAR Stories

Action Research . . . was recruiting people for a focus group. A man was disqualified toward the end of the screener, due to a lack of knowledge about the business being studied. But this was after being told about the $40 incentive. The man became very irate and demanded $40 for his time. A supervisor spent half an hour on the phone politely explaining that he was disqualified and that the stipend was for actual participants. The individual then stated he would visit Action Research headquarters in the morning to make sure it was a "legit" business.

The next morning, the man did show up, entered an employee's office, and refused to leave until he was paid $40. The staff once again explained to the person he had been disqualified on the phone for the focus group and that he should leave. The man refused to leave and started shouting, and following staff around the building. The office manager called the police while staff attempted to reason with the man.

The police arrived and warned the man to leave the premises. He refused, instead choosing to head up the stairs, prepared to smash the windows. Needless to say, the police arrested the man and were forced to literally carry him away. It was later learned that when the man appeared before a judge (he had to be carried in), he laid on the floor and refused to speak or enter a plea. The judge ordered him taken away for psychiatric evaluation . . . where he presently remains. It is assumed he is still demanding $40.

Source: "War Stories: True Life Tales in Marketing Research," by Art Shulman, *Quirk's Marketing Research Review* (October 1999). Reprinted by permission of Art Shulman.

3. Good listening skills: The ability both to hear what is being said and to identify what is not being said.
4. Good observation skills: The ability to see in detail what is happening or not happening and to interpret body language.
5. Interest in a wide range of topics and the ability to immerse yourself in the topic and learn the necessary knowledge and language quickly.
6. Good oral and written communication skills: The ability to clearly express yourself and to do so confidently in groups of all types and sizes.
7. Objectivity: The ability to set your personal ideas and feelings aside and remain open to the ideas and feelings of others.
8. Sound knowledge of the basic principles, foundations, and applications of research, marketing, and advertising.
9. Flexibility, ability to live with uncertainty, make fast decisions, and think on your feet (or the part of your anatomy that is seated in the moderator's chair).
10. Good attention to detail and organizational ability.[7]

In addition to the above, a moderator needs the following client-focused skills:

1. An ability to understand the client's business in more than just a cursory fashion, to become an integral part of the project team, and to have credibility with senior management.
2. The ability to provide the strategic leadership in both the planning and the execution phases of a project in order to improve the overall research design and provide more relevant information on which to base decisions.
3. Providing feedback to and being a sounding board for the client at every stage of the research process, including before, during, and after the groups. This includes being able to turn the research findings into strategically sound implications for the client at the end of the project.
4. Reliability, responsiveness, trustworthiness, independence, and a dogged determination to remove obstacles in order to get the job done.
5. A personal style that is a comfortable match with the client.[8]

In the past few years, there has been an increase in the number of formal moderator training courses offered by advertising agencies, research firms, and manufacturers with large marketing research departments. Most programs are strictly for employees, but a few are open to anyone.

A second, more informal school of thought on moderator training emphasizes personality, empathy, sensitivity, and good instincts. It assumes that some people just have a "feel" for con-

PART 2:
Creating a Research Design

I'm going to read you a few statements. After I read each one, I'd like you to tell me whether it describes you "very well," "pretty well," "not too well" or "not at all."

Figure 5.4

Sample Scaling Question to Screen for Creativity

CIRCLE ONE NUMBER PER ROW

	Very well	Pretty well	Not too well	Not at all
I enjoy discussing new ideas.	4	3	2	1
I am open about expressing my thoughts around strangers.	4	3	2	1
I am open about expressing my thoughts around people I know.	4	3	2	1
I'm a good listener.	4	3	2	1
I enjoy/enjoyed participating in brainstorming sessions at work or when I was in school.	4	3	2	1
I enjoy coming up with new ideas.	4	3	2	1
I consider myself creative and imaginative.	4	3	2	1
I tend to be willing to change old habits.	4	3	2	1
I have good ideas.	4	3	2	1
I'm usually the first among my friends to try something new (movies, clothes, restaurants, foods).	4	3	2	1
	(MUST RESPOND "VERY WELL" OR "PRETTY WELL" TO THE SECOND STATEMENT AND AT LEAST 6 OF THE OTHER STATEMENTS)		(IF THEY RESPOND "NOT TOO WELL" OR "NOT AT ALL" TO MORE THAN 2 STATEMENTS, THANK AND TERMINATE)	

Source: Merrill Shugoll and Nancy Kolkebeck, "You Get What You Ask For," *Quirk's Marketing Research Review* (December 1999), pp. 61–65.

Dilbert

Dilbert © UFS. Reprinted by Permission.

ducting groups—individuals who observe long enough and have these innate abilities can become good group moderators. With this approach, trainees watch an established moderator conduct a few focus groups and then find themselves in a room with 8 or 10 people. Emerging an hour and a half later, they realize that they have conducted their first focus group.

Not only should the moderators be well trained and prepared, but clients must be prepared for observing a group from behind a mirror. A series of suggestions are offered in the In Practice feature to help ensure that clients get maximum benefit out of each session.

In **PRACTICE**

How Clients Can Get the Most Out of Focus Groups

DONA VITALE, OWNER OF STRATEGIC FOCUS, INC., A QUALITATIVE research consulting firm in Chicago, offers the following tips on how clients can get more out of focus groups.

1. *Participate in pre-group planning.* Set your personal information objectives for the groups. Think in advance about the topic and have a clear idea of what you hope to learn. Then make sure you communicate your questions to the project manager. Let him or her know what you see as the important issues or objectives to be explored. If possible, help shape the way objectives get articulated by attending a planning meeting with the qualitative researcher who will moderate the groups.

2. *Put yourself in the proper frame of mind.* Before the focus groups, familiarize yourself with the discussion guide. Highlight the topics or discussion areas you're particularly interested in. Make

notes to remind yourself of what you want to find out. Arrive at the research facility about a half-hour before the scheduled start of the groups. Give yourself time to settle in and get acclimated.

3. *Get to know the moderator.* If you haven't previously met the moderator, introduce yourself and explain your role and responsibilities in relation to the project. Take a moment to discuss how the groups are expected to progress. Don't ask for last-minute revisions of the discussion guide, but point out the parts of the discussion you are particularly interested in and provide a little background about what you'd like to know. Familiarize yourself with any stimuli that will be presented. Read the concepts. Look at the visuals.

4. *Be an active listener and observer.* Get involved with each group right from the beginning. As the moderator makes introductory remarks, look at the respondents. Observe their expressions, their dress and the way they are reacting to the situation. Turn those couple of minutes into an opportunity to

PART 2:
Creating a Research Design

begin learning about the respondents before they start talking.

Make a drawing of the shape of the table at the beginning of your notes. As respondents introduce themselves, jot down first names to show where they are sitting. Along with their names, note any relevant personal information such as number and ages of children, occupation, place of residence, or whatever else the moderator has included in the introduction to provide background and context. Having this information to refer to during the course of the discussion will help you understand what you hear.

5. *Try new ways of taking notes.* Divide your note-taking page into two columns. Head one column, "Things I already know or believe or have heard before" and the other, "Things that are new to me." Record comments and notes accordingly.

6. *Be an active part of the debriefing.* Be prepared to stay at the end of the last group and have a brief discussion with the moderator and the other observers. Don't expect instant analysis or deep insights from the moderator at this session. He or she is probably exhausted, and needs some time to think about what happened in the groups. Help the process by sharing your reactions. What did you think was important? What seemed new? What contradicts past research or experience? Be ready to share your observations, while striving to keep an open mind as to what it all means.

7. *After active observation, step back and think.* Unless the groups were conducted for purely tactical purposes, take some time to think before acting on what you learn. Go ahead and revise the language of concepts that respondents didn't understand, or change a visual element people found offensive, but don't forge ahead with plans to change your whole distribution strategy or revamp next year's marketing plan the day after the last group.[9] ■

The Discussion Guide Regardless of how well trained and personable the moderator is, a successful focus group requires a well-planned discussion guide. A **discussion guide** is a written outline of the topics to be covered during the session. Usually the guide is generated by the moderator based on the research objectives and client information needs. It serves as a checklist to ensure that all salient topics are covered and in the proper sequence. For example, an outline might begin with attitudes and feelings toward eating out, then move to fast foods, and conclude with a discussion of the food and decor of a particular chain. It is important to get the research director and other client observers, such as a brand manager, to agree that the topics listed in the guide are the most important ones to be covered. It is not uncommon for a team approach to be used in generating a discussion guide.

The guide tends to lead the discussion through three stages. In the first stage, rapport is established, the rules of group interactions are explained, and objectives are given. In the second stage, the moderator attempts to provoke intensive discussion. The final stage is used for summarizing significant conclusions and testing the limits of belief and commitment.

discussion guide
A written outline of topics to be covered during a focus group discussion.

Figure 5.5 shows an actual discussion guide (more detailed than most) used by a moderator to explore the credit card usage of college students, their reactions to different concepts for tabletop displays that might be used in student unions to entice students to sign up for cards, their reactions to different product

Figure 5.5

Discussion Guide on Credit Card Concepts for College Student Groups

I. **Warm-Up Explanation of Focus Group/Rules** (10–12 minutes)

A. Explain focus groups.
B. No correct answers—only your opinions. You are speaking for many other people like yourself.
C. Need to hear from everyone.
D. Some of my associates are watching behind mirror. They are very interested in your opinions.
E. Audiotapes—because I want to concentrate on what you have to say—so I don't have to take notes. Video, too.
F. Please—only one person talking at a time. No side discussions—I'm afraid I'll miss some important comments.
G. Don't ask me questions because what I know and what I think are not important—it's what you think and how you feel that are important. That's why we're here.
H. Don't feel bad if you don't know much about some of the things we'll be talking about— that's OK and important for us to know. If your view is different from that of others in the group, that's important for us to know. Don't be afraid to be different. We're not looking for everyone to agree on something unless they really do.
I. We need to cover a series of topics, so I'll need to move the discussion along at times. Please don't be offended.
J. *Any questions?*

II. **Credit Card History** (15 minutes)

First of all, I am interested in your attitudes toward, and usage of, credit cards.
A. How many have a major credit card? Which credit card/cards do you have? When did you acquire these cards?
B. Why/how did you get that credit card/cards?
C. Which credit card do you use most often? Why do you use that credit card most often? For what purpose/purposes do you use your credit card/cards most often?
D. Is it difficult for college students to get credit cards? Are some cards easier to get? Which ones? Is it difficult for college students to get a "good" or "desirable" credit card?
E. What is your current attitude toward credit cards and their use? Have your attitudes toward credit cards changed since you got one? How have they changed?

III. **Tabletop Concepts** (15 minutes)

Now I am going to show you several concepts for tabletop displays for credit cards that might be set up on campus in places where students congregate, such as student union and student activities buildings. Each display would be one of several displays for different products and services. I am interested in your reactions to the different displays. After I show you each display, I would like for you to write down your initial reactions on this form (*show and pass out form*). I am interested in your initial reactions. After we take a minute for you to write down your reactions, we will discuss each concept in more detail.
A. SHOW FIRST CONCEPT.
   1. HAVE THEM WRITE FIRST REACTION.
   2. DISCUSSION.
      a. What was your first reaction to this tabletop display? What, if anything, do you particularly *like* about this display?
      b. Would you stop to find out more? Are you drawn to this display? Why? Why not? What, if anything, is interesting about it?

    c. What is your reaction to ENVIRONMENTAL/EDUCATION/MUSIC OFFER? Likes/dislikes?

B. REPEAT FOR SECOND CONCEPT.

C. REPEAT FOR THIRD CONCEPT.

D. SHOW ALL THREE CONCEPTS.
    1. Which of these concepts, if any, would be *most likely* to attract your attention? Get you to stop for more information? Why?
    2. Which one would be *least likely* to attract your attention? Get you to stop for more information? Why?

IV.   **Brochures and Offers** (25 minutes)

Now I would like for you to see the credit card offers that might go with each of the displays we just discussed. First of all, I will show you a sample brochure and offer. Next, I would like for you to indicate your first reaction to the offer on the sheet provided. Finally, we will discuss your reactions to each offer.

A. SHOW FIRST BROCHURE AND OFFER.
    1. ASK THEM TO RECORD THEIR FIRST REACTION.
    2. DISCUSSION.
        a. What was your first reaction to this offer?
        b. What, if anything, do you particularly *like* about this offer? What, if anything, do you particularly *dislike* about this offer?
        c. Do you understand the offer?
        d. Do you feel it is an important benefit?
        e. Would you sign up for this offer? Why?
        f. Would this card displace an existing card?
        g. Would this be your card of choice?
        h. Would you continue to use this product after college?
        i. How does this card, described in this offer, compare with the card you use most frequently?
        j. How likely would you be to apply for this card? Why/why not? Would you plan to actually use this card, or just have it? Would you plan to keep it after college?

B. REPEAT FOR SECOND BROCHURE AND OFFER.

C. REPEAT FOR THIRD BROCHURE AND OFFER.

D. SHOW ALL THREE BROCHURES AND OFFERS.
    1. Which of these is the best offer? Why do you say that?
    2. Which, if any, of the cards described in these offers would you apply for? Why?

V.   **Designs** (10 minutes)

Finally, I would like for you to see three alternative designs for the credit card that would go with the environmental offer. As with the two previous sections of the discussion, I will show each design, ask for you to write down your initial reaction to the design, and then we will discuss each design. Please use the form provided earlier to write down your initial reactions.

A. SHOW FIRST DESIGN.
    1. ASK THEM TO WRITE DOWN FIRST REACTION.
    2. DISCUSSION.
        a. What is your first reaction to this design? Is there anything you particularly *like* about this design? *Dislike* about it?
        b. Is there anything about this design that would make you uncomfortable about using it while you are in college? How about after you get out of college?

B. REPEAT FOR SECOND DESIGN.

C. REPEAT FOR THIRD DESIGN.

D. SHOW ALL THREE DESIGNS.
    1. Which, if any, of these cards would you use? Prefer?
    2. Are there any of these cards you would not use? Why?

Thanks for your participation.

WAR Stories

instant analysis
Moderator debriefing, offering a forum for brainstorming by the moderator and client observers.

concepts for credit cards, and, finally, their reactions to different designs for credit cards. The displays and offers are built around three concepts:

1. *CDs.* When a student signs up, he or she chooses a free CD from a list. Students can earn points toward more free CDs via card usage.
2. *Environment.* The card issuer donates money to plant a certain number of trees based on card usage. The money is given to an internationally recognized environmental organization.
3. *Credit education.* Educational material on credit use and abuse is provided periodically. Credit reports are provided free of charge once per year. A gold card is provided after graduation if the user's credit history is good.

The groups were conducted in several areas of the country, with students from a variety of universities and colleges. In general, students did not find the education approach to be attractive. Participants were split in their preference for a free CD and contributions toward environmental causes. However, none of the concepts tested particularly well.

The Focus Group Report   Typically, after the final group in a series is completed, there will be a moderator debriefing, sometimes called **instant analysis.** This tradition has both pros and cons. Arguments for instant analysis include the idea that it serves as a forum for combining the knowledge of the marketing specialists who viewed the group with that of the moderator. It gives the client an opportunity to hear and react to the moderator's initial perceptions, and it harnesses the heightened awareness and excitement of the moment to generate new ideas and implications in a brainstorming environment.

The shortcomings include the possibility of biasing future analysis on the part of the moderator with this "hip-shooting commentary," conducted without the benefit of time to reflect on what transpired. Instant analysis will be influenced by recency, selective recall, and other factors associated with limited memory capabilities; it does not allow the moderator to hear all that was said in a less than highly involved and anxious state. There is nothing wrong with a moderator debriefing as long as the moderator explicitly reserves the right to change her or his opinion after reviewing the tapes.

Today, a formal focus group report is typically a PowerPoint presentation. The written report is nothing more than a copy of the PowerPoint slides.[10]

Benefits and Drawbacks of Focus Groups

The benefits and drawbacks of qualitative research in general also apply to focus groups. But focus groups have some unique pros and cons that deserve mention.

Focus Group Myths

JUDITH LANGER, PRESIDENT OF LANGER ASSOCIATES, A QUALITATIVE marketing research firm based in New York, offers several myths of focus group research.

Myth: Focus groups should never have more than six or seven respondents so each one gets more "air time."

The ideal number of respondents depends on the type of respondents, the subject and the moderator's style. Most of the focus groups my company conducts with consumers have eight to 10 respondents. The smaller the group, the lower the odds of good chemistry, which sometimes results in less energy. However, mini-focus groups of four to six respondents have their place. Examples include groups of executives, who are highly opinionated, sometimes self-important; teenagers, who can be very shy or, conversely, hard to control; for detailed probes of decision-making; and, in some cases, to explore reactions to advertising.

Myth: Lots of good ideas die in focus groups because consumers are not ready to accept new concepts.

Qualitative research offers researchers the opportunity to probe what underlies consumers' reactions. If an idea meets immediate respondent rejection, a good researcher explores the reasons why, whether the product might fit a real need and what, if anything, could change the respondents' minds. Do the respondents lack knowledge? Are they anxious about newness, or rejecting specific features? Is there a deeper resistance? The moderator can explore respondents' reactions to getting additional information, learning of advantages they haven't yet seen, changes in the product or service or the communication.

Myth: The sign of a good moderator is that he or she says very little in a focus group.

True enough in the ideal focus group, in which respondents speak one at a time, stick to the subject, offer detailed explanations of their answers without going on too long, and offer constructive criticism of the client's ideas. But the ideal focus group doesn't occur often. If respondents were so well-behaved, moderators might not be needed. We see the moderator's role as active—both responsive and creative. That role includes guiding the group dynamics. In addition, moderators should offer nonleading feedback by reflecting back to respondents what the moderator picks up to probe further. For example, a moderator can ask, "What I seem to be hearing is . . . . Is that true?

An experienced moderator can sense when respondents are open, following up with questions to reach a deeper level. Also, moderators should follow up on hypotheses developed before the research or from earlier focus groups if those issues did not arise unaided. A good moderator does not simply ask the questions in the topic guide but follows up on interesting or new ideas relevant to the research issues. And moderators should look for solutions to the client's problems. If respondents reject the product or concept statement, the moderator should first ask for suggestions open-ended, then probe reactions to possible ideas that come to mind.

Active moderating is not the same as asking leading questions. When probing questions are asked in a neutral manner, respondents feel free to say what they believe and will give more information.

Myth: Sending notes to the moderator during the focus group enables clients to be involved in the process, ensuring that the research provides answers to their questions.

Notes brought into the interviewing room—especially repeated ones—can be quite disruptive. Clients need and deserve to be part of the process, but unless the client is convinced the moderator is going in the wrong direction or providing incorrect information, it's best to resist the temptation because:

1. Respondents tend to forget about the one-way mirror quickly and interact with the moderator and one another. Notes are reminders that unseen people are watching, which can make respondents self-conscious.
2. Repeated notes raise questions in respondents' minds about whether the observers trust the moderator, creating a tense and awkward situation.
3. Reminders are usually superfluous when a question is later in the topic guide. Unless it is clear that the moderator has not asked the question at a particularly critical juncture, he or she will probably ask it later. And, the moderator may have a good reason for holding off.
4. Many handwritten notes, scribbled in the darkened clients' room, are hard to read. The moderator has to stop and struggle with the handwriting, slowing down the group. Better to arrange in advance for the moderator to come into the back room once or twice to see whether the client has any questions. Agreeing ahead of time on the rough timing of different sections of the topic guide also helps.

Myth: A discussion guide for focus groups is referred to by some clients as "a script," a term that implies that the moderator should follow it pretty much verbatim.

A topic guide should be just that—a general guide of the topics that should be covered, the order in which they should be covered and some ideas on possible probes or techniques the moderator might use. Certain aspects of the guide should be kept in sequence, while others are not as important. For instance, general questions usually are best asked before specific ones. The sequence is merely a guideline, though, when there is no significant research reason for holding off on a subject until another one has been discussed.

Each focus group has its own rhythm and the moderator should try to harness its energy. If respondents become animated about a subject, an effective moderator follows up right away. To cut respondents off and move on to another question can dissipate energy that the group may not regain. The "seize-the-moment" style of moderating feels more spontaneous and conversational to respondents, and because it seems natural and unforced, they are more likely to open up. Clients should not expect questions to be asked in the exact order they appear in the topic guide. Some may not even be asked in the phrasing of the topic guide.[11] ■

PART 2:

Creating a Research Design

Advantages of Focus Groups The interactions among respondents can stimulate new ideas and thoughts that might not arise during one-on-one interviews. And group pressure can help challenge respondents to keep their thinking realistic. Energetic interactions among respondents also make it likely that observation of a group will provide first-hand consumer information to client observers in a shorter amount of time and in a more interesting way than will individual interviews.

Another advantage focus groups offer is the opportunity to observe customers or prospects from behind a one-way mirror. In fact, there is growing use of focus groups to expose a broader range of employees to customer comments and views. "We have found that the only way to get people to really understand what customers want is to let them see customers, but there are few people who actually come in contact with customers," says Bonnie Keith, corporate market research manager at Compaq Computer Corporation. "Right now, we are getting people from our manufacturing and engineering operations to attend and observe focus groups."

Another advantage of focus groups is that they can be executed more quickly than many other research techniques. In addition, findings from groups tend to be easier to understand and to have a compelling immediacy and excitement. "I can get up and show a client all the charts and graphs in the world, but it has nowhere near the impact of showing 8 or 10 customers sitting around a table and saying that the company's service isn't good," says Jean-Anne Mutter, director of marketing research at Ketchum Advertising.[12]

Disadvantages of Focus Groups Unfortunately, some of the strengths of focus groups also can become disadvantages. For example, the immediacy and apparent understandability of focus group findings can cause managers to be misled instead of informed. Mutter says, "Even though you're only getting a very small slice, a focus group gives you a sense that you really understand the situation." She adds that focus groups can strongly appeal to "people's desire for quick, simple answers to problems, and I see a decreasing willingness to go with complexity and to put forth the effort needed to really think through the complex data that will be yielded by a quantitative study."[13]

This sentiment is echoed by Gary Willets, director of marketing research for NCR Corporation. He notes, "What can happen is that you will do the focus group, and you will find out all of these details, and someone will say, 'OK, we've found out all that we need to know.' The problem is that what is said in a focus group may not be all that typical. What you really want to do is do a qualitative study on the front end and follow it up with a quantitative study."[14] Focus groups, like qualitative research in general, is essentially inductive in approach. The research is data-driven, with findings and conclusions being drawn directly from the information provided. In contrast, quantitative studies generally follow a deductive approach, in which formulated ideas and hypotheses are tested with data collected specifically for that purpose.

Other disadvantages relate to the focus group process itself. For example, focus group recruiting may be a problem if the type of person recruited responds differently to the issues being discussed than do other target segments. White middle-class individuals, for example, participate in qualitative research in numbers disproportionate to their presence in the marketplace. Also, some focus group facilities create an impersonal feeling, making honest conversation unlikely. Corporate or formal settings with large boardroom tables and unattractive or plain decor may make it difficult for respondents to relax and share their feelings.

The greatest potential for distortion is during the group interview itself. As a participant in the social interaction, the moderator must take care not to behave in ways that prejudice responses. The moderator's style may contribute to bias. For example, an aggressive, confronting style may lead respondents to say whatever they think the moderator wants them to say, to avoid attack. Or "playing dumb" may create the perception that the moderator is insincere or phony and cause respondents to withdraw.

Respondents also can be a problem. Some individuals are simply introverted and do not like to speak out in group settings. Other people may attempt to dominate the discussion. These are people who know it all—or think they do—and answer every question first, without giving others a chance to speak. A dominating participant may succeed in swaying other group members. If a moderator is abrupt with a respondent, it can send the wrong message to other group members—"You'd better be cautious, or I will do the same thing to you." Fortunately, a good moderator can stifle a dominant group member and not the rest of the group. Simple techniques used by moderators include avoiding eye contact with a dominant person; reminding the group that "we want to give everyone a chance to talk"; saying "Let's have someone else go first"; or if someone else is speaking and the dominant person interrupts, looking at the initial speaker and saying, "Sorry, I cannot hear you."

Conducting focus groups in an international setting raises a number of other issues, as the Global Issues feature explains.

Online Focus Groups

online focus groups
Focus groups conducted via the Internet.

Perhaps the hottest controversy in qualitative research today is over the rapidly growing popularity of **online focus groups.** Many marketing researchers, such as Greenfield Online, NFO Interactive, and Harris Black International, believe that Internet focus groups can replace face-to-face focus groups, although they acknowledge that online research has limitations. Others that are moving aggressively into online marketing research, such as Millward Brown International and Digital Marketing Services (DMS), are avoiding online focus groups.

Advantages of Online Focus Groups   Marketers who have used online focus groups, and the marketing researchers conducting them, say that benefits far outweigh limitations. Those benefits include lack of geographic barriers, much lower costs (about half as much), faster turnaround time, and intangibles such as increased openness on the part of respondents when they do not have an interviewer staring them in the face.

"I think [the panelists] were more definite about things they didn't like than they'd be in front of a moderator," said Lisa Crane, vice president of sales and marketing for Universal Studios Online, which used an online focus group to test a redesigned site it's developing for Captain Morgan Original Spiced Rum, a brand of its parent company, Seagram Company. Rudy Nadilo, president and

PART 2:
Creating a Research Design

Japanese Focus Groups Are Different

INTERNATIONAL FOCUS GROUP WORK DEMANDS SOME VERY SPECIAL AWARENESS AND adaptations. The major issues that confront the project manager on the international front can be reduced to four basic categories:

- Socio-cultural differences
- Linguistic differences
- Differences in business practices
- World events and economic differences

Japan will be used as an example. Some countries might be a challenge on one or two fronts but Japan is a challenge on all of them! How are Japanese research companies different? There are relatively few research companies to choose from, even in cities the size of Tokyo. This creates booking problems, especially when you realize that the facilities are very tiny by American standards.

The cultural and linguistic differences between the U.S. and Japan require that your discussion guide and other materials be translated by your host organization and then translated back to English by an independent source to make sure that the correct nuances are getting across. This takes time. Often, direct translation is impossible, and you have to rely on interpretation—getting the general idea across without word-for-word equivalence.

Another time constraint is that you can really only accomplish one group per evening instead of the two to which we are accustomed. The Japanese in urban areas like Tokyo must commute from one to three hours home.

The cost of doing foreign focus groups is invariably higher than similar work undertaken domestically. As a general rule you can expect a project to cost 2 to 2½ times more in Europe than it would in the U.S., and 4 to 6 times more in Japan. Higher real estate costs and salaries make the cost of doing business in Japan very high for your subcontractors.

Japanese consumers still display a deference to seniority, power, and status as defined by their culture. Within moments of arrival, everyone in the group will know where they stand and will tend to defer to the most powerful person. As a result, the moderator has a daunting task with many groups. Female executives and decision makers are still rare in Japan. In most groups, it is best not to mix women and men because the women may just sit and smile nervously and defer to the men.[15] ∎

CEO of Greenfield Online, which conducted the online focus groups for Universal, said they are meant "to complement, not replace" traditional panels.[16]

Greenfield Product Manager Susan Roth said she received 2,700 responses within one day of sending out a so-called screener email to approximately 6,000 users in Greenfield's database of 500,000 Internet homes. She then formed two groups of eight panelists each for the client, which needed to make sure respondents were over 21 and had certain drinking preferences.

During the online focus group, held in a private chat room on Greenfield's site, a moderator fielded questions and answers on one side of a split screen, while clients made suggestions—instantly, by typing—on the left side of the screen. "I loved the way I was able to influence what the moderator said instantly," said Ms. Crane. Greenfield charges about $6,000 plus incentives for this type of two-group project. A conventional two-group package costs about $10,000.[17]

Not only are the costs lower for online focus groups, but there are substantial travel savings for the client as well. Expenditures for round-trip airline tickets to distant cities, meals, hotels, and taxis are avoided. Clients merely log on in their own office, or even at home, to observe the research in progress.

Another advantage of online focus groups lies in access to the hard-to-reach target population. Online, it's possible to reach populations that are traditionally inaccessible because of time or professional constraints—groups such as physicians, lawyers, and senior business executives. Chances are higher that they will be available to participate, too, since they do not need to take time from their busy schedules to visit a focus group facility but, rather, can participate from the privacy of their own homes.[18]

Online focus group advocates claim that inability to see a focus group participant doesn't necessarily mean that the observer cannot sense emotion. Certainly, numerous nonverbal cues (e.g., the way one is sitting, leaning, smirking, etc.) are sacrificed, but some nonverbal cues, called "emoticons," can occur in an online chat environment. Emotions are text-based "pictures" that result from the use of punctuation marks which, in combination, look like expression-bearing faces. In addition to emoticons, online focus group respondents tend to rely more on words and complete sentences (versus hand movements or expressions) to express their thoughts and tend to express these thoughts in more concise ways—without depending on the pauses and hesitations that occur during spoken communications.[19]

Another advantage claimed for online focus groups is efficient moderator–client interaction. During the traditional focus group, the client observes the discussion from behind a one-way glass; communication with the moderator is impossible without interfering with the discussion. An online focus group, though, offers a remarkable opportunity for two-way interaction between the moderator and the client. This direct interaction, while the moderator conducts the group, has become a necessity in operating a fully effective online focus group discussion. Rather than sneaking into the room with a note scribbled on a piece of paper, the client can address the moderator directly, clearly, and efficiently, without interrupting the group dynamic.[20]

Traditional focus groups always include "natural talkers," who dominate the discussion, despite a good moderator's attempt to equalize participant contributions. Other participants will be less comfortable voicing opinions in a group; they may express themselves more freely when not face to face with their peers. The online focus group has a built-in leveling effect, in the sense that shy participants can express themselves as freely as more outgoing participants. One participant points out why he likes participating in online focus groups, explaining, "I can be honest without the face-to-face peer pressure of focus groups"; another offers, "I get to express my opinion without having to hear someone's reaction."[21] At least in terms of honesty and willingness to offer genuine ideas and opinions, respondents tend to feel more comfortable participating from the privacy of their own homes.

In fact, the likelihood of distraction is lower when participants must focus on reading a computer screen than when they are sitting in a focus group room watching the moderator, listening to other respondents, thinking about their answers, wondering what they'll say next, and envisioning what's going on behind the one-way mirror.

Occasionally, problems with domineering or obnoxious participants can worsen when people aren't sitting face to face. When Jeff Walkowski began moderating online focus groups, he wasn't prepared for the "Animal House" behavior of the people involved: Women in a detergent focus group ganged up on each other; college students traded crude comments. "I didn't realize people would sling mud at each other online," said Walkowski, president of group moderator service QualCore.com, who has moderated offline and online focus groups for clients such as American Honda Motor Company's Acura Division, PowerBar, and Procter & Gamble. He believes that "they'd be more civil in a face-to-face environment." Recently, he found the Virtual Research Room, called Vrroom (http://www.vrroom.com), which has an instant ejection feature for unruly participants. He hasn't used that feature yet but is glad to know that it's there if needed.[22]

Disadvantages of Online Focus Groups   Critics say that the research community does itself an injustice by calling qualitative research sessions conducted over the Internet "focus groups." Their criticisms include the following:

- *Group dynamics.* One of the key reasons for using traditional focus groups is to view the interactions among the group participants, as they can provide excellent insights. In cyberspace, it is difficult, if not impossible, to create any real group dynamics, particularly when the participants are reading from computer screens rather than interacting verbally.
- *Nonverbal inputs.* Experienced moderators use nonverbal inputs from participants while moderating and analyzing sessions. It is not possible to duplicate the nonverbal input in an online environment.
- *Client involvement.* Many organizations use the focus group methodology because it gives clients an opportunity to experience some direct interface with consumers in an objective environment. Nothing can replace the impact of watching focus groups from behind a one-way mirror, no matter how good the videotapes, remote broadcast facilities, or reports written by moderators. With online focus groups, clients can only monitor written responses on a computer screen.
- *Security.* With a traditional focus group, the moderator and client know who is in the room, assuming that appropriate screening has been done. With online focus groups, there is no way to be sure who is sitting at the computer terminal. Without the ability to see the person, how do the moderator and client know who he or she really is?
- *Attention to the topic.* Another important benefit of the traditional focus group process is that the participants in the group understand that they are

expected to stay in the room for the full two hours of the session and contribute to the discussion. It is very difficult for a participant in a well-moderated focus group to do something that could distract him or her from the proceedings. However, in an online environment, the moderator can never be sure that the participants are not watching TV, reading a book, or eating dinner while the session is proceeding.

■ *Exposure to external stimuli.* A key use of focus groups is to present advertising copy, new product concepts, prototypes, or other stimuli to the participants in order to get their reactions. In an online chat situation, it is almost impossible to duplicate the kind of exposure to external stimuli that occurs in the live focus group environment. As a result, the value of the input received online is more questionable than that of input coming from a live environment.

■ *Role and skill of the moderator.* Most marketing professionals agree that the most important factor in the quality of traditional focus group research is the skill of the moderator. Experienced moderators do more than simply ask questions of participants. A good moderator uses innovative techniques to draw out quiet or shy participants, energize a slow group, and delve a little deeper into the minds of the participants. The techniques available to a moderator sitting alone at a computer terminal are much more limited because of the lack of face-to-face involvement with participants.[23]

Table 5.2 summarizes the advantages and disadvantages of traditional and online focus groups.

Other Trends in Focus Group Research

A number of fads have come and gone in focus group research over the past decade. No longer do we hear much about replicated groups, mega groups, multivariate groups, video thematic apperception test groups, or sensitivity groups.

There is, however, continued growth in the use of focus groups. Commensurate with this growth is an expansion in the number (more than 700) and quality of focus group facilities in the United States. Most cities with a population of more than 100,000 have at least one group facility. Tiny viewing rooms with small one-way mirrors are rapidly disappearing. Instead, field service firms are installing plush two-tiered observation areas that wrap around the conference room to provide an unobstructed view of all respondents. Built-in counters for taking notes, padded chairs, and a fully stocked refreshment center (which can create problems) are becoming commonplace.

videoconferencing
Televising a focus group session at a focus group facility or company site so that more staff can view customer opinions.

Videoconferencing   One new trend is **videoconferencing.** Why send a group of staffers to a distant city—and pay for their airfare, lodging, and meals—when you can shuttle them either to a local focus group facility or to a conference room down the hall to watch a focus group session on a TV monitor?[24]

While rates and capabilities vary, services that specialize in serving the research market, such as VideoConferencing Alliance Network (VCAN), FocusVision, VideoFocus Direct, and Direct Window, all allow clients to view groups remotely. Some clients view groups on their own equipment, while others buy or lease from the services.

Table 5.2

Advantages and Disadvantages of Traditional and Online Focus Groups

	Traditional Focus Groups	Online Focus Groups
Basic costs	More expensive	Cheaper
Participants	Participants are locally based, because of travel time and expense.	Anyone in the world with a computer and modem can participate.
Time commitment	Approximately 3½-hour time commitment. Busy respondents are less likely to be available.	No driving to facility, approximately 60-minute time commitment. Busy respondents are more likely to be available.
Openness of respondents	Some respondents are intimidated and afraid to speak openly in a face-to-face group setting.	Lack of face-to-face contact may lead respondents to express true feelings in writing.
Group dynamics	What one person says and does (gestures and expressions) can lead others to react.	None, according to critics
Nonverbal communication	Body language can be observed.	Body language cannot be observed. Participants can use emoticons to enhance communication.
Transcripts	Transcript is time-consuming and expensive to obtain; often not in complete sentences or thoughts.	Word-for-word transcripts are available almost immediately; usually in complete sentences/thoughts.
Respondent recruiting	Recruiting certain types of respondents (e.g., physicians, top managers) is difficult.	It is easier to obtain all types of respondents.
Client travel costs	Very expensive when client must go to several cities for one or two days each	None
Communication with moderator	Observers can send notes into focus group room.	Observers can communicate privately with moderator on a split screen.
Respondent security	Participants are accurately identified.	It is more difficult to ascertain who is participating.
Attention to topic	Respondents' attentiveness can be observed.	Respondents may be engaged in other activities.
Client involvement	Client can observe flesh-and-blood consumers interacting.	Client can read live dialogue and transcripts.
Exposure to external stimuli	Package designs, advertising copy, and product prototypes with demonstrations can be shown to participants.	Ability to show stimuli is currently quite limited.

At its Basking Ridge, New Jersey, offices, AT&T uses GroupNet, a service provided by VCAN. VCAN is a network of research firms that provide videoconferencing of focus groups in 20 U.S. markets, using Picture Tel equipment. AT&T has set up viewing rooms in its offices and in the offices of its ad agency partners in New York City.[25]

Nancy Canali Lucas, vice president of research for TBS Superstation, in Atlanta, Georgia, believes that videoconferencing has helped expose more TBS staffers to the live research process. "It allows us to get a larger audience of people

Videoconferencing gives researchers and customers a chance to view a focus group from a remote location or at a later time. More people can be exposed to the focus group. Visit http://www.vcan.com or http://www.focusvision.com to find out more about video-conferencing.

who don't normally attend focus groups, people like the head of the network, for example, or the head of the entertainment division, who may not be interested in the micro-issues that we deal with but who can step in and take a look at the group because it's being shown right here."[26]

Viewing Focus Groups Online   A second trend, closely related to the first, is viewing focus groups on the Internet. Although streaming video suffers from a lack of quality due to bandwidth problems on most computers, advocates of online viewing argue that it is insights, not entertainment, that clients are seeking. And in terms of access, showing a focus group session online offers a number of advantages. Clients have the flexibility to watch the event either live or on demand, whenever they have the time to do so. This flexibility is particularly appreciated by viewers in other time zones or other countries, who can watch the session when they are ready, rather than having to get up at 5 A.M. and drive to a facility to watch a live videoconferencing event. If the groups are indexed, clients also have the flexibility to jump directly to a specific segment of each session.

The Internet broadcasting of focus group sessions allows more people to be involved in the event. Traditionally, the client representatives who attend focus groups are middle management. This is because top managers don't have the time to travel to the groups, and junior employees do not have the seniority—or the budget. Broadcasting the groups on the Web gives junior staff members and senior managers access on their own computers—at the office or at home. In fact, pieces of the video can even be sent as email attachments. In other words, a researcher can send a manager an email with a two-minute segment of the interview that reinforces the items learned in the focus group. And when it comes from the mouths of customers whom managers can see and hear, it has a big impact.

With Internet broadcasting of focus groups, the client has the ability to keep track of all the brainstorming that goes on behind the mirror, even though the viewers may be located all over the world. Client Lounge, a chat room maintained by Active Group, a Norcross, Georgia, research firm, offers an online viewing interface. The company embeds the video in a chat room so that all of the people who are logged on can interact with each other and discuss ideas as the group is occurring.[27]

Another benefit of watching focus groups online is that the digitized content can be easily incorporated in PowerPoint presentations. Immediately following the sessions, clients at the facility get a CD containing all of the content.

Other Qualitative Methodologies

Most of this chapter has been devoted to focus groups because of their pervasive use in marketing research. However, several other qualitative techniques are also used, albeit on a much more limited basis.

Depth Interviews

Depth interviews are relatively unstructured one-on-one interviews. The interviewer is thoroughly trained in the skill of probing and eliciting detailed answers to each question. Sometimes psychologists are used as depth interviewers: they employ nondirective clinical techniques to uncover hidden motivations.

The direction of a depth interview is guided by the responses of the interviewee. As the interview unfolds, the interviewer thoroughly probes each answer and uses the replies as a basis for further questioning. For example, a depth interview might begin with a discussion of snack foods. The interviewer might follow each answer with "Can you tell me more?" "Would you elaborate on that?" or "Is that all?" The interviewer might then move into the pros and cons of various ingredients, such as corn, wheat, and potatoes. The next phase could delve into the sociability of the snack food. Are Fritos, for example, more commonly eaten alone or in a crowd? Are Wheat Thins usually reserved for parties? When should you serve Ritz crackers?

The advantages of depth interviews over focus groups are as follows:

1. Group pressure is eliminated, so the respondent reveals more honest feelings, not necessarily those considered most acceptable among peers.
2. The personal one-on-one situation gives the respondent the feeling of being the focus of attention—that his or her thoughts and feelings are important and truly wanted.
3. The respondent attains a heightened state of awareness because he or she has constant interaction with the interviewer and there are no group members to hide behind.
4. The longer time devoted to individual respondents encourages the revelation of new information.
5. Respondents can be probed at length to reveal the feelings and motivations that underlie statements.
6. Without the restrictions of cultivating a group process, new directions of questioning can be improvised more easily. Individual interviews allow greater flexibility to explore casual remarks and tangential issues, which may provide critical insights into the main issue.

depth interviews
One-on-one interviews that probe and elicit detailed answers to questions, often using nondirective techniques to uncover hidden motivations.

7. The closeness of the one-on-one relationship allows the interviewer to become more sensitive to nonverbal feedback.
8. A singular viewpoint can be obtained from a respondent without influence from others.
9. The interview can be conducted anywhere, in places other than a focus group facility.
10. Depth interviews may be the only viable technique for situations in which a group approach would require that competitors be placed in the same room. For example, it might be very difficult to do a focus group on systems for preventing bad checks with managers from competing department stores or restaurants.

The disadvantages of depth interviews relative to focus groups are as follows:

1. Depth interviews are much more expensive than focus groups, particularly when viewed on a per-interview basis.
2. Depth interviews do not generally get the same degree of client involvement as focus groups. It is difficult to convince most client personnel to sit through multiple hours of depth interviews so as to benefit firsthand from the information.
3. Because depth interviews are physically exhausting for the moderator, they do not cover as much ground in one day as do focus groups. Most moderators will not do more than four or five depth interviews in a day, whereas they can involve 20 people in a day in two focus groups.
4. Focus groups give the moderator an ability to leverage the dynamics of the group to obtain reactions that might not be generated in a one-on-one session.[28]

The success of any depth interview depends mainly on the skills of the interviewer. Good depth interviewers, whether psychologists or not, are hard to find and expensive. A second factor that determines the success of depth research is proper interpretation. The unstructured nature of the interview and the clinical nature of the analysis increase the complexity of the task. Small sample sizes, the difficulty of making comparisons, the subjective nature of the researcher's interpretations, and high costs have all contributed to the lack of popularity of depth interviewing. Classic applications of depth interviews include

- Communication checks (e.g., review of print, radio, or TV advertisements or other written materials)
- Sensory evaluations (e.g., reactions to varied formulations for deodorants or hand lotions, sniff tests for new perfumes, or taste tests for a new frosting)
- Exploratory research (e.g., defining baseline understanding or a product, service, or idea)
- New product development, prototype stage
- Packaging or usage research (e.g., when clients want to "mirror" personal experience and obtain key language descriptors)[29]

N. W. Ayer Partners, one of the nation's largest advertising agencies, had conducted several market segmentation studies of baby boomers but still felt that it lacked a good understanding of these consumers. Ayer's research director decided to conduct depth interviews. The depth interviews generated four market segments: Satisfied Selves, who are optimistic, and achievement-oriented; Contented Traditionalists, who are home-oriented and socially very conservative; Worried Traditionalists, anticipating disaster on all fronts; and '60s in the '90s People, who are aimless, feel unfulfilled, and have no direction in life.

Behavioral differences translated down to brand use. In the alcohol category, for example, Satisfied Selves use upscale brands and are the target for imported wine sales. Contented Traditionalists consume little alcohol; but when they drink, they favor brown liquors, such as whiskey. Worried Traditionalists drink an average amount, but their consumption patterns are very different from those of the other segments. For each type of liquor, people in this segment reported a dual brand-use pattern; they use an upscale brand as well as a lower-priced one. "Maybe they have one brand on hand for when they entertain guests, the socially visible brands, and a cheaper brand they consume when home alone," the research director said. Members of the '60s in the '90s segment are heavy liquor consumers, especially of vodka and beer.[30]

Projective Tests

Projective techniques are sometimes incorporated into depth interviews. The origins of projective techniques lie in the field of clinical psychology. In essence, the objective of any **projective test** is to delve below surface responses to obtain true feelings, meanings, and motivations. The rationale behind projective tests comes from the knowledge that people are often reluctant or unable to reveal their deepest feelings. In some instances, they are unaware of those feelings because of psychological defense mechanisms.

Projective tests are techniques for penetrating a person's defense mechanisms to allow true feelings and attitudes to emerge. Generally, a respondent is presented with an unstructured and nebulous situation and asked to respond. Because the situation is ill-defined and has no true meaning, the respondent must impose her or his own frame of reference. In theory, the respondent "projects" personal feelings into the unstructured situation, bypassing defense mechanisms because the respondent is not referring directly to herself or himself. As the individual talks about something or someone else, her or his inner feelings are revealed.

Most projective tests are easy to administer and are tabulated like other open-ended questions. They are often used in conjunction with nonprojective open- and closed-ended questions. A projective test may gather "richer," and perhaps more revealing, data than do standard questioning techniques. Projective techniques are used often in image questionnaires and concept tests, and occasionally in advertising pretests. It is also common to apply several projective techniques during a depth interview.

The most common forms of projective techniques used in marketing research are word association tests, sentence and story completion tests, cartoon tests, photo sorts, consumer drawings, storytelling, and third-person techniques. Other techniques, such as psychodrama tests and the Thematic Apperception Test (TAT), have been popular in treating psychological disorders but of less help in marketing research.

Word Association Tests
Word association tests are among the most practical and effective projective tools for marketing researchers. An interviewer

projective test
A technique for tapping respondents' deepest feelings by having them project those feelings into an unstructured situation.

word association test
A projective test in which the interviewer says a word and the respondent must mention the first thing that comes to mind.

reads a word to a respondent and asks him or her to mention the first thing that comes to mind. Usually, the individual will respond with a synonym or an antonym. The words are read in quick succession to avoid allowing time for defense mechanisms to come into play. If the respondent fails to answer within three seconds, some emotional involvement with the word is assumed.

Word association tests are used to select brand names, advertising campaign themes, and slogans. For example, a cosmetic manufacturer might ask consumers to respond to the following words as potential names for a new perfume: infinity, encounter, flame, desire, precious, erotic. One of these words or a synonym suggested by respondents might then be selected as the brand name.

sentence and story completion tests
Projective tests in which respondents complete sentences or stories in their own words.

Sentence and Story Completion Tests   **Sentence and story completion tests** can be used in conjunction with word association tests. The respondent is furnished with an incomplete story or group of sentences and asked to complete it. A few examples of incomplete sentences follow:

1. Marshall Fields is . . .
2. The people who shop at Marshall Fields are . . .
3. Marshall Fields should really . . .
4. I don't understand why Marshall Fields doesn't . . .

Here's an example of a story completion test:

Sally Jones just moved to Chicago from Los Angeles, where she had been a salesperson for IBM. She is now a district manager for the Chicago area. Her neighbor Rhonda Smith has just come over to Sally's apartment to welcome her to Chicago. A discussion of where to shop ensues. Sally notes, "You know, I've heard some things about Marshall Fields . . . ." What is Rhonda's reply?

As you can see, story completion tests provide a more structured and detailed scenario for the respondent. Again, the objective is for the interviewees to put themselves in the role of the imaginary person mentioned in the scenario.

Sentence and story completion tests have been considered by some researchers to be the most useful and reliable of all the projective tests.

cartoon test
Projective test in which the respondent fills in the dialogue of one of two characters in a cartoon.

Cartoon Tests   The typical **cartoon test** consists of two characters with balloons, similar to those seen in comic books; one balloon is filled with dialogue, and the other balloon is blank (see Figure 5.6). The respondent is asked to fill in the blank balloon. Note that the cartoon figures in Figure 5.6 are left vague and without expression so that the respondent is not given clues regarding a suggested type of response. The ambiguity is designed to make it easier for the respondent to project his or her feelings into the cartoon situation.

Cartoon tests are extremely versatile and highly projective. They can be used to obtain differential attitudes toward two types of establishments and the congruity or lack of congruity between these establishments and a particular product. They can also be used to measure the strength of an attitude toward a particular product or brand; or to ascertain what function is being performed by a given attitude.

photo sort
A projective technique in which a respondent sorts photos of different types of people, identifying those people who she or he feels would use the specified product or service.

Photo Sorts   With **photo sorts,** consumers express their feelings about brands by manipulating a specially developed photo deck depicting different types of

Figure 5.6

Cartoon Test

people, from business executives to college students. Respondents connect the individuals in the photos with the brands they think they would use.

BBDO Worldwide, one of the country's largest advertising agencies, has developed a trademarked technique called Photosort. A Photosort conducted for General Electric found that consumers thought the brand attracted conservative, older, business types. To change that image, GE adopted the "Bring Good Things to Life" campaign. A Photosort for Visa found the credit card to have a wholesome, female, middle-of-the-road image in customers' minds. The "Everywhere You Want to Be" campaign was devised to interest more high-income men.[31]

Using Photosort, BBDO interviewed 100 members of the primary target market for beer: men, ages 21 to 49, who drink at least six beers weekly. Researchers showed each respondent 98 photographs and asked him to match each picture with the brand of beer that the photo subject probably drank. A Bud drinker, as viewed by the respondents, is not exactly the corporate type: He appears tough, grizzled, blue collar. A Miller drinker, in contrast, comes off as light-blue collar, civilized, and friendly looking. Coors has a somewhat more feminine image—not necessarily a plus in a business in which 80 percent of the product gets consumed by men.[32]

Another photo sort technique, entitled Pictured Aspirations Technique (PAT), was created by Grey Advertising, also a large New York advertising agency. The technique attempts to uncover how a product fits into a consumer's aspirations. Consumers sort a deck of photos according to how well the pictures describe their aspirations. In research done for Playtex's 18-hour bra, this technique revealed that the product was out of sync with the aspirations of potential customers. The respondents chose a set of pictures that depicted "the me they wanted to be" as very energetic, slim, youthful, and vigorous. But the pictures they used to express their sense of the product were a little more old-fashioned, a little stouter, and less vital and energetic looking. Out went the "Good News for

Full-Figured Gals" campaign, with Jane Russell as spokesperson, and in came the more sexy, fashionable concept of "Great Curves Deserve 18 Hours."

Consumer Drawings   Researchers sometimes ask consumers to draw what they are feeling or how they perceive an object. **Consumer drawings** can unlock motivations or express perceptions. For example, McCann-Erickson advertising agency wanted to find out why Raid roach spray outsold Combat insecticide disks in certain markets. In interviews, most users agreed that Combat is a better product because it kills roaches without any effort on the user's part. So the agency asked the heaviest users of roach spray—low-income women from the southern United States—to draw pictures of their prey (see Figure 5.7). The goal was to get at their underlying feelings about this dirty job.

consumer drawings
A projective technique in which respondents draw what they are feeling or how they perceive an object.

Figure 5.7

Consumer Drawings That Helped Identify Respondents' Need for Control

Source: Courtesy of McCann-Erickson, New York.

"One night I just couldn't take the horror of these bugs sneaking around in the dark. They are always crawling when you can't see them. I had to do something. I thought wouldn't it be wonderful if when I switch on the light the roaches would shrink up and die like vampires to sunlight. So I did, but they just all scattered. But I was ready with my spray so it wasn't a total loss. I got quite a few . . . continued tomorrow night when nighttime falls."

"A man likes a free meal you cook for him; as long as there is food he will stay."

"I tiptoed quietly into the kitchen, perhaps he wasn't around. I stretched my arm up to turn on the light. I hoped I'd be alone when the light went on. Perhaps he is sitting on the table I thought. You think that's impossible? Nothing is impossible with that guy. He might not even be alone. He'll run when the light goes on I thought. But what's worse is for him to slip out of sight. No, it would be better to confront him before he takes control and 'invites a companion'."

All of the 100 women who participated in the agency's interviews portrayed roaches as men. "A lot of their feelings about the roach were very similar to the feelings that they had about the men in their lives," said Paula Drillman, executive vice president at McCann-Erickson. Many of the women were in common-law relationships. They said that the roach, like the man in their life, "only comes around when he wants food." The act of spraying roaches and seeing them die was satisfying to this frustrated, powerless group. Setting out Combat disks may have been less trouble, but it just didn't give them the same feeling. "These women wanted control," Drillman said. "They used the spray because it allowed them to participate in the kill."[33]

Storytelling As the name implies, **storytelling** requires consumers to tell stories about their experiences. It is a search for subtle insights into consumer behavior.

Gerald Zaltman, a Harvard Business School professor, has created a metaphor laboratory to facilitate the storytelling process. (A metaphor is a description of one thing in terms that are usually used to describe another; it can be used to represent thoughts that are tacit, implicit, and unspoken.) Zaltman elicits metaphors from consumers by asking them to spend time over several weeks thinking about how they would visually represent their experiences with a company. To help them with the process, he asks them to cut out magazine pictures that somehow convey those experiences. Then, consumers come to his lab and spend several hours telling stories about all of the images they chose and the connections between the images and their experiences with the firm.

One metaphor study was conducted on pantyhose. "Women in focus groups have always said that they wear them because they have to, and they hate it," says Glenda Green, a marketing research manager at DuPont, which supplies the raw material for many pantyhose manufacturers. "We didn't think we had a completely accurate picture of their feelings, but we hadn't come up with a good way to test them."[34] DuPont turned to storytelling for better insights. Someone brought a picture of a spilled ice cream sundae, capturing the rage she feels when she spots a run in her hose. Another arrived with a picture of a beautiful woman with baskets of fruit. Other photos depicted a Mercedes and Queen Elizabeth. "As we kept probing into the emotions behind the choice of these photos, the women finally began admitting that hose made them feel sensual, sexy, and more attractive to men," says Green. "There's no way anyone would admit that in a focus group." Several stocking manufacturers used this information to alter their advertising and package design.

Third-Person Technique Perhaps the easiest projective technique to apply, other than word association, is the **third-person technique.** Rather than directly asking respondents what they think, researchers couch the question in terms of "your neighbor," "most people," or some other third party. Rather than asking a mother why she typically does not fix a nutritionally balanced breakfast for her children, a researcher might ask, "Why don't many people provide their families nutritionally balanced breakfasts?" The third-person technique is often used to avoid questions that might be embarrassing or evoke hostility if posed directly to a respondent.

storytelling
A projective technique in which respondents are required to tell stories about their experiences, with a company or product, for example; also known as the *metaphor technique.*

third-person technique
A projective technique in which the interviewer learns about respondents' feelings by asking them to answer for a third party, such as "your neighbor" or "most people."

The Future of Qualitative Research

The rationale behind qualitative research tests is as follows:

1. The criteria employed and the evaluations made in most buying and usage decisions have emotional and subconscious content, which is an important determinant of buying and usage decisions.
2. Such content is adequately and accurately verbalized by the respondent only through *indirect* communicative techniques.

To the extent that these tenets remain true or even partially correct, the demand for qualitative applications in marketing research will continue to exist. But the problems of small sample sizes and subjective interpretation will continue to plague some forms of qualitative research. Inability to validate and replicate qualitative research will further deter its use.

On the positive side, the use of online focus groups will grow. Focus group research can provide data and insights not available through any other techniques. Low cost and ease of application will lend even greater impetus to use online focus groups in the 21st century. Finally, the qualitative–quantitative split will begin to close as adaptations and innovations allow researchers to enjoy the advantages of both approaches simultaneously.

Summary

Qualitative research refers to research whose findings are not subject to quantification or quantitative analysis. It is often used to examine consumer attitudes, feelings, and motivations. Qualitative research, particularly the use of focus groups, continues to grow in popularity for three reasons. First, qualitative research is usually cheaper than quantitative studies. Second, it is an excellent means of understanding the in-depth motivations and feelings of consumers. Third, it can improve the efficiency of quantitative research.

Qualitative research is not without its disadvantages. Sometimes, qualitative research does not distinguish small differences in attitudes or opinions about a marketing mix as well as large-scale quantitative studies do. Also, respondents in qualitative studies are not necessarily representative of the population of interest to the researcher. And, the quality of the research may be questionable, given the number of individuals who profess to be experts in the field, yet lack formal training.

Focus groups are the most popular type of qualitative research. A focus group typically consists of 8 to 12 paid participants who are led by a moderator in an in-depth discussion on a particular topic or concept. The goal of the focus group is to learn and understand what people have to say and why. The emphasis is on getting people to talk at length and in detail about the subject at hand. The interaction associated with group dynamics is essential to the success of focus group research. The idea is that a response from one person will become a stimulus for another person, thereby generating an interplay of responses that will yield more information than if the same number of people had contributed independently.

Most focus groups are held in a group facility, which is typically set up in a conference room, with a large one-way mirror built into one wall. Microphones are placed in unobtrusive locations to record the discussion. Behind the mirror is a viewing room. The moderator plays a critical role in the success or failure of the group and is aided in his or her efforts by a well-planned discussion guide. More and more focus groups are being conducted online because online focus groups are fast and cost effective; they also reach populations that are typically inaccessible. However, there are a number of problems associated with online focus groups, the most important being the inability to create any real group dynamics.

A number of other qualitative research methodologies are used, but on a much more infrequent basis. One such technique is depth interviews. Depth interviews are unstructured one-on-one interviews. The interviewer is thoroughly trained in the skill of probing and eliciting detailed answers to each question. He or she often uses nondirective clinical techniques to uncover hidden motivations. The use of projective techniques represents another form of qualitative research. The objective of any projective test is to delve below the surface responses to obtain true feelings, meanings, or motivations. Some common forms of projective techniques are word association tests, sentence and story completion tests, cartoon tests, photo sorts, consumer drawings, storytelling, and third-person techniques.

Key Terms and Definitions

qualitative research Research whose findings are not subject to quantification or quantitative analysis.

quantitative research Research that uses mathematical analysis.

focus group A group of 8 to 12 participants who are led by a moderator in an in-depth discussion on one particular topic or concept.

group dynamics The interaction among people in a group.

focus group facility Research facility consisting of a conference room or living room setting and a separate observation room with a one-way mirror or live audiovisual feed.

focus group moderator A person hired by the client to lead the focus group; this person should have a background in psychology or sociology or, at least, marketing.

discussion guide A written outline of topics to be covered during a focus group discussion.

instant analysis Moderator debriefing, offering a forum for brainstorming by the moderator and client observers.

online focus groups Focus groups conducted via the Internet.

videoconferencing Televising a focus group session at a focus group facility or company site so that more staff can view customer opinions.

depth interviews   One-on-one interviews that probe and elicit detailed answers to questions, often using nondirective techniques to uncover hidden motivations.

projective test   A technique for tapping respondents' deepest feelings by having them project those feelings into an unstructured situation.

word association test   A projective test in which the interviewer says a word and the respondent must mention the first thing that comes to mind.

sentence and story completion tests   Projective tests in which respondents complete sentences or stories in their own words.

cartoon test   A projective test in which the respondent fills in the dialogue of one of two characters in a cartoon.

photo sort   A projective technique in which a respondent sorts photos of different types of people, identifying those people who she or he feels would use the specified product or service.

consumer drawings   A projective technique in which respondents draw what they are feeling or how they perceive an object.

storytelling   A projective technique in which respondents are required to tell stories about their experiences, with a company or product, for example; also known as the *metaphor technique.*

third-person technique   A projective technique in which the interviewer learns about respondents' feelings by asking them to answer for a third party, such as "your neighbor" or "most people."

Questions for Review & Critical Thinking

1. What are the major differences between quantitative and qualitative research?
2. What are some of the possible disadvantages of using focus groups?
3. What are some of the trends in focus group research? Why do you think these trends have evolved?
4. What can the client do to get more out of focus groups?
5. What is the purpose of a projective test? What major factors should be considered in using a projective technique?
6. Conduct a focus group in your class on one of the following three topics:
   a. Student experiences at the student union
   b. The quality of existing frozen dinners and snacks and new items that would be desired by students
   c. How students spend their entertainment dollars and what additional entertainment opportunities they would like to see offered
7. What are some major issues in conducting international focus groups?

8. What are the advantages and disadvantages of online focus groups? Should they really be considered focus groups?
9. Take a consumer drawing test—draw a typical Pepsi drinker and a typical Coke drinker. What do the images suggest about your perceptions of Coke and Pepsi drinkers?
10. Use the metaphor technique to tell a story about going to the supermarket.

Working the Net

Go to http://www.researchconnections.com. Under "Live Demos," look at the information available at Focus Connect. Report your findings to the class.

Real-Life Research • 5.1

DaimlerChrysler's PT Cruiser

At first glance, DaimlerChrysler AG's new PT Cruiser looks like a massive gamble. It's part 1920s gangster car, part 1950s hot rod and part London taxicab. DaimlerChrysler touts the vehicle as a sure-fire "segment buster" that combines the room of a minivan with the flair of a sport-utility vehicle and the practicality of a small car.

In the latest focus groups, 41% of consumers who saw the PT Cruiser loved it and 26% hated it, according to Joseph N. Caddell, DaimlerChrysler's general product manager for small-car operations. That's a high negative for such an important product.

But that volatile response is exactly what the former Chrysler Corp. intended. The PT Cruiser—the initials stand for Personal Transportation—is the company's first vehicle designed entirely through an unconventional market-research process known as "archetype research." It is overseen by a 57-year-old French-born medical anthropologist named G. Clotaire Rapaille. It was developed by Dr. Rapaille when he was working with autistic children in Europe and has been used by such companies as Procter & Gamble Co. and General Motors Corp.

Development of the PT Cruiser began with a series of free-wheeling, three-hour focus-group sessions in the U.S. and Europe. Participants were asked, with lights dimmed and mood music playing, to drift back to their childhoods and jot down the memories invoked by the prototype PT Cruiser parked in the room. After the sessions, Dr. Rapaille and a team from Chrysler pored over the stories with orange and yellow highlighter pens, sleuthing for the emotion sparked by the vehicle. Dr. Rapaille calls it "the reptilian hot button."

All this struck many on the PT Cruiser team, accustomed to traditional focus groups with direct questions and concrete answers, as more than a little strange. "Everyone was skeptical," recalls the principal designer of the vehicle's exterior, Bryan Nesbitt, who was in his late 20s during the sessions and had never traveled abroad. "The results seemed so vague." Yet the research led to major design changes that made the car look more outlandish and the company more confident it would sell.

Dr. Rapaille and about a dozen other members of the PT Cruiser team took the designer's first prototypes and hit the road. Over several months, they held a series of three-hour sessions in cities across the U.S. and Europe. Unlike in traditional focus groups, where participants are chosen because they fit into a particular demographic segment, the members were picked by Dr. Rapaille to represent an entire culture.

In the first hour, after showing the group a PT Cruiser, Dr. Rapaille would stand up and tell the participants, seated in a circle: "I'm from another planet and I don't even know what you do with that. What is the purpose of this thing?"

One early prototype, a variant on the one that resembled the Golf, was described by many participants as too toylike. "They said, 'I'm grown up, so I don't want a toy,'" recalls Dr. Rapaille. "So we knew that was wrong."

In the second hour, the participants were asked to sit down on the floor, like children, and use scissors and a pile of magazines to cut out collages of words they thought described the vehicle. At that point their chief concern about the prototype became clearer: It looked insubstantial and unsafe.

The discomfort was particularly notable with the focus groups in the U.S., where hatchbacks don't sell as well as they do in Europe. In the conversation following the collage making, many participants suggested the rear hatch's large window would let prying outsiders see in and make the car dangerous if hit from behind.

A group in Paris had a different reaction. Accustomed to hatchbacks, the French group was more concerned about the car's utility than its safety. It described the prototype . . . as a tantalizingly wrapped box under a Christmas tree that promised a great gift but didn't deliver one.

The result: The Chrysler team went back to the drawing board and, at a later session, introduced a foam model of removable seats. That and a front passenger seat that folds forward to make a tray that can hold a laptop have become among the PT Cruiser's most talked-about features.

The third hour was perhaps the most bizarre—but also the most productive. Dr. Rapaille asked the participants to lie down on the floor. Then he dimmed the lights, began playing tapes of soothing music and told the group to relax their bodies. The researcher-turned-consultant wanted to lull them into a semisleeping state, when the intellectual part of the brain hasn't yet seized control from the "reptilian," or instinctive, part. The goal was to figure out what "reptilian hot button" the PT Cruiser pushed.

Dr. Rapaille gave the participants pen and paper and asked them to write stories triggered by the prototype they had just seen. In the first focus groups, the stories centered again on toys. In later groups, when Dr. Rapaille asked the participants to write about what they hoped the PT Cruiser would become, the stories contrasted a dangerous outside world with a secure interior of the car.

The general sentiment was that the participants wanted more of a sport-utility vehicle. "It's a jungle out there," says Dr. Rapaille, recalling the message. "It's Mad Max. People want to kill me, rape me." The consultant's message to the designers: "Give me a big thing like a tank."

So the designers went to work to make the PT Cruiser more tough looking. They bulked up the fenders, giving the car a "kind of bulldog stance from the rear," says Mr. Nesbitt, the designer. And they made the rear window smaller, increasing the amount of sheet metal in the hatch to make it look stronger. The result: a vehicle that thrills some and puts off others. "We have what we call a healthy level of dislike," says David Bostwick, Director of Corporate Marketing Research, who thinks that's a good sign that "we didn't make a generic vehicle."[35]

Questions

1. Is Dr. Rapaille really conducting focus groups? Is it qualitative research?
2. Would this technique work for the following?
   a. new frozen foods
   b. furniture
   c. computer chips
   d. business jet design
3. Is there any need to follow up Dr. Rapaille's work with quantitative research?

PART 2:
Creating a Research Design

Real-Life Research • 5.2

Pillsbury Cake Mixes

To learn more about its client's product, Pillsbury cake mixes, McCann-Erickson Advertising Agency decided to conduct some qualitative research. It brought 50 consumers into the agency and asked them to sketch likely buyers of two different brands of cake mixes: Pillsbury and Duncan Hines. Examples of the sketches are shown in the figure. Consistently, the group portrayed Pillsbury customers as apron-clad, grandmotherly types, whereas they pictured Duncan Hines customers as svelte, contemporary women.

Questions

1. You are the account executive for Pillsbury. What kind of changes in its advertising program for cake mixes would you recommend? Why?
2. What other projective techniques could have been used to ascertain consumers' perceptions of these two products? Describe how one of these techniques might be applied to explore images of Pillsbury and Duncan Hines cake mixes.
3. How might quantitative studies be used to confirm or invalidate the findings of the qualitative research?

Who Baked the Cake?

Chapter Six

Survey Research: The Profound Impact of the Internet

Learning Objectives

To understand the reasons for the popularity of survey research.

To learn about the types of error in survey research.

To learn about the types of surveys.

To understand the advantages and disadvantages of online surveys.

To gain insight into the ways online surveys can be conducted.

To learn about recruiting sources for online surveys.

To recognize the special issues that arise in designing online questionnaires.

To gain insight into the factors that determine the choice of particular survey methods.

*F*AST COMPANY—ONE OF TODAY'S HOTTEST BUSINESS MAGAZINES—HAS won a National Magazine Award for general excellence, as well as numerous other awards. In the summer of 1999, the *Fast Company*–Roper Starch Survey series was launched with the mission of exploring a range of business and workplace issues in the new economy. These online surveys are conducted among college-educated employed adults, with data collection across the AOL subscriber base by Digital Marketing Services (DMS), one of Roper's online research partners. The polls focus on topics ranging from achieving balance between work and home to envisioning the role of the e-world and technology in business during the new millennium.

THE RESULTS OF *FAST COMPANY*–ROPER Starch Surveys have appeared in *Fast Company* magazine, giving insight into the psyche of America's labor force. The new economy has forced people to redefine their relationships with work—and so, with life. This rapid reordering is a work in progress, and most people feel some ambiguity or even angst about the result. Despite talk about achieving balance, these college-educated workers are still driven by a desire to have it all: more fulfilling work; more money; and more time for a personal life. In explaining their sacrifices to succeed at their jobs, they say they are working hard today for gains tomorrow—avoiding as best they can the tough choices necessary to achieve real "balance." The *Fast Company*–Roper Starch Surveys will continue to track workers' attitudes and observations as they struggle with career and business issues.[1] ■

The Roper Starch Survey series launched by *Fast Company* magazine—one of today's hottest business magazines—explores a range of issues in the new economy. Online surveys are a new way of doing research that offers insight into the psyche of America's labor force.

Find out more about *Fast Company* surveys at

http://www.
fastcompany.com

Survey research is the use of a questionnaire to gather facts, opinions, and attitudes; it is the most popular way to gather primary data. What are the various types of survey research? As noted previously, not everyone is willing to participate in a survey. What kinds of errors does that create? What are the other types of errors encountered in survey research? Why has Internet survey research become so popular and what are its drawbacks? These questions are answered in this chapter.

The Popularity of Survey Research

Some 126 million Americans have been interviewed at some point in their lives. Each year, about 70 million people are interviewed in the United States, which is the equivalent of over 15 minutes per adult per year. Surveys have a high rate of usage in marketing research compared to other means of collecting primary data, for some very good reasons.

■ *The need to know why.* In marketing research, there is a critical need to have some idea about why people do or do not do something. For example, why did they buy or not buy a particular brand? What did they like or dislike about it? Who or what influenced them? We do not mean to imply that surveys can prove causation, only that they can be used to develop some idea of the causal forces at work.
■ *The need to know how.* At the same time, the marketing researcher often finds it necessary to understand the process consumers go through before taking some action. How did they make the decision? What time period passed? What did they examine or consider? When and where was the decision made? What do they plan to do next?
■ *The need to know who.* The marketing researcher also needs to know who the person is, from a demographic or lifestyle perspective. Information on age, income, occupation, marital status, stage in the family life cycle, education, and other factors is necessary for the identification and definition of market segments.

Types of Errors in Survey Research

When assessing the quality of information obtained from survey research, the manager must make some determination of the accuracy of those results. This requires careful consideration of the research methodology employed in relation to the various types of error that might result (see Figure 6.1).

Sampling Error

Two major types of errors may be encountered in connection with the sampling process. They are random error and systematic error, sometimes referred to as bias.

random error, or **random sampling error**
Error that results from chance variation.

chance variation
The difference between the sample value and the true value of the population mean.

Surveys often attempt to obtain information from a representative cross section of a target population. The goal is to make inferences about the total population based on the responses given by respondents sampled. Even when all aspects of the sample are investigated properly, the results are still subject to a certain amount of **random error** (or **random sampling error**) because of chance variation. **Chance variation** is the difference between the sample value and the true value of the population mean. This error cannot be eliminated, but it can be reduced by increasing the sample size. It is possible to estimate the range of random error at a particular level of confidence. Random error and the procedures for estimating it are discussed in detail in Chapters 12 and 13.

PART 2:
Creating a Research Design

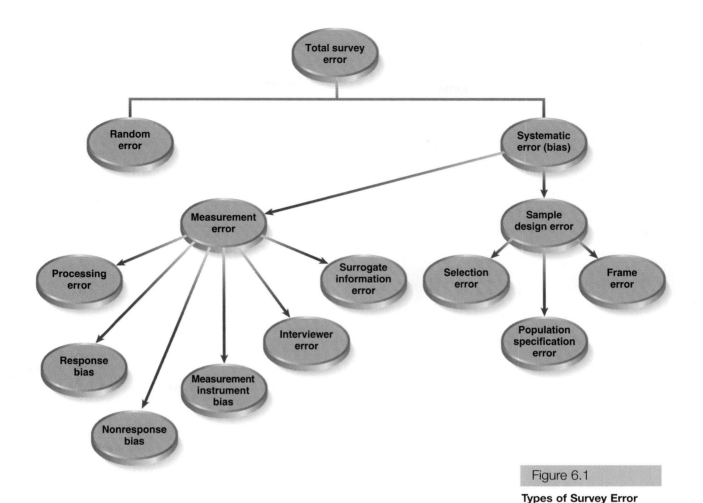

Figure 6.1

Types of Survey Error

Systematic Error

Systematic error, or **bias,** results from mistakes or problems in the research design or from flaws in the execution of the sample design. Systematic error exists in the results of a sample if those results show a consistent tendency to vary in one direction (consistently higher or consistently lower) from the true value of the population parameter. Systematic error includes all sources of error except those introduced by the random sampling process. Therefore, systematic errors are sometimes called *nonsampling errors*. The nonsampling errors that can systematically influence survey answers can be categorized as *sample design error* and *measurement error.*

Sample Design Error   **Sample design error** is systematic error that results from a problem in the sample design or sampling procedures. Types of sample design errors include frame errors, population specification errors, and selection errors.

systematic error, or **bias**
Error that results from problems or flaws in the execution of the research design; sometimes called *nonsampling error.*

sample design error
Systematic error that results from an error in the sample design or sampling procedures.

A population must be defined before research can begin. Errors can occur if a population is not defined correctly or if selection procedures are not followed properly.

sampling frame
The list of population elements or members from which units to be sampled are selected.

frame error
Error resulting from an inaccurate or incomplete sampling frame.

population specification error
Error that results from incorrectly defining the population or universe from which a sample is chosen.

Frame Error.   The **sampling frame** is the list of population elements or members from which units to be sampled are selected. **Frame error** results from using an incomplete or inaccurate sampling frame. The problem is that a sample drawn from a list that is subject to frame error may not be a true cross section of the target population. A common source of frame error in marketing research is the use of a published telephone directory as a sampling frame for a telephone survey. Many households are not listed in a current telephone book because they do not want to be listed or are not listed accurately because they have recently moved or changed their telephone number. Research has shown that those people who are listed in telephone directories are systematically different from those who are not listed in certain important ways, such as socioeconomic levels.[2] This means that if a study purporting to represent the opinions of all households in a particular area is based on listings in the current telephone directory, it will be subject to frame error.

Population Specification Error.   **Population specification error** results from an incorrect definition of the population or universe from which the sample is to be selected. For example, suppose a researcher defined the population or universe for a study as people over the age of 35. Later, it was determined that younger individuals should have been included and that the population should have been defined as people 20 years of age or older. If those younger people who were excluded are significantly different in regard to the variables of interest, then the sample results will be biased.

Selection Error.   Selection error can occur even when the analyst has a proper sampling frame and has defined the population correctly. **Selection error** occurs when sampling procedures are incomplete or improper or when appropriate selection procedures are not properly followed. For example, door-to-door interviewers might decide to avoid houses that do not look neat and tidy because they think the inhabitants will not be agreeable to doing a survey. If people who live in messy houses are systematically different from those who live in tidy houses, then selection error will be introduced into the results of the survey. Selection error is a serious problem in nonprobability samples, a subject discussed in Chapter 12.

Measurement Error   Measurement error is often a much more serious threat to survey accuracy than is random error. When the results of public opinion polls are given in the media and in professional marketing research reports, an error figure is frequently reported (say, plus or minus 5%). The television viewer or the user of a marketing research study is left with the impression that this figure refers to total survey error. Unfortunately, this is not the case. This figure refers only to random sampling error. It does not include sample design error and speaks in no way to the measurement error that may exist in the research results. **Measurement error** occurs when there is variation between the information being sought (true value) and the information actually obtained by the measurement process. Our main concern in this text is with systematic measurement error. Various types of error may be caused by numerous deficiencies in the measurement process. These errors include surrogate information error, interviewer error, measurement instrument bias, processing error, nonresponse bias, and response bias.

Surrogate Information Error. **Surrogate information error** occurs when there is a discrepancy between the information actually required to solve a problem and the information being sought by the researcher. It relates to general problems in the research design, particularly failure to properly define the problem. A classic and well-known case of surrogate information error relates to the New Coke fiasco. Apparently, the research for New Coke focused on the taste of the product and failed to consider the attitudes of consumers toward a product change. The failure of New Coke strongly suggests, as the producers of Coke should have understood, that people purchase Coke for many reasons other than taste.

Interviewer Error. **Interviewer error,** or **interviewer bias,** results from the interviewer's influencing a respondent—consciously or unconsciously—to give untrue or inaccurate answers. The dress, age, gender, facial expressions, body language, or tone of voice of the interviewer may influence the answers given by some or all respondents. This type of error is caused by problems in the selection and training of interviewers or by the failure of interviewers to follow instructions. Interviewers must be properly trained and supervised to appear neutral at all times. Another type of interviewer error occurs when deliberate cheating takes place. This can be a particular problem in door-to-door interviewing, where interviewers may be tempted to falsify interviews and get paid for work they did not actually do. The procedures developed by the researcher must include safeguards to ensure that this problem will be detected (see Chapter 14).

Measurement Instrument Bias. **Measurement instrument bias** (sometimes called *questionnaire bias*) results from problems with the measurement instrument or questionnaire (see Chapter 9). Examples of such problems include leading questions or elements of the questionnaire design that make recording responses difficult and prone to recording errors (see Chapter 11). Problems of this type can be avoided by paying careful attention to detail in the questionnaire design phase and by using questionnaire pretests before field interviewing begins.

Processing Error. **Processing errors** are primarily due to mistakes that occur when information from survey documents is entered into the computer. For example, a data entry operator might enter the wrong response to a particular question. Errors of this type are avoided by developing and strictly adhering to quality control procedures when processing survey results. This process is discussed in detail in Chapter 14.

selection error
Error that results from following incomplete or improper sampling procedures or not following appropriate procedures.

measurement error
Systematic error that results from a variation between the information being sought and what is actually obtained by the measurement process.

surrogate information error
Error that results from a discrepancy between the information needed to solve a problem and that sought by the researcher.

interviewer error, or **interviewer bias**
Error that results from the interviewer's influencing—consciously or unconsciously—the answers of the respondent.

measurement instrument bias
Error that results from the design of the questionnaire or measurement instrument; also known as *questionnaire bias*.

processing error
Error that results from the incorrect transfer of information from a survey document to a computer.

Nonresponse Bias. Ideally, if a sample of 400 people is selected from a particular population, all 400 of those individuals should be interviewed. As a practical matter, this will never happen. Response rates of 5 percent or less are common in mail surveys. The question is "Are those who did respond to the survey systematically different in some important way from those who did not respond?" Such differences lead to **nonresponse bias.** We recently examined the results of a study conducted among customers of a large savings and loan association. The response rate to the questionnaire, included in customer monthly statements, was slightly under 1 percent. Analysis of the occupations of those who responded revealed that the percentage of retired people among respondents was 20 times higher than in the local metropolitan area. This overrepresentation of retired individuals raised serious doubts about the accuracy of the results.

Yet this experience may be the exception rather than the rule. One researcher reviewed 14 studies in which differences between respondents and nonrespondents (or earlier or later respondents) to mail surveys were reportedly found.[3] When the raw data were recalculated to address the question of whether differences between respondents and the entire sample were large enough to be meaningful, the less complete returns were found to closely approximate the more complete returns. Of all the reported studies that have looked for such differences, none has found meaningful, practical differences between respondents and the entire sample or between early respondents and respondents as a whole.

Obviously, the higher the response rate, the less the possible impact of nonresponse, because nonrespondents then represent a smaller subset of the overall picture. If the decrease in bias associated with improved response rates is trivial, then allocating resources to obtain higher response rates might be wasteful in studies in which resources could be used for better purposes.

Thomas Danbury, chairman of Survey Sampling, Incorporated, reports that his firm conducted one study in which 65,000 telephone interviews were completed. Interviewers made up to seven attempts over a four-week period to reach each household and then up to seven more to interview a randomly selected adult. At the end of the project, the researchers looked at what they would have found if only one attempt had been made, then two attempts, all the way to seven. Danbury noted, "To our surprise, the results would have been very similar had we made no callbacks at all!"[4] Table 6.1 shows the incidence of several demographic characteristics measured by one attempt versus seven attempts. Despite these findings, Danbury still recommends three callback attempts.

Nonresponse error occurs when the following happens:

- A person cannot be reached at a particular time.
- A potential respondent is reached but cannot or will not participate at that time (for example, the telephone request to participate in a survey comes just as the family is sitting down to dinner).
- A person is reached but refuses to participate in the survey. This is the most serious problem because it may be possible to achieve future participation in the first two circumstances.

The **refusal rate** is the percentage of persons contacted who refused to participate in a survey. Today, the overall refusal rate is approximately 60 percent—up from 52 percent in 1992, according to the Council for Marketing and Opinion

Differences in Demographic Characteristics Based on One Callback Attempt versus Seven in a Survey of 65,000 Adults

Demographic Characteristic	One Call	Seven Calls
Income $50K+	45%	47%
Some college+	47%	49%
Employed full time	76%	78%
Married	65%	63%
Unlisted number	35%	37%
1–2 person household	52%	52%
Rent home	29%	30%
Moved in 5 years	48%	50%
Male	45%	46%

Source: Courtesy of Survey Sampling, Inc.

Research (CMOR). Most refusals (68%) occur before the survey introduction (initial refusals); only one-quarter (26%) occur after the introduction is read (qualified refusals). Few (6%) terminate once the survey is under way. While most individuals (71%) express a willingness to participate in future surveys, this willingness is lukewarm (nearly three times as many are "fairly willing" compared to "very willing").[5] While these percentages are based on a study by the CMOR and are not necessarily reflective of the entire industry, they do reflect the significant increase in the refusal rate.

Response Bias.   If there is a tendency for people to answer a particular question in a certain way, then there is **response bias.** Response bias can result from deliberate falsification or unconscious misrepresentation.

Deliberate falsification occurs when people purposefully give untrue answers to questions. There are many reasons why people might knowingly misrepresent information in a survey. They may wish to appear intelligent, not reveal information that they feel is embarrassing, or conceal information that they consider to be personal. For example, in a survey about fast-food buying behavior, the respondents may have a fairly good idea of how many times they visited a fast-food restaurant in the past month. However, they may not remember which fast-food restaurants they visited or how many times they visited each restaurant. Rather than answering "Don't know" in response to a question regarding which restaurants they visited, the respondents may simply guess.

Unconscious misrepresentation occurs when a respondent is legitimately trying to be truthful and accurate but gives an inaccurate response. This type of bias may occur because of question format, question content, or various other reasons.

Strategies for minimizing survey errors are summarized in Table 6.2.

response bias
Error that results from the tendency of people to answer a question incorrectly through either deliberate falsification or unconscious misrepresentation.

Threats to Survey Research

Telemarketing

Telemarketing calls have become ubiquitous. As of 2001, virtually all U.S. households had been reached by telemarketers; 93 percent reported having received a call, and 84 percent having received a call in the past year. (In 1992, when telemarketing was first measured, 81% reported having ever received a call, and 68% having received a call in the past year.) And, households are being called repeatedly, with an average (median) of 20 calls in the past year (up from 8 in 1995).

Consumers are becoming increasingly annoyed by telemarketing calls. A majority (51%) consider them unpleasant (up from 47% in 1992), and 77 percent terminated their last telemarketing call (up from 62% in 1992). Only 5 percent agreed to the last telemarketing request they received (down from 8% in 1992 and 11% in 1995).

Despite industry efforts to combat "sugging" (selling under the guise of research), this activity appears to be continuing at a constant level. As many people say they have been asked to answer "survey questions" that turned out to be for sales purposes.

Answering Machine Usage

Growth over time in answering machine ownership appears to have slowed. Three-quarters (74%) indicated ownership as of 2000, up slightly from 68 percent in 1995, and up substantially from 37 percent in 1990. While many answering machine owners are reachable for telephone surveys, extra effort is required. The proportion of people using answering machines to "ever" screen their calls has remained stable at half of all owners, who only screen an average of 25 percent of their calls.

Call Screening Services

Call Blocking, Caller ID, and Distinctive Ringing are all increasing threats to telephone surveys. The combined numbers of those saying that they "currently subscribe" or "plan to subscribe" for all three services have doubled since 1995, with Caller ID being the most popular.

One-third (34%) of respondents report currently subscribing to Caller ID, while another 8 percent plan to subscribe. One-fifth (17%) currently subscribe to Call Blocking, while another 3 percent plan to subscribe. Distinctive Ringing is the least popular of the three services; only 8 percent currently subscribe, and 2 percent report that they plan to subscribe. Use of each of the three services is significantly higher among those with unlisted phone numbers than among those with listed numbers.

Privacy and Confidentiality Concerns

While many individuals are very concerned about personal privacy (85% are "very" or "somewhat" concerned), most do not feel that surveys are an invasion of privacy (75%). However, a majority do not believe that research firms maintain confidentiality (52%). As would be expected, individuals from households with unlisted phone numbers have somewhat higher concerns about privacy issues than those from listed households.[6] ■

Table 6.2

Types of Errors and Strategies for Minimizing Errors

I. Random error	This error can be reduced only by increasing sample size.
II. Systematic error	This error can be reduced by minimizing sample design and measurement errors.
A. Sample design error	
Frame error	This error can be minimized by getting the best sampling frame possible and doing preliminary quality control checks to evaluate the accuracy and completeness of the frame.
Population specification error	This error results from incorrect definition of the population of interest. It can be reduced or minimized only by more careful consideration and definition of the population of interest.
Selection error	This error results from using incomplete or improper sampling procedures or not following appropriate selection procedures. It can occur even with a good sampling frame and an appropriate specification of the population. It is minimized by developing selection procedures that will ensure randomness and by developing quality control checks to make sure that these procedures are followed in the field.
B. Measurement error	
Surrogate information error	This error results from seeking and basing decisions on the wrong information. It results from poor design and can be minimized only by paying more careful attention to specification of the types of information required to fulfill the objectives of the research.
Interviewer error	This error occurs because of interactions between the interviewer and the respondent that affect the responses given. It is minimized by careful interviewer selection and training. In addition, quality control checks should involve unobtrusive monitoring of interviewers to ascertain whether they are following prescribed guidelines.
Measurement instrument bias	Also referred to as *questionnaire bias,* this error is minimized only by careful questionnaire design and pretesting.
Processing error	This error can occur in the process of transferring data from questionnaires to the computer. It is minimized by developing and following rigid quality control procedures for transferring data and supporting quality control checks.
Nonresponse bias	This error results from the fact that those people chosen for the sample who actually respond are systematically different from those who are chosen and do not respond. It is particularly serious in connection with mail surveys. It is minimized by doing everything possible (e.g., shortening the questionnaire, making the questionnaire more respondent friendly, doing callbacks, providing incentives, contacting people when they are most likely to be at home) to encourage those chosen for the sample to respond.
Response bias	This error occurs when something about a question leads people to answer it in a particular way. It can be minimized by paying special attention to questionnaire design. In particular, questions that are hard to answer, might make the respondent look uninformed, or deal with sensitive issues should be modified (see Chapter 11).

Types of Surveys

Asking people questions is the essence of the survey approach. But what type of survey is best for a given situation? The non-Internet survey alternatives discussed in this chapter are door-to-door interviews, executive interviews, mall-intercept interviews, telephone interviews, self-administered questionnaires, and mail surveys.

Door-to-Door Interviews

door-to-door interviews
Interviews conducted face to face with consumers in their homes.

Door-to-door interviews, in which consumers are interviewed in person in their homes, were at one time thought to be the best survey method. This conclusion was based on a number of factors. First, the door-to-door interview is a personal, face-to-face interaction with all the attendant advantages—immediate feedback from the respondent, the ability to explain complicated tasks, the ability to use special questionnaire techniques that require visual contact to speed up the interview or improve data quality, and the ability to show the respondent product concepts and other stimuli for evaluation. Second, the participant is at ease in a familiar, comfortable, secure environment.

This approach to interviewing has a number of drawbacks that explain its virtual disappearance. Jerry Rosenkranz, chairman of Data Development, a large New York–based custom research firm, lists the disadvantages of door-to-door interviewing:

- The growth of the two-adult working family and other changes in family composition mean less availability of potential respondents.
- Although response rates for in-home interviews were historically higher than for other approaches, they are gradually deteriorating.
- Unsafe (high crime) areas, distance, and lack of accessibility sometimes negated reaching the desired sample.
- The drop in qualified interviewing personnel, whether because of a drop in education or the increase in other options with better pay, has become a factor over time.
- The special characteristics required of a field interviewer, that is, the "chutz-pah to make a cold call," limit the potential pool of interviewers.
- The client and field service's unease due to the lack of "hands-on" control of a field force that is out there somewhere (in direct comparison to a permanent workforce in a centralized location under supervision—clocking in 9 to 5).
- The lack of communication between the home office, the field office, and the interviewing staff (except at the end of day) is a serious handicap if one wishes to execute questionnaire changes, examine incidence rate, or hasten data retrieval.
- The effects of such old bugaboos as weather (too good or too bad), car problems, broken-in[to] cars, sickness, etc.
- Cheating, fudging, or shortcutting by the interviewers, interviewing the wrong respondent, etc., promote low levels of validation. This postfield check may be too late to permit us to replace the necessary data. In any case, it is very costly to go back for it.[7]

PART 2:
Creating a Research Design

The door-to-door approach to survey data collection may soon disappear altogether from the marketing research scene.

Executive Interviews

Executive interviews are used by marketing researchers as the industrial equivalent of door-to-door interviews. This type of survey involves interviewing businesspeople at their offices concerning industrial products or services. For example, if Hewlett-Packard wants information about user preferences for features that might be offered in a new line of computer printers, it needs to interview prospective user-purchasers of the printers. It would thus be appropriate to locate and interview these people at their offices.

This type of interviewing is expensive. First, individuals involved in the purchasing decision for the product in question must be identified and located. Sometimes lists can be obtained from various sources, but more frequently screening must be conducted over the telephone. A particular company may indeed have individuals of the type being sought, but locating them within a large organization can be expensive and time-consuming. Once a qualified person is located, the next step is to get that person to agree to be interviewed and to set a time for the interview. This is not usually as hard as it might seem, because most professionals seem to enjoy talking about topics related to their work.

Finally, an interviewer must go to the particular place at the appointed time. Long waits are frequent; cancellations are common. This type of survey requires highly skilled interviewers because they are frequently interviewing on topics they know little about. Executive interviews have essentially the same advantages and disadvantages as door-to-door interviews.

executive interviews
The industrial equivalent of door-to-door interviewing.

Mall-Intercept Interviews

Mall-intercept interviews are a popular survey method accounting for approximately one-third of all personal interviews. This survey approach is relatively simple. Shoppers are intercepted in public areas of shopping malls and either interviewed on the spot or asked to come to a permanent interviewing facility in the mall. Approximately 500 malls throughout the country have permanent survey facilities operated by marketing research firms. An equal or greater number of malls permit marketing researchers to interview on a daily basis. Many malls do not permit marketing research interviewing, however, because they view it as an unnecessary nuisance to shoppers.

Mall interviewing is of relatively recent origin. The greatest growth in the use of this technique occurred in the 1970s. The mall-intercept interview is a low-cost substitute for the door-to-door interview. In fact, this approach has grown primarily at the expense of door-to-door interviewing.

Mall surveys are less expensive than door-to-door interviews because respondents come to the interviewer rather than the other way around. Interviewers spend more of their time actually interviewing and less of their time hunting for someone to interview. Also, mall interviewers do not have the substantial travel time and mileage expenses associated with door-to-door inter-

mall-intercept interviews
Interviews conducted by intercepting mall shoppers (or shoppers in other high-traffic locations) and interviewing them face to face.

viewing. In addition to low cost, mall-intercept interviews have many of the advantages associated with door-to-door interviews in that respondents can try test products on the spot.

However, a number of serious disadvantages are associated with mall-intercept interviewing. First, it is virtually impossible to get a sample representative of a large metropolitan area from shoppers at a particular mall. Even though malls may be large, most of them draw shoppers from a relatively small local area. In addition, malls tend to attract certain types of people, based on the stores they contain. Studies also show that some people shop more frequently than others and therefore have a greater chance of being selected. Finally, many people refuse mall interviews. In summary, mall-intercept interviewing cannot produce a good or representative sample except in the rare case in which the population of interest is coincident with or is a subset of the population who shops at a particular mall.

Second, the mall environment is not always viewed as a comfortable place to conduct an interview. Respondents may be ill at ease, in a hurry, or preoccupied by various distractions outside the researcher's control. These factors may adversely affect the quality of the data obtained. Even with all its problems, the popularity of mall-intercept interviews has held steady in recent years.[8]

Rather than interview in the public areas of malls, some researchers are conducting surveys in stores at the point-of-purchase. The notion is that in-store research gets the consumer as he or she reaches for the product on the shelf. "The closer you can take the research to the point of decision, whether it's at the store shelf or in the pantry, the more actionable it is," says Karen Snepp, vice president of consumer insights at Frito-Lay.[9] Various companies, including Procter & Gamble, General Mills, Starbucks, McDonald's, and Walgreens, currently conduct in-store studies.

In-store research can sometimes determine the future of new product concepts. Quaker State asked Elrick & Lavidge to investigate the viability of a new product for its Slick 50 engine-treatment brand. The study was conducted in three locations—Dallas, Miami, and Tulsa—all with different levels of Slick 50 sales. Since Quaker State couldn't advertise the product because it was still in secret development, Elrick & Lavidge conducted phone surveys in the three markets to identify category users. Those consumers, mostly young men, were then offered a financial incentive to participate in the study at their local store.

At the store, they were shown the Slick 50 product on the shelf and in end-of-aisle displays. Researchers peppered them with questions: Did they like the package design? Could it be improved? Was it a product they would buy? Purchase likelihood was key for Quaker State to understand. However, the merger of Quaker State and Pennzoil has squelched further development of the product for now.[10]

Telephone Interviews

Until 1990, telephone interviewing was the most popular form of survey research. The advantages of telephone interviewing are compelling. First, telephoning is a relatively inexpensive way to collect survey data. Second, the telephone interview has the potential to produce a high-quality sample. *Random-digit sampling*, or *random-digit dialing*, is a frequently used sampling approach (see

PART 2:
Creating a Research Design

Chapter 12). The basic idea is simple: Instead of drawing a sample from the phone book or other directory, researchers use telephone numbers generated via a random-number procedure. This approach ensures that people with unlisted numbers and those who have moved or otherwise changed their telephone numbers since the last published phone book are included in the sample in the correct proportion.

The telephone survey approach has several inherent disadvantages. First, respondents cannot be shown anything in a typical telephone interview. This shortcoming ordinarily eliminates the telephone survey as an alternative in situations that require respondents to comment on visual product concepts, advertisements, and the like.

Second, some critics have suggested that telephone interviewers are unable to make the various judgments and evaluations that can be made by in-home interviewers (e.g., evaluations concerning income, based on what the respondent's home looks like and other outward signs of economic status). In reality, marketing research interviewers are almost never called on to make such judgments.

A third disadvantage of the telephone interview is that it limits the quantity and types of information that can be obtained. A respondent's patience wears thin more easily over the phone, and it is easy to hang up the phone. The telephone is also a poor vehicle for conducting a depth interview or a long interview with many open-ended questions.

A fourth disadvantage of telephone interviewing, discussed earlier in the chapter, is associated with the increased use of screening devices. On the average, for every hour an interviewer spends on the phone, 30 minutes is spent just trying to find a person who will agree to be surveyed.[11] This, of course, drives up the cost of telephone surveys.

A fifth disadvantage is that research has shown the potential for personality bias in phone surveys. That is, persons who agree to participate in a telephone interview may be more outgoing, confident, conscientious, and agreeable than those who will not.[12]

Today, nearly all telephone interviews are central-location telephone interviews. In some cases, firms are further centralizing the process by conducting completely automated telephone surveys.

Central-Location Telephone Interviews

Central-location telephone interviews are conducted from a facility set up for that purpose. The reason for the popularity of central-location phone interviews is fairly straightforward—in a single word, control. First, the interviewing process can be monitored; most central-location telephone interviewing facilities have unobtrusive monitoring equipment that permits supervisors to listen in on interviews as they are being conducted. Interviewers who are not doing the interview properly can be corrected, and those who are incapable of conducting a proper interview can be terminated. One supervisor can monitor from 10 to 20 interviewers. Ordinarily, each interviewer is monitored at least once per shift. Second, completed interviews are edited on the spot as a further quality control check. Interviewers can be immediately informed of any deficiencies in their work. Finally, interviewers' working hours are controlled.

central-location telephone interviews
Interviews conducted by calling respondents from a centrally located marketing research facility.

WAR Stories

computer-assisted telephone interviews (CATI)
Central-location telephone interviews in which interviewers enter respondents' answers directly into a computer.

completely automated telephone surveys (CATS)
Interviews that use interactive voice response (IVR) technology to ask the questions.

Most research firms have computerized the central-location telephone interviewing process. In **computer-assisted telephone interviews (CATI),** each interviewer is seated in front of a computer terminal or a personal computer. When a qualified respondent gets on the line, the interviewer starts the interview by pressing a key or series of keys on the keyboard. The questions and multiple-choice answers appear on the screen one at a time. The interviewer reads the question and enters the response, and the computer skips ahead to the appropriate next question. For example, the interviewer might ask whether the respondent has a dog. If the answer is yes, there might be a series of questions regarding what type of dog food the person buys. If the answer is no, those questions would be inappropriate. The computer takes into account the answer to the dog ownership question and skips ahead to the next appropriate question.

In addition, the computer can help customize questionnaires. For example, in the early part of a long interview, a respondent is asked the years, makes, and models of all the cars he or she owns. Later in the interview, questions might be asked about each specific car owned. The question might come up on the interviewer's screen as follows: "You said you own a 2000 GMC truck. Which family member drives this vehicle most often?" Other questions about this vehicle and others owned would appear in similar fashion.

Another advantage of CATI is that computer tabulations can be run at any point in the study. This luxury is not available with a pencil-and-paper interview. Based on preliminary tabulations, certain questions might be dropped, saving time and money in subsequent interviewing. If, for example, 98.3 percent of those interviewed answer a particular question in the same manner, there is probably no need to continue asking the question. Tabulations may also suggest the need to add questions to the survey. If an unexpected pattern of product use is uncovered in the early stages of interviewing, questions can be added that delve further into this behavior. Finally, management may find the early reporting of survey results useful in preliminary planning and strategy development.

Completely Automated Telephone Surveys A recent development that simplifies telephone surveys by harnessing interactive voice response (IVR) technology to conduct interviews is called **completely automated telephone surveys (CATS).** Instead of using a human interviewer to read questions and key responses, CATS uses the recorded voice of a professional interviewer. Respondents answer closed-ended questions by pushing numbers on their push-button phones. Open-ended responses are recorded on tape for verbatim transcription and coding.

There are two versions of CATS: outbound calling and inbound calling. Outbound calling requires an accurate list of respondents' telephone numbers because the computer dials a sample of phone numbers and a recording solicits participation from whoever answers. This method tends to get lower response rates because people find it easier to hang up on a machine. With the inbound calling version, respondents are given a phone number to call after they have been recruited, usually by mail.

CATI Systems Improve the Survey Data Gathering Process

CATI SYSTEMS DEVELOPED IN RESPONSE TO NEEDS OF MARKETING researchers, including the following:

Disk-based recode. Automobile studies were being conducted that required an interviewer to choose from over 1,500 makes/models/styles of automobile. Each choice had to be presented quickly to the interviewer with only 24 lines on the screen to display these items.

Large number of quotas. At first there were only 20 to 30 quotas (required characteristics or responses in order to continue the interview) in a typical survey. Gradually these became used as counters of all kinds of cells that could be used to trigger different activities. For example, people with large dogs, living in Texas should answer questions 33, 34 and 35 but not 37. When joined together with custom-designed systems such as "Commander," developed by Maritz Marketing Research, these counters would permit users to streamline interviewing and tabulation with minimal training. Consequently, the software was enhanced to support many thousands of quotas.

Dialing systems. Eventually, telephone technology evolved to a point where interfaces between CATI software and telephone switches were possible. Because of the variation in phone rates, Custom Research Inc. installed a "least-cost routing" system to steer calls along the cheapest lines. Interviewers that dialed 10 or more calls per hour were losing some productivity, so "auto-dialers" were introduced that would enable the computer to dial the number displayed on the screen to prevent dialing errors. Still, some interviews are less than five minutes in length, and it may take much longer than that just to reach a respondent. A "predictive dialer" system was developed for Nielsen Media Research that automatically handled all the busy and no-answer calls, so interviewers were always presented with a live respondent.

Calls to multiple questionnaires. It is sometimes desirable to switch from one questionnaire to another in the middle of an interview, for example, to survey other members of a family in addition to the head of household. Being able to spawn a new questionnaire easily avoids interruption and makes it possible to access common information from the head of household questionnaire.

Ownership. Respondents who are very difficult to reach, such as doctors, top executives, or frequent travelers, may need to suspend the interview to take care of urgent business. When the interview resumes later, it is often desirable for the respondent to talk to the same interviewer. So on inbound calls, The Gallup Organization wanted the caller to be connected to the original interviewer who "owns" that call.[13] ∎

Companies using CATS have found that they are getting data fast and at low cost. The system is flexible and can be adapted to particular research needs. It has been used for several different types of studies: customer satisfaction, service quality monitoring, product/warranty registration, in-home product testing, and election day polling. Although CATS will never replace traditional methods, it does offer researchers another choice.[14]

Self-Administered Questionnaires

The self-administered and mail survey methods explained in this section have one thing in common. They differ from the other survey methods discussed in that no interviewer—human or computer—is involved. The major disadvantage of **self-administered questionnaires** is that no one is present to explain things to the respondent and clarify responses to open-ended questions. For example, if someone were asked via an open-ended question why he or she does not buy a particular brand of soft drink, a typical answer might be "because I don't like it." From a managerial perspective, this answer is useless. It provides no information that can be used to alter the marketing mix and thereby make the product more attractive. An interviewer conducting the survey, however, would "probe" for a response— after receiving and recording the useless response, the interviewer would ask the respondent what it was that he or she did not like about the product. The interviewee might then indicate a dislike for the taste. The interviewer would then ask what it was about the taste that the person did not like. Here the interviewer might finally get something useful, with the respondent indicating that the product in question was, for example, "too sweet." If many people give a similar response, management might elect to reduce the sweetness of the drink. The point is that, without probing, management would have only the useless first response.

Some have argued that the absence of an interviewer is an advantage in that it eliminates one source of bias. There is no interviewer whose appearance, dress, manner of speaking, or failure to follow instructions may influence respondents' answers to questions.

Kiosk-based computer interviewing is a relatively new and successful way of capturing data on consumers' recent experiences. Go to http://www.modalis.com/english/technologies/cati.html to find out more about one company's kiosk-based offerings.

Self-administered interviews are often used in malls or other central locations where the researcher has access to a captive audience. Airlines, for example, often have programs in which questionnaires are administered during the flight. Passengers are asked to rate various aspects of the airline's services, and the results are used to track passenger perceptions of service over time. Many hotels, restaurants, and other service businesses provide brief questionnaires to patrons to find out how they feel about the quality of service provided (see Figure 6.2).

A recent development in the area of direct computer interviewing is kiosk-based computer interviewing. Kiosks are developed with multimedia, touch-screen computers contained in freestanding cabinets. These computers can be

PART 2:
Creating a Research Design

Figure 6.2

Self-Administered Questionnaire

Source: Courtesy of Accent Marketing & Research, Ltd., London.

GATWICK EXPRESS

Customer Survey

0 1 2 3 4 5 6 7 8 R

Please complete this questionnaire by ticking the appropriate boxes or by writing in your answer in the space provided. A separate questionnaire should be completed by EACH member of your travelling party aged 14 and over.

Veuillez compléter le questionnaire suivant en cochant les cases appropriées ou en écrivant votre réponse dans l'espace prévu. Un questionnaire séparé devrait être complété par CHAQUE membre de votre groupe de voyage âgé de 14 ans et au-delà.

Bitte füllen Sie den nachfolgenden Fragebogen durch Ankreuzen der entsprechendenb Kästchen bzw. schriftlich an den vorgesehenen Stellen aus. JEDES Mitglied Ihrer Reisegruppe über 14 Jahren sollte einen separaten Fragebogen ausfüllen.

Q1 Are you sitting in Club (1st) class or Express (2nd) class on this train?
Etes-vous assis en classe Club (1ère) ou Express (2ème) dans ce train?
Sitzen Sie in der Club-Klasse (1. Kl) oder in der Express-Klasse (2. Kl) dieses Zuges?
Club (1st) ☐
Express (2nd) ☐

Q2 Are you flying or have you flown today?
Est-ce vous partez en voyage ou avez-vous voyagé par avion aujourd'hui?
Fliegen Sie heute oder Sie heute schon geflogen?
I will fly /*Je vais voyager par avion /Ich fliege* ☐
I have flown / *J'ai voyagé par avion /Ich bin geflogen* ☐
I am not flying (GO TO Q11) ☐
Je ne voyage pas par avion /Ich fliege nicht (ALLEZ A /WEITER ZU Q11)

Q3a Please write in the origin and destination of your flight and the scheduled arrival and departure times.
Veuillez inscrire l'origine et la destination de votre vol ainsi que les heures prévues de départ et d'arrivée.
Bitte geben Sie Ihren Abflug- und Zielort und die planmäßige Abflug- und Ankunftszeit an.
From / *De /Von* ....
To / *A /Zu* ....
Departure time / *Départ /Abflugzeit* ....
Arrival time /*Arrivée /Ankunftzeit* ....

Q3b Do you know your flight number?
Connaissez-vous le numéro de votre vol?
Wissen Sie Ihre Flugnummer?
If yes PLEASE WRITE IN ....

Q3c Which airline will/did you fly with?
Avec quelle compagnie aérienne volerez-vous/avez-vous volé?
Mit welcher Fluggesellschaft fliegen Sie/sind Sie geflogen?
....

Q4 Are/were you on the outward or return leg of your air journey?
Outward ☐ Return ☐
Single leg journey ☐

Q5a Is/was this flight a direct one or will/did you change planes en route?
Direct flight (GO TO Q6) ☐
Will/did change planes en route ☐

Q5b Please write in your ultimate origin and ultimate destination airports of this trip.
Origin ☐ Destination ☐

Q6 What flight ticket type do/did you have?
Economy Full Fare ☐ First Class ☐
Stand-by/Apex ☐ Business/Club ☐
Staff-Discount ☐ Don't know ☐
Other discount ☐ Other ☐

Q7 What is the UK origin/destination of your journey today?
Central London ☐ Outer London (North) ☐
Outer London (South) ☐ Other South East ☐
East Anglia ☐ South West ☐
Midlands ☐ Northern England ☐
Scotland ☐ Wales ☐
N.Ireland ☐ Other ☐
Don't know ☐

Q8 What is your usual country of residence?
Mainland UK ☐ Northern Ireland/Eire ☐
Channel Islands ☐ Other ☐

Q9 How many **adults** are in your party (including yourself)?
One adult ☐ Two adults ☐
Three adults ☐ More than three adults ☐

OFFICE USE ONLY
0 1 2 3 4 5 6 7 8 9
1000
100
10
1
0 1 2 3 4 5 6 7 8 9
100
10
1

PLEASE TURN OVER

(continued)

programmed to administer complex surveys, show full-color scanned images (products, store layouts), and play sound and video clips. Kiosks have been used successfully at trade shows and conventions and are now being tested in retail environments, where they have many applications. From a research standpoint, kiosk-based interviewing can be used in place of exit interviews to capture data on recent experiences. Kiosks have other definite advantages: This form of interviewing tends to be less expensive, people tend to give more honest answers than they would to a human interviewer, and internal control is higher because the survey is preprogrammed.

Figure 6.2

Self-Administered Questionnaire

(continued)

Q10 How many **children** (aged 2-14) are in your party?
- None ☐
- One child ☐
- Two children ☐
- Three children ☐
- More than three ☐

Q11 What is/was the nature of your journey today?
- Flying on business ☐
- Flying for a conference/trade fair/exhibition ☐
- Flying for a holiday (package) ☐
- Flying for a holiday (arranged independently) ☐
- Flying to visit friends/relatives ☐
- Flying to/from work ☐
- Flying for other purposes ☐

- Meeting friends/relatives at the airport ☐
- Business at the airport ☐
- Travel to/from work at the airport ☐
- Travel to/from work in London ☐
- Other reason, but not flying ☐

Q12 How many times in the last 12 months have you travelled by air? (PLEASE INCLUDE ALL YOUR FLIGHTS TO/FROM ANY AIRPORT)
- None ☐
- Once only ☐
- 2-3 times ☐
- 4-5 times ☐
- 6-10 times ☐
- 11-40 times ☐
- 41-50 times ☐
- More than 50 times ☐

Q13 Where did you hear about Gatwick Express?
- In Britain ☐
- Outside Britain ☐

Q14 How did you **first** hear about the Gatwick Express? (TICK ONE BOX ONLY)
- Advert in newspaper/magazine ☐
- Poster/Leaflet ☐
- Article in newspaper/magazine ☐
- British Rail ☐
- Word of mouth ☐
- Signs at Gatwick Airport ☐
- Signs at Victoria Station ☐
- Travel guide ☐
- Travel Agency information ☐
- Airline leaflet or Airline Offices ☐
- In-flight magazine ☐
- In-flight announcement or flight staff ☐
- Other ☐

Q15 Did you consider an alternative way of travelling between London and Gatwick Airport?
- Yes ☐
- No (GOTO Q17) ☐

Q16 Which alternative(s) did you consider? (YOU MAY TICK MORE THAN ONE BOX)
- Taxi ☐
- Car ☐
- Coach ☐
- South Central Trains ☐
- Thameslink Trains ☐
- Other ☐

Q17 What was the **main** reason you chose to travel **by rail** to/from Gatwick for your journey today? (TICK ONE BOX ONLY)
- Speed ☐
- Convenience ☐
- Comfort ☐
- Reliability ☐
- Cost ☐
- Other ☐

Q18 Why did you choose to travel **on the Gatwick Express** rather than any other train service between London and Gatwick Airport? (YOU MAY TICK MORE THAN ONE BOX)
- Speed ☐
- Convenience ☐
- Comfort ☐
- Reliability ☐
- Frequency ☐
- Cost ☐
- Always a train ready to join ☐
- Didn't know about other train service ☐
- Other ☐

Q19 What is your age?
- Under 14 ☐
- 14-17 ☐
- 18-24 ☐
- 25-34 ☐
- 35-44 ☐
- 45-54 ☐
- 55-64 ☐
- 65 or over ☐

Q20 Are you male or female?
- Male ☐
- Female ☐

Q21 Do you have any other comments to make about the Gatwick Express service?

THANK YOU FOR YOUR COOPERATION, PLEASE HAND THIS QUESTIONNAIRE TO THE INTERVIEWER WHEN THEY RETURN OR LEAVE IT ON YOUR SEAT WHEN YOU LEAVE THE TRAIN.
MERCI DE VOTRE COOPERATION, VEUILLEZ REMETTRE CE QUESTIONNAIRE A L'ENQUETEUR A SON RETOUR OU LE LAISSER SUR VOTRE SIEGE AVANT DE SORTIR DU TRAIN.
WIR DANKEN IHNEN FÜR IHRE FREUNDLICHE HILFE. BITTE HÄNDIGEN SIE DIESEN FRAGEBOGEN AN DEN INTERVIEWER ZURÜCK, WENN DIESE/R ZU IHREM ABTEIL ZURÜCKKEHRT ODER LASSEN SIE IHN AUF DEM SITZ LIEGEN, WENN SIE SIE DEN ZUG VERLASSEN.

ad hoc mail surveys
Questionnaires sent to selected names and addresses without prior contact by the researcher; sometimes called *one-shot mail surveys.*

mail panels
Precontacted and pre-screened participants who are periodically sent questionnaires.

Mail Surveys

Two general types of mail surveys are used in marketing research: ad hoc mail surveys and mail panels. In **ad hoc mail surveys** (sometimes called *one-shot mail surveys*), the researcher selects a sample of names and addresses from an appropriate source and mails questionnaires to the people selected. Ordinarily, there is no prior contact, and the sample is used only for a single project. However, the same questionnaire may be sent to nonrespondents several times to increase the overall response rate. In contrast, **mail panels** operate in the following manner:

PART 2:
Creating a Research Design

1. A sample group is precontacted by letter. In this initial contact, the purpose of the panel is explained, and people are usually offered a gratuity.

2. As part of the initial contact, consumers are asked to fill out a background questionnaire on the number of family members, their ages, education level, income, types of pets, types of vehicles and ages, types of appliances, and so forth.

3. After the initial contact, panel participants are sent questionnaires from time to time. The background data collected on initial contact enable researchers to send questionnaires only to appropriate households. For example, a survey about dog food usage and preferences would be sent only to dog owners.

A mail panel is a type of longitudinal study. A **longitudinal study** is one that questions the same respondents at different points in time. Several companies, including Market Facts, NPD Research, and National Family Opinion Research, operate large (more than 100,000 households) consumer mail panels.

On first consideration, mail appears to be an attractive way to collect survey data. There are no interviewers to recruit, train, monitor, and pay. The entire study can be sent out and administered from a single location. Hard-to-reach respondents can be readily surveyed. Mail surveys appear to be convenient, efficient, and inexpensive.

Like self-administered questionnaires, mail surveys of both types encounter the problems associated with not having an interviewer present. In particular, no one is there to probe responses to open-ended questions, a real constraint on the types of information that can be sought. The number of questions—and, consequently, the quantity of obtainable information—is usually more limited in mail surveys than in surveys involving interviewers.

Ad hoc mail surveys suffer from a high rate of nonresponse and attendant systematic error. Nonresponse in mail surveys is not a problem as long as everyone has an equal probability of not responding. However, numerous studies have shown that certain types of people—such as those with more education, those with high-level occupations, women, those less interested in the topic, and students—have a greater probability of not responding than other types.[15] Response rates in ad hoc mail surveys may run anywhere from less than 5 percent to more than 50 percent, depending on the length of the questionnaire, its content, the group surveyed, the incentives employed, and other factors.[16] Those who operate mail panels claim response rates in the vicinity of 70 percent.

Many strategies designed to enhance response rates have been developed. Some of the more common ones are summarized in Table 6.3. The question must always be "Is the cost of the particular strategy worth the increased response rate generated?" Unfortunately, there is no clear answer to this question that can be applied to all procedures in all situations.

Even with its shortcomings, mail surveying remains a popular data collection technique in commercial marketing research. In fact, more people participate in mail surveys than in any other type of survey research.

WAR Stories

At the end of October I was briefing a study at a telephone bank which was conducting a number of studies in addition to mine. Late in the afternoon, all work was temporarily interrupted while the company took an hour for a Halloween party. Everybody except me was in costume.

While waiting in line for Halloween cake, the fellow in front of me wondered aloud how his respondents would feel if they knew the person conducting the interview, a survey for a blood bank, was dressed as a vampire.

Source: "War Stories: True Life Tales in Marketing Research," by Art Shulman, *Quirk's Marketing Research Review* (January 1999). Reprinted by permission of Art Shulman.

longitudinal study
Study in which the same respondents are resampled over time.

Table 6.3

Tactics Employed to Increase Mail Survey Response Rates

- Advance postcard or telephone call alerting respondent to survey

- Follow-up postcard or phone call

- Monetary incentives (nickel, dime, quarter, half-dollar)

- Premiums (pencil, pen, keychain, etc.)

- Postage stamps rather than metered envelopes

- Self-addressed, stamped return envelope

- Personalized address and well-written cover letter

- Promise of contribution to favorite charity

- Entry into drawings for prizes

- Emotional appeals

- Affiliation with universities or research institutions

- Personally signed cover letter

- Multiple mailings of the questionnaire

- Reminder that respondent participated in previous studies (for mail panel participants)

Non-Internet survey alternatives discussed in this section are summarized in Table 6.4.

Survey Research on the Internet

The way survey research is conducted has changed forever because of the Internet. It is projected that by 2005 online research will account for 50 percent of all marketing research revenue—over $3 billion.[17] The reason for this phenomenal growth is straightforward: The advantages far outweigh the disadvantages.

Advantages of Online Surveys

Most companies today face shorter product life cycles, increased competition, and a rapidly changing business environment. Management decision makers are having to make complex, rapid-fire decisions, and Internet research can help by providing timely information. The specific advantages of online surveys include the following.[18]

Table 6.4

Non-Internet Forms of Survey Research

Type of Interview	Description
Door-to-door interviews	Interviews are conducted in respondents' homes (rarely used today).
Executive interviews	Interviews of industrial product users (e.g., engineers, architects, doctors, executives) or decision makers are conducted at their place of business.
Mall-intercept interviews	Interviews with consumers are conducted in a shopping mall or other high-traffic location. Interviews may be done in a public area of the mall, or respondents may be taken to a private test area.
Central-location telephone interviews	Interviews are conducted from a telephone facility set up for that purpose. These facilities typically have equipment that permits supervisors to unobtrusively monitor the interviewing while it is taking place. Many of these facilities do national sampling from a single location. An increasing number have computer-assisted interviewing capabilities. At these locations, the interviewer sits in front of a computer terminal attached to a mainframe or a personal computer. The questionnaire is programmed into the computer, and the interviewer uses the keyboard to directly enter responses.
Completely automated telephone surveys (CATS)	CATS has all the advantages and disadvantages of telephone interviews, but the respondent answers questions read by a recorded voice. Respondents may dial local or 800 numbers and respond to voice prompts (multiple-choice questions) by pressing the buttons on their touch-tone telephones. This approach has been successfully used with physicians and other difficult-to-reach populations. Respondents can call when it is convenient for them, 24 hours per day, 365 days per year.
Self-administered questionnaires	Self-administered questionnaires are most frequently employed at high-traffic locations such as shopping malls or in captive audience situations such as classrooms and airplanes. Respondents are given general information on how to fill out the questionnaire and expected to fill it out on their own. Kiosk-based point-of-service touch screens provide a way to capture information from individuals in stores, health clinics, and other shopping or service environments. Sometimes software-driven questionnaires on diskettes are sent to individuals who have personal computers.
Ad hoc (one-shot) mail surveys	Questionnaires are mailed to a sample of consumers or industrial users, without prior contact by the researcher. Instructions are included; respondents are asked to fill out the questionnaire and return it via mail. Sometimes a gift or monetary incentive is provided. Software-driven questionnaires on diskettes are sometimes sent to individuals who have personal computers.
Mail panels	Questionnaires are mailed to a sample of individuals who have been precontacted. The panel concept has been explained to them, and they have agreed to participate for some period of time, in exchange for gratuities. Mail panels typically generate much higher response rates than do ad hoc mail surveys.

■ *Rapid deployment, real-time reporting.* Online surveys can be broadcast to thousands of potential respondents simultaneously. Respondents complete surveys, and the results are tabulated and posted for corporate clients to view as the returns arrive. Thus, Internet survey results can be in the decision maker's hands in significantly less time than traditional survey results.

■ *Dramatically reduced costs.* The use of electronic survey methods can cut costs by 25 percent to 40 percent and provide results in half the time it takes to do traditional telephone surveys. Data collection costs account for a large proportion of any traditional marketing research budget. Telephone surveys are labor-intensive efforts incurring training, telecommunications, and management costs. Online surveys eliminate these costs almost completely. While the costs of traditional survey techniques rise in proportion to the number of interviews desired, electronic solicitations can grow in volume with little increase in project costs.

■ *Ready personalization.* Internet surveys can be highly personalized for greater relevance to each respondent's own situation, thus speeding up the response process. Respondents appreciate being asked only pertinent questions, being able to pause and then resume the survey as needed, and having the ability to see previous responses and correct inconsistencies.

■ *High response rates.* Busy respondents may be growing increasingly intolerant of "snail mail" or telephone-based surveys. Online surveys take half the time to complete that phone interviews do, can be accomplished at the respondent's convenience (after work hours), and are much more stimulating and engaging. Graphics, interactivity, links to incentive sites, and real-time summary reports make the interview more enjoyable. The result: much higher response rates.

■ *Ability to contact the hard-to-reach.* Certain groups are among the most surveyed on the planet and the most difficult to reach (doctors, high-income professionals, CIOs in Global 2000 firms). Many of these groups are well represented online. Internet surveys provide convenient anytime/anywhere access that makes it easy for busy professionals to participate.

■ *Simplified and enhanced panel management.* Internet panels are electronic communities, linked via the Internet, that are committed to providing feedback and counsel to research firms and their clients. They may be large or small, syndicated or proprietary, and they may consist of customers, potential customers, partners, or employees. Internet panels can be built and maintained at a fraction of the cost and time required for traditional panels. Once a panel is created and a questionnaire is finalized, surveys can be deployed, data collected, and top-level results reported within days.

A sophisticated database tracks panelist profile data and survey responses, facilitating longitudinal studies and data mining to yield insights into attitudes and behaviors over time and across segments. Response rates are high, typically 30 to 60 percent, because respondents have agreed in advance to participate in the survey. These participants tend to provide more detailed and thoughtful answers than do those in traditional surveys, because they don't have to provide demographic and technographic information (it's already been captured) and because they become engaged in the panel community over time.

■ *Profitability for research firms.* Online surveys can be very profitable. Gordon Black, CEO of Harris Interactive, says profit margins can go as high as 90 percent.[19]

Internet panels are already huge. Harris Interactive has a database of 4 million Internet users. By agreeing to take part in periodic Harris poll online surveys, subjects receive the chance to win various prizes and cash awards. When a survey is ready, the company sends email to target individuals inviting them to visit the Harris poll Web site and answer questions.

PART 2:

Creating a Research Design

Target individuals are given unique passwords to ensure that they respond to the survey one time only. The company hopes to have 6 million potential respondents in its database by the end of 2001.

NFO Interactive, NPD Online, and Decision Analyst also have large Internet panels. For example, Decision Analyst has over one million in its American Consumer Opinion Online panel. The firm also has a technology panel of scientists, engineers, and information technology professionals; a physicians' panel; and a building contractors' panel. All of these online panels have members from all over the world.

Disadvantages of Online Surveys

The most common complaint about the use of online surveys is that Internet users are not representative of the population as a whole. One retort, of course, is that most managers aren't interested in the population as a whole. Also, over 45 percent of the population now uses the Internet at home, work, school, or other locations.

In Table 6.5, Dennis Gonier, president of Digital Marketing Services (DMS), a subsidiary of America Online (AOL), offers a comparison of U.S. Census data,

Table 6.5

A Demographic Comparison among U.S. Census Data, America Online Users, and Participants in the Opinion Place

	U.S. Census	AOL	Opinion Place
Gender			
■ Male	48%	48%	46%
■ Female	52	52	54
Age			
■ 18–24	12%	19%	12%
■ 25–34	20	25	25
■ 35–44	21	28	28
■ 45–54	15	19	20
■ 55+	32	9	11
Income			
■ Less than $50K	71%	42%	56%
■ More than $50K	29	58	44
Marital Status			
■ Married	61%	69%	57%
Children in Household			
■ Yes	35%	53%	45%

Source: Dennis Gonier, "The Research Emperor Gets New Clothes," *1999 CASRO Marketing Research Journal,* p. 111. Reprinted with permission from the Council of American Survey Research Organizations.

AOL users, and the demographics of Opinion Place, an opt-in survey research site on AOL managed by DMS. Note that AOL's profile is not that different from that of the U.S. Census. And Opinion Place is becoming more like both of them. More importantly, when DMS made an extensive comparability study between Opinion Place results and the same survey administered by mall-intercept or telephone interviews, the comparability study documented a consistent business direction finding.[20] In other words, the same business strategies were developed using data from mall-intercept and telephone surveys as using data from the Opinion Place.

In the In Practice feature, Douglas Rivers, CEO of InterSurvey in Palo Alto, California, argues that population coverage is just part of the problem.

In PRACTICE

The Problem Is Not Just Representativeness of the Web Population

OKAY, THE WEB POPULATION DOESN'T LOOK LIKE AMERICA, but it will soon, so people argue it's just a matter of time before the population coverage problem goes away. But there is a more fundamental problem with Web surveys that won't disappear even if everyone has Internet access: there is no direct way to sample e-mail addresses.

In telephone surveys, households can be selected by random digit dialing (RDD). Because every phone number has exactly 10 digits, it is easy to generate a random set of phone numbers. There are some complications because households can have more than one phone line and different numbers of people, but it is well understood how to handle these issues.

Unfortunately, there is no analog of RDD for e-mail addresses. Nor is there any listing of e-mail addresses that could serve as a sampling frame. Even if such a listing existed, it would be considered spamming to send out survey requests to a sample of such e-mail addresses.

Today most Web surveys recruit "samples" of Web users employing banner ads, pop-up windows, opt-in e-mail lists, and similar devices. These are "convenience samples," chosen haphazardly and with no theoretical underpinnings. It is tempting to believe that Web surveys, because they are conducted on the Internet, are representative of Web users.

The people who accept these invitations, however, are not randomly selected and are demonstrably unrepresentative of Web users. For example, teenagers are much more likely to frequent on-line game sites and chat rooms than to fill out surveys. Web survey takers tend to be older and better educated than average Web users. For some reason, men are more likely to take Web surveys than women, even though the gender gap on the Web has almost disappeared. Thus these samples don't represent anything in particular.[21] ■

PART 2:
Creating a Research Design

A second problem is security on the Internet. Users today are quite understandably worried about privacy issues. This fear has been fueled by sensational media accounts of cyberstalkers and con artists who prey on Internet users. A solution to the security issue already exists in the form of **SSL (secure socket layer) technology.** Most responsible organizations collecting sensitive information over the Internet use this technology. The major problem is that consumers do not understand that this type of 128-bit encryption provides an extremely high level of security for all their sensitive information. It is up to the industry to communicate this fact to potential users.

A third problem exists when an **unrestricted Internet sample** is set up on the Internet. This means anyone who wishes to complete the questionnaire can do so. It is fully self-selecting and probably representative of no one except Web surfers. The problem gets worse if the same Internet user can access the questionnaire over and over. For example, the first time *InfoWorld,* a computer user magazine, conducted its Readers' Choice survey on the Internet, the results were so skewed by repeat voting for one product that the entire survey was publicly abandoned and the editor had to ask for readers' help to avoid the problem again. All responsible organizations conducting surveys over the Internet easily guard against this problem by providing unique passwords to those individuals they invite to participate. These passwords permit one-time access to the survey.

SSL (secure socket layer) technology
A computer encryption system that secures sensitive information.

unrestricted Internet sample
A self-selected sample group consisting of anyone who wishes to complete an Internet survey.

Methods of Conducting Online Surveys

There are several basic methods for conducting online surveys: email questionnaires, converted CATI systems, Web survey systems, bulletin boards, downloadable surveys, and survey design Web sites. Each of these methods is briefly discussed below.

Email Questionnaires The questionnaire is prepared like a simple email message and sent to a list of known email addresses. The respondent fills in the answers and emails the form with her or his replies back to the research organization. A computer program is typically used to prepare the questionnaire and the email address list and to extract the data from the responses.

Email questionnaires are simple to construct and fast to distribute. By showing up in the respondent's email inbox, they demand immediate attention. Although they are generally limited to plain text, graphics can be sent as e-mail attachments that are decoded separately from the questionnaire text.

Recent research has compared email surveys with so-called snail-mail (U.S. Post Office) surveys. Of course, the researchers found cost and time savings available through email surveys. They also found that respondents were more likely to answer open-ended questions in email surveys. Nonresponse rate for the email survey was 42 percent.[22]

Converted CATI Systems In a converted CATI system, a software translator program takes questionnaires programmed in the CATI vendor's questionnaire construction language and translates them for distribution over the Web. The Web server may be located in the research supplier's facility, or time may be rented from a service bureau that has the CATI system installed. The Web server is linked to a database that receives and stores the respondents' replies.

Converted CATI systems have the good sample and quota management typical of CATI programs. They also inherit the ability to set up complex skip patterns for screening and to adapt to respondents' replies. They can do data verification at the time of entry and request re-entry of illegal data immediately. Converted CATI systems provide quick migration to Internet interviewing for current users of a particular CATI system and permit reuse of existing programmed questionnaires.

On the negative side, the CATI systems on which these Internet survey products are based were designed for a telephone interviewer working from a computer screen; respondent screen formatting is somewhat limited as a result. In addition, the CATI languages frequently do not take advantage of the Web's ability to present graphics and audiovisual material.[23]

Web Survey Systems

Web survey systems are software systems specifically designed for Web questionnaire construction and delivery. They consist of an integrated questionnaire designer, Web server, database, and data delivery program, designed for use by nonprogrammers.

In a typical use, the questionnaire is constructed with an easy-to-use editor, using a visual interface, and then automatically transmitted to the Web server system. The Web server distributes the questionnaire and files responses in a database. The user can query the server at any time via the Web for completion statistics, descriptive statistics on responses, and graphical displays of data.

Web survey systems typically have a lower cost per completed interview than converted CATI systems, although they are more expensive than email surveys for small surveys (under 500 respondents). The lower cost results from the efficiencies of using software tools designed specifically for Web use and from the sharing of Internet access costs and hardware costs that a central server system provides.[24]

Bulletin Boards

Another form of online research is bulletin board research. Bulletin board conferences are useful for collecting responses over time. The technique involves inviting people to a specific Web site where a discussion topic is posted. As people respond to the question(s), they can see what others have written and reply to the original responses. In this way, the conversation gradually moves back and forth, much like the discussion of a focus group in slow motion.

Putting up a bulletin board is not difficult, but it does take more skill than creating an email survey. Unlike other research forms, bulletin boards have no means of automated data accumulation. Consequently, costs are somewhat higher than those for email, in large part because of the time needed to handle the comment transcripts and code responses for any quantitative appraisal. Although graphics and other visual stimuli can be incorporated in the original question, the format of the bulletin board reply system is fixed and not very flexible.

This technology is good when a panel of experts or beta testers need to post quick reactions or discuss impressions with others. The method combines elements of both quantitative and qualitative techniques, and the conversational transcript can provide extremely rich data.[25]

Downloadable Surveys

When surveys are downloaded from the Web and then run on previously installed software provided by the researcher, the computing tasks are shifted from the online server to the respondent's PC. Once preloaded, the survey software can read the much smaller files that the respondent downloads from the Internet. The result is that the surveys run much like fixed-form, interactive surveys. Once the survey has "played" on the respondent's PC, the data file created can be uploaded the next time the Internet is accessed.

Downloadable surveys tend to be more costly and time-intensive than other forms of online research. In some instances, they also require a greater level of respondent sophistication for software installation and the correct handling of the data upload process. If the survey software must be downloaded in order to take the survey, the time requirement (from 20 minutes to 2 hours) may discourage some respondents. Having the respondent complete the survey offline (rather than collecting the data live) and then re-establish the data upload connection can also lead to delays and lost surveys. This form of online research is used primarily with panels or prerecruited groups who regularly communicate with the survey organizer.[26]

Survey Design Web Sites Several Web sites allow the researcher to design a survey online without loading design software. The survey is then administered on the design site's server. Some offer tabulation and analysis packages as well. South-Western Publishing Company, the publisher of this text, has made arrangements for your class to use WebSurveyor. This is the same survey design Web site used by marketing research professionals. Your class can conduct an Internet survey, using friends and classmates as the population, and analyze the data for free! You can preview the site at http://www.websurveyor.com. This system will permit you to create a new survey, entering and arranging questions as you wish (a library of questions is available); preview the survey; make final edits; publish the survey; analyze the results; and even generate a report that you can output to your printer or to a series of html pages for Web publication. The emergence of these integrated Web surveying tools permits even the smallest organizations to participate in Web interviewing.

Internet Samples

Developing a good questionnaire is only half the battle in conducting online surveys. The researcher must also find respondents.[27] We have already discussed unrestricted samples as a disadvantage of conducting surveys online.

Screened Internet Samples In **screened internet samples,** the researcher adjusts for the unrepresentativeness of the self-selected respondents by imposing quotas based on some desired sample characteristics. These are often demographic characteristics, such as gender, income, or geographic region, or product-related criteria, such as past purchase behavior, job responsibilities, or

WAR Stories

A researcher preferring anonymity tells about being an interviewer early in his career, conducting a survey sponsored by a particular regional brand of beer. The brand's advertising was based on the fact that the beer was made using pure water from a particular lake. One respondent, when asked if he found anything hard to believe about the advertising, said he did. The cause of his skepticism? "I once visited that lake and saw a man standing on the shore using it as a toilet," he said.

Source: "War Stories: True Life Tales in Marketing Research," by Art Shulman, *Quirk's Marketing Research Review* (November 1999). Reprinted by permission of Art Shulman.

screened Internet sample
A self-selected sample group in which quotas are imposed, based on some desired sample characteristics.

current product use. The applications for screened samples are generally similar to those for unrestricted samples.

Screened sample questionnaires typically use a branching, or skip, pattern for asking screening questions to determine whether or not the full questionnaire should be presented to the respondent. Some Web survey systems can make immediate market segment calculations that assign a respondent to a particular segment based on screening questions, then select the appropriate questionnaire to match the respondent's segment.

Alternatively, some Internet research providers maintain a "panel house" that recruits respondents, who fill out a preliminary classification questionnaire. This information is used to classify respondents into demographic segments. Clients specify the desired segments, and the respondents who match the desired demographics are permitted to fill out the questionnaires of all clients who specify that segment.

recruited Internet sample
A sample group recruited to ensure representativeness of a target population.

Recruited Internet Samples

Recruited Internet samples are used in surveys that require more control over the makeup of the sample. Recruited samples are ideal for applications in which there is already a database from which to recruit the sample. For example, a good application would be a survey that used a customer database to recruit respondents for a purchaser satisfaction study.

Respondents are recruited by telephone, mail, or email or in person. After qualification, they are sent the questionnaire by email, or are directed to a Web site that contains a link to the questionnaire. At Web sites, passwords are normally used to restrict access to the questionnaire to only recruited sample members. Since the makeup of the sample is known, completions can be monitored and, to improve the participation rate, follow-up messages can be sent to those who have not completed the questionnaire.

Sources of recruited Internet samples include recruited panels, opt-in list rentals, opt-in panels, numerous Web-based incentive marketing programs (see Chapter 4), random intercepts of Web site visitors, and Web sites that have collected personal information about their visitors.[28] The advantages and disadvantages of each are discussed below.

Recruited Panels.   In the early days of Internet recruiting, panels were created by means of Web-based advertising, or posting, that offered compensation for participation in online studies. This method allowed research firms to build large pools of individuals who were available to respond quickly to the demands of online marketing research.

These specially constructed panels had certain drawbacks. There were unavoidable expenses associated with advertising to recruit the panel and then collecting, storing, and updating the associated data. To keep the panel members satisfied, research firms had to provide them with a certain number of studies, or else they were likely to drop out of the program. Many panels experienced rapid growth but also massive churn rates, as unmotivated prospective respondents moved on to other panels for compensation or changed email addresses. Some recruited panelists were "professional" survey takers and would supply whatever information they thought would make them more attractive for stud-

PART 2:
Creating a Research Design

ies. Personal Web sites and newsletters promoted these panels as a way to earn easy money.

Research firms discovered that, to prevent panel members from becoming oversensitized, it was important to limit the number or frequency of studies, even if it resulted in higher attrition. Using contests with cash awards or prizes instead of paying for a completed study helped establish a fixed incentive cost for a study. However, it also reduced the number of people willing to participate, as respondents no longer received instant gratification for time invested.

A number of panels have been created specifically for marketing research studies. In evaluating such panels, it is important to have a good understanding of how often they update member data and remove duplicate listings and how they validate the accuracy of supplied information.

Opt-in List Rentals.   With the widespread use of email, a new opportunity for recruiting has emerged. Although email offers an excellent way to reach online users, unsolicited email, or *spam,* has proved to be a negative method of recruiting. An acceptable alternative is the use of opt-in lists of email users, who sign up for various Web-based services and agree to receive selective emails from the provider when they register. A number of highly targeted opt-in email lists, containing the names of individuals willing to participate in online studies, are available. The cost of renting such lists adds to the basic cost of recruiting, however, and may increase the time required for both screening and validation. The privacy agreements associated with these lists usually put strict limitations on their usage, and access to personal information is restricted.

A researcher planning to use an opt-in list for recruiting should investigate the company providing the list carefully. He or she should find out how long the company has been compiling the list and verify that it is using only opt-in individuals.

Opt-in Panels.   The emergence of Internet-based loyalty marketing or incentive programs (see Chapter 4) has led to the creation of large databases that are rich in personal information, making it easy to locate highly targeted individuals. In these programs, users earn points, frequent flier mileage, credits, and other types of Internet currency by visiting Web sites, reading targeted emails, and purchasing from participating sponsors. These rapidly growing, self-sustaining programs, featuring built-in incentive programs, are potential sources of highly targeted online users. Incentives for marketing research study participation can provide members with additional opportunities to earn points and can provide programs with a new revenue stream. It would be difficult and time-consuming to recruit many of these individuals using other methods.

Researchers considering using opt-in panels must determine how reliable the databases are and how fast providers can respond for studies requiring fast turnaround. There is usually a set-up charge to use the panel, and the conversion rate of dollars to incentive points will vary widely. Another consideration is the time and effort required to establish a relationship with the company and negotiate terms for use of the panel in marketing research studies. Unless the researcher is able to capture personal information from the respondent, conducting longitudinal studies (in which the same respondents are re-interviewed over time) is somewhat complicated.

Random Web Site Intercepts.   A valuable way to elicit research data from existing Web site traffic evolved with the use of random intercept banners inviting visitors to participate in surveys. These banners, which pop up in a preset random pattern, ask whether the visitor would like to participate in a short survey. A visitor who accepts is linked to a page where he or she fills out screening questions that can be used to identify and qualify potential respondents. The survey has to be short, since most people will not be motivated to participate in a long survey without compensation. (One exception is when the individual feels strongly about the subject and wants to provide input.) A number of methods exist for capturing this information on an ongoing basis for a variety of applications.

Random Web site intercepts may not be the most effective way to recruit for certain types of studies. Unless site traffic is substantial, it may not be possible to determine the amount of time required to locate samples of adequate size. Also, it is important to determine where in a site the visitors are when the banner is presented, as the reasons people come to the Web site may be important in the design of the study.

One recent study using banner ads on Yahoo! and several other search engines generated approximately 63,000 exposures. The ads posed two different appeals. The first was intrinsic ("Your opportunity to contribute to an important study"), and the second was extrinsic ("Your opportunity to win valuable prizes"). On all four servers, the intrinsic appeal had a higher click-through rate to the questionnaire than did the extrinsic ad. If this finding could be generalized to the entire Internet population, marketing researchers could save a lot of money in prizes and incentives. However, both types of banner ads produced extremely low click-through rates (.28% for the intrinsic appeal and .20% for the extrinsic appeal).[29] Given the cost of banner ads, either approach can be an expensive way to generate a sample.

Data Capture of Visitors.   As company Web sites grow more sophisticated and more valuable, studying their visitors becomes increasingly important. These visitors can be organized and utilized to study a multitude of issues, including customer service, consumer needs, customer satisfaction, proposed site redesign and developments, and core customer concerns. Methods exist that can help a Web site better serve its visitors while at the same time building a variety of prospective panels for future studies. These panels will grow ever more important in contributing to companies' understanding of their customers in the digital age.

Creating Online Questionnaires

Questionnaire writing will be discussed in detail in Chapter 11. However, some issues unique to Internet questionnaires are more appropriately addressed here. The simplest way to create an Internet survey is to use a survey design Web site such as WebSurveyor or Internet survey research software such as Survey Assistant, The Survey System, Stat Pac, or Inquisite.

Surveys need to load quickly in order to achieve a good response. People won't wait; they'll move on to another Web site. Graphics increase the time required for a survey to load. Although it's tempting to make beautiful back-

PART 2:
Creating a Research Design

grounds, all those graphics can be a problem. What will the background and text look like on different browsers and at different font sizes? Whatever graphics are selected should look good and load quickly, no matter what kind of computer set-up the respondent has.

"Our own reaction at the beginning was to design a fairly fancy question-naire," says Bob Tortora, chief methodologist at The Gallup Organization. "You're much better off using a very plain questionnaire—something that looks like a mail questionnaire. When you start getting fancy, you start slowing down transmission times."[30]

The survey should be easy to respond to as well. It's a lot easier to click on a response than to type one in. The entry mechanism should be matched to the question—buttons or drop-down menus for a single response, check boxes for multiple answers. It's useful to include an option for "Other" responses, but few people will use it, so it should be considered supplemental, not part of the core response data.

Buttons are best when there are five or fewer answers to choose from; a drop-down menu is easier to use with more than five answers. For really lengthy lists with short identifiers, such as the 50 states, it's wise to allow respondents the option of typing in the two-letter abbreviation rather than forcing them to scroll through the list.

Researchers must be aware of any default answers (No Opinion, Don't Know, None of the Above). A common mistake among inexperienced Internet survey programmers is to unintentionally make the first response in a list the default answer; this can seriously skew the results. It isn't a problem if you use survey design software, as it avoids such errors automatically, but if you're doing the programming yourself, you'll need to check the default values when you're working on online surveys.

The Interactive Marketing Research Organization

In 2000, a new organization called the **Interactive Marketing Research Organization (IMRO)** was formed. The first objective of IMRO is to be "a confederation of world leaders among firms involved in new technology marketing research, to lead in the development, dissemination and implementation of interactive marketing research concepts, practice and information."[31] Thirteen Internet marketing research suppliers, including Modalis Research Technologies, Greenfield Online, Market Facts, NPD Online, NFO Interactive, and Cyber Dialogue, along with eight client companies, including Dell Computer, IBM, Intel, and Time Warner, helped to found the new organization.

IMRO's initial efforts will focus on spam and the misuse of personal data. The organization expects to host conferences, debates, and workshops. It is also planning a quarterly newsletter and eventually a journal.[32]

Interactive Marketing Research Organization (IMRO)
An organization dedicated to the development, dissemination, and implementation of interactive marketing research concepts, practice, and information.

Determination of the Survey Method

A number of factors may affect the choice of a survey method in a given situation. The researcher should choose the survey method that will provide data of the desired types, quality, and quantity at the lowest cost. The major considerations in the selection of a survey method are summarized in Table 6.6.

Sampling Precision

The required level of sampling precision is an important factor in determining which survey method is appropriate in a given situation. Some projects by their very nature require a high level of sampling accuracy, whereas this may not be a critical consideration in other projects. If sampling accuracy were the only criterion, the appropriate data collection technique would probably be central-location telephone interviewing, an online survey of a sample drawn from a huge Internet panel, or some other form of polling of a sample drawn from customer lists. The appropriate survey method for a project not requiring a high level of sampling accuracy might be the mail approach or some type of Internet survey.

The trade-off between the central-location telephone survey and the mail survey methods in regard to sampling precision is one of accuracy versus cost. A central-location telephone survey employing a random-digit dialing sampling procedure will probably produce a better sample than the mail survey method. However, the mail survey will most likely cost less. In some cases, Internet samples will provide both lower cost and greater accuracy.

Table 6.6

Factors That Determine the Selection of a Particular Survey Method

Factor	Comment
Sampling precision	If the need for accuracy in the study results is not great, less rigorous and less expensive sampling procedures may be appropriate.
Budget	It is important to determine how much money is available for the survey portion of the study.
Need to expose respondent to various stimuli and have respondent perform specialized tasks	Taste tests and prototype usage tests require face-to-face contact. Card sorts, certain visual scaling methods, and the like require either face-to-face contact or the Internet.
Quality of data required	It is important to determine how accurate the results of the study need to be.
Length of questionnaire	Long questionnaires are difficult to do by mail, over the phone, or in a mall.
Incidence rate	Are you looking for people who make up 1 percent of the total population or 50 percent of the population? If you are looking for a needle in a haystack, you need an inexpensive way to find it. The Internet is probably the best source.
Degree of structure of questionnaire	Highly unstructured questionnaires may require data collection by personal interview.
Time available to complete survey	There may not be time to wait for responses via snail-mail. The Internet is the fastest way to go.

PART 2:
Creating a Research Design

Budget

The commercial marketing researcher frequently encounters situations in which the budget available for a study has a strong influence on the survey method used. For example, assume that for a particular study the budgetary constraint for interviewing is $10,000 and the sample size required for the necessary accuracy is 1,000. If the cost of administering the questionnaire using the mall-intercept method would be $27.50 per interview and the cost of administering it via Internet survey would be $.50 per interview, the choice is fairly clear—assuming that nothing about the survey absolutely requires face-to-face contact.

Requirements for Respondent Reactions

In some studies, the marketing researcher needs to get respondent reactions to various marketing stimuli—perhaps product prototype usage (a new style of PC keyboard) or a taste test. In these cases, the need to get respondent reactions to stimuli requires personal contact between interviewer and respondent.

Taste tests typically require food preparation. This preparation must be done under controlled conditions so that the researcher can be certain that each person interviewed is responding to the same stimulus. The only viable survey alternative for tests of this type is the mall-intercept approach or some variant. One variant, for example, is recruiting people to come to properly equipped central locations, such as community centers, to sample products and be interviewed.

Some surveys require face-to-face interviewing because of the need to use special measurement techniques or obtain specialized forms of information. The tasks are so complex that the interviewer must be available to explain the tasks and ascertain whether the respondents understand what is required of them.

Quality of Data

The quality of data required is an important determinant of the survey method. Data quality is measured in terms of validity and reliability. (These two concepts are discussed in detail in Chapter 9.) *Validity* refers to the degree to which a measure reflects the characteristic of interest. In other words, a valid measure provides an accurate reading of whatever the researcher is trying to measure. *Reliability* refers to the consistency with which a measure produces the same results with the same or comparable populations.

Many factors beyond the interviewing method affect data quality. Sampling methods, questionnaire design, specific scaling methods, and interviewer train-

Taste tests are most often conducted in a group setting because of their unique requirements. Can you imagine conducting this type of research through a mall-intercept survey? Visit http://kelloggs.com to see whether Kellogg's conducts Internet surveys.

ing are a few of them. However, each of the various interviewing methods has certain inherent strengths and weaknesses in terms of data quality. These strengths and weaknesses are summarized in Table 6.7.

The important point here is that the issue of data quality may override other considerations such as cost. For example, although the least expensive way to get responses to a long questionnaire with many open-ended questions might be via a mall-intercept interview, the data obtained by this method might be so biased—because of respondent fatigue, distraction, and carelessness—that the results would be worthless at best and misleading at worst.

Length of the Questionnaire

The length of the questionnaire—the amount of time it takes the average respondent to complete the survey—is an important determinant of the appropriate survey method to use. If the questionnaire for a particular study takes an hour to complete, the choices of survey method are extremely limited.

Table 6.7

Strengths and Weaknesses of Selected Data Collection Methods in Terms of Quality of Data Produced

Method	Strengths	Weaknesses
Mall-intercept interview	Interviewer can show, explain, and probe.	Many distractions are inherent in the mall environment; respondent may be in a hurry, not in proper frame of mind to answer survey questions; there is more chance for interviewer bias; nonprobability sampling problems arise.
Central-location telephone interview	Supervisor can monitor the interviewing process easily; excellent samples can be obtained; interviewer can explain and probe.	Respondent may be distracted by things going on at their location; problems arise in long interviews and interviews with many open-ended questions.
Self-administered questionnaire	Interviewer and associated biases are eliminated; respondent can complete the questionnaire when convenient; respondent can look up information and work at own pace.	There is no interviewer to show, explain, or probe; sample may be poor because of nonresponse; who actually completes the questionnaire cannot be controlled.
Mail survey	Same strengths as for self-administered method.	Same weaknesses as for self-administered questionnaire; sample quality is better with mail panel.
Online survey	Administration is inexpensive; data can be gathered quickly; questions can be readily personalized; response rates are high, especially for the hard-to-reach; panel management is easy.	Users are not representative of whole population; privacy concerns may arise; unrestricted sample may provide skewed results.

PART 2:
Creating a Research Design

Telephone, mall-intercept, and most other types of surveys, with the exception of personal interviews, will not work. People shopping at a mall ordinarily do not have an hour to spend being interviewed. Terminations increase and tempers flare when interviewers must try to keep respondents on the phone for an hour. Response rates plummet when people receive through the mail questionnaires that take an hour or more to complete. The trick is to match the survey technique to the length of the questionnaire.

Incidence Rate

Incidence rate refers to the percentage of people or households in the general population that would qualify as interviewees in a particular study. For example, assume that you are doing a taste test for a new stovetop stuffing mix. It has been decided that only people who have purchased a stovetop stuffing mix in the last 30 days should be interviewed. It is estimated that out of the general population only 5 percent of all adults fall into this category. The incidence rate for this study is 5 percent. In marketing research, it is typical to seek people with an incidence rate of 5 percent or lower.

> **incidence rate**
> Percentage of people or households in the general population that fit the qualifications to be sampled.

Search costs, which correlate with the time spent trying to locate qualified respondents, sometimes exceed the costs of interviewing. In situations where the researcher expects incidence rates to be low and search costs high, it is important to select the method or combination of methods that will provide the desired survey results at a reasonable cost.

Doing a low-incidence rate study on a door-to-door basis would be very expensive. This approach should be taken only if there is some compelling reason for doing so—a long depth interview, for example. The lowest-cost survey alternative for the low-incidence study is probably the Internet panel or some other form of online survey, assuming that this approach meets the other data collection requirements of the study. One advantage of the Internet panel is that is can be prescreened; people can be asked a number of questions, usually including some on product usage, when the panel is set up. For example, if panel members were asked during prescreening whether anyone in their household participated in downhill or alpine skiing, the Internet panel operator could—at very low cost—pull out only those households with one or more skiers for a survey of Alpine skiers.

Structure of the Questionnaire

In addition to the length of the questionnaire, the degree of structure required in the questionnaire may be a factor in determining which survey method is most appropriate for a given study. *Structure* refers to the extent to which the questionnaire follows a set sequence or order, has a predetermined wording of questions, and relies on closed-ended (multiple-choice) questions. A questionnaire that does all these things would be structured; one that deviates from these set patterns would be considered unstructured. A questionnaire with little structure is likely to require a face-to-face interview. Very brief, highly structured questionnaires do not require face-to-face contact between interviewer and

respondent. Mail, telephone, self-administered, and online surveys are viable options for studies of this type.

Time Available to Complete the Survey

If the client needs to have survey results quickly, the Internet is the best choice. Generally, central-location telephone and mall-intercept interviews can also be completed in a timely manner.

The Marketing Research Interviewer

No discussion of survey research in marketing would be complete without considering the person who actually does the interviewing. As noted in Chapter 2, most marketing research interviewing is still done under the direct supervision of field service firms. The actual interviewing is conducted, to a large extent, by individuals who work part-time for relatively low wages. A new, totally inexperienced interviewer works at a rate somewhere between minimum wage and minimum wage plus 20 percent. It is unusual to find even the most experienced interviewers earning more than minimum wage plus 50 percent. The pay is not good, and fringe benefits are minimal. Ordinarily, an interviewer's involvement with an interviewing assignment begins when he or she is asked by a supervisor at a field service firm to work on a particular job. If the interviewer accepts the assignment, he or she will be given a date and time for a briefing about the job. At the briefing, the questionnaire for the study and all deadlines and requirements for the job are discussed.

Interviewers are typically the main interface with consumers and are, therefore, a vital link to consumer cooperation. Their skill level and pay level are areas of concern now being addressed by the Marketing Research Association, which has several suggestions for developing and strengthening interviewers' consumer interaction skills: good training programs that cover ways to establish consumer rapport and a basic understanding of "cooperation turning points," frequent monitoring of interviewers' interaction skills to evaluate their impact on consumer cooperation, and feedback to interviewers on monitoring results.

Summary

Surveys are popular for several reasons. First, managers need to know why people do or do not do something. Second, managers need to know how decisions are made. Third, managers need to know what kind of person, from a demographic or lifestyle perspective, is making the decision to buy or not buy a product.

There are two major categories of errors in survey research: random error and systematic error, or bias. Systematic error can be further broken down into measurement error and sample design error. Types of sample design error include selection, population specification, and frame errors. Frame error results from the use of an incomplete or inaccurate sampling frame. Population specification error results from an incorrect definition of the universe or population from which the sample is to be selected. Selection error results from adopting incomplete or improper sampling procedures or not properly following appropriate selection procedures.

The second major category of systematic error is measurement error. Measurement error occurs when there is a discrepancy between the information being sought (true value) and the information actually obtained by the measurement process. Measurement error can be created by a number of factors, including surrogate information error, interviewer error, measurement instrument bias, processing error, nonresponse bias, and response bias. Surrogate information error results from a discrepancy between the information actually required to solve a problem and the information sought by the researcher. Interviewer error occurs when an interviewer influences a respondent to give untrue or inaccurate answers. Measurement instrument bias is caused by problems within the questionnaire itself. Processing error results from mistakes in the transfer of information from survey documents to the computer. Nonresponse bias occurs when a particular individual in a sample cannot be reached or refuses to participate in the survey. Response bias arises when interviewees tend to answer questions in a particular way, whether out of deliberate falsification or unconscious misrepresentation.

There are several types of surveys. Mall-intercept interviews are conducted with shoppers in public areas of shopping malls, either by interviewing them in the mall or by asking them to come to a permanent interviewing facility within the mall. Executive interviews are the industrial equivalent of door-to-door interviews; they involve interviewing professional people at their offices, typically concerning industrial products or services. Central-location telephone interviews are conducted from a facility set up for the specific purpose of doing telephone survey research. Computer-assisted telephone interviewing (CATI) is a form of central-location interviewing. Each interviewer is seated in front of a computer terminal or personal computer. The computer guides the interviewer and the interviewing process by exhibiting appropriate questions on the computer screen. The data are entered into the computer as the interview takes place. In completely automated telephone surveys (CATS), IVR technology is used to conduct interviews. A self-administered questionnaire is filled out by the respondent. The big disadvantage of this approach is that probes cannot be used to clarify responses. Mail surveys can be divided into ad hoc, or one-shot, surveys and mail panels. In ad hoc mail surveys, questionnaires are mailed to potential respondents without prior contact. The sample is used for only a single survey project. In a mail panel, consumers are precontacted by letter and are offered an incentive for participating in the panel for a period of time. If they agree, they fill out a background questionnaire. Then, periodically, panel participants are sent questionnaires.

The Internet is beginning to dominate survey research. Internet surveys offer rapid deployment and real-time reporting, dramatically reduced costs, ready personalization, high response rates, the ability to reach low-incidence respondents, simplified and enhanced panel management, and profitability for survey research firms. The disadvantages are the potential nonrepresentativeness of Internet users, privacy and security concerns, and the poor quality of unrestricted Internet samples.

The types of Internet samples are unrestricted, screened, and recruited. Online surveys can be conducted through email, converted CATI systems, Web survey systems, bulletin boards, downloadable surveys, and survey design Web sites. Sources for Internet surveys are recruited panels, opt-in list rentals, opt-in panels, random Web site intercepts, and data capture of Web site visitors.

Creating online questionnaires requires special attention to the number and type of graphics. Long downloads cause respondents to terminate surveys. Whether and how to use "buttons," dropdown menus, and default answers must also be considered.

The factors that determine which survey method to use include the degree of sampling precision required, budget, whether respondents need to react to various stimuli or to perform specialized tasks, the quality of data required, the length of the questionnaire, the degree of structure of the questionnaire, and the time available to complete the survey.

Key Terms & Definitions

random error, or **random sampling error**   Error that results from chance variation.

chance variation   The difference between the sample value and the true value of the population mean.

systematic error, or **bias**   Error that results from problems or flaws in the execution of the research design; sometimes called nonsampling error.

sample design error   Systematic error that results from an error in the sample design or sampling procedures.

sampling frame   The list of population elements or members from which units to be sampled are selected.

frame error   Error resulting from an inaccurate or incomplete sampling frame.

population specification error   Error that results from incorrectly defining the population or universe from which a sample is chosen.

selection error   Error that results from following incomplete or

PART 2:
Creating a Research Design

improper sampling procedures or not following appropriate procedures.

measurement error   Systematic error that results from a variation between the information being sought and what is actually obtained by the measurement process.

surrogate information error   Error that results from a discrepancy between the information needed to solve a problem and that sought by the researcher.

interviewer error, or **interviewer bias**   Error that results from the interviewer's influencing—consciously or unconsciously—the respondent.

measurement instrument bias Error that results from the design of the questionnaire or measurement instrument; also known as questionnaire bias.

processing error   Error that results from the incorrect transfer of information from a survey document to a computer.

nonresponse bias   Error that results from a systematic difference between those who do and those who do not respond to a measurement instrument.

refusal rate   The percentage of persons contacted who refused to participate in a survey.

response bias   Error that results from the tendency of people to answer a question incorrectly through either deliberate falsification or unconscious misrepresentation.

door-to-door interviews   Interviews conducted face to face with consumers in their homes.

executive interviews   The industrial equivalent of door-to-door interviewing.

mall-intercept interviews   Interviews conducted by intercepting mall shoppers (or shoppers in other high-traffic locations) and interviewing them face to face.

central-location telephone interviews   Interviews conducted by calling respondents from a centrally located marketing research facility.

computer-assisted telephone interviews (CATI)   Central-location telephone interviews in which interviewers enter respondents' answers directly into a computer.

completely automated telephone surveys (CATS)   Interviews that use interactive voice response (IVR) technology to ask the questions.

self-administered questionnaires Questionnaires filled out by respondents with no interviewer present.

ad hoc mail surveys   Questionnaires sent to selected names and addresses without prior contact by the researcher; sometimes called one-shot mail surveys.

mail panels   Precontacted and pre-screened participants who are periodically sent questionnaires.

longitudinal study   Study in which the same respondents are resampled over time.

SSL (secure socket layer) technology   A computer encryption system that secures sensitive information.

unrestricted Internet sample   A self-selected sample group consisting of anyone who wishes to complete an Internet survey.

screened Internet sample A self-selected sample group in which quotas are imposed, based on some desired sample characteristics.

recruited Internet sample A sample group recruited to ensure representativeness of a target population.

Interactive Marketing Research Organization (IMRO) An organization dedicated to the development, dissemination, and implementation of interactive marketing research concepts, practice, and information.

incidence rate Percentage of people or households in the general population that fit the qualifications to be sampled.

Questions for Review & Critical Thinking

1. The owner of a hardware store in Eureka, California, is interested in determining the demographic characteristics of people who shop at his store versus those of people who shop at competing stores. He also wants to know what his image is relative to the competition. He would like to have the information within three weeks and is working on a limited budget. Which survey method would you recommend? Why?

2. Discuss this statement: "A mall-intercept interview is representative only of people who shop in that particular mall. Therefore, only surveys that relate to shopping patterns of consumers within that mall should be conducted in a mall-intercept interview."

3. A colleague is arguing that the best way to conduct a study of attitudes toward city government in your community is through a mail survey because it is the cheapest method. How would you respond to your colleague? If time were not a critical factor in your decision, would your response change? Why?

4. Discuss the various types of sample design error and give examples of each.

5. Why is it important to consider measurement error in survey research? Why is this typically not discussed in professional marketing research reports?

6. What types of error might be associated with the following situations?
   a. Conducting a survey about attitudes toward city government, using the telephone directory as a sample frame.
   b. Interviewing respondents only between 8:00 A.M. and 5:00 P.M. on features they would like to see in a new condominium development.
   c. Asking people if they have visited the public library in the past two months.
   d. Asking people how many tubes of toothpaste they used in the past year.
   e. Telling interviewers they can probe using any particular example they wish to make up.

7. What are the advantages and disadvantages of conducting surveys on the Internet?

8. Explain the three types of Internet samples, and discuss why a researcher might choose one over the others.

PART 2:
Creating a Research Design

9. Divide the class into teams. Each team should go to a different opt-in survey site on the Web and participate in an online survey. A spokesperson for each team should report the results to the class.
10. What are various ways to obtain respondents for online surveys?
11. Describe the advantages and disadvantages of online surveys.

Working the Net

1. Go to http://www.websurveyor.com/home_intro.asp and explain how the company's software allows users to distribute questionnaires over the Internet.
2. Go to American Consumer Opinion's Web site at http://www.acop.com. Describe the type of Internet samples being drawn and the types of surveys being conducted.
3. Participate in a survey at one of the following URLs and report on your experience to the class:
   a. Personality test:
      http://www.users.interport.net/~zang/personality.html
   b. Emotional intelligence test:
      http://www.utne.com/azEQ.tmpl
   c. Values and Lifestyles (VALS) test:
      http://future.sri.com/vals/valsindex.shtml
   d. Various online surveys on topics such as politics and consumer trends:
      http://www.survey.net
   e. Prudential Securities Investment Personality Quiz:
      http://www.prusec.com/financial_concerns/quiz.htm
   f. Miscellaneous surveys:
      http://www.dssresearch.com/mainsite/surveys.htm

Real-Life Research • 6.1

Unilever

Unilever is a giant consumer products company with annual sales of over $43 billion. Long fascinated with the Internet, the company launched a pioneering Website for the Ragu brand in the mid-1900s. The global conglomerate sunk $210 million into e-commerce and interactive marketing in 2000 with greater spending in 2001. So far, Unilever spends only a small percentage of its roughly $5.7 billion annual advertising and promotions budget on interactive marketing. But that small percentage can make a world of difference, especially as Unilever turns its eye to online markets in Europe, Asia, and Latin America, where the economic power of the Internet is only beginning to spread. Indeed, although Unilever's products—from Dove soap to Lipton tea—reach nearly every U.S. household, North America is not the company's primary market. It sells most of its products in Europe, and the company does business in 88 countries—from Austria to Zimbabwe.

"It's almost like the Internet was built for us," says Tony Romeo, co-founder and Chairman of the Unilever Interactive Brand Center in New York. "It's an international medium, and we are probably the most global of consumer companies."

Unilever has experimented with interactive marketing since the mid-1900s. But the establishment of its Interactive Brand Center (IBC) in 1998 was the first sign that Unilever was truly committed to making the Internet part of its marketing strategy. The center, which employs about 20 people in the United States, has been replicated in the Netherlands and in Singapore.

The IBC serves as a research and development center and shares its findings with interactive marketers assigned to specific business units. New technologies and techniques in the United States—where use of the Internet reached critical mass first—will eventually be rolled out around the world, after they've been tweaked to suit local tastes.

What they've learned in the past few years has now become conventional wisdom. Consumers aren't particularly interested in visiting a Website centered around Wisk laundry detergent, for example, but they do turn to the Internet when they're looking for information—such as how to get a stain out of a favorite shirt.

"From our point of view, people are looking for something that can add utility to their lives," says Unilever's Romeo. That "utility first" principle guided Unilever in consumer tests it orchestrated with Excite@Home beginning in 1999. Unilever ran a broadband ad for Lipton Recipe Secrets on Excite@Home's site. With broadband, Unilever discovered that it could not only show a product, but that it could also provide practical demonstrations of its use—online cooking lessons, if you will. The click-through rate was incredible. The Recipe Secrets banner prompted 8 percent of consumers who saw it to visit the site; of those, 62 percent obtained a recipe. Of total site visitors, 11 percent actually went to the store to buy a Recipe Secrets product and used it to prepare a meal.[33]

Questions

1. How might Unilever use online survey research at its Interactive Brand Center to build its Web presence?
2. What type of online surveys might be most effective?
3. What are some respondent sources that the IBC might draw on? Which might be most effective for existing products? New products?

Real-Life Research • 6.2

Your Personal Consultant, Incorporated

Like a genie in a bottle or a janitor in a drum, management support software captures a consultant on a floppy disk. By using a computer program to simulate a discussion with a human expert, a user can pick up negotiating tips, forecast a financial future, or devise a marketing strategy. These software productivity tools often are loosely grouped into two categories: decision support and expert systems. Decision support software addresses the individual situation with prepackaged responses culled from the experience of experts. Expert systems offer a blend of enlightened guidance and subjective judgment that allows the user to arrive at her or his own answers. Your Personal Consultant, Incorporated was organized in October 2000 as a $500,000 research and development limited partnership. The five founders kicked in $230,000 more, raised an additional $500,000 through a private placement, and netted $1.5 million in a public offering. Their first product, an expert system for picking a store location, went to market in January of the following year.

Gaining visibility in this market has not been easy. Major distributors are not interested in carrying a lot of additional software lines. Big advertising campaigns are beyond the means of this start-up operation. With approximately 100 companies already in the field, a shake-out is bound to occur. At this point in time, Your Personal Consultant could use a consultant of its own! It has no marketing plan per se.

Questions

1. What marketing problems are facing Your Personal Consultant, and what are its informational needs?
2. Can survey research be of benefit to the organization? If so, what survey methodology would you recommend?
3. What sources of survey error might be encountered in the type of survey methodology you recommended? Why?
4. What can be done to help minimize the possibility of this survey error?

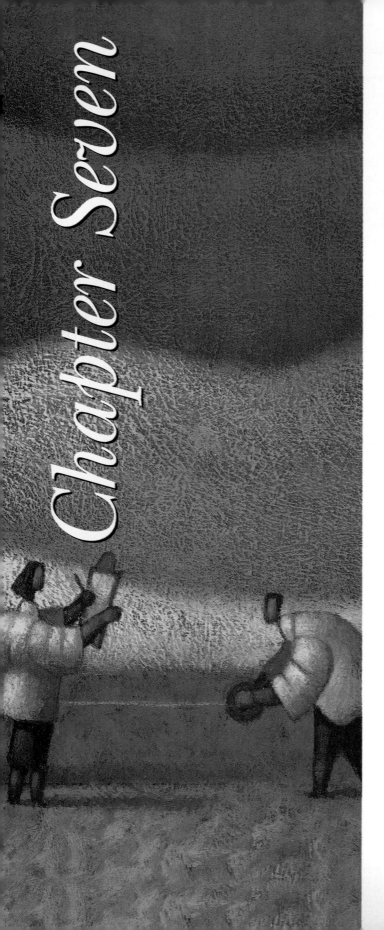

Chapter Seven

Primary Data Collection: Observation

Learning Objectives

To develop a basic understanding of observation research.

To learn the approaches to observation research.

To understand the advantages and disadvantages of observation research.

To explore the types of human observation.

To understand the types of machine observation and their advantages and disadvantages.

To explore the tremendous impact of scanner-based research on the marketing research industry.

To learn about observation research on the Internet

A S A MANUFACTURER OF TOP QUALITY LOUDSPEAKERS AND OTHER AUDIO equipment, Bose Corporation has a reputation for excellence. Thanks to the firm's strong belief in R&D, audiophiles and the general public alike know that the Bose name is synonymous with technological innovation and great sound.

TO MAKE SURE EMPLOYEES EXTEND THE PURsuit of excellence to the retail setting, Bose has been using mystery shopping since 1995 to monitor performance of salespeople at its factory stores—which sell new and factory-renewed products—and at its Bose showcase stores—which sell new merchandise. Mystery shops are also conducted at department stores and electronics superstores where Bose products are sold.

THE BOSE STORE MYSTERY SHOPS ARE TWOpart. They begin with a phone call, in which the shopper calls to ask questions on specific products. Shoppers indicate if the employee performed tasks such as answering questions clearly. Employees are also rated on their friendliness, helpfulness, etc., using an excellent–satisfactory–unsatisfactory scale. Finally, shoppers have space to write about their interaction and support the ratings they gave the employee. "We ask our shoppers specifically what we could have done to improve. We have a lot of yes/no questions so that it can be as objective as possible but we also want them to express in their own words how we did and what we could do to make them feel more welcome," John Pazol says.

FOR THE IN-PERSON VISIT, SHOPPERS DESCRIBE HOW/IF THEY WERE GREETED, their evaluation of the employee in charge of the theater presentation (Bose stores contain a theater for presenting a short audio-visual show which highlights Bose equipment), the employee's selling and closing skills and exploration of customer needs (Did the employee use language which helped you picture having the product in your home?), product demonstration and knowledge (Did the employee describe and demonstrate the benefits?), and overall impressions (Did the Bose representative make you feel important, provide a comfortable environment?). At the factory stores, shoppers must note if the employee volunteered an explanation of factory-renewed products during their visit.

EACH STORE RECEIVES A QUARTERLY SUMMARY SHOWING THE STAFF'S OVERALL performance. The district and store managers also get copies of the shops. The stores use the mystery shopping data as a tool to bring awareness of where they're doing well and where there are opportunities to do better. Depending on

Bose uses mystery shoppers to monitor the performance of salespeople at its factory stores, as well as at department stores and electronic superstores where Bose products are sold. Mystery shopping data provide employees with information on areas where they are doing well and where there is opportunity to do better.

Find out more about Bose's commitment to excellence at

 http://www. bose.com

each store's overall performance, the employee team, including managers, are awarded a customer satisfaction bonus. Outstanding mystery shopping reports are often posted at the individual stores so employees can celebrate. Individual employees are noted only for outstanding service (they're not singled out if they perform poorly) and can win points in the Bose employee recognition program.[1] ∎

The Bose story describes a form of observation research. What is observation research? What are its advantages and limitations? Are mechanical devices used in observation research? These are some of the questions we will consider in this chapter.

The Nature of Observation Research

observation research
The systematic process of recording patterns of occurrences or behaviors without normally communicating with the people involved.

Instead of asking people questions, as a survey does, observation research depends on watching what people do. Specifically, **observation research** can be defined as the systematic process of recording patterns of occurrences or behaviors without questioning or normally communicating with the people involved. (Mystery shopping is an exception.) A marketing researcher using the observation technique witnesses and records events as they occur or compiles evidence from records of past events. The observation may involve watching people or watching phenomena, and it may be conducted by human observers or by machines. Table 7.1 gives examples of these various observation situations.

Conditions for Using Observation

Three conditions must be met before observation can be successfully used as a data collection tool for marketing research:

1. The needed information must be either observable or inferable from behavior that is observable. For example, if a researcher wants to know why an

Table 7.1

Observation Situations

	Example
People watching people	Observers stationed in supermarkets watch consumers select frozen Mexican dinners, with the purpose of seeing how much comparison shopping people do at the point of purchase.
People watching phenomena	Observers stationed at an intersection count vehicles moving in various directions to establish the need for a traffic light.
Machines watching people	Movie or video cameras record consumers selecting frozen Mexican dinners.
Machines watching phenomena	Traffic-counting machines monitor the flow of vehicles at an intersection.

individual purchased a new Jeep rather than an Explorer, observation research will not provide the answer.

2. The behavior of interest must be repetitive, frequent, or in some manner predictable. Otherwise, the costs of observation may make the approach prohibitively expensive.

3. The behavior of interest must be of relatively short duration. Observation of the entire decision-making process for purchasing a new home, which might take several weeks or months, is not feasible.

Approaches to Observation Research

Researchers have a variety of observation approaches to choose from. They are faced with the task of choosing the most effective approach for a particular research problem, from the standpoint of cost and data quality. The five dimensions along which observation approaches vary are (1) natural versus contrived situations, (2) open versus disguised observation, (3) structured versus unstructured observation, (4) human versus machine observers, and (5) direct versus indirect observation.

Natural versus Contrived Situations   Counting how many people use the drive-in window at a particular bank during certain hours is a good example of a completely natural situation. The observer plays no role in the behavior of interest. Those being observed should have no idea that they are under observation. At the other extreme is recruiting people to do their shopping in a simulated supermarket (rows of stocked shelves set up in a field service's mall facility) so that their behavior can be carefully observed. In this case, the recruited people must be given at least some idea that they are participating in a study. The participants might be given grocery carts and told to browse the shelves and pick out items that they might normally use. The researchers might use alternative point-of-purchase displays for several products under study. To test the effectiveness of the various displays, the observers would note how long the shopper paused in front of the test displays and how often the product was actually selected.

A contrived environment enables the researcher to better control extraneous variables that might have an impact on a person's behavior or the interpretation of that behavior. Use of such an environment also tends to speed up the data-gathering process. The researcher does not have to wait for natural events to occur but instead instructs the participants to perform certain actions. Because more observations can be collected in the same length of time, the result will be either a larger sample or faster collection of the targeted amount of data. The latter should lower the costs of the project.

The primary disadvantage of a contrived setting is that it is artificial, and thus the observed behavior may be different from what would occur in a real-world situation. The more natural the setting, the more likely it is that the behavior will be normal for the individual being observed.

Open versus Disguised Observation   Does the person being observed know that he or she is being observed? It is well known that the presence of an observer may have an influence on the phenomena being observed.[2] Two general mechanisms work to bias the data. First, if people know they are being observed (as in **open observation**), they may behave differently. Second, the appearance and behavior of the observer offers a potential for bias similar to that associated with the presence of an interviewer in survey research.

Disguised observation is the process of monitoring people who do not know they are being watched. A common form of disguised observation is observing behavior from behind a one-way mirror. For example, a product manager may observe respondent reactions to alternative package designs from behind a one-way mirror during a focus group discussion.

Structured versus Unstructured Observation   Observation can be structured or unstructured much in the same manner as surveys can. In a **structured observation,** the observer fills out a questionnaire-like form on each person or event observed. In totally **unstructured observation,** the observer simply makes notes on the behavior or activity being observed. In general, the same considerations that determine how structured a survey should be also determine how structured an observation should be. If you already know a good deal about the behavior of interest, structured observation probably makes more sense. If you know very little, unstructured observation is the proper approach or at least an appropriate preliminary approach.

Structured observation often consists of simply counting the number of times a particular activity or behavior occurs. For example, suppose a researcher is interested in testing two sets of instructions on a new cake mix recipe. To develop a baseline of behavior, the researcher could have participants prepare their own favorite recipes, using the cake mix. One-half of the group would get one set of instructions, and the remainder the other set. Variables recorded might include the number of times the instructions were read, the number of trips to the cabinet to retrieve bowls and other instruments, the number of strokes that the mix is beaten, and oven temperatures.

Human versus Machine Observers   In some situations, it is possible and even desirable to replace human observers with machines—when machines can do the job less expensively, more accurately, or more readily. Traffic-counting devices are probably more accurate, definitely cheaper, and certainly more willing than human observers. It would not be feasible, for example, for ACNielsen to have human observers in people's homes to record television viewing habits. Movie cameras and audiovisual equipment record behavior much more objectively and in greater detail than human observers ever could. Finally, the electronic scanners found in a growing number of retail stores provide more accurate and timely data on product movement than human observers ever could.

Direct versus Indirect Observation   Most of the observation carried out for marketing research is direct observation of current behavior. However, in some cases, past behavior must be observed. To do this, the researcher must turn to some record of the behavior. Archaeologists dig up sites of old settlements and attempt to determine the nature of life in early societies from the physical evidence they find. **Garbologists** sort through people's garbage to analyze household consumption patterns. Marketing research usually is much more mundane.

PART 2:
Creating a Research Design

In a product prototype test, it may be important to learn how much of the test product the consumer used. The most accurate way to find this out is to have the respondent return the unused product so that the researcher can see how much is left. If a study involved the in-home use of a laundry soil and stain remover, it would be important to know how much of the remover each respondent actually used. All of the respondents' answers to questions would be considered from this usage perspective.

Advantages of Observation Research

Watching what people actually do rather than depending on their reports of what they did has one very significant and obvious advantage: First-hand information is not subject to many of the biasing factors associated with the survey approach. Specifically, the researcher avoids problems associated with the willingness and ability of respondents to answer questions. Also, some forms of data are gathered more quickly and accurately by observation. Letting a scanner record the items in a grocery bag is much more efficient than asking the shopper to enumerate them. Similarly, rather than asking young children which toys they like, major toy manufacturers prefer to invite target groups of children into a large playroom and observe via a one-way mirror which toys are chosen and how long each holds the child's attention.

Disadvantages of Observation Research

The primary disadvantage of observation research is that only behavior and physical personal characteristics usually can be examined. The researcher does not learn about motives, attitudes, intentions, or feelings. Also, only public behavior is observed; private behavior—such as dressing for work or committee decision making within a company—is beyond the scope of observation research. A second problem is that present observed behavior may not be projectable into the future. The fact that a consumer purchases a certain brand of milk after examining several alternatives does not mean that he or she will continue to do so in the future.

Observation research can be time-consuming and costly if the observed behavior occurs rather infrequently. For example, if observers in a supermarket are waiting to watch the purchase behavior of persons selecting Lava soap, they may have a long wait. And if the choice of consumers to be observed is biased (for example, shoppers who go grocery shopping after 5:00 P.M.), distorted data may be obtained.

Human Observation

As noted in Table 7.1, people can be employed to watch other people or certain phenomena. For example, people can act as mystery shoppers, observers behind one-way mirrors, or recorders of shopper traffic and behavior patterns. Researchers also can conduct retail and wholesale audits, which are types of observation research.

WAR Stories

ethnographic research
The study of human behavior in its natural context, involving observation of behavior and physical setting coupled with depth interviews to obtain participants' perspectives.

mystery shoppers
People who pose as consumers and shop at a company's own stores or those of its competitors to collect data about customer–employee interactions and to gather observational data; they may also compare prices, displays, and the like.

Ethnographic Research

Ethnographic research comes to marketing from the field of anthropology. The popularity of the technique in commercial marketing research is increasing. **Ethnographic research,** or the study of human behavior in its natural context, involves observation of behavior and physical setting, along with depth interviews to obtain participants' perspectives. Thus, ethnographic research incorporates observation techniques, depth interviews, and sometimes audio- and videotapes to record people in their natural settings.[3] Ethnographic studies can cost anywhere from $5,000 to as much as $800,000, depending on how deeply a company wants to delve into its customers' lives.[4]

Knowing what consumers do with beef is vital to the National Cattlemen's Beef Association (NCBA). Even though sales of steaks have been rising, two-thirds of the beef industry's product line has been losing market share. So NCBA turned to ethnographic research for help. A scene from the study follows:

A woman in suburban Baltimore is shopping for her family's meals for the week. She cruises past the poultry section, stopping only momentarily to drop a couple of packages of boneless chicken breasts into her cart. Then, the dreaded sea of red looms before her. Tentatively, she picks up a package of beef. "This cut looks good, not too fatty," she says, juggling her two-year-old on her hip. "But I don't know what it is. I don't know how to cook it," she confesses, and trades it for a small package of sirloin and her regular order of ground beef.[5]

The researchers found that the above scenario was replayed daily in supermarkets across the country. Using the research findings, many grocers rearranged their meat cases to display beef by cooking method, rather than by cuts of meat. Simple, three-step cooking instructions will soon be printed on the packages.

Mystery Shoppers

Mystery shoppers are used to gather observational data about a store (e.g., are the shelves neatly stocked?) and to collect data about customer–employee interactions. In the latter case, of course, there is communication between the mystery shopper and the employee. The mystery shopper may ask, "How much is this item?" "Do you have this in blue?" or "Can you deliver this by Friday?" The interaction is not an interview, and communication occurs only so that the mystery shopper can observe the actions and comments of the employee. Mystery shopping is, therefore, classified as an observational marketing research method, even though communication is often involved.

The mystery shopping concept has four basic levels, which differ in the depth and type of information collected:

■ *Level 1*—The mystery shopper conducts a mystery telephone call. Here, the mystery shopper calls the client location and evaluates the level of service received over the phone, following a scripted conversation.

- *Level 2*—The mystery shopper visits an establishment and makes a quick purchase; little or no customer–employee interaction is required. For example, in a Level 2 mystery shop, a mystery shopper purchases an item (e.g., gas, a hamburger, or a lottery ticket) and evaluates the transaction and image of the facility.
- *Level 3*—The mystery shopper visits an establishment and, using a script or scenario, initiates a conversation with a service and/or sales representative. Level 3 mystery shopping usually does not involve an actual purchase. Examples include discussing different cellular telephone packages with a sales representative, reviewing services provided during an oil change, etc.
- *Level 4*—The mystery shopper performs a visit that requires excellent communication skills and knowledge of the product. Discussing a home loan, the process for purchasing a new car, or visiting apartment complexes serve as examples.[6]

Mystery shopping can have any one of several objectives. These objectives include measuring employee training, preparing for new competition, monitoring the competition through comparison shopping, and recognizing good employees.

Measuring Employee Training   The most common use of mystery shopping is to measure employee training. The evaluation is best done in three phases.

In phase one, shoppers are sent in to evaluate the existing level of customer service. This provides a benchmark—a place to start in assessing what areas need to be addressed in a training program, as well as what positive performance needs to be reinforced.

In phase two, the evaluations are analyzed, and a training program is developed, based on identified weaknesses and company standards. The training program is implemented, either company-wide or as a test in a targeted location or region.

In phase three, shoppers return to evaluate the customer service post-training. The effectiveness of the training program can be measured using a custom-designed evaluation form developed to highlight the areas in which training took place.

Areas of continuing weakness can then be addressed, and trainers can determine which techniques worked well in getting the message across to employees and which didn't. Over a period of several months—or longer—continued improvement in specific areas can be documented, as can persistent weaknesses.[7]

Suppose a national bookstore chain, such as Barnes & Noble, has a service policy stating that, when a customer enters the store, a floor employee should (1) ask questions to determine the customer's area of interest, (2) take the customer to the appropriate section of the store, (3) show the customer several alternative titles, (4) help the customer decide which one(s) to buy, and (5) ask if there is something else he or she can do to help the customer.[8] To evaluate compliance with this policy, the chain might use a sample mystery shopper evaluation form like the one shown in Figure 7.1.

Figure 7.1

Excerpt from a Mystery Shopper's Scoring Sheet

Source: Dan Prince, "How to Ensure an Objective Mystery Shop," *Quirk's Marketing Research Review* (January 1996). Reprinted by permission of *Quirk's Marketing Research Review*.

BOOKSTORE EVALUATION

Store _____ Date _____

Employee _____ Shopper _____

Time entered store _____ Time exited store _____

Time spent waiting for employee _____

Does employee . . .

_____ Greet customer with a smile?

_____ Ask "Is there something in particular I can help you with today?"

_____ Ask at least one additional follow-up question to assist customer?

_____ Take customer to appropriate section?

_____ Show customer two more titles?

Preparing for New Competition   When a mid-sized department store, with seven locations in two states, learned that two national chains were locating in or near the same mall as its flagship store, the client asked for an intensive, two-month mystery shopping program designed to accomplish two things. The first was to take a snapshot of the state of its employees' customer service skills. The client wanted to make sure that customers were being greeted, helped, and thanked. The second was to determine if employees' stress levels were being communicated to the customer (it was the December holiday season). This evaluation was designed to identify strengths and weaknesses, which could then be addressed in a bid to stave off new competition.[9]

Monitoring the Competition through Comparison Shopping   Comparing one's own store with that of a competitor is another goal of mystery shopping reports. Many companies ask mystery shopping organizations to shop not only their own locations but also those of their closest competitors. By using the same evaluation form and the same shopper at each establishment, the organization can tell how the firm is doing compared to the competition.

Recognizing Good Employees   Service affects sales, customer satisfaction, and ultimately customer loyalty, which in turn affects a company's profits. Service is, of course, delivered by a company's employees. Many firms have found that recognizing employees who provide customers with outstanding service builds employee morale and better customer satisfaction.

Sonic operates more than 2,200 drive-in restaurants in 27 states. The company is the largest chain of drive-in restaurants in the nation and is known for its

Undercover with a Hotel Spy

J. C. SCHAEFER UNSCREWS A LIGHT BULB FROM A BEDSIDE LAMP IN THE posh Windsor Court Hotel in New Orleans and begins violently whacking it against the bedspread. He shakes the light bulb to make sure the filament inside is broken and then carefully screws it back into the lamp.

Mr. Schaefer isn't your average hotel guest. in fact, he isn't even J. C. Schaefer. His real name is David Richey, and he's a hotel spy who uses a variety of aliases to check out luxury hotels all over the world. Over two days, he'll employ an extensive bag of tricks to see if the Windsor Court—rated as the top hotel in the world in a *Condé Nast Traveler* magazine poll—is as good as its reputation. The "burnt-out light bulb" test is one of the toughest. Only 11% of hotels tested by Mr. Richey's Chevy Chase, Md., firm, Richey International, detect the burnt-out bulb on the housekeeping staff's first pass.

The Windsor Court is a member of Preferred Hotels & Resorts Worldwide, a group of 120 independent luxury hotels that share a common reservations system. Preferred requires that all its hotels meet at least 80% of its standards in a test conducted annually by Richey International.

After checking in, Mr. Richey heads off to lunch while his room is being prepared. The Windsor Court has a five-star dining room, but the mystery shopper decides to eat at the hotel bar, the Polo Club Lounge. Mr. Richey orders crab cakes from the menu, then orders french fries to see if the bar readily accommodates off-menu orders. It does.

The food is good, and the service is friendly. But the waiters get marked down for not making eye contact and for not busing away the ketchup after the meal is done. "They're nice guys," Mr. Richey says, "But they're not real polished."

A little after 2 P.M. Mr Richey walks into a sprawling $295-a-night suite at the Windsor Court. He pulls out a disposable camera and begins taking pictures. Overall, the room gets high marks for cleanliness and creature comforts. But Mr. Richey spots scuff marks on the baseboard and a snag in one of the curtains.

Then it's on to the bathroom. "Forty percent of hotels have hair in either the sink, the tub or on the floor," Mr. Richey announces as he begins his inspection. This room, it turns out, does not.

Before leaving for dinner, Mr. Richey sets up a test to see how well the housekeeping staff will pick up the room when they turn down the covers on the bed later that evening. He leaves some magazines askew in the magazine rack, puts a cup of pistachio shells on the table and disables the light bulb.

After dinner, Mr. Richey heads downstairs for another test. "I have changed my travel plans and will be going to New York tomorrow," Mr. Richey informs the concierge. "Can you make reservations for me?" "Unfortunately we can't do that," the concierge replies. "You either have to do it yourself or call a travel agent." Mr. Richey, as always, takes the news calmly. "That was awful," he says later. "I'm sure the general manager will be horrified."

Back in the room, Mr. Richey finds a neatly turned-down bed. However, the housekeeper hasn't done a very good job of tidying the room. And the defective light bulb hasn't been replaced. Mr. Richey takes copious photos. It's 10 P.M., but Mr. Richey will be up for another couple of hours preparing his report.[11] ■

nostalgic eat-in-your-car burgers, coneys, fries, and shakes. Food is delivered by carhops, some even on roller skates, or customers can walk up and place an order.

One of Sonic's employee recognition programs, the Dr Pepper Sonic Games, begins with in-store competition among crew members to become "station champs." A station is where a specific food such as french fries is prepared. After the drive-in manager determines a drive-in's station champs, mystery shopping takes over.

Mystery shoppers anonymously evaluate each drive-in on service, cleanliness, quality, and concept integrity. Each year, 10 drive-ins are selected to become Sonic Games finalists and their crew members flown in, all expenses paid, to the site of Sonic's national convention, where they compete for national recognition.

Sonic has found that recognizing employees for outstanding customer service builds morale and increases customer satisfaction. Go to http://www.sonicdrivein.com to find some fun facts about Sonic.

The contestants are evaluated in their individual stations and as a team by a panel of 18 judges over a two-day period on service, quality, accuracy, and speed. Bronze, silver, and gold medals, as well as cash prizes, are awarded to the top three winning teams and the top three contestants in each station position—all of which are presented on stage at Sonic's national convention. Approximately 2,500 managers, franchisees, and supervisors, representing Sonic Drive-Ins across the country, attend the annual meeting.[10]

One-Way Mirror Observations

The discussion of focus groups in Chapter 5 noted that focus group facilities almost always provide **one-way mirror observation,** which allows clients to observe the group discussion as it unfolds. New product development managers, for example, can note consumers' reactions to various package prototypes as they are demonstrated by the moderator. (One researcher spent 200 hours watching mothers change diapers to gather information for the redesign of disposable diapers.) In addition, the clients can observe the degree of emotion exhibited by the consumer as he or she speaks. One-way mirrors are also sometimes used by child psychologists and toy designers to observe children at play.

one-way mirror observation
The practice of watching behaviors or activities from behind a one-way mirror.

The lighting level in the observation room must be very dim relative to that in the focus group room. Otherwise, the focus group participants can see into the observation room. Several years ago, we (the authors) were conducting a focus group of orthopedic surgeons in St. Louis, Missouri. One physician arrived approximately 20 minutes early and was ushered into the group room. A young assistant product manager for the pharmaceutical manufacturer was already seated in the observation room. The physician, being alone in the group room, decided to take advantage of the large framed mirror on the wall for some last-minute grooming. He walked over to the mirror and began combing his hair. At the same time, the assistant product manager, sitting about a foot away on the other side of the mirror, decided to light a cigarette. As the doctor combed his hair, there was suddenly a bright flash of light, and another face appeared through the mirror. What happened next goes beyond the scope of this text. In recent years, the trend has been to inform participants of the one-way mirror and to explain who is in the other room watching and why.

Shopper Pattern and Behavior Studies

Shopper pattern studies are used by retailers to trace the flow of shoppers through a store. Normally, the researcher uses a pen to trace the footsteps of the shopper on a diagram of the store aisles. By comparing the traffic flows of a representative sample of shoppers, store managers can determine where to place such items as impulse goods. Alternatively, the store can change layouts over time and see how the change modifies shopping patterns. Generally speaking, retailers want shoppers to be exposed to as much merchandise as possible while in the store. Supermarkets, for example, typically put necessities toward the rear of the store, hoping that shoppers will place more items in their basket on impulse as they move down the aisle to reach the milk, bread, or other necessities.

shopper pattern studies
Drawings that record the footsteps of a shopper through a store's aisles.

Shopper behavior research involves observing consumers—or perhaps videotaping them and then watching the tape—in a variety of shopping settings. Starbucks, Anheuser-Busch, McDonald's, and Procter & Gamble, among others, have hired Envirosell, a marketing research firm, to observe shopper behavior. The company creates about 15,000 hours of videotape of shoppers each year, and these videos are then analyzed for behavioral tendencies. Some of Envirosell's findings include the following:

shopper behavior research
Observation of consumers, either in person or on video-tape, in a variety of shopping settings.

- Installing ledges for customer pocketbooks cut a store's checkout time 15 percent.
- Pedestrians can take 25 feet to slow down, so a store just past an establishment without visual appeal may be missed.
- Special displays just inside stores will be seen by more people if moved back, near the end of the "decompression zone" where customers adjust to light and surroundings.
- Older people tend to shop in couples or larger groups and should have access to chairs in stores and something to look at while their more active friends browse.
- Large toy stores have ignored a wealth of potential business from grandparents who will not shop there because they cannot find good advice on what toys are popular and appropriate for various age groups.
- Average number of times a product is handled by shoppers before it is bought: lipsticks, 6; towels, 6.6; compact discs and toys, 11.[12]

Classic retailing blunders observed by Envirosell include positioning junk food on high shelves out of the reach of kids; keeping hearing-aid batteries on

Observation Research Is Used Sparingly in Many Countries

OBSERVATION RESEARCH IS USED EXTENSIVELY IN THE UNITED STATES and Japan, but less so in Europe. For example, little observation research is conducted in Ireland. Where it is used, it tends to be as a generalized technique to get a research idea or to help the researcher decide what aspects of the problem are worth researching. It may be used as a check on other research techniques. Many researchers avoid using the method due to its inability to observe such factors as attitudes, motivations, and plans.

There is a reluctance on the part of Irish business to allow the researcher to come on-site and observe behaviors over a period of time. Many Irish researchers would question the reliability of what they are observing. There is a tendency for many people to act differently than they would otherwise. Most of the observation that is used is of the natural, direct, and unobtrusive type.[13] ∎

bottom shelves, where the elderly have to bend over to get at them; and marketing hair products for blondes in a Washington, D.C., neighborhood that is 95 percent African American.[14]

Audits

audit
The examination and verification of the sales of a product.

Audits are another category of human observation research. An **audit** is the examination and verification of sales of a product. Audits generally fall into two categories: retail audits, which measure sales to final consumers, and wholesale audits, which determine the amount of product movement from warehouses to retailers. Wholesalers and retailers allow auditors into their stores and stockrooms to examine the company's sales and order records in order to verify product flows. In turn, the retailers and wholesalers receive cash compensation and basic reports about their operations from the audit firms.

Because of the availability of scanner-based data (discussed later in this chapter), physical audits at the retail level may someday all but disappear. The largest nonscanner-based wholesale audit company, SAMI, has already gone out of business. Its client list was sold to Information Resources, Incorporated (IRI), a company that specializes in providing scanner-based data. ACNielsen, the largest retail audit organization, no longer uses auditors in grocery stores. The data are entirely scanner-based. Currently, ACNielsen uses both auditors and scanner-based data for other types of retail outlets. However, the data probably will be scanner-based only once a large majority of individual retailers within a store category (e.g., hardware stores, drugstores) install scanners.

PART 2:
Creating a Research Design

Machine Observation

The observation methods discussed so far have involved people observing things or consumers. Now we turn our attention to observation by machines, including traffic counters, physiological measurement devices, opinion and behavior management devices, and scanners.

Traffic Counters

Among the most common and popular machines in observation research are **traffic counters**. As the name implies, traffic counters measure vehicular flow over a particular stretch of roadway. Outdoor advertisers rely on traffic counts to determine number of exposures per day to a specific billboard. Retailers use the information to ascertain where to locate a particular type of store. Convenience stores, for example, require a moderately high traffic volume to reach target levels of profitability.

Physiological Measurement Devices

When an individual is aroused or feels inner tension or alertness, his or her condition is referred to as *activation*.[15] Activation is stimulated via a subcortical unit called the *reticular activation system (RAS)*, located in the human brain stem. The sight of a product or advertisement, for example, can activate the RAS. When the arousal processes in the RAS are directly provoked, the processing of information increases. Researchers have used a number of devices to measure the level of a person's activation.

Electroencephalograph   An **electroencephalograph (EEG)** is a machine that measures electric pulses on the scalp and generates a record of electrical activity in the brain. Although electroencephalography probably is the most versatile and sensitive procedure for detecting arousal, it involves expensive equipment, a laboratory environment, and complex data analysis requiring special software programs. Using EEG technology developed by NASA to monitor astronauts' alertness levels, Capita Corporation has begun measuring respondents' reactions to advertisements. Capita uses a headset that reads electrical signals coming from a subject's scalp five times per second, as the person interacts with media such as a television program, a commercial, a Web page, or a banner ad. These brain waves are converted into a scrolling graph synchronized with the visual stimuli on the screen, giving the marketer a play-by-play view of which segments excite the viewer and which ones don't.

Recently, Capita, with the help of U.S. Interactive, an Internet services company that tracks Web ads, tested the system's reliability. Capita monitored the brain waves of 48 respondents as they confronted four banner ads with strong click-through rates and four ads with low rates. In three of four tests, Capita's measure correctly identified the "strong" banners.[16]

The ability to accurately translate the data is what troubles one cable network executive. "An ad might get someone to perspire or their eyes to dilate or their brain waves to peak, but the resounding issue is, what does that really tell you?" he says. "Just because the needles are moving does not mean that it will affect their behavior, get them to purchase something, or improve their brand awareness."[17]

galvanic skin response (GSR)
A change in the electric resistance of the skin associated with activation responses; also called *electrodermal response.*

Galvanic Skin Response   **Galvanic skin response (GSR),** also known as *electrodermal response,* is a change in the electric resistance of the skin associated with activation responses. A small electric current of constant intensity is sent into the skin through electrodes attached to the palmar side of the fingers. The changes in voltage observed between the electrodes indicate the level of stimulation. Because the equipment is portable and not expensive, measuring GSR is the most popular way to assess emotional reaction to a stimulus. GSR is used primarily to measure stimulus response to advertisements but is sometimes used in packaging research.

Inner Response, Incorporated uses GSR to evaluate commercials. In tests of an Eastman Kodak Company film-processing ad, Inner Response determined that viewers' interest levels built slowly in the opening scenes, rose when a snapshot of an attractive young woman was shown, but spiked highest when a picture appeared of a smiling, pigtailed girl. Knowing which scenes had the highest impact helped Kodak in making changes in the spot's content and cutting its length.[18]

pupilometer
A machine that measures changes in pupil dilation.

Pupilometer   The **pupilometer** measures changes in pupil dilation as subjects view an advertisement, while brightness and distance from the screen are held constant. The basic assumption is that increased pupil size reflects positive attitudes, interest, and arousal. The pupilometer has fallen from favor among many researchers because pupil dilation appears to measure some combination of arousal, mental effort, processing load, and anxiety.[19] Arousal alone is much better measured by GSR.

voice pitch analysis
Studying changes in the relative vibration frequency of the human voice to measure emotion.

Voice Pitch Analysis   **Voice pitch analysis** measures emotion by examining changes in the relative vibration frequency of the human voice. In voice pitch analysis, the normal, or baseline, pitch of an individual's speaking voice is charted by engaging the subject in an unemotional conversation. Then, the more pitch deviates from the baseline, the greater is said to be the emotional intensity of the person's reaction to a stimulus, such as a question. Voice pitch analysis has several advantages over other forms of physiological measurement:

■ One can record without physically connecting wires and sensors to the subject.
■ The subject need not be aware of the recording and analysis.
■ The nonlaboratory setting avoids the weaknesses of an artificial environment.
■ It provides instantaneous evaluation of answers and comments.[20]

Voice pitch analysis has been used in package research, to measure consumers' emotional responses to advertising, to predict consumer brand preference for dog food, and to determine which consumers from a target group would be most predisposed to try a new product. Validity of the studies to date has been subject to serious question.[21]

The devices just discussed are used to measure involuntary changes in an individual's physiological makeup. Arousal produces adrenaline, which

PART 2:
Creating a Research Design

enhances the activation process via a faster heart rate, increased blood flow, an increase in skin temperature and perspiration, pupil dilation, and an increase in brain-wave frequency. Researchers often infer information about attitudes and feelings from these measures.

Opinion and Behavior Measurement Devices

Radio Listenership Tracking A device called **MOBILTRAK** is now being used to determine which FM radio stations people are listening to as they are driving. Jim Spahn, marketing director of the Riverchase Galleria in Hoover, Alabama, has a MOBILTRAK device at each of his mall's five entrances. The information has allowed him to target ads for the 200-store shopping mall on local radio and track the results.[22]

The People Reader, an opinion and behavior measurement device developed by the PreTesting Company, unobtrusively records reading material and readers' eye activity to determine readers' habits as well as the stopping power and brand-name recall associated with different-sized ads. Go to http://www. pretesting.com to learn about the products and services this company offers.

People Reader The PreTesting Company has invented a device called the **People Reader,** which looks like a lamp. When respondents sit in front of it, they are not aware that it is simultaneously recording both their reading material and the activity of their eyes. The self-contained unit is totally automatic and can record any respondent—with or without glasses—without the use of attachments, chin rests, helmets, or special optics. It allows respondents to read any size magazine or newspaper and lets them spend as much time as they want reading and rereading the publication. Through use of the People Reader and specially designed hidden cameras, the PreTesting Company has been able to document both reading habits and the results of different sized ads in terms of stopping power and brand-name recall. The company's research has found the following:

- Nearly 40 percent of all readers either start from the back of a magazine or "fan" a magazine for interesting articles and ads. Fewer than half the readers start from the very first page of a magazine.
- Rarely does a double-page ad provide more than 15 percent additional top-of-mind awareness than a single-page ad. Usually, the benefits of a double-page spread are additional involvement and communication, not top-of-mind awareness.
- In the typical magazine, nearly 35 percent of each of the ads receives less than two seconds' worth of voluntary examination.
- The strongest involvement power recorded for ads has been three or more successive single-page ads on the right-hand side of a magazine.
- Because most ads "hide" the name of the advertisers and do not show a close-up view of the product package, brand-name confusion is greater than 50 percent on many products such as cosmetics and clothing.
- A strong ad that is above average in stopping power and communication will work regardless of which section in the magazine it is placed. It will also work well in any type of ad or editorial environment. However, an ad that is below average in stopping power and involvement will be seriously affected by the surrounding environment.[23]

MOBILTRAK
A device that picks up radio signals to determine which FM radio stations people are listening to in their cars.
People Reader
A machine that simultaneously records the respondent's reading material and eye reactions.

Rapid Analysis Measurement System (RAMS)

A hand-held device that allows respondents to record how they are feeling by turning a dial.

Rapid Analysis Measurement System   The **Rapid Analysis Measurement System (RAMS)** is a hand-held device, about the size of a cell phone, with a dial in the center. Respondents turn the dial to the right when they are feeling favorable toward a subject, and to the left to indicate more negative feelings.

Best Western is the world's largest hotel system. Its image, however, was that of a mom-and-pop motel along the highway. The company was afraid that its existing "Best Places . . . Best Bet" advertising campaign was not communicating the notion that Best Western is a global chain with hotels in attractive locations. An audience was equipped with RAMS and shown commercials for Holiday Inn, Ramada, and Best Western. RAMS scores were highest for Best Western commercials, resulting in the firm's decision to keep its "Best Places . . . Best Bet" campaign. The company estimates that it saved as much as $750,000 by staying with the old campaign instead of developing a new one.[24]

people meters

Components of a microwave computerized rating system, used to measure national TV audiences, that transmits demographic information overnight.

People Meter   Several years ago, ACNielsen announced that it would use its **people meters** to measure the size of national television audiences. The people meter system is a microwave computerized rating system that transmits demographic information overnight. It provides information on what TV shows are being watched, the number of households watching, and which family members are watching. The type of activity is recorded automatically; household members merely have to indicate their presence by pressing a button. Nielsen currently has people meters in 5,000 homes across the country. The devices provide ratings data for 7 broadcast networks, 50 cable networks, and hundreds of national syndicators. An additional 20,000 homes in 47 markets have set tuners, which tell Nielsen what network a set is tuned to but not who is watching.

Four times a year, Nielsen sends more than one million diaries to participating families, who record their viewing habits. It is the only way networks can get detailed demographic information about who sees their programs in different parts of the country, and the data are used to set local advertising rates. As a result, networks tend to clog those four "sweeps" months—February, May, July, and November—with high-profile programming. In 2000, Nielsen announced that, starting with Boston, it would begin installing people meters in large local markets to measure local viewing habits year around.[25]

Ultimately, digital television will do away with the need for people meters, as it contains the technology for audience measurement. Digital cable has already arrived, and Nielsen has entered into a contract with Time Warner (which has 13 million cable-wired homes) to jointly develop methods for analyzing the so-called clickstream data that will be generated by digital cable set-top boxes. In fact, many insiders believe that clickstream programming will ultimately replace channel television, since the set-top device is really a computer with an operating system that can serve up various content, be it a TV show or a Web site. Channels disappear in a digital TV environment.

Digital technology raises some fundamental issues about what constitutes viewing. If, for example, a viewer is watching a basketball game on one-third of the television screen, is doing personal finances with Quicken on another third, and has the Internet running on yet another third, how should viewing be rated? Nielsen has turned to its own clients for the answer. To help redefine "viewing"

PART 2:
Creating a Research Design

Real-Time Marketing Is on the Way

J. WALKER SMITH, VICE PRESIDENT OF MARKETING SPECTRUM IN Atlanta, Georgia, sees the marriage of various electronic programs and devices as leading to "real-time marketing." As the gap in time between marketplace activity and marketplace response shrinks and disappears, marketing will become a real-time activity, no longer constrained to wait for batches of data before actions can be taken. Improvements in marketing strategy and tactics will be initiated the instant any weaknesses or opportunities become apparent and, in this world, advantages will accrue to firms with superior and more secure communications networks and to those with better ways of instantly evaluating, verifying, testing, and acting on marketplace data.

This scenario is not as far-fetched as it may seem. Already on Wall Street, real-time marketing is being implemented under the guise of program trading (an observation owed to Doug Haley of Yankelovich Clancy Shulman). In industries more dependent on physical distribution and delivery systems (as opposed to the electronic transfers possible in the financial industry), developments like just-in-time inventory are overcoming the barriers to real-time marketing.

Blair Peters, group research manager of Kraft General Foods Marketing Information Department, sees the future this way:

It does not take much imagination to weave a future scenario in which businesses base most of their decisions on robots and self-calibrating models. Such models will be robust in that the information takes into account every aspect of human behavior (e.g., purchasing, media) and product movement through the company's distribution channel (from plant, to warehouse, to store take-away). The models will be self-calibrating because of expert systems powered by artificial intelligence. This futuristic scenario is both exciting and frightening. It is exciting in that it represents a world that every information professional has dreamed about. Most problems could be analyzed. However, the scenario is frightening in that many people will be left behind in the wake of these changes. Professionals will have to retool in terms of their mind-set and technical skills or become obsolete.[26] ■

in the digital age, Nielsen has initiated a PC/TV committee, including such visionaries as Microsoft media research czar Andy Fessel.[27]

Scanner-Based Research

Two electronic monitoring tools comprise the scanner-based research system: television meters and **laser scanners,** which "read" the UPC codes on products and produce instantaneous information on sales. Separately, each monitoring device provides marketers with current information on the advertising audience

laser scanners
Devices that read the UPC codes on products and produce instantaneous information on sales.

and on sales and inventories of products. Together, television meters and scanners measure the impact of marketing. Has scanner-based research been of much benefit to marketers? The top executive of one manufacturer estimates that one-third to one-half of its gains in profitability in the past several years can be attributed to scanner-based research.[28]

The marriage of scanners, database management, telecommunications, artificial intelligence, and computing gives hope for a "brave new world" of marketing. Scenarios for this possible new world are presented in the In Practice feature, first by a marketing researcher and then by a major user of scanner-based data.

The two major scanner-based research suppliers are Information Resources, Incorporated (IRI) and ACNielsen; each has about half the market. So that you can gain an appreciation of scanner-based research, we will discuss the product offerings of IRI in detail.[29]

BehaviorScan   IRI is the founder of scanner-based research and the developer of **BehaviorScan**, which has a household panel in each of six markets. The BehaviorScan markets are geographically dispersed cities: Pittsfield, Massachusetts; Eau Claire, Wisconsin; Cedar Rapids, Iowa; Grand Junction, Colorado; Midland, Texas; and Visalia, California (see Figure 7.2). Panel members shop with an ID card, which is presented at checkouts in supermarkets, drugstores, and mass merchandisers. This card allows IRI to electronically track each household's purchases, item by item, over time. With such a measure of household purchasing, it is possi-

BehaviorScan

A scanner-based research system that can manipulate the marketing mix for household panels in geographically dispersed markets and then electronically track consumer purchases.

Figure 7.2

BehaviorScan Market Map

Source: www.infores.com/
public/prodserv/images/
bsmktmap.gif

BehaviorScan Market Map

PART 2:
Creating a Research Design

ble to analyze real changes in consumer buying behavior associated with manipulating marketing variables (such as TV advertising or consumer promotions) or introducing a new product.

For strategic tests of alternative marketing plans, the BehaviorScan household panels are split into two or more subgroups, balanced on past purchasing, demographics, and stores shopped. A test commercial can be broadcast over the cable network to one group of households, while the other group gets a control ad, without the consumer even realizing that the commercial is only a test ad. This feature makes BehaviorScan the most effective means of evaluating changes in advertising. In each market, IRI maintains permanent warehouse facilities and staff to control distribution, price, and promotions. Competitive activity is monitored, and a record of pricing, displays, and features permits an assessment of the responsiveness to a brand promotion.

For testing consumer promotions such as coupons, product samples, and refund offers, balanced panel subsamples are again created within each market. Then, through direct mail or split newspaper-route targeting, a different treatment is delivered to each group. Both sales and profits are analyzed.

In-store variables may also be tested. Within the markets, split groups of stores are used to read the effect on sales of a change in packaging, shelf placement, or pricing. Tests are analyzed primarily on a store movement basis, but purchasing by panel shoppers in the test and control stores can also be analyzed. With the BehaviorScan system, it is possible to evaluate alternative advertising levels while simultaneously varying in-store prices or consumer promotions, thereby testing a completely integrated marketing plan.

In summary, BehaviorScan allows marketing managers to answer critical marketing questions such as the following:

- What is the impact of our new advertising program?
- How can we minimize incremental media costs?
- What happens to sales if we change the ad frequency or day part?
- How many units of our new product will we sell in a year?
- How many units will be cannibalized from existing products by the new product?
- What is the effectiveness of each marketing mix element in driving trial and repeat purchasing?
- What is the impact of an alternative marketing program on results?

InfoScan **InfoScan tracking service** is an all-store, census scanner data system, which collects data weekly from more than 31,000 supermarkets, drugstores, and mass merchandisers. Coverage is now being expanded to include convenience stores and liquor stores. Through the use of IRI identification cards and television viewing monitors, IRI maintains the largest multi-outlet consumer panel in America, with 55,000 households (see Figure 7.3).

The continual collection of huge amounts of scanner panel data has created a mammoth secondary database. The database can be used to examine the impact of each element of the marketing mix on sales. It can also be used to discern consumer consumption trends. For example, Joe Durrett, chairman and CEO of IRI, discussed seven recent consumer trends that have created significant growth opportunities for astute consumer package goods marketers.

InfoScan tracking service
A scanner-based data system that collects information on consumer packaged goods.

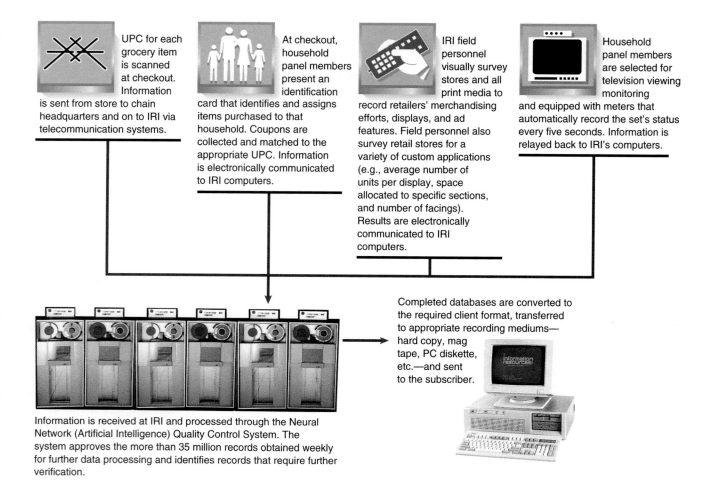

UPC for each grocery item is scanned at checkout. Information is sent from store to chain headquarters and on to IRI via telecommunication systems.

At checkout, household panel members present an identification card that identifies and assigns items purchased to that household. Coupons are collected and matched to the appropriate UPC. Information is electronically communicated to IRI computers.

IRI field personnel visually survey stores and all print media to record retailers' merchandising efforts, displays, and ad features. Field personnel also survey retail stores for a variety of custom applications (e.g., average number of units per display, space allocated to specific sections, and number of facings). Results are electronically communicated to IRI computers.

Household panel members are selected for television viewing monitoring and equipped with meters that automatically record the set's status every five seconds. Information is relayed back to IRI's computers.

Completed databases are converted to the required client format, transferred to appropriate recording mediums—hard copy, mag tape, PC diskette, etc.—and sent to the subscriber.

Information is received at IRI and processed through the Neural Network (Artificial Intelligence) Quality Control System. The system approves the more than 35 million records obtained weekly for further data processing and identifies records that require further verification.

Figure 7.3

How InfoScan Works

1. *Convenience and portability.* Products such as bottled water, moist towelettes, and lunch kits have seen average sales increases of 98 percent since 1994.
2. *Ready-to-eat consumption.* There has been over $4 billion of growth in categories such as frozen pizza and appetizers, refrigerated dinners, and fresh salad kits in the past five years.
3. *Natural/organic foods.* An ever-growing number of products bear nutritional claims; natural/organic products accounted for $10 billion in 2000.
4. *Functional foods.* Sales of high-protein meals, energy bars, and herbal-enhanced products have grown in excess of 75 percent since 1994.
5. *Health and self-care.* Nine categories, including hair growth and hair coloring products, nutritional supplements, antacids, and anti-smoking products, grew from $3.5 billion in 1994 to over $7 billion in 2000.
6. *Extra care and indulgence rewards.* Sales of premium ice creams and premium-priced toothbrushes are growing rapidly; aromatherapy helped boost candle sales to over $833 million in 2000.

PART 2:
Creating a Research Design

7. *Female influence.* With 60 percent of adult females working outside the home, sales of many beauty categories are up over 55 percent; conversely, hosiery sales have declined in today's casual workplace.

The InfoScan tracking service includes total outlet information, used to benchmark a retailer's performance against that of other retailers in the same trading area. Figure 7.4 compares a Chicago supermarket retailer's cookie category performance to total supermarket sales in the Chicago market. The retailer's share of the total Chicago market indicates that the account is not getting its fair share of sales for the cookie category or for Brand A. This topline analysis suggests that problems could stem from a number of factors, including low category item assortment (index of 89), a higher price for Brand A (index of 125), and fewer weeks of promotional support (indices of 90 and 72).

InfoScan Reviews is a syndicated data service that offers retail scanner-based information for manufacturers, retailers, and brokers. The Reviews provides aggregate data on 266 InfoScan consumer package goods product categories. The data can help a researcher monitor trends across categories, products, and competitive factors, as well as analyze historical sales and promotion trends and identify market opportunities.

Shoppers' Hotline The Shoppers' Hotline multi-outlet panel comprises 55,000 households. Using IRI's proprietary ScanKey in-home scanner, each member household records its purchase information on an ongoing basis. By combining this information with demographic data on each panel household, **Shoppers' Hotline** monitors consumer purchase behavior, answering such questions as who buys what, when, and why. Shoppers' Hotline panel households are also available for attitudinal surveys. Combining survey and panel data adds even more depth to clients' understanding of consumers.

One of the seven recent consumer trends that have created significant growth opportunities for consumer package goods marketers is the trend toward convenience and portability. Bottled water sales have increased 98% since 1994.

Shoppers' Hotline
A scanner-based research system that comprises 55,000 households, which use an in-home scanner to record purchase information on an ongoing basis.

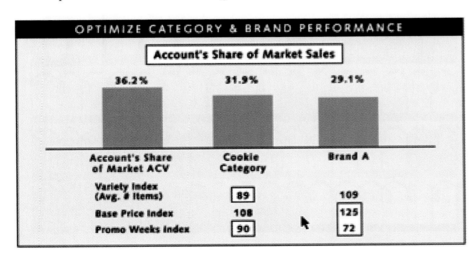

Managers want decision-making information, not data. The key to IRI's success is not the millions of new scanner records it obtains each week, but rather the useful information it derives from those records through powerful software. For example, IRI's Apollo Space Management software helps answer one of the most fundamental questions faced by manufacturers and retailers: What is the optimal use of retail shelf space (the most valuable asset in any store)? Apollo analyzes scanner data from the InfoScan database to review the amount of shelf space, price, and profit components of product category shelf sets such as dishwashing soaps or cereals. It then provides actionable suggestions for optimizing shelf allocations for each item in the section. The new Apollo 7.0 provides merchandising realism with 3-D shelving views. The software produces color-coded planograms (see Figure 7.5) and custom reports.

The Future of Scanning   The next generation of scanners, to be known as Scanner Plus, will have abilities far beyond those of today's machines. These scanners will be able to communicate with personal computers in homes. One function might be to analyze an individual household's consumption based on its prior purchase patterns and offer menu or product use suggestions with an associated shopping list. To encourage the use of that shopping list, companies

Figure 7.5

Color-Coded Planograms Help Pinpoint Sales and Profit Opportunities with Optimal Shelf Plans

Source: Reprinted by permission of Information Resources, Inc. (IRI)

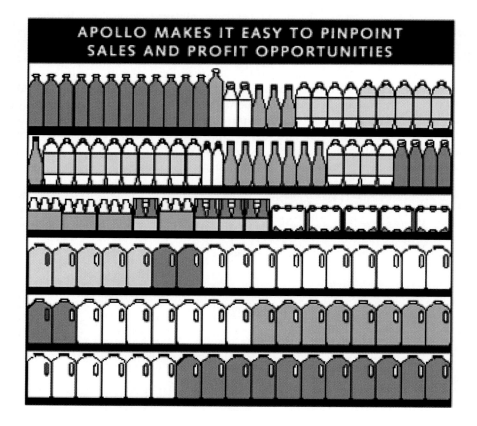

APOLLO MAKES IT EASY TO PINPOINT SALES AND PROFIT OPPORTUNITIES

PART 2:
Creating a Research Design

could make special offers on certain listed items. Rather than offering everyone the same promotion, they could design special offers for each household.

Scanner Plus also may keep track of each household's coupons and other special offers received directly from advertisers. These offers would be entered into the household's electronic account, both in the household's personal computer and in its Scanner Plus "promotion" bank.

An example of a similar system already in use is the Vision Value card offered by Big Bear Supermarkets in Ohio. It combines product scanning with the computerized equivalent of "green stamps," to provide consumers with coupons for products they actually use.

How will this new development affect marketing research? Advertisers will want to test the previously untestable—for example, how a product's acceptance is affected by a household's menu or what the optimum menu scenario is for a product's particular set of attributes. Advertisers will want to test promotional values as a function of menu mix and repeat consumption rather than use today's criterion of simply covering the cost of the promotion.[30]

Observation Research on the Internet

In Chapter 4, we discussed how the ability to track online surfers had enabled Double Click and other organizations to build huge databases on Internet surfing and online shopping behavior. Although privacy concerns are being raised by both consumer advocacy groups and members of Congress, new Internet tracking companies are being created on a regular basis. One such company is Boston-based Predictive Networks, Incorporated.

Predictive Networks

Predictive Networks has developed software that can track every site a Web surfer visits and build a "digital silhouette," or profile, of him or her based on those movements. If someone were to visit an online sailing site, say, then a travel site and a scuba site, Predictive's profile model might immediately send that person sunscreen or snorkel ads in pop-up windows. The company also plans to target news content to a user's profile.

Predictive believes that Web users will be willing to let the company track their every move online in exchange for a cheaper rate from their Internet service provider. Today, IDT Corporation of Hackensack, New Jersey, uses Predictive's software for its free Internet service called freeatlast.com.

Predictive will share ad revenue with IDT and other Internet service providers it signs up in the future. Advertisers, who will place their ads through Predictive, are so eager for this sort of precision targeting that some have already agreed to pay ad rates as much as six times higher than usual.[31]

Virgin Entertainment

Similar to Predictive, Virgin Entertainment gives free Internet appliances to customers willing to be tracked online. These Web devices, which cost Virgin about

$500 each, allow users to surf the Net and send email, but cannot be used for computing functions such as word processing and spreadsheets.

To get the devices, customers must log on to a Web site—http://www.virginconnectme.com—and fill out a questionnaire designed to determine their fit with the so-called Virgin lifestyle. Questions cover shopping preferences; music and entertainment interests; where and how customers generally get online; and how they spend their time once they get on the Web. Answers are rated and scored, then evaluated. If the person is accepted, he or she must spend at least 10 hours per month surfing the Internet or return the machine.

Vividence Corporation

Yet a third type of online observation research coupled with an incentive is offered by Vividence Corporation. Vividence recruits Web surfers to fill out a profile sheet which includes demographic and lifestyle information. The data are then stored in the Vividence database.

One service Vividence offers to companies is evaluation of the quality of their beta Web sites or existing Web sites. Vividence uses its database to select site testers whose profiles match those of the firm's target customers. Vividence sends testers to a firm's Web site with a set of tasks to accomplish. As testers navigate through the firm's Web site, Vividence technology monitors and captures all of their actions. One form of output provided to the client by Vividence comes from ClickStreams, a visual depiction tool that maps out both aggregate and individual tester navigation through a Web site. ClickStreams pinpoints the primary sources of both user confusion and user success on a Web site, allowing clients to understand which paths contribute most to tester success, which paths contribute most to tester confusion, and where on a site testers get lost or stuck. Testers are paid a minimum of $15 per site visit and are entered into a monthly drawing for a $3,000 prize.[32]

Digimarc Corporation

In 2000, magazines such as *Forbes, Wired,* and *GQ* began planting codes in advertisements that, when scanned with a hand-held device, whisk a reader directly to specifically tailored Web sites. These sites might offer for sale the products being advertised or just provide a fast way to get more information. The new Web technology "gives an absolute measure of reader response," because companies can count the number of online hits generated by each print ad, says Dan Brewster, chief executive of American Express Publishing Corporation.[33]

Digimarc Corporation offers this new technology to advertisers. Eventually, the same kind of codes could appear on the side of packaged goods or be embedded in magazine articles, helping people get additional information on a purchase or a topic of interest. The disadvantage of this technology is that a reader must either go to a computer or already be sitting at one to scan the code. A key question is "If a person doesn't opt to visit a Web site after seeing an ad, does this mean that the ad is not effective?" The answer, of course, is "not necessarily."

Summary

Observation research is the systematic process of recording patterns of occurrences or behaviors without questioning or normally communicating with the people involved. For observation to be used successfully, the needed information must be observable and the behavior of interest must be repetitive, frequent, or in some manner predictable. The behavior of interest also should be of a relatively short duration. There are five dimensions along which observation approaches vary: (1) natural versus contrived situations, (2) open versus disguised observation, (3) structured versus unstructured observation, (4) human versus machine observers, and (5) direct versus indirect observation.

The biggest advantage of observation research is that researchers can see what people actually do rather than having to rely on what they say they did, thereby avoiding many biasing factors. Also, some forms of data are more quickly and accurately gathered by observation. The primary disadvantage of this type of research is that the researcher learns nothing about motives, attitudes, intentions, or feelings.

People watching people or objects can take the form of ethnographic research, mystery shopping, one-way mirror observations (for example, child psychologists might watch children play with toys), shopper pattern and behavior studies, and audits.

Machine observation may involve traffic counters, physiological measurement devices, opinion and behavior measurement devices, or scanners. The use of scanners in carefully controlled experimental settings enables the marketing researcher to accurately and objectively measure the direct causal relationship between different kinds of marketing efforts and actual sales. The leaders in scanner-based research are Information Resources, Incorporated and ACNielsen.

In the future, scanners will be able to communicate with home computers. One function may be to offer menu and product use suggestions.

Observation research on the Internet consists largely of tracking the surfing patterns of Internet users. Internet users may receive cash and prizes in return for consenting to be tracked.

Key Terms & Definitions

observation research The systematic process of recording patterns of occurrences or behaviors without normally communicating with the people involved.

open observation The process of monitoring people who know they are being watched.

disguised observation The process of monitoring people who do not know they are being watched.

structured observation A study in which the observer fills out a questionnaire-like form on each person or event observed or counts the number of times a behavior or activity occurs.

unstructured observation A study in which the observer simply makes notes on the behavior or activity being observed.

garbologists Researchers who sort through people's garbage to analyze household consumption patterns.

ethnographic research The study of human behavior in its natural context, involving observation of behavior and physical setting coupled with depth interviews to obtain participants' perspectives.

mystery shoppers People who pose as consumers and shop at a company's own stores or those of its competitors to collect data about customer–employee interactions and to gather observational data; they may also compare prices, displays, and the like.

one-way mirror observation The practice of watching behaviors or activities from behind a one-way mirror.

shopper pattern studies Drawings that record the footsteps of a shopper through a store's aisles.

shopper behavior research Observation of consumers, either in person or on videotape, in a variety of shopping settings.

audit The examination and verification of the sales of a product.

traffic counters Machines used to measure vehicular flow over a particular stretch of roadway.

electroencephalograph (EEG) A machine that measures electrical pulses on the scalp and generates a record of electrical activity in the brain.

galvanic skin response (GSR) A change in the electric resistance of the skin associated with activation responses; also called *electrodermal response*.

pupilometer A machine that measures changes in pupil dilation.

voice pitch analysis Studying changes in the relative vibration frequency of the human voice to measure emotion.

MOBILTRAK A device that picks up radio signals to determine which FM radio stations people are listening to in their cars.

People Reader A machine that simultaneously records the respondent's reading material and eye reactions.

Rapid Analysis Measurement System (RAMS) A hand-held device that allows respondents to record how they are feeling by turning a dial.

people meters Components of a microwave computerized rating system, used to measure national TV audiences, that transmits demographic information overnight.

laser scanners Devices that read the UPC codes on products and produce instantaneous information on sales.

BehaviorScan A scanner-based research system that can manipulate the marketing mix for household panels in geographically dispersed markets and then electronically track consumer purchases.

InfoScan tracking service A scanner-based data system that collects information on consumer packaged goods.

Shoppers' Hotline A scanner-based research system that comprises 55,000 households, which use an in-home scanner to record purchase information on an ongoing basis.

PART 2:
Creating a Research Design

Questions for Review & Critical Thinking

1. You are charged with the responsibility of determining whether men are brand-conscious when shopping for racquetball equipment. Outline an observation research procedure for making that determination.
2. Fisher-Price has asked you to develop a research procedure for determining which of its prototype toys is most appealing to four- and five-year-olds. Suggest a methodology for making this determination.
3. What are the biggest drawbacks of observation research?
4. Compare the advantages and disadvantages of observation research with those of survey research.
5. It has been said that "people buy things not for what they will do, but for what they mean." Discuss this statement in relation to observation research.
6. You are a manufacturer of a premium brand of ice cream. You want to know more about your market share, competitors' pricing, and the types of outlets where your product is selling best. What kind of observation research data would you purchase? Why?
7. How might a mystery shopper be valuable to the following organizations?
   a. Delta Airlines
   b. Marshall Field's
   c. H&R Block
8. Use ethnographic research to evaluate the dining experience at your student center. What did you learn?
9. Why has scanner-based research been seen as "the ultimate answer" for marketing researchers? Do you see any disadvantages of this methodology?

Working on the Net

1. Go to http://acnielsen.com and http://www.infores.com and determine what ACNielsen and IRI are saying on the Web about their latest scanner-based research technology.

Real-Life Research • 7.1

Procter & Gamble's Bibsters

Procter & Gamble has been developing and testing disposable baby bibs called "Bibsters." Since some focus group attendees can't articulate their feelings about a product and often are reluctant to talk about how they use it (especially if it involves their child), P&G decided to observe how consumers would use this product in daily life.

By watching people from the moment of purchase to when they threw Bibsters into the trash, P&G learned that there was no such thing as the average consumer, says Jan-Patrick Kuehlwein, manager of global strategic planning. For instance, busy working mothers were quick to embrace Bibsters. Since these women valued the time they spent with their child, they didn't want to waste time on lower-value activities such as clean-up. "It was a no-brainer [for them] to go to a disposable bib," Kuehlwein says. Although the convenience of Bibsters appealed to stay-at-home moms, they couldn't justify the higher cost, he adds.

On a less emotional level, P&G found that cloth bibs were often scattered all over the house—and usually ended up in places where they weren't needed, such as an upstairs bedroom. "People had about a 20-minute window to feed their child, and they either had to roam around to find a bib or wash one because they were all dirty," Kuehlwein notes. The company has yet to roll out Bibsters (Kuehlwein would not say when the product might hit the shelves), but some of the insights gleaned from the study have already been applied to P&G's marketing of disposable diapers.

Questions

1. Do you consider P&G's research to be ethnographic research? Why or why not?
2. Bibsters are to be a global product. Does P&G need to conduct observation research in other countries, or is the huge U.S. market sufficient? Why?
3. Should quantitative research also be undertaken for Bibsters? Why?
4. What are some of the reasons that the product might not already be on the market?

Real-Life Research • 7.2

Sara Lee

Anita Scott has just been promoted to brand manager of frozen bakery products for Sara Lee. Her first new product introductions will be a line of frozen pastries. Currently, the company plans to introduce three flavors: chocolate, strawberry, and apricot. The pastries can be heated in a conventional oven or microwaved for quick preparation. Anita is considering using coupons in coordination with the introduction of the pastries. She has recently acquired some scanner data on coupon usage for new products. That information is presented in the following tables and figures.

Information on Coupon Usage on New Products

Issues	Values versus established brands Use of coupons on trial versus repeat purchase Coupon-related purchases versus other purchases
The Data Base	*Markets:* Evansville, IN Portland, ME
Time Period	39 weeks from introduction

Categories, Brands	*Ready-to-Eat Cereal* *Cookies*
	  Sun Flakes Soft Batch
	  S'Mores Duncan Hines
	  Fiber One Puddin Creme
	  OJ's Almost Home
	  Bran Muffin Crisp
	  Almond Delight *Cereal Meal Bars*
	            S'Mores Chewy
	Soluble Coffee Dandy Bran
	  Classic Rice Krispies
	  Silka Whipps
	  Brava
	  Decaf *Crackers*
	            Great Crisps
	            Stone Creek

Sample Size	3,912 households

Average Coupon Values

Coupons on new brands are slightly higher in absolute face value than coupons on established brands. The percentage discount spread is greater since the average dollar transaction on new products purchased with a coupon is lower.

Average Coupon Value

Established Brands		New Brands	
Value	% Redeemed	Value	% Redeemed
$.346	17.6%	$.380	22.0%

Average Retail Price

Established Brands	New Brands
$1.96	$1.73

The Effect of Face Value on Speed of Redemption

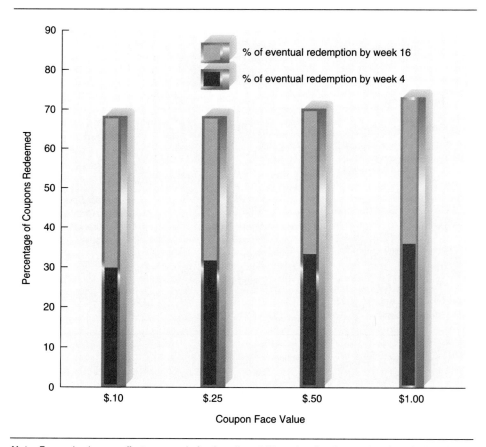

Note: Face value has no effect on speed of redemption at 16 weeks after the coupon drop. At 4 weeks after, higher value coupons have achieved only a slightly higher percentage of eventual redemption than have lower value coupons.

Percentage of Volume with Coupon Redemption

Category	All Brands	New Brands
Cereal	16.2%	24.8%
Soluble coffee	30.5	17.8
Cookies	6.7	17.6
Cereal meal bars	13.0	18.1
Crackers	7.1	14.8
Average	14.7%	18.6%

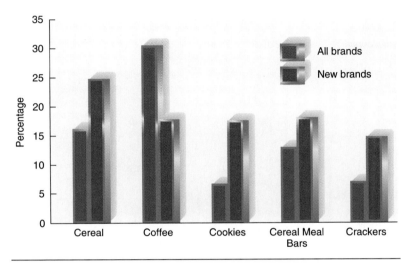

Note: For all new brands studied except soluble coffee, the percentage of volume with redemption for new brands substantially exceeded that for existing brands. The relative difference is greatest in the cookie category.

Index of Coupon Triers to Noncoupon Triers

Category	Volume	Purchase Occasions
Cereal	93%	91%
Soluble coffee	76	77
Cookies	83	82
Cereal meal bars	97	95
Crackers	84	88
Average	87*	87*

Note: The buyer attracted by a coupon did not purchase as much or as often as a buyer who tried without a coupon. This is particularly true for the coffee brands studied.

*The households that initially tried with a coupon purchased only 87 percent as much as the households that tried without a coupon. This is linked to the fact that triers with coupons purchased only on 87 percent as many occasions.

All Brands

	Ounces (000)	Percentage of Total Volume	Percentage of Trial or Repeat Volume
Total Volume	414.7	100.0%	
Trial volume	145.8	35.1	
with coupon	29.6	7.1	20.2
without coupon	116.2	28.0	79.8
Repeat volume	268.9	64.9	
with coupon	46.7	11.3	17.4
without coupon	222.2	53.6	82.6

Note: When all brands are combined, the coupon trial was 20 percent of the total trial and peaked in period 2. Coupon repeat equals 17 percent of total repeat volume and grew consistently as a percentage of total volume.

PART 2:
Creating a Research Design

Percentage of Buying Households Redeeming Coupons

Category	All Brands	New Brands
Cereal	73.2%	45.8%
Soluble coffee	57.4	37.1
Cookies	42.0	49.0
Cereal meal bars	41.8	38.8
Crackers	46.3	26.8
Average	52.1%	39.5%

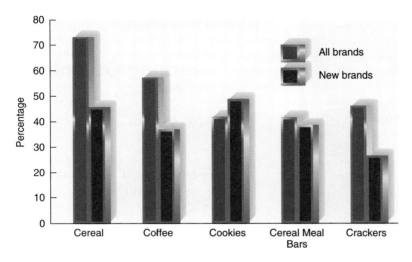

Note: For all categories but cookies, a higher percentage of households buying existing brands redeem coupons. This seeming discrepancy in cookies was probably caused by the coupon activity associated with the "Soft Cookie Wars."

Questions

1. After examining the scanner data, recommend a couponing strategy, including price, for the pastry line.
2. What additional data would be useful to Anita in planning her couponing strategy?
3. What are some limitations that Anita should be aware of in using the scanner data?

Chapter Eight

Primary Data Collection: Experimentation

Learning Objectives

To understand the nature of experiments.

To gain insight into requirements for proving causation.

To learn about the experimental setting.

To examine experimental validity.

To learn the limitations of experimentation in marketing research.

To compare types of experimental designs.

To gain insight into test marketing.

D VDS.COM SELLS AUDIO AND VIDEO CDS OVER THE INTERNET. IT OFFERS a comprehensive catalog of music and videos, which it sells at exceptionally low prices. The company has experienced phenomenal growth and, unlike many dot.com organizations, is already making a substantial profit as a percentage of sales. However, its marketing director, Suzy Chan, believes the firm's current graphic look is dated and should be replaced. Working with an advertising agency that specializes in graphic design for e-commerce Web sites, she developed a number of alternative designs. These designs were tested in a series of focus groups with consumers who said they purchase music and/or video CDs over the Internet. One design emerged as the clear winner; it was seen by the focus group participants as superior to the other design concepts and to the current design used by DVDs.com.

SHEMEKA THOMAS, CEO OF DVDS.COM, HAS just completed a review of Chan's written report on the redesign effort, including the recommendation that the company switch to the new design. Thomas is not convinced, as she is reluctant to move away from a formula that has been very successful. She wonders whether stated preferences for a Web site design by consumers in a focus group will translate into higher sales. Thomas had previously been marketing director for a packaged goods manufacturer. In that organization, new advertising and product concepts that passed testing in focus groups and surveys were evaluated in test markets before being accepted for market introduction. She believes that the test market approach will provide more valid estimates of the effectiveness of the new graphic treatment than those provided by the focus groups. After checking possible methods of test marketing the design with the technical department, Thomas decides to use the following approach for testing the effectiveness of the new graphic design for the DVDs.com Web site:

DVDs are a growing part of the home video market. How might a researcher experiment to find out what percentage of DVDs are bought online?

- For a period of one month, visitors to the DVDs.com Web site will randomly see either the current design or the new design. An approximately equal number of people will be exposed to each design.

- Everything else—price, featured DVDs and CDs, etc.—will be kept the same under both graphic treatments.

- The following information will be recorded for each visitor: whether he/she purchases anything, total music purchases, total video purchases, total combined purchases, and whether or not the visitor has made purchases from DVDs.com in the preceding 30 days.

- At the end of the one-month period, aggregate results of the above measurements will be reported for those exposed to the old design and those exposed to the new design. Differences will be tested for statistical significance and evaluated for managerial significance. ■

Find out about a simulated test marketing system offered by ACNielsen at

http://acnielsen. com/services/ custom/p06.htm

CHAPTER 8:
Primary Data Collection: Experimentation

When you finish this chapter, you should be able to determine whether Thomas's concerns about focus group results and her preference for test marketing are well founded. In addition, you should be able to evaluate the alternative research plan she has proposed.

What Is an Experiment?

experiment
Research approach in which one variable is manipulated and the effect on another variable is observed.

Research based on experimentation is fundamentally different from research based on surveys or observation.[1] In the case of both survey and observation research, the researcher is, in essence, a passive assembler of data. The researcher asks people questions or observes what people or objects do. In experimental research, the situation is very different: The researcher becomes an active participant in the process.

In concept, an **experiment** is straightforward. The researcher changes or manipulates one thing (called an *experimental, treatment, independent,* or *explanatory variable*) to observe what effect the change has on something else (referred to as a *dependent variable*). In marketing experiments, the dependent variable is frequently some measure of sales, such as total sales, market share, or the like; experimental variables are typically marketing mix variables, such as price, amount or type of advertising, and changes in product features.

Demonstrating Causation

causal research
Research designed to determine whether a change in one variable likely caused an observed change in another.

Experimental research is often referred to as **causal** (not casual) **research** because it is the only type of research that has the potential to demonstrate that a change in one variable *causes* some predictable change in another variable. To demonstrate causation (that *A* likely caused *B*), one must be able to show three things:

1. Concomitant variation (correlation)
2. Appropriate time order of occurrence
3. Elimination of other possible causal factors

Please note that we are using the terms *causation* and *causality* in the scientific sense.[2] The scientific view of causation is quite different from the popular view, which implies that there is a single cause of an event. For example, when someone says in everyday conversation that *X* is the cause of some observed change in *Y*, he or she generally means that *X* is the only cause of the observed change in *Y*. But the scientific view holds that *X* is only one of a number of determining conditions that caused the observed change in *Y*.

PART 2:
Creating a Research Design

In addition, the everyday view of causality implies a completely deterministic relationship, while the scientific view implies a probabilistic relationship. The popular view is that if X is the cause of Y, then X must always lead to Y. The scientific view holds that X can be a cause of Y if the presence of X makes the occurrence of Y more probable, or likely.

Finally, the scientific view holds that one can never definitively prove that X is a cause of Y but only infer that a relationship exists. In other words, causal relationships are always inferred and never demonstrated conclusively beyond a shadow of a doubt. Three types of evidence—concomitant variation, appropriate time order of occurrence, and elimination of other possible causal factors—are used to infer causal relationships.

Concomitant Variation

To provide evidence that a change in A caused a particular change in B, one must first show that there is **concomitant variation,** or correlation, between A and B; in other words, A and B must vary together in some predictable fashion. This might be a *positive* or an *inverse* relationship. Two variables that might be related in a positive manner are advertising and sales. They would be positively related if sales increased by some predictable amount when advertising increased by a certain amount. Two variables that might be related in an inverse manner are price and sales. They would be inversely (negatively) related if sales increased when price decreased and decreased when price increased. The researcher can test for the existence and direction of statistical relationships by means of a number of statistical procedures, including chi-square analysis, correlation analysis, regression analysis, and analysis of variance. All of these statistical procedures are discussed later in the text (chi-square in Chapter 15, correlation analysis and regression analysis in Chapter 16, and analysis of variance in Chapter 17).

However, concomitant variation by itself does not prove causation. Simply because two variables happen to vary together in some predictable fashion does not prove that one causes the other. For example, suppose you found a high degree of correlation between sales of a product in the United States and the GDP (gross domestic product) of Germany. This might be true simply because both variables happened to be increasing at a similar rate. Further examination and consideration might show that there was no true link between the two variables. To infer causation, you must be able to show correlation—but correlation alone is not proof of causation.

concomitant variation
A predictable statistical relationship between two variables.

Appropriate Time Order of Occurrence

The second requirement for demonstrating that a causal relationship likely exists between two variables is showing that there is an **appropriate time order of occurrence.** To demonstrate that A caused B, one must be able to show that A occurred before B occurred. For example, to demonstrate that a price change had an effect on sales, you must be able to show that the price change occurred before the change in sales was observed. However, showing that A and B vary concomitantly and that A occurred before B still does not provide evidence strong enough to permit one to conclude that A is the likely cause of an observed change in B.

appropriate time order of occurrence
The occurrence of a change in an independent variable before an observed change in the dependent variable.

Elimination of Other Possible Causal Factors

The most difficult thing to demonstrate in many marketing experiments is that the change in *B* was not caused by some factor other than *A*. For example, suppose a company increased its advertising expenditures and observed an increase in the sales of its product. Correlation and appropriate time order of occurrence are present. But has a likely causal relationship been demonstrated? The answer is "no." It is possible that the observed change in sales is due to some factor other than the increase in advertising. For example, at the same time advertising expenditures were increased, a major competitor may have decreased advertising expenditures, or increased price, or pulled out of the market. Even if the competitive environment did not change, one or a combination of other factors may have influenced sales. For example, the economy in the area might have received a major boost for some reason that has nothing to do with the experiment. For any of these reasons or others, the observed increase in sales might have been caused by some factor or combination of factors other than or in addition to the increase in advertising expenditures. Much of the discussion in this chapter is related to designing experiments so as to eliminate or adjust for the effects of other possible causal factors.

The Experimental Setting

Experiments can be conducted in a laboratory or a field setting.[3] Most experiments in the physical sciences are conducted in a laboratory setting; many marketing experiments are field experiments.

Laboratory Experiments

laboratory experiments
Experiments conducted in a controlled setting.

Laboratory experiments provide a number of important advantages.[4] The major advantage of conducting experiments in a laboratory is the ability to control many extraneous causal factors—temperature, light, humidity, and so on—and focus on the effect of a change in *A* on *B*. In the lab, the researcher can effectively deal with the third element of proving causation (elimination of other possible causal factors) and focus on the first two elements (concomitant variation and appropriate time order of occurrence). This additional control strengthens the researcher's ability to infer that an observed change in the dependent variable was caused by a change in the experimental, or treatment, variable. As a result, laboratory experiments generally are viewed as having greater internal validity (discussed in greater detail in the next section). On the other hand, the controlled and possibly sterile environment of the laboratory may not be a good analog of the marketplace. For this reason, the findings of laboratory experiments sometimes do not hold up when transferred to the actual marketplace. Therefore, laboratory experiments are often seen as having greater problems with external validity (see the next section). However, laboratory experiments are probably being used to a greater extent today than in the past, because of their many advantages.

Field Experiments

Field experiments are conducted outside the laboratory in an actual market environment. Test markets, discussed later in this chapter, are a frequently used type of field experiment. Field experiments solve the problem of the realism of the environment but open up a whole new set of problems. The major problem is that in the field the researcher cannot control all the spurious factors that might influence the dependent variable, such as the actions of competitors, the weather, the economy, societal trends, and the political climate. Therefore, field experiments have more problems related to internal validity, whereas lab experiments have more problems related to external validity.

field experiments
Tests conducted outside the laboratory in an actual environment, such as a market.

Experimental Validity

Validity is defined as the degree to which an experiment actually measures what the researcher was trying to measure (see Chapter 9). The validity of a measure depends on the extent to which the measure is free from both systematic and random error. Two specific kinds of validity are relevant to experimentation: internal validity and external validity.

Internal validity refers to the extent to which competing explanations for the experimental results observed can be ruled out. If the researcher can show that the experimental, or treatment, variable actually produced the differences observed in the dependent variable, then the experiment can be said to be internally valid. This kind of validity requires evidence demonstrating that variation in the dependent variable was caused by exposure to the treatment variable and not other possible causal factors.

internal validity
The extent to which competing explanations for the experimental results observed can be ruled out.

External validity refers to the extent to which the causal relationships measured in an experiment can be generalized to outside persons, settings, and times.[5] The issue here is how representative the subjects and the setting used in the experiment are of other populations and settings to which the researcher would like to project the results. As noted earlier, field experiments offer a higher degree of external validity and a lower degree of internal validity than do laboratory experiments.

external validity
The extent to which causal relationships measured in an experiment can be generalized to outside persons, settings, and times.

Experimental Notation

In our discussion of experiments, we will use a standard system of notation, described below:

- X is used to indicate the exposure of an individual or a group to an experimental treatment. The experimental treatment is the factor whose effects we want to measure and compare. Experimental treatments may be factors such as different prices, package designs, point-of-purchase displays, advertising approaches, or product forms.

The Difference between Internal and External Validity

THE PROBLEM OF INTERNAL VERSUS EXTERNAL VALIDITY WAS RECENTLY addressed in a research project on the effectiveness of racially exclusive real estate advertising. A field experiment found that using African Americans in real estate advertisements produced a positive effect for African-American readers in terms of liking the models pictured in the photographs, and African-American respondents could identify with the models pictured in the photographs.

In discussing the results, the researchers said that they would have liked to have conducted a laboratory experiment. However, they were more concerned about issues of external validity because of recent court decisions and opted to conduct a study that would more closely reflect what happens when actual housing prospects view real estate advertising. Therefore, they employed a field experiment approach using a mail survey, rather than the artificial laboratory situation.[6] ∎

- O (for observation) is used to refer to the process of taking measurements on the test units. *Test units* are individuals, groups of individuals, or entities whose response to the experimental treatments is being tested. Test units might include individual consumers, groups of consumers, retail stores, total markets, or other entities that might be the targets of a firm's marketing program.
- Different time periods are represented by the horizontal arrangement of the Xs and Os. For example,

$$O_1 \qquad X \qquad O_2$$

would describe an experiment in which a preliminary measurement O_1 was taken of one or more test units, then one or more test units were exposed to the experimental variable X, and then a measurement O_2 of the test units was taken. The Xs and Os can be arranged vertically to show simultaneous exposure and measurement of different test units. For example, the following design involves two different groups of test units:

$$\begin{array}{cc} X_1 & O_1 \\ X_2 & O_2 \end{array}$$

The two groups of test units received different experimental treatments at the same time (X_1 and X_2), and then the two groups were measured simultaneously (O_1 and O_2).[7]

Extraneous Variables

In interpreting experimental results, the researcher would like to be able to conclude that the observed response is due to the effect of the experimental variable. However, many things stand in the way of the ability to reach this conclusion. In anticipation of possible problems in interpretation, the researcher needs to design the experiment so as to eliminate as many extraneous factors as possible as causes of the observed effect.

Examples of Extraneous Variables

Examples of extraneous factors or variables that pose a threat to experimental validity are history, maturation, instrument variation, selection bias, mortality, testing effects, and regression to the mean.[8]

History **History** refers to the intervention, between the beginning and end of the experiment, of any variable or event—other than those manipulated by the researcher (experimental variables)—that might affect the value of the dependent variable. Early tests of Prego Spaghetti Sauce by the Campbell Soup Company provide an example of a possible problem with extraneous variables. Campbell executives claim that Ragu greatly increased its advertising levels and use of cents-off deals during their tests. They believe that this increased marketing activity was designed to get shoppers to stock up on Ragu and make it impossible for Campbell to get an accurate reading of potential sales for its Prego product.

Maturation **Maturation** refers to changes in subjects throughout the course of the experiment that are a function of time; it includes getting older, hungrier, more tired, and the like. Throughout the course of an experiment, the responses of people to a treatment variable may change because of these maturation factors and not because of the treatment variable. The likelihood that maturation will be a serious problem in a particular experiment depends on the length of the experiment. The longer the experiment runs, the more likely it is that maturation will present problems for interpreting the results.

Instrument Variation **Instrument variation** refers to any changes in measurement instruments that might explain differences in the measurements taken. It is a serious problem in marketing experiments where people are used as interviewers or observers to measure the dependent variable. If measurements on the same subject are taken by different interviewers or observers at different points in time, differences between measurements may reflect variations in the way the interviewing or observation was done by different interviewers or observers. On the other hand, if the same interviewer or observer is used to take measurements

Harry Heller, CEO of Harry Heller Research, relates an experience he had some time ago while testing commercials in the Los Angeles area. It seems that just as the test commercial was being shown in the theater, a minor but quite palpable earthquake rolled across the city. When Harry inquired about a retest, the representative of the research company replied, "That won't be necessary. We'll just compare the results to our earthquake norms."

Source: "War Stories: True Life Tales In Marketing Research," by Art Shulman, *Quirk's Marketing Research Review* (December 1994). Reprinted by permission of Art Shulman.

history
The intervention, between the beginning and end of an experiment, of outside variables or events that might change the dependent variable.

maturation
Changes in subjects occurring during the experiment that are not related to the experiment but may affect subjects' response to the treatment factor.

instrument variation
Changes in measurement instruments (e.g., interviews or observers) that might explain differences in measurements.

on the same subject over time, differences may reflect the fact that the particular observer or interviewer has become less interested and is doing a sloppier job.

selection bias
Systematic differences between the test group and the control group due to a biased selection process.

Selection Bias   The threat to validity posed by **selection bias** is encountered in situations where the experimental or test group is systematically different from the population to which the researcher would like to project the experimental results or from the control group. In projecting the results to a population that is systematically different from the test group, the researcher may get results very different from those we got in the test because of differences in the makeup of the two groups. Similarly, an observed difference between a test group and an untreated control group (not exposed to the experimental variable) may be due to differences between the two groups and not to the effect of the experimental variable. Researchers can ensure equality of groups through either randomization or matching. *Randomization* involves assigning subjects to test groups and control groups at random. *Matching* involves what the name suggests—making sure that there is a one-to-one match between people or other units in the test and control groups in regard to key characteristics (e.g., age). Specific matching procedures are discussed later in this chapter.

mortality
Loss of test units or subjects during the course of an experiment, which may result in a nonrepresentative experimental group.

Mortality   **Mortality** refers to the loss of test units during the course of an experiment. It is a problem because there is no easy way to know whether the lost units would have responded to the treatment variable in the same way as those units that remained throughout the entire experiment. An experimental group that was representative of the population or that matched a control group may become nonrepresentative because of the systematic loss of subjects with certain characteristics. For example, in a study of music preferences of the population, if nearly all the subjects under the age of 25 were lost during the course of the experiment, then the researcher would likely get a biased picture of music preferences at the end of the experiment. In this case, the results probably would lack external validity.

testing effect
An effect that is a byproduct of the research process itself.

Testing Effects   **Testing effects** result from the fact that the process of experimentation may produce its own effect on the responses observed. For example, measuring attitude toward a product before exposing subjects to an ad may act as a treatment variable, influencing perception of the ad. Testing effects come in two forms:

- *Main testing effects* are the possible effects of earlier observations on later observations. For example, students taking the GMAT for the second time tend to do better than those taking the test for the first time, even though the students have no information about the items they actually missed on the first test. This effect also can be reactive in the sense that responses to the first administration of an attitude test have some actual effect on subjects' attitudes that is reflected in subsequent applications of the same test.
- *Interactive testing effect* is the effect of a prior measurement on a subject's response to a later measurement. For example, if subjects are asked about their awareness of advertising for various products (pre-exposure measurement) and then exposed to advertising for one or more of these products

PART 2:
Creating a Research Design

(treatment variable), postmeasurements would likely reflect the joint effect of the pre-exposure and the treatment condition.

Regression to the Mean   **Regression to the mean** refers to the observed tendency of subjects with extreme behavior to move toward the average for that behavior during the course of an experiment. Test units may exhibit extreme behavior because of chance, or they may have been specifically chosen because of their extreme behavior. The researcher might, for example, have chosen people for an experimental group because they were extremely heavy users of a particular product or service. In such situations, their tendency to move toward the average behavior may be interpreted as having been caused by the treatment variable when in fact it has nothing to do with the treatment variable.

regression to the mean
Tendency of subjects with extreme behavior to move toward the average for that behavior during the course of an experiment.

Controlling Extraneous Variables

Causal factors that threaten validity must be controlled in some manner to establish a clear picture of the effect of the manipulated variable on the dependent variable. Extraneous causal factors are ordinarily referred to as *confounding variables* because they confound the treatment condition, making it impossible to determine whether changes in the dependent variable are due solely to the treatment conditions.

Four basic approaches are used to control extraneous factors: randomization, physical control, design control, and statistical control.

Randomization is carried out by randomly assigning subjects to treatment conditions so that extraneous causal factors related to subject characteristics can reasonably be assumed to be represented equally in each treatment condition, thus canceling out extraneous effects.

Physical control of extraneous causal factors may involve somehow holding constant the value or level of the extraneous variable throughout the experiment. Another approach to physical control is matching respondents in regard to important personal characteristics (e.g., age, income, lifestyle) before assigning them to different treatment conditions. The goal is to make sure there are no important differences between characteristics of respondents in the test and control groups.

Design control is the control of extraneous factors by means of specific types of experimental designs developed for this purpose. Such designs are discussed later in this chapter.

Finally, **statistical control** can be used to account for extraneous causal factors if these factors can be identified and measured throughout the course of the experiment. Procedures such as analysis of covariance can adjust for the effects of a confounded variable on the dependent variable by statistically adjusting the value of the dependent variable for each treatment condition.

randomization
The random assignment of subjects to treatment conditions to ensure equal representation of subject characteristics.

physical control
Holding constant the value or level of extraneous variables throughout the course of an experiment.

design control
Use of the experimental design to control extraneous causal factors.

statistical control
Adjusting for the effects of confounded variables by statistically adjusting the value of the dependent variable for each treatment condition.

Experimental Design, Treatment, and Effects

In an **experimental design,** the researcher has control over and manipulates one or more independent variables. In the experiments we discuss, typically only one

experimental design
A test in which the researcher has control over and manipulates one or more independent variables.

independent variable is manipulated. Nonexperimental designs, which involve no manipulation, are often referred to as *ex post facto* (after the fact) *research*—an effect is observed, and then some attempt is made to attribute this effect to some causal factor.

An experimental design includes four factors:

1. The *treatment,* or experimental, *variable* (independent variable) that is manipulated
2. The *subjects* who participate in the experiment
3. A *dependent variable* that is measured
4. Some *plan or procedure* for dealing with extraneous causal factors

treatment variable
The independent variable that is manipulated in an experiment.

The **treatment variable** is the independent variable that is manipulated. *Manipulation* refers to a process in which the researcher sets the levels of the independent variable to test a particular causal relationship. To test the relationship between price (independent variable) and sales of a product (dependent variable), a researcher might expose subjects to three different levels of price and record the level of purchases at each price level. As the variable that is manipulated, price is the single treatment variable, with three treatment conditions or levels.

An experiment may include a test, or treatment, group and a control group. A *control group* is a group in which the independent variable is not changed during the course of the experiment. A *test group* is a group that is exposed to manipulation (change) of the independent variable.

experimental effect
The effect of the treatment variable on the dependent variable.

The term **experimental effect** refers to the effect of the treatment variable on the dependent variable. The goal is to determine the effect of each treatment condition (level of treatment variable) on the dependent variable. For example, suppose that three different markets are selected to test three different prices, or treatment conditions. Each price is tested in each market for three months. In market 1, a price 2 percent lower than existing prices for the product is tested; in market 2, a price 4 percent lower is tested; and in market 3, a price 6 percent lower is tested. At the end of the three-month test, sales in market 1 are observed to have increased by less than 1 percent over sales for the preceding three-month period. In market 2, sales increased by 3 percent; and in market 3, sales increased by 5 percent. The change in sales observed in each market is the experimental effect.

The Limitations of Experimental Research

As the preceding discussion shows, experiments are an extremely powerful form of research—the only type of research that can truly explore the existence and nature of causal relationships between variables of interest. Given these obvious advantages over other research designs for primary data collection, you might ask why experimental research is not used more often. There are many reasons, including the cost of experiments, the issue of security, and problems associated with implementing experiments.

PART 2:
Creating a Research Design

The High Cost of Experiments

To some degree, when making comparisons of the costs of experiments with the costs of surveys or observation-based research, we are comparing apples to oranges. Experiments can be very costly in both money and time. In many cases, managers may anticipate that the costs of doing an experiment would exceed the value of the information gained. Consider, for example, the costs of testing three alternative advertising campaigns in three different geographic areas. Three different campaigns must be produced; airtime must be purchased in all three markets; the timing in all three markets must be carefully coordinated; some system must be put into place to measure sales before, during, and after the test campaigns have run; measurements of other extraneous variables must be made; extensive analysis of the results must be performed; and a variety of other tasks must be completed in order to execute the experiment. All of this might well cost more than $1 million.

Security Issues

Conducting a field experiment in a test market involves exposing a marketing plan or some key element of a marketing plan in the actual marketplace. Undoubtedly, competitors will find out what is being considered well in advance of full-scale market introduction. This advance notice gives competitors an opportunity to decide whether and how to respond. In any case, the element of surprise is lost. In some instances, competitors have actually "stolen" concepts that were being tested in the marketplace and gone into national distribution before the company testing the product or strategy element completed the test marketing.

Implementation Problems

Problems that may hamper the implementation of an experiment include difficulty gaining cooperation within the organization, contamination problems, differences between test markets and the total population, and the lack of an appropriate group of people or geographic area for a control group.

It can be extremely difficult to obtain cooperation within the organization to execute certain types of experiments. For example, a regional marketing manager might be very reluctant to permit her market area to be used as a test market for a reduced level of advertising or a higher price. Quite naturally, her concern would be that the experiment might lower sales for the area.

Contamination occurs when buyers from outside the test area come into the area to purchase the product being tested, thereby distorting the results of the experiment. Outside buyers might live on the fringes of the test market area and receive TV advertisements—intended only for those in the test area—that offer a lower price, a special rebate, or some other incentive to buy a product. Their purchases will indicate that the particular sales-stimulating factor being tested is more effective than actually is the case.

In some cases, test markets may be so different, and the behavior of consumers in those markets so different, that a relatively small experimental effect is difficult to detect. This problem can be dealt with by careful matching of test

contamination
The inclusion in a test of a group of respondents who are not normally there—for example, outside buyers who see an advertisement intended only for those in the test area and enter the area to purchase the product being tested.

markets and other similar strategies designed to ensure a high degree of equivalency of test units.

Finally, in some situations, no appropriate geographic area or group of people may be available to serve as a control group. This may be the case in a test of industrial products, whose very small number of purchasers are concentrated geographically. An attempt to test a new product among a subset of such purchasers would almost certainly be doomed to failure.

Selected Experimental Designs

This section presents examples of pre-experimental, true experimental, and quasi-experimental designs.[9] In outlining these experimental designs, we will use the system of notation introduced earlier.

Pre-Experimental Designs

pre-experimental designs
Designs that offer little or no control over extraneous factors.

Studies using **pre-experimental designs** generally are difficult to interpret because such designs offer little or no control over the influence of extraneous factors. As a result, these studies often are not much better than descriptive studies when it comes to making causal inferences. With these designs, the researcher has little control over aspects of exposure to the treatment variable (such as to whom and when) and measurements. However, these designs frequently are used in commercial test marketing because they are simple and inexpensive. They are useful for suggesting new hypotheses but do not offer strong tests of existing hypotheses. The reasons for this will be clear after you review the discussion of pre-experimental designs that follows. Examples of pre-experimental designs are shown in Table 8.1.

one-shot case study design
Pre-experimental design with no pretest observations, no control group, and an after-measurement only.

One-Shot Case Study Design   The **one-shot case study design** involves exposing test units (people or test markets) to the treatment variable for some period of time and then taking a measurement of the dependent variable. Symbolically, the design is shown as follows:

$$X \qquad O_1$$

There are two basic weaknesses in this design. No pretest observations are made of the test units that will receive the treatment, and no control group of test units that did not receive the treatment is observed. As a result of these deficiencies, the design does not deal with the effects of any of the extraneous variables discussed previously. Therefore, the design lacks internal validity and, most likely, external validity as well. This design is useful for suggesting causal hypotheses but does not provide a strong test of such hypotheses. Many test markets for new products (not previously on the market) are based on this design.

one-group pretest–posttest design
Pre-experimental design with pre- and postmeasurements but no control group.

One-Group Pretest–Posttest Design   The **one-group pretest–posttest design** is the design employed most frequently for testing changes in established products or marketing strategies. The fact that the product was on the market before the change provides the basis for the pretest measurement (O_1). The design is shown symbolically as follows:

$$O_1 \qquad X \qquad O_2$$

PART 2:
Creating a Research Design

Table 8.1

Examples of Pre-Experimental Designs

Situation: Blue Cross/Blue Shield is in the process of instituting a new sales training program for its existing sales force. The program is designed to increase the productivity of individual salespersons and, thus, the entire sales force. Butler Moore, vice president of sales, wants to do a small-scale research project to determine whether the program is producing the desired results. Billy Marion, director of marketing research, has proposed three pre-experimental designs, as follows.

One-Shot Case Study Design	Static-Group Comparison Design	One-Group Pretest–Posttest Design
Basic design: $X \quad O_1$	Basic design: Experimental group: $X \quad O_1$ Control group: $\qquad O_2$	Basic design: $O_1 \quad X \quad O_2$
Sample: Ask for volunteers from among those who have taken the course.	Sample: Volunteers for both test and control groups.	Sample: Ask for volunteers from among those who took the course.
Treatment (X): Taking the course.	Treatment: Taking the course.	Treatment: Taking the course.
Measurement (O_1): Actual sales performance for the six-month period after the course.	Measurements (O_1, O_2): O_1 is actual sales performance of experimental group for six months after the course. O_2 is the same for control group that did not take the course (treatment).	Measurement (O_1, O_2): O_1 is actual sales performance for the six months prior to the course; O_2 is actual sales performance for the six months after the course.
Weaknesses: No conclusive inferences can be drawn from the results. The posttest measurement of sales may be the result of many uncontrolled factors. It cannot be judged better or worse in the absence of pretest observation of sales performance. There is no control group of salespersons who did not receive the treatment (take the course).	Weaknesses: There is no pretest measure to help us deal with threats to validity, such as history and maturation. Because subjects were not assigned to the two groups at random, differences in performance between the two groups may be attributed to differences in the groups (one group had better salespersons to begin with) rather than the sales training course.	Comparison: Same as in one-shot case study design except that a pretest measure of sales performance (O_2) is taken. Weaknesses: This design is better than the one-shot case study design but still has many serious problems. Differences between pretest and posttest measures may be attributable to factors other than the sales training course. For example, economic conditions (better or worse) may contribute to the observed change in the dependent variable (history); salespersons may improve in ways that have nothing to do with the course over the period (maturation); the pretest measure and the fact that the salespersons knew their performance was being monitored may affect the performance (testing effect); and some salespersons may leave the company over the period (mortality).

Pretest observations are made of a single group of subjects or a single test unit (O_1) that then receives the treatment. Finally, a posttest observation is made (O_2). The treatment effect is estimated by $O_2 - O_1$.

History is a threat to the internal validity of this design because an observed change in the dependent variable might be caused by an event that took place outside the experiment between the pretest and posttest measurements. In laboratory experiments, this threat can be controlled by insulating respondents from outside influences. Unfortunately, this type of control is impossible in field experiments.

Maturation is another threat to this type of design. An observed effect might be caused by the fact that subjects have grown older, smarter, more experienced, or the like between the pretest and the posttest.

This design has only one pretest observation. As a result, the researcher knows nothing of the pretest trend in the dependent variable. The posttest score may be higher because of an increasing trend of the dependent variable in a situation where this effect is not the treatment of interest.

static-group comparison design
Pre-experimental design that utilizes an experimental and a control group, but subjects or test units are not randomly assigned to the two groups and no premeasurements are taken.

Static-Group Comparison Design   The **static-group comparison design** uses two treatment groups: the experimental group is exposed to the treatment, while the control group is not. The two groups must be considered as nonequivalent because subjects are not randomly assigned to the groups. The design can be shown symbolically as follows:

$$\text{Experimental Group:} \quad X \quad O_1$$

$$\text{Control Group:} \qquad\qquad\quad O_2$$

The treatment effect is estimated by $O_1 - O_2$. The most obvious flaws in this design are the absence of pretests and the fact that any posttest differences between the groups may be due to the treatment effect, selection differences between the nonequivalent groups, or many other reasons.

True Experimental Designs

true experimental design
Research using an experimental group and a control group, to which test units are randomly assigned.

In a **true experimental design,** the experimenter randomly assigns treatments to randomly selected test units. In our notation system, the random assignment of test units to treatments is denoted by (R). Randomization is an important mechanism that makes the results of true experimental designs more valid than the results of pre-experimental designs. True experimental designs are superior because randomization takes care of many extraneous variables. The principal reason for choosing randomized experiments over other types of research designs is that they clarify causal inference.[10] Three true experimental designs are discussed in this section: before and after with control group design, Solomon four-group design, and after-only with control group design.

before and after with control group design
True experimental design that involves random assignment of subjects or test units to experimental and control groups and pre- and post-measurements of both groups.

Before and After with Control Group Design   The **before and after with control group design** can be presented symbolically as follows:

$$\text{Experimental Group:} \quad (R) \quad O_1 \quad X \quad O_2$$

$$\text{Control Group:} \qquad\quad (R) \quad O_3 \qquad\quad O_4$$

Because the test units in this design are randomly assigned to the experimental and control groups, the two groups can be considered equivalent. Therefore, they are likely to be subject to the same extraneous causal factors, except for the treatment of interest in the experimental group. For this reason, the difference between the pre- and postmeasurements of the control group $(O_4 - O_3)$ should provide a good estimate of the effect of all the extraneous influences experienced by each group. The true impact of the treatment variable X can be known only when the extraneous influences are removed from the difference between the pre- and postmeasurements of the experimental group. Thus, the true impact of X is estimated by $(O_2 - O_1) - (O_4 - O_3)$. This design generally controls for all but two major threats to validity: mortality and history.

Mortality will be a problem if units drop out during the study and these units differ systematically from the ones that remain. This results in a selection bias because the experimental and control groups are composed of different subjects at the posttest than they were at the pretest. History will be a problem in those situations where factors other than the treatment variable affect the experimental group but not the control group, or vice versa. Examples of this design and the after-only with control group design are provided in Table 8.2.

Solomon Four-Group Design

The **Solomon four-group design** is similar to the before and after with control group design, with the addition of a second set of experimental and control groups to control for all extraneous variable threats to internal validity and the interactive testing effect. This design is presented symbolically as follows:

Solomon four-group design
Research in which two experimental groups and two control groups are used to control for all extraneous variable threats.

Experimental Group 1:	(R)	O_1	X	O_2
Control Group 1:	(R)	O_3		O_4
Experimental Group 2:	(R)		X	O_5
Control Group 2:	(R)			O_6

The second experimental group receives no pretest but is otherwise identical to the first experimental group. The second control group receives only a posttest measurement.

This design provides several measures of the experimental treatment effect of X. They are $(O_2 - O_1) - (O_4 - O_3)$, $O_6 - O_5$, and $O_2 - O_4$. Agreement among these measures allows inferences made about the effect of the treatment to be much stronger. In addition, this design allows direct measurement of the interaction of the treatment and before measure effects $[(O_2 - O_4) - (O_5 - O_6)]$.

After-Only with Control Group Design

The **after-only with control group design** differs from the static-group comparison design (the pre-experimental design with nonequivalent groups) in regard to the assignment of the test units. In the static-group comparison design, test units are not randomly assigned to treatment groups. As a result, it is possible for the groups to differ in regard to the dependent variable before presentation of the treatment. The after-only with control group design deals with this shortcoming; it can be shown symbolically as follows.

after-only with control group design
True experimental design that involves random assignment of subjects or test units to experimental and control groups, but no premeasurement of the dependent variable.

Table 8.2

Examples of True Experimental Designs

Situation: A shampoo marketer wants to measure the sales effect of a point-of-purchase display. The firm is considering two true experimental designs.

After-Only with Control Group Design	Before and After with Control Group Design
Basic design: Experimental Group: (R) X O_1 Control Group: (R) O_2 Sample: Random sample of stores that sell shampoo. Stores are randomly assigned to test and control groups. Groups can be considered equivalent. Treatment (X): Placing the point-of-purchase display in stores in the experimental group for one month. Measurements (O_1, O_2): Actual sales of company's brand during the period that the point-of-purchase displays are in test stores. Comments: Because of random assignment of stores to groups, the test group and control group can be considered equivalent. Measure of the treatment effect of X is $O_1 - O_2$. If $O_1 = 125,000$ units and $O_2 = 113,000$ units, then treatment effect $= 12,000$ units.	Basic design: Experimental Group: (R) O_1 X O_2 Control Group: (R) O_3 O_4 Sample: Same as after-only design. Treatment (X): Same as after-only design. Measurements $(O_1$ to $O_4)$: O_1 and O_2 are pre- and postmeasurements for the experimental group; O_3 and O_4 are the same for the control group. Results: $O_1 = 113,000$ units $O_2 = 125,000$ units $O_3 = 111,000$ units $O_4 = 118,000$ units Comments: Random assignment to groups means that the groups can be considered equivalent. Because groups are equivalent, it is reasonable to assume that they will be equally affected by the same extraneous factors. The difference between pre- and postmeasurements for the control group $(O_4 - O_3)$ provides a good estimate of the effects of all extraneous factors on both groups. Based on these results, $O_4 - O_3 = 7,000$ units. The estimated treatment effect is $(O_2 - O_1) - (O_4 - O_3) =$ $(125,000 - 113,000) - (118,000 - 111,000) =$ $5,000$ units.

$$\text{Experimental Group:} \quad (R) \qquad X \qquad O_1$$
$$\text{Control Group:} \qquad\quad (R) \qquad\qquad O_2$$

Essentially, this design consists of the last two groups of the Solomon four-group design.

Notice that the test units are randomly (R) assigned to experimental and control groups. This random assignment should produce experimental and control groups that are approximately equal in regard to the dependent variable before presentation of the treatment to the experimental group. It can reasonably be assumed that test unit mortality (one of the threats to internal validity) will affect each group in the same way.

Considering this design in the context of the shampoo example described in Table 8.2, we can see a number of problems. Events other than the treatment variable may have occurred during the experimental period in one or a few stores in the experimental group. If a particular store in the experimental group

PART 2:
Creating a Research Design

ran a sale on certain other products and, as a result, had a larger than average number of customers in the store, shampoo sales might have increased because of the heavier traffic. Events such as these, which are store-specific (history), may distort the overall treatment effect. Also, there is a possibility that a few stores may drop out during the experiment (mortality threat), resulting in selection bias because the stores in the experimental group will be different at the posttest.

Quasi-Experiments

When designing a true experiment, the researcher often must create artificial environments to control independent and extraneous variables. Because of this artificiality, questions are raised about the external validity of the experimental findings. Quasi-experimental designs have been developed to deal with this problem. They generally are more feasible in field settings than are true experiments.

In **quasi-experiments,** the researcher lacks complete control over the scheduling of treatments or must assign respondents to treatments in a *nonrandom* fashion. These designs frequently are used in marketing research studies because cost and field constraints often do not permit the researcher to exert direct control over the scheduling of treatments and the randomization of respondents. Examples of quasi-experiments are interrupted time-series designs and multiple time-series designs.

quasi-experiments
Studies in which the researcher lacks complete control over the scheduling of treatment or must assign respondents to treatments in a nonrandom manner.

Interrupted Time-Series Designs
Interrupted time-series designs involve repeated measurement of an effect both before and after a treatment is introduced that "interrupts" previous data patterns. Interrupted time-series experimental designs can be shown symbolically as follows:

interrupted time-series design
Research in which repeated measurement of an effect "interrupts" previous data patterns.

$$O_1 \quad O_2 \quad O_3 \quad O_4 \quad X \quad O_5 \quad O_6 \quad O_7 \quad O_8$$

A common example of this type of design in marketing research involves the use of consumer purchase panels. A researcher might use such a panel to make periodic measurements of consumer purchase activity (the Os), introducing a new promotional campaign (the X) and examining the panel data for an effect. The researcher has control over the timing of the promotional campaign but cannot be sure when the panel members were exposed to the campaign or whether they were exposed at all.

This design is very similar to the one-group pretest–posttest design

$$O_1 \quad X \quad O_2$$

However, time-series experimental designs have greater interpretability than the one-group pretest–posttest design because the many measurements allow more understanding of extraneous variables. If, for example, sales of a product were on the rise and a new promotional campaign were introduced, the true effect of this campaign could not be estimated if a pretest–posttest design were used. However, the rising trend in sales would be obvious if a number of pretest and posttest observations had been made. Time-series designs help determine the underlying trend of the dependent variable and provide better interpretability in regard to the treatment effect.

There are two fundamental weaknesses of the interrupted time-series design. The primary weakness is the experimenter's inability to control history.

Although maintaining a careful log of all possibly relevant external happenings can reduce this problem, the researcher has no way of determining the appropriate number and timing of pretest and posttest observations.

The other weakness of this design comes from the possibility of interactive effects of testing and evaluation apprehension resulting from the repeated measurements taken on test units. For example, panel members may become "expert" shoppers or simply become more conscious of their shopping habits. Under these circumstances, it may be inappropriate to make generalizations to other populations.

Multiple Time-Series Designs If a control group can be added to an interrupted time-series design, then researchers can be more certain in their interpretation of the treatment effect. This design, called the **multiple time-series design,** can be shown symbolically as follows:

Experimental Group:	O_1	O_2	O_3	X	O_4	O_5	O_6
Control Group:	O_1	O_2	O_3		O_4	O_5	O_6

The researcher must take care in selecting the control group. For example, if an advertiser were testing a new advertising campaign in a test city, that city would constitute the experimental group and another city that was not exposed to the new campaign would be chosen as the control group. It is important that the test and control cities be roughly equivalent in regard to characteristics related to the sale of the product (e.g., competitive brands available).

multiple time-series design
An interrupted time-series design with a control group.

Test Markets

test market
Testing of a new product or some element of the marketing mix using an experimental or quasi-experimental design.

A common form of experimentation used by marketing researchers is test marketing. The term **test market** is used rather loosely to refer to any research that involves testing a new product or change in an existing marketing strategy (e.g., product, price, place promotion) in a single market, group of markets, or region of the country through the use of experimental or quasi-experimental designs.[11]

New product introductions play a key role in a firm's financial success or failure. The conventional wisdom in the corporate world is that new products will have to be more profitable in the future than they were in the past because of higher levels of competition and a faster pace of change. However, the estimated failure rate of new products varies greatly; the rate has been estimated at anywhere from 66 percent to almost 90 percent. The results of a 1991 survey by Weston (Connecticut) Researcher Group EFO, Ltd. indicate that marketers expected 86 percent of their new products to fail. The estimate in 1984 was 80 percent.[12] In addition, data reported by Burke Marketing Research Services indicate that 65 percent of all new product dollars are spent on marginal or losing brands. To make up for the failures and maintain corporate profitability at necessary levels, successful products must produce a return on investment averaging greater than 30 percent.

As you probably already recognize, test market studies have the goal of helping marketing managers make better decisions about new products and additions or changes to existing products or marketing strategies. A test market study does this by providing a real-world test for evaluating products and marketing programs. Marketing managers use test markets to evaluate proposed national programs with many separate elements on a smaller, less costly scale. The basic idea is to determine whether the estimated profits from rolling the product out on a national basis justify the potential risks. Test market studies are designed to provide information in regard to the following issues:

- Estimates of market share and volume that can be projected to the total market.
- The effects that the new product will have on sales of similar products (if any) already marketed by the company. The extent to which the new product takes business away from the company's existing products is referred to as the *cannibalization rate*.
- Characteristics of consumers who buy the product.

Lifestyle data are often collected to find out about the characteristics of possible consumers. This information helps a firm refine the marketing strategy for its product. What might lifestyle data reveal about consumers who would purchase this ring?

Demographic data will almost surely be collected, and lifestyle, psychographic, and other types of classification data may also be collected. This information is useful in helping the firm refine the marketing strategy for the product. For example, knowing the demographic characteristics of likely purchasers will help in developing a media plan that will effectively and efficiently reach target customers. Knowing the psychographic and lifestyle characteristics of target customers will provide valuable insights into how to position the product and the types of promotional messages that will appeal to them.

- The behavior of competitors during the test. This may provide some indication of what competitors will do if the product is introduced nationally.

An alternative to traditional test markets is the growing area of simulated test markets (STMs). STMs use survey data and mathematical models to simulate test market results at much lower cost. Details on how STMs are actually conducted are provided later in this section.

Test markets employ various experimental designs. Traditional test markets, by definition, are field experiments, whereas STMs rely on laboratory approaches. Traditional test markets rely almost exclusively on pre-experimental and time-series designs. STMs use pre-experimental, time-series, and, in some cases, true experimental designs.

Costs of Test Marketing

Test marketing is expensive. It is estimated that a simple two-market test can cost $300,000 to $400,000 and that a long-running, complex test in four or more markets can cost more than $1 million. These estimates refer only to *direct costs*, which may include the following:

- Production of commercials
- Payments to an advertising agency for services

- Media time, charged at a higher rate because of low volume
- Syndicated research information
- Customized research information and associated data analysis
- Point-of-purchase materials
- Coupons and sampling
- Higher trade allowances to obtain distribution[13]

Many *indirect costs* are also associated with test marketing, including the following:

- Cost of management time spent on the test market
- Diversion of sales activity from existing products
- Possible negative impact of a test market failure on other products with the same family brand
- Possible negative trade reactions to products if the firm develops a reputation for not doing well
- Cost of letting competitors know what the firm is doing, thereby allowing them to develop a better strategy or beat the firm to the national market.[14]

The cost of test markets is high, and, as a result, they should be used only as the last step in a research process that has shown the new product or strategy to have considerable potential. In some situations, it may be cheaper to go ahead and launch the product, even if it fails.

The Decision to Conduct Test Marketing

From the preceding discussion, you can see that test markets offer at least two important benefits to the firm conducting the test.[15]

- First and foremost, the test market provides a vehicle by which the firm can obtain a good estimate of a product's sales potential under realistic market conditions. A researcher can develop estimates of the product's national market share on the basis of these test results and use this figure to develop estimates of future financial performance for the product.
- Second, the test should identify weaknesses of the product and the proposed marketing strategy for the product and give management an opportunity to correct any weaknesses. It is much easier and less expensive to correct these problems at the test market stage than after the product has gone into national distribution.

On the other hand, these benefits must be weighed against a number of costs and other negatives associated with test markets.[16] The financial costs of test markets are not insignificant. And test markets give competitors an early indication of what the firm is planning to do. They thus share the opportunity to make adjustments in their marketing strategy; or, if the idea is simple and not legally protected, they may be able to copy the idea and move into national distribution faster than the original firm can.

Four major factors should be taken into account in determining whether to conduct a test market:

1. Weigh the cost and risk of failure against the probability of success and associated profits. If estimated costs are high and you are very uncertain about

PART 2:
Creating a Research Design

the likelihood of success, then you should lean toward doing a test market. On the other hand, if both expected costs and the risk of product failure are low, then an immediate national rollout without a test market may be the appropriate strategy.

2. Consider the likelihood and speed with which competitors can copy your product and introduce it on a national basis. If the product can be easily copied, then it may be appropriate to go ahead and introduce the product without a test market.

3. Consider the investment required to produce the product for the test market versus the investment required to produce the product in the quantities necessary for a national rollout. In cases where the difference in investment required is very small, it may make sense to introduce the product nationally without a test market. However, in cases where a very large difference exists between the investment required to produce the product for test market and that required for a national rollout, conducting a test market before making a decision to introduce the product nationally makes good sense.

4. Consider how much damage an unsuccessful new product launch would inflict on the firm's reputation. Failure may hurt the firm's reputation with other members of the channel of distribution (retailers) and impede the firm's ability to gain their cooperation in future product launches.[17]

The Wide Variety of Products and Services in Test Markets

In PRACTICE

A SAMPLING OF PRODUCTS IN TEST MARKETING IN 2000 GIVES some idea of the flexibility and adaptability of the test market approach.

Campbell Soup Company is testing "Supper" soups in a glass jar. This line, inspired by family dinner favorites, is being tested in four varieties—Pasta Primavera with White Meat Chicken, Pot Roast with Vegetables, Vegetable Lasagna, and Oriental-Style Chicken and Vegetables. This line was developed in response to the growing demand for quick and easy meal solutions. A recent *Restaurants and Institutions* survey shows that about 70 percent of Americans don't decide what they are serving for dinner until that evening.[18]

Blockbuster announced an agreement with NetActive to place PC games in selected stores to test consumer acceptance. The test began in April, 1999, in 14 cities. The program is being extended to Austin, Boston, Detroit, Cleveland, Hartford, Houston, Indianapolis, Jacksonville, Los Angeles, Orlando, Raleigh, Sacramento, Salt Lake City, and San Diego. The new service enables members to rent a PC game for five evenings for $5.99. Members can extend their rentals for an additional five evenings for $3.99 by either using a credit card online or purchasing "e-tickets" at the Blockbuster store.

Participating Blockbuster stores will carry approximately 20 PC games spanning a range of interests.[19]

Tropicana, a unit of PepsiCo, is in the early stages of a test of a kid-targeted juice line in upstate New York and Iowa. The product, called Tropicana Drenchers, is a 30 percent juice beverage fortified with vitamins A, C, and E and calcium. It comes in orange, strawberry, and tropical flavors. It is intended to compete against offerings such as Procter & Gamble's Sunny Delight, Minute Maid's Hi-C, and Campbell Soup's V-8 Splash. Hi-C and V-8 Splash are also calcium-fortified.[20]

Shell Oil Company is test marketing its robotic fuel pump in Westfield, Indiana, an Indianapolis suburb. The product has been in development for eight years. Over 1,000 customers have signed up to use the robotic pumps at selected stations where they will be available. Shell is offering a free 90-day trial. After that, stations will charge customers $1 to use the robotic system. To use the pump, a car must have a special spring-loaded gas cap, which costs $20, and a coded computer chip containing vehicle information on the windshield. When a car approaches the SmartPump, sensors read the computer chip and let the robotic arm know what type of car to fuel. After that, the consumer swipes a credit card and selects the desired grade of fuel. A soft suction device on a robotic arm opens the gas tank's door, removes the special gas cap, and begins filling the tank. The entire process takes about three minutes.[21]

Japan's Storage Battery Company has begun test marketing automotive batteries that use 100 percent recycled lead and recycled polypropylene plastic. The environment-friendly batteries, available in three types, are guaranteed for 24 months and 40,000 kilometers of driving. They sell for about the same price as traditional batteries.[22]

Procter & Gamble recently announced plans for the global test marketing of a unique new floor cleaning system in Canada, beginning in fall 2000. The Swiffer WetJet is an appliance-like product that is a true innovation in floor cleaning. Swiffer WetJet combines P&G's cleaning expertise with its paper products technology in a durable, battery-operated device. Prior to product research and development, extensive attitudinal studies were carried out globally. The findings highlighted a common desire for an aid that would eliminate the strain and fatigue of floor cleaning, which was rated throughout the world as one of the most tiring and unpleasant household tasks.[23]

The Miller Brewing Company is continuing to test plastic beer bottles in 16 markets around the United States, including Los Angeles, Phoenix, Miami, Dallas, Cleveland, Raleigh, and San Antonio. The plastic bottles are also being tested at several sports stadiums in the United States, including Veteran's Stadium in Philadelphia and the Houston Astrodome. Anheuser Busch terminated its testing of plastic bottles in Dallas and Phoenix and at New York's Madison Square Garden in 1999. A survey conducted by Young & Rubicam's Brand Futures Group found that consumer attitudes toward plastic beer bottles varied. Some thought they were a great idea, while at the other extreme many were horrified at the idea of drinking beer from plastic bottles.[24] ■

PART 2:
Creating a Research Design

Steps in a Test Market Study

Once the decision has been made to conduct test marketing, a number of steps must be carried out if we are to achieve a satisfactory result.

Step One: Define the Objective

As always with these kinds of lists, the first step in the process is to define the objectives of the test. Typical test market objectives include the following:

- Develop share and volume estimates.
- Determine the characteristics of people who are purchasing the product.
- Determine frequency and purpose of purchase.
- Determine where (retail outlets) purchases are made.
- Measure the effect of sales of the new product on sales of similar existing products in the line.

Step Two: Select a Basic Approach

After specifying the objectives of the test market exercise, the next step is to decide on the appropriate type of test market method, given the stated objectives. Three basic approaches are available: simulated test market; standard, or traditional, test market; and controlled test market.

- *Simulated test market.* STMs do not involve actual testing in the marketplace. Under this approach, a sample of individuals, representative of the target group, are exposed to various stimuli (new product concepts) and asked to make simulated purchase choices from among these stimuli. Results are used as input to mathematical models to make projections of how the new product would sell nationally.
- *Standard, or traditional, test market.* This approach involves an actual market test on a limited basis.
- *Controlled test market.* Under this approach, the test market is handled by an outside research company such as Information Resources, Inc. (see Chapter 7 for a more detailed discussion). Minimarkets operated by the testing company may be used, as well as controlled store panels. Companies conducting test market studies typically guarantee distribution of the new product in stores that cover some percentage of the minimarkets. They also usually provide warehouse facilities and have their own field representatives to sell the product to retailers. And they are typically responsible for stocking shelves and tracking sales either manually or electronically.

Step Three: Develop Detailed Test Procedures

After the objectives and a basic approach for the test have been developed, the researcher must develop a detailed plan for conducting the test. Manufacturing and distribution decisions must be made to ensure that adequate product is available and that it is available in most stores of the type that sell that particular product class. In addition, the detailed marketing plan to be used for the test must be specified. The basic positioning approach must be selected, the actual commercials must be developed, a pricing strategy must be chosen, a media plan must be developed, and various promotional activities must be specified.

Selecting markets for a test is an important decision. Significant regional differences should be considered in choosing cities as test markets. To find some readily apparent regional differences between Seattle and Miami, visit http://www.ci.seattle.wa.us and http://www.miami.com.

Step Four: Select Test Markets   The selection of markets for the test is an important decision. A number of factors must be taken into account in making this decision.

- The market should not be overtested. Markets that have been used extensively by other companies for testing purposes may not respond in the same way as those that have not been used before.
- The market should have normal development in the particular product class. Sales should be typical, not unusually high or unusually low.
- Markets with unusual demographic profiles should be avoided. For example, college towns and retirement areas are not particularly good areas for testing most new products.

PART 2:
Creating a Research Design

- Cities selected should reflect significant regional differences. If sales of the product type vary significantly by region, then each major region should be represented in the test by at least one city.
- The markets chosen should have little media spillover into other markets and receive relatively little media from outside the area. For example, if television stations in a particular market reach a very large area outside that market, the advertising used for the test product may pull in a large number of consumers from outside the market. This will make the product appear more successful than it really is.
- Media usage patterns for the market should closely reflect national norms. For example, if television viewership differs significantly from national patterns, this might bias the estimates made for the national market.
- The markets chosen should be large enough to provide meaningful results, but not so large that testing becomes too expensive.
- Distribution channels in the chosen markets should reflect national patterns. For example, all types of stores that sell the particular product should be present in the market in their approximate national proportions.
- The competitive situation in the markets chosen should be similar to the national situation for the product category. For example, it would not be a good idea to use a market in which one or more of the firm's national competitors were not present.
- The demographic profiles of the cities used should be similar to one another and similar to the national demographic profile.[25]

As you can see, many of the criteria relate to using cities that are microcosms of the country or a region of the country where the product ultimately will be sold. The basic motivation for taking this approach is to make sure that the test market results can be projected to the total area where the product will be sold. This is critical if a test market is to satisfy one of its important objectives—developing reliable estimates of sales of the new product. A list of the most typical metropolitan areas in the United States is provided in Table 8.3.[26] The cumulative index in the table is an index of similarity to the national market, considering housing value, age, and race characteristics of the market simultaneously. A value of 0.0 indicates a perfect match to the national market on these characteristics.

Step Five: Execute the Plan   Once the plan is in place, the researcher can begin execution. At this point, a key decision has to be made: How long should the test run? The average test runs for 6 to 12 months. However, shorter and longer tests are not uncommon. The test must run long enough for an adequate number of repeat purchase cycles to be observed, in order to provide a measure of the "staying power" of a new product or marketing program. The shorter the average period is, the shorter the test needs to be. Cigarettes, soft drinks, and packaged goods are purchased every few days, while such products as shaving cream and toothpaste are purchased only every few months. The latter products would require a longer test. Whatever the product type, the test must be continued until the repeat purchase rate stabilizes. There is a tendency for the percentage of people making repeat purchases to drop for some period of time before reaching a relatively constant level.

Most Typical Metropolitan Areas

Rank	Metropolitan Area	1990 Population	Housing Cumulative Index	Value Index	Age Index	Race Index
1	Detroit, MI	4,382,000	22.8	11.8	1.5	9.5
2	St. Louis, MO-IL	2,444,000	22.8	15.1	1.6	6.2
3	Charlotte-Gastonia Rock Hill, NC-SC	1,162,000	24.1	13.5	2.7	7.9
4	Forth Worth-Arlington, TX	1,332,000	25.1	17.0	5.9	2.2
5	Kansas City, MO-KS	1,566,000	25.4	17.9	2.7	4.8
6	Indianapolis, IN	1,250,000	25.5	16.7	2.4	6.3
7	Philadelphia, PA-NJ	4,857,000	26.7	18.0	1.7	7.1
8	Wilmington, NC	120,000	27.2	15.1	4.1	8.0
9	Cincinnati, OH-KY-IN	1,453,000	27.2	19.1	1.6	6.6
10	Nashville, TN	985,000	27.6	18.5	2.9	6.2
11	Dayton-Springfield, OH	951,000	27.6	19.5	1.9	6.2
12	Jacksonville, FL	907,000	27.6	17.2	2.5	7.9
13	Toledo, OH	614,000	27.9	20.0	2.4	5.5
14	Greensboro-Winston-Salem- High Point, NC	942,000	27.8	17.6	2.9	7.3
15	Columbus, OH	1,377,000	28.4	19.0	3.8	5.7
16	Charlottesville, VA	131,000	28.5	16.9	6.3	5.2
17	Panama City, FL	127,000	28.6	20.1	2.6	6.0
18	Pensacola, FL	344,000	28.7	21.8	2.2	4.7
19	Milwaukee, WI	1,432,000	28.8	23.4	1.4	4.1
20	Cleveland, OH	1,831,000	28.9	18.2	3.4	7.4

Source: Judith Waldrop, "All-American Markets," *American Demographics,* January 1992. Reprinted from *American Demographics* magazine with permission. Copyright © 1992, Cowles Business Media, Ithaca, New York.

Repeat purchase rate is critical to the process of estimating ultimate sales of the product. If the test is ended too soon, sales will be overestimated.

Two other considerations in determining the length of the test relate to the expected speed of competitor reaction and the costs of running the test. If there is reason to expect that competitors will react quickly to the test marketing (introduce their own versions of the new product), then the test should be as short as possible. Minimizing the length of the test reduces the amount of time competitors have to react. Finally, the value of additional information to be gained from the test must be balanced against the cost of continuing to run the test. At some point, the value of additional information will be outweighed by its cost.

Step Six: Analyze the Test Results   The data produced by an experiment should be evaluated throughout the test period. However, after completion of the experiment, a more careful and thorough evaluation of the data must be performed. This analysis will focus on four areas:

- *Purchase data.* The purchase data are often the most important data produced by an experiment. The levels of initial purchase (trial) throughout the course of the experiment provide an indication of how well the advertising and promotion program worked. The repeat rate (percentage of initial triers who made second and subsequent purchases) provides an indication of how well the product met the expectations created through advertising and promotion. Of course, the trial and repeat purchase results provide the basis for estimating sales and market share if the product were distributed nationally.
- *Awareness data.* How effective were the media expenditures and media plan in creating awareness of the product? Do consumers know how much the product costs? Do they know its key features?
- *Competitive response.* Ideally, the responses of competitors should be monitored during the period of the test market. For example, competitors may try to distort test results by offering special promotions, price deals, and quantity discounts. Their actions may provide some indication of what they will do if the product moves into national distribution and some basis for estimating the effect of these actions on their part.
- *Source of sales.* If the product is a new entry in an existing product category, it is important to determine where sales are coming from. In other words, which brands did the people who purchased the test product previously purchase? This information provides a true indication of real competitors. If the firm has an existing brand in the market, it also indicates to what extent the new product will take business from existing brands and from the competition.

Based on the evaluation, a decision will be made to improve the marketing program or the product, drop the product, or move the product into national or regional distribution.

Simulated Test Markets

Although the use of traditional test markets has been declining, there has been a corresponding increase in the use of **simulated test markets (STMs),** sometimes referred to as *pretest markets.* STMs do not involve actual test markets; they rely instead on laboratory approaches and mathematical modeling. Under the STM approach, a model of consumer response to a new product is developed. This model is used to generate volume estimates and to provide information for evaluating features of the product and the anticipated marketing mix.[27] The typical STM includes the following steps:

simulated test market (STM)
Use of survey data and mathematical models to simulate test market results at a much lower cost; also called *pretest market.*

1. Intercept consumers at shopping malls (the mall-intercept approach is discussed in Chapter 6).
2. Screen them for category use or target market membership, via a separate questionnaire or initial questions on the main questionnaire.
3. Expose those who qualify to the new product concept or prototype and, in many cases, prototype advertising.
4. Give participants an opportunity to buy the new product in a real or laboratory setting.

5. Interview those who purchased the new product (after an appropriate time interval) to determine their assessment of it and their likelihood of making further purchases.

6. Using the trial and repeat purchase estimates as input into a mathematical model, project share or volume for the product if it were distributed on a national basis. (Management must supply information regarding proposed advertising, distribution, and other elements of the proposed marketing strategy for the new product.)

There are four major reasons for the popularity of STMs. First, they are relatively surreptitious. Because laboratory designs are employed, competitors are unlikely to know that a test is being conducted, no less any details of the test or the nature of the new product being tested. Second, STMs can be completed more quickly than standard test markets, usually within a maximum of three to four months. Third, STMs are much cheaper than standard test markets. A typical STM can be conducted for $50,000 to $100,000, whereas the cost of a typical standard test market may approach $1 million. Finally, and perhaps most importantly, evidence has shown that STMs can be very accurate. For example, on the basis of a published validation study, ASSESSOR (The M/A/R/C Group) has been shown to produce predictions of market share that are, on average, within 0.8 share point of the actual shares achieved by the products.[28] In terms of the variance of the estimates produced by ASSESSOR, this study shows that 70 percent of the predictions fell within 1.1 share points of actual results.

Other Types of Test Marketing

In addition to traditional test marketing and STMs, there are other means by which companies can gauge a product's potential. One alternative is a *rolling rollout,* which usually follows a pretest. A product is launched in a certain region rather than in one or two cities. Within a matter of days, scanner data can provide

General Mills used the "rolling rollout" when it introduced MultiGrain Cheerios to the public. Visit http://www. generalmills.com to find out what new products the company may be introducing.

PART 2:
Creating a Research Design

Virtual Shopping

RECENT ADVANCES IN COMPUTER GRAPHICS AND THREE-DIMENsional modeling have brought simulated test marketing to a much broader range of companies, products, and applications. How? By allowing the marketer to recreate—quickly and inexpensively—the atmosphere of an actual retail store on a computer screen using virtual reality. For example, a consumer can view shelves stocked with any kind of product. The shopper can "pick up" a package from the shelf by touching its image on the monitor. In response, the product moves to the center of the screen, where the shopper can use a three-axis trackball to turn the package so that it can be examined from all sides. To "purchase" the product, the consumer touches an image of a shopping cart, and the product moves to the cart. Just as in a physical store, products pile up in the cart as the customer shops. During the shopping process, the computer unobtrusively records the amount of time the consumer spends shopping in each product category, the time the consumer spends examining each side of a package, the quantity of product the consumer purchases, and the order in which items are purchased.

Computer-simulated environments like the one just described offer a number of advantages over older research methods. First, unlike focus groups, concept tests, and other laboratory approaches, the virtual store duplicates the distracting clutter of an actual market to a greater extent. Consumers can shop in an environment with a more realistic level of complexity and variety.

Second, researchers can implement and modify the tests very quickly. Once images of the product are scanned into the computer, the researcher can make changes in the assortment of brands, product packaging, pricing, promotions, and shelf space within a matter of minutes. Data collection is also fast and error-free because the information generated by the purchase is automatically captured and stored by the computer. Third, test costs are low because displays are created electronically. Once the hardware and software are in place, the cost of a test is largely a function of the number of respondents. Respondents generally are given a small incentive to participate. Fourth, the simulation has a high degree of flexibility. It can be used to test entirely new marketing concepts or to fine-tune existing programs. The simulation also makes it possible to eliminate or, at least, control much of the noise that exists in field experiments.

The most important benefit of the methodology, however, is the opportunity it gives to market researchers and marketers to exercise their imaginations. It transforms the simulated test market from a go-or-no-go hurdle that occurs late in the planning process to an efficient marketing laboratory for experimenting with new ideas. Product managers can test new concepts before incurring manufacturing or advertising costs, paying slotting allowances to the trade, alerting competitors, or knowing whether the new ideas are good, bad, terrible, or fantastic.[29] ■

Source: Raymond R. Burke reprinted by permission of *Harvard Business Review.* Excerpt from "Virtual Shopping: Breakthrough in Marketing Research" by Raymond R. Burke, *Harvard Business Review,* March–April 1996. Copyright © 1996 by Harvard Business School Publishing Corporation.

information on how the product is doing. The product can then be launched in additional regions; ads and promotions can be adjusted along the way to a national introduction. General Mills has used this approach for products like MultiGrain Cheerios.

Another alternative is to try a product out in a foreign market before rolling it out globally. Specifically, one or a few countries can serve as a test market for a continent or even the world. This *lead country strategy* has been used by Colgate-Palmolive Company. In 1991, the company launched Palmolive Optims shampoo and conditioner in the Philippines, Australia, Mexico, and Hong Kong. Later, the products were rolled out in Europe, Asia, Latin America, and Africa.

Some marketers think that classic test marketing will make a comeback. It may be that for totally new products, more thorough testing will be necessary, whereas for other types of product introductions, such as line extensions, an alternative approach is more appropriate.[30]

Global ISSUES

The Japanese and Test Marketing

THE JAPANESE DOWNPLAY THE IMPORTANCE OF TEST MARKETING. They tend to rush products into commercialization and let the market decide on winners and losers. Japanese competitors believe in product covering—rushing out instant imitations. These rival manufacturers hurry to produce their own versions just in case the pioneer's should prove to be a best seller. Western firms use the rifle approach; they thoroughly test the market and revise products until they meet customers' needs before launching them.[31] ∎

Source: Originally published in *Marketing Intelligence & Planning,* MCB UP Ltd. From P. Herbig, A. Genestra, and A. T. Shao, "What Does Marketing Really Mean to the Japanese?", *Marketing Intelligence & Planning,* Vol. 13, Iss. 9, 1995, MCB UP Ltd., Bradford, England. Reprinted by permission.

PART 2:
Creating a Research Design

Summary

Experimental research provides evidence of whether a change in an independent variable causes some predictable change in a dependent variable. To show that a change in *A* likely caused an observed change in *B,* one must show three things: concomitant variation, appropriate time order of occurrence, and the elimination of other possible causal factors. Experiments can be conducted in a laboratory or a field setting. The major advantage of conducting experiments in a laboratory is that the researcher can control extraneous factors. However, in marketing research, laboratory settings often do not appropriately replicate the marketplace. Experiments conducted in the actual marketplace are called field experiments. The major difficulty with field experiments is that the researcher cannot control all the other factors that might influence the dependent variable.

In experimentation, we are concerned with internal and external validity. Internal validity refers to the extent to which competing explanations of the experimental results observed can be ruled out. External validity refers to the extent to which causal relationships measured in an experiment can be generalized to other settings. Extraneous variables are other independent variables that may affect the dependent variable and thus stand in the way of the ability to conclude that an observed change in the dependent variable was due to the effect of the experimental, or treatment, variable. Extraneous factors include history, maturation, instrument variation, selection bias, mortality, testing effects, and regression to the mean. Four basic approaches are used to control extraneous factors: randomization, physical control, design control, and statistical control.

In an experimental design, the researcher has control over and manipulates one or more independent variables. Nonexperimental designs, which involve no manipulation, are referred to as *ex post facto* research. An experimental design includes four elements: the treatment, subjects, a dependent variable that is measured, and a plan or procedure for dealing with extraneous causal factors. An experimental effect is the effect of the treatment variable on the dependent variable.

Experiments have an obvious advantage in that they are the only type of research that can demonstrate the existence and nature of causal relationships between variables of interest. Yet the amount of actual experimentation done in marketing research is limited because of the high cost of experiments, security issues, and implementation problems. There is evidence to suggest that the use of experiments in marketing research is growing.

Pre-experimental designs offer little or no control over the influence of extraneous factors and are thus generally difficult to interpret. Examples include the one-shot case study design, the one-group pretest–posttest design, and the static-group comparison design. In a true experimental design, the researcher is able to eliminate all extraneous variables as competitive hypotheses to the treatment. Examples of true experimental designs are the before and after with control group design, the Solomon four-group design, and the after-only with control group design.

In quasi-experiments, the researcher has control over data collection procedures but lacks complete control over the scheduling of treatments. The treatment groups in a quasi-experiment normally are formed by assigning respondents to treatments in a nonrandom fashion. Examples of quasi-experimental designs are the interrupted time-series design and the multiple time-series design.

Test marketing involves testing a new product or some element of the marketing mix by using experimental or quasi-experimental designs. Test markets are field experiments, and they are extremely expensive to conduct. The steps in conducting a test market study include defining the objectives for the study, selecting a basic approach to be used, developing detailed procedures for the test, selecting markets for the test, executing the plan, and analyzing the test results.

Key Terms & Definitions

experiment Research approach in which one variable is manipulated and the effect on another variable is observed.

causal research Research designed to determine whether a change in one variable likely caused an observed change in another.

concomitant variation A predictable statistical relationship between two variables.

appropriate time order of occurrence The occurrence of a change in an independent variable before an observed change in the dependent variable.

laboratory experiments Experiments conducted in a controlled setting.

field experiments Tests conducted outside the laboratory in an actual environment, such as a market.

internal validity The extent to which competing explanations for the experimental results observed can be ruled out.

external validity The extent to which causal relationships measured in an experiment can be generalized to outside persons, settings, and times.

history The intervention, between the beginning and end of an experiment, of outside variables or events that might change the dependent variable.

maturation Changes in subjects occurring during the experiment that are not related to the experiment but may affect subjects' response to the treatment factor.

instrument variation Changes in measurement instruments (e.g., interviews or observers) that might explain differences in measurements.

selection bias Systematic differences between the test group and the control group due to a biased selection process.

mortality Loss of test units or subjects during the course of an experiment, which may result in a nonrepresentative experimental group.

testing effect An effect that is a byproduct of the research process itself.

regression to the mean Tendency of subjects with extreme behavior to move toward the average for that behavior during the course of an experiment.

randomization The random assignment of subjects to treatment conditions to ensure equal representation of subject characteristics.

physical control Holding constant the value or level of extraneous variables throughout the course of an experiment.

design control Use of the experimental design to control extraneous causal factors.

statistical control Adjusting for the effects of confounded variables by statistically adjusting the value of the dependent variable for each treatment condition.

experimental design A test in which the researcher has control over and manipulates one or more independent variables.

treatment variable The independent variable that is manipulated in an experiment.

experimental effect The effect of the treatment variable on the dependent variable.

contamination The inclusion in a test of a group of respondents who are not normally there—for example, outside buyers who see an advertisement intended only for those in the test area and enter the area to purchase the product being tested.

pre-experimental designs Designs that offer little or no control over extraneous factors.

one-shot case study design Pre-experimental design with no pretest observations, no control group, and an after-measurement only.

one-group pretest–posttest design Pre-experimental design with pre- and postmeasurements but no control group.

static-group comparison design Pre-experimental design that utilizes an experimental and a control group, but subjects or test units are not randomly assigned to the two groups and no premeasurements are taken.

true experimental design Research using an experimental group and a control group, to which test units are randomly assigned.

before and after with control group design True experimental design that involves random assignment of subjects or test units to experimental and control groups and pre- and postmeasurements of both groups.

Solomon four-group design Research in which two experimental groups and two control groups are used to control for all extraneous variable threats.

after-only with control group design True experimental design that involves random assignment of subjects or test units to experimental and control groups, but no premeasurement of the dependent variable.

quasi-experiments Studies in which the researcher lacks complete control over the scheduling of treatment or must assign respondents to treatments in a nonrandom manner.

interrupted time-series design Research in which repeated measurements of an effect "interrupts" previous data patterns.

multiple time-series design An interrupted time-series design with a control group.

test market Testing of a new product or some element of the marketing mix using an experimental or quasi-experimental design.

simulated test market (STM) Use of survey data and mathematical models to simulate test market results at a much lower cost; also called *pretest market*.

Questions for Review & Critical Thinking

1. Petorama is considering offering a new service to its customers: home delivery of pet food for orders of $50 or more. Management is weighing the pros and cons of immediately introducing the concept nationally as opposed to testing it in two or three markets. What are the advantages and disadvantages of each approach? What would you recommend that Petorama do? Justify your recommendation.

2. Tico Taco, a national chain of Mexican fast-food restaurants, has developed the "Super Sonic Taco," which is the largest taco in the market and sells for $1.19. Tico Taco has identified its target customers for this new product as men under 30 who are not concerned about health issues, such as fat content or calories. It wants to test the product in at least four regional markets before making a decision to introduce it nationally. What criteria would you use to select test cities for this new product? Which cities would you recommend using? Why would you recommend those cities?

3. Of the primary data collection techniques available to the researcher (survey, observation, experiment), why is the experiment the only one that can provide conclusive evidence of causal relationships? Of the various types of experiments, which type or types provide the best evidence of causation or noncausation?

4. What are some important independent variables that must be dealt with in an experiment to test consumer reactions to the XFL? Explain why those variables are important.

5. Managers of the student center at your university or college are considering three alternative brands of frozen pizza to be offered on the menu. They want to offer only one of the three and want to find out which brand students prefer. Design an experiment to determine which brand of pizza the students prefer.

6. Night students at the university or college are much older than day students. Introduce an explicit control for day versus night students in the preceding experiment.

7. Why are quasi-experiments much more popular in marketing research than true experiments?

8. How does history differ from maturation? What specific actions might you take to deal with each in an experiment?

9. A manufacturer of microwave ovens has designed an improved model that will reduce energy costs and cook food evenly throughout. However, this new model will increase the product's price by 30 percent because of extra components and engineering design changes. The company wants to determine what effect the new model will have on sales of its microwave ovens. Propose an appropriate experimental design that can provide the desired information for management. Why did you select this design?

10. Discuss various methods by which extraneous causal factors can be controlled.

11. Explain how various measurements of the experimental effect in a Solomon four-group design can provide estimates of the effects of certain extraneous variables.

12. Discuss the alternatives to traditional test marketing. Explain their advantages and disadvantages.

Using WebSurveyor

XYZ Marketing Research recently conducted a survey in a local college town. The goal of the survey was to identify the television networks most popular among adults over the age of 18. XYZ used the same questionnaire and general instructions to conduct interviews via both email and telephone.

XYZ sent invitations for the email version of the survey to 1,000 people selected at random from an email list provider using the local zip code. XYZ also drew a random sample of 1,000 names from the local telephone directory and completed 200 interviews.

Install the WebSurveyor Desktop software by inserting the CD-ROM provided with this textbook in your CD-ROM drive and selecting the INSTALL option (an overview of the software is provided in Chapter 10). After you install the software, run the program by selecting Start, Programs, WebSurveyor, and then WebSurveyor Desktop from the Windows Start bar. If the survey builder wizard appears, click Cancel.

Using the WebSurveyor Desktop software you just installed, open the CHAPTER08 survey by selecting File and then Open from the main menu and navigating to the SURVEYS subdirectory under the directory where you installed the WebSurveyor Desktop software (usually c:\program files\websurveyor desktop 3).

Next, navigate to the analysis page by selecting View, Survey Results, and then Analysis from the main menu. Now click the Update Results button at the bottom of the Analysis page and follow the prompts to load the survey results from the CD-ROM included with this textbook. Use the last question of the survey to group responses based on the interview technique.

Exercises

1. How do the telephone and email surveys differ in terms of the demographic characteristics of the two samples? How would you explain the differences?
2. How do the two samples differ in terms of the television shows watched most frequently? How would you explain these differences?
3. Based on your analysis of the two samples, why do you think they are different? How did the different data collection approaches for the two samples affect the results?

Real-Life Research • 8.1

Market Analysts and Promotional Specialists, Incorporated

Market Analysts and Promotional Specialists, Incorporated (M.A.P.S.) is a marketing consulting firm that specializes in the development of promotional campaigns. The firm was formed five years ago by two young marketing graduate students, David Roth and Lisa Ryan, who soon overcame their initial lack of experience and have since become known for their innovativeness and creativity. Their clients include industrial wholesalers, retail product manufacturers, food brokers, and distributors, as well as retail outlets.

In 1994, Dixie Brewing Company enlisted M.A.P.S. to develop a new promotional campaign for its line of beers. At the time, Dixie was the last of the microbreweries in New Orleans and distributed its products within a 200-mile radius of the city. The company had enjoyed a good reputation for a number of years, but its image had recently been tarnished by the accidental distribution of a shipment of bad beer. Dixie also was losing market share because of increased competition from national brewers. Miller High Life had purchased Cresent Distributors, a large liquor distributor in the New Orleans area, and was beginning to implement aggressive promotional tactics in the local market.

Dixie was concerned primarily with its retail merchandising methods. David and Lisa immediately began to study Dixie's product line and its present shelf space allocations in various stores throughout the market area. M.A.P.S.'s previous work with food brokers helped them realize that proper shelf placement was extremely important in supermarket merchandising.

The company's product line consisted of two beers, Dixie and Dixie Light. Both beers were sold in 32-ounce glass bottles, 12-ounce glass-bottle six-packs, and 12-ounce can six-packs.

In New Orleans, beer may be purchased in supermarkets and convenience stores. Also, in most stores, beer can be purchased either warm or cold. In studying the refrigerated closets holding beverages, David and Lisa noticed that most were small—8 to 12 feet in length—and had glass doors on the front. Because of the relatively small size of the entire cold beer display, they believed that the typical consumer would view the case from left to right; therefore, they believed Dixie should place its products on the extreme left side of all cold beer cases.

Warm beer was displayed in a much different manner. Most stores displayed beverage products in bulk and usually devoted an entire aisle to such displays. David and Lisa reasoned that the normal consumer could not view all the brands at once and thus would have to "shop," or walk into the aisle. For this reason, they recommended that Dixie place its beer in the middle of the other brands.

Because Dixie Light was produced in response to Miller Lite, David and Lisa recommended that it be placed to the left of Miller Lite in both warm and cold beer displays. Traditionally, Dixie Light had been placed next to its standard beer brand. Dixie had noticed a significant decrease in its regular brand's market share after the introduction of Dixie Light.

To test their theories, David and Lisa selected a convenience store, located in a suburb of New Orleans, that contained both warm and cold beer displays. This store was then used in an experiment to measure the effect of shelf placement on beer sales. One treatment consisted of setting up the displays as they were currently being used in stores across town. The second treatment arranged the displays according to the new M.A.P.S. plan. All other factors, such as price and number of bottles, were held constant throughout the experiment. The first version of the setup was used for the first two weeks in April, and the second treatment was run for the last two weeks of the month.

The following data show the percentage of beer purchased by brand for each treatment:

	Treatment #1	Treatment #2
Dixie	18%	23%
Miller	18%	15%
Bud	19%	18%
Coors	13%	13%
Dixie Light	10%	8%
Miller Lite	13%	14%
Coors Light	9%	9%

Questions

1. Critique the research design with respect to internal and external validity considerations.
2. Discuss the advantages and disadvantages of using the convenience store in this experiment.
3. Based on the information given, what conclusions can be reached regarding the M.A.P.S. plan?
4. Recommend a research design that would produce more interpretable results.

Real-Life Research • 8.2

DVDs.com

Review the opening vignette for this chapter. Pay special attention to the research design proposed by Shemeka Thomas. The results of the test are summarized in the following table:

Item	Exposed to:	
	Current Graphic	**New Graphic**
Visitors	57,233	56,788
Percentage who made a purchase	33.40%	34.50%
Average music purchase	$22.45	$24.65
Average video purchase	$44.74	$49.50
Average total purchase	$67.19	$74.15
Percentage of repeat purchasers, last 30 days	22.40%	18.50%

Questions

1. Comment on the basic research design proposed by Thomas. What are its strengths? What are its weaknesses? How might it be modified to improve the quality of the information obtained?
2. Compose the differences between the various measures for the current graphic treatment and the new graphic treatment. What would you conclude on the basis of this analysis?
3. Evaluate the differences between measures of the two graphic approaches from a managerial perspective.
4. Based on the above results and the research design used, what recommendation would you make? Should the current graphic approach be retained, or should it be replaced with the new graphic? Or are the results inconclusive?

1. Texas Instruments has manufacturing plants all over the world. It has found that plant managers need marketing research data related to "benchmarking data" to distribute to their employees. What other marketing research information might be helpful to plant managers ? Could the Internet play a role in distributing the information? How?
2. Qualitative research findings are not projectable to target market populations. Numbers-oriented employees, such as those found in finance or engineering, often criticize qualitative research as "not real research" and "too touchy-feely." How can qualitative research be valuable to engineers and accountants? How might a researcher sell skeptical employees on qualitative research?
3. "Customer visits" refers to a program of individually interviewing a dozen business customers of the organization to determine how they use products and what new product features are desired. Customer visits are conducted at the client's location. The visit always includes representatives of both marketing and engineering as an interviewing team. Why would customer visits be conducted in this manner?

Ethical Dilemma

Using Survey Research to Measure the Perceived Ethical Standards and Social Responsibility of Business

A RECENT *BUSINESS WEEK*/HARRIS POLL EVALUATED HOW Americans view the ethics and social responsibilities of business. The sample was made up of 1035 adults nationwide. Some of the key findings are presented below.

American business should be given most of the credit for the prosperity that has prevailed during most of the 1990s.

	Agree Strongly	Somewhat Agree	Somewhat Disagree	Disagree Strongly	Not Sure/ No Answer
2000	26%	42%	19%	10%	2%
1996	55%*		44%*		

*Respondents were asked only to agree or disagree with the statement.

Business has gained too much power over too many aspects of American life.

	Agree Strongly	Somewhat Agree	Somewhat Disagree	Disagree Strongly	Not Sure/ No Answer
2000	52%	30%	12%	4%	2%
1996	71%*		28%*		

*Respondents were asked to only agree or disagree with the statement.

In general, what is good for business is good for most Americans.

	Agree Strongly	Somewhat Agree	Somewhat Disagree	Disagree Strongly	Not Sure/ No Answer
2000	17%	35%	23%	24%	1%
1996	32%	39%	20%	8%	1%

How much confidence do you have in those running big business?

	Great Deal	Only Some	Hardly Any	Not Sure/ No Answer
2000	19%	58%	17%	5%
1999	15%	69%	13%	3%

Having large profits is more important to big business than developing safe, reliable, quality products for consumers.

	Agree Strongly	Somewhat Agree	Somewhat Disagree	Disagree Strongly	Not Sure/ No Answer
2000	38%	28%	14%	17%	3%

How would you rate these industries in serving their consumers?

	Poor	Only Fair	Pretty Good	Excellent	Don't Know/ No Answer
HMOs	43%	28%	15%	3%	11%
Tobacco companies	43%	30%	14%	5%	8%
Oil companies	39%	35%	16%	3%	7%
Insurance companies	32%	41%	21%	3%	3%
Pharmaceutical companies	27%	37%	26%	5%	5%
Airlines	22%	41%	25%	3%	9%
Telephone companies	20%	42%	31%	6%	1%
News organizations	18%	38%	33%	6%	5%
Hospitals	15%	35%	38%	9%	3%
Entertainment companies	14%	33%	38%	9%	6%
Automobile companies	12%	42%	37%	6%	3%
Financial services firms	12%	40%	34%	5%	9%
Computer companies	4%	30%	40%	10%	16%

How would you rate large U.S. companies on each of the following?

Making good products and competing in a global economy

	Excellent	Pretty Good	Only Fair	Poor	Don't Know/ No Answer
2000	18%	50%	26%	5%	1%
1996	14%	44%	33%	9%	

Treating all of their employees well

	Excellent	Pretty Good	Only Fair	Poor	Don't Know/ No Answer
2000 (Aug.)	6%	25%	42%	21%	6%

Educating their consumers on the health and safety of their products

	Excellent	Pretty Good	Only Fair	Poor	Don't Know/ No Answer
2000 (Aug.)	8%	31%	38%	19%	4%

Having fair and reasonable prices, relative to their profits

	Excellent	Pretty Good	Only Fair	Poor	Don't Know/ No Answer
2000 (Aug.)	5%	22%	46%	23%	4%

Providing job security for employees

	Excellent	Pretty Good	Only Fair	Poor	Don't Know/ No Answer
2000 (Aug.)	7%	25%	36%	29%	3%

How would you assess compensation of top officers of large U.S. companies?

	Too Much	Too Little	Just About the Right Amount	Not Sure/ No Answer
2000	73%	3%	21%	3%
1996	73%	5%	19%	3%

How would you rate the power of different business groups in influencing government policy, politicians, and policymakers in Washington?

		Too Much	Too Little	About Right	Not Sure/ No Answer
Big companies	**2000**	74%	5%	20%	1%
	1999	82%	8%	3%	7%
Small business	**2000**	2%	78%	19%	1%
	1999	3%	89%	2%	4%

Entertainment and popular culture are dominated by corporate money which seeks mass appeal over quality.

	Agree Strongly	Somewhat Agree	Somewhat Disagree	Disagree Strongly	Not Sure/ No Answer
2000	45%	37%	11%	4%	4%

Entertainment and media companies do a good job of creating products that many people want to buy and enjoy.

	Agree Strongly	Somewhat Agree	Somewhat Disagree	Disagree Strongly	Not Sure/ No Answer
2000	32%	46%	13%	8%	1%

Which of the following statements do you agree with more strongly?

	2000	**1999**
U.S. corporations should have only one purpose—to make the most profit for their shareholders—and their pursuit of that goal will be best for America in the long run.	4%	5%
U.S. corporations should have more than one purpose. They also owe something to their workers and the communities in which they operate, and they should sometimes sacrifice some profit for the sake of making things better for their workers and communities.	95%	95%
Not Sure/No Answer	1%	0%

Source: "How Business Rates: By the Numbers," *Business Week* (September 11, 2000), pp. 148–149.

Questions

1. You have been asked to give a five-minute oral summary of the above survey to the corporate ethics committee. Carefully review the data and make your report.
2. What trends, if any, do you see developing between 1996 and 2000?
3. If you worked for a large HMO, what actions might you suggest based on this survey?
4. Why do you think that large corporations are perceived as being too powerful?

PART 2:
Creating a Research Design

Check it out!

Go to the Center for Marketing Resources at http://mcdaniel.swcollege.com where you will find additional marketing resources and study hints to help you with the material covered in Part Three.

Chapter Nine

The Concept of Measurement

Learning Objectives

To understand the concept of measurement.

1

To learn about the measurement process and how to develop a good measurement scale.

2

To understand the four levels of scales and their typical usage.

3

To explore the concepts of reliability and validity.

4

"**H**OW DO WE CREATE THE RIGHT GLOBAL STRATEGY?" REMAINS, FOR many brands and marketers, one of the toughest questions. To shed needed light on the "going global" quandary, Roper Starch Worldwide offers Roper Reports Worldwide, an annual tracking study conducted in 30 countries.

THE GOOD NEWS IS THAT THINKING GLOBALLY AND ACTING LOCALLY STILL works, but with a powerful twist: The link between personal values and consumers' affinities for other cultures needs to be better understood, because such understanding is critical to gaining maximum success for global marketing strategies.

AS ROPER STARCH CONDUCTED SURVEYS IN EACH COUNTRY, IT measured how close consumers feel to different cultures around the world. The researchers asked consumers—a sample of 30,000 respondents, projectable to more than 1.3 billion—which cultures share the values that are most important to them as individuals.

THEIR ANSWERS ARE TELLING, ESPECIALLY TO COMPANIES TRYING to figure out whether they should be marketing as global, American, or local entities. Based on the answers, Roper Starch divided consumers into three main groups:

- *Nationalists,* comprising 26% of the survey, feel close to their own cultures but not to others. Nationalists are somewhat older, with more in the 40–65 age bracket. They also are skewed slightly more toward females who are likely to be homemakers, while the men are more likely to hold blue-collar jobs. Key personal values are duty, respect for ancestors, wealth, power, status, and social stability.

Into what Roper Starch consumer category would this young lady most likely fit? Would she be categorized as a Nationalist or an Internationalist?

- *Internationalists,* or 15% of the sample, feel somewhat close to three or more outside cultures. Internationalists are younger, many between 13 and 29. More male than female, they tend to be better educated, hold better jobs, and enjoy a higher income and better living standard. Key personal values are openmindedness and social tolerance, learning, creativity, freedom, knowledge, and wisdom.

- *Disengaged,* 7% of the sample, consider themselves somewhat distant from their cultures. They also are younger but less educated than Nationalists and Internationalists and more likely than Nationalists to be blue-collar workers. They earn less income and have a lower standard of living. Personal values include having fun, music, living for today, romance, and enjoying life.

Find out more about Roper Reports Worldwide and global marketing strategies at

 http://www. roper.com

TO ENSURE THAT STRATEGIES WORK OPTIMALLY ACROSS ALL GLOBAL MARKETS, marketers must seek a high level of agreement between personal values and the cultural attributes of products. Marketers need to distinguish between overarching global strategies and messages—the core of their campaigns—and the components intimately tied to local values.

MARKETERS SEEKING TO RAMP UP THEIR GLOBAL STRATEGIES SHOULD CAREFULLY examine both sides of the cultural coin. Marketers who get the message—and who can convey it with sensitivity and impact—are destined to be the top players on the global stage, while those who do not are likely to find themselves in the wings.[1] ■

The concepts of "globally oriented," "nationalist," "internationalist," and even "disengaged" can be measured. What is a construct, and how can it be measured? How does one determine the reliability and validity of the information? These are some of the issues we will explore in this chapter.

The Measurement Process

measurement
The process of assigning numbers or labels to persons, objects, or events in accordance with specific rules for representing quantities or qualities of attributes.

rule
A guide, a method, or a command that tells a researcher what to do.

Measurement is the process of assigning numbers or labels to persons, objects, or events in accordance with specific rules for representing quantities or qualities of attributes. Measurement, then, is a procedure used to assign numbers that reflect the amount of an attribute possessed by a person, object, or event. Note that it is not the person, object, or event that is being measured, but rather its attributes. A researcher, for example, does not measure a consumer per se but rather measures that consumer's attitudes, income, brand loyalty, age, and other relevant factors.

The concept of rules is key to measurement. A **rule** is a guide, a method, or a command that tells a researcher what to do. For example, a rule of measurement might state, "Assign the numbers 1 through 5 to people according to their disposition to do household chores. If they are extremely willing to do any and all household chores, assign them a 1. If they are not willing to do any household chores, assign them a 5." The numbers 2, 3, and 4 would be assigned based on the *degree* of their willingness to do chores, as it relates to the absolute endpoints of 1 and 5.

A problem often encountered with rules is a lack of clarity or specificity. Some things are easy to measure because rules are easy to create and follow. The measurement of gender, for example, is quite simple, as the researcher has concrete criteria to apply in assigning a 1 for a male and a 2 for a female. Unfortunately, many characteristics of interest to a marketing researcher—such as brand loyalty, purchase intent, and total family income—are much harder to measure because of the difficulty of devising rules to assess the true value of these consumer attributes. The steps a researcher should take to measure a phenomenon appear in Figure 9.1.

Step One: Identify the Concept of Interest

The measurement process begins with identification of the concept of interest. A *concept* is an abstract idea generalized from particular facts. It is a category of

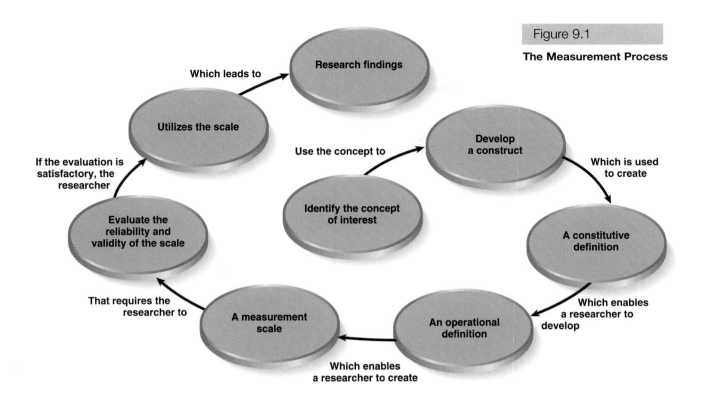

Figure 9.1

The Measurement Process

thought used to group sense data together "as if they were all the same." All perceptions regarding a stoplight at the intersection of South and Main Streets form a category of thought, although a relatively narrow one. Perceptions of all stoplights, regardless of location, would be a broader concept, or category of thought.

Step Two: Develop a Construct

Constructs are specific types of concepts that exist at higher levels of abstraction than do everyday concepts. Constructs are invented for theoretical use and thus are likely to cut across various preexisting categories of thought. The value of specific constructs depends on how useful they are in explaining, predicting, and controlling phenomena, just as the value of everyday concepts depends on how helpful are in everyday affairs. Generally, constructs are not directly observable. Instead, they are inferred by some indirect method from results such as findings on a questionnaire. Examples of marketing constructs include brand loyalty, high-involvement purchasing, social class, personality, and channel power. Constructs aid researchers by simplifying and integrating the complex phenomena found in the marketing environment.

constructs
Specific types of concepts that exist at higher levels of abstraction.

Step Three: Define the Concept Constitutively

constitutive definition
A statement of the meaning of the central idea or concept under study, establishing its boundaries; also known as *theoretical,* or *conceptual, definition.*

The third step in the measurement process is to define the concept constitutively. A **constitutive** (or *theoretical,* or *conceptual*) **definition** is a statement of the meaning of the central idea or concept under study, establishing its boundaries. Constructs of a scientific theory are defined constitutively. Thus, all constructs, to be capable of being used in theories, must possess constitutive meaning. Like a dictionary definition, a constitutive definition should fully distinguish the concept under investigation from all other concepts, making the study concept readily discernible from very similar but different concepts. A vague constitutive definition can cause an incorrect research question to be addressed. For instance, to say that researchers are interested in studying marital roles would be so general as to be meaningless. To say that they want to examine the marital roles of newlyweds (married less than 12 months) from 24 to 28 years of age with four years of college may not even suffice. While one researcher may be interested in communication patterns as partners assume certain roles, a second researcher may be interested in parenting roles.

Step Four: Define the Concept Operationally

operational definition
A statement of precisely which observable characteristics will be measured and the process for assigning a value to the concept.

A precise constitutive definition makes the operational definition task much easier. An **operational definition** specifies which observable characteristics will be measured and the process for assigning a value to the concept. In other words, it assigns meaning to a construct in terms of the operations necessary to measure it in any concrete situation.

Because it is overly restrictive in marketing to insist that all variables be operationally defined in directly measurable terms, many variables are stated in more abstract terms and measured indirectly, based on theoretical assumptions about their nature. For example, it is impossible to measure an attitude directly, because an attitude is an abstract concept that refers to things inside a person's mind. It is possible, nonetheless, to give a clear theoretical definition of an attitude as an enduring organization of motivational, emotional, perceptual, and cognitive processes with respect to some aspect of the environment. On the basis of this definition, instruments have been developed for measuring attitudes indirectly, by asking questions about how a person feels, what the person believes, and how the person intends to behave.

In summary, an operational definition serves as a bridge between a theoretical concept and real-world events or factors. Constructs such as "attitude" and "high-involvement purchasing" are abstractions that cannot be observed. Operational definitions transform such constructs into observable events. In other words, they define or give meaning to a construct by spelling out what the researcher must do to measure it. There are many different potential operational definitions for any single concept, regardless of how exact the constitutive definition may be. The researcher must choose the operational definition that fits most appropriately with the objectives of the research.

An example of a constitutive definition, a corresponding operational definition, and a resultant measurement scale are shown in Table 9.1. The operational definition of role ambiguity was developed by two marketing professors for use with salespeople and customer service personnel. The theoretical notion is that role ambiguity leads to job stress and impedes a worker's ability to improve performance and obtain job-based rewards, leading to job dissatisfaction.

Construct equivalence deals with how people see, understand, and develop measurements of a particular phenomenon. The problem confronting the global marketing researcher is that, because of sociocultural, economic, and political differences, construct perspectives may be neither identical nor equivalent. The examples provided in the Global Issues feature highlight the construct equivalence problem faced by global marketing researchers.

scale
A set of symbols or numbers so constructed that the symbols or numbers can be assigned by a rule to the individuals (or their behaviors or attitudes) to whom the scale is applied.

Step Five: Develop a Measurement Scale

Table 9.1 includes a scale that ranges from "very certain" to "very uncertain." A **scale** is a set of symbols or numbers so constructed that the symbols or numbers

Table 9.1	**Constitutive and Operational Definitions of Role Ambiguity**	
	Constitutive Definition	Role ambiguity is a direct function of the discrepancy between the information available to the person and that which is required for adequate performance of a role. It is the difference between a person's actual state of knowledge and the knowledge that provides adequate satisfaction of that person's personal needs and values.
	Operational Definition	Role ambiguity is the amount of uncertainty (ranging from very uncertain to very certain on a five-point scale) an individual feels regarding job role responsibilities and expectations from other employees and customers.
	Measurement Scale	The measurement scale consists of 45 items, with each item assessed by a five-point scale with category labels *1* = very certain, *2* = certain, *3* = neutral, *4* = uncertain, *5* = very uncertain. Samples of the 45 items follow:

- How much freedom of action I am expected to have
- How I am expected to handle nonroutine activities on the job
- The sheer amount of work I am expected to do
- To what extent my boss is open to hearing my point of view
- How satisfied my boss is with me
- How managers in other departments expect me to interact with them
- What managers in other departments think about the job I perform
- How I am expected to interact with my customers
- How I should behave (with customers) while on the job
- If I am expected to lie a little to win customer confidence
- If I am expected to hide my company's foul-ups from my customers
- About how much time my family feels I should spend on the job
- To what extent my family expects me to share my job-related problems
- How my coworkers expect me to behave while on the job
- How much information my coworkers expect me to convey to my boss

Source: Adapted from Jagdip Singh and Gary K. Rhoads, "Boundary Role Ambiguity in Marketing-Oriented Positions: A Multidimensional, Multifaceted Operationalization," *Journal of Marketing Research* 28 (August 1991), pp. 328–338. Reprinted by permission of the American Marketing Association.

Construct Equivalence Problems Often Occur in Global Marketing Research

CONSTRUCT EQUIVALENCE PROBLEMS IN GLOBAL MARKETING RESEARCH may relate to functional equivalence, conceptual equivalence, or definitional equivalence. Some examples of each type of problem follow.

Functional Equivalence. In England, Germany, and Scandinavia, beer is generally perceived as an alcoholic beverage. In Mediterranean lands, however, beer is considered akin to soft drinks. Therefore, a study of the competitive status of beer in Northern Europe would have to build in questions on wine and liquor. In Italy, Spain, or Greece, the comparison would have to be with soft drinks.

In Italy, it's common for children to have a bar of chocolate between two slices of bread as a snack. In France, bar chocolate is often used in cooking. But a German housewife would be revolted by either practice.

Conceptual Equivalence. A researcher using the concepts "out-group" and "in-group" would be dealing with very different groups in the United States and Greece. In the United States, the in-group includes people from one's own country, and the out-group includes foreigners. In Greece, the out-group includes coun-trymen with whom one is not closely associated. (When Athenians were asked to help fellow Greeks and foreigners mail letters, the Greeks received worse treatment than did the foreigners.)

Personality traits such as aggressiveness or assertiveness may not be relevant in all countries or cultures. The concept may be absent from the culture and language or may have an entirely different meaning.

As a final example, Japanese and Western concepts of decision making differ considerably. Whereas the Westerner sees decision making as a discrete event, the Japanese cannot make that distinction.

Definitional Equivalence. In France, fragrance is measured on a hot–cold continuum. In the United States and the United Kingdom, hot and cold are not attributes assigned to fragrances. That is, an attribute used to categorize product classes may vary from one country or culture to another.

Perceptions of beer, as cited under functional equivalence, also provide an example of problems in achieving definitional equivalence. In the United Kingdom, beer would be classified as an alcoholic drink. In Mediterranean cultures, it would be classified as a soft drink.[2] ∎

can be assigned by a rule to the individuals (or their behaviors or attitudes) to whom the scale is applied. The assignment on the scale is indicated by the individual's possession of whatever the scale is supposed to measure. Thus, a salesperson who feels he knows exactly how he is supposed to interact with customers would mark *very certain* for that item on the scale in Table 9.1.

Creating a measurement scale begins with determining the level of measurement desirable or possible. Table 9.2 describes the four basic levels of measurement: nominal, ordinal, interval, and ratio.

Nominal Level of Measurement

Nominal scales are among those most commonly used in marketing research. A nominal scale partitions data into categories that are mutually exclusive and collectively exhaustive, implying that every bit of data will fit into one and only one category and that all data will fit somewhere on the scale. The term *nominal* means "name-like," indicating that the numbers assigned to objects or phenomena are naming or classifying them but have no true number value; that is, the numbers cannot be ordered, added, or divided. The numbers are simply labels or identification numbers and nothing else. Examples of two nominal scales follow:

nominal scales
Scales that partition data into mutually exclusive and collectively exhaustive categories.

| **Sex:** | (1) Male | (2) Female | |
| **Geographic area:** | (1) Urban | (2) Rural | (3) Suburban |

Table 9.2

The Four Basic Levels of Measurement

Level	Description*	Basic Empirical Operations	Typical Usage	Typical Descriptive Statistics
Nominal	Uses numerals to identify objects, individuals, events, or groups	Determination of equality/inequality	Classification (male/female; buyer/non-buyer)	Frequency counts, percentages/modes
Ordinal	In addition to identification, provides information about the relative amount of some characteristic possessed by an event, object, etc.	Determination of greater or lesser	Rankings/ratings (preferences for hotels, banks, etc., social class; ratings of foods based on fat content, cholesterol)	Median (mean and variance metric)
Interval	Possesses all the properties of nominal and ordinal scales plus equal intervals between consecutive points	Determination of equality of intervals	Preferred measure of complex concepts/constructs (temperature scale, air pressure scale, level of knowledge about brands)	Mean/variance
Ratio	Incorporates all the properties of nominal, ordinal, and interval scales plus an absolute zero point	Determination of equality of ratios	Preferred measure when precision instruments are available (sales, number of on-time arrivals, age)	Geometric mean/harmonic mean

*Because higher levels of measurement contain all the properties of lower levels, higher level scales can be converted into lower level ones (i.e., ratio to interval or ordinal or nominal, or interval to ordinal or nominal, or ordinal to nominal).

Source: Adapted from S. S. Stevens, "On the Theory of Scales of Measurement," *Science 103* (June 7, 1946), pp. 677–680.

The only quantifications in numerical scales are the number and percentage of objects in each category—for example, 50 males (48.5 percent) and 53 females (51.5 percent). Computing a mean of 2.4 for geographic area would be meaningless; only the mode, the value that appears most often, would be appropriate.

Ordinal Level of Measurement

ordinal scales
Scales that maintain the labeling characteristics of nominal scales and have the ability to order data.

Ordinal scales have the labeling characteristics of nominal scales plus an ability to order data. Ordinal measurement is possible when the transitivity postulate can be applied. (A *postulate* is an assumption that is an essential prerequisite to carrying out an operation or line of thinking.) The *transitivity postulate* is described by the notion that "if *a* is greater than *b*, and *b* is greater than *c*, then *a* is greater than *c*." Other terms that can be substituted for *is greater than* are *is preferred to, is stronger than,* and *precedes.* An example of an ordinal scale follows:

Please rank the following brands of fax machines from *1* to *5,* with *1* being the most preferred and *5* the least preferred.

Panasonic   _____
Toshiba   _____
Sharp   _____
Savin   _____
Ricoh   _____

Ordinal numbers are used strictly to indicate rank order. The numbers do not indicate absolute quantities, nor do they imply that the intervals between the numbers are equal. For example, a person ranking the fax machines might like Toshiba only slightly more than Savin and view Ricoh as totally unacceptable. Such information would not be obtained from an ordinal scale.

Because ranking is the objective of an ordinal scale, any rule prescribing a series of numbers that preserves the ordered relationship is satisfactory. In other words, Panasonic could have been assigned a value of 30; Sharp, 40; Toshiba, 27; Ricoh, 32; and Savin, 42. Or any other series of numbers could have been used, as long as the basic ordering was preserved. In the case just cited, Savin is 1; Sharp, 2; Ricoh, 3; Panasonic, 4; and Toshiba, 5. Common arithmetical operations such as addition and multiplication cannot be used with ordinal scales. The appropriate measure of central tendency is the mode or the median. A percentile or quartile measure is used for measuring dispersion.

A controversial (yet rather common) use of ordinal scales is to rate various characteristics. In this case, the researcher assigns numbers to reflect the relative ratings of a series of statements, then uses these numbers to interpret relative distance. Recall that the marketing researchers examining role ambiguity used a scale ranging from *very certain* to *very uncertain.* The following values were assigned:

(1)	**(2)**	**(3)**	**(4)**	**(5)**
Very Certain	**Certain**	**Neutral**	**Uncertain**	**Very Uncertain**

If a researcher can justify the assumption that the intervals are equal within the scale, then the more powerful parametric statistical tests can be applied.

PART 3:
Data Acquisition

(Parametric statistical tests will be discussed in Chapters 15 and 16.) Indeed, some measurement scholars argue that equal intervals should be normally assumed.

The best procedure would seem to be to treat ordinal measurements as though they were interval measurements but to be constantly alert to the possibility of gross inequality of intervals. As much as possible about the characteristics of the measuring tools should be learned. Much useful information has been obtained by this approach, with resulting scientific advances in psychology, sociology, and education. In short, it is unlikely that researchers will be led seriously astray by heeding this advice, if they are careful in applying it.[3]

Interval Level of Measurement

Interval scales contain all the features of ordinal scales with the added dimension that the intervals between the points on the scale are equal. The concept of temperature is based on equal intervals. Marketing researchers often prefer interval scales over ordinal scales because they can measure how much of a trait one consumer has (or does not have) over another. An interval scale enables a researcher to discuss differences separating two objects. The scale possesses properties of order and difference but with an arbitrary zero point. Examples are the Fahrenheit and Celsius scales; the freezing point of water is zero on one scale and 32 degrees on the other.

The arbitrary zero point of interval scales restricts the statements that a researcher can make about the scale points. One can say that 80°F is hotter than 32°F or that 64°F is 16 degrees cooler than 80°F. However, one cannot say that 64°F is twice as warm as 32°F. Why? Because the zero point on the Fahrenheit scale is arbitrary. To understand this point, consider the transformation of the two Fahrenheit temperatures to Celsius using the formula Celsius = $(F - 32)(5/9)$; 32°F equals 0°C, and 64°F equals 17.8°C. The statement we made about the Fahrenheit temperatures (64° is twice as warm as 32°) does not hold for Celsius. The same would be true of rankings of fax machines on an interval scale. If Toshiba is given a 20 and Sharp a 10, we cannot say that Toshiba is liked twice as much as Sharp, because a point defining the absence of liking has not been identified and assigned a value of zero on the scale.

Interval scales are amenable to computation of an arithmetic mean, standard deviation, and correlation coefficients. The more powerful parametric statistical tests such as *t*-tests and *F*-tests can be applied. In addition, researchers can take a more conservative approach and use nonparametric tests if they have concern about the equal intervals assumption.

Ratio Level of Measurement

Ratio scales have all the characteristics of those scales previously discussed as well as a meaningful absolute zero or origin. Because there is universal agreement as to the location of the zero point, comparisons among the magnitudes of ratio-scaled values are acceptable. Thus, a ratio scale reflects the actual amount of a variable. Physical characteristics of a respondent such as age, weight, and height are examples of ratio-scaled variables. Other ratio scales are based on area, distance, money values, return rates, population counts, and lapsed periods of time.

Commonly used temperature scales are based on equal intervals and an arbitrary zero point. Marketing researchers often prefer interval scales because they can measure how much more of a trait one consumer has than another.

interval scales
Scales that have the characteristics of ordinal scales, plus equal intervals between points to show relative amounts; they may include an arbitrary zero point.

ratio scales
Scales that have the characteristics of interval scales, plus a meaningful zero point so that magnitudes can be compared arithmetically.

Because some objects have none of the property being measured, a ratio scale originates at a zero point with absolute empirical meaning. For example, an investment (albeit a poor one) can have no rate of return, or a census tract in New Mexico could be devoid of any persons. An absolute zero implies that all arithmetic operations are possible, including multiplication and division. Numbers on the scale indicate the actual amounts of the property being measured. A large bag of McDonald's french fries weighs eight ounces and a regular bag at Burger King weighs four ounces; thus, a large McDonald's bag of fries weighs twice as much as a regular Burger King bag of fries.

Step Six: Evaluate the Reliability and Validity of the Measurement

An ideal marketing research study would provide information that is accurate, precise, lucid, and timely. Accurate data imply accurate measurement, or $M = A$, where M refers to measurement and A stands for complete accuracy. In marketing research, this ideal is rarely, if ever, achieved. Instead,

$$M = A + E$$

where E = errors

Errors can be either random or systematic, as noted in Chapter 6. Systematic error results in a constant bias in the measurements, caused by faults in the measurement instrument or process. For example, if a faulty ruler (on which one inch is actually one and a half inches) is used in Pillsbury's test kitchens to measure the height of chocolate cakes cooked with alternative recipes, all cakes will be recorded at less than their actual height. *Random error* also influences the measurements but not systematically. Thus, random error is transient in nature. A person may not answer a question truthfully because he is in a bad mood that day.

Two scores on a measurement scale can differ for a number of reasons.[4] Only the first of the following eight reasons does not involve error. A researcher must determine whether any of the remaining seven sources of measurement differences are producing random or systematic error.

1. *A true difference in the characteristic being measured.* A perfect measurement difference is solely the result of actual differences. For example, John rates McDonald's service as 1 (excellent) and Sandy rates its service as 4 (average), and the variation is due only to actual attitude differences.
2. *Differences due to stable characteristics of individual respondents,* such as personality, values, and intelligence. Sandy has an aggressive, rather critical personality, and she gives no one and nothing the benefit of the doubt. She actually was quite pleased with the service she received at McDonald's, but she expects such service and so gave it an average rating.
3. *Differences due to short-term personal factors,* such as temporary mood swings, health problems, time constraints, or fatigue. Earlier on the day of the study, John had won $400 in a "Name That Tune" contest on a local radio station. He stopped by McDonald's for a burger after he picked up his winning

check. His reply on the service quality questionnaire might have been quite different if he had
been interviewed the previous day.

4. *Differences caused by situational factors,* such as distractions or others present in the interview situation.
Sandy was giving her replies while trying to watch
her four-year-old nephew, who was running amok
on the McDonald's playground; John had his new
fiancée along when he was interviewed. Replies of
both people might have been different if they had
been interviewed at home while no other friend or
relative was present.

5. *Differences resulting from variations in administering the
survey.* Interviewers can ask questions with different
voice inflections, causing response variation. And
because of such factors as rapport with the interviewee, manner of dress, sex, or race, different interviewers can cause responses to vary. Interviewer bias

can be as subtle as a nodding of the head. One interviewer who tended to
nod unconsciously was found to bias some respondents. They thought that
the interviewer was agreeing with them when he was, in fact, saying, "OK,
I'm recording what you say—tell me more."

6. *Differences due to the sampling of items included in the questionnaire.* When
researchers attempt to measure the quality of service at McDonald's, the scales
and other questions used represent only a portion of the items that could have
been used. The scales created by the researchers reflect their interpretation of
the construct (service quality) and the way it is measured. If the researchers
had used different words or if items had been added or removed, the scale values reported by John and Sandy might have been different.

7. *Differences due to a lack of clarity in the measurement instrument.* A question may
be ambiguous, complex, or incorrectly interpreted. A survey that asked
"How far do you live from McDonald's?" and then gave choices "(1) less than
5 minutes, (2) 5 to 10 minutes," and so forth, would be ambiguous; someone walking would undoubtedly take longer to get to the restaurant than a
person driving a car or riding a bike. This topic is covered in much greater
detail in Chapter 10.

8. *Differences due to mechanical or instrument factors.* Blurred questionnaires, lack
of space to fully record answers, missing pages in a questionnaire, or a balky
pen can result in differences in responses.

Martin Weinberger, executive vice president of Oxtoby-Smith, Incorporated,
offers his perspectives on measurement in the In Practice feature.

Reliability

A measurement scale that provides consistent results over time is reliable. If a
ruler consistently measures a chocolate cake as nine inches high, then the ruler
is said to be reliable. Reliable scales, gauges, and other measurement devices can
be used with confidence and with the knowledge that transient and situational

Two scores on a measurement
scale can differ for a number
of reasons. McDonald's may
score higher on one person's
survey than on another person's because of real differences in perceptions of the
service or because of a variety
of random or systematic
errors. The reliability and validity of the type of measurement
should always be checked.

The Truth about What Respondents Say

MARTIN WEINBERGER IS EXECUTIVE VICE PRESIDENT OF OXTOBY-Smith, Incorporated, New York, one of America's largest and oldest marketing research companies. His 25 years of experience in the research industry has led him to develop certain perspectives regarding measurement in consumer research. Several of those perspectives are described below.

1. Sometimes Consumers Don't Tell the Truth; Sometimes They Are Willing to Reveal It. Several years ago, a major catalog company was having trouble with its boys' slacks—it was getting an unusually large number of returns. Consumers were writing that the reason for the return was that the slacks did not fit properly. On the basis of that information, the catalog sales company believed something must be wrong with the diagrams and instructions it provided to consumers for ordering the right size slacks. Oxtoby-Smith was asked to find out what was wrong with the diagrams or the instructions so the client could fix them. We were given the names of consumers who had returned the boys' slacks.

We sent our interviewers into the field, carrying the heavy catalog, with the diagrams and the instructions. What we found was not what we had expected to find. The consumers told us the slacks had fit perfectly well. The mothers had ordered three or four pairs of slacks for their teenage sons in the hope that the son would find *one* pair he would be willing to wear. Then the mother had to face returning the other two or three pairs. The mothers felt uncomfortable giving any explanation for the return of the slacks other than "poor fit." This finding indicated that the diagrams were not the problem. The instructions were not the problem. The catalog company had to learn to live with the returns in the same way the mothers had to live with the habits of their teenage sons.

2. Sometimes Consumers Claim More Than They Know; Sometimes They Are Just Confused. It has been well established that consumers sometimes claim awareness of brands that do not exist. That is why it is important to include fictitious brand names in studies of brand awareness to see how much claiming is going on. In fact, I have done a study in which a fictitious brand name had *more* brand awareness than the client's brand and the client considered changing the name of its brand to the fictitious brand name!

3. Sometimes Consumers Don't Know Why They Buy the Brands They Buy. This section could be subtitled, "Why you should not ask why." I have conducted a large number of studies asking consumers, at the client's request, *why* they buy the products they buy, and I have looked at their answers to that question. At the same time, I have looked at their answers to other questions. I have found that consumers often do not really *know* why they buy the brands they buy.

A simple case in point is a food or beverage product. Ask consumers why they buy a brand, and they usually will tell you "because it tastes good." If you give a consumer a blind product test, you may find out that this individual cannot differentiate between his or her preferred Brand X and Brand Y. If you use a double-blind paired comparison, in one paired blind test a consumer will prefer X and in another paired blind test the same individual will prefer Y.

4. Consumers Not Only Have Opinions, They Have Passions. Generally, consumers are very cooperative. They will answer almost any questions you ask them. But, my experience teaches me that you need to know more than just their opinions; you need to know their passions.

For example, a manufacturer of toilet paper that is thinking of introducing a scented version might ask us to find out which of a series of scents is preferred by consumers. We could test the scents and tell them scent A is more widely preferred than scent B. However, we would be remiss in our job if we failed to find out whether consumers would be disposed toward toilet paper *with any scent at all* and what the scent preferences are of those who *like* the idea of scented toilet paper. Possibly those who are interested in toilet paper with scents prefer scent B over scent A, whereas scent A appeals to those who, in the marketplace, would be buying *unscented* paper.[5] ∎

factors are not interfering with the measurement process. Reliable instruments provide stable measures at different times under different conditions. A key question regarding reliability is "If we measure some phenomenon over and over again with the same measurement device, will we get the same or highly similar results?" An affirmative answer means that the device is reliable.

Thus, **reliability** is the degree to which measures are free from random error and, therefore, provide consistent data. The less error there is, the more reliable the observation is, so a measurement that is free of error is a correct measure. A reliable measurement, then, does not change when the concept being measured remains constant in value. However, if the concept being measured does change in value, the reliable measure will indicate that change. How can a measuring instrument be unreliable? If your weight stays constant at 150 pounds but repeated measurements on your bathroom scale show your weight to fluctuate, the scale's lack of reliability may be due to a weak spring.

There are three ways to assess reliability: test-retest, the use of equivalent forms, and internal consistency.

reliability
The degree to which measures are free from random error and, therefore, provide consistent data.

Test-Retest Reliability **Test-retest reliability** is obtained by repeating the measurement with the same instrument, approximating the original conditions as closely as possible. The theory behind test-retest is that if random variations are present, they will be revealed by differences in the scores between the two tests. **Stability** means that very few differences in scores are found between the first and second administrations of the test; the measuring instrument is said to be stable. For example, assume that a 30-item department store image measurement scale was administered to the same group of shoppers at two different times. If the correlation between the two measurements was high, the reliability would be assumed to be high.

test-retest reliability
The ability of the same instrument to produce consistent results when used a second time under conditions as similar as possible to the original conditions.
stability
Lack of change in results from test to retest.

equivalent form reliability
The ability of two very similar forms of an instrument to produce closely correlated results.

internal consistency reliability
The ability of an instrument to produce similar results when used on different samples during the same time period to measure a phenomenon.

split-half technique
A method of assessing the reliability of a scale by dividing the total set of measurement items in half and correlating the results.

There are several problems with test-retest reliability. First, it may be very difficult to locate and gain the cooperation of respondents for a second testing. Second, the first measurement may alter a person's response on the second measurement. Third, environmental or personal factors may change, causing the second measurement to change.

Equivalent Form Reliability   The difficulties encountered with the test-retest approach can be avoided by creating equivalent forms of a measurement instrument. For example, assume that the researcher is interested in identifying inner-directed versus outer-directed lifestyles. Two questionnaires can be created containing measures of inner-directed behavior (see Table 9.3) and measures of outer-directed behavior. These measures should receive about the same emphasis on each questionnaire. Thus, although the questions used to ascertain the lifestyles are different on the two questionnaires, the number of questions used to measure each lifestyle should be approximately equal. The recommended interval for administering the second equivalent form is two weeks, although in some cases the two forms are given one after the other or simultaneously. **Equivalent form reliability** is determined by measuring the correlation of the scores on the two instruments.

There are two problems with equivalent forms that should be noted. First, it is very difficult, and perhaps impossible, to create two totally equivalent forms. Second, if equivalence can be achieved, it may not be worth the time, trouble, and expense involved. The theory behind the equivalent forms approach to reliability assessment is the same as that of the test-retest. The primary difference between the test-retest and the equivalent forms methods is the testing instrument itself. Test-retest uses the same instrument, whereas the equivalent forms approach uses a different, but highly similar, measuring instrument.

Internal Consistency Reliability   **Internal consistency reliability** assesses the ability to produce similar results when different samples are used to measure a phenomenon during the same time period. The theory of internal consistency rests on the concept of equivalence. *Equivalence* is concerned with how much error may be introduced by using different samples of items to measure a phenomenon; it focuses on variations at one point in time among samples of items. A researcher can test for item equivalence by assessing the homogeneity of a set of items. The total set of items used to measure a phenomenon, such as inner-directed lifestyles, is divided into two halves; the total scores of the two halves are then correlated. Use of the **split-half technique** typically calls for scale items to be randomly assigned to one half or the other. The problem with this method is that the estimate of the coefficient of reliability is totally dependent on how the items were split. Different splits result in different correlations when, ideally, they should not.

To overcome this problem, many researchers now use the *Cronbach alpha technique,* which involves computing mean reliability coefficient estimates for all

Table 9.3

Statements Used to Measure Inner-Directed Lifestyles

I often don't get the credit I deserve for things I do well.
I try to get my own way regardless of others.
My greatest achievements are ahead of me.
I have a number of ideas that someday I would like to put into a book.
I am quick to accept new ideas.
I often think about how I look and what impression I am making on others.
I am a competitive person.
I feel upset when I hear that people are criticizing or blaming me.
I'd like to be a celebrity.
I get a real thrill out of doing dangerous things.
I feel that almost nothing in life can substitute for great achievement.
It's important for me to be noticed.
I keep in close touch with my friends.
I spend a good deal of time trying to decide how I feel about things.
I often think I can feel my way into the innermost being of another person.
I feel that ideals are powerful motivating forces in people.
I think someone can be a good person without believing in God.
The Eastern religions are more appealing to me than Christianity.
I feel satisfied with my life.
I enjoy getting involved in new and unusual situations.
Overall, I'd say I'm happy.
I feel I understand where my life is going.
I like to think I'm different from other people.
I adopt a commonsense attitude toward life.

possible ways of splitting a set of items in half. A lack of correlation of an item with other items in the scale is evidence that the item does not belong in the scale and should be omitted. One limitation of the Cronbach alpha is that the scale items require equal intervals. If this criterion cannot be met, another test called the KR-20 can be used. The *KR-20 technique* is applicable for all dichotomous or nominally scaled items.

Validity

Recall that the second characteristic of a good measurement device is validity. **Validity** addresses the issue of whether what the researcher was trying to measure was actually measured. When Coke first brought out "New Coke," it had conducted more than 5,000 interviews that purported to show New Coke was favored over original Coke. Unfortunately, its measurement instrument was not valid. This led to one of the greatest marketing debacles of all time! The validity of a measure refers to the extent to which the measurement instrument and procedure are free from both systematic and random error. Thus, a measuring device is valid only if differences in scores reflect true differences on the characteristic being measured rather than systematic or random error. You should recognize that a necessary precondition for validity is that the measuring instrument be reliable. An instrument that is not reliable will not yield consistent results when measuring the same phenomenon over time.

validity
The degree to which what was being measured was actually measured.

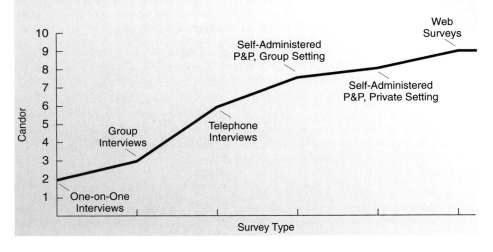

The Anonymity Gradient

BILL MACELROY, PRESIDENT OF SOCRATIC TECHNOLOGIES, SAN Francisco, discusses the concept of the importance of anonymous responses to respondents:

We feel that the privacy of the interviewee's environment may play a key role in the types of answers given because the change in the characteristics of answers doesn't stop when no specific interviewer is present. Even within self-administered interviewing situations, the degree to which the respondent feels "secure and alone" appears to produce more candor. We have called this observed phenomenon the anonymity gradient.

Over the past three years, we have had several opportunities to run side-by-side studies in which the same questions were asked using different modes of field methodology (e.g., one-on-one interviewing, CATI telephone, paper and pencil, disk-by-mail, and Web-based interviewing). As we examined the answers to identi-

cally worded questions, a curious pattern began to emerge. Increased human presence had the distinctive effect of producing kinder, less frank answers. This difference was also noted between paper and pencil surveys conducted with and without other people in the area.

The most candid answers (based on the degree to which people reported known problems, complained about service that was known to be a concern and gave in-depth responses when probed for areas that needed improvement) came from people using their own personal computers. Researchers have reported that when people use computers they tend to enter a "cool and immersive, womb-like environment" in which the level of engagement can produce exaggerated levels of perceived privacy. The anonymity gradient can be thought of as a pattern of candor that changes with the perceived level of privacy. This relationship is shown in the chart.

By itself, the anonymity gradient might be an interesting anomaly, but without much practical value. We

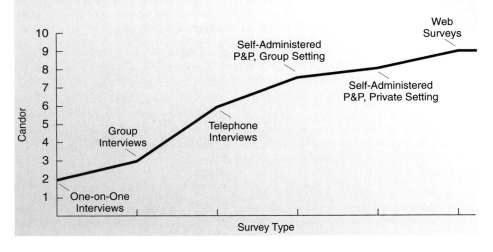

PART 3:
Data Acquisition

have, however, found some distinctive characteristics that may be helpful to people as they are planning conversions from certain forms of research to others. This is particularly important if your company has been tracking satisfaction, performance, problem resolution, and other similar topics using telephone, paper and pencil, or one-on-one interviewing techniques. There can be an unpleasant shock to the system when, after many periods of hearing from your customers that they are completely satisfied with no problems to report, you suddenly find out that they are less satisfied and have a whole list of demands for improvement. You may encounter this when converting traditional methodologies to newer technologies.

For example, most data related to purchase interest tends to be overstated when actual purchases are tallied. Although we haven't had the benefit of tracking actual results, we suspect that some data related to purchase interest collected using a more anonymous technology may be closer to what will really happen when the product actually ships.[6] ■

A scale or other measuring device is basically worthless to a researcher if it lacks validity, because it is not measuring what it is supposed to. On the surface, this seems like a rather simple notion, yet validity often is based on subtle distinctions. Assume that your teacher gives an exam that he has constructed to measure marketing research knowledge, and the test consists strictly of applying a number of formulas to simple case problems. A friend receives a low score on the test and protests to the teacher that she "really understands marketing research." Her position, in essence, is that the test was not valid. She maintains that, rather than measuring knowledge of marketing research, the test measured memorization of formulas and the ability to use simple math to find solutions. The teacher could repeat the exam only to find that student scores still fell in the same order. Does this mean that the protesting student was incorrect? Not necessarily; the teacher may be systematically measuring the ability to memorize rather than a true understanding of marketing research.

Unlike the teacher attempting to measure marketing research knowledge, a brand manager is interested in successful prediction. The manager, for example, wants to know if a purchase intent scale successfully predicts trial purchase of a new product. Thus, validity can be examined from a number of different perspectives, including face, content, criterion-related, and construct validity (see Table 9.4).

Face Validity   **Face validity** is the weakest form of validity. It is concerned with the degree to which a measurement seems to measure what it is supposed to. It is a judgment call by the researcher, made as the questions are designed. Thus, as each question is scrutinized, there is an implicit assessment of its face validity. Revisions enhance the face validity of the question until it passes the researcher's subjective evaluation. Alternatively, *face validity* can refer to the subjective agreement of researchers, experts, or people familiar with the market, product, or industry that a scale logically appears to be accurately reflecting what it is supposed

face validity
The degree to which a measurement seems to measure what it is supposed to measure.

Table 9.4

Assessing the Validity of a Measurement Instrument

Face validity	The degree to which a measurement instrument seems to measure what it is supposed to, as judged by researchers.
Content validity	The degree to which measurement items represent the universe of the concept under study.
Criterion-related validity	The degree to which a measurement instrument can predict a variable that is designated a criterion. a. Predictive validity: The extent to which a future level of a criterion variable can be predicted by a current measurement on a scale. b. Concurrent validity: The extent to which a criterion variable measured at the same point in time as the variable of interest can be predicted by the measurement instrument.
Construct validity	The degree to which a measurement instrument confirms a hypothesis created from a theory based on the concepts under study. a. Convergent validity: The degree of association among different measurement instruments that purport to measure the same concept. b. Discriminant validity: A measure of the lack of association among constructs that are supposed to be different.

to measure. A straightforward question such as "What is your age?" followed by a series of age categories generally is agreed to have face validity. Most scales used in marketing research attempt to measure attitudes or behavioral intentions, which are much more elusive.

content validity
The representativeness, or sampling adequacy, of the content of the measurement instrument.

Content Validity **Content validity** is the representativeness, or sampling adequacy, of the content of the measurement instrument. In other words, does the scale provide adequate coverage of the topic under study? Say that McDonald's has hired you to measure its image among adults 18 to 30 years of age who eat fast-food hamburgers at least once a month. You devise the following scale:

modern building	1	2	3	4	5	old-fashioned building
beautiful landscaping	1	2	3	4	5	poor landscaping
clean parking lots	1	2	3	4	5	dirty parking lots
attractive signs	1	2	3	4	5	unattractive signs

A McDonald's executive would quickly take issue with this scale, claiming that a person could evaluate McDonald's on this scale and never have eaten a McDonald's hamburger. In fact, the evaluation could be made simply by driving past a McDonald's. The executive could further argue that the scale lacks content validity because many important components of image—such as the quality of the food, cleanliness of the eating area and restrooms, and promptness and courtesy of service—were omitted.

The determination of content validity is not always a simple matter. It is very difficult, and perhaps impossible, to identify all the facets of McDonald's image. Content validity ultimately becomes a judgmental matter. One could approach content validity by first carefully defining precisely what is to be measured.

PART 3:
Data Acquisition

Second, an exhaustive literature search and focus groups could be conducted to identify all possible items for inclusion on the scale. Third, a panel of experts could be asked their opinions on whether an item should be included. Finally, the scale could be pretested and an open-ended question asked that might identify other items to be included. For example, after a more refined image scale for McDonald's has been administered, a follow-up question could be "Do you have any other thoughts about McDonald's that you would like to express?" Answers to this pretest question might provide clues for other image dimensions not previously considered.

Criterion-Related Validity   **Criterion-related validity** examines the ability of a measuring instrument to predict a variable that is designated a criterion. Suppose that we wish to devise a test to identify marketing researchers who are exceptional at moderating focus groups. We begin by having impartial marketing research experts identify from a directory of researchers those they judge to be best at moderating focus groups. We then construct 300 items to which all the group moderators are asked to reply yes or no, such as "I believe it is important to compel shy group participants to speak out" and "I like to interact with small groups of people." We then go through the responses and select the items that the "best" focus group moderators answered one way and the rest of the moderators answered the other way. Assume that this process produces 84 items, which we put together to form what we shall call the Test of Effectiveness in Focus Group Moderating (TEFGM). We feel that this test will identify good focus group moderators. The criterion of interest here is the ability to conduct a good focus group. We might explore further the criterion-related validity of TEFGM by administering it to another group of moderators, each of whom has been designated as either "best" or "not as good." Then we could determine how well the test identifies the section to which each marketing researcher is assigned. Thus, criterion-related validity is concerned with detecting the presence or absence of one or more criteria considered to represent constructs of interest.

Two subcategories of criterion-related validity are predictive validity and concurrent validity. **Predictive validity** is the extent to which a future level of a criterion variable can be predicted by a current measurement on a scale. A voter-motivation scale, for example, is used to predict the likelihood that a person will vote in the next election. A savvy politician is not interested in what the com-

A politician is interested in what issues those likely to vote perceive as important. The predictive validity of the politician's measures may determine whether or not he or she is elected.

criterion-related validity
The degree to which a measurement instrument can predict a variable that is designated a criterion.

predictive validity
The degree to which a future level of a criterion variable can be forecast by a current measurement scale.

concurrent validity
The degree to which another variable, measured at the same point in time as the variable of interest, can be predicted by the measurement instrument.

construct validity
The degree to which a measurement instrument represents and logically connects, via the underlying theory, the observed phenomenon to the construct.

convergent validity
The degree of correlation among different measurement instruments that purport to measure the same construct.

discriminant validity
A measure of the lack of association among constructs that are supposed to be different.

munity as a whole perceives as important problems but only in what persons who are likely to vote perceive as important problems. These are the issues that the politician would address in speeches and advertising. Another example of predictive validity is the extent to which a purchase intent scale for a new Pepperidge Farm pastry predicts actual trial of the product.

Concurrent validity is concerned with the relationship between the predictor variable and the criterion variable, both of which are assessed at the same point in time—for example, the ability of a home pregnancy test to accurately determine whether a woman is pregnant right now. Such a test with low concurrent validity could cause a lot of undue stress.

Construct Validity Construct validity, although not often consciously addressed by many marketing researchers on a day-to-day basis, is extremely important to marketing scientists. Assessing construct validity involves understanding the theoretical foundations underlying the obtained measurements. A measure has **construct validity** if it behaves according to the theory behind the prediction. Purchase behavior can be observed directly; someone either buys product A or does not. Yet scientists have developed constructs on lifestyle, involvement, attitude, and personality that help explain why someone does or does not purchase something. These constructs are largely unobservable. Researchers can observe behavior related to the constructs—that is, the purchase of a product. However, they cannot observe the constructs themselves—such as an attitude. Constructs help scientists communicate and build theories to explain phenomena.

Two statistical measures of construct validity are convergent and discriminant validity. **Convergent validity** reflects the degree of correlation among different measures that purport to measure the same construct. **Discriminant validity** reveals the lack of—or low—correlation among constructs that are supposed to be different. Assume that we develop a multi-item scale that measures the propensity to shop at discount stores. Our theory suggests that this propensity is caused by four personality variables: high level of self-confidence, low need for status, low need for distinctiveness, and high level of adaptability. Further, our theory suggests that propensity to shop at discount stores is not related to brand loyalty or high-level aggressiveness.

Evidence of construct validity exists if our scale does the following:

- Correlates highly with other measures of propensity to shop at discount stores, such as reported stores patronized and social class (convergent validity)
- Has a low correlation with the unrelated constructs of brand loyalty and a high level of aggressiveness (discriminant validity)

All the types of validity discussed here are somewhat interrelated in both theory and practice. Predictive validity is obviously very important on a scale to predict whether a person will shop at a discount store. A researcher developing a discount store patronage scale probably would first attempt to understand the constructs that provide the basis for prediction. The researcher would put forth a theory about discount store patronage—that, of course, is the foundation of

PART 3:
Data Acquisition

construct validity. Next, the researcher would be concerned with which specific items to include on the discount store patronage scale and whether these items relate to the full range of the construct. Thus, the researcher would ascertain the degree of content validity. The issue of criterion-related validity could be addressed in a pretest by measuring scores on the discount store patronage scale and actual store patronage.

Reliability and Validity—A Concluding Comment

The concepts of reliability and validity are illustrated in Figure 9.2. Situation 1 shows holes all over the target, which could be caused by the use of an old rifle, being a poor shot, or many other factors. This complete lack of consistency means there is no reliability. Because the instrument lacks reliability, thus creating huge errors, it cannot be valid. Measurement reliability is a necessary condition for validity.

Situation 2 denotes a very tight pattern (consistency), but the pattern is far removed from the bull's-eye. This illustrates that an instrument can have a high level of reliability (little variance) but lack validity. The instrument is consistent, but it does not measure what it is supposed to measure. The shooter has a steady eye, but the sights are not adjusted properly. Situation 3 shows the reliability and validity that researchers strive to achieve in a measurement instrument; it is on target with what the researcher is attempting to measure.

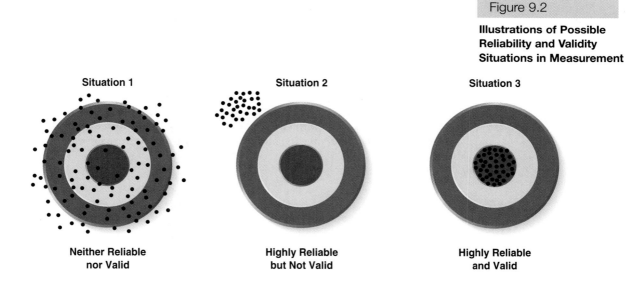

Figure 9.2

Illustrations of Possible Reliability and Validity Situations in Measurement

Situation 1 — **Neither Reliable nor Valid**

Situation 2 — **Highly Reliable but Not Valid**

Situation 3 — **Highly Reliable and Valid**

Summary

Measurement consists of using rules to assign numbers or labels to objects in such a way as to represent quantities or qualities of attributes. A measurement rule is a guide, a method, or a command that tells a researcher what to do. Accurate measurement requires rules that are both clear and specific.

The measurement process comprises the following steps: (1) identify the concept of interest, (2) develop a construct, (3) define the concept constitutively, (4) define the concept operationally, (5) develop a measurement scale, and (6) evaluate the reliability and validity of the scale. A constitutive definition is a statement of the meaning of the central concept under study, establishing its boundaries. An operational definition specifies which observable characteristics will be measured and the process for assigning a value to the concept.

There are four basic levels of measurement: nominal, ordinal, interval, and ratio. A nominal scale partitions data into categories that are mutually exclusive and collectively exhaustive. The numbers assigned to objects or phenomena have no true numerical meaning; they are simply labels. Ordinal scales have the labeling characteristics of nominal scales plus an ability to order data. Interval scales contain all the features of ordinal scales with the added dimension that the intervals between the points on the scale are equal. Interval scales enable the researcher to discuss differences separating two objects. They are amenable to computation of an arithmetic mean, standard deviation, and correlation coefficients. Ratio scales have all the characteristics of previously discussed scales as well as a meaningful absolute zero or origin, thus permitting comparison of the absolute magnitude of the numbers and reflecting the actual amount of the variable.

Measurement data consist of accurate information and errors. Systematic error results in a constant bias in the measurements. Random error also influences the measurements but is not systematic; it is transient in nature. Reliability is the degree to which measures are free from random error and therefore provide consistent data. There are three ways to assess reliability: test-retest, internal consistency, and use of equivalent forms. Validity addresses whether the attempt at measurement was successful. The validity of a measure refers to the extent to which the measurement device or process is free from both systematic and random error. Types of validity include face, content, criterion-related, and construct validity.

Key Terms & Definitions

measurement The process of assigning numbers or labels to persons, objects, or events in accordance with specific rules for representing quantities or qualities of attributes.

rule A guide, a method, or a command that tells a researcher what to do.

constructs Specific types of concepts that exist at higher levels of abstraction.

constitutive definition   A statement of the meaning of the central idea or concept under study, establishing its boundaries; also known as *theoretical,* or *conceptual, definition.*

operational definition   A statement of precisely which observable characteristics will be measured and the process for assigning a value to the concept.

scale   A set of symbols or numbers so constructed that the symbols or numbers can be assigned by a rule to the individuals (or their behaviors or attitudes) to whom the scale is applied.

nominal scales   Scales that partition data into mutually exclusive and collectively exhaustive categories.

ordinal scales   Scales that maintain the labeling characteristics of nominal scales and have the ability to order data.

interval scales   Scales that have the characteristics of ordinal scales, plus equal intervals between points to show relative amounts; they may include an arbitrary zero point.

ratio scales   Scales that have the characteristics of interval scales, plus a meaningful zero point so that magnitudes can be compared arithmetically.

reliability   The degree to which measures are free from random error and, therefore, provide consistent data.

test-retest reliability   The ability of the same instrument to produce consistent results when used a second time under conditions as similar as possible to the original conditions.

stability   Lack of change in results from test to retest.

equivalent form reliability   The ability of two very similar forms of an instrument to produce closely correlated results.

internal consistency reliability   The ability of an instrument to produce similar results when used on different samples during the same time period to measure a phenomenon.

split-half technique   A method of assessing the reliability of a scale by dividing the total set of measurement items in half and correlating the results.

validity   The degree to which what was being measured was actually measured.

face validity   The degree to which a measurement seems to measure what it is supposed to measure.

content validity   The representativeness, or sampling adequacy, of the content of the measurement instrument.

criterion-related validity   The degree to which a measurement instrument can predict a variable that is designated a criterion.

predictive validity   The degree to which a future level of a criterion variable can be forecast by a current measurement scale.

concurrent validity   The degree to which another variable, measured at the same point in time as the variable of interest, can be predicted by the measurement instrument.

construct validity   The degree to which a measurement instrument represents and logically connects, via the underlying theory, the observed phenomenon to the construct.

convergent validity The degree of correlation among different measurement instruments that purport to measure the same construct.

discriminant validity A measure of the lack of association among constructs that are supposed to be different.

Questions for Review & Critical Thinking

1. What is measurement?
2. Differentiate among the four types of measurement scales, and discuss the types of information obtained from each.
3. How does reliability differ from validity? Give examples of each.
4. Give an example of a scale that would be reliable but not valid. Also give an example of a scale that would be valid but not reliable.
5. What are three methods of assessing reliability?
6. What are three methods of assessing validity?

Working the Net

Go to a Web search engine and look up "validity and reliability." Describe to the class the new insights you gain into these important concepts.

Real-Life Research • 9.1

The Great Life?

What do you give to a person that has everything? With the nation rolling in good times, it's not an unthinkable question. A number of the traditional aspirations of "the good life" appear to be hitting a wall. There have been decreases in the percentages of Americans saying various items historically associated with success are part of their personal idea of "the good life, the life you'd like to have." Americans still have a fairly expansive concept of the good life. Twenty items are cited by one-quarter or more of the public as part of their vision of it, led by "a home you own" (88%), "a happy marriage" (76%), and "one or more children" (70%). But a number of items are down from 1996, from products like a car (69%, down 6) or color TV (53%, down 5) to a job that pays much more than average (54%, down 8) and a college education for the kids (52%, down

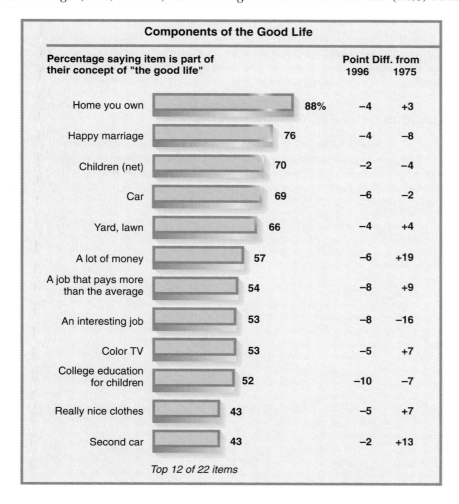

Components of the Good Life

Percentage saying item is part of their concept of "the good life"		Point Diff. from	
		1996	1975
Home you own	88%	−4	+3
Happy marriage	76	−4	−8
Children (net)	70	−2	−4
Car	69	−6	−2
Yard, lawn	66	−4	+4
A lot of money	57	−6	+19
A job that pays more than the average	54	−8	+9
An interesting job	53	−8	−16
Color TV	53	−5	+7
College education for children	52	−10	−7
Really nice clothes	43	−5	+7
Second car	43	−2	+13

Top 12 of 22 items

10). Given the high aspirations evident in other research findings—such as the public's fascination with the Internet, cell phones, and other new technologies, the increasing priority people place on money and financial independence, and the return of status symbols—it doesn't seem likely that Americans have lowered their expectations. Perhaps instead people have different aspirations. At a time when people drop out of college to become Internet millionaires, the stock market is creating vast sums of wealth, and "ditching the Joneses" has replaced "keeping up with the Joneses," the old aspirations may not be enough. The good life may be giving way to the *great* life.

The Good Life Is Now. More people feel the good life is within their grasp: 28% feel their chances are "very good" of reaching it, up 4 points from 1996 and 8 points higher than 1994. Another 11%, up 5 from 1996, say they've "already achieved it." People aged 18–29 have had the biggest increase in feeling their prospects are "very good" (39%, up 16 from 1996). The biggest gain in attaining the good life: people 60 and older (31%, up 18).

What People Have. Progress toward getting the items on the good life list is still mixed. Majorities have a car (71%), a color TV (68%), kids (61%), a home they own (57%), and a yard (53%). Increasing percentages have "good life" gadgets such as a second color TV (40%, up 4 from 1996 and 31 higher than 1975). But there's been slippage in some areas. In what seems to be another sign of the time squeeze today, one of the most notable decreases is in having a five-day workweek (21%, down 6 from 1996 and down 12 from 1975).[7]

Questions

1. Create a constitutive definition of the concept of "the good life."
2. Create an operational definition of the concept of "the good life."
3. At what measurement level are the data shown in the graph?
4. Illustrate how each level of measurement (see Table 9.2) could be used in a survey of "the good life."

Real-Life Research • 9.2

Evaluating Service Quality

The service industry accounts for 70 percent of the gross national product, absorbs approximately 72 percent of the total workforce, and is responsible for more than one-half of all consumer spending. *The Atlanta Journal* and *The Atlanta Constitution* invited their readers to fill out a questionnaire printed in the newspapers regarding service quality. A total of 610 readers filled out and mailed the questionnaire. The results are in the following table.

Responses to a Questionnaire on Survey Quality

Industry	Atlanta readers believe service is . . .		
	Good	Bad	No Response
Airlines	55.7%	16.2%	28.0%
Auto dealers	15.6	52.1	32.3
Auto service	8.7	71.5	19.8
Banks	44.6	36.4	19.0
Brokerage firms	20.3	13.8	65.9
Car rentals	27.2	16.2	56.4
Department stores	29.3	46.2	24.4
Discount brokers	18.0	50.5	31.3
Doctor/dentist	47.9	26.6	25.6
Dry cleaning	47.9	15.9	36.2
Electric hookup	23.9	12.6	63.4
Fast food	35.1	36.1	28.9
Grocery stores	45.4	25.6	29.0
Hospitals	27.1	34.4	38.5
Insurance companies	19.8	44.3	35.9
Local governments	9.0	59.3	31.5
Motels/hotels	44.4	16.7	38.9
Newspapers	49.7	20.0	30.3
Restaurants	35.9	27.2	36.9
Small appliance repair	9.2	29.7	61.2
Telephone hookup	26.1	30.0	43.9

Questions

1. What are the constructs? What are the constitutive definitions in this case? Are they sufficient? If not, what are the implications?
2. What kind of scale probably was used? What is the highest level of scaling that could have been used? Give an example.
3. Describe four possible sources of error in the data.
4. Do you think that the scale is reliable? Why or why not? What could be done to test for reliability?
5. Is the scale valid in your opinion? Why? How might you determine validity?

Chapter Ten

Using Measurement Scales to Build Marketing Effectiveness

Learning Objectives

To understand the linkage among attitudes, behavior, and marketing effectiveness.

1

To become familiar with the concept of scaling.

2

To learn about the various types of attitude scales.

3

To examine some basic considerations in selecting a type of scale.

4

To realize the importance of attitude measurement scales in management decision making.

5

THOUGH ITS LODGING PROPERTIES HAVE A DISTINCTLY TRADITIONAL FEEL, La Quinta Inns is taking an untraditional approach to analyzing and distributing the data from its customer satisfaction research. Founded in 1968 and still based in Texas, La Quinta owns and operates over 300 limited-service, mid-price hotels, primarily in warm-weather regions of the United States.

LA QUINTA IS USING A DESKTOP COMPUTER system to give its regional and general managers a lot more control over the kind of information they can extract from survey results and allowing them to understand satisfaction by customer segment and individualize key drivers from each hotel. Now they can go into the database themselves and look at the most recent data right down to the property level.

THE SURVEY COVERS THE BASICS OF A lodging stay chronologically, including check-in, the condition of the room, any problems the guest may have encountered, and La Quinta's continental breakfast. "We

start from the minute they drove up to the property," says Jim Gard, La Quinta's Director of Relationship Marketing and Research, "and we take them back through the experience. When you drove up, was the exterior appealing? Were you greeted warmly? Were your reservations in order? Was the staff friendly and helpful? We put the questions right in the order they experienced things so that they can really reconstruct it from memory, because people are probably getting the survey about 10 to 17 days after checkout. That approach works very well for us."

THE SURVEY GIVES LA QUINTA A WAY TO DEVELOP A LIST OF BEST PRACTICES BY looking at the properties that score highly and examining how their practices differ from properties that don't do so well. (It's been effective enough to allow La Quinta to eliminate its mystery shopping program.) Also, the scores are incorporated into manager bonuses—not at a high percentage, but enough to add a little extra incentive to strive for excellence.[1] ∎

La Quinta's approach to distributing data from its customer satisfaction survey allows regional and general managers to extract key data. The survey helps La Quinta develop a list of best practices.

Find out more about La Quinta's commitment to customer satisfaction at

http://www. laquinta.com

La Quinta's customer satisfaction research is based on the concept of measurement—for example, "How would you rate your overall experience with La Quinta during your last visit?" La Quinta's customer satisfaction survey encompasses several different types of attitude scales. Why is it useful to measure attitudes? What tools are available for measuring attitudes? What factors should be considered in selecting an attitude scale? These questions will be answered in this chapter.

An attitude is a psychological construct, a way of conceptualizing an intangible. Attitudes cannot be observed or measured directly; their existence is inferred from their consequences. An **attitude** is an enduring organization of motivational, emotional, perceptual, and cognitive processes with respect to some aspect of a person's environment. In marketing research, it is a learned predisposition to respond in a consistently favorable or unfavorable manner toward an object or concept. Attitudes tend to be long lasting and consist of clusters of interrelated beliefs. They encompass a person's value system, which represents her or his standards of good and bad, right and wrong, and so forth. Thus, an individual may have a specific attitude toward Disney World, based on beliefs about need for entertainment, cartoon characters, fantasy, crowds of people, waiting in lines, and many other things. Disney World also may be highly valued as good, clean, wholesome fun.

The Link between Attitudes and Behavior

The link between attitudes and behavior is complex. Predictions of future behavior for a group of consumers tend to be more accurate than those for a single consumer. Specifically, researchers have identified the following links:

1. The more favorable the attitude of consumers, the higher the incidence of product usage; the less favorable the attitude, the lower the incidence of product usage.
2. The less favorable people's attitudes toward a product, the more likely they are to stop using it.
3. The attitudes of people who have never tried a product tend to be distributed around the mean in the shape of a normal distribution.[2]
4. When attitudes are based on actually trying and experiencing a product, attitudes predict behavior quite well. Conversely, when attitudes are based on advertising, attitude–behavior consistency is significantly reduced.[3]

Some marketing researchers have become rather pessimistic about the ability of attitude research to predict behavior.[4] The present view of most researchers, however, is that one must learn to recognize the factors that influence the extent to which measured attitudes accurately predict behavior. Six factors should be considered in assessing whether attitude research findings will predict behavior:[5]

1. *Involvement of the consumer.* Attitudes are likely to predict purchase behavior only under conditions of high involvement.

2. *Attitude measurement.* The measure of attitude has to be reliable, valid, and at the same level of abstraction as the measure of behavior. For example, if the behavior involves contributing to a specific charity, such as the American Cancer Society, the attitude measure cannot ask less specific (i.e., more abstract) questions about consumers' attitudes toward charities in general. A similar consistency must be applied to the variable of time. If the behavior involves buying a new Porsche within the next six months, the measure should include a time parameter. The longer the time between attitude measurement and the behavior, the weaker the relationship is.

3. *Effects of other people.* The feelings of other people toward the purchase and the consumer's motivation to comply with these feelings influence the extent to which attitudes predict behavior.

4. *Situational factors.* If situational factors, such as holidays, time pressures, or sickness, intervene, measured attitudes may fail to predict behavior well.

5. *Effects of other brands.* Even though a consumer's attitude toward a brand may be quite favorable, if that consumer's attitude toward another brand is even more favorable, the other brand will probably be purchased. One of the reasons the "attitude toward the object" model is often unable to accurately predict behavior is that it fails to include measures of attitudes toward other objects.

6. *Attitude strength.* For an attitude to influence behavior, it must be held with sufficient strength and conviction to be activated in memory.[6] The degree of association between an attitude and an object varies across a continuum. At one end of the continuum is the nonattitude: The consumer has neither positive nor negative feelings about a particular brand. At the other end of the continuum is the extreme attitude: The consumer feels very strongly about the brand.

Attitude measurement must be reliable, valid, and specific to the particular behavior. If the behavior is contributing to the American Cancer Society, the questions asked should refer only to that charity. Go to http://www.cancer.org to find out what information is available to help in framing such questions.

attitude
An enduring organization of motivational, emotional, perceptual, and cognitive processes with respect to some aspect of a person's environment.

Enhancing Marketing Effectiveness

Attitudes are truly the essence of the "human change agent" that all marketers strive to influence. Marketing managers realize that there is not a perfect correlation between attitudes and behavior. Yet in designing or modifying a marketing mix, managers know that attitude measures are often the best tool available for finding an effective mix. When Chrysler is trying to decide which of three potential new grill designs will sell the most Jeeps, it relies on attitude research. The implicit assumption is the grill most preferred in attitude research testing will sell the most Jeeps, all other things being equal. Thus, marketing managers measure attitudes in an attempt to predict behavior; correct predictions will enable managers to bring the "right" new product to the marketplace. This new product will be accompanied by the "right" marketing mix, again usually based to some extent on attitude research. Demographic data and past purchase patterns also are important data sources in deciding on a new marketing mix.

Kevin Bokeno, president of Keynote Consulting in Advance, North Carolina, notes that Baby Boomers may be altering the traditional hierarchy-of-effects

Gimme What You've Got Now

WE'VE HEARD OF A COUPLE WHO BOUGHT A BRAND new van in slightly over an hour. Did they comparison shop on the Net? Collect sell sheets to pinpoint the desired and required features prior to the purchase? Nope. They needed the van and had from 9:00 to 11:00 on Saturday morning open before another weekend crammed with soccer, dance, and alas, work spillover from the week before.

Did they get a good deal? Probably not. Did they get all the features they wanted? Doubtful.

However, this couple made a very conscious, and increasingly very typical, tradeoff. Even in this traditionally high-involvement purchase, they were willing to risk making a sub-optimal purchase decision in order to "get it over and done with and get on with our lives."

Our search clearly suggests that an increasing number of consumers are willing to shorten the purchase decision time and act without the facts. For more and more of us, if a true need exists, behavior occurs after a very minimum level of product familiarity and actually before attitude formation. We call this the "microwave process" because there is a willingness to risk getting a less than optimal product to get it quicker.

Although somewhere in the back of our minds, we consumers recognize that we should do our buying homework (and it's even easier given the availability of information), an increasing number of us simply want to fit the process into the allotted time.

Another reason we are willing to squeeze our buying decision process into a few in-store seconds is our relative affluence. Our haste does not allow us to critically evaluate the value/price equation, but we willingly acknowledge this shortcoming going in; and, more importantly, we know that if we make a mistake, we have the resources to cover it later.[7] ■

purchase model of (1) awareness, (2) familiarity, (3) attitude formation, (4) belief, and (5) behavior. Bokeno shares some of his thoughts in the In Practice feature.

Scaling Defined

scaling
Procedures for assigning numbers (or other symbols) to properties of an object in order to impart some numerical characteristics to the properties in question.

The term **scaling** refers to procedures for attempting to determine quantitative measures of subjective and sometimes abstract concepts. It is defined as a procedure for assigning numbers (or other symbols) to properties of an object in order to impart some numerical characteristics to the properties in question. Actually, numbers are assigned to *indicants* of the properties of objects. The rise and fall of mercury in a glass tube (a thermometer) is an indicant of temperature variations.

A scale is a measurement tool. Scales are either unidimensional or multidimensional. **Unidimensional scales** are designed to measure only one attribute of a concept, respondent, or object. Thus, a unidimensional scale measuring consumers' price sensitivity might include several items to measure price sensitivity, but combined into a single measure; all interviewees' attitudes are then placed along a linear continuum, called *degree of price sensitivity*. **Multidimensional scales** are based on the premise that a concept, respondent, or object might be better described using several dimensions. For example, target customers for Jaguar automobiles may be defined in three dimensions: level of wealth, degree of price sensitivity, and appreciation of fine motor cars.

unidimensional scales
Scales designed to measure only one attribute of a concept, respondent, or object.

multidimensional scales
Scales designed to measure several dimensions of a concept, respondent, or object.

Attitude Measurement Scales

Measurement of attitudes relies on less precise scales than those found in the physical sciences and hence is much more difficult. Because an attitude is a construct that exists in the mind of the consumer, it is not directly observable—unlike, for example, weight in the physical sciences. In many cases, attitudes are measured at the nominal or ordinal level. Some more sophisticated scales enable the marketing researcher to measure at the interval level. One must be careful not to attribute the more powerful properties of an interval scale to the lower-level nominal or ordinal scales.

Graphic Rating Scales

Graphic rating scales offer respondents a graphic continuum, typically anchored by two extremes. Figure 10.1 depicts three types of graphic rating

graphic rating scales
Measurement scales that include a graphic continuum, anchored by two extremes.

Potential Jaguar customers may be defined in three dimensions on a multidimensional scale. Go to http://www.jaguar.com to find out what new customers Jaguar might be targeting.

scales that might be used to evaluate La-Z-Boy recliners. Scale A represents the simplest form of a graphic scale. Respondents are instructed to mark their response on the continuum. After respondents have done so, scores are ascertained by dividing the line into as many categories as desired and assigning a score based on the category into which the mark has been placed. For example, if the line were six inches long, every inch might represent a category. Scale B offers the respondent slightly more structure by assigning numbers along the scale.

Responses to graphic rating scales are not limited to simply placing a mark on a continuum, as scale C illustrates. Scale C has been used successfully by many researchers to speed up self-administered interviews. Respondents are asked to touch the thermometer on the computer screen that best depicts their feelings.

Graphic rating scales can be constructed easily and are simple to use. They enable a researcher to discern fine distinctions, assuming that the rater has adequate discriminatory abilities. Numerical data obtained from the scales are typically treated as interval data.

One disadvantage of graphic rating scales is that overly extreme anchors tend to force respondents toward the middle of the scale. Also, some research has suggested that such scales are not as reliable as itemized rating scales.

Figure 10.1

**Three Types of
Graphic Rating Scales**

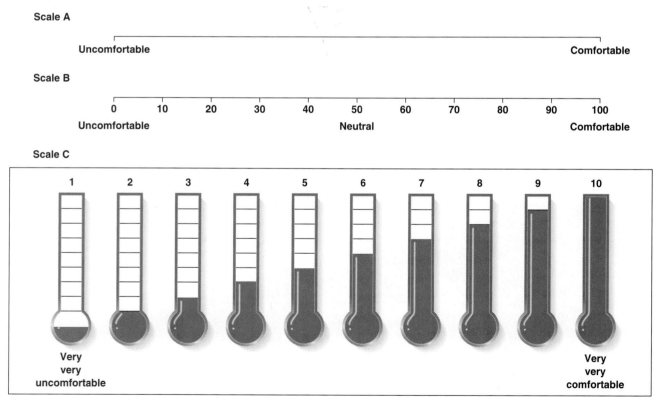

PART 3:
Data Acquisition

Itemized Rating Scales

Itemized rating scales are similar to graphic rating scales, except that respondents must select from a limited number of ordered categories rather than placing a mark on a continuous scale. (Purists would argue that scale C in Figure 10.1 is an itemized rating scale.) Figure 10.2 shows some examples of itemized rating scales taken from nationwide marketing research surveys. Starting items are rotated on each questionnaire to eliminate the order bias that might arise from starting with the same item each time.

Scale A was used by a dot-com company in determining what features and services it should add to its Web site. Scale B was used in a mall-intercept survey on the public's attitudes toward airline safety. Scale C was used by an e-commerce music retailer to better understand how people select a music Web site. Scale D was also an Internet survey, conducted by a producer of customer relationship management software. Examples of other itemized rating scales are shown in Table 10.1.

Although itemized rating scales do not allow for the fine distinctions that can be achieved in a graphic rating scale, they are easy to construct and administer. And the definitive categories found in itemized rating scales usually produce more reliable ratings.

Rank-Order Scales

Itemized and graphic scales are considered to be **noncomparative scales** because the respondent makes a judgment without reference to another object, concept, or person. **Rank-order scales,** on the other hand, are **comparative scales** because the respondent is asked to compare two or more items and rank each item. Rank-order scales are widely used in marketing research for several reasons. They are easy to use and give ordinal measurements of the items evaluated. Instructions are easy to understand, and the process typically moves at a steady pace. Some researchers claim that rank-order scales force respondents to evaluate concepts in a realistic manner. Figure 10.3 illustrates a series of rank-order scales taken from a study on eye shadows.

Rank-order scales possess several disadvantages. If all of the alternatives in a respondent's choice set are not included, the results could be misleading. For example, a respondent's first choice on all dimensions in the eye shadow study might have been Max Factor, which was not included. A second problem is that the concept being ranked may be completely outside a person's choice set, thus producing meaningless data. Perhaps a respondent doesn't use eye shadow and feels that the product isn't appropriate for any woman. Another limitation is that the scale gives the researcher only ordinal data. Nothing is learned about how far apart the items stand or how intensely the respondent feels about the ranking of an item. Finally, the researcher does not know why the respondent ranked the items as he or she did.

Q-Sorting

Q-sorting is basically a sophisticated form of rank ordering. A respondent is given cards listing a set of objects—such as verbal statements, slogans, product

---

itemized rating scales
Measurement scales in which the respondent selects an answer from a limited number of ordered categories.

noncomparative scales
Measurement scales in which judgment is made without reference to another object, concept, or person.

rank-order scales
Measurement scales in which the respondent compares two or more items and ranks them.

comparative scales
Measurement scales in which one object, concept, or person is compared with another on a scale.

Q-sorting
A measurement scale employing a sophisticated form of rank ordering using card sorts.

Figure 10.2

Itemized Rating Scales Used in Internet and Mall Surveys

If offered, how likely would you be to use the following areas on this site?

Scale A

a.) Auctions								
Not at all likely to use	○1	○2	○3	○4	○5	○6	○7	**Extremely likely to use**
b.) Fee-based education tools								
Not at all likely to use	○1	○2	○3	○4	○5	○6	○7	**Extremely likely to use**
c.) Event registration								
Not at all likely to use	○1	○2	○3	○4	○5	○6	○7	**Extremely likely to use**
d.) Online shopping markets								
Not at all likely to use	○1	○2	○3	○4	○5	○6	○7	**Extremely likely to use**
e.) Recruiting								
Not at all likely to use	○1	○2	○3	○4	○5	○6	○7	**Extremely likely to use**
f.) Research subscription								
Not at all likely to use	○1	○2	○3	○4	○5	○6	○7	**Extremely likely to use**
g.) Trading community								
Not at all likely to use	○1	○2	○3	○4	○5	○6	○7	**Extremely likely to use**
h.) Training/seminars								
Not at all likely to use	○1	○2	○3	○4	○5	○6	○7	**Extremely likely to use**

Scale B

When you fly, how often, if ever, are you frightened—always, most of the time, sometimes, or never? [BASED ON THOSE WHO HAVE EVER FLOWN]

Always	**Most of the time**	**Sometimes**	**Never**
(1)	(2)	(3)	(4)

How much confidence do you have in the following to do all they can to maintain air safety—a great deal, a fair amount, not too much, or none at all? How much confidence do you have in . . . [RANDOM ORDER]

	Great deal	**Fair amount**	**Not too much**	**None at all**
Pilots	(1)	(2)	(3)	(4)
Air traffic controllers	(1)	(2)	(3)	(4)
International airlines	(1)	(2)	(3)	(4)
Regional airlines	(1)	(2)	(3)	(4)
Federal government agencies	(1)	(2)	(3)	(4)

How confident do you feel about the safety standards of the major commercial airlines, in general—very confident, somewhat confident, not too confident, or not confident at all?

Very confident	**Somewhat confident**	**Not too confident**	**Not confident at all**
(1)	(2)	(3)	(4)

Scale C

What factors influence your choice of music Web sites? (Rate the importance of each item.)

	Not at all important				Very important
Customer benefits or rewards for shopping	○	○	○	○	○
Customer service or delivery options	○	○	○	○	○
Ease of use of Web site	○	○	○	○	○
Low prices	○	○	○	○	○
Real-time audio sampling of CDs	○	○	○	○	○
Reviews and artist information	○	○	○	○	○

Scale D

How interested would you be in obtaining additional information about this customer relationship management solution for your business?

- ○ Extremely interested
- ○ Very interested
- ○ Somewhat interested
- ○ Not very interested
- ○ Not at all interested

How likely is it that your business will invest in this type of customer relationship management solution within the next 12 months?

- ○ Extremely likely
- ○ Very likely
- ○ Somewhat likely
- ○ Not very likely
- ○ Not at all likely

Table 10.1

Selected Itemized Rating Scales

Characteristic of Interest	Rating Choices				
Purchase Intent	Definitely will buy	Probably will buy	Probably will not buy	Definitely will not buy	
Level of Agreement	Strongly agree	Somewhat agree	Neither agree nor disagree	Somewhat disagree	Strongly disagree
Quality	Very good	Good	Neither good nor bad	Fair	Poor
Dependability	Completely dependable	Somewhat dependable	Not very dependable	Not dependable at all	
Style	Very stylish	Somewhat stylish	Not very stylish	Completely unstylish	
Satisfaction	Completely satisfied	Somewhat satisfied	Neither satisfied nor dissatisfied	Somewhat dissatisfied	Completely dissatisfied
Cost	Extremely expensive	Expensive	Neither expensive nor inexpensive	Slightly inexpensive	Very inexpensive
Ease of Use	Very easy to use	Somewhat easy to use	Not very easy to use	Difficult to use	
Color Brightness	Extremely bright	Very bright	Somewhat bright	Slightly bright	Not bright at all
Modernity	Very modern	Somewhat modern	Neither modern nor old-fashioned	Somewhat old-fashioned	Very old-fashioned

Please rank the following eye shadows, with 1 being the brand that best meets the characteristic being evaluated and 6 the worst brand on the characteristic being evaluated. The six brands are listed on card C. (HAND RESPONDENT CARD C.) Let's begin with the idea of having high-quality compacts or containers. Which brand would rank as having the highest-quality compacts or containers? Which is second? (RECORD BELOW.)

	Q.48. Having High-Quality Container	Q.49. Having High-Quality Applicator	Q.50. Having High-Quality Eye Shadow
Avon	_____	_____	_____
Cover Girl	_____	_____	_____
Estee Lauder	_____	_____	_____
Maybelline	_____	_____	_____
Natural Wonder	_____	_____	_____
Revlon	_____	_____	_____

Card C		
Avon	Cover Girl	Estee Lauder
Maybelline	Natural Wonder	Revlon

features, or potential customer services—and asked to sort them into piles according to specified rating categories. For example, the cards might each describe a feature that could be incorporated into a new automobile design, and the respondent might be asked to sort the cards according to how well he or she likes the potential feature. Q-sorts usually contain a large number of cards—from 60 to 120 cards. For statistical convenience, the respondent is instructed to put varying numbers of cards in several piles, the whole making up a normal statistical distribution.

Here is a Q-sort distribution of 90 items:

Excellent feature										Poor feature
3	4	7	10	13	16	13	10	7	4	3
10	9	8	7	6	5	4	3	2	1	0

This is a rank-order continuum from Excellent Feature (10) to Poor Feature (0), with varying degrees of approval and disapproval between the extremes.

The numbers 3, 4, 7, . . ., 7, 4, 3 are the numbers of cards to be placed in each pile. The numbers below the line are the values assigned to the cards in each pile. That is, the three cards on the left ("Excellent Feature") are each assigned 10, the four cards in the next pile are assigned 9, and so on through the distribution, to the three cards on the extreme right ("Poor Feature"), which are assigned 0. The center pile, containing 16 cards, is a neutral pile. The respondent is told to put into the neutral pile cards that are left over after other choices have been made; these include cards that seem ambiguous or about which he or she cannot make a decision. In brief, this Q-sort will contain 11 piles of varying numbers of cards, and the cards in each pile will be assigned a value from 0 through 10. A Q-sort can be used to determine the relative ranking of items by individuals and to identify clusters of individuals who exhibit the same preferences. These clusters may then be analyzed as a potential basis for market segmentation. (Factor analysis, discussed in Chapter 17, is used to identify clusters of individuals.) Thus, Q-sorts have a much different objective than other types of scaling—the goal is to uncover groups of individuals who possess similar attitudes.

Paired Comparisons

Paired comparison scales ask a respondent to pick one of two objects from a set, based on some stated criteria. The respondent, therefore, makes a series of paired judgments between objects. Figure 10.4 shows a paired comparison scale used in a national study for sun care products. Only part of the scale is shown; the data collection procedure typically requires the respondent to compare all possible pairs of objects.

Paired comparisons overcome several problems of traditional rank-order scales. First, it is easier for people to select one item from a set of two than to rank a large set of data. Second, the problem of order bias is overcome; there is no pattern in the ordering of items or questions to create a source of bias. On the negative side, because all possible pairs are evaluated, the number of paired comparisons increases geometrically as the number of objects to be evaluated increases arithmetically. Thus, the number of objects to be evaluated should remain fairly small to prevent interviewee fatigue.

Constant Sum Scales

To avoid long lists of paired items, marketing researchers use **constant sum scales** more often than paired comparisons. Constant sum scales require the respondent to divide a given number of points, typically 100, among two or more attributes based on their importance to him or her. Respondents must value each item relative to all other items. The number of points allocated to each alternative indicates the ranking assigned to it by the respondent, as well as the relative magnitude of each alternative as perceived by the respondent. A constant sum scale used in a national study of tennis sportswear is shown in Figure 10.5. Another advantage of the constant sum scale over a rank-order or paired comparison scale is that if the respondent perceives two characteristics to have equal value, he or she can so indicate.

WAR Stories

Kevin Reilly of KCR/CREATIVE reports conducting a focus group with five-year-olds and explaining a five-point rating scale utilizing the familiar face of Snoopy from the "Peanuts" comic strip. On this scale, the emotive expressions on Snoopy's face ran from "elated" to "sad." In order to test kids' understanding of the rating scale, Reilly first gave them a few throw-away questions, usually extremes on the emotional spectrum. First, he asked them to, "Point to the face that tells me how much you like boiled broccoli." Understandably, the responses were mostly negative all around.

Then, to check the high end of the scale, he asked kids to, "Point to the face that tells me how you'd feel if every day were Christmas." As expected, responses were very enthusiastic—except for one boy who offered a more neutral rating. When asked why, his response was quite matter-of-fact: "It wouldn't really be a big deal to me. . . . I'm Jewish."

Source: "War Stories: True Life Tales in Marketing Research," by Art Shulman, *Quirk's Marketing Research Review*. Reprinted by permission of Art Shulman.

paired comparison scales
Measurement scales that ask the respondent to pick one of two objects in a set, based on some stated criteria.

constant sum scales
Measurement scales that ask the respondent to divide a given number of points, typically 100, among two or more attributes, based on their importance to him or her.

Figure 10.4

A Paired Comparison Scale for Sun Care Products

Here are some characteristics used to describe sun care products in general. Please tell me which characteristic in each pair is more important to you when selecting a sun care product.

a. Tans evenly	**b.** Tans without burning
a. Prevents burning	**b.** Protects against burning and tanning
a. Good value for the money	**b.** Goes on evenly
a. Not greasy	**b.** Does not stain clothing
a. Tans without burning	**b.** Prevents burning
a. Protects against burning and tanning	**b.** Good value for the money
a. Goes on evenly	**b.** Tans evenly
a. Prevents burning	**b.** Not greasy

Figure 10.5

A Constant Sum Scale Used in a Tennis Sportswear Study

Below are seven characteristics of women's tennis sportswear. Please allocate 100 points among the characteristics such that the allocation represents the importance of each characteristic to you. The more points that you assign to a characteristic, the more important it is. If the characteristic is totally unimportant, you should not allocate any points to it. When you've finished, please double-check to make sure that your total adds to 100.

Characteristics of Tennis Sportswear	**Number of Points**
Is comfortable to wear	_____
Is durable	_____
Is made by well-known brand or sports manufacturers	_____
Is made in the U.S.A.	_____
Has up-to-date styling	_____
Gives freedom of movement	_____
Is a good value for the money	_____
	100 points

A major disadvantage of this scale is that the respondent may have difficulty allocating the points to total 100 if there are a lot of characteristics or items. Most researchers feel that 10 items is the upper limit on a constant sum scale.

Semantic Differential Scales

semantic differential scales Measurement scales that examine the strengths and weaknesses of a concept by having the respondent rank it between dichotomous pairs of words or phrases that could be used to describe it; the means of the responses are then plotted as a profile, or image.

The semantic differential was developed by Charles Osgood, George Suci, and Percy Tannenbaum.[8] The focus of their original research was on the measurement of meaning of an object to a person. The object might be a savings and loan association and the meaning its image among a certain group of people.

The construction of a **semantic differential scale** begins with determination of a concept to be rated, such as the image of a company, brand, or store. The researcher selects dichotomous (opposite) pairs of words or phrases that could be used to describe the concept. Respondents then rate the concept on a scale

Adjective 1	Mean of Each Adjective Pair							Adjective 2
	1	2	3	4	5	6	7	
Modern	*	*	*	*	*	*	*	Old-fashioned
Aggressive	*	*	*	*	*	*	*	Defensive
Friendly	*	*	*	*	*	*	*	Unfriendly
Well-established	*	*	*	*	*	*	*	Not well-established
Attractive exterior	*	*	*	*	*	*	*	Unattractive exterior
Reliable	*	*	*	*	*	*	*	Unreliable
Appeals to small companies	*	*	*	*	*	*	*	Appeals to big companies
Makes you feel at home	*	*	*	*	*	*	*	Makes you feel uneasy
Helpful services	*	*	*	*	*	*	*	Indifferent to customers
Nice to deal with	*	*	*	*	*	*	*	Hard to deal with
No parking or transportation problems	*	*	*	*	*	*	*	Parking or transportation problems
My kind of people	*	*	*	*	*	*	*	Not my kind of people
Successful	*	*	*	*	*	*	*	Unsuccessful
Ads attract a lot of attention	*	*	*	*	*	*	*	Haven't noticed ads
Interesting ads	*	*	*	*	*	*	*	Uninteresting ads
Influential ads	*	*	*	*	*	*	*	Not influential

Figure 10.6

A Semantic Differential Profile of an Arizona Savings and Loan Association

(usually 1 to 7). The mean of the responses for each pair of adjectives is computed, and the means are plotted as a profile, or image.

Figure 10.6 is an actual profile of an Arizona savings and loan association as perceived by noncustomers with family incomes of $45,000 and above. A quick glance shows that the firm is viewed as somewhat old-fashioned, with rather plain facilities. It is viewed as well-established, reliable, successful, and probably very nice to deal with. The institution has parking problems and perhaps entry and egress difficulties. Its advertising is viewed as dismal.

The semantic differential is a quick and efficient means of examining the strengths and weaknesses of a product or company image versus those of the competition. More importantly, however, the semantic differential has been shown to be sufficiently reliable and valid for decision making and prediction in marketing and the behavioral sciences.[9] Also, the semantic differential has proved to be statistically robust (generalizable from one group of subjects to another) when applied to corporate image research.[10] This makes possible the measurement and comparison of images held by interviewees with diverse backgrounds.

Although these advantages have led many researchers to use the semantic differential as an image measurement tool, it is not without disadvantages. First, the semantic differential suffers from a lack of standardization. It is a highly generalized technique that must be adapted for each research problem. There is no single set of standard scales, and hence the development of customized scales becomes an integral part of the research.

The number of divisions on the semantic differential scale also presents a problem. If too few divisions are used, the scale is crude and lacks meaning; if

Global ISSUES

Be Cautious in Interpreting Scales Used in Global Research

Sabra Brock, vice president of Citicorp, notes that devising scales and other types of questions requires careful planning when conducting marketing research in Asia. In Asia, many countries have the capability of conducting some kinds of Western-style marketing research. Japan, Hong Kong, Singapore, and the Philippines have fairly advanced research industries. Other countries in Asia such as China, South Korea, Indonesia, and India have research capabilities, but they are so underdeveloped as to require special supervision. Asia also has fewer research and marketing firms that can act as data "translators," people who can transform computer tables and research results into specific marketing directions.

Attitudes toward research vary from country to country in Asia, as do reactions to pricing, distribution, and promotion strategies. Most Asians respond differently to being interviewed than Americans. They frequently have less patience with the abstract and rational phrasing commonly used in questionnaires, particularly where literacy rates are low.

The interpretation of research tools like scales is different among educated Asians. The Japanese desire not to contradict, for example, makes for more yea-saying and upward scale bias than in a Western culture.

Apart from the varying reactions to research, there also are design implications to the distinct pricing and distribution strategies employed in Asia. For example, when querying Asians about pricing, the researcher must realize that they are especially prone to equating high price with high quality. In countries where imports are restricted or highly taxed, like South Korea and the Philippines, "imported" and especially "made in USA" are strong product claims.

Among the Chinese countries in Asia, many distinct dialects are spoken. A Hong Kong native speaks the Cantonese dialect and must study Mandarin to communicate easily in Taiwan. These language dissimilarities are critical in questionnaire development. In Hong Kong, written and oral Cantonese are different enough to necessitate rewriting a questionnaire when the methodology changes from self-administered to interviewer-read.[11] ∎

too many are used, the scale goes beyond the ability of most people to discriminate. Researchers have found the seven-point scale to be the most satisfactory.

Another disadvantage of the semantic differential is the *halo effect*. The rating of a specific image component may be dominated by the interviewee's overall impression of the concept being rated. Bias may be significant if the image is hazy in the respondent's mind. To partially counteract the halo effect, the researcher should randomly reverse scale adjectives so that all the "good" ones are not placed on one side of the scale and the "bad" ones on the other. This forces the interviewee to evaluate the adjectives before responding. After the data have been gathered, all the positive adjectives are placed on one side and the negative ones on the other to facilitate analysis.

In analysis of a seven-point semantic differential scale, care must be taken in interpreting a score of 4. A response of 4 indicates one of two things—the respondent either is unable to relate the given pair of adjectives to the concept or is simply neutral or indifferent. Image studies frequently contain a large number of 4 responses. This phenomenon tends to pull the profiles toward the neutral position. Thus, the profiles lack clarity, and little distinction appears.

Stapel Scales

The **Stapel scale** is a modification of the semantic differential. A single adjective is placed in the center of the scale, which typically is a 10-point scale ranging from +5 to −5. The technique is designed to measure both the direction and the intensity of attitudes simultaneously. (The semantic differential, on the other hand, reflects how closely the descriptor adjective fits the concept being evaluated.) An example of a Stapel scale is shown in Figure 10.7.

The primary advantage of the Stapel scale is that it enables the researcher to avoid the arduous task of creating bipolar adjective pairs. The scale may also permit finer discrimination in measuring attitudes. A drawback is that descriptor adjectives can be phrased in a positive, neutral, or negative vein, and the choice of phrasing has been shown to affect the scale results and the person's ability to respond.[12] The Stapel scale has never had much popularity in commercial research and is used less frequently than the semantic differential.

Stapel scales
Measurement scales that require the respondent to rate, on a scale ranging from +5 to −5, how closely and in what direction a descriptor adjective fits a given concept.

Cheap Prices	Easy to Navigate
+5	+5
+4	+4
+3	+3
+2	+2
+1	+1
Cheap Prices	Easy to Navigate
−1	−1
−2	−2
−3	−3
−4	−4
−5	−5

Figure 10.7

A Stapel Scale Used to Measure a Retailer's Web Site

Select a "plus" number for words you think describe the Web site accurately. The more accurately you think the word describes the Web site, the larger the "plus" number you should choose. Select a "minus" number for words you think do not describe the Web site accurately. The less accurately you think the word describes the Web site, the larger the "minus" number you should choose. Therefore, you can select any number from +5 for words you think are very accurate all the way to −5 for words you think are very inaccurate.

Likert Scales

The **Likert scale** is another scale that avoids the problem of developing pairs of dichotomous adjectives. The scale consists of a series of statements expressing either a favorable or an unfavorable attitude toward the concept under study. The respondent is asked to indicate the level of her or his agreement or disagreement with each statement by assigning it a numerical score. The scores are then totaled to measure the respondent's attitude.

Figure 10.8 shows two Likert scales for Mygame.com, an Internet game site targeted toward teenagers. Scale A measures attitudes toward the Mygame registration process; scale B evaluates users' attitudes toward advertising on the Mygame Web site.

With the Likert scale, the respondent is required to consider only one statement at a time, with the scale running from one extreme to the other. A series of statements (attitudes) can be examined, yet there is only a single set of uniform replies for the respondent to choose from.

Rensis Likert created this scale to measure a person's attitude toward concepts (e.g., unions), activities (e.g., swimming), and so forth. He recommended the following steps in building the scale:

People's attitudes toward activities like skiing can be measured using Likert scales.

Likert scales
Measurement scales in which the respondent specifies a level of agreement or disagreement with statements expressing either a favorable or an unfavorable attitude toward the concept under study.

1. The researcher identifies the concept, activity, etc., to be scaled.
2. The researcher assembles a large number of statements (75 to 100) concerning the public's sentiments toward the concept, activity, etc.
3. Each test item is classified by the researcher as generally "favorable" or "unfavorable" with regard to the attitude under study. No attempt is made to scale the items; however, a pretest is conducted that involves the full set of statements and a limited sample of respondents.
4. In the pretest, the respondent indicates agreement (or not) with *every* item, checking one of the following direction-intensity descriptors:
   a. Strongly agree
   b. Agree
   c. Undecided
   d. Disagree
   e. Strongly disagree
5. Each response is given a numerical weight (e.g., 5, 4, 3, 2, 1).
6. The individual's *total attitude score* is represented by the algebraic summation of weights associated with the items checked. In the scoring process, weights are assigned so that the direction of attitude—favorable to unfavorable—is consistent over items. For example, if 5 were assigned to "strongly agree" for favorable items, 5 should be assigned to "strongly disagree" for unfavorable items.
7. After seeing the results of the pretest, the researcher selects only those items that appear to discriminate well between high and low *total* scorers. This may be done by first finding the highest and lowest quartiles of subjects on the basis of *total* score and then comparing the mean differences on each *specific* item for these high and low groups (excluding the middle 50 percent of subjects).

Figure 10.8

Likert Scales Used by Mygame.com

Scale A

How did you feel about the Mygame.com registration process when you became a new user?

	Strongly disagree	Somewhat disagree	Neutral	Somewhat agree	Strongly agree
The registration was simple.	○	○	○	○	○
The registration questions were "non-threatening."	○	○	○	○	○
The registration on Mygame.com will protect my privacy.	○	○	○	○	○
The registration did not take a long time to complete.	○	○	○	○	○
The registration informed me about the site.	○	○	○	○	○

Scale B

How do you feel about the following statements?

	Strongly disagree	Disagree	Neutral	Somewhat agree	Strongly agree
Allowing companies to advertise on the Internet allows me to access free services.	○	○	○	○	○
I do not support advertising on Mygame.com even though it provides me with free entertainment.	○	○	○	○	○
There is extremely too much advertising on the Internet.	○	○	○	○	○
There is extremely too much advertising on Mygame.com.	○	○	○	○	○
It's easy for me to ignore the advertising on Mygame.com and just play the game.	○	○	○	○	○

8. The 20 to 25 items finally selected are those that have discriminated "best" (i.e., exhibited the greatest differences in mean values) between high and low total scorers in the pretest.

9. Steps 3 through 5 are then repeated in the main study.

Likert created the scale so that a researcher could look at a summed score and tell whether a person's attitude toward a concept was positive or negative. For example, the maximum favorable score on a 20-item scale would be 100; therefore, a person scoring 92 would be presumed to have a favorable attitude. Of course, two people could both score 92 and yet have rated various statements differently. Thus, specific components of their overall attitude could differ markedly. For example, if respondent A strongly agreed (5) that a particular bank had good parking and strongly disagreed (1) that its loan programs were the best in town and respondent B had the exact opposite attitude, both would have summed scores of 6.

In the world of marketing research, Likert-like scales are very popular. They are quick and easy to construct and can be administered by telephone or via the Internet. Commercial researchers rarely follow the textbook-like process just outlined. Instead, the scale usually is developed jointly by a client project manager and a researcher. Many times, the scale is created following a focus group.

Developing and administering scales in the real world of marketing research sometimes presents problems not emphasized in textbooks. E. B. Feltser, a freelance marketing researcher, discusses several of these problems in the In Practice feature.

In PRACTICE

Setting the Number of Scale Points Is Not Always Easy

A MULTI-POINT SCALE IS A WONDERFUL THING. SUBTLE, NICELY OBjective, neatly quantifiable. Interviewers appreciate them because they're fast and don't entail all the typing or handwriting work associated with open-ends. It's easy to understand why they are so common in surveys.

Consider the basic, garden-variety five-point scale:

5. Extremely satisfied
4. Satisfied
3. Neither satisfied nor dissatisfied
2. Dissatisfied
1. Extremely dissatisfied
6. Don't know (DO NOT READ)
7. Refused (DO NOT READ)

Read it aloud, at speed. You're in an echo chamber, right? That's thanks to numbers 2 and 4. The easy fix is to add an adjective to 2 and 4: somewhat satisfied, maybe, or mildly satisfied or routinely satisfied or whatever. That kind of parallel construction gets a rhythm going that respondents seem to remember more easily. It also cuts down on the "I'm quite satisfied." "Would you say you're extremely satisfied or satisfied?" "Quite satisfied" round-and-round that drives interviewers up the wall and inspires them to key in 5 or 4 as the mood strikes, just to get on with the survey. And in fact, "satisfied" and "dissatisfied" are open-ended emotional states that logically include all other levels of satisfaction or dissatisfaction, including the "extremely" level. It's no wonder some respondents have a tough time nailing that one. Incidentally, why does the midpoint have to be so user-unfriendly? Why not a simple "I'm neutral about it"? It takes less time to say, and surveys, especially long ones, are like Olympic track events: Seconds count, and they add up fast.

Don't know (DO NOT READ) and the mid-point paradox. "Gee. I've never tried it. I guess I'd give it a 3. That's neutral, right?" Thus does the respondent valiantly try to fit the square peg into the round hole. But what's a poor interviewer to do? The classic instruction is to go with the respondent's numerical rating. And yet, it must be important from a marketing standpoint to distinguish between potential devoted consumers (I've never tried it) and experienced but disenchanted ones (It's OK, nothing special. Give it a 3.).

Perhaps it's time to replace the classic instruction with something more useful to an interviewer. Treating "don't know" as a naughty little secret instead of a viable response forces interviewers to make subjective (often highly subjective) choices, and that turns mid-point quantification into mush. Besides, the endearing thing about most respondents is that they truly do try to give honest opinions within the response framework. Even those who are aware that "don't know" is an option tend to ignore it whenever they can. Tipping the respondent to the "don't know" option cuts down on such pleasant responses as "I've already told you three times I never heard of it. I don't want to answer any more of these stupid questions. Good-bye!" Anything that cuts down on mid-terms is a thing of joy and delight to an interviewer.

Multi multi-point scales.

(Q.22) Now, using a seven-point scale where 7 means very satisfied . . . .

(Q.24) Now, using a five-point scale, where 5 means liked very much . . . .

(Q.26) Now, using a seven-point scale where 7 means disliked very much . . . .

Well, OK, in truth it's been a while since I've done a survey where the multi-pointers reversed polarity in mid-stream (thank heaven for small favors!). But why do some topics warrant a cruder response than others— a five-pointer set like a grubby medieval serf amongst the aristocratic, fine-tuned seven-pointers? From the interviewer's point of view, it means using time to explain the new scale, and then using more time to reintroduce the returning seven-pointer. Most respondents grasp the concept of a multi-point scale quite easily, but too much shifting around gives even the sharpest of them whiplash. Worse, they get confused, and even more time is used up explaining the scale yet again to bewildered respondents ("5. No, 7. 7? Is 7 the top this time?").[13] ∎

Purchase Intent Scales

Perhaps the single scale used most often in marketing research is the **purchase intent scale.** The ultimate issue for marketing managers is, Will they buy the product or not? If so, what percentage of the market can I expect to obtain? The purchase intent question normally is asked for all new products and services and product and service modifications, by manufacturers, retailers, and even nonprofit organizations.

purchase intent scales
Scales used to measure a respondent's intention to buy or not buy a product.

During new product development, the purchase intent question is first asked during concept testing to get a rough idea of demand. The manager wants to quickly eliminate potential turkeys, take a careful look at those products for which purchase intent is moderate, and push forward the products that seem to have star potential. At this stage, investment is minimal and product modification or concept repositioning is an easy task. As the product moves through development, the product itself, promotion strategy, price levels, and distribution channels become more concrete and focused. Purchase intent is evaluated at each stage of development, and demand estimates are refined. The crucial go–no go decision for national or regional rollout typically comes after test marketing. Immediately before test marketing, commercial researchers have another critical stage of evaluation. Here, the final or near-final version of the product is placed in consumers' homes in test cities around the country. After a period of in-home use (usually two to six weeks), a follow-up survey is conducted among participants to find out their likes and dislikes, how the product compares with what they use now, and what they would pay for it. The critical question near the end of the questionnaire is purchase intent.

Question 21 in Figure 10.9 is a purchase intent question taken from a follow-up study on in-home placement of a fly trap. The trap consisted of two three-inch discs held about one-quarter inch apart by three plastic pillars; it looked somewhat like a large, thin yo-yo. The trap contained a pheromone to attract the flies and a glue that would remain sticky for six months. Supposedly, the flies flew in but never out. Centered on the back side of one of the disks was an adhesive tab so that the disk could be attached to a kitchen window. The concept was to eliminate flies in the kitchen area without resorting to a pesticide. Question 22 was designed to aid in positioning the product, and question 23 traditionally was used by the manufacturer as a double check on purchase intent. If 60 percent of the respondents claimed that they definitely would buy the product and 90 per-

---

Figure 10.9	21. If a set of three traps sold for approximately $1.00 and was available in the stores where you normally shop, would you:
Purchase Intent Scale and Related Questions for In-Home Product Placement of Fly Traps	

21. If a set of three traps sold for approximately $1.00 and was available in the stores where you normally shop, would you:

	(51)
definitely buy the set of traps	1
probably buy	2
probably not buy—SKIP TO Q23	3
definitely not buy—SKIP TO Q23	4

22. Would you use the traps (a) instead of or (b) in addition to existing products?

	(52)
instead of	1
in addition to	2

23. Would you recommend this product to your friends?

	(53)
definitely	1
probably	2
probably not	3
definitely not	4

PART 3:
Data Acquisition

cent said they definitely would not recommend the product to their friends, the researcher would question the validity of the purchase intent.

The purchase intent scale has been found to be a good predictor of consumer choice of frequently purchased and durable consumer products.[14] The scale is very easy to construct, and consumers are simply asked to make a subjective judgment of their likelihood of buying a new product. From past experience in the product category, a marketing manager can translate consumer responses on the scale to estimates of purchase probability. Obviously, everyone who "definitely will buy" the product will not do so; in fact, a few who state that they definitely will not buy actually will buy the product. The manufacturer of the fly trap is a major producer of both pesticide and nonpesticide pest control products. Assume that, based on historical follow-up studies, the manufacturer has learned the following about purchase intent of nonpesticide home-use pest-control products:

- 63 percent of the "definitely will buy" actually purchase within 12 months.
- 28 percent of the "probably will buy" actually purchase within 12 months.
- 12 percent of the "probably will not buy" actually purchase within 12 months.
- 3 percent of the "definitely will not buy" actually purchase within 12 months.

Suppose that the fly trap study resulted in the following:

- 40 percent—definitely will buy
- 20 percent—probably will buy
- 30 percent—probably will not buy
- 10 percent—definitely will not buy

Assuming that the sample is representative of the target market,

$$(.4)(63\%) + (.2)(28\%) + (.3)(12\%) + (.1)(3\%)$$
$$= 34.7\% \text{ market share}$$

Most marketing managers would be deliriously happy at such a high market share prediction for a new product. Unfortunately, because of consumer confusion, the product was killed after the in-home placement despite the high prediction.

It is not uncommon for marketing research firms to conduct studies containing a purchase intent scale in cases where the client does not have historical data to use as a basis for weighing the results. A reasonable but conservative estimate would be 70 percent of the "definitely will buy," 35 percent of the "probably will buy," 10 percent of the "probably will not buy," and zero of the "definitely will not buy."[15] Higher weights are common in the industrial market.

Some companies use the purchase intent scale to make go–no go decisions in product development without reference to market share. Typically, managers simply add the "definitely will buy" and "probably will buy" percentages and compare that total to a predetermined go–no go threshold. One consumer goods manufacturer, for example, requires a combined score of 80 percent or higher at the concept testing stage and 65 percent for a product to move from in-home placement tests to test marketing.

Considerations in Selecting a Scale

Most non-image studies include a purchase intent scale. But many other questions arise in selecting a scale. Considerations include type of scale, balanced versus nonbalanced scale, number of scale categories, and forced versus nonforced choice.

Type of Scale

Most commercial researchers lean toward scales that can be administered over the telephone or via the Internet, to save interviewing expense. Ease of administration and development also are important considerations. For example, a rank-order scale can be quickly created, whereas developing a semantic differential (rating) scale is often a long and tedious process. Decision-making needs of the client are always of paramount importance. Can the decision be made using ordinal data, or must the researcher provide interval information? Researchers also must consider the respondents, who usually prefer nominal and ordinal scales because of their simplicity. Ultimately, the choice of which type of scale to use will depend on the problem at hand and the questions that must be answered. It is not uncommon to find several types of scales in one research study. For example, an image study for a grocery chain might have a ranking scale of competing chains and a semantic differential to examine components of the chain's image.

Balanced versus Nonbalanced Scale

A **balanced scale** has the same number of positive and negative categories; a **nonbalanced scale** is weighted toward one end or the other. If the researcher expects a wide range of opinions, then a balanced scale probably is in order. If past research or a preliminary study has determined that most opinions are positive, then using a scale with more positive gradients than negative ones will enable the researcher to ascertain the degree of positiveness toward the concept being researched. We have conducted a series of studies for the YMCA and know that its overall image is positive. Thus, we used the following categories to track the YMCA's image: (1) outstanding, (2) very good, (3) good, (4) fair, (5) poor.

Number of Scale Categories

The number of categories to be included in a scale is another issue that must be resolved by the marketing researcher. If the number of categories is too small— for example, good, fair, poor—the scale is crude and lacks richness. A three-category scale does not reveal the intensity of feeling that, say, a ten-category scale offers. Yet, a ten-category scale may go beyond a person's ability to accurately discriminate among categories. Research has shown that rating scales typically should have from five to nine categories.[16] When a scale is being

Past research has indicated that the YMCA has an overall positive image. This means that a nonbalanced scale with more positive gradients than negative can be used in future research about the YMCA. Go to http://www.ymca.com to see how the YMCA is using research to reach new customers.

balanced scales
Measurement scales that have the same number of positive and negative categories.

nonbalanced scales
Measurement scales that are weighted toward one end or the other of the scale.

PART 3:
Data Acquisition

administered over the telephone, the maximum that most respondents can adequately handle is five categories.

With an even number of scale categories, there is no neutral point. Without a neutral point, respondents are forced to indicate some degree of positive or negative feelings on an issue. Persons who are truly neutral are not allowed to express their neutrality. On the other hand, some marketing researchers say that putting a neutral point on a scale gives the respondent an easy way out, allowing the person with no really strong opinion to avoid concentrating on his or her

Solving the Scale Ratings Problem

ARITHMETIC WORKS ON REAL NUMBERS LIKE PHYSICAL counts and measures. Real numbers form both an ordinal series (each number is higher than the preceding one) and a cardinal one (each number is exactly one higher than the preceding one, an equal-interval scale). Scale ratings are ordinal, but we don't know, and cannot tell, whether they are equal-interval scales. We just hope they are because all our statistical manipulations, from averaging to multivariate analysis, depend on it.

We don't know how respondents use the scale. Do they select their rating in terms of how far it is below the top of the scale, or how far above the bottom or relative to the midpoint (which they easily misidentify in an even-numbered scale like one-to-10)? They may agonize over the choice between ratings of eight or nine but be cavalier about ratings at the low end. And when we say "they," we don't mean a group—we have to deal with each respondent individually.

A yea-sayer's rating of nine or 10 may be equal in meaning to a nay-sayer's seven or eight. In monadic tests, differences in aggregate ratings may reflect differing yea-sayer/nay-sayer ratios rather than real differences in perception or attitude.

We can solve the problem, but it means extra work.

Each respondent is asked three questions at the start of the interview: (1) On this scale, how do you rate the brand you now use, or that you know best? (2) How do you rate the best brand you know about? and (3) What rating represents the minimum acceptable level? The answers give us three meaningful anchor points for that respondent's ratings. Their actual ratings can be translated into responses relative to one or more of these reference points to produce real-meaning relative ratings that can be reliably aggregated and analyzed statistically without depending on dubious assumptions.

The answers to these three questions also provide useful information on their own. For example, how is the present brand rated relative to the minimum acceptable level? If those ratings are close, that identifies a potential brand-switching prospect. So does a wide spread between the present-brand rating and the best-brand rating. The responses offer a greater range of analytic potential.[17] ∎

actual feelings. Of course, it is rather unusual for any individual to be highly emotional about a new flavor of salad dressing, a package design, or a test commercial for a pickup truck!

Forced versus Nonforced Choice

As mentioned in the discussion of semantic differential scales, if a neutral category is included, it typically will attract those who are neutral and those who lack adequate knowledge to answer the question. Some researchers have resolved this issue by adding a "Don't know" response as an additional category. For example, a semantic differential might be set up as follows:

Friendly	1	2	3	4	5	6	7	**Unfriendly**	Don't Know
Unexciting	1	2	3	4	5	6	7	**Exciting**	Don't Know

A "Don't know" option, however, can be an easy out for the lazy respondent.

If it has a neutral point, a scale without a "Don't know" option does not force a respondent to give a positive or negative opinion. A scale without a neutral point or a "Don't know" option forces even those persons with no information about an object to state an opinion. The argument for forced choice is that the respondent has to concentrate on his or her feelings. The arguments against forced choice are that inaccurate data are recorded and that some respondents may refuse to answer the question. A questionnaire that continues to require respondents to provide an opinion when, in fact, they lack the necessary information to do so can create ill will and result in early termination of the interview.

Attitude Measures and Management Decision Making

So far in this chapter we have discussed the nature of attitudes, various types of measurement scales, and some considerations in creating a scale. We now turn our attention to making attitude research more valuable for management decision making.

In the wide spectrum of features of a product or brand, there are some that predispose consumers to action (that is, to preference for the product, to actual purchase, to making recommendations to friends, etc.) and others that do not. Attitudes that are most closely related to preference or to actual purchase decisions are said to be **determinant attitudes.** Other attitudes—no matter how favorable—are not determinant. Obviously, marketers need to know which features lead to attitudes that "determine" buying behavior, for these are the features around which marketing strategy must be built.[18]

With reference to determinant attitudes, Nelson Foote, manager of the consumer and public relations research program for General Electric, commented: "In the electrical appliance business, we have been impressed over and over by the way in which certain characteristics of products come to be taken for granted by consumers, especially those concerned with basic functional performance or with values like safety."

"If these values are missing in a product, the user is extremely offended," he said. "But if they are present, the maker or seller gets no special credit or pref-

determinant attitudes
Those consumer attitudes most closely related to preferences or to actual purchase decisions.

PART 3:
Data Acquisition

erence because, quite logically, every other maker and seller is assumed to be offering equivalent values. In other words, the values that are salient in decision making are the values that are problematic—that are important, to be sure, but also those which differentiate one offering from another."

In proprietary studies evaluating such automobile attributes as power, comfort, economy, appearance, and safety, for example, consumers often rank safety as first in importance. However, these same consumers do not see various makes of cars as differing widely with respect to safety; therefore, safety is not a determinant feature in the actual purchase decision. This fact should rightly lead the company to concentrate on raising its performance in features other than safety. However, if safety is totally ignored, the brand may soon be perceived as being so unsafe that it loses some of its share of the market. At this point, safety would achieve determinance, a quality it would hold until concentration on safety by the "unsafe" company brought its product back into line with those of other companies.

To identify determinant attitudes and discern their relative degree of determinance, researchers must go beyond the scaling of respondents' attitudes. The study design must include a methodology for measuring determinance, for it will not naturally develop in the course of scaling. There are three major approaches to identifying determinant attitudes: (1) direct questioning, (2) indirect questioning, and (3) observation.

Direct Questioning

The most obvious way to approach determinant attitudes is to ask consumers directly what factors they consider important in a purchasing decision. Through direct questioning, respondents may be asked to explain their reasons for preferring one product or brand over another. Or, they may be asked to rate their "ideal brand" for a given product in terms of several product attributes so that a model profile can be constructed (see the discussion of semantic differential scales).

This approach has the appeal of seeming to get directly to the issue of "Why do you buy?" Unfortunately, it rests on two very questionable assumptions: (1) Respondents know why they buy or prefer one product over another, and (2) they will willingly explain what these reasons are.

Another direct questioning approach is "dual questioning," which involves asking two questions concerning each product attribute that might be determinant. Consumers are first asked what factors they consider important in a purchasing decision and then asked how they perceive these factors as differing among the various products or brands.

Tables 10.2 and 10.3 illustrate this approach through ratings of attitudes toward savings and loan associations, given during a survey of the general public in the Los Angeles area. (The various benefits or claims are ranked in descending order in each table so that comparisons between the tables can be made more easily.) Notice that some items are high in rated importance but are

Table 10.2

Importance Ratings of Savings and Loan Characteristics

Benefit or Claim	Average Ratings*
Safety of money	1.4
Interest rate earned	1.6
Government insurance	1.6
Financial strength	2.0
Ease of withdrawing money	2.0
Management ability	2.0
Attitude of personnel	2.1
Speed/efficiency of service	2.2
Compounding frequency	2.2
Branch location convenience	2.3
Time required to earn interest	2.3
Parking convenience	2.4
Years in business	2.5
Other services offered	3.1
Building/office attractiveness	3.4
Premiums offered	4.0

*1—"extremely important"; 2—"very important"; 3—"fairly important"; 4—"slightly important," etc.

Source: James Myers and Mark Alpert, "Determinant Buying Attitudes: Meaning and Measurement," *Marketing Management* (Summer 1997), p. 52. Reprinted by permission of the American Marketing Association.

Table 10.3

Difference Ratings of Savings and Loan Characteristics

Benefit or Claim	Big Difference	Small Difference	No Difference	Don't Know
Years in business	53%	31%	10%	6%
Financial strength	40	32	22	6
Parking convenience	37	35	22	6
Safety of money	36	15	47	2
Management ability	35	26	27	12
Government insurance	35	11	51	3
Branch location convenience	34	36	28	2
Attitude of personnel	34	28	33	5
Interest rate earned	33	30	35	2
Speed/efficiency of service	32	28	35	5
Ease of withdrawing money	29	18	48	5
Compounding frequency	28	36	31	5
Time required to earn interest	26	34	33	7
Building/office attractiveness	24	44	30	2
Other services offered	21	34	29	16
Premiums offered	15	36	38	11

Source: James Myers and Mark Alpert, "Determinant Buying Attitudes: Meaning and Measurement," *Marketing Management* (Summer 1997), p. 53. Reprinted by permission of the American Marketing Association.

not thought to differ much among the various savings and loan associations (for example, safety of money, interest rate earned). Thus, while safety of money is ranked first in importance, about half of all respondents feel there is no difference among savings and loan associations in terms of safety; therefore, safety of funds is probably not a determinant feature. Conversely, some items show big differences among the various associations but are considered to be of relatively little importance in determining the choice of a savings and loan (for example, years in business, parking convenience).

On the other hand, "interest rate earned" has a very high importance ranking, and far fewer respondents feel there is no difference among the various associations relative to interest rate. Financial strength is rated somewhat lower in importance but is second highest in terms of the difference between associations. Therefore, financial strength appears to be relatively determinant of attitudes. Similarly, the researcher can proceed through the rest of the ratings to identify those attitudes that seem to influence the choice among various savings and loans most strongly and thus, presumably, are determinant attitudes.

Indirect Questioning

Another approach to identifying determinant attitudes is indirect questioning, of which there are many forms. Recall from Chapter 5 that indirect questioning is any interviewing approach that does not directly ask respondents to indicate the reasons why they bought a product or service or which features or attributes are most important in determining choice.

Observation

A third technique for identifying buying motives is observation research (see Chapter 7). For example, in one study, supermarket shoppers were observed, and detailed reports were recorded of their movements and statements while interacting with certain products on display in several different stores. The authors drew conclusions concerning who does the shopping, the influence of children and adult males on purchasing decisions, the effect of pricing, where brand choices seem to be made, and how much package study is involved. One of the findings of this study was that shoppers seemed to reject certain candy packaging in favor of other packaging. This finding suggests that package design might be a determinant feature, though by no means the only one.[19] (The disadvantages of observation research were discussed in Chapter 7.)

Choosing a Method for Identifying Determinant Attitudes

Direct questioning, indirect questioning, and observation each have some limitations in identifying determinant attitudes. Therefore, the marketing researcher should use two or more of the techniques. Convergent findings will offer greater assurance that the attitudes identified are indeed determinant attitudes. Several statistical tools can aid the researcher in this process; they will be discussed in Part Four.

Summary

An attitude is an enduring organization of motivational, emotional, perceptual, and cognitive processes with respect to some aspect of a person's environment. In marketing research, it is a learned predisposition to respond in a consistently favorable or unfavorable manner toward an object or concept.

The term *scaling* refers to procedures for attempting to determine quantitative measures of subjective and somtimes abstract concepts. It is defined as a procedure for assigning numbers or other symbols to properties of an object in order to impart some numerical characteristics to the properties in question. Scales are either unidimensional or multidimensional. A unidimensional scale is designed to measure only one attribute of a concept, respondent, or object. Multidimensional scaling is based on the premise that a concept, respondent, or object might be better described using several dimensions.

One type of scale is called a graphic rating scale. Respondents are presented with a graphic continuum, typically anchored by two extremes. Itemized rating scales are similar to graphic rating scales except that respondents must select from a limited number of categories rather than placing a mark on a continuous scale. A rank-order scale is a comparative scale because respondents are asked to compare two or more items with each other. Q-sorting is a sophisticated form of rank ordering. Respondents are asked to sort a large number of cards into piles of predetermined size according to specified rating categories. Paired comparison scales ask the respondent to pick one of two objects from a set, based on some stated criteria. Constant sum scales require the respondent to divide a given number of points, typically 100, among two or more attributes, based on their importance to him or her. Respondents must value each item relative to all other items. The number of points allocated to each alternative indicates the ranking assigned to it by the respondent.

The semantic differential was developed to measure the meaning of an object to a person. The construction of a semantic differential scale begins with determination of a concept to be rated, such as a brand image; then the researcher selects dichotomous pairs of words or phrases that could be used to describe the concept. Respondents then rate the concept on a scale, usually 1 to 7. The mean of the responses is computed for each pair of adjectives, and the means are plotted as a profile, or image. In the Stapel scale, a single adjective is placed in the center of the scale. Typically, a Stapel scale is designed to simultaneously measure both the direction and the intensity of attitudes. The Likert scale is another scale that avoids the problem of developing pairs of dichotomous adjectives. The scale consists of a series of statements expressing either a favorable or an unfavorable attitude toward the concept under study. The respondent is asked to indicate the level of his or her agreement or disagreement with each statement by assigning it a numerical score. Scores are then totaled to measure the respondent's attitude.

The scale that is used most often and perhaps is most important to marketing researchers is the purchase intent scale. This scale is used to measure a respondent's intention to buy or not buy a product. The purchase intent question usually asks a person to state whether he would definitely buy, probably buy,

PART 3:
Data Acquisition

probably not buy, or definitely not buy the product under study. The purchase intent scale has been found to be a good predictor of consumer choice of frequently purchased consumer durable goods.

Several factors should be considered in selecting a particular scale for a study. The first is the type of scale to use: rating, ranking, sorting, or purchase intent. Next, consideration must be given to the use of a balanced scale versus a nonbalanced scale. The number of categories also must be determined. A related factor is whether to use an odd or even number of categories. Finally, the researcher must consider whether to use forced or nonforced choice sets.

Attitudes that predispose consumers to action are called determinant attitudes. Marketing researchers need to identify which attitudes, of all those measured, are determinant. This can be accomplished by direct questioning, indirect questioning, and observation research.

Key Terms & Definitions

attitude   An enduring organization of motivational, emotional, perceptual, and cognitive processes with respect to some aspect of a person's environment.

scaling   Procedures for assigning numbers (or other symbols) to properties of an object in order to impart some numerical characteristics to the properties in question.

unidimensional scales   Scales designed to measure only one attribute of a concept, respondent, or object.

multidimensional scales   Scales designed to measure several dimensions of a concept, respondent, or object.

graphic rating scales   Measurement scales that include a graphic continuum, anchored by two extremes.

itemized rating scales   Measurement scales in which the respondent selects an answer from a limited number of ordered categories.

noncomparative scales   Measurement scales in which judgment is made without reference to another object, concept, or person.

rank-order scales   Measurement scales in which the respondent compares two or more items and ranks them.

comparative scales   Measurement scales in which one object, concept, or person is compared with another on a scale.

Q-sorting   A measurement scale employing a sophisticated form of rank ordering using card sorts.

paired comparison scales   Measurement scales that ask the respondent to pick one of two objects in a set, based on some stated criteria.

constant sum scales   Measurement scales that ask the respondent to divide a given number of points, typically 100, among two or more attributes, based on their importance to him or her.

semantic differential scales Measurement scales that examine the strengths and weaknesses of a concept by having the respondent rank it between dichotomous pairs of words or phrases that could be used to describe it; the means of the responses are then plotted as a profile, or image.

Stapel scales Measurement scales that require the respondent to rate, on a scale ranging from +5 to −5, how closely and in what direction a descriptor adjective fits a given concept.

Likert scales Measurement scales in which the respondent specifies a level of agreement or disagreement with statements expressing either a favorable or an unfavorable attitude toward the concept under study.

purchase intent scales Scales used to measure a respondent's intention to buy or not buy a product.

balanced scales Measurement scaes that have the same number of positive and negative categories.

nonbalanced scales Measurement scales that are weighted toward one end or the other of the scale.

determinant attitudes Those consumer attitudes most closely related to preferences or to actual purchase decisions.

Questions for Review & Critical Thinking

1. Discuss some of the considerations in selecting a rating, ranking, or purchase intent scale.
2. What are some of the arguments for and against having a neutral point on a scale?
3. Compare and contrast the semantic differential scale, Stapel scale, and Likert scale. Under what conditions would a researcher use each one?
4. The local department store in your home town has been besieged by competition from the large national chains. What are some ways that target customers' attitudes toward the store could be changed?
5. Develop a Likert scale to evaluate the parks and recreation department in your city.
6. Develop a purchase intent scale for students eating at the university's cafeteria. How might the reliability and validity of this scale be measured? Why do you think purchase intent scales are so popular in commercial marketing research?
7. When might a researcher use a graphic rating scale rather than an itemized rating scale?
8. What are the disadvantages of a graphic rating scale?
9. Develop a rank-order scale for soda preferences of college students. What are the advantages and disadvantages of this type of scale?
10. What are some adjective pairs or phrases that could be used in a semantic differential to measure the image of your college or university?
11. What are determinant attitudes, and why are they important?

PART 3:
Data Acquisition

Working the Net

Using a Web search engine, search for "attitude scales" and "marketing research." Did you find any new scales or new information about scales discussed in this chapter? Report your findings to the class.

Using WebSurveyor

WebSurveyor enables you to quickly and efficiently gather information via the Internet without becoming an "expert" in Web design or HTML programming.

How It Works

WebSurveyor is composed of two components:

- *WebSurveyor Desktop.* This Windows application provides all the tools you need to design, distribute, and analyze Web surveys.
- *WebSurveyor Account.* Our exclusive survey hosting service provides a unique Web address for your survey and a dedicated environment for collecting your responses.

Our unique hybrid approach gives you the optimal mix of speed, control, availability, and security. Knowing that you will spend most of your online survey project time on survey design and analysis, we have put these tools on your desktop to give you total control, faster turnaround, and perpetual data access. When coupled with our hosting service, these tools will enable you to quickly and confidently gather critical information via the Web without waiting for your IT department or Webmaster.

WebSurveyor Process

The following steps illustrate the workflow of a typical survey with WebSurveyor.

Step 1: Assemble. You build a survey using WebSurveyor Desktop and "publish" it to your WebSurveyor Account on the WebSurveyor.NET network.

Step 2: Ask. You tell people about your survey by using WebSurveyor Desktop's email notification manager, placing a hypertext link on an existing Web page, using a banner ad, sending out flyers, or using any other practical method. Participants take the survey, using a standard Web browser. When they press the submit button, their answers are sent to WebSurveyor.NET, where they are stored.

web**S**URVEYOR™
When you need to know. Now.

Ask

Analyze

Step 3: Analyze. You retrieve responses from your WebSurveyor Account and perform analysis using WebSurveyor Desktop.

Exercises

Using the WebSurveyor Desktop software, open the CHAPTER10 survey by selecting File and then Open from the main menu and navigating to the SURVEYS subdirectory under the directory where you installed the WebSurveyor Desktop software (usually c:\program files\websurveyor desktop 3).

1. Review each question by highlighting the question and clicking the Edit button at the left or by previewing the survey (F9). Identify the type of scale used for each question.
2. Change the scale for question 4 to a positive nonbalanced scale.
3. Click on Help in the main menu and locate the section Matrix Questions. After reading this information, exit Help. Add a matrix question to the survey to compare the respondent's view of product quality for American-Made Blue jeans and four other brands. Use the "Quality" itemized rating scale from Table 10.1.

Real-Life Research • 10.1

Roper Reports

Roper Reports are used by business executives throughout the world to keep abreast of business and social trends. Below are three figures from a recent *Roper Report,* dealing with attitudes toward advertising, consumer awareness of certain new products, and the type of beverages people consume most.[20]

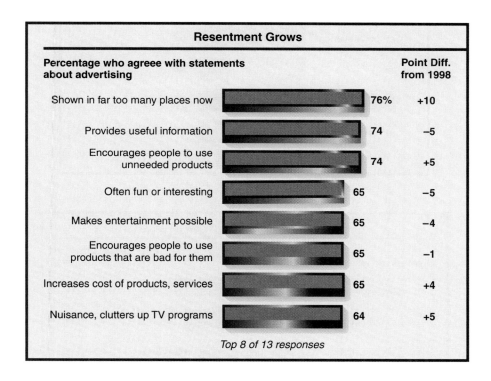

Resentment Grows		
Percentage who agree with statements about advertising		**Point Diff. from 1998**
Shown in far too many places now	76%	+10
Provides useful information	74	–5
Encourages people to use unneeded products	74	+5
Often fun or interesting	65	–5
Makes entertainment possible	65	–4
Encourages people to use products that are bad for them	65	–1
Increases cost of products, services	65	+4
Nuisance, clutters up TV programs	64	+5
Top 8 of 13 responses		

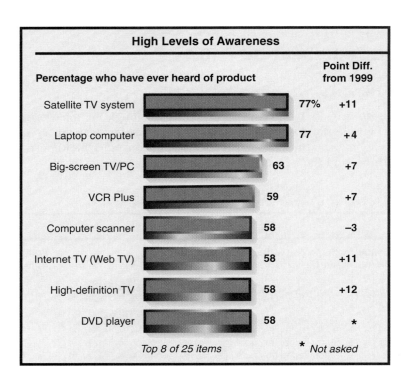

High Levels of Awareness

Percentage who have ever heard of product — Point Diff. from 1999

Product	%	Point Diff. from 1999
Satellite TV system	77%	+11
Laptop computer	77	+4
Big-screen TV/PC	63	+7
VCR Plus	59	+7
Computer scanner	58	–3
Internet TV (Web TV)	58	+11
High-definition TV	58	+12
DVD player	58	*

Top 8 of 25 items   * *Not asked*

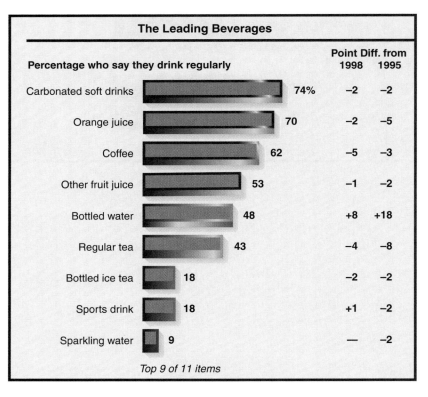

The Leading Beverages

Percentage who say they drink regularly

Beverage	%	Point Diff. from 1998	Point Diff. from 1995
Carbonated soft drinks	74%	–2	–2
Orange juice	70	–2	–5
Coffee	62	–5	–3
Other fruit juice	53	–1	–2
Bottled water	48	+8	+18
Regular tea	43	–4	–8
Bottled ice tea	18	–2	–2
Sports drink	18	+1	–2
Sparkling water	9	—	–2

Top 9 of 11 items

PART 3:
Data Acquisition

Questions

1. Re-create the scales that might have been used to develop the figures.
2. Develop three new scales that will elicit additional information about the topics discussed in the three figures. For example, what else might a researcher want to know (in a scaled question) about a regular drinker of bottled water?

Real-Life Research • 10.2

Frigidaire Refrigerators

Frigidaire Refrigerators was interested in comparing its image with those of a number of other appliance corporations. Some of the questions used on the questionnaire follow.

Q.1 We are interested in your overall opinion of five companies that manufacture refrigerators. Please rank them from 1 to 5, with 1 being the best and 5 the worst (READ LIST. WRITE IN NUMBER GIVEN FOR *EACH* COMPANY LISTED. BE SURE *ONE* ANSWER IS RECORDED FOR EACH COMPANY.)

Companies	Rank
General Electric	_____
Westinghouse	_____
Frigidaire	_____
Sears	_____
Whirlpool	_____

Q.2 Now, I would like to have your opinion on a few statements that could be used to describe Frigidaire and the refrigerators it makes.

For each statement I read, please tell me how much you *agree* or *disagree* with the statement about Frigidaire. If you *agree completely* with the statement made, you should give it a *10* rating. If you *disagree completely* with the statement made, you should give it a *0* rating. Or, you can use any number in between which best expresses your opinion on each statement about Frigidaire. (READ LIST. BEGIN WITH STATEMENT CHECKED AND WRITE IN NUMBER GIVEN FOR *EACH* STATEMENT LISTED. BE SURE *ONE* ANSWER IS RECORDED FOR EACH.)

Statements	Rating
( ) They are a modern, up-to-date company.	_____
( ) Their refrigerators offer better value than those made by other companies.	_____
( ) Their refrigerators last longer than those made by other companies.	_____
( ) They are a company that stands behind their products.	_____
(✓) Their refrigerators have more special features than those made by other companies.	_____
( ) They are a well-established, reliable company.	_____
( ) Their refrigerators are more dependable than those made by other companies.	_____
( ) Their refrigerators offer higher-quality construction than those made by other companies.	_____
( ) Their refrigerators have a better guarantee or warranty than those made by other companies.	_____

Q.3 If you were buying a (READ APPLIANCE) today, what make would be your first choice? Your second choice? Your third choice? (DO *NOT* READ LIST. CIRCLE NUMBER BELOW APPROPRIATE APPLIANCE. *BEGIN WITH APPLIANCE CHECKED.*)

( ) **Refrigerator**   (✓) **Electric Range**

Brands	First Choice	Second Choice	Third Choice	First Choice	Second Choice	Third Choice
General Electric	1	1	1	1	1	1
Westinghouse	2	2	2	2	2	2
Frigidaire	3	3	3	3	3	3
Sears	4	4	4	4	4	4
Whirlpool	5	5	5	5	5	5
Other (SPECIFY)						

Q.4 If you were in the market for a refrigerator today, how interested would you be in having the 2000 Frigidaire refrigerator that was described in the commercial in your home? Would you say you would be . . . (READ LIST)

	Very interested	1
(CIRCLE	Somewhat interested	2
ONE	Neither interested or disinterested	3
NUMBER)	Somewhat disinterested, or	4
	Very disinterested	5

Q.5 Why do you feel that way? (PROBE FOR COMPLETE AND MEANINGFUL ANSWERS.)

_____
_____
_____
_____
_____

Q.6 Now, I would like to ask you a few questions for statistical purposes only:

(A) Do you currently own any major appliances made by Frigidaire?

(CIRCLE ONE NUMBER)	Yes	1
	No	2

(B) Is the head of household male or female?

(CIRCLE ONE NUMBER)	Male	1
	Female	2

(C) Which letter on this card corresponds to your age group?

	A. Under 25	1
(CIRCLE	B. 25 to 34	2
ONE	C. 35 to 44	3
NUMBER)	D. 45 to 54	4
	E. 55 and over	5

Questions

1. What types of scales are represented in the questionnaire? What is the purpose of each scale? What other scales could have been substituted to obtain the same data?
2. Could a semantic differential scale have been used in this questionnaire? If so, what are some of the adjective pairs that might have been used?
3. Do you think the managers of Frigidaire have the necessary information now to evaluate the company's competitive position as perceived by consumers? If not, what additional questions should be asked?

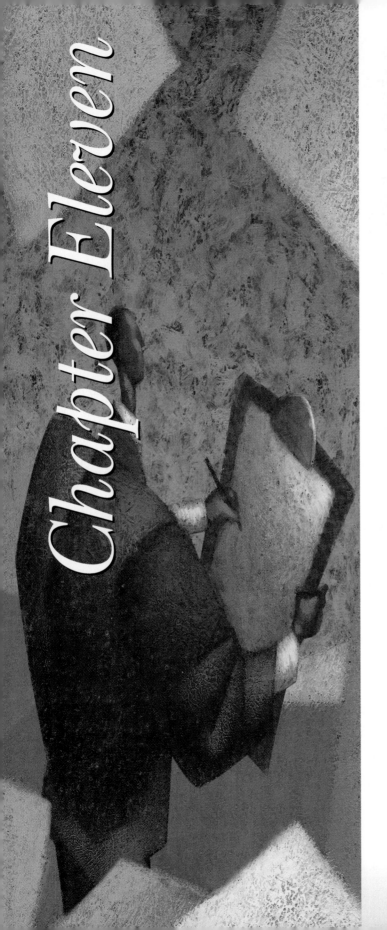

Chapter Eleven

Questionnaire Design

Learning Objectives

To understand the role of the questionnaire in the data collection process.

To become familiar with the criteria for a good questionnaire.

To learn the process for questionnaire design.

To become knowledgeable about the three basic forms of questions.

To learn the necessary procedures for successful implementation of a survey.

To understand how software and the Internet are influencing questionnaire design.

To understand the impact of the questionnaire on data collection costs.

K RAFT FOODS ALREADY KNEW THAT CONSUMERS THINK FROZEN PIZZA tastes like cardboard. Carryout from the local pizzeria, they believe, will always beat a pie that heats in the oven. How could Kraft change that mind-set with its new product, DiGiorno Rising Crust Pizza? Kraft had to pinpoint why people eat pizza, regardless of whether it's frozen or carryout. SMI-Alcott mailed a survey to 1,000 pizza lovers and asked them about their habits. When did they eat pizza? Could they describe the last two times they had it? Results showed that people ate pizza during fun social occasions or at home, when no one—especially mom—wanted to be stuck in the kitchen. Other activities, maybe a party, a big sports game on TV, or just a quiet night with their mate, were more important than making a five-course meal. People said they mostly ate frozen pizza for convenience, when time was short, but called for delivery for a variety of reasons. They also questioned the quality of frozen pizza, saying it couldn't offer the same taste as carryout.

FOCUS GROUPS WITH WOMEN AGES 25–54, conducted by Loran Marketing Group, supported the findings. Participants said they wanted a frozen pizza with a fresh-baked taste, but so far hadn't found one in the grocery store. Then the groups watched a demonstration of DiGiorno, its crust rising as it baked in the oven. The image clicked—and convinced skeptical consumers that even a frozen pizza could really deliver.

OF COURSE, IT HAD TO TASTE GOOD, TOO. PRODUCT DYNAMICS RAN A SERIES of blind taste tests with consumers to rate DiGiorno against both frozen and carryout pies. No problem there: It scored the highest among frozen brands and placed second to only one carryout product. Ideas for the ad campaign were presented to a group of consumers in a series of interviews. Again, Kraft heard that people wanted a frozen pizza with the taste and crust of carryout. And, these folks added, they'd need proof that DiGiorno was for real before picking it up in the frozen-foods aisle. This insight underscored the need to actually show DiGiorno rising in the oven during the commercials.

KRAFT ALSO LEARNED THAT PEOPLE HAD TROUBLE PRONOUNCING "DIGIORNO," the Italian name chosen to lend authenticity to the product. If they couldn't say it, how would they remember it? A simple solution: Final copy for the TV spots made sure that the brand name was repeated several times.

Kraft used good questionnaire design to help find out how to get customers to overcome their skepticism that a frozen pizza could be just as good as a delivered pizza. As a result of this and other types of marketing research, DiGiorno pizza has been a success.

Find out whether Kraft Foods has any other questionnaires that might lead to new products at

 http://www. kraftfoods.com

NIELSEN DATA SHOWS A STEADY RISE IN SALES FOR DIGIORNO SINCE ITS LAUNCH in 1996. It now boasts $300 million in revenues, placing it second in its category (Tombstone, another Kraft brand, ranks number one). Brand awareness, according to Millward Brown, has jumped significantly, too—from 23 percent in 1996 to 77 percent. And watch out, pizza man: 49 percent of Millward Brown participants say that DiGiorno is a worthy substitute for carryout.[1] ■

Survey research and focus groups enabled Kraft Foods to build demand for DiGiorno. The cornerstone of survey research is the questionnaire. What are the objectives of questionnaire design? A poor questionnaire can lead to interviewer frustration and respondent confusion, in turn causing interviews to be terminated by the respondent. What makes for a good questionnaire? What steps are involved in questionnaire development? What impact does the Internet have on questionnaires? We will explore these and other issues in this chapter.

The Role of a Questionnaire

questionnaire
A set of questions designed to generate the data necessary to accomplish the objectives of the research project; also called an *interview schedule* or *survey instrument*.

Every form of survey research relies on the use of a questionnaire, the common thread in almost all data collection methods. A **questionnaire** is a set of questions designed to generate the data necessary to accomplish the objectives of the research project; it is a formalized schedule for collecting information from respondents. You have most likely seen or even filled out a questionnaire recently. Creating a good questionnaire requires both hard work and imagination.

A questionnaire standardizes the wording and sequencing of questions and imposes uniformity on the data-gathering process. Every respondent sees or hears the same words; every interviewer asks identical questions. Without such standardization, interviewers could ask whatever they wanted, and researchers would be left wondering whether respondents' answers were a consequence of interviewer influence or interpretation; a valid basis for comparing respondents' answers would not exist. The jumbled mass of data would be unmanageable from a tabulation standpoint. In a very real sense, then, the questionnaire is a control device, but it is a unique one, as you will see.

The questionnaire (sometimes referred to as an *interview schedule* or *survey instrument*) plays a critical role in the data collection process. An elaborate sampling plan, well-trained interviewers, proper statistical analysis techniques, and good editing and coding are all for naught if the questionnaire is poorly designed. Improper design can lead to incomplete information, inaccurate data, and, of course, higher costs. The questionnaire and the interviewer are the production line of marketing research. It is here that the product, be it good or bad, is created. The questionnaire is the workers' (interviewers') tool that creates the basic product (respondent information).

Figure 11.1 illustrates the pivotal role of the questionnaire. It is positioned between survey objectives (drawn from the manager's problem) and respondent information. In this position, it must translate the objectives into specific questions to solicit the required information from respondents.

PART 3:
Data Acquisition

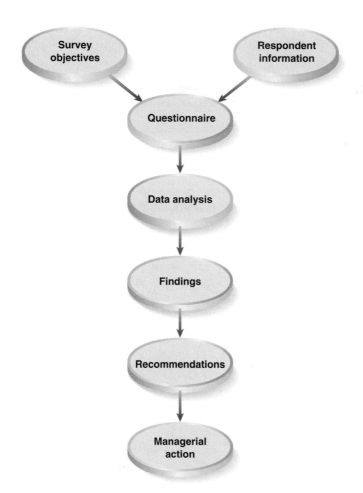

Figure 11.1

The Questionnaire's Pivotal Role in the Research Process

Survey objectives

Respondent information

Questionnaire

Data analysis

Findings

Recommendations

Managerial action

Assume that Swatch is considering the development of a child's wristwatch. The timepiece would have a plastic casing with printed circuits inside. Swatch's engineering staff believes that it can come up with a watch that will withstand the potential abuse from the normal activities of a child between 8 and 13 years old. Preliminary marketing research is called for to determine the acceptability of the watch to the target market. One objective is to determine children's reactions to the watch. The marketing researchers must translate the objectives into language understandable to child respondents, as a child of eight probably won't be able to respond to questions that use such terms as *acceptability, efficiency,* and *likelihood of purchase.*

This example illustrates the pivotal role of the questionnaire: It must translate the survey objectives into a form understandable to respondents and "pull" the requisite information from them. At the same time, it must recover their responses in a form that can be easily tabulated and translated into findings and recommendations that will satisfy a manager's information requirements.

Questionnaires also play a key role in survey costs, which will be discussed in detail later in the chapter.

Criteria for a Good Questionnaire

To design a good questionnaire, the researchers must consider a number of issues: Does it provide the necessary decision-making information for management? Does it consider the respondent? Does it meet editing, coding, and data processing requirements?

Does It Provide the Necessary Decision-Making Information?

The primary role of any questionnaire is to provide the information required for management decision making. Any questionnaire that fails to provide important insights for management or decision-making information should be discarded or revised. Therefore, the managers who will be using the data should always approve the questionnaire. By signing off on the questionnaire, the manager is saying, "Yes, this instrument will supply the data I need to reach a decision." If the manager does not sign off, then the marketing researcher must continue to revise the questionnaire.

A questionnaire should always fit the respondent. Though parents typically purchase cereal, children often make the decision about what kind to buy. A taste test questionnaire for children should be worded in language they can understand.

Does It Consider the Respondent?

As companies have recognized the importance of marketing research, the number of surveys taken annually has mushroomed. Poorly designed, confusing, and lengthy surveys have literally turned off thousands of potential respondents. It is estimated that more than 50 percent of all persons contacted refuse to participate in surveys.

The researcher designing a questionnaire must consider not only the topic and the type of respondent, but the interviewing environment and questionnaire length as well. One recent study found that when a respondent attaches little interest or importance to the survey topic, questionnaire length is relatively unimportant.[2] In other words, people are not going to participate in the survey no matter how long or short the questionnaire is. The study also found that respondents will answer somewhat longer questionnaires when they are interested in the topic and when they perceive that they will have little difficulty in responding to the questions.

A questionnaire should be designed explicitly for the intended respondents. For example, although a parent typically is the purchaser of cold cereals, the child, either directly or indirectly, often makes the decision as to which brand. Thus, a taste test questionnaire about cold cereals should be formulated in children's language. On the other hand, a survey about *purchasing* cold cereals should be worded in language suitable for adult interviewees. One of the most important tasks of questionnaire design is to fit the questions to the prospective respondent. The questionnaire designer must strip away any marketing jargon and business terminology that may be misunderstood by the respondent. In fact, it is best to use simple, everyday language, as long as the result is not insulting or demeaning to the respondent.

Does It Meet Editing, Coding, and Data Processing Requirements?

Once the information has been gathered, it will have to be edited and then coded for data processing. A questionnaire should be designed with these later processes in mind.

Editing refers to going through each questionnaire to make certain that skip patterns were followed and required questions were filled out. The **skip pattern** is the sequence in which questions are asked, based on a respondent's answer. Figure 11.2 shows a clearly defined skip pattern from question 4a to question 5a for persons who answer "No" to question 4a.

In mall and telephone interviews, replies to all open-ended questions (which ask respondents to answer in their own words) are recorded verbatim by the interviewer (see later discussion). Sometimes the responses are then **coded** by listing the answers from a number of randomly selected completed questionnaires; however, if at all possible, responses to open-ended questions should be precoded. Those responses occurring with the greatest frequency are listed on a coding sheet (such as the one in Table 11.1), which the editor uses to code all other responses to the open-ended question. Today, sophisticated neural network systems software is decreasing the necessity for manually coding responses

editing
Going through each questionnaire to ensure that skip patterns were followed and the required questions filled out.

skip pattern
Sequence in which questions are asked, based on a respondent's answer.

coding
The process of grouping and assigning numeric codes to the various responses to a question.

4a. Do you usually use a cream rinse or a hair conditioner on your child's hair?
    (1) ( ) No (SKIP TO 5a)   (2) ( ) (ASK Q. 4b)

4b. Is that a cream rinse that you pour on or a cream rinse that you spray on?
    (1) ( ) Cream rinse that you pour on
    (2) ( ) Cream rinse that you spray on

4c. About how often do you use a cream rinse or a hair conditioner on your child's hair? Would you say less than once a week, once a week, or more than once a week?
    (1) ( ) Less than once a week
    (2) ( ) Once a week
    (3) ( ) More than once a week

5a. Thinking of the texture of your child's hair, is it . . . . (READ LIST)
    (1) ( ) Fine   (2) ( ) Coarse   (3) ( ) Regular

5b. What is the length of your child's hair? (READ LIST)
    (1) ( ) Long   (2) ( ) Medium   (3) ( ) Short

Figure 11.2

An Example of a Questionnaire Skip Pattern

Table 11.1	Coding Sheet for the Question "What Is Your Occupation?"	
	Category	**Code**
	Professional/technical	1
	Manager/official/self-employed	2
	Clerical/sales	3
	Skilled worker	4
	Service worker	5
	Unskilled laborer	6
	Farm operator or rancher	7
	Unemployed or student	8
	Retired	9

to open-ended questions. Software is also used by many researchers to check the editing of questionnaires.

In summary, a questionnaire serves many masters. First, it must accommodate all the research objectives in sufficient depth and breadth to satisfy the information requirements of the manager. Next, it must "speak" to the respondent in understandable language and at the appropriate intellectual level. Furthermore, it must be convenient for the interviewer to administer, and it must allow the interviewer to quickly record the respondent's answers. At the same time, the questionnaire must be easy to edit and check for completeness. It also should facilitate coding and data entry. Finally, the questionnaire must be translatable into findings that respond to the manager's original questions.

WAR Stories

Freelance moderator Paul Schneller recalls reviewing screeners [screening questions] for a focus group he was to conduct. One of the questions asked was, "What do you like to do in your spare time?" (INTERVIEWER: RECORD VERBATIM IN SPACE PROVIDED.)

The replies were a bit briefer than Schneller had hoped. On every screener, the recruiter had written "VERBATIM," neglecting to record anything the respondent had said.

Source: "War Stories: True Life Tales in Marketing Research," by Art Shulman, *Quirk's Marketing Research Review* (April 1997). Reprinted by permission of Art Shulman.

The Questionnaire Design Process

Designing a questionnaire involves a series of logical steps, as shown in Figure 11.3. The steps may vary slightly when performed by different researchers, but all researchers tend to follow the same general sequence. Committees and lines of authority can complicate the process, so it is wise to clear each step with the individual who has the ultimate authority for the project. This is particularly true for the first step: determining survey objectives, resources, and constraints. Many work hours have been wasted because a researcher developed a questionnaire to answer one type of question and the "real" decision maker wanted something entirely different. It also should be noted that the design process itself—specifically, question wording and format—can raise additional issues or unanswered questions. This, in turn, can send the researcher back to step one for a clearer description of the information sought.

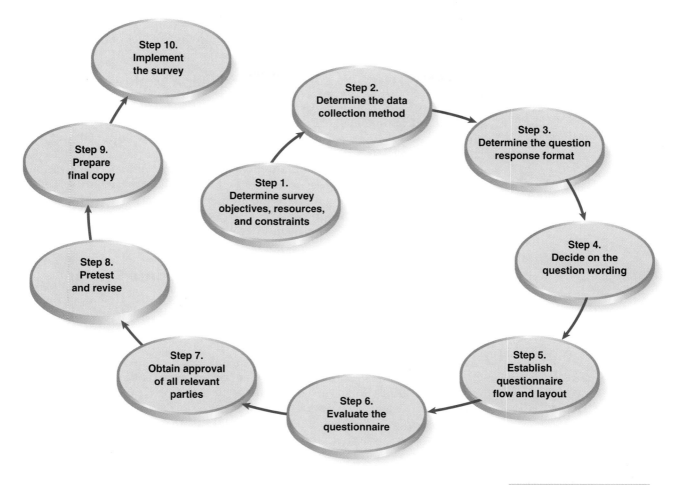

Figure 11.3

The Questionnaire Design Process

Step One: Determine Survey Objectives, Resources, and Constraints

The research process often begins when a marketing manager, brand manager, or new product development specialist has a need for decision-making information that is not available. In some firms, it is the manager's responsibility to evaluate all secondary sources to make certain that the needed information has not already been gathered. In other companies, the manager leaves all research activities, primary and secondary, to the research department. The discussion of uses of marketing research in Chapter 2 covers this issue in more detail.

Although a brand manager may initiate the research request, everyone affected by the project—including the assistant brand manager, the group product manager, and even the marketing manager—should provide input into exactly what data are needed. **Survey objectives** (outlining the decision-making

survey objectives
An outline of the decision-making information sought through the questionnaire.

information required) should be spelled out as clearly and precisely as possible. If this step is completed carefully and thoroughly, the rest of the process will follow more smoothly and efficiently.

Step Two: Determine the Data Collection Method

Given the variety of ways in which survey data can be gathered, such as via the Internet, telephone, mail, or self-administration, the research method will have an impact on questionnaire design. An in-person interview in a mall will have constraints (such as a time limitation) not encountered with an Internet questionnaire. A self-administered questionnaire must be explicit and usually rather short; because no interviewer will be present, respondents will not have the opportunity to clarify a question. A telephone interview may require a rich verbal description of a concept to make certain the respondent understands the idea being discussed. In contrast, an Internet survey can show the respondent a picture or video or demonstrate a concept.

Step Three: Determine the Question Response Format

Once the data collection method has been determined, a decision must be made regarding the types of questions to be used in the survey. Three major types of questions are used in marketing research: open-ended, closed-ended, and scale-response questions.

open-ended questions
Questions to which the respondent replies in her or his own words.

Open-Ended Questions   **Open-ended questions** are those to which the respondent replies in her or his own words. In other words, the researcher does not limit the response choices.

Often, open-ended questions require probes from the interviewer. In a *probe,* the interviewer encourages the respondent to elaborate or continue the discussion. The interviewer may say, "Is there anything else?" or "Would you elaborate on that?" in order to clarify the respondent's interests, attitudes, and feelings. Computers are playing an increasingly important role in analyzing and recording probes to open-ended questions.

Open-ended questions offer several advantages to the researcher. They enable respondents to give their general reactions to questions like the following:

1. What advantages, if any, do you think ordering from an e-commerce company offers compared with buying from local retail outlets? (*Probe:* What else?)
2. Why do you have one or more of your rugs or carpets professionally cleaned rather than cleaning them yourself or having someone else in the household clean them?
3. What do you think is most in need of improvement here at the airport?
4. What is there about the color of _____ [product] that makes you like it the best? (*Probe:* What color is that?)
5. Why do you say that brand [the one you use most often] is better?

Each of the preceding questions was taken from a different nationwide survey covering five products and services. Note that open-ended questions 2 and 4 are

PART 3:
Data Acquisition

part of a skip pattern. Before being asked question 2, the respondent has already indicated that he or she uses a professional carpet cleaning service and does not depend on members of the household.

Open-ended responses have the advantage of providing the researcher with a rich array of information. The respondent's answers are based on his or her personal frame of reference and described in real-world terminology rather than laboratory or marketing jargon. Often, this is helpful in designing promotion themes and campaigns; it enables copywriters to use the consumer's language. This rich array of information can now be captured even in computer-assisted interviews and Internet surveys.

The inspection of open-ended responses also can serve as a means of interpreting closed-ended questions. Analysis often sheds additional light on the motivations or attitudes behind closed-ended response patterns. It is one thing to know that color ranks second in importance out of five product attributes—but it might be much more valuable to know why color is important. For example, a recent study of mobile home park residents identified a great deal of dissatisfaction with the trash pick-up service, but further inspection of the open-ended responses uncovered the reason: Neighbors' dogs were allowed to run free and were overturning the receptacles.

Similarly, open-ended questions may suggest additional alternatives, not listed in a closed-ended response format. For example, a previously unrecognized advantage of using an e-commerce company might be uncovered in responses to question 1. A closed-ended question on the same subject would not have this advantage.

One manufacturer for which we consult always ends product placement questionnaires with the following: "Is there anything else that you would like to tell us about the product that you have tried during the past three weeks?" This probe seeks any final tidbit of information that might provide additional insight for the researcher.

Open-ended questions are not without their problems. Editing and coding consume great amounts of time and money. Editing open-ended responses requires collapsing the many response alternatives into some reasonable number. If too many categories are used, data patterns and response frequencies may be difficult to interpret. Even if a proper number of categories is used, editors may still have to interpret what the interviewer has recorded and force the data into a category. If the categories are too broad, the data may be too general and important meaning may be lost.

A related problem of open-ended questions is the potential for interviewer bias. Although training sessions continually stress the importance of verbatim recording of open-ended questions, interviewers in the field often take shortcuts. Also, slow writers may unintentionally miss important comments. Good probes that ask "Can you tell me a little more?" or "Is there anything else?" are helpful in dealing with this problem.

Precoding open-ended questions can partially overcome these problems. Assume that this question was to be asked in a food study: "What, if anything, do you normally add to a taco that you have prepared at home, besides meat?" Coding categories for this open-ended question might be as follows.

Response	Code
Avocado	1
Cheese (Monterey Jack, cheddar)	2
Guacamole	3
Lettuce	4
Mexican hot sauce	5
Olives (black or green)	6
Onions (red or white)	7
Peppers (red or green)	8
Pimento	9
Sour cream	0
Other	X

These answers would be listed on the questionnaire, and a space would be provided to write in any nonconforming reply in the "Other" category. In a telephone interview, the question would still qualify as open-ended because the respondents would not see the categories and the interviewer would be instructed not to divulge them. Precoding necessitates that the researcher have sufficient familiarity with previous studies of a similar nature to anticipate respondents' answers. Otherwise, a pretest with a fairly large sample is needed.

If a food study on tacos asked "What, if anything besides meat, do you normally add to a taco you have prepared at home?" coding categories would need to be determined to categorize answers to this open-ended question.

Open-ended questions may be biased toward the articulate interviewee. A person with elaborate opinions and the ability to express them may have much greater input than a shy, inarticulate, or withdrawn respondent. Yet, both might be equally likely prospective consumers of a product.

Suppose an editor confronted the following responses to the taco question: "I usually add a green, avocado-tasting hot sauce." "I cut up a mixture of lettuce and spinach." "I'm a vegetarian; I don't use meat at all. My taco is filled only with guacamole." How should the editor code these?

A basic problem with open-ended questions lies in the interpretation-processing area. A two-phase judgment must be made. First, the researcher must decide on an appropriate set of categories, and then each response must be evaluated to determine which category it falls into.

A final difficulty with open-ended questions is their inappropriateness on some self-administered questionnaires. With no interviewer there to probe, respondents may give a shallow, incomplete, or unclear answer. On a self-administered questionnaire without precoded choices, answers to the taco question might read "I use a little bit of everything" or "I use the same things they use in restaurants." These answers would have virtually no value to a researcher.

closed-ended questions
Questions that require the respondent to choose from a list of answers.

Closed-Ended Questions   A **closed-ended question** requires the respondent to make a selection from a list of responses. The primary advantage of closed-ended questions is simply the avoidance of many of the problems associated with open-ended questions. Reading response alternatives may jog a person's memory and

PART 3:
Data Acquisition

generate a more realistic response. Interviewer bias is eliminated because the interviewer is simply checking a box, circling a category, recording a number, or punching a key. Because the option of expounding on a topic is not given to a respondent, there is no bias toward the articulate. Finally, coding and data entry can be done automatically with questionnaire software programs.

It is important to realize the difference between a precoded open-ended question and a multiple-choice question. A precoded open-ended question allows the respondent to answer in a freewheeling format; the interviewer simply checks coded answers as they are given. Probing is used, but a list is never read. If the answer given is not one of the precoded ones, it is written verbatim in the "Other" column. In contrast, a closed-ended question requires that a list of alternatives be read by the respondent or interviewer.

Using Technology to Record Open-Ended Responses

AUDITS AND SURVEYS HAS DEVELOPED A SYSTEM CALLED A&S Voice/CATI. When an open-ended question comes up on the screen, the interviewer has the capability to record the entire response in the respondent's own voice onto PC disk rather than a tape recorder. The assumption is that the interview is taking place via a PC rather than a dumb terminal. The system affords some important new benefits for analysts of open-ended responses:

- By recording the entire open-ended response, the interviewer does not break spontaneity by interrupting to clarify and write or type the response.
- How a thing is said is captured along with what is said.
- It's even possible to record how the interviewers ask the questions

and the give-and-take between the interviewer and the respondent.

The system stores the response on a computer as a digital file on hard disk or floppies. Hence, the verbatim response can be sorted like any other computer file. The data can be transmitted via telephone lines like any other data or the floppies can be mailed to researchers at the client firm.

In analyzing a customer satisfaction study, for example, the analyst can sort respondents who are satisfied and those who are dissatisfied and listen to each group's actual comments as to why. During analysis and report presentation or preparation, actual-voice, open-ended responses can be sorted by answers to any other question in the questionnaire and by traditional classification questions (sex, age, income, etc.).[3] ■

In PRACTICE

Traditionally, marketing researchers have separated closed-ended questions into two types: **dichotomous questions,** with a two-item response option, **multiple-choice** (or multichotomous) **questions,** with a multi-item response option.

Dichotomous Questions.   In a dichotomous question, the two response categories are sometimes implicit. For instance, the implicit response options to the question "Did you buy gasoline for your automobile in the last week?" are "Yes" and "No." Even if the respondent says, "I rented a car last week, and they filled it up for me. Does that count?" the question would still be classified as dichotomous. A few examples of dichotomous questions follow:

1. Did you heat the Danish roll before serving it?
   Yes   1
   No   2

2. The federal government doesn't care what people like me think.
   Agree   1
   Disagree   2

3. Do you think that inflation will be greater or less than it was last year?
   Greater than   1
   Less than   2

Because the respondent is limited to two fixed alternatives, dichotomous questions are easy to administer and tabulate and usually evoke a rapid response. Many times, a neutral response option is added to dichotomous questions; if it is omitted, interviewers may jot down "DK" for "Don't know" or "NR" for "No response."

Dichotomous questions are prone to a large amount of measurement error. Because alternatives are polarized, the wide range of possible choices between the poles is omitted. Thus, appropriate wording is critical to obtaining accurate responses. Questions phrased in a positive form may well result in opposite answers from questions expressed in a negative form. For example, responses may depend on whether "Greater than" or "Less than" is listed first. These problems can be overcome by using a split ballot technique: One-half of the questionnaires have "Greater than" listed first, and the other half have "Less than" first. This procedure aids in reducing potential order bias.

Another problem with the dichotomous question is that responses frequently fail to communicate any intensity of feeling on the part of the respondent. In some cases, like the gasoline purchasing example, the matter of intensity does not apply. But in some instances, strong feelings about an issue may be lost in the dichotomous response form. If the gasoline purchasing interview continued with the question "Would you purchase gasoline priced $1.00 per gallon above current prices if you were guaranteed twice the miles per gallon?" responses would likely range in intensity from "No; absolutely not" to "You bet!"

Multiple-Choice Questions.   With multiple-choice questions, replies do not have to be coded as they do with open-ended questions, but the amount of information provided is more limited. The respondent is asked to give one alternative that correctly expresses his or her opinion or, in some instances, to indicate all alternatives that apply. Some examples of multiple-choice questions follow:

1. I'd like you to think back to the last footwear of any kind that you bought. I'll read you a list of descriptions and would like for you to tell me which category it falls into. (READ LIST AND CHECK THE PROPER CATEGORY)

Dress and/or formal	1	Specialized athletic shoes	4
Casual	2	Boots	5
Canvas-trainer-gym shoes	3		

2. (HAND RESPONDENT CARD) Please look at this card and tell me the letter that indicates the age group you belong to.

A.	Under 17	1	D.	35–49 years	4
B.	17–24 years	2	E.	50–64 years	5
C.	25–34 years	3	F.	65 and over	6

3. In the last three months, have you used Noxzema Skin Cream . . . (CHECK ALL THAT APPLY)

as a facial wash?	1
for moisturizing the skin?	2
for treating blemishes?	3
for cleansing the skin?	4
for treating dry skin?	5
for softening skin?	6
for sunburn?	7
for making the facial skin smooth?	8

Question 1 may not cover all possible alternatives and, thus, may not capture a true response. Where, for example, would an interviewer record work shoes? The same thing can be said for question 3. Not only are all possible alternatives not included, but respondents cannot elaborate or qualify their answers. The problem could be easily overcome by adding an "Any other use?" alternative to the question.

The multiple-choice question has two additional disadvantages. First, the researcher must spend time generating the list of possible responses. This phase may require brainstorming or intensive analysis of focus group tapes or secondary data. Second, the researcher must settle on a range of possible answers. If the list is too long, the respondent may become confused or lose interest. A related problem with any list is *position bias*. Respondents typically will choose either the first or the last alternative, all other things being equal. When questionnaire software and CATI systems are used, however, position bias is eliminated by automatically rotating response order.

Scaled-Response Questions　　The last response format to be considered is **scaled-response questions,** which are closed-ended questions where the response choices are designed to capture intensity of feeling. Consider the following questions.

1. Now that you have used the product, would you say that you would buy it or not?
   (CHECK ONE)
   Yes, would buy it
   No, would not buy it

scaled-response questions
Closed-ended questions in which the response choices are designed to capture the intensity of the respondent's feeling.

2. Now that you have used the product, would you say that you . . .
(CHECK ONE)
definitely would buy it?
probably would buy it?
might or might not buy it?
probably would not buy it?
definitely would not buy it?

The first question fails to capture intensity. It determines the direction ("Yes" versus "No"), but it cannot compare with the second question in completeness or sensitivity of response. The latter also has the advantage of being ordinal in nature.

A primary advantage of using scaled-response questions is that scaling permits measurement of the intensity of respondents' answers. Also, many scaled-response forms incorporate numbers which can be used directly as codes. Finally, the marketing researcher can use much more powerful statistical tools with some scaled-response questions (see Chapter 17).

The most significant problems with scaled-response questions arise from respondent misunderstanding. Scaled questions sometimes tax respondents' abilities to remember and answer. First, the questionnaire must explain the response category options; then, the respondent must translate these options into his or her own frame of reference. Interviewers usually are provided with a detailed description of the response categories allowed and often are instructed to have the respondent state that he or she understands the scale before they ask any questions. Take a look at Figure 11.4 for examples of a telephone interviewer's instructions to respondents. In the case of self-administered questionnaires or Internet surveys, the researcher often presents the respondent with an example of how to respond to a scale as part of the instructions.

Step Four: Decide on the Question Wording

Once the marketing researcher has decided on the specific types of questions and the response formats, the next task is the actual writing of the questions. Wording specific questions can require a significant investment of the researcher's time unless questionnaire software or a survey Web site like WebSurveyor is used. Four general guidelines about the wording of questions are useful to bear in mind: (1) The wording must be clear, (2) the wording must not bias the respondent, (3) the respondent must be able to answer the questions, and (4) the respondent must be willing to answer the questions.

Make Sure the Wording Is Clear Once the researcher has decided that a question is absolutely necessary, the question must be stated so that it means the same thing to all respondents. Ambiguous terminology—for example, "Do you live within five minutes of here?" or "Where do you usually shop for clothes?"—should be avoided. The respondent's answer to the first question will depend on such factors as mode of transportation (maybe the respondent walks), driving speed, and perceptions of elapsed time. (The interviewer

WAR Stories

Market research interviewers always record responses verbatim, don't they? Ask that of a certain researcher, who prefers anonymity, who tells about reading the recorded response to one of the open-end questions in his study. "None of my business," the questionnaire said.

Source:"War Stories: True Life Tales in Marketing Research," by Art Shulman, *Quirk's Marketing Research Review* (January 1997). Reprinted by permission of Art Shulman.

would do better to display a map with certain areas delineated and ask whether the respondent lives within the area outlined.) The second question depends on the type of clothing being purchased and the meaning of the word "Where."

Clarity also calls for the use of reasonable terminology. A questionnaire is not a vocabulary test. Jargon should be avoided, and verbiage should be geared to the target audience. The question "What is the level of efficacy of your preponderant dishwashing liquid?" probably would be greeted by a lot of blank stares. It would be much simpler to ask "Are you (1) very satisfied, (2) somewhat satisfied, or (3) not satisfied with your current brand of dishwashing liquid?" Words with precise meanings, universal usage, and minimal connotative confusion should be selected. When respondents are uncertain of what a question means, the incidence of "No response" answers increases.

A further complication in wording questions is the need to tailor the language to the target respondent group, whether it is lawyers or construction laborers. This advice may seem painfully obvious, but there are instances in which failure to relate to respondents' frames of reference has been disastrous. A case in point is the use of the word *bottles* (or *cans*) in this question: "How many bottles of beer do you drink in a normal week?" Because in some southern states

---

Figure 11.4

Sample Telephone Interviewer's Instructions for a Scaled-Response Question Form

---

Example #1

I have some statements that I will read to you. For each one, please indicate whether you "strongly agree," "agree," "disagree," "strongly disagree," or have no opinion. I will read the statement, and you indicate *your* opinion as accurately as possible. Are the instructions clear?

(IF THE RESPONDENT DOES NOT UNDERSTAND, REPEAT RESPONSE CATEGORIES. THEN GO ON TO READ STATEMENTS AND RECORD RESPONSES. CIRCLE RESPONDENT'S OPINION IN EACH CASE.)

Example #2

Now I'm going to read you a list of statements that may or may not be important to you in deciding where to shop for computer equipment. Let's use your telephone dial as a scale. #1 would mean "definitely disagree," and #6 would mean "definitely agree." Or you can pick any number in between that best expresses your feelings.
Let's begin. To what extent do you agree or disagree that (INSERT STATEMENT) is an important aspect when deciding where to shop for computer equipment?

Example #3

Now I shall read a list of statements about automotive servicing which may or may not be important to you when servicing your car.

Let's use your telephone dial as a scale. . . .
Number 1 would mean you *disagree completely* with the statement.
Number 2 would mean you *disagree* with the statement.
Number 3 would mean you *somewhat disagree* with the statement.
Number 4 would mean you *somewhat agree* with the statement.
Number 5 would mean you *agree* with the statement.
Number 6 would mean you *agree completely* with the statement.

Do you have any questions about the scale?

1. To what extent do you agree or disagree that (INSERT STATEMENT) is a feature you consider when selecting a place to have your car serviced?

---

beer is sold in 32-, 12-, 8-, 7-, 6-, and even 4-ounce bottles, a "heavy" drinker (defined as someone who consumes eight bottles of beer per week) may drink as little as 32 ounces while a "light" drinker (defined as someone who consumes up to three bottles) may actually drink as much as 96 ounces.

Clarity can be improved by stating the purpose of the survey at the beginning of the interview. To put the questions in the proper perspective, the respondent needs to understand the nature of the study and what is expected of him or her but not necessarily who is sponsoring the project.

To achieve clarity in wording, the researcher should avoid asking two questions in one, sometimes called a *double-barreled question*. For example, "How did you like the taste and texture of the coffee cake?" should be broken into two questions, one concerning taste and the other texture. Each question should address only one aspect of evaluation.

Avoid Biasing the Respondent

Questions such as "Do you often shop at lower-class stores like Kmart?" and "Have you purchased any high-quality Black & Decker tools in the past six months?" show an obvious bias. Leading questions, such as "Weren't you pleased with the good service you received last night at the Holiday Inn?" is also quite obviously biased. However, bias may be much more subtle than that illustrated in these examples.

Sponsor identification early in the interviewing process can distort answers. An opening statement such as "We are conducting a study on the quality of banking for Northeast National Bank and would like to ask you a few questions" should be avoided. Similarly, it will not take long, for example, for a person to recognize that the survey is being conducted for Miller beer if, after the third question, every question is related to this product.

Consider the Respondent's Ability to Answer the Questions

In some cases, a respondent may never have acquired the information needed to answer the question. For example, a husband may not know which brand of sewing thread is preferred by his wife, and respondents will know nothing about a brand or store that they have never encountered. A question worded so as to imply that the respondent should be able to answer it will often elicit a reply that is nothing more than a wild guess. This creates measurement error, since uninformed opinions are being recorded.

A second problem is forgetfulness. For example, you probably cannot remember the answers to all these questions: What was the name of the last movie you saw in a theater? Who were the stars? Did you have popcorn? How many ounces were in the container? What price did you pay for the popcorn? Did you purchase any other snack items? Why or why not? The same is true for the typical respondent. But if a brand manager for Mars, Incorporated wants to know what brand of candy you purchased last, what alternative brands you considered, and what factors led you to the brand selected, marketing researchers will ask, constructing questions that create measurement error. Often respondents will give the name of a well-known brand, like Milky Way or Hershey. In other cases, respondents will mention a brand that they often purchase, but it may not be the last brand purchased.

To avoid the problem of a respondent's inability to recall, the researcher should keep the referenced time periods relatively short. For example, if the respondent says "Yes" to the question "Did you purchase a candy bar within the past seven days?" then brand and purchase motivation questions can be asked. A poor question like "How many movies have you rented in the past year to view at home on your VCR?" might be replaced with the following:

a. How many movies have you rented in the past month to view on your VCR?

b. Would you say that, in the last month, you rented more movies, fewer movies, or about the average number of movies you rent per month? (IF "MORE" OR "LESS," ASK THE FOLLOWING QUESTION)

c. What would you say is the typical number of movies you rent per month?

Consider the Respondent's Willingness to Answer the Question   A respondent may have a very good memory, yet not be willing to give a truthful reply. If an event is perceived as embarrassing, sensitive in nature, threatening, or divergent from the respondent's self-image, it is likely either not to be reported at all or to be distorted in a socially desirable direction.

Embarrassing questions that deal with topics such as borrowing money, personal hygiene, sexual activities, and criminal records must be phrased carefully to minimize measurement error. One technique is to ask the question in the third person—for example, "Do you think that most people charge more on their credit cards than they should? Why?" By generalizing the question to "most people," the researcher may be able to learn more about individual respondents' attitudes toward credit and debt.

Another method for soliciting embarrassing information is for the interviewer to state, prior to asking the question, that the behavior or attitude is not unusual—for example, "Millions of Americans suffer from hemorrhoids; do you or any member of your family suffer from this problem?" This technique, called *using counterbiasing statements,* makes embarrassing topics less intimidating for respondents to discuss.

Step Five: Establish Questionnaire Flow and Layout

After the questions have been properly formulated, the next step is to sequence them and develop a layout for the questionnaire. Questionnaires are not constructed haphazardly; there is a logic to the positioning of each section (see Table 11.2). Experienced marketing researchers are well aware that good questionnaire development is the key to obtaining a completed interview. A well-organized questionnaire usually elicits answers that are more carefully thought out and detailed. Researcher wisdom has led to the following general guidelines concerning questionnaire flow.

Use Screening Questions to Identify Qualified Respondents   Most marketing research employs some type of quota sampling. Only qualified respon-

WAR Stories

Art Shulman, President of Art Shulman Research, conducted a survey among subscribers to a biker magazine, where 10 percent of the respondents (heavily skewed to riding Harley-Davidsons) indicated they were currently in jail and responding from there. "That sure messed up our question on household size. One subscriber indicated he was part of a throng of 8,000 (all of his fellow inmates), while another reported there were two in his cell, 'including yourself.'"

Source: "War Stories: True Life Tales in Marketing Research," by Art Shulman, *Quirk's Marketing Research Review* (November 1996). Reprinted by permission of Art Shulman.

How a Questionnaire Should Be Organized

Location	Type	Examples	Rationale
Screeners	Qualifying questions	"Have you been snow skiing in the past 12 months?" "Do you own a pair of skis?"	The goal is to identify target respondents.
First few questions	Warm-ups	"What brand of skis do you own?" "How many years have you owned them?"	Easy-to-answer questions show the respondent that the survey is simple.
First third of questions	Transitions	"What features do you like best about the skis?"	Questions related to research objectives require slightly more effort.
Second third	Difficult and complicated questions	"Following are 10 characteristics of snow skis. Please rate your skis on each characteristic, using the scale below."	The respondent has committed to completing the questionnaire and can see that just a few questions are left.
Last third	Classifing and demographic questions	"What is the highest level of education you have attained?"	The respondent may leave some "personal" questions blank, but they are at the end of the survey.

dents are interviewed, and specific minimum numbers (quotas) of various types of qualified respondents may be sought. For example, a food products study generally has quotas of users of specific brands, a magazine study screens for readers, and a cosmetic study screens for brand awareness.

screeners

Questions used to identify appropriate respondents.

Screeners (screening questions) may appear on the questionnaire, or a screening questionnaire may be filled out for everyone who is interviewed. Any demographics obtained provide a basis against which to compare persons who qualify for the full study. A long screening questionnaire can significantly increase the cost of the study, as more information must be obtained from every contact with a respondent. But it may provide important data on the nature of nonusers, nontriers, and persons unaware of the product or service being researched. Short screening questionnaires, such as the one in Figure 11.5, quickly eliminate unqualified persons and enable the interviewer to move immediately to the next potential respondent.

Most importantly, screeners provide a basis for estimating the costs of a survey. A survey in which only qualified respondents are interviewed is going to be much cheaper to conduct than one with a 5 percent incidence rate, all else being equal. Many surveys are placed with field services at a flat rate per completed questionnaire. The rate is based on a stated average interview time and incidence rate. Screeners are used to determine whether, in fact, the incidence rate holds true in a particular city. If it does not, the flat rate is adjusted accordingly.

Begin with a Question That Gets the Respondent's Interest After introductory comments and screens to find a qualified respondent, the initial questions should be simple, interesting, and nonthreatening. To open a questionnaire with an income or age question could be disastrous. These are often

Hello. I'm from Data Facts Research. We are conducting a survey among men, and I'd like to ask you a few questions.

1. Do you or does any member of your family work for an advertising agency, a marketing research firm, or a company that manufactures or sells shaving products?

(TERMINATE)   Yes ( )
(CONTINUE WITH Q. 2)   No ( )

2. How old are you? Are you . . . (READ LIST)

(TERMINATE)   Under 15 yrs. old? ( )

(CHECK QUOTA CONTROL FORM—IF QUOTA GROUP FOR   15 to 34 yrs. old? ( )
WHICH THE RESPONDENT QUALIFIES *IS NOT* FILLED,
CONTINUE, IF QUOTA GROUP *IS* FILLED, THEN TERMINATE.)   Over 34 yrs. old? ( )

3. The last time you shaved, did you use an electric razor or a razor that uses blades?

(TERMINATE)   Electric Razor ( )
(CONTINUE WITH Q. 4)   Blade Razor ( )

4. How many times have you shaved in the past seven days?
(IF LESS THAN THREE TIMES, TERMINATE. IF THREE OR MORE TIMES, CONTINUE WITH THE MAIN QUESTIONNAIRE.)

Figure 11.5

A Screening Questionnaire That Seeks Men 15 Years of Age and Older Who Shave at Least Three Times a Week with a Blade Razor

Some Problems and Potential Solutions with Screening Questions

In PRACTICE

BASED ON THE RECOMMENDED METHODS FOR SCREENING, A RESEARCHER who has the unfortunate task of conducting a phone survey of bus commuters who earn over $50,000 a year and live in ZIP Code 23456, might start the survey by asking if the person on the phone earns over $50,000 a year, lives in ZIP Code 23456, and has commuted to work by bus in the past week. Such a method might be used despite the fact that researchers usually ask about income at the end of the survey, after some rapport has been established.

While having to screen for three characteristics may be an extreme example for a phone survey, needing to screen for multiple characteristics is very common when recruiting for focus groups. In fact, a review of 68 recent focus group screeners used by clients of Continental Research found an income screener on the first page of over 70% of them.

Sometimes, researchers can reduce the number of screening questions or eliminate them altogether by narrowing the initial sample frame. In the above example, the need to ask ZIP Code could be eliminated by using a sampling frame that contains only households in the desired ZIP Code. Similarly, if the researcher purchased a list of people living in that ZIP Code who earned over $50,000 a year, then two of the "screeners" could be asked at the end of the survey as confirmation questions (anticipating a very high incidence). While only one screening question, bus ridership, would be necessary, one does have to weigh any possible biases caused by the list source.

Some problem screeners and solutions created by Continental Research of Norfolk, Virginia, are shown below.

The Career Choice Survey

The purpose of this telephone survey was to learn more about how women between ages 20 and 29 made certain career decisions. To minimize costs, the questionnaire started with:

Hello, I'm with Acme Research in (city). We're doing a survey this evening with women in their twenties.

IF MALE SAY: Does anyone in your home fit this description? (Get female, repeat introduction)

IF FEMALE SAY: May I ask your age?

At the close of the first evening of interviewing, we found a female in the age group in only 23 (12.8%) of 180 households contacted. Researchers began to suspect that some people were using the screening criteria to politely end the interview. The survey was revised by placing three opinion questions after a brief introduction. The newly revised survey read:

Hello, I'm with Acme Research in (city). We're doing a brief opinion survey this evening.

IF MALE SAY: We alternate who we ask for in our surveys; may I speak with an adult female?

IF FEMALE SAY: Do you think that employees should be allowed to smoke in ALL workplaces, SOME, or in NO workplaces?

(THEN, TWO OTHER OPINION ITEMS WERE ASKED BEFORE THE AGE QUESTION.)

Using this survey format, the improved incidence rate was 26.6%. The difference was found to be statistically significant.

Pet Product Survey

A client who was considering creating an infomercial for a pet product had identified his target market as dog and/or cat owners who held a major credit card. He wanted these prospects to evaluate various features of his new product. To minimize cost, the questionnaire started with:

1) Hello, I'm with (company). We're doing a survey this evening with pet owners, do you have a dog or cat?

2) And, do you have a major credit card such as MasterCard or VISA?

Based on other research done previously, the client said that we should expect an incidence rate of between 30% and 40%. Unfortunately, the incidence rate we found when using this survey format was only 8.9%.

To help account for the lower-than-expected incidence rate, we split the sample frame and reworded some surveys as follows:

1) Hello, I'm with (company). We're doing a brief lifestyle survey tonight and we'd like to know how many refrigerators and televisions you have in your home.

2) Do you have a VCR?

3) Do you have a dog or cat?

4) Do you have more than one car?

5) Do you have a major credit card?

By the end of the project, the incidence rate was 11.4% using the first, more direct questioning method and 31.8% using the second, more indirect technique. The difference between these two percentages was found to be statistically significant.[4] ∎

considered threatening and immediately put the respondent on the defensive. The initial question should be easy to answer without much forethought.

Ask General Questions First Once the interview progresses beyond the opening warm-up questions, the questionnaire should proceed in a logical fashion. First, general questions are asked to get the person thinking about a concept, company, or type of product; then the questionnaire moves to the specifics. For example, a questionnaire on shampoo might begin with "Have you purchased a hair spray, hair conditioner, or hair shampoo within the past six weeks?" Then it would ask about the frequency of shampooing, brands purchased in the past three months, satisfaction and dissatisfaction with brands purchased, repurchase intent, characteristics of an "ideal" shampoo, respondent's hair characteristics, and finally demographics.

Ask Questions That Require "Work" in the Middle Initially, the respondent will be only vaguely interested in and understanding of the nature of the survey. As the interest-building questions transpire, momentum and commitment to the interview will build. When the interview shifts to questions with scaled-response formats, the respondent must be motivated to understand the response categories and options. Alternatively, questions might necessitate some recall or opinion formation on the part of the respondent. Established interest and commitment must sustain the respondent in this part of the interview.

Insert "Prompters" at Strategic Points Good interviewers can sense when a respondent's interest and motivation sag and will attempt to build them back up. However, it is always worthwhile for the questionnaire designer to insert short encouragements at strategic locations in the questionnaire. These may be simple statements such as "There are only a few more questions to go" or "This next section will be easier." Encouraging words may also be inserted as part of an introduction to a section: "Now that you have helped us with those comments, we would like to ask a few more questions."

Position Sensitive, Threatening, and Demographic Questions at the End As mentioned earlier, the objectives of a study sometimes necessitate questions on topics about which respondents may feel uneasy. These topics should be covered near the end of the questionnaire to ensure that most of the questions are answered before the respondent becomes defensive or breaks off the interview. Another argument for placing sensitive questions toward the end is that by the time these questions are asked, interviewees have been conditioned to respond. In other words, the respondent has settled into a pattern of seeing or hearing a question and giving an answer.

WAR Stories

Mark Snowden is a media strategist for a large Christian missions organization. He tells about participating on a team conducting a media preference survey across the Americas that included several Indian groups. They were really pleased with the response, netting more than 6,000 surveys. However, when they received the 100 completed questionnaires from the K'ekchi in Guatemala, they quickly noticed that they were all filled out identically! At first they suspected tampering by a leader or a missionary, but each form (translated from K'ekchi) had been meticulously completed by a different person who boldly signed his or her name at the end. Later, his team determined that the ancient Mayan custom still lingered—for a group consensus to be reached on every question, even in a questionnaire. And, yes, his team included each of the 100 completed questionnaires in their survey results.

Source: "War Stories: True Life Tales in Marketing Research," by Art Shulman, *Quirk's Marketing Research Review.* Reprinted by permission of Art Shulman.

Allow Plenty of Space for Open-Ended Responses   An open-ended question that allows half a line for a reply usually will receive a reply of that length and nothing more. Generally speaking, three to five lines of blank space are deemed sufficient for open-ended replies. The researcher must judge how much detail is desirable in an open-ended reply. "Which department store did you visit most recently?" requires much less answer space than the follow-up question "What factors were most important in your decision to go to [name of department store]?"

Put Instructions in Capital Letters   To avoid confusion and to clarify what is a question and what is an instruction, all instructions should be in capital letters—for example, "IF 'YES' TO QUESTION 13, SKIP TO QUESTION 17." Capitalizing helps bring the instructions to the interviewer's or respondent's attention.

Step Six: Evaluate the Questionnaire

Once a rough draft of the questionnaire has been designed, the marketing researcher is obligated to take a step back and critically evaluate it. This phase may seem redundant, given the careful thought that went into each question. But recall the crucial role played by the questionnaire. At this point in the questionnaire development, the following issues should be considered: (1) Is the question necessary? (2) Is the questionnaire too long? (3) Will the questions provide the information needed to accomplish the research objectives?

Is the Question Necessary?   Perhaps the most important criterion for this phase of questionnaire development is the necessity for a given question. Sometimes researchers and brand managers want to ask questions because "they were on the last survey we did like this" or because "it would be nice to know." Excessive numbers of demographic questions are very common. Asking for education data, numbers of children in multiple age categories, and extensive demographics on the spouse simply is not warranted by the nature of many studies.

Each question must serve a purpose. Unless it is a screener, an interest generator, or a required transition, it must be directly and explicitly related to the stated objectives of the particular survey. Any question that fails to satisfy at least one of these criteria should be omitted.

Is the Questionnaire Too Long?   At this point, the researcher should role-play the survey, with volunteers acting as respondents. Although there is no magic number of interactions, the length of time it takes to complete the questionnaire should be averaged over a minimum of five trials. Any questionnaire to be administered in a mall or over the telephone should be a candidate for cutting if it averages longer than 20 minutes. Sometimes mall-intercept interviews can run slightly longer if an incentive is provided to the respondent. Most Internet surveys should take less than 15 minutes to complete.

Common incentives are movie tickets, pen and pencil sets, and cash or checks. The use of incentives often actually lowers survey costs because response rates increase and terminations during the interview decrease. If checks are given out instead of cash, the canceled checks can be used to create a list of survey participants for follow-up purposes.

Will the Questions Provide the Information Needed to Accomplish the Research Objectives?   The researcher must make certain that sufficient numbers and types of questions are contained within the questionnaire to meet the decision-making needs of management. A suggested procedure is to carefully review the written objectives for the research project and then write each question number next to the objective that the particular question will address. For example, question 1 applies to objective 3, question 2 to objective 2, and so forth. If a question cannot be tied to an objective, the researcher should determine whether the list of objectives is complete. If the list is complete, the question should be omitted. If the researcher finds an objective with no questions listed beside it, appropriate questions should be added. Lynn Newman, vice president of Maritz Marketing Research, discusses the difficulties of writing a good questionnaire in the In Practice feature.

Step Seven: Obtain Approval of All Relevant Parties

After the first draft of the questionnaire has been completed, copies should be distributed to all parties who have direct authority over the project. Practically speaking, managers may step in at any time in the design process with new information, requests, or concerns. When this happens, revisions are often necessary. It is still important to get final approval of the first draft even if managers have already intervened in the development process.

Managerial approval commits management to obtaining a body of information via a specific instrument (questionnaire). If the question is not asked, the data will not be gathered. Thus, questionnaire approval tacitly reaffirms what decision-making information is needed and how it will be obtained. For example, assume that a new product questionnaire asks about shape, material, end use, and packaging. By approving the form, the new product development manager is implying, "I know what color the product will be" or "It is not important to determine color at this time."

Step Eight: Pretest and Revise

When final managerial approval has been obtained, the questionnaire must be pretested. No survey should be conducted without a pretest. Moreover, a pretest does not mean one researcher's administering the questionnaire to another researcher. Ideally, a pretest is done by the best interviewers who will ultimately be working on the job and is administered to target respondents for the study. In a **pretest,** interviewers are told to look for misinterpretations by respondents, lack of continuity, poor skip patterns, additional alternatives for precoded and closed-ended questions, and general respondent reaction to the interview. The pretest should be conducted in the same mode as the final interview—that is, if the study is to be an Internet survey, then the pretest should be too.

pretest
A trial run of a questionnaire.

After completion of the pretest, any necessary changes should be made. Managerial approval should then be reobtained before going into the field. If the original pretest results in extensive design and question alterations, a second pretest is in order.

In PRACTICE

Tips for Writing a Good Questionnaire

IF YOU HAVE EVER SENT WHAT YOU THOUGHT WAS A "FINAL" QUESTIONNAIRE to a marketing research supplier, only to have it returned to you full of wording changes, deletions, and other editorial comments, you're not alone. Writing a questionnaire does not, at first glance, appear to be a very difficult task: Just figure out what you want to know, and write questions to obtain that information. But although writing questions is easy, writing good questions is not. Here are some do's and don'ts when writing questions.

1. *Avoid abbreviations, slang, or uncommon words that your audience might not understand.* For example: What is your opinion of PPOs? It is quite possible that everyone does not know that PPO stands for Preferred Provider Organization. If the question targets the general public, the researcher might run into problems. On the other hand, if the question is for physicians or hospital administrators, then the acronym PPO is probably acceptable.

2. *Be specific.* The problem with vague questions is that they generate vague answers. For example: What is your household income? As respondents come up with numerous interpretations to this question, they will give all kinds of answers—income before taxes, income after taxes, etc. Another example: How often did you attend sporting events during the past year? (1) Never, (2) Rarely, (3) Occasionally, (4) Regularly. Again, this question is open for interpretation. people will interpret "sporting event" and the answer list differently—does "regularly" mean weekly, monthly, or what?

3. *On the other hand, don't overdo it.* When questions are too precise, people cannot answer them. They will either refuse or guess. For example: How many books did you read [last year]? You need to give them some ranges: (1) None, (2) 1–10, (3) 11–25, (4) 26–50, (5) More than 50.

4. *Make sure your questions are easy to answer.* Questions that are too demanding will also lead to refusals or guesses. For example: Please rank the following 20 items in order of importance to you when you are shopping for a new car. You're asking respondents to do a fair amount of calculating. Don't ask people to rank 20 items; have them pick the top 5.

5. *Don't assume too much.* This is a fairly common error, in which the question-writer infers something about people's knowledge, attitudes, or behavior. For example: Do you tend to agree or disagree with the president's position on gun control? This question assumes that the respondent is aware that the president has a position on gun control and knows what that position is. To avoid this error, the writer must be prepared to do some educating. For example: "The president has

recently stated his position on gun control. Are you aware that he has taken a stand on this issue?" If the answer is yes, then continue with: "Please describe in your own words what you understand his position on gun control to be." And, finally, "Do you tend to agree or disagree with his stand?"

6. *Watch out for double questions and questions with double negatives.* Combining questions or using a double negative leads to ambiguous questions and answers. For example: "Do you favor the legalization of marijuana for use in private homes but not in public places?" If this question precisely describes the respondent's position, then a "yes" answer is easily interpreted. But a "no" could mean the respondent favors use in public places but not in private homes, or opposes both, or favors both. Similarly, here is an example of a question with a double negative: "Should the police chief not be directly responsible to the mayor?" The question is ambiguous; almost any answer will be even more so.

7. *Check for bias.* A biased question can influence people to respond in a manner that does not accurately reflect their positions. There are several ways in which questions can be prejudiced. One is to imply that respondents should have engaged in a certain behavior. For example: "The movie, *XYZ*, was seen by more people than any other movie this year. Have you seen this movie?" So as not to appear "different," respondents may say yes even though they haven't seen the movie. The question should be: "Have you ever seen the movie, *XYZ*?" Another way to bias a question is to have unbalanced answer choices. For example: "Currently our country spends XX billion dollars a year on foreign aid. Do you feel this amount should be (1) increased, (2) stay the same, (3) decreased a little, (4) decreased somewhat, (5) decreased a great deal?" This set of responses encourages respondents to select a "decrease" option, since there are three of these and only one increase option.

Pretesting: The Survey before the Survey

All the rewriting and editing in the world won't guarantee success. However, pretesting is the least expensive way to make sure your questionnaire research project is a success. The primary purpose of a pretest is to make certain that the questionnaire gives the respondent clear, understandable questions that will evoke clear, understandable answers.[5] ∎

Step Nine: Prepare Final Questionnaire Copy

Even the final copy phase does not allow the researcher to relax. Precise instructions for typing, spacing, numbering, and precoding must be set up, and the results proofread. In a mail survey, compliance and subsequent response rates may be affected positively by a professional-looking questionnaire. For telephone interviews, the copy is typically read from a computer screen.

Step Ten: Implement the Survey

Completion of the questionnaire establishes the basis for obtaining the desired decision-making information from the marketplace. As discussed in Chapter 2, most research interviewing is conducted by field service firms. It is the firm's job to complete the interviews and send them back to the researcher. In essence, field services are the production line of the marketing research industry. A series of forms and procedures must be issued with the questionnaire to make certain that the field service firm gathers the data correctly, efficiently, and at a reasonable cost. Depending on the data collection method, these may include supervisor's instructions, interviewer's instructions, screeners, call record sheets, and visual aids.

supervisor's instructions
Written directions to the field service firm on how to conduct the survey.

Supervisor's Instructions
Supervisor's instructions inform the field services firm of the nature of the study, start and completion dates, quotas, reporting times, equipment and facility requirements, sampling instructions, number of interviewers required, and validation procedures. In addition, detailed instructions are required for any taste test that involves food preparation. Quantities typically are measured and cooked using rigorous measurement techniques and devices.

A vital part of any study handled by a field service, supervisor's instructions establish the parameters for conducting the research. Without clear instructions, the interview may be conducted 10 different ways in 10 cities. A sample page from a set of supervisor's instructions is shown in Figure 11.6.

call record sheets
Interviewers' logs, listing the number of contacts and the results of each contact.

Call Record Sheets
Call record sheets are used to measure the efficiency of the interviewers. The form normally indicates the number of contacts and the results of each contact (see Figure 11.7). A supervisor can examine calls per hour, contacts per completed interview, average time per interview, and so forth to analyze an interviewer's efficiency. If, for example, the number of contacts per completed interview is high, the field supervisor should examine the reasons why. The interviewer may not be using a proper approach, or the mall area may be difficult to cover.

A researcher can use aggregated data for all field service interviewers to measure the firm's efficiency. A high cost per interview might be traced to a large number of contacts per completed interview. This, in turn, may be due to poor interviewer selection and training by the field service firm.

Field Management Companies

field management companies
Firms that provide such support services as questionnaire formatting, screener writing, and coordination of data collection.

Conducting fieldwork is much easier today than it was in years past. The stereotypical "kitchen table" field service firm is passing into history. In its place are companies that specialize in field management. **Field management companies,** such as QFact, On-Line Communications, and Direct Resource, generally provide questionnaire formatting, screener writing, development of instructional and peripheral materials, shipping services, field auditing, and all coordination of data collection, coding, and tab services required for the project. On com-

Purpose	To determine from diet soft drink users their ability to discriminate among three samples of Diet Dr Pepper and give opinions and preferences between two of the samples
Staff	3–4 experienced interviewers per shift
Location	One busy shopping center in a middle to upper-middle socioeconomic area. The center's busiest hours are to be worked by a double shift of interviewers.
	In the center, 3–4 private interviewing stations are to be set up and a refrigerator and good counterspace made available for product storage and preparation.
Quota	192 completed interviews broken down as follows:
	A minimum of 70 Diet Dr Pepper users
	A maximum of 122 other diet brand users
Project materials	For this study, you are supplied the following:
	250 Screening Questionnaires
	192 Study Questionnaires
	4 Card A's
Product/preparation	For this study, our client shipped to your refrigerated facility 26 cases of soft drink product. Each case contains 24 10-oz. bottles—312 coded with an *F* on the cap, 312 with an *S*.
	Each day, you are to obtain from the refrigerated facility approximately 2–4 cases of product—1–2 of each code. Product must be transported in coolers and kept refrigerated at the location. It should remain at approximately 42°F.
	In the center, you are to take one-half of the product coded *F* and place the #23 stickers on the bottles. The other half of the *F* product should receive #46 stickers.
	The same should be done for product *S*—one-half should be coded #34, the other half #68. A supervisor should do this task before interviewing begins. Interviewers will select product by *code number.* Code number stickers are enclosed for this effort.
	Each respondent will be initially testing three product samples as designated on the questionnaire. Interviewers will come to the kitchen, select the three designated bottles, open and pour 4 oz. of each product into its corresponding coded cup. The interviewer should cap and *refrigerate* leftover product when finished pouring and take only the three *cups* of product on a tray to respondent.

Figure 11.6

A Sample Page of Supervisor's Instructions for a Diet Soft Drink Taste Test

pletion of a study, they typically submit a single, comprehensive invoice for the project. Generally lean on staff, these companies provide the services clients need without attempting to compete with the design and analytical capabilities of full-service companies and ad agency research staffs.

Figure 11.7

Sample Call Record Sheet

	Date	Date	Date	Date
Total completions	_____	_____	_____	_____
Quota A	_____	_____	_____	_____
Quota B	_____	_____	_____	_____
Terminate at	_____	_____	_____	_____
Q. A	_____	_____	_____	_____
Q. B	_____	_____	_____	_____
Q. C–No deodorant/antiperspirant	_____	_____	_____	_____
Q. D–No roll-on	_____	_____	_____	_____
Q. E–Ban full	_____	_____	_____	_____
Q. E–"Other" full	_____	_____	_____	_____
Q. F–Refusal	_____	_____	_____	_____
Q. G–No telephone	_____	_____	_____	_____
Total incomplete contacts	_____	_____	_____	_____
No one home	_____	_____	_____	_____
No woman available	_____	_____	_____	_____
Refused	_____	_____	_____	_____
Language/hearing	_____	_____	_____	_____
Respondent break-off	_____	_____	_____	_____
Other	_____	_____	_____	_____
Briefing hours	_____	_____	_____	_____
Interviewing hours	_____	_____	_____	_____
Travel hours	_____	_____	_____	_____
Mileage	_____	_____	_____	_____

A number of full-service companies and qualitative professionals have discovered that using field management companies can be cost-effective; it can increase productivity by allowing them to take on more projects while using fewer of their internal resources. One example of this trend is the business relationship between Heakin Research and MARC, which hired Heakin to handle field management on particular types of studies. Likewise, several qualitative researchers have developed ongoing relationships with field management companies, whose personnel function as extensions of the consultant's staff, setting up projects and freeing up the researcher to conduct groups, write reports, and consult with clients.

Of course, like any other segment of the research industry, field management has its limitations. By definition, field management companies generally do not have design and analytical capabilities. This means that their clients may, on occasion, need to seek other providers to meet their full-service needs. Additionally, because this is a relatively new segment of the industry, experience, services, and standards vary tremendously from firm to firm. It's advisable to carefully screen prospective companies and check references. These limitations notwithstanding, field management companies provide a way for researchers to increase their productivity in a cost-effective manner, while maintaining the quality of the information on which their company's decisions and commitments are based.

PART 3:
Data Acquisition

The Impact of the Internet on Questionnaire Development

As with most other aspects of marketing research, the Internet has affected questionnaire development and use in several ways. For example, a marketing research company can now create a questionnaire and send it as an email attachment to management for comments and approval; once approved, it can be placed on the client's server to be used as an Internet survey. Or researchers can simply use an Internet company like WebSurveyor to create a survey on the Internet.

WebSurveyor is a leading Internet self-service questionnaire-building site. It allows marketing researchers to create online surveys quickly and then view real-time results anytime and anywhere, using remote access. The advantage of WebSurveyor is that the marketing research client has no questionnaire software to install, and no programming or administration is required. All operations are automated and performed through WebSurveyor's Web site. This includes survey design, respondent invitation, data collection, analysis, and results reporting.

WebSurveyor uses a combination of desktop software and an Internet service to enable decision makers to conduct online surveys. The WebSurveyor Desktop software provides all the tools needed to design, distribute, and analyze surveys. WebSurveyor's unique hosting service provides the user with a Web site to host the survey, a unique Web address to access the survey, and a dedicated environment for receiving survey responses.

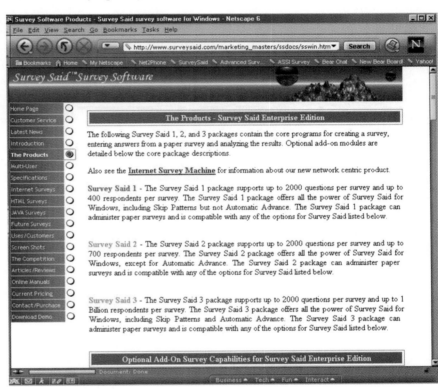

With Survey Said, researchers can create PC- and Internet-based surveys. The editing and modifying of a survey are actually done in Survey Said's Survey Creator. Visit http://www.surveysaid.com to find out more about this software.

Software for Questionnaire Development

Software for questionnaire development has advanced at a rapid rate over the past several years. Sensus Multimedia by Sawtooth Technologies is a multimedia PC-based package.[6] Along with a traditional questionnaire, researchers can use sounds, images, and animations or movie clips. Sensus can also incorporate earlier responses into later questions. It can even do calculations that follow

In the global market of today, a product may be tested in many countries at the same time. The need for questionnaires in several different languages has grown considerably in the last decade.

through to later answers. For instance, suppose you fill out a survey on tractors and say that you have two Fords, three John Deeres, and four International Harvesters. The software might then introduce a later question with "Thinking about your nine tractors . . . ." It could go on to ask you questions about your Ford, your John Deeres, and your International Harvesters. Sensus Multimedia costs about $2,000.

A second software program for questionnaire development is Survey Said. With this software, researchers can create PC-based and Internet-based surveys. The Internet surveys require HTML (hypertext markup language) or Java "applets." HTML allows the researcher to create links (which move the user to other pages when the user clicks on them). HTML also allows the researcher to embed pictures, sounds, and movies into a page created for the Web.

In a program it calls the "Survey Creator," Survey Said allows the marketing researcher to create and modify survey content. Once the researcher calls up the survey, an editing window appears, which provides the researcher with all the question alternatives available. Survey Said cannot do calculations or feed sums from earlier answers back to the respondent. However, a detailed skip pattern is available to guide respondents to different questions depending on their answers.

In summary, Survey Said is a versatile program that is easy to use. Its data collection facilities allow several surveys to be up and running on one Web site. At a price of $1,690, it is a real value.

Today's global marketers offer a variety of products to their customers throughout the world. Many times, a new product concept is tested simultaneously in a number of different countries, requiring questionnaires in a variety of languages. Fortunately, new software programs ease the "language problem," as the Global Issues feature explains.

Costs, Profitability, and Questionnaires

A discussion of questionnaires would not be complete without mentioning their impact on costs and profitability. Marketing research suppliers typically bid against one another for a client's project. A supplier who overestimates costs will usually lose the job to a lower-cost competitor. In all survey research, the questionnaire and incidence rate (see Chapter 6) are the core determinants of a proj-

Consistency Is the Key in Global Research

WHEN COLLECTING AND PROCESSING DATA FOR INTERnational research, consistency is paramount. If the data are not collected and processed consistently, then the results cannot be compared regionally, and eventually project cost and turnaround time will increase. Attention to details and their standardization is imperative.

Specialized software packages for survey design can be tremendously helpful, allowing a library of standard questions, responses, and even routing logic to be compiled. They can be easily retrieved and used to create the different versions of the survey, to achieve consistency in the wording of questions and responses.

Some of these software packages also interface to, or contain, translation utilities. Using these utilities, a researcher can create a database of commonly used phrases, translated into different languages and easily retrieved and used.[7] ∎

Global ISSUES

ect's estimated costs. When one of America's largest research suppliers examined costs and bids for all of its projects conducted by central-location telephone interviewing, it found that it had overestimated project costs 44 percent of the time during as recent 18-month period. The resulting overbidding had translated into millions of dollars of lost sales opportunities.

To avoid overbidding, managers must better understand questionnaire costs. In one central-location telephone study with a 50 percent incidence rate and calls lasting an average of 15 minutes, MARC, a large international marketing research firm, found that only 30 percent of the data collection costs involved asking the questions. Seventy percent of the data collection costs were incurred trying to reach a qualified respondent.[8]

Table 11.3 depicts the numerous roadblocks an interviewer can encounter trying to get a completed interview. Each roadblock adds to the costs. MARC, for example, has found that simply adding a security screener to a questionnaire can increase the cost of interviewing by as much as 7 percent.

Another major source of extra cost in survey research is premature termination of interviews. People terminate interviews for four major reasons: the subject matter, redundant or difficult-to-understand questions, questionnaire length, and changing the subject during an interview. People like to talk about some subjects and not others. For example, the subject of gum is no problem, but bringing up mouthwash results in many terminations. Figure 11.8 reveals that a 20+-minute interview on gum results in few terminations (actual data). However, many people terminate a mouthwash interview within 3 minutes or in

Table 11.3	Difficulties in Finding a Qualified Respondent in a Central-Location Telephone Interview

1. Failed Attempts
   - Busy
   - No answer
   - Answering machine
   - Business number
   - Phone/language problem
   - Discontinued line

2. Cooperation Problems
   - Respondent not at home
   - Respondent refused to be interviewed

3. Screener Determines Respondent Not Eligible
   - Failed security test (works for marketing research firm, advertising agency, or the client)
   - Doesn't use the product
   - Demographic disqualification (wrong gender, age, etc.)
   - Quota filled (For example, survey has a quota of 500 users of Tide and 500 users of other clothes washing powders. Interviewer already has 500 Tide users; the current respondent uses Tide.)

4. Respondent Terminated during Interview

Figure 11.8

Actual Respondent Termination Patterns for Interviews in Three Different Product Categories

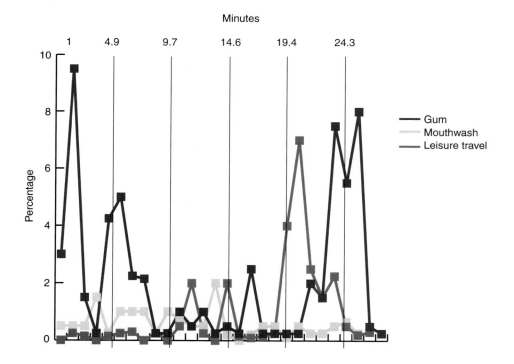

PART 3:
Data Acquisition

the 19- to 22-minute range. Terminations of a leisure travel interview don't become a serious problem until the interview reaches 20 minutes in length. Terminations usually mean that the interview must be redone and all the time spent interviewing the respondent was wasted. However, preliminary research has found that callbacks on terminated interviews can sometimes result in a completed interview.[9] (The same research on callbacks to persons who originally refused to be surveyed was not productive.)

Once managers understand the actual costs of data collection, they should be in a better position to bid on jobs with a high degree of cost accuracy. Better information should result in less overbidding and therefore more contracts.

Summary

The questionnaire plays a critical role in the data collection process. The criteria for a good questionnaire may be categorized as follows: (1) providing the necessary decision-making information, (2) fitting the respondent, and (3) meeting editing, coding, and data processing requirements.

The process of developing a questionnaire is a sequential one:

Step One. Determine survey objectives, resources, and constraints.

Step Two. Determine the data collection method.

Step Three. Determine the question response format.

Step Four. Decide on the question wording.

Step Five. Establish questionnaire flow and layout.

Step Six. Evaluate the questionnaire.

Step Seven. Obtain approval of all relevant parties.

Step Eight. Pretest and revise.

Step Nine. Prepare final questionnaire copy.

Step Ten. Implement the survey.

The three different types of questions—open-ended, closed-ended, and scaled-response questions—each have advantages and disadvantages. In establishing the wording and positioning of questions within the questionnaire, the researcher must try to ensure that the wording is clear and does not bias the respondent and that the respondent will be able and willing to answer the questions.

During the implementation of survey research, procedures must be followed to ensure that the data are gathered correctly, efficiently, and at a reasonable cost. These include preparing supervisor's instructions, interviewer's instructions, screeners, call record sheets, and visual aids. Many research organizations are now turning to field management companies to actually conduct the interviews.

Questionnaire software and the Internet are having a major impact on survey design. Sensus Multimedia software enables researchers to incorporate sounds, images, animations, and movie clips into questionnaires. Survey Said facilitates the creation of PC-based and Internet surveys. WebSurveyor enables researchers to go to its Web site and create online surveys.

The role of the questionnaire in survey research costs can be a decisive one. If a research firm overestimates data collection costs, chances are that it will lose the project to another supplier. Most data collection costs are associated not with conducting the actual interview, but with finding a qualified respondent. A respondent's propensity to terminate an interview, which can be costly, is often based on the nature of the topic discussed.

Key Terms & Definitions

questionnaire A set of questions designed to generate the data necessary to accomplish the objectives of the research project; also called an *interview schedule* or *survey instrument.*

editing Going through each questionnaire to ensure that skip patterns were followed and the required questions filled out.

skip pattern Sequence in which questions are asked, based on a respondent's answer.

coding The process of grouping and assigning numeric codes to the various responses to a question.

survey objectives An outline of the decision-making information sought through the questionnaire.

open-ended questions Questions to which the respondent replies in her or his own words.

closed-ended questions Questions that require the respondent to choose from a list of answers.

dichotomous questions Closed-ended questions that ask the respondents to choose between two answers.

multiple-choice questions Closed-ended questions that ask the respondent to choose among several answers; also called *multichotomous questions.*

scaled-response questions Closed-ended questions in which the response choices are designed to capture the intensity of the respondent's feeling.

screeners Questions used to identify appropriate respondents.

pretest A trial run of a questionnaire

supervisor's instructions Written directions to the field service firm on how to conduct the survey.

call record sheets Interviewers' logs, listing the number of contacts and the results of each contact.

field management companies Firms that provide such support services as questionnaire formatting, screener writing, and coordination of data collection.

Questions for Review & Critical Thinking

1. Explain the role of the questionnaire in the research process.
2. How do respondents influence the design of a questionnaire? Give some examples (e.g., questionnaires designed for engineers, baseball players, army generals, migrant farmworkers).
3. Discuss the advantages and disadvantages of open-ended questions and closed-ended questions.
4. Assume that you are developing a questionnaire about a new sandwich for McDonald's. Use this situation to outline the procedure for designing a questionnaire.
5. Give examples of poor questionnaire wording, and explain what is wrong with each question.
6. Once a questionnaire has been developed, what other factors need to be considered before the questionnaire is put into the hands of interviewers?
7. Why is pretesting a questionnaire important? Are there some situations in which pretesting is not necessary?
8. Design three open-ended and three closed-ended questions to measure consumers' attitudes toward BMW automobiles.
9. What's wrong with the following questions?
   a. How do you like the flavor of this high-quality Maxwell House coffee?
   b. What do you think of the taste and texture of this Sara Lee coffee cake?
   c. We are conducting a study for Bulova watches. What do you think of the quality of Bulova watches?
10. What do you see as the major advantages of using a field management company? What are the drawbacks?

Working the Net

1. How might the Internet affect questionnaire design in the future?
2. Using Infoseek or another search engine, type in "questionnaire design." Report to the class on two questionnaire design software programs you find on the Internet.

Using WebSurveyor

Using the WebSurveyor Desktop software, open the CHAPTER11 survey by selecting File and then Open from the main menu and navigating to the SURVEYS subdirectory under the directory where you installed the WebSurveyor Desktop software (usually c:\program files\websurveyor desktop 3).

Exercises

1. Rewrite each question and identify any problems with wording, scales, or format.
2. Using WebSurveyor, rewrite the questions to eliminate the problems you identify.
3. Using the WebSurveyor Desktop software, create a new questionnaire with a minimum of 20 questions to evaluate the student services at your school. The questionnaire should measure the following:
   a. The quality of student services
   b. Student's knowledge of student services
   c. Usage rate of student services
   d. Satisfaction with student services
   e. Additional student services desired
   f. Student demographics

Real-Life Research • 11.1

Transborder Airline Passenger Study

The following survey was administered to passengers flying across the U.S.–Canadian border.

ABOUT YOUR FLIGHT TODAY . . .
In the following questions, please tell us about your Canada–U.S. (transborder) flight today . . .

1. **Where will/did the flight take off?** (Airport/City)

    _____

2. **Where will/did the flight land?** (Airport/City)

    _____

	Mo.	Day	Yr.

3. **What was the date of the flight?** __ __ __ __ __ __

4a. **Airline flown:** _____ **Flight number:** _____

4b. **How many days before this trip did you . . .**

    Begin to plan the trip?   _____
    Make your reservation?   _____

5a. **Did you, yourself, make your reservation directly with the airline?**

    ☐ Yes   ☐ No

5b. **How many nights will you be away this trip?** _____

6. **In which cabin in the airplane were you seated?**

    ☐ First Class   ☐ Business/Executive Class   ☐ Coach/Economy

7. **(IF FIRST or BUSINESS/EXECUTIVE) Were you upgraded?**
    ☐ Yes   ☐ No

8. **Please check which applies to this trip. (CHECK ALL THAT APPLY)**

    ☐ Flying on a purchased ticket
    ☐ Upgrading (Complimentary/mileage award/purchased upgrade)
    ☐ Flying on a frequent flyer award ticket

9. **About how full was your section of the airplane?**

    ☐ Less than 1/2 full   ☐ More than 3/4 full
    ☐ 1/2 to 3/4 full   ☐ 100% full

10. **What was the <u>primary</u> purpose of this flight? (CHECK ONLY ONE)**

    ☐ Business   ☐ Leisure   ☐ Visit friends or relatives

11. **How close to the scheduled departure time did your plane leave the gate?**

    ☐ Within 5 min   ☐ 16–30 min   ☐ 46–59 min
    ☐ 6–15 min   ☐ 31–45 min   ☐ One hour or more

12. **Who <u>made the decision</u> regarding the airline flown on this trip?**

    ☐ I primarily chose the airline   ☐ Secretary/Assistant
    ☐ Travel agent/Company travel department   ☐ Someone else

If you do not know why this airline was chosen, check here and go to Q. 14. ⟶ ☐

13. **Please divide 10 points among the five items listed below to indicate how important each of them was to you in selecting this flight on this airline. <u>The more imporant an item was to you in selecting the flight, the more points you should give it.</u> You may give any item as many or as few points as you like, but the total number of points you give must add to 10.**

Schedule convenience   _____

Ticket price   _____

Frequent flier/Mileage program   _____

Nationality of airline   _____

Service quality   _____

10 points

14. **Where did you check in at the airport? (CHECK ONE ANSWER)**

☐ At the ticket counter   ☐ At the gate

15. **Please rate the <u>overall</u> services you received on this flight using a scale where:**

5=Excellent; 4=Very good; 3=Good; 2=Fair; and 1=Poor

Overall rating of travel experience with this airline today   _____

Overall airline ground services   _____

Overall seating comfort   _____

Overall rating of aircraft   _____

Overall rating of on-board services   _____

Overall value for money   _____

16. **Thinking about the details of this flight, please rate the following using the same scale:**

5=Excellent; 4=Very good; 3=Good; 2=Fair; and 1=Poor

Check here if not
used/not applicable ➘

Airline reservations services (if used)   _____   ☐

Speed of check-in (where you checked in)   _____   ☐

Helpfulness/Courtesy of airline check-in personnel   _____   ☐

Efficiency of boarding   _____   ☐

Cleanliness of aircraft interior   _____   ☐

Condition of aircraft interior   _____   ☐

Cabin appearance (e.g. attractiveness, lighting)   _____   ☐

Air quality in aircraft cabin   _____   ☐

Space for carry-on baggage   _____   ☐

Arm and shoulder room   _____   ☐

Legroom   _____   ☐

Amount of personal space when seated   _____   ☐

Food quality   _____   ☐

Amount of food   _____   ☐

Courtesy/Friendliness of flight attendants   _____   ☐

Responsiveness of flight attendants   _____   ☐

Entertainment (reading material, audio, video)   _____   ☐

On-board telecommunication services
   (e.g. voice/data/fax)   _____   ☐

Aircraft quietness during flight   _____   ☐

Smoothness of flight   _____   ☐

On-time performance   _____   ☐

Keeping passengers informed before/during flight   _____   ☐

Promptness of baggage delivery   _____   ☐

17. **If all airlines flying between the U.S. and Canada had the same flight schedules and fares, which airline would you use as your first choice?**

_____

PART 3:

Data Acquisition

18. **What type of food was on this flight?**

    ☐ Meal   ☐ Snack (e.g. peanuts/pretzels)   ☐ Neither

19. **Which type of airplane was used for the flight you are evaluating? (CHECK ONE ANSWER ONLY)**

☐ A310	☐ F28	☐ 747
☐ A319	☐ F100	☐ 757
☐ A320	☐ MD80	☐ 767
☐ CRJ/Canadair Jet/CL-5	☐ MD90	☐ 777
☐ DC-9	☐ 727	☐ Other
☐ DC-10	☐ 737	

20. **Please rate the airport where the transborder portion of your flight originated on a scale where:**
    5=Excellent; 4=Very good; 3=Good; 2=Fair; and 1=Poor

Clear, easy to follow signs	_____
Cleanliness	_____
Quality of restaurants	_____
Ease of reaching departure gates	_____

ABOUT FLYING IN GENERAL . . .

21a. **In which airlines frequent flyer/mileage programs are you actively collecting miles? If "none," check here** ⟶ ☐

21b. **And, in which airlines frequent flyer/mileage program are you collecting miles for this flight? If "none," check here** ⟶ ☐

	Actively collecting miles	Collecting for this flight
Air Canada	☐	☐
Alaska Airlines	☐	☐
America West	☐	☐
American Airlines	☐	☐
Canadian Airlines	☐	☐
Continental Airlines	☐	☐
Delta Air Lines	☐	☐
Southwest Airlines	☐	☐
United Airlines	☐	☐
Other _____	☐	☐

22a. **Including this trip, how many <u>round trips</u> by air have you flown in the past 12 months <u>primarily</u> for . . .**

    Business _____   Leisure _____

22b. **And how many of these were flown between Canada and the U.S.?**

    _____

22c. **Of all your trips between Canada and the U.S., how many were on the airline used for your current flight?**

    _____

23a. **Which airline do you fly most often <u>within</u> your home country?**

    _____

23b. **And which airline do you fly most often when you fly between the U.S. and Canada?**

    _____

23c. **When flying between the U.S. and Canada, do you prefer to fly . . . (CHECK ONE)**

    ☐ A Canadian carrier   ☐ A U.S. carrier   ☐ Doesn't matter

24. Thinking about airlines that fly between the U.S. and Canada, please choose the ONE airline that is best for each of the following:

	Air Canada	Alaska	American	Canadian	Continental	Delta	United
Convenient schedules/routes	☐	☐	☐	☐	☐	☐	☐
Low fares	☐	☐	☐	☐	☐	☐	☐
Frequent flyer program	☐	☐	☐	☐	☐	☐	☐
Customer service	☐	☐	☐	☐	☐	☐	☐
On-time performance	☐	☐	☐	☐	☐	☐	☐
Airline reputation	☐	☐	☐	☐	☐	☐	☐

25a. Some airlines are codeshare partners with others. A codeshare is an agreement between two or more airlines to share seats on one airline's aircraft. A codeshare flight has two or more flight numbers, one for each airline sharing the flight.

25b. Are you on a codeshare flight?

☐ Yes   ☐ No   ☐ Don't know

→ **Were you informed that you would be traveling on a codeshare?**

☐ Yes   ☐ No

How satisfied are you with this codeshare arrangement?

☐ Very satisfied   ☐ Not very satisfied
☐ Somewhat satisfied   ☐ Not at all satisfied

26a. Please look at your ticket and indicate which airline appears on your ticket.

_____

26b. And what airline are you actually flying on? _____

FOR CLASSIFICATION PURPOSES . . .

27. a. Are you . . .   ☐ Male   ☐ Female

b. Age: _____ years

c. Approximate total annual household income before taxes:

Canadian $ ☐
$_____   U.S. $ ☐

d. Occupation
☐ Sr Executive/CEO   ☐ Sales/Buyer   ☐ Retired
☐ Executive/Mngmt   ☐ Self-employed   ☐ Student
☐ Administrative/Office   ☐ Govt./Military   ☐ Other
☐ Professional   ☐ Unskilled laborer
☐ Technical/Craftsperson   ☐ Homemaker

Questions

1. What do you think were the objectives of this research study?
2. Critique the questionnaire flow.
3. Identify the various types of questions used in the survey.
4. How would the questionnaire have been different if it had been a telephone survey? An Internet survey? Be specific.

Real-Life Research • 11.2

S. T. Arrow

S. T. Arrow owned a chain of dry cleaners in Portland, Oregon. Competition from One-Hour Martinizing and a regional chain had lowered Arrow's market share from 14 percent to 12 percent. Moreover, his overall profits had fallen 11 percent from the previous year. Arrow decided that an aggressive marketing strategy was in order. Before establishing such a strategy, he felt that a thorough study of the dry cleaning market was needed. The following questionnaire was created by Arrow and given to each customer as the customer left one of Arrow's stores.

Dry Cleaning Questionnaire

Name _____

Address _____

Phone number _____

Where do you take your dry cleaning and laundry?

How much do you spend on dry cleaning/laundry? _____

Sex: Male _____   Female _____

Age Group: Under 30_____ 30–40_____ 40–50_____ 50–60_____ Over 60_____

Marital Status: Single _____   Married _____

Income: Under $5,000 _____ $5,000–25,000 _____ $25,000–60,000 _____

Over $60,000 _____

Number living in home: Alone _____   2 people _____   3 people _____

4 people _____   5 people or more _____

Home: Rent _____   Own _____   What type of housing? _____

Education: High school graduate _____   Associate degree _____

Bachelor's degree _____   Master's degree _____   More _____

1. How long have you been using your dry cleaner? _____
2. How would you rate it? Great _____   Good _____   OK _____
   Not too good _____   Bad _____
3. The dry cleaning establishment

	I now use offers	I would like to use if would offer
Convenience		
—All work done on premises	_____	_____
—Wash'n'wear cleaning services	_____	_____
—Pressing while you wait	_____	_____
—Washing while you wait	_____	_____
—A drive-through window	_____	_____
—Computerized receipts and organization	_____	_____
—Shirt laundry service	_____	_____
—An outlet for drop off/pick up	_____	_____
—Machines to pick up/drop off after hours	_____	_____
—A special for people moving into a new location where the cleaners pick up, clean, and deliver rugs and drapes for new home	_____	_____

	I now use offers	I would like to use if would offer

4. Services
—Shoe repair
—Shoe shining
—Mending
—Altering and tailoring
—Hand pressing
—Dyeing
—Summer/winter clothing storage
—Hand laundering
—Sponged and pressed
—Fur storage

5. For Sale
—Ties and other accessories
—Spot removers, lint brushes, etc.
—Buttons, thread, zippers, etc.
—Woolite

6. Who in your home drops off/picks up the dry cleaning/laundry?
—Wife/mother/self
—Husband/father/self
—Each decides their own clothing is ready
—We take turns

7. Who within the household decides that the clothing is in need of dry cleaning?
—Wife/mother/self
—Husband/father/self
—Each decides their own clothing is ready
—Other family member/self

8. Please check one for each topic.

	A) I am this type	B) I would like to remain as this type

—I hate housework. I just hate having to do it.

—I'd rather pay more to enjoy more. It's easier to pay someone to clean my home and clothes so that I'm free to do what I want to do.

—I enjoy being at home. I was brought up believing a woman's place is in the home and that's where I'm happy.

—I like cleaning my home. It gives me a good feeling.

—Since I have small children, I'm at home, so I clean. But if I were working, it would be easier to have someone come in.

—I don't feel right having someone else cleaning up after me. I find myself cleaning before they come and after they leave. They don't clean the way I do.

PART 3:
Data Acquisition

9. Check the phrase in each group that best describes

(Check one for each column)

	Your present dry cleaner	The way you would like your dry cleaner to be or remain
a. Makes me feel like an intruder.	_____	_____
Keeps me waiting.	_____	_____
Is businesslike.	_____	_____
Always has a friendly word.	_____	_____
b. Gives the feeling he's too busy for me.	_____	_____
Forgets my name when they're crowded.	_____	_____
Always says hello even when they're busy.	_____	_____
Takes the time to treat me individually no matter what.	_____	_____
c. There's a chemical odor, and the posters are outdated and curled at the ends.	_____	_____
There's nothing noticeable about the shop good or bad.	_____	_____
The shop smells clean, the clothes are scientifically racked, and the posters are helpful.	_____	_____
d. Standardized service	_____	_____
Efficient, but distant	_____	_____
Interested in personal requirements	_____	_____
Go out of their way to please.	_____	_____
e. The shop leaves an unkempt impression.	_____	_____
Store is neat, but cluttered.	_____	_____
There is space to move around.	_____	_____
Shop has a warm, cared-for look.	_____	_____
f. The store could use a thorough cleaning.	_____	_____
The shop is acceptably clean.	_____	_____
Store is assuringly sanitary.	_____	_____
g. There's never an answer to questions.	_____	_____
I must point out spots, belts, loose buttons.	_____	_____
We discuss whether it can be cleaned.	_____	_____
The dry cleaner explains particular processes and new chemicals.	_____	_____

Questions

1. Critique S. T. Arrow's questionnaire.
2. What additional topics should have been covered?
3. Discuss the sampling procedure.
4. Did S. T. Arrow develop his questionnaire in a scientific manner?

Chapter Twelve

Basic Sampling Issues

Learning Objectives

To understand the concept of sampling.

To learn the steps in developing a sampling plan.

To understand the concepts of sampling error and nonsampling error.

To understand the differences between probability samples and nonprobability samples.

To understand sampling implications of surveying over the Internet.

S YLVIA MCCORMICK, DIRECTOR OF MARKETING RESEARCH FOR TEXAS
Electric Power (TEP), is in the process of reviewing the results of a survey
just completed over the Internet. The survey targeted household decision
makers for energy needs in the state of Texas. McCormick conducted the
Internet survey at the urging of her boss, the senior marketing officer for
TEP, who was concerned about the increasing cost of marketing research
studies and the length of time it took to complete them. As the electric
power industry in Texas is deregulated, energy producers like TEP feel
pressured to develop strategies to hold on to current residential electric
customers in their traditional service areas and to attract new customers
from other areas. The need to develop new strategies and make decisions
for the post-regulation era has necessitated spending large sums of money
on marketing research—much more than TEP was accustomed to spending.
A research firm marketing the Internet approach to data collection had convinced McCormick's boss that its approach offered a solution to the cost
and time problems.

FOR THIS FIRST STUDY, THE RESEARCH FIRM HAD OBTAINED 12,435 COM-
pleted surveys at a cost of just under $20,000 in less than four days. The
survey was hosted on the research firm's Web site, and TEP was not identified as its sponsor. No comprehensive list of email addresses for Texas
homeowners was available, so the research firm placed banner ads on the
sites of AOL, Yahoo!, Northern Light, and Excite. They argued that these
banner ads were seen by millions of people every day, and therefore the
resulting sample would be representative of the population of all Texas
household decision makers for energy needs. The banner ads made it clear
that the survey was for Texas homeowners only and that a prize drawing
would be held from among those who responded. Top prizes were five high-
definition televisions and five DVD players.

In this vignette, Texas Electric
Power's director of marketing
research must decide on the
best sampling approach to
determine how to keep traditional customers and gain new
customers.

LOOKING AT THE SURVEY RESULTS, MCCORMICK IS CONCERNED THAT THE
sample may not be totally representative of the target population and therefore
the results could be misleading. First of all, the survey questions provided no
means of determining whether individual respondents are Texas homeowners;
they may not be from Texas, and, if they are from Texas, they may not be homeowners. She has compared the demographic characteristics of the Internet sample to the demographic characteristics of random telephone samples from prior
studies, and the Internet sample appears to be significantly younger, better educated, more affluent, and more male. She is concerned that some demographic
groups have been excluded or, at least, undersampled and that the opinions of
these groups are not adequately reflected in the sample. She wants to discuss
these issues with her boss, but given his current excitement about the new survey medium, she knows that she must be well prepared to argue her case. In
addition, the cost savings are dramatic. A telephone survey with a similar sample size would have cost over $200,000. ∎

**Find articles on sampling
issues at**

http://www.
quirks.com

The issues confronting McCormick directly relate to a number of the central themes of this chapter. As in other areas, the question is one of choosing the best sampling approach in a given situation, based on resource constraints and accuracy requirements. As the vignette suggests, different sampling approaches have different costs, data quality levels, and sampling accuracy levels associated with them. The job for the researcher is to obtain the necessary information, at the appropriate levels of quality and accuracy, at the lowest possible cost. After you have had an opportunity to read this chapter, which will provide you with a solid working knowledge of modern scientific sampling procedures, consider what you would say to McCormick's boss.

The Concept of Sampling

sampling
The process of obtaining information from a subset of a larger group.

Sampling refers to the process of obtaining information from a subset (a sample) of a larger group (the universe or population). A user of marketing research then takes the results from the sample and makes estimates of the characteristics of the larger group. The motivation for sampling is to be able to make these estimates more quickly and at a lower cost than would be possible by any other means. It has been shown time and again that sampling a small percentage of a population can result in very accurate estimates. An example that you are probably familiar with is polling in connection with a presidential election. Most major polls use samples of 1,000 to 1,500 people to make predictions regarding the voting behavior of tens of millions of people, and their predictions have proven to be remarkably accurate.

The key to making accurate predictions about the characteristics or behavior of a large population on the basis of a relatively small sample lies in the way in which individuals are selected for the sample. It is critical that they be selected in a scientific manner, which ensures that the sample is representative—that it is a true miniature of the population. All of the major types of people who make up the population of interest should be represented in the sample in the same proportions in which they are found in the larger population. This sounds simple, and as a concept, it is simple. However, achieving this goal in sampling from a human population is not easy.

Population

population
The entire group of people about whom information is needed; also called *universe* or *population of interest.*

In discussions of sampling, the terms *population* and *universe* are often used interchangeably.[1] In this textbook, we will use the term *population*. The **population,** or *population of interest,* is the entire group of people about whom the researcher needs to obtain information. One of the first steps in the sampling process is defining the population of interest. This often involves defining the target market for the product or service in question.

Consider a product concept test for a new nonprescription cold symptom–relief product, such as Contac. You might take the position that the population of interest includes everyone, because everyone suffers from colds from time to time. Although this is true, not everyone buys a nonprescription cold symptom–relief product when he or she gets a cold. In this case, the first task in

PART 3:
Data Acquisition

the screening process would be to determine whether people have purchased or used one or more of a number of competing brands during some time period. Only those who had purchased or used one of these brands would be included in the population of interest.

Defining the population of interest is a key step in the sampling process. There are no specific rules to follow in defining the population of interest. What the researcher must do is apply logic and judgment in addressing the basic issue: Whose opinions are needed in order to satisfy the objectives of the research? Often, the definition of the population is based on the characteristics of current or target customers.

Sample versus Census

In a **census,** data are obtained from or about every member of the population of interest. Censuses are seldom employed in marketing research, as populations of interest to marketers normally include many thousands or even millions of individuals. The cost and time required to collect data from a population of this magnitude are so great that censuses are usually out of the question. It has been demonstrated repeatedly that a relatively small but carefully chosen sample can very accurately reflect the characteristics of the population from which it is drawn. A **sample** is a subset of all the members of a population. Information is obtained from or about a sample and used to make estimates about various characteristics of the total population. Ideally, the sample from or about which information is obtained is a representative cross-section of the total population.

Although censuses are used infrequently in marketing research, there are instances in which they are appropriate and feasible. For example, a census may be useful to an industrial products firm that has only a small number of customers for some highly specialized product it sells. In such a situation, it may be possible to obtain information from the entire population of customers.

Note that the popular belief that a census provides more accurate results than a sample is not necessarily true. In a census of a human population, there are many impediments to actually obtaining information from every member of the population. The researcher may not be able to obtain a complete and accurate list of the entire population, or certain members of the population may refuse to provide information. Because of these barriers, the ideal census is seldom attainable, even with very small populations. You may have read or heard about these types of problems in connection with the 1990 and 2000 U.S. Census.[2]

census
A collection of data obtained from or about every member of the population of interest.

sample
A subset of all the members of a population of interest.

Developing a Sampling Plan

The process of developing an operational sampling plan can be summarized by the seven steps shown in Figure 12.1. These steps are defining the population, choosing a data collection method, identifying a sampling frame, selecting a sampling method, determining sample size, developing operational procedures, and executing the sampling plan.

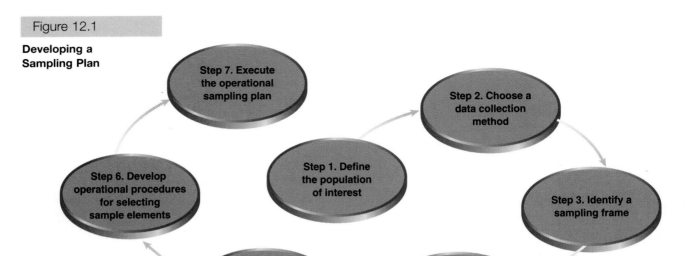

Figure 12.1

Developing a Sampling Plan

Step 7. Execute the operational sampling plan

Step 2. Choose a data collection method

Step 1. Define the population of interest

Step 6. Develop operational procedures for selecting sample elements

Step 3. Identify a sampling frame

Step 5. Determine sample size

Step 4. Select a sampling method

Step One: Define the Population of Interest

The basic issue in developing a sampling plan is to specify the characteristics of those individuals or things (e.g., customers, companies, stores) from whom or about whom information is needed to meet the research objectives. The population of interest is often specified in terms of geographic area, demographic characteristics, product or service usage characteristics, and/or awareness measures (see Table 12.1). In surveys, the question of whether a particular individual does or does not belong to the population of interest is often dealt with by means of screening questions. Even with a list of the population and a sample from that list, researchers still need screening questions to qualify potential respondents. Figure 12.2 on page 400 provides a sample sequence of screening questions.

In addition to defining who will be included in the population of interest, researchers should also define the characteristics of individuals who should be excluded. For example, most commercial marketing research surveys exclude some individuals for so-called security reasons. Very frequently, one of the first questions on a survey asks whether the respondent or anyone in the respondent's immediate family works in marketing research, advertising, or the product or service area at issue in the survey (see, for example, question 5 in Table 12.2). If the individual answers "Yes" to this question, the interview is terminated. This type of question is called a *security question* because those who work in the industries in question are viewed as security risks. They may be competitors or work for competitors, and managers do not want to give them any indication of what their company may be planning to do.

PART 3:
Data Acquisition

Table 12.1	**Some Bases for Defining the Population of Interest**	
	Geographic Area	What geographic area is to be sampled? This is usually a question of the client's scope of operation. The area could be a city, a county, a metropolitan area, a state, a group of states, the entire United States, or a number of countries.
	Demographics	Given the objectives of the research and the target market for the product, whose opinions, reactions, and so on are relevant? For example, does the sampling plan require information from women over 18; women 18–34; women 18–34 with household incomes over $35,000 per year who work and who have preschool children?
	Usage	In addition to geographic area and/or demographics, the population of interest frequently is defined in terms of some product or service use requirement. This is usually stated in terms of use versus nonuse or use of some quantity of the product or service over a specified period of time. The following examples of use screening questions illustrate the point: • Do you drink five or more cans, bottles, or glasses of diet soft drinks in a typical week? • Have you traveled to Europe for vacation or business purposes in the past two years? • Have you or has anyone in your immediate family been in a hospital for an overnight or extended stay in the past two years?
	Awareness	The researcher may be interested in surveying those individuals who are aware of the company's advertising, to explore what the advertising communicated about the characteristics of the product or service.

There may be reasons to exclude individuals for other reasons. For example, the Dr Pepper Company might wish to do a survey among individuals who drink five or more cans, bottles, or glasses of soft drink in a typical week but do not drink Dr Pepper, because the company is interested in developing a better understanding of heavy soft drink users who do not drink their product. Therefore, researchers would exclude those who drank one or more cans, bottles, or glasses of Dr Pepper in the past week.

Step Two: Choose a Data Collection Method

The selection of a data collection method has implications for the sampling process. As noted in the vignette, for example, both telephone interviews and Internet surveys have certain inherent disadvantages in regard to sampling.

Step Three: Identify a Sampling Frame

The third step in the process is to identify the **sampling frame,** which is a list of the members or elements of the population from which units to be sampled are to be selected. Identifying the sampling frame may simply mean specifying a procedure for generating such a list. In the ideal situation, the list of population members is complete and accurate. Unfortunately, there usually is no such list. For example, the population for a study may be defined as those individuals who have spent two or more hours on the Internet in the past week; there can be no complete listing of these individuals. In such instances, the sampling frame

sampling frame
A list of population elements from which units to be sampled can be selected or a specified procedure for generating such a list.

Hello. I'm _____ with _____ Research. We're conducting a survey about products used in the home. May I ask you a few questions?

1. Have you been interviewed about any products or advertising in the past 3 months?
   Yes   (TERMINATE AND TALLY)
   No   (CONTINUE)

2. Which of the following hair care products, if any, have you used in the past month? (HAND PRODUCT CARD TO RESPONDENT; CIRCLE ALL MENTIONS)
   1 Regular shampoo
   2 Dandruff shampoo
   3 Creme rinse/instant conditioner
   4 "Intensive" conditioner
   (INSTRUCTIONS: IF "4" IS CIRCLED—SKIP TO Q. 4 AND CONTINUE FOR "INTENSIVE" QUOTA; IF "3" IS CIRCLED BUT NOT "4"—ASK Q. 3 AND CONTINUE FOR "INSTANT" QUOTA)

3. You said that you have used a creme rinse/instant conditioner in the past month. Have you used either a creme rinse or an instant conditioner in the past week?
   Yes (used in the past week)   (CONTINUE FOR "INSTANT" QUOTA)
   No (not used in past week)   (TERMINATE AND TALLY)

4. Into which of the following groups does your age fall? (READ LIST, CIRCLE AGE)
   X   Under 18   (CHECK AGE QUOTAS)
   1   8–24
   2   25–34
   3   35–44
   X   45 or over

5. Previous surveys have shown that people who work in certain jobs may have different reactions to certain products. Now, do you or does any member of your immediate family work for an advertising agency, a marketing research firm, a public relations firm, or a company that manufactures or sells personal care products?
   Yes   (TERMINATE AND TALLY)
   No   (CONTINUE)
   (IF RESPONDENT QUALIFIES, INVITE HIM OR HER TO PARTICIPATE AND COMPLETE NAME GRID BELOW)

specifies a procedure that will produce a representative sample with the desired characteristics. Thus, there seldom is a perfect correspondence between the sampling frame and the population of interest.

For example, a telephone book might be used as the sample frame for a telephone survey sample in which the population of interest was all households in a particular city. However, the telephone book does not include households that do not have telephones and those with unlisted numbers. It is well established that those with listed telephone numbers are significantly different from those with unlisted numbers in regard to a number of important characteristics. Subscribers who voluntarily unlist their phone numbers are more likely to be renters, live in the central city, have recently moved, have larger families, have younger children, and have lower incomes than their counterparts with listed numbers.[3] There are also significant differences between the two groups in terms of purchase, ownership, and use of certain products.

Unlisted numbers are more prevalent in the western United States, in metropolitan areas, among nonwhites, and among those in the 18–34 age group. These findings have been confirmed in a number of studies.[4] The extent of the problem is suggested by the data in Table 12.2. The implications are clear: If representative samples are to be obtained in telephone surveys, researchers should use procedures that will produce samples including appropriate proportions of households with unlisted numbers.

One possibility is **random-digit dialing,** which generates lists of telephone numbers at random. This procedure can become fairly complex. Fortunately, companies

such as Survey Sampling offer random-digit samples at a very attractive price. Details on the way such companies draw their samples can be found at http://www.ssisamples.com/random_digit.html. Developing an appropriate sampling frame is often one of the most challenging problems facing the researcher.[5]

Step Four: Select a Sampling Method

The fourth step in developing a sampling plan is selection of a sampling method, which will depend on the objectives of the study, the financial resources available, time limitations, and the nature of the problem under investigation. The major alternative sampling methods can be grouped under two headings: probability sampling methods and nonprobability sampling methods.

Probability samples are selected in such a way that every element of the population has a known, nonzero likelihood of selection.[6] Simple random sampling is the best known and most widely used probability sampling method. With probability sampling, the researcher must closely adhere to precise selection procedures that avoid arbitrary or biased selection of sample elements. When these procedures are followed strictly, the laws of probability hold, allowing calculation of the extent to which a sample value can be expected to differ from a population value. This difference is referred to as *sampling error.*

Nonprobability samples are those in which specific elements from the population have been selected in a nonrandom manner. *Nonrandomness* results when population elements are selected on the basis of convenience—because they are easy or inexpensive to reach. *Purposeful nonrandomness* occurs when a sampling

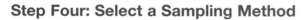

The population for a study must be defined. For example, a population for a study may be defined as those individuals who have spent two or more hours on the Internet in the past week.

random-digit dialing
A method of generating lists of telephone numbers at random.

probability samples
Samples in which every element of the population has a known, nonzero likelihood of selection.

nonprobability samples
Samples in which specific elements from the population have been selected in a nonrandom manner.

Table 12.2

Metropolitan Statistical Areas (MSAs) with Highest Incidence of Unlisted Phones in 1997

MSA Name	Total MSA Households	Percent Households with Phone	Percent Estimated Phone Households Unlisted*	MSA Rank Based on Percent Unlisted Households
Sacramento, CA	563,000	97.6%	71.6	1
Oakland, CA	822,700	98.0	71.4	2
Fresno, CA	284,300	95.8	71.1	3
Los Angeles–Long Beach, CA	3,023,300	96.7	69.8	4
San Diego, CA	940,100	97.8	68.9	5
San Jose, CA	540,500	98.8	68.9	6
Orange County, CA	875,300	98.5	67.0	7
Riverside–San Bernardino, CA	987,200	96.0	65.5	8
Bakersfield, CA	203,400	94.7	64.8	9
San Francisco, CA	665,100	98.3	64.4	10
Ventura, CA	228,000	98.4	63.5	11
Las Vegas, NV–AZ	465,100	96.2	59.8	12
Portland–Vancouver, OR–WA	668,100	97.2	44.9	13
Tacoma, WA	239,700	97.1	44.4	14
Honolulu, HI	283,800	98.0	42.6	15
Jersey City, NJ	205,100	93.3	42.0	16
Tucson, AZ	301,700	94.5	40.1	17
El Paso, TX	205,200	91.9	39.5	18
Seattle–Bellevue–Everett, WA	880,100	98.2	38.8	19
San Antonio, TX	510,900	93.4	38.4	20
Detroit, MI	1,607,000	96.6	38.1	21
Phoenix–Mesa, AZ	986,000	94.7	36.8	22
Chicago, IL	2,774,200	96.1	35.9	23
Miami, FL	718,600	95.2	33.6	24
Houston, TX	1,328,900	93.7	33.0	25

*The unlisted rate is determined by comparing the estimated number of telephone households with the actual number of households found in telephone directories. Estimated telephone households are computed by taking projected household estimates at the county level and applying a figure from the U.S. Census that indicates the percentage of households with a telephone.

Source: Reprinted by permission of Survey Sampling, Inc.

plan systematically excludes or overrepresents certain subsets of the population. For example, if a sample designed to solicit the opinions of all women over the age of 18 were based on a telephone survey conducted during the day on weekdays, it would systematically exclude working women.

Probability samples offer several advantages over nonprobability samples, including the following:

■ The researcher can be sure of obtaining information from a representative cross-section of the population of interest.
■ Sampling error can be computed.

Gallup Pioneers Modern Sampling Methods

"A NEW TECHNIQUE FOR OBJECTIVE METHODS FOR Measuring Reader Interest in Newspapers" was the title of George Gallup's Ph.D. thesis at the University of Iowa. Working the *Des Moines Register* and *Tribune* and the 200-year-old statistical theory probabilities of Swiss mathematician Jakob Bernoulli, Gallup developed sampling techniques. He showed that you did not have to talk to everybody as long as you randomly selected respondents according to a sampling plan that takes into account whatever diversity was relevant in the universe of potential respondents—geographic, ethnic, economic. Although not everybody understood or believed his ideas then—or now—this intellectual invention was a big deal.

On many occasions, Gallup used a particular example to explain what he was talking about and doing. "Suppose there are 7,000 white beans and 3,000 black beans well churned in a barrel. If you scoop out 100 of them, you'll get approximately 70 white beans and 30 black beans in your hand, and the range of your possible error can be computed mathematically. As long as the barrel contains many more beans than your handful, the proportion will remain within that margin of error 997 times out of 1,000."

In the early 1930s, George Gallup was in great demand around the country. He became head of the journalism department at Drake University and then switched to Northwestern. During this period he was doing readership surveys for newspapers throughout the northeastern United States. In the summer of 1932, a new advertising agency, Young and Rubicam, invited him to New York to create a research department and procedures for evaluating the effectiveness of advertising. In that same year, he used his polling techniques to help his mother-in-law get elected secretary of state of Iowa. Based on this experience, he was confident that his sampling methodology was valid not only for beans and newspaper readers, but for voters also. As long as you understood the sampling universe—white, black, male, female, rich, poor, urban, rural, Republican, Democratic—you could predict elections or calculate public attitudes on public opinion questions by interviewing a relatively small number of people as long as that small number of people was representative of the total population from which they were drawn. Gallup proved that population values could be accurately estimated by means of scientific samples and made a fortune in the process.[7] ∎

■ The survey results can be projected to the total population. For example, if 5 percent of the individuals in a probability sample give a particular response, the researcher can project this percentage, plus or minus the sampling error, to the total population.

Examples of Frame Errors

KELLEY FISH, JAMES BARNES, AND BENJAMIN BANAHAN PROvide two interesting examples of sample frame error. The first example involves a poll conducted by *The Literary Digest* in 1936. This publication predicted that Alf Landon would win the election over Franklin Roosevelt on the basis of the results of a very large (more than two million) sample of voters chosen from telephone directories and automobile ownership lists. Unfortunately, the sample frames used (telephone directories and automobile lists) were not representative of the population of American voters in 1936. Many people did not have telephones, and many did not have cars. These individuals tended to have lower incomes. Therefore, the frames chosen were heavily weighted in favor of the affluent, who were more likely to vote Republican (for Landon). *The Literary Digest* went out of business shortly after the election because of the severe loss of credibility associated with its erroneous prediction.

The case of a dog food manufacturer who conducted extensive market research among dog owners provides a more humorous example. The manufacturer made demand estimates, tested the packaging style and size, and designed and tested an advertising campaign—all with dog owners. The product was launched with a big campaign and experienced tremendous initial sales. However, a few months later sales came to a virtual standstill. The company brought in a consultant, who took the dog food out to the local dog pound and put it in front of the dogs. They would not touch it. Despite all the marketing research with dog owners, the manufacturer did not see the potential for sample frame error.[8] ∎

On the other hand, probability samples have a number of disadvantages, the most important of which is that they are usually more expensive than nonprobability samples of the same size. The rules for selection increase interviewing costs and professional time spent in signing and executing the sample design.[9]

The disadvantages of nonprobability samples are essentially the reverse of the advantages of probability samples:

- The researcher does not know the degree to which the sample is representative of the population from which it was drawn.
- Sampling error cannot be computed.
- The results cannot and should not be projected to the total population.

Given the disadvantages of nonprobability samples, you may wonder why they are used so frequently by marketing researchers. The reasons for their use relate to their inherent advantages, which include the following:

PART 3:
Data Acquisition

- Nonprobability samples cost less than probability samples. Lower costs have considerable appeal in those situations where accuracy is not of critical importance. Exploratory research is an example of such a situation.
- Nonprobability samples ordinarily can be gathered more quickly than probability samples can.
- Nonprobability samples of the population are reasonably representative if collected in a careful, thorough manner.[10]

In addition to choosing between probability and nonprobability sampling methods, the researcher must choose among sampling procedures. These procedures are summarized in Figure 12.3 and discussed in greater detail later in the chapter.

Issues related to the beliefs of the public in regard to sampling issues are summarized in the In Practice feature on 900-number polls.

Step Five: Determine Sample Size

Once a sampling method has been chosen, the next step is to determine the appropriate sample size. (The issue of sample size determination is covered in detail in Chapter 13.) In the case of nonprobability samples, researchers tend to rely on such factors as available budget, rules of thumb, and number of subgroups to be analyzed in their determination of sample size. However, with probability samples, researchers use formulas to calculate the sample size required, given target levels of *acceptable error* (the difference between sample result and population value) and *levels of confidence* (the likelihood that the confidence interval—sample result plus or minus the acceptable error—will take in the true population value). As noted earlier, the ability to make statistical inferences about population values based on sample results is a major advantage of probability samples.

Figure 12.3

Classification of Sampling Methods

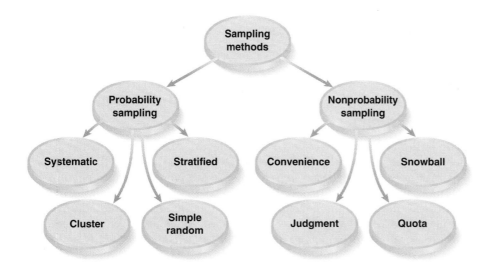

In PRACTICE

"900 Polls" Produce Biased Results

YOU HAVE PROBABLY SEEN THE 900 NUMBER TELEPHONE POLLS on CNN and other news programs. These polls violate all the statistical principles on which legitimate research surveys are based. The responses from self-selected 900 number polls are not projectable to any definable population group because they are biased due to the fact that they are based on responses from only those aware of the poll, interested enough to respond, willing and able to pay to respond, and able to reach the given number. There is also the possibility that a given individual may make multiple calls to such a 900 number poll.

Although these polls are clearly not representative, a recent poll conducted by the R. H. Bruskin Company, based on a national telephone probability survey of 1,000 adults, indicates that substantial proportions of the general population believe these polls are legitimate and representative in certain respects:

- 45 percent believe that the results of these call-in polls are believable.
- 40 percent believe that the results of these polls should be believed because thousands of people participated in the poll.
- 40 percent believe that those who call in on these kinds of polls have the same opinions as those who do not call in.
- 38 percent believe that those who respond to these kinds of polls are typical of the entire U.S. population.
- 36 percent believe that the results of these polls would not be reported if they were not accurate.
- 34 percent believe that the results of these polls should be believed because they are sponsored by major television, newspaper, or magazine organizations.
- 24 percent believe that these polls are scientific.
- 24 percent believe that the results of these polls accurately represent what the country as a whole thinks.[11] ∎

Step Six: Develop Operational Procedures for Selecting Sample Elements

The operational procedures to be used in selecting sample elements in the data collection phase of a project should be developed and specified, whether a probability or a nonprobability sample is being used.[12] However, the procedures are much more critical to the successful execution of a probability sample, in which case they should be detailed, clear, and unambiguous and should eliminate any interviewer discretion regarding the selection of specific sample elements. Failure to develop a proper operational plan for selecting sample elements can jeopardize the entire sampling process. Figure 12.4 provides an example of an operational sampling plan.

PART 3:
Data Acquisition

In the instructions that follow, reference is made to follow your route around a block. In cities, this will be a city block. In rural areas, a block is a segment of land surrounded by roads.

1. If you come to a dead end along your route, proceed down the opposite side of the street, road, or alley, traveling in the other direction. Continue making right turns, where possible, calling at every third occupied dwelling.

2. If you go all the way around a block and return to the starting address without completing four interviews in listed telephone homes, attempt an interview at the starting address. (This should seldom be necessary.)

3. If you work an entire block and do not complete the required interviews, proceed to the dwelling on the opposite side of the street (or rural route) that is *nearest* the starting address. Treat it as the next address on your Area Location Sheet and interview that house only if the address appears next to an "X" on your sheet. If it does not, continue your interviewing to the left of that address. Always follow the right turn rule.

4. If there are no dwellings on the street or road opposite the starting address for an area, circle the block opposite the starting address, following the right turn rule. (This means that you will circle the block following a clockwise direction.) Attempt interviews at every third dwelling along this route.

5. If, after circling the adjacent block opposite the starting address, you do not complete the necessary interviews, take the next block found, *following a clockwise direction*.

6. If the third block does not yield the dwellings necessary to complete your assignment, proceed to as many blocks as necessary to find the required dwellings; these blocks follow a clockwise path around the primary block.

Source: From "Belden Associates Interviewer Guide," 1986. Reprinted by permission. The complete guide is over 30 pages long and contains maps and other aids for the interviewer.

Figure 12.4

Example of Operational Sampling Plan

Step Seven: Execute the Operational Sampling Plan

The final step in the sampling process is execution of the operational sampling plan. This step requires adequate checking to ensure that specified procedures are adhered to.

Sampling and Nonsampling Errors

Consider a situation in which the goal is to determine the average gross income of the members of a particular population.[13] If the researcher could obtain accurate information about all members of the population, he or she could simply compute the population parameter average gross income. A *population parameter* is a value that defines a true characteristic of a total population. Assume that μ (the population parameter, average gross income) is \$42,300. As already noted, it is almost always impossible to measure an entire population (take a census). Instead, the researcher selects a sample and makes inferences about population parameters from sample results. In this case, the researcher might take a sample of 400 from a population of 250,000. An estimate of the average age of the members of the population ($\overline{X}$) would be calculated from the sample values. Assume that the average gross income of the sample members is \$41,100. A second random sample of 400 might be drawn from the same population, and the average again computed. In the second case, the average might be $43,400. Additional samples might be chosen, and a mean calculated for each sample. The researcher would find that the means computed for the various samples would be fairly close but not identical to the true population value in most cases.

The accuracy of sample results is affected by two general types of error: sampling error and nonsampling (measurement) error. The following formula represents the effects of these two types of error on estimating a population mean:

$$\overline{X} = \mu \pm \epsilon_s \pm \epsilon_{ns}$$

where $\overline{X}$ = sample mean
μ = true population mean
ϵ_s = sampling error
ϵ_{ns} = nonsampling, or measurement, error

sampling error
Error that occurs because the sample selected is not perfectly representative of the population.

nonsampling error
All error other than sampling error; also called *measurement error.*

Sampling error results when the sample selected is not perfectly representative of the population. There are two types of sampling error: administrative and random. *Administrative error* relates to the problems in the execution of the sample—that is, flaws in the design or execution of the sample that cause it to not be representative of the population. These types of error can be avoided or minimized by careful attention to the design and execution of the sample. *Random sampling error* is due to chance and cannot be avoided. This type of error can be reduced, but never totally eliminated, by increasing the sample size. **Nonsampling,** or measurement **error,** includes all factors other than sampling error that may cause inaccuracy and bias in the survey results.

Probability Sampling Methods

As discussed earlier, every element of the population has a known and equal likelihood of being selected for a probability sample. There are four types of probability sampling methods: simple random sampling, systematic sampling, stratified sampling, and cluster sampling.

Simple Random Sampling

Simple random sampling is the purest form of probability sampling. For a simple random sample, the known and equal probability is computed as follows:

$$\text{Probability of selection} = \frac{\text{Sample size}}{\text{Population size}}$$

For example, if the population size is 10,000 and the sample size is 400, the probability of selection is 4 percent:

$$.04 = \frac{400}{10,000}$$

PART 3:
Data Acquisition

If a sampling frame (listing of all the elements of the population) is available, the researcher can select a **simple random sample** as follows:

1. Assign a number to each element of the population. A population of 10,000 elements would be numbered from 1 to 10,000.
2. Using a table of random numbers (such as Table 1 in Appendix 2, "Statistical Tables"), begin at some arbitrary point and move up, down, or across until 400 (sample size) five-digit numbers between 1 and 10,000 have been chosen. The numbers selected from the table identify specific population elements to be included in the sample.

Simple random sampling is appealing because it seems easy and meets all the necessary requirements of a probability sample. It guarantees that every member of the population has a known and equal chance of being selected for the sample. Simple random sampling begins with a current and complete listing of the population. Such listings, however, are extremely difficult, if not impossible, to obtain. Simple random samples can be obtained in telephone surveys through the use of random digit dialing. They can also be generated from computer files such as customer lists; software programs are available or can be readily written to select random samples that meet all necessary requirements.

Systematic Sampling

Because of its simplicity, **systematic sampling** is often used as a substitute for simple random sampling. It produces samples that are almost identical to those generated via simple random sampling.

To obtain a systematic sample, the researcher first numbers the entire population, as in simple random sampling. Then the researcher determines a *skip interval* and selects names based on this interval. The skip interval can be computed very simply through use of the following formula:

$$\text{Skip interval} = \frac{\text{Population size}}{\text{Sample size}}$$

For example, if you were using a local telephone directory and had computed a skip interval of 100, every one-hundredth name would be selected for the sample. The use of this formula would ensure that the entire list was covered.

A random starting point should be used in systematic sampling. For example, if you were using a telephone directory, you would need to draw a random number to determine the page on which to start—say, page 53. You would draw another random number to determine the column to use on that page—for example, the third column. You would draw a final random number to determine the actual starting element in that column—say, the 17th name. From that beginning point, you would employ the skip interval until the desired sample size had been reached.

The main advantage of systematic sampling over simple random sampling is economy. Systematic sampling is often simpler, less time-consuming, and less expensive to use than simple random sampling. The greatest danger lies in the possibility that hidden patterns within the population list may inadvertently be

simple random sample
Probability sample selected by assigning a number to every element of the population and then using a table of random numbers to select specific elements for inclusion in the sample.

systematic sampling
Probability sampling in which the entire population is numbered and elements are selected using a skip interval.

pulled into the sample. However, this danger is remote when alphabetical listings are used.

Stratified Sampling

Stratified samples are probability samples that are distinguished by the following procedural steps:

1. The original, or parent, population is divided into two or more mutually exclusive and exhaustive subsets (e.g., male and female).
2. Simple random samples of elements from the two or more subsets are chosen independently of each other.

Although the requirements for a stratified sample do not specify the basis on which the original or parent population should be separated into subsets, common sense dictates that the population be divided on the basis of factors related to the characteristic of interest in the population. For example, if you are conducting a political poll to predict the outcome of an election and can show that there is a significant difference in the way men and women are likely to vote, then gender is an appropriate basis for stratification. If you do not do stratified sampling in this manner, then you do not get the benefits of stratification, and you have expended additional time, effort, and resources for no benefit. With gender as the basis for stratification, one stratum, then, would be made up of men and one of women. These strata are mutually exclusive and exhaustive in that every population element can be assigned to one and only one (male or female) and no population elements are unassignable. The second stage in the selection of a stratified sample involves drawing simple random samples independently from each stratum.

Researchers prefer stratified samples over simple random samples because of their potential for greater statistical efficiency.[14] That is, if two samples are drawn from the same population—one a properly stratified sample and the other a simple random sample—the stratified sample will have a smaller sampling error. Also, reduction of a sampling error to a certain target level can be achieved with a smaller stratified sample. Stratified samples are statistically more efficient because one source of variation has been eliminated.

If stratified samples are statistically more efficient, why are they not used all the time? There are two reasons. First, the information necessary to properly stratify the sample frequently may not be available. For example, little may be known about the demographic characteristics of consumers of a particular product. To properly stratify the sample and to get the benefits of stratification, the researcher must choose bases for stratification that yield significant differences between the strata in regard to the measurement of interest. When such differences are not identifiable, the sample cannot be properly stratified. Second, even if the necessary information is available, the potential value of the information may not warrant the time and costs associated with stratification.

In the case of a simple random sample, the researcher depends entirely on the laws of probability to generate a representative sample of the population. With stratified sampling, the researcher, to some degree, forces the sample to be representative by making sure that important dimensions of the population are represented in the sample in their true population proportions. For example, the researcher may know that although men and women are equally likely to be users of a particular product, women are much more likely to be heavy users. In a study designed to analyze consumption patterns of the product, failure to properly represent women in the sample would result in a biased view of consumption patterns. Assume that women make up 60 percent of the population of interest and men account for 40 percent. Because of sampling fluctuations, a properly executed simple random sampling procedure might produce a sample made up of 55 percent women and 45 percent men. This is the same kind of error you would obtain if you flipped a coin 10 times. The ideal result of 10 coin tosses would be five heads and five tails, but more than half the time you would get a different result. In similar fashion, a properly drawn and executed simple random sample from a population made up of 60 percent women and 40 percent men is not likely to consist of exactly 60 percent women and 40 percent men. However, the researcher can force a stratified sample to have 60 percent women and 40 percent men.

Three steps are involved in implementing a properly stratified sample:

1. *Identify salient (important) demographic or classification factors*—factors that are correlated with the behavior of interest. For example, there may be reason to believe that men and women have different average consumption rates of a particular product. To use gender as a basis for meaningful stratification, the researcher must be able to show with actual data that there are significant differences in the consumption levels of men and women. In this manner, various salient factors are identified. Research indicates that, as a general rule, after the six most important factors have been identified, the identification of additional salient factors adds little in the way of increased sampling efficiency.[15]

2. *Determine what proportions of the population fall into the various subgroups under each stratum* (e.g., if gender has been determined to be a salient factor, determine what proportion of the population is male and what proportion is female). Using these proportions, the researcher can determine how many respondents are required from each subgroup. However, before a final determination is made, a decision must be made as to whether to use proportional allocation or disproportional, or optimal, allocation.

Under **proportional allocation,** the number of elements selected from a stratum is directly proportional to the size of the stratum in relation to the size of the population. With proportional allocation, the proportion of elements to be taken from each stratum is given by the formula n/N, where n = the size of the stratum and N = the size of the population.

Disproportional, or **optimal, allocation** produces the most efficient samples and provides the most precise or reliable estimates for a given sample size. This

A stratified sample may be used in certain cases. For example, if a political poll is being done to predict who will win an election, a difference in the way men and women are likely to vote would make gender an appropriate basis for stratification.

proportional allocation
Sampling in which the number of elements selected from a stratum is directly proportional to the size of the stratum relative to the size of the population.

disproportional, or **optimal, allocation**
Sampling in which the number of elements taken from a given stratum is proportional to the relative size of the stratum and the standard deviation of the characteristic under consideration.

approach requires a double weighting scheme. Under this scheme, the number of sample elements to be taken from a given stratum is proportional to the relative size of the stratum and the standard deviation of the distribution of the characteristic under consideration for all elements in the stratum. This scheme is used for two reasons. First, the size of a stratum is important because those strata with greater numbers of elements are more important in determining the population mean. Therefore, such strata should have more weight in deriving estimates of population parameters. Second, it makes sense that relatively more elements should be drawn from those strata having larger standard deviations (more variation) and relatively fewer elements should be drawn from those strata having smaller standard deviations. Allocating relatively more of the sample to those strata where the potential for sampling error is greatest (largest standard deviation) is cost-effective and improves the overall accuracy of the estimates. There is no difference between proportional allocation and disproportional allocation if the distributions of the characteristic under consideration have the same standard deviation from stratum to stratum.[16]

3. *Select separate simple random samples from each stratum.* This process is implemented somewhat differently than traditional simple random sampling. Assume that the stratified sampling plan requires that 240 women and 160 men be interviewed. The researcher will sample from the total population and keep track of the number of men and women interviewed. At some point in the process, when 240 women and 127 men have been interviewed, the researcher will interview only men until the target of 160 men is reached. In this manner, the process generates a sample in which the proportion of men and women conforms to the allocation scheme derived in step 2.

Stratified samples are not used as often as one might expect in marketing research. The reason is that the information necessary to properly stratify the sample is usually not available in advance. Stratification cannot be based on guesses or hunches but must be based on hard data regarding the characteristics of the population and the relationship between these characteristics and the behavior under investigation. Stratified samples are frequently used in political polling and media audience research. In those areas, the researcher is more likely to have the information necessary to implement the stratification process.

Cluster Sampling

The types of samples discussed so far have all been single unit samples, in which each sampling unit is selected separately. In the case of **cluster samples,** the sampling units are selected in groups.[17] There are two basic steps in cluster sampling:

cluster sample
Probability sample in which the sampling units are selected in groups to reduce data collection costs.

1. The population of interest is divided into mutually exclusive and exhaustive subsets.
2. A random sample of the subsets is selected.

If the sample consists of all the elements in the selected subsets, it is called a *one-stage cluster sample.* However, if the sample of elements is chosen in some probabilistic manner from the selected subsets, the sample is a *two-stage cluster sample.*

PART 3:
Data Acquisition

Both stratified and cluster sampling involve dividing the population into mutually exclusive and exhaustive subgroups. However, in stratified samples the researcher selects a sample of elements from each subgroup, while in cluster samples, the researcher selects a sample of subgroups and then collects data either from all the elements in the subgroup (one-stage cluster sample) or from a sample of the elements (two-stage cluster sample).

All the probability sampling methods discussed to this point require sampling frames that list or provide some organized breakdown of all the elements in the target population. Under cluster sampling, the researcher develops sampling frames that specify groups or clusters of elements of the population without actually listing individual elements. Sampling is then executed by taking a sample of the clusters in the frame and generating lists or other breakdowns for only those clusters that have been selected for the sample. Finally, a sample is chosen from the elements of the selected clusters

The most popular type of cluster sample is the area sample, in which the clusters are units of geography (e.g. city blocks). A researcher, conducting a door-to-door survey in a particular metropolitan area, might randomly choose a sample of city blocks from the metropolitan area, select a sample of clusters, and then interview a sample of consumers from each cluster. All interviews would be conducted in the clusters selected, dramatically reducing interviewers' travel time and expenses. Cluster sampling is considered to be a probability sampling technique because of the random selection of clusters and the random selection of elements within the selected clusters.

Cluster sampling assumes that the elements in a cluster are as heterogeneous as those in the total population. If the characteristics of the elements in a cluster are very similar, then that assumption is violated and the researcher has a problem. In the city-block sampling just described, there may be little heterogeneity within clusters because the residents of a cluster are very similar to each other and different from those of other clusters. Typically, this potential problem is dealt with in the sample design by selecting a large number of clusters and sampling a relatively small number of elements from each cluster.

Another possibility is *multistage area sampling*, or *multistage area probability sampling*, which involves three or more steps. Samples of this type are used for national surveys or surveys that cover large regional areas. Here, the researcher randomly selects geographic areas in progressively smaller units. For example, a statewide door-to-door survey might include the following steps:

1. Choose counties within the state to make sure that different areas are represented in the sample. Counties should be selected with a probability proportional to the number of sampling units (households) within the county. Counties with a larger number of households would have a higher probability of selection than would counties with a smaller number of households.

The most popular type of cluster sample is the area sample in which the clusters are units of geography (e.g., city blocks). Cluster sampling is considered to be a probability sampling technique because of the random selection of clusters and the random selection of elements within the selected clusters.

2. Select residential blocks within those counties.
3. Select households within those residential blocks.

A more detailed example of developing a national probability sample is provided in the In Practice feature.

Developing a National Probability Sample

O PINION RESEARCH CORPORATION (ORC) DEVELOPS PROBABIL-ity sampling plans in the context of its national probability sample. This is a permanent sampling framework that eliminates the need and expense of repeating some of the basic and most complex steps in drawing a sample in such assignments.

Step 1. Selecting counties. The first step in developing the national probability sample used by ORC in nationwide studies is to list the approximately 3,000 counties in the United States. The list is grouped on the basis of the nine U.S. Census Bureau regions. Within each region, the list is ordered by size of population. Counties are selected from the list so that each county has a probability of being selected proportionate to its population.

Step 2. Towns. Within each county selected, all minor civil divisions (e.g., towns or cities) are then listed in order of population, and the selection procedure described previously for selecting counties is repeated. That is, each town has a probability of selection proportionate to its population.

Step 3. Actual interviewing locations. Once the towns are selected, starting points for the interviews are selected. These starting points are determined from telephone directories covering the towns selected.

Step 4. Individual households. The households to be surveyed within a town are determined by selecting one or more telephone numbers at random from the local telephone book. Because some people have listed telephones and others do not, the actual interviewing starts next door to the address of the telephone number selected. In this way, every household in the United States can enter into the sample.

Step 5. Individual respondents. The selection of individual respondents is also completely predesignated by the sampling plan. When the study requires that information be obtained from a particular person in a household, such as a man or a woman, that person is specified. In other cases, when any of a number of persons in a household might be eligible (e.g., the study might require interviews with persons 21 and over), random methods are used to preselect the person to be interviewed.

In this situation, the interviewer lists on a form all the residents of a household and their ages in a predetermined order (e.g., from oldest to youngest). Each individual is assigned a number. Finally, the interviewers refer to a selection table to determine which person to interview.[18] ∎

From the standpoint of statistical efficiency, cluster samples are generally less efficient than other types of probability samples. In other words, a cluster sample of a certain size will have a larger sampling error than a simple random sample or a stratified sample of the same size. To see the greater cost efficiency and lower statistical efficiency of a cluster sample, consider the following example. A researcher needs to select a sample of 200 households in a particular city for in-home interviews. If she selects these 200 households via simple random sampling, they will be scattered across the city. Cluster sampling might be implemented in this situation by selecting 20 residential blocks in the city and randomly choosing 10 households on each block to interview. It is easy to see that interviewing costs will be dramatically reduced under the cluster sampling approach. Interviewers do not have to spend as much time traveling and their mileage is dramatically reduced. In regard to sampling error, however, you can see that simple random sampling has the advantage. Interviewing 200 households scattered across the city increases the chance of getting a representative cross-section of respondents. If all interviewing is conducted in 20 randomly selected blocks within the city, certain ethnic, social, or economic groups might be missed or over- or underrepresented.

As noted previously, cluster samples are, in nearly all cases, statistically less efficient than simple random samples. It is possible to view a simple random sample as a special type of cluster sample, in which the number of clusters is equal to the total sample size, with one sample element selected per cluster. At this point, the statistical efficiency of the cluster sample and that of the simple random sample are equal. From this point on, as the researcher decreases the number of clusters and increases the number of sample elements per cluster, the statistical efficiency of the cluster sample declines. At the other extreme, the researcher might choose a single cluster and select all the sample elements from that cluster. For example, he or she might select one relatively small geographic area in the city where you live and interview 200 people from that area. How comfortable would you be that a sample selected in this manner would be representative of the entire metropolitan area where you live?

Nonprobability Sampling Methods

In a general sense, any sample that does not meet the requirements of a probability sample is, by definition, a nonprobability sample. We have already noted that a major disadvantage of nonprobability samples is the inability to calculate sampling error for them. This suggests the even greater difficulty of evaluating the overall quality of nonprobability samples. How far do they deviate from the standard required of probability samples? The user of data from a nonprobability sample must make this assessment, which should be based on a careful evaluation of the methodology used to generate the nonprobability sample. Is it likely that the methodology employed will generate a cross-section of individuals from the target population? Or, is the sample hopelessly biased in some particular direction? These are the questions that must be answered. Four types of nonprobability samples are frequently used: convenience, judgment, quota, and snowball samples.

Convenience Samples

convenience samples
Nonprobability samples used primarily for reasons of convenience.

Convenience samples are primarily used, as their name implies, for reasons of convenience. Companies like Frito-Lay often use their own employees for preliminary tests of new product formulations developed by their R&D departments. At first, this may seem to be a highly biased approach. However, these companies are not asking employees to evaluate existing products or to compare their products with a competitor's products. They are asking employees only to provide gross sensory evaluations of new product formulations (e.g., saltiness, crispness, greasiness). In such situations, convenience sampling may represent an efficient and effective means of obtaining the required information. This is particularly true in an exploratory situation, where there is a pressing need to get an inexpensive approximation of true value.

Some believe that the use of convenience sampling is growing at a faster rate than the growth in the use of probability sampling.[19] The reason, as suggested in the In Practice feature on SSI-LITe, is the growing availability of databases of consumers in low-incidence and hard-to-find categories. For example, suppose a company has developed a new athlete's foot remedy and needs to conduct a survey among those who suffer from the malady. Because these individuals make up

In **PRACTICE**

SSI Provides Useful Convenience Samples

SURVEY SAMPLING INCORPORATED (SSI) CURRENTLY OFFERS OVER 3,000 low-incidence consumer and business lists. SSI-LITe is a form of convenience sampling, which the research industry can use to assist in screening for low-incidence segments of the population. To the degree that SSI's sampling services act as a barometer of research activity, SSI-LITe sales suggest that the use of convenience samples is growing at a faster rate than the use of probability samples.

Probability sampling in the strictest sense allows each potential respondent an opportunity to be selected for a study. The probabilities of selection can be controlled and calculated as a result of sample selection. Research results can serve both enumerative

and analytical purposes. This is not the case when a subjective selection of respondents is used, as with SSI-LITe and other nonprobability samples. Yet the practical constraints of time and budgets clearly make a case for the use of nonprobability samples.

When less than 1 percent of U.S. households purchase a certain brand, research options may become quite limited, and targeted samples, such as SSI-LITe, provide researchers with the opportunity to gain an understanding of attitudes and behaviors that they could not otherwise gain. The problem occurs when the researcher or research user attempts to project the findings to the total population, which can lead to costly wrong decisions. The researcher must understand the limitations of a research design that employs anything other than a probability sample. ∎

only 4 percent of the population, researchers conducting a telephone survey would have to talk with 25 people to find 1 individual who suffered from the problem. Purchasing a list of individuals known to suffer from the problem can dramatically reduce the cost of the survey and the time necessary to complete it. Though such a list might be made up of individuals who used coupons when purchasing the product or sent in for manufacturers' rebates, companies are increasingly willing to make the tradeoff of lower cost and faster turnaround for a lower-quality sample. Figure 12.5 provides some examples of the more than 3,000 lists available from Survey Sampling, Incorporated.

Judgment Samples

The term **judgment sample** is applied to any sample in which the selection criteria are based on the researcher's judgment about what constitutes a representative sample. Most test markets and many product tests conducted in shopping malls are essentially judgment sampling. In the case of test markets, one or a few markets are selected based on the judgment that they are representative of the population as a whole. Malls are selected for product taste tests based on the researcher's judgment that the particular malls attract a reasonable cross-section of consumers who fall into the target group for the product being tested.

judgment samples
Nonprobability samples in which the selection criteria are based on the researcher's personal judgment about representativeness of the population under study.

Quota Samples

Quota samples are typically selected in such a way that demographic characteristics of interest to the researcher are represented in the sample in target proportions. Thus, many people confuse quota samples and stratified samples. There are, however, two key differences between a quota sample and a stratified sample. First, respondents for a quota sample are not selected randomly, as they must be for a stratified sample. Second, the classification factors used for a stratified sample are selected based on the existence of a correlation between the factor

quota samples
Nonprobability samples in which quotas, based on demographic or classification factors selected by the researcher, are established for population subgroups.

Sports/Boating/Fishing/Outdoor Activities

Bicycling
Boating: Power
Boating: Sailing
Bow Hunting
Camping
Cycling
Environmental Concerns
Exercise Equipment
Fishing
Fly Fishing
Golf
Hiking
Horseback Riding
Hunting/Shooting
Motorcycles, Interest in
Motorcycling, Participation in
NASCAR Enthusiast

Outdoor Enthusiast
Outdoor Recreation
Outdoor Sports Lover
Physical Fitness
Running/Jogging
Sailing
Scuba Diving
Snow Boarding
Snow Skiing
Soccer
Sports
Sports Cards
Sports Equipment
Sports Items
Tennis
Walking for Health
Watching Sports on TV

Figure 12.5

Examples from the Activities List of Survey Sampling, Incorporated

and the behavior of interest. There is no such requirement in the case of a quota sample. The demographic or classification factors of interest in a quota sample are selected on the basis of researcher judgment.

Snowball Samples

In **snowball samples,** sampling procedures are used to select additional respondents on the basis of referrals from initial respondents. This procedure is used to sample from low-incidence or rare populations—that is, populations that make up a very small percentage of the total population.[20] The costs of finding members of these rare populations may be so great that the researcher is forced to use a technique such as snowball sampling. For example, suppose an insurance company needed to obtain a national sample of individuals who have switched from the indemnity form of health care coverage to a health maintenance organization in the past six months. It would be necessary to sample a very large number of consumers to identify 1,000 that fall into this population. It would be far more economical to obtain an initial sample of 200 people from the population of interest and have each of them provide the names of an average of four other people to complete the sample of 1,000.

The main advantage of snowball sampling is a dramatic reduction in search costs. However, this advantage comes at the expense of sample quality. The total sample is likely to be biased because the individuals whose names were obtained from those sampled in the initial phase are likely to be very similar to those initially sampled. As a result, the sample may not be a good cross-section of the total population. There is general agreement that some limits should be placed on the number of respondents obtained through referrals, although there are no specific rules regarding what these limits should be. This approach may also be hampered by the fact that respondents may be reluctant to give referrals.

Internet Sampling

Conducting marketing research surveys over the Internet is a relatively new phenomenon. At first, it was an experimental curiosity, with various researchers tinkering with the mechanics of the process. Recently, however, some major mainstream research organizations, such as Harris Black, have announced that they plan to migrate much of their survey data collection to the Internet in a relatively short period of time. Harris Black notes that it has built a panel of over 3 million consumers willing to be surveyed via the Internet.[21]

The advantages of Internet interviewing are compelling:

- *Target respondents can complete the survey at their convenience*—late at night, over the weekend, and at any other convenient time.
- *Data collection is inexpensive.* Once basic overhead and other fixed costs are covered, interviewing is essentially volume-insensitive. Thousands of interviews can be conducted at an actual data collection cost of less than $1 per survey. This low cost may, to some extent, be offset by the need to use incentives to encourage responses. By comparison, a 10-minute telephone interview targeting people who make up 50 percent of the population may cost

$15 or more per survey. Data entry and data processing costs are dramatically reduced because respondents essentially do the data entry for the researcher.

- *The interview can be administered under software control,* which allows the survey to follow skip patterns and do other "smart" things.
- *The survey can be completed quickly.* Hundreds or thousands of surveys can be completed in a day or less.[22]

Unfortunately, there is no large body of scientific research regarding the representativeness of Internet samples, as there is for other data collection approaches. Those who have carefully evaluated Internet surveying are most concerned that the pool of people available in cyberspace does not correctly represent the general population. The group of Internet respondents tend to be richer, whiter, more male, and more tech-savvy.[23] The biases are becoming less pronounced over time as the percentage of the population connected to the Internet increases.[24] However, the nonrepresentativeness of Internet respondents will exist for some time into the future. This general problem is compounded by the fact that no comprehensive and reliable source of email addresses exists.

Companies such as Survey Sampling, Incorporated are busily building email databases, but the problems are great. For example, although SSI claims to have 7 million email addresses in its database, this number is small in relation to the total U.S. population. The problem is compounded by the fact that email addresses are easily and frequently changed as people switch jobs, change Internet service providers, and open or close accounts at Yahoo!, Hotmail, and other email providers. This means that any list of email addresses will be constantly changing. For the foreseeable future, it will be virtually impossible to get an inclusive sampling frame of email addresses for almost any generalized population, such as new car buyers, new home buyers, people with cable TV service, or fast food users.

In some cases, researchers recruit samples of consumers via Internet bulletin board postings or banner advertising on search engines (Yahoo!, Google, Hotbot, and others). Once again, the biases are obvious. Those who do not use the Internet have no chance of being included in the sample, even though they might be part of the target population. Among Internet users, consumers who do not visit the sites in question or who do not visit those sites during the time that the banner ads are running have no chance of being included in the sample. In addition, those who visit the sites infrequently have less chance of being included than those who visit them frequently.

Finally, research firms such as Harris Black and Greenfield Online tout the fact that they have developed large panels of individuals who have responded to their solicitations and have agreed to accept and complete

WAR Stories

Jewel Alderton of Facts Consolidated tells about a telephone survey her company was conducting about shopping habits, where the quota for respondents over the age of 55 had already been filled. So at this point in the study the screener read, "We're conducting a short survey about shopping habits and would like to include your opinions. Are you the male/female head of the household and between the ages of 18 and 54?"

The female on the other end of the phone replied, "No, I am 81 years old, but I would like to do your survey."

The interviewer tried to explain about quota sampling, but the woman insisted on being interviewed. Finally, the interviewer referred the matter to the supervisor. When the supervisor got on the line, the consumer asked for all pertinent information about Facts Consolidated and informed the supervisor that their practices were discriminatory. She further informed the supervisor that she would take the necessary steps to report Facts Consolidated to the AARP and the President's Council on Aging.

So far, no one has been arrested, and the President's Council on Aging has not been heard from.

Source: "War Stories: True Life Tales in Marketing Research," by Art Shulman, *Quirk's Marketing Research Review* (May 1998). Reprinted by permission of Art Shulman.

email surveys.[25] Again, the biases are fairly obvious, and the lack of representativeness of their panels can be clearly seen. These firms counter criticism by claiming that they weight survey results to make them representative. For example, suppose a population is known to be 60 percent female and 40 percent male. If an Internet survey produces a sample that is 70 percent male and 30 percent female, the results can be weighted to align them with the known population proportions. However, this approach fails to recognize that other biases may lurk below the surface and only be distorted by such weighting.

There are cases where Internet surveys, with all their other inherent advantages, may produce excellent samples. Those cases involve situations where the client organization or the researcher has email addresses for all members of a particular population. For example, high-technology firms such as Texas Instruments may have lists of essentially all individuals who make decisions regarding the purchase of their products for incorporation in other products. These industrial buyers are probably fairly heavy users of the Internet, both at home and at work. Selecting a true random sample of all members of such a population is relatively easy. At minimal cost, all the individuals can be sent invitations to participate and reminders to complete the survey. Response rates in excess of 70 percent are not uncommon for surveys of this type, especially if incentives are offered to encourage responses. Internet surveys are an emerging form of data collection that will probably become dominant at some point in the future. Their advantages are numerous and compelling. However, until the sampling issues discussed above can be resolved, the results of Internet surveys will be suspect because of lack of survey representativeness.

A last word of caution must be expressed here: Don't post surveys in public areas. Posting surveys in public areas such as the Internet or a Web site, with no control over access, is an invitation for disaster in the form of highly biased samples—as *BYTE* magazine found out.[26] A single advocate for a specific outcome may stumble across the survey and post a notice about the existence of the survey to a particular news or advocacy group, thereby rallying a large population segment to vote a certain way on the survey. Based on the results of three questions from the *BYTE* survey, one might conclude that UNIX and OS/2 are surprisingly popular (see Figure 12.6). Analysis of the locations of respondents, however, indicated that they were 12 times more likely to come from IBM.com (OS/2 is an IBM product) than were typical *BYTE* site visitors. They were OS/2 and UNIX supporters who wanted to make sure that their favorites did well in the survey. One way to avoid a biased response is to invite individuals to participate via email or other means and provide each person invited with a unique password and/or ID number.

Figure 12.6

Operating System Used

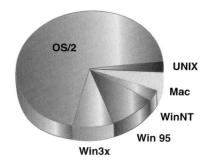

PART 3:
Data Acquisition

Summary

The population, or universe, is the total group of people in whose opinions one is interested. A census involves collecting desired information from every member of the population of interest. A sample is simply a subset of a population. The steps in developing a sampling plan are as follows: Define the population of interest, choose the data collection method, identify the sampling frame, select the sampling method, determine sample size, develop and specify an operational plan for selecting sampling elements, and execute the operational sampling plan. The sampling frame is a list of the elements of the population from which the sample will be drawn or a specified procedure for generating the list.

In probability sampling methods, samples are selected in such a way that every element of the population has a known, nonzero likelihood of selection. Nonprobability sampling methods select specific elements from the population in a nonrandom manner. Probability samples have several advantages over nonprobability samples, including reasonable certainty that information will be obtained from a representative cross-section of the population, a sampling error that can be computed, and survey results that can be projected to the total population. However, probability samples are more expensive than nonprobability samples and usually take more time to design and execute.

The accuracy of sample results is determined by both sampling error and nonsampling error. Sampling error occurs because the sample selected is not perfectly representative of the population. There are two types of sampling error: random sampling error and administrative error. Random sampling error is due to chance and cannot be avoided; it can only be reduced by increasing sample size.

Probability samples include simple random samples, systematic samples, stratified samples, and cluster samples. Nonprobability samples include convenience samples, judgment samples, quota samples, and snowball samples. At the present time, Internet samples tend to be convenience samples. That may change in the future as better email sampling frames become available.

Key Terms & Definitions

sampling   The process of obtaining information from a subset of a larger group.

population   The entire group of people about whom information is needed; also called *universe* or *population of interest.*

census   A collection of data obtained from or about every member of the population of interest.

sample   A subset of all the members of a population of interest.

sampling frame   A list of population elements from which units to be sampled can be selected or a specified procedure for generating such a list.

random-digit dialing   A method of generating lists of telephone numbers at random.

probability samples   Samples in which every element of the population has a known, nonzero likelihood of selection.

nonprobability samples   Samples in which specific elements from the population have been selected in a nonrandom manner.

sampling error   Error that occurs because the sample selected is not perfectly representative of the population.

nonsampling error   All error other than sampling error; also called *measurement error.*

simple random sample   Probability sample selected by assigning a number to every element of the population and then using a table of random numbers to select specific elements for inclusion in the sample.

systematic sampling   Probability sampling in which the entire population is numbered and elements are selected using a skip interval.

stratified sample   Probability sample that is forced to be more representative though simple random sampling of mutually exclusive and exhaustive subsets.

proportional allocation   Sampling in which the number of elements selected from a stratum is directly proportional to the size of the stratum relative to the size of the population.

disproportional, or optimal, allocation   Sampling in which the number of elements taken from a given stratum is proportional to the relative size of the stratum and the standard deviation of the characteristic under consideration.

cluster sample   Probability sample in which the sampling units are selected in groups to reduce data collection costs.

convenience samples   Nonprobability samples used primarily for reasons of convenience.

judgment samples   Nonprobability samples in which the selection criteria are based on the researcher's personal judgment about representativeness of the population under study.

quota samples   Nonprobability samples in which quotas, based on demographic or classification factors selected by the researcher, are established for population subgroups.

snowball samples   Nonprobability samples in which additional respondents are selected based on referrals from initial respondents.

Questions for Review & Critical Thinking

1. What are some situations in which a census would be better than a sample? Why are samples usually employed rather than censuses?

2. Develop a sampling plan for examining undergraduate business students' attitudes toward Internet advertising.

3. Give an example of a perfect sampling frame. Why is a telephone directory usually not an acceptable sampling frame?

4. Distinguish between probability and nonprobability samples. What are the advantages and disadvantages of each? Why are nonprobability samples so popular in marketing research?

5. Distinguish among a systematic sample, a cluster sample, and a stratified sample. Give examples of each.

6. What is the difference between a stratified sample and a quota sample?

7. American National Bank has 1,000 customers. The manager wishes to draw a sample of 100 customers. How could this be done using systematic sampling? What would be the impact on the technique, if any, if the list were ordered by average size of deposit?

8. Do you see any problem with drawing a systematic sample from a telephone book, assuming that the telephone book is an acceptable sample frame for the study in question?

9. Describe snowball sampling. Give an example of a situation in which you might use this type of sample. What are the dangers associated with this type of sample?

10. Name some possible sampling frames for the following:
    a. Patrons of sushi bars
    b. Smokers of high-priced cigars
    c. Snowboarders
    d. Owners of DVD players
    e. People who have visited one or more countries in Europe in the last year
    f. People who emigrated to the United States within the last two years
    g. People with allergies

11. Identify the following sample designs:
    a. The names of 200 patrons of a casino are drawn from a list of visitors for the last month, and a questionnaire is administered to them.
    b. A radio talk show host invites listeners to call in and vote yes or no on whether handguns should be banned.
    c. A dog food manufacturer wants to test a new dog food. It decides to select 100 dog owners who feed their dogs canned food, 100 who feed their dogs dry food, and 100 who feed their dogs semimoist food.
    d. A poll surveys men who play golf to predict the outcome of a presidential election.

Working the Net

1. Go to the Survey Sampling site at http://www.ssisamples.com. Find the information on its LITe samples. What lists does it offer for "Families"? What lists does it have under the category "Electronics"?

2. Go to Survey Sampling at http://www.ssisamples.com/products.html. What does it offer in the way of random-digit telephone samples? When would you use samples of this type? What does SSI offer in regard to business samples? Provide examples of two situations in which you might use its business samples.

Using WebSurveyor

Using the list of companies provided on the CD-ROM included with this text-book ⟨[cddrive]:\Exercises\Chapter12\companies.txt⟩, generate a random sample of 100 names. Assume that the names are from the population of interest.

Exercises

1. What procedure did you use? Why did you use that procedure? What other procedure or procedures might you have used to accomplish the same goal?
2. Defend the premise that the procedure you used generated a sample in which every name had an equal and known chance of being included.
3. What is the known chance of inclusion in this case?

Real-Life Research • 12.1

The Research Group

The Research Group has been hired by the National Internet Service Providers Association to determine the following:

- What specific factors motivate people to choose a particular Internet service provider (ISP)?
- How do these factors differ between choosing an ISP for home use and choosing an ISP for business use?
- Why do people choose one ISP over the others?
- How many have switched ISPs in the past year?
- Why did they switch ISPs?
- How satisfied are they with their current ISP?
- Do consumers know or care whether an ISP is a member of the National Internet Service Providers Association?
- What value-added services do consumers want from ISPs (e.g., telephone support for questions and problems)?

The Research Group underbid three other research companies to get the contract. In fact, its bid was more than 25 percent lower than the next lowest bid. The primary way in which The Research Group was able to provide the lowest bid related to its sampling methodology. In its proposal, The Research Group specified that college students would be used to gather the survey data. Its plan called for randomly selecting 20 colleges from across the country, contacting the chairperson of the marketing department, and asking her or him to submit a list of 10 students who would be interested in earning extra money. Finally, The Research Group would contact the students individually with the goal of identifying five students at each school who would ultimately be asked to get 10 completed interviews. Students would be paid $10 for each completed survey. The only requirement imposed in regard to selecting potential respondents was that they had to be ISP subscribers at the time of the survey. The Research Group proposal suggested that the easiest way to do this would be for the student interviewers to go to the student union or student center during the lunch hour and ask those at each table whether they might be interested in participating in the survey.

Questions

1. How would you describe this sampling methodology?
2. What problems do you see arising from this technique?
3. Suggest an alternative sampling method that might give the National Internet Service Providers Association a better picture of the information it desired.

Real-Life Research • 12.2

Florida National Bank

Florida National Bank (FNB) operates branches in 65 cities and towns throughout Florida. The bank offers a complete range of financial services, including Visa and MasterCard credit cards. FNB has 62,500 people in the state using its credit cards. Based on their original applications, it has certain information about these individuals, including name, address, zip code, telephone number, income, education, and assets. FNB is interested in determining whether there is a relationship between the volume of purchases charged on credit cards and demographic characteristics of the individual cardholder. For example, are individuals in certain parts of the state more or less likely to be heavy users of the card? Is there a relationship between a person's income and his or her level of card usage? Is there a relationship between the person's level of education and card usage? The data could be used to more effectively target offerings sent through the mail if significant relationships are found. Paul Bruney is research director for FNB, and he is currently in the process of developing a design for the research. If you were Bruney, how would you answer the following questions?

Questions

1. How would you define the population of interest for the study?
2. What sampling frame(s) might you use for the project?
3. What procedure would you use to select a simple random sample from the sampling frame you chose above?
4. Would it make sense to use a stratified sample in this situation? Why or why not? How would you approach the process of developing a stratified sample from the sampling frame you chose?
5. Could you use the sampling frame to draw a cluster sample? How would you go about it? Would it make any sense to do this?
6. Which of the three probability sampling methods just mentioned would you choose for this study? Why would you choose that option?

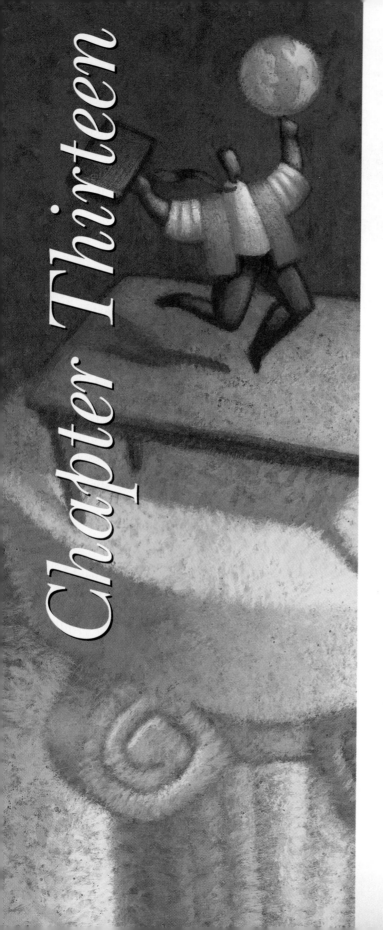

Chapter Thirteen

Sample Size Determination

Learning Objectives

To learn the financial and statistical issues in the determination of sample size.

To discover methods for determining sample size.

To gain an appreciation of a normal distribution.

To understand population, sample, and sampling distributions.

To distinguish between point and interval estimates.

To recognize problems involving sampling means and proportions.

TOM KING, MARKETING DIRECTOR FOR AUSTEX CABLE, HAS JUST FINISHED reviewing a proposal from Data Dimensions, a research firm he has worked with in the past. He had invited Data Dimensions to submit a proposal on conducting a customer satisfaction survey with current Austex customers in Austin. King had stressed the fact that he had a limited budget for the research and had asked his account rep at Data Dimensions to come up with a solid research design at a "value" price.

THE RESEARCH FIRM PROPOSES TO EMPLOY a telephone survey, with all interviews conducted from its central-location telephone interviewing facility. It recommends that a random sample of 384 customers, selected from Austex's current list of customers, be surveyed. In the proposal, Data Dimensions indicates that a random sample of 384 will produce estimates that are within ±5 percent of true population values, with 95 percent confidence.

KING HAS SEVERAL BASIC QUESTIONS REGARDING THE SAMPLE DESIGN. FIRST, given that Austex has 37,500 customers in Austin, the recommended sample size seems relatively small. Second, he is wondering whether the stated error range and confidence level will apply to results for different subgroups. In particular, analysis of complaints received from customers shows that Austex gets a disproportionately large number of complaints from customers over the age of 50. Approximately half of all its customers are over 50, and approximately half are 50 or younger. King believes that it is important to have estimates for each group that are within ±5 percent of the true value for the group, with 95 percent confidence. On the one hand, he wonders whether 384 respondents are enough. On the other hand, if a larger sample size is required, he is concerned about the adequacy of his budget.

FINALLY, KING IS INTERESTED IN THE PROCEDURES THAT DATA DIMENSIONS WILL use to get a representative sample of his customers. Its proposal says that it will employ a simple random sample. King would like some additional explanation of how a random sample will ensure representativeness. ■

Sample size is an important consideration when Austex Cable, an Austin, Texas cable television provider, is reviewing proposals for a customer satisfaction survey.

Find out more about customer satisfaction surveys at

 http://www. guidestarco. com/customer- satisfaction- online-surveys.HTM

These common issues, which researchers and those who buy research must deal with on a regular basis, are addressed in this chapter. After reading this chapter, you should be able to respond to all of King's concerns.

Determining Sample Size for Probability Samples

The process of determining sample size for probability samples involves financial, statistical, and managerial issues. As a general rule, the larger the sample is, the smaller the sampling error. However, larger samples cost more money, and the resources available for a project are always limited. Though the cost of increasing sample size tends to rise on a linear basis (double the sample size, almost double the cost), sampling error decreases at a rate equal to the square root of the relative increase in sample size. If sample size is quadrupled, data collection cost is almost quadrupled, but the level of sampling error is reduced by only 50 percent.

Managerial issues must be reflected in sample size calculations. How accurate do estimates need to be, and how confident must managers be that true population values are included in the chosen confidence interval? Some cases require high levels of precision (small sampling error) and confidence that population values fall in the small range of sampling error (the confidence interval). Other cases may not require the same level of precision or confidence.

Budget Available

The sample size for a project is often determined, at least indirectly, by the budget available. Thus, it is frequently the last project factor determined. A brand manager may have $50,000 available in the budget for a new product test. After deduction of other project costs (e.g., research design, questionnaire development, data processing), the amount remaining determines the size of the sample that can be surveyed. Of course, if the dollars available will not produce an adequate sample size, then management must make a decision: Either additional funds must be found, or the project should be canceled.

Although this approach may seem highly unscientific and arbitrary, it is a fact of life in a corporate environment. Financial constraints challenge the researcher to develop research designs that will generate data of adequate quality for decision-making purposes at low cost. This "budget available" approach forces the researcher to explore alternative data collection approaches and to carefully consider the value of information in relation to its cost.[1] In the In Practice feature, Thomas Semon discusses the potential dangers in cutting costs when it comes to sample size.

Rule of Thumb

Potential clients may specify in the RFP (request for proposal) that they want a sample of 200, 400, 500, or some other size. Sometimes, this number is based on desired sampling error. In other cases, it is based on nothing more than past experience. The justification for the specified sample size may boil down to a "gut feeling" that a particular sample size is necessary or appropriate.

If the researcher determines that the sample size requested is not adequate to support the objectives of the proposed research, then she or he has a professional responsibility to present arguments for a larger sample size to the client and let the client make the final decision. If the client rejects arguments for a

Sample Costs versus the Costs of an Invalid Survey

MARKETERS, ALL TOO OFTEN, TRY TO SAVE A FEW bucks on sample size and risk millions in opportunity loss. This is according to Thomas Semon, expert columnist for *Marketing News*. He noted that an ad agency that he once worked for bragged about using samples of 120 for copy research. Samples of this size can be adequate in some cases but not in others. There is not a one-size-fits-all sample size for any type of research. The really critical factor is the size of the expected difference or change to be measured—the smaller that is, the larger the sample must be, squared.

In testing two versions of an ad, a current or control version and a new version, we might adopt the rule that the new version will be adopted if it scores significantly higher than the current or control version. "Significance" might be set at either the 90 percent or 95 percent confidence level.

This type of decision criterion protects against the risk that random sampling error results in an overestimate of the favorable response and leads to the false conclusion that the new version should be adopted. However, the opposite problem (underestimate of the favorable response, leading to the false conclusion that the new version should be rejected) is just as likely, and the decision criterion specified does not protect against this possibility. In this example, a sample size of 120 does not have the statistical power to protect against the opportunity loss that may result from failure to recognize superiority of the new version.

When the effect size, the needed or expected difference, is large (e.g., more than 10 percentage points), then statistical power is typically not a problem. However, very small effect sizes (e.g., 2 percentage points) may require such large sample sizes as to be impractical from a cost perspective.[2] ∎

larger sample size, then the researcher may decline to submit a proposal based on the belief that an inadequate sample size will produce results with so much error that they may be misleading.[3]

Number of Subgroups to Be Analyzed

In any sample size determination problem, consideration must be given to the number and anticipated size of various subgroups of the total sample that must be analyzed and about which statistical inferences must be made. For example, a researcher might decide that a sample of 400 is quite adequate overall. However, if male and female respondents must be analyzed separately and the sample is expected to be 50 percent male and 50 percent female, then the expected sample size for each subgroup is only 200. Is this number adequate for making the desired statistical inferences about the characteristics of the two groups? If the results are to be analyzed by both sex and age, then the problem gets even more complicated.

Assume that it is important to analyze four subgroups of the total sample: men under 35, men 35 and over, women under 35, and women 35 and over. If each group is expected to make up about 25 percent of the total sample, a sample of 400 will include only 100 respondents in each subgroup. The problem is that as sample size gets smaller, sampling error gets larger and it becomes more difficult to tell whether an observed difference between two groups is a real difference or simply a reflection of sampling error.

Other things being equal, the larger the number of subgroups to be analyzed is, the larger the required total sample size. It has been suggested that a sample should provide, at a minimum, 100 or more respondents in each major subgroup and 20 to 50 respondents in each of the less important subgroups.[4]

Traditional Statistical Methods

You probably have been exposed in other classes to traditional approaches for determining sample size for simple random samples. These approaches are reviewed in this chapter. Three pieces of information are required to make the necessary calculations for a sample result:

- An estimate of the population standard deviation
- The acceptable level of sampling error
- The desired level of confidence that the sample result will fall within a certain range (result ± sampling error) of true population values

With these three pieces of information, the researcher can calculate the size of the simple random sample required.[5]

The Normal Distribution

General Properties

central limit theorem
The idea that a distribution of a large number of sample means or sample proportions will approximate a normal distribution, regardless of the distribution of the population from which they were drawn.

The normal distribution is crucial to classical statistical inference. There are several reasons for its importance. First, many variables encountered by marketers have probability distributions that are close to the normal distribution. Examples include the number of cans, bottles, or glasses of soft drink consumed by soft drink users, the number of times that people who eat at fast food restaurants go to such restaurants in an average month, and the average hours per week spent viewing television. Second, the normal distribution is useful for a number of theoretical reasons; one of the more important of these relates to the central limit theorem. According to the **central limit theorem,** for any population, regardless of its distribution, the distribution of sample means or sample proportions approaches a normal distribution as sample size increases. The importance of this tendency will become clear later in the chapter. Third, the normal distribution is a useful approximation of many other discrete probability distributions.

If, for example, a researcher measured the heights of a large sample of men in the United States and plotted those values on a graph, a distribution similar to the one shown in Figure 13.1 would result. This distribution is a **normal distribution,** and it has a number of important characteristics, including the following:

1. The normal distribution is bell-shaped and has only one mode. The mode is a measure of central tendency and is the particular value that occurs most frequently. (A bimodal, or two-mode, distribution would have two peaks or humps.)
2. The normal distribution is symmetric about its mean. This is another way of saying that it is not skewed and that the three measures of central tendency (mean, median, and mode) are all equal.
3. A particular normal distribution is uniquely defined by its mean and standard deviation.
4. The total area under a normal curve is equal to one, meaning that it takes in all observations.
5. The area of a region under the normal distribution curve between any two values of a variable equals the probability of observing a value in that range when an observation is randomly selected from the distribution. For example, on a single draw, there is a 34.13 percent chance of selecting from the distribution shown in Figure 13.1 a man between 5'7" and 5'9" in height.
6. The area between the mean and a given number of standard deviations from the mean is the same for all normal distributions. The area between the mean and plus or minus one standard deviation takes in 68.26 percent of the area under the curve, or 68.26 percent of the observations. This **proportional property of the normal distribution** provides the basis for the statistical inferences we will discuss in this chapter.

normal distribution
A continuous distribution that is bell-shaped and symmetric about the mean; the mean, median, and mode are equal.

proportional property of the normal distribution
The feature that the area between the mean and a given number of standard deviations from the mean is the same for all normal distributions.

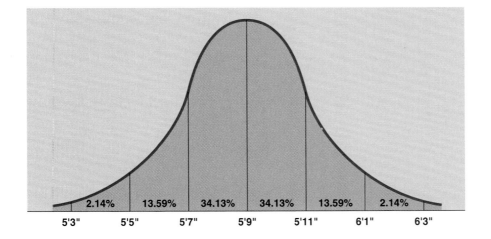

Figure 13.1

A Normal Distribution for Heights of Men

The Standard Normal Distribution

standard normal distribution

A normal distribution with a mean of zero and a standard deviation of one.

Any normal distribution can be transformed into what is known as a standard normal distribution. The **standard normal distribution** has the same features as any normal distribution. However, the mean of the standard normal distribution is always equal to zero, and the standard deviation is always equal to one. The probabilities provided in Table 2 in Appendix 2 are based on a standard normal distribution. A simple transformation formula, based on the proportional property of the normal distribution, is used to transform any value X from any normal distribution to its equivalent value Z from a standard normal distribution:

$$Z = \frac{\text{Value of the variable} - \text{Mean of the variable}}{\text{Standard deviation of the variable}}$$

Symbolically, the formula can be stated as follows:

$$Z = \frac{X - \mu}{\sigma}$$

where X = value of the variable
μ = mean of the variable
σ = standard deviation of the variable

standard deviation

A measure of dispersion calculated by subtracting the mean of the series from each value in a series, squaring each result, summing the results, dividing the sum by the number of items minus 1, and taking the square root of this value.

The areas under a standard normal distribution (reflecting the percent of all observations) for various Z values **(standard deviations)** are shown in Table 13.1. The standard normal distribution is shown in Figure 13.2.

Figure 13.2

Standard Normal Distribution

Note: The term Pr(Z) is read "the probability of Z."

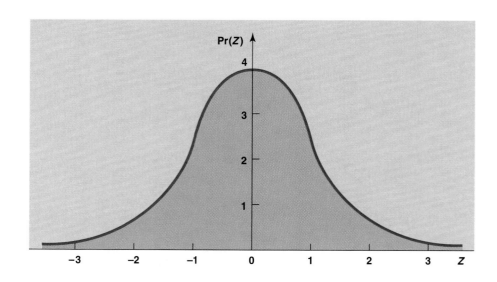

PART 3:
Data Acquisition

Table 13.1

Area under Standard Normal Curve for *Z* Values (Standard Deviations) of 1, 2, and 3	
Z Values (Standard Deviation)	**Area under Standard Normal Curve (%)**
1	68.26
2	95.44
3	99.74

Population and Sample Distributions

The purpose of conducting a survey based on a sample is to make inferences about the population, not to describe the sample. The population, as defined earlier, includes all possible individuals or objects from whom or about which information is needed to meet the objectives of the research. A sample is a subset of the total population.

A **population distribution** is a frequency distribution of all the elements of the population. It has a mean, usually represented by the Greek letter μ, and a standard deviation, usually represented by the Greek letter σ.

A **sample distribution** is a frequency distribution of all the elements of an individual (single) sample. In a sample distribution, the mean is usually represented by $\bar{X}$ and the standard deviation is usually represented by S.

population distribution
A frequency distribution of all the elements of a population.
sample distribution
A frequency distribution of all the elements of an individual sample.

Sampling Distribution of the Mean

At this point, it is necessary to introduce a third distribution, the sampling distribution of the sample mean. Understanding this distribution is crucial to understanding the basis for our ability to compute sampling error for simple random samples. The **sampling distribution of the mean** is a conceptual and theoretical probability distribution of the means of all possible samples of a given size drawn from a given population. Although this distribution is seldom calculated, its known properties have tremendous practical significance. Actually deriving a distribution of sample means involves drawing a large number of simple random samples (e.g., 25,000) of a certain size from a particular population. Then, the means for the samples are computed and arranged in a frequency distribution. Because each sample is composed of a different subset of sample elements, all the sample means will not be exactly the same. If the samples are sufficiently large and random, then the resulting distribution of sample means will approximate a normal distribution. This assertion is based on the central limit theorem, which states that as sample size increases, the distribution of the means of a large number of random samples taken from virtually any population approaches a normal distribution with a mean equal to μ and a standard deviation (referred to as *standard error*) $S_{\bar{x}}$, where n = sample size and

sampling distribution of the mean
A theoretical frequency distribution of the means of all possible samples of a given size drawn from a particular population; it is normally distributed.

$$S_{\bar{x}} = \frac{\sigma}{\sqrt{n}}$$

The **standard error of the mean** ($S_{\bar{x}}$) is computed in this way because the variance, or dispersion, within a particular distribution of sample means will be smaller if it is based on larger samples. Common sense tells us that with larger samples individual sample means will, on the average, be closer to the population mean.

It is important to note that the central limit theorem holds regardless of the shape of the population distribution from which the samples are selected. This means that, regardless of the population distribution, the sample means selected from the population distribution will tend to be normally distributed.

The notation ordinarily used to refer to the means and standard deviations of population and sample distributions and sampling distribution of the mean is summarized in Table 13.2. The relationships among the population distribution, sample distribution, and sampling distribution of the mean are shown graphically in Figure 13.3.

The results of a simple random sample of fast food restaurant patrons could be used to compute the mean number of visits for the period of one month for each of the 1,000 samples.

standard error of the mean
The standard deviation of a distribution of sample means.

Basic Concepts

Consider a case in which a researcher takes 1,000 simple random samples of size 200 from the population of all consumers who have eaten at a fast food restaurant at least once in the past 30 days. The purpose is to estimate the average number of times these individuals eat at a fast food restaurant in an average month.

If the researcher computes the mean number of visits for each of the 1,000 samples and sorts them into intervals based on their relative values, the frequency distribution shown in Table 13.3 might result. Figure 13.4 graphically illustrates these frequencies in a histogram, on which a normal curve has been superimposed. As you can see, the histogram closely approximates the shape of a normal curve. If the researcher draws a large enough number of samples of size 200, computes the mean of each sample, and plots these means, the resulting distribution will be a normal distribution. The normal curve shown in Figure

Table 13.2	Notation for Means and Standard Deviations of Various Distributions		
	Distribution	**Mean**	**Standard Deviation**
	Population	μ	σ
	Sample	$\bar{X}$	S
	Sampling	$\mu_{\bar{x}} = \mu$	$S_{\bar{x}}$

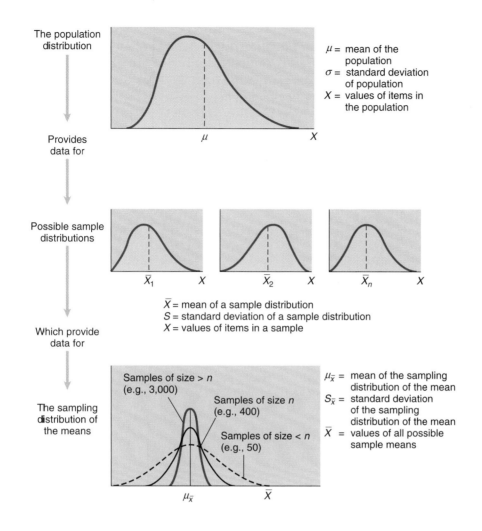

The population distribution

Provides data for

μ = mean of the population
σ = standard deviation of population
X = values of items in the population

Possible sample distributions

Which provide data for

$\bar{X}$ = mean of a sample distribution
S = standard deviation of a sample distribution
X = values of items in a sample

The sampling distribution of the means

Samples of size > n (e.g., 3,000)
Samples of size n (e.g., 400)
Samples of size < n (e.g., 50)

$\mu_{\bar{x}}$ = mean of the sampling distribution of the mean
$S_{\bar{x}}$ = standard deviation of the sampling distribution of the mean
$\bar{X}$ = values of all possible sample means

Figure 13.3

Relationships of the Three Basic Types of Distribution

Source: Adapted from *Statistics, A Fresh Approach,* 4E, by D. H. Sanders et al. © 1990 McGraw-Hill, Inc. Reprinted with permission of the McGraw-Hill Companies.

13.4 is the sampling distribution of the mean for this particular problem. The sampling distribution of the mean for simple random samples that are large (30 or more observations) has the following characteristics:

- The distribution is a normal distribution.
- The distribution has a mean equal to the population mean.
- The distribution has a standard deviation (the standard error of the mean), equal to the population standard deviation divided by the square root of the sample size:

$$\sigma_{\bar{x}} = \frac{\sigma}{\sqrt{n}}$$

This statistic is referred to as the standard error of the mean (instead of the standard deviation) to indicate that it applies to a distribution of sample means

Table 13.3	Frequency Distribution of 1,000 Sample Means: Average Number of Times Respondent Ate at a Fast Food Restaurant in the Past 30 Days	
	Number of Times	**Frequency of Occurrence**
	2.6–3.5	8
	3.6–4.5	15
	4.6–5.5	29
	5.6–6.5	44
	6.6–7.5	64
	7.6–8.5	79
	8.6–9.5	89
	9.6–10.5	108
	10.6–11.5	115
	11.6–12.5	110
	12.6–13.5	90
	13.6–14.5	81
	14.6–15.5	66
	15.6–16.5	45
	16.6–17.5	32
	17.6–18.5	16
	18.6–19.5	9
	Total	1,000

Figure 13.4

Actual Sampling Distribution of Means for Number of Times Respondent Ate at Fast Food Restaurant in Past 30 Days

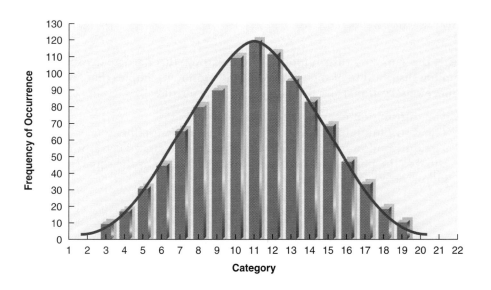

PART 3:
Data Acquisition

rather than to the standard deviation of a sample or a population. Keep in mind that this calculation applies *only* to a simple random sample. Other types of probability samples (e.g., stratified samples and cluster samples) require more complex formulas for computing standard error.

Making Inferences on the Basis of a Single Sample

In practice, there is no call for taking all possible random samples from a particular population

and generating a frequency distribution and histogram like those shown in Table 13.3 and Figure 13.4. Instead, the researcher wants to take one simple random sample and make statistical inferences about the population from which it was drawn. The question is, what is the probability that any one simple random sample of a particular size will produce an estimate of the population mean that is within one standard error (plus or minus) of the true population mean? The answer, based on the information provided in Table 13.1, is that there is a 68.26 percent probability that any one sample from a particular population will produce an estimate of the population mean that is within plus or minus one standard error of the true value, because 68.26 percent of all sample means fall in this range. There is a 95.44 percent probability that any one simple random sample of a particular size from a given population will produce a value that is within plus or minus two standard errors of the true population mean, and a 99.74 percent probability that such a sample will produce an estimate of the mean that is within plus or minus three standard errors of the population mean.

The sampling distribution of the proportion is used to estimate the percentage of the population that watches a particular television program.

Point and Interval Estimates

The results of a sample can be used to generate two kinds of estimates of a population mean: point and interval estimates. The sample mean is the best **point estimate** of the population mean. Inspection of the sampling distribution of the mean shown in Figure 13.4 suggests that a particular sample result is likely to produce a mean that is relatively close to the population mean. However, the mean of a particular sample could be any one of the sample means shown in the distribution. A small percentage of these sample means are a considerable distance from the true population mean. The distance between the sample mean and the true population mean is the sampling error.

Given that point estimates based on sample results are exactly correct in only a small percentage of all possible cases, interval estimates generally are preferred. An **interval estimate** is a particular interval or range of values within

point estimate
A particular estimate of a population value.

interval estimate
An interval or range of values within which the true population value is estimated to fall.

confidence level
The probability that a particular interval will include the true population value; also called *confidence coefficient.*
confidence interval
The interval that, in all probability, includes the true population value.

which the true population value is estimated to fall. In addition to stating the size of the interval, the researcher usually states the probability that the interval will include the true value of the population mean. This probability is referred to as the **confidence level,** or *confidence coefficient,* and the interval is called the **confidence interval.**

Interval estimates of the mean are derived by first drawing a random sample of a given size from the population of interest and calculating the mean of that sample. This sample mean is known to lie somewhere within the sampling distribution of all possible sample means, but exactly where this particular mean falls in that distribution is not known. There is a 68.26 percent probability that this particular sample mean lies within one standard error (plus or minus) of the true population mean. Based on this information, the researcher states that he or she is 68.26 percent confident that the true population value is equal to the sample value plus or minus one standard error. This statement can be shown symbolically, as follows:

$$\bar{X} - 1\sigma_{\bar{x}} \leq \mu \leq \bar{X} + 1\sigma_{\bar{x}}$$

By the same logic, the researcher can be 95.44 percent confident that the true population value is equal to the sample estimate plus or minus two (technically 1.96) standard errors, and 99.74 percent confident that the true population value falls within the interval defined by the sample value plus or minus three standard errors.

These statements assume that the standard deviation of the population is known. However, in most situations, this is not the case. If the standard deviation of the population were known, by definition the mean of the population would also be known, and there would be no need to take a sample in the first place. Because information on the standard deviation of the population is lacking, its value is estimated based on the standard deviation of the sample.

Sampling Distribution of the Proportion

Marketing researchers frequently are interested in estimating proportions or percentages rather than or in addition to estimating means. Common examples include estimating the following:

- The percentage of the population that is aware of a particular ad
- The percentage of the population that accesses the Internet one or more times in an average week
- The percentage of the population that has visited a fast food restaurant four or more times in the past 30 days
- The percentage of the population that watches a particular television program

In situations in which a population proportion or percentage is of interest, the sampling distribution of the proportion is used.

sampling distribution of the proportion
A relative frequency distribution of the sample proportions of many random samples of a given size drawn from a particular population; it is normally distributed.

The **sampling distribution of the proportion** is a relative frequency distribution of the sample proportions of a large number of random samples of a given size drawn from a particular population. The sampling distribution of a proportion has the following characteristics:

- It approximates a normal distribution.
- The mean proportion for all possible samples is equal to the population proportion.
- The standard error of a sampling distribution of the proportion can be computed with the following formula:

$$S_p = \sqrt{\frac{P(1 - P)}{n}}$$

where S_p = standard error of sampling distribution of proportion

        P = estimate of population proportion

        n = sample size

Consider the task of estimating the percentage of all adults who have purchased something over the Internet in the past 90 days. As in generating a sampling distribution of the mean, the researcher might select 1,000 random samples of size 200 from the population of all adults and compute the proportion of all adults who have purchased something over the Internet in the past 90 days for all 1,000 samples. These values could then be plotted in a frequency distribution, and this frequency distribution would approximate a normal distribution. The estimated standard error of the proportion for this distribution can be computed using the formula provided earlier.

For reasons that will be clear to you after you read the next section, marketing researchers have a tendency to prefer dealing with sample size problems as problems of estimating proportions rather than means.

Determining Sample Size

Problems Involving Means

Consider once again the task of estimating how many times the average fast food restaurant user visits a fast food restaurant in an average month. Management needs an estimate of the average number of visits to make a decision regarding a new promotional campaign that is being developed. To make this estimate, the marketing research manager for the organization intends to survey a simple random sample of all fast food users. The question is, what information is necessary to determine the appropriate sample size for the project? The formula for calculating the required sample size for problems that involve the estimation of a mean is as follows:[6]

$$n = \frac{Z^2 \sigma^2}{E^2}$$

where Z = level of confidence expressed in standard errors
σ = population standard deviation
E = acceptable amount of sampling error

Three pieces of information are needed to compute the sample size required:

1. The acceptable or allowable level of sampling error E
2. The acceptable level of confidence Z. In other words, how confident does the researcher want to be that the specified confidence interval includes the population mean?
3. An estimate of the population standard deviation σ

allowable sampling error
The amount of sampling error the researcher is willing to accept.

The level of confidence Z and **allowable sampling error** E for this calculation must be set by the researcher in consultation with his or her client. As noted earlier, the level of confidence and the amount of error are based not only on statistical criteria, but also on financial and managerial criteria. In an ideal world, the level of confidence would always be very high and the amount of error very low. However, because this is a business decision, cost must be considered. An acceptable tradeoff among accuracy, level of confidence, and cost must be developed. High levels of precision and confidence may be less important in some situations than in others. For example, in an exploratory study, you may be interested in developing a basic sense of whether attitudes toward your product are generally positive or negative. Precision may not be critical. However, in a product concept test, you would need a much more precise estimate of sales for a new product before making the potentially costly and risky decision to introduce that product in the marketplace.

population standard deviation
The standard deviation of a variable for the entire population.

Making an estimate of the **population standard deviation** presents a more serious problem. As noted earlier, if the population standard deviation were known, the population mean also would be known (the population mean is needed to compute the population standard deviation), and there would be no need to draw a sample. How can the researcher estimate the population standard deviation before selecting the sample? One or some combination of the following four methods might be used to deal with this problem:

1. *Use results from a prior survey.* In many cases, the firm may have conducted a prior survey dealing with the same or a similar issue. In this situation, a possible solution to the problem is to use the results of the prior survey as an estimate of the population standard deviation.
2. *Conduct a pilot survey.* If this is to be a large-scale project, it may be possible to devote some time and some resources to a small-scale pilot survey of the population. The results of this pilot survey can be used to develop an estimate of the population standard deviation that can be used in the sample size determination formula.
3. *Use secondary data.* In some cases, secondary data can be used to develop an estimate of the population standard deviation.

4. *Use judgment.* If all else fails, an estimate of the population standard deviation can be developed based solely on judgment. Judgments might be sought from a variety of managers in a position to make educated guesses about the required population parameters.

It should be noted that after the survey has been conducted and the sample mean and sample standard deviation have been calculated, the researcher can assess the accuracy of the estimate of the population standard deviation used to calculate the required sample size. At this time, if appropriate, adjustments can be made in the initial estimates of sampling error.

Let's return to the problem of estimating the average number of fast food visits made in an average month by users of fast food restaurants:

■ After consultation with managers in the company, the marketing research manager determines that an estimate is needed of the average number of times that fast food consumers visit fast food restaurants. She further determines that managers believe that a high degree of accuracy is needed, which she takes to mean that the estimate should be within .10 (one-tenth) of a visit of the true population value. This value (.10) should be substituted into the formula for the value of E.

■ In addition, the marketing research manager decides that, all things considered, she needs to be 95.44 percent confident that the true population mean falls in the interval defined by the sample mean plus or minus E (as just defined). Two (technically, 1.96) standard errors are required to take in 95.44 percent of the area under a normal curve. Therefore, a value of 2 should be substituted into the equation for Z.

■ Finally, there is the question of what value to insert into the formula for σ. Fortunately, the company conducted a similar study one year ago. The standard deviation in that study for the variable—the average number of times a fast food restaurant was visited in the past 30 days—was 1.39. This is the best estimate of s available. Therefore, a value of 1.39 should be substituted into the formula for the value of σ. The calculation follows:

$$n = \frac{Z^2\sigma^2}{E^2}$$

$$n = \frac{2^2(1.39)^2}{(.10)^2}$$

$$n = \frac{4(1.93)}{.01}$$

$$n = \frac{7.72}{.01}$$

$$n = 772$$

Based on this calculation, a simple random sample of 772 is necessary to meet the requirements outlined.

Problems Involving Proportions

Now let's consider the problem of estimating the proportion or percentage of all adults who have purchased something via the Internet in the past 90 days. The goal is to take a simple random sample from the population of all adults to estimate this proportion.[7]

■ As in the problem involving fast food users, the first task in estimating the population mean on the basis of sample results is to decide on an acceptable value for E. If, for example, an error level of ± 4 percent is acceptable, a value of .04 should be substituted into the formula for E.

■ Next, assume that the researcher has determined a need to be 95.44 percent confident that the sample estimate is within ± 4 percent of the true population proportion. As in the previous example, a value of 2 should be substituted into the equation for Z.

■ Finally, in a study of the same issue conducted one year ago, 5 percent of all respondents indicated they had purchased something over the Internet in the past 90 days. Thus, a value of .05 should be substituted into the equation for P.

The resulting calculations are as follows:

$$n = \frac{Z^2[P(1 - P)]}{E^2}$$

$$n = \frac{2^2[.05(1 - .05)]}{.04^2}$$

$$n = \frac{4(.0475)}{.0016}$$

$$n = \frac{.19}{.0016}$$

$$n = 119$$

Given the requirements, a random sample of 475 respondents is required. It should be noted that, in one respect, the process of determining the sample size necessary to estimate a proportion is easier than the process of determining the sample size necessary to estimate a mean: If there is no basis for estimating P, the researcher can make what is sometimes referred to as the most pessimistic, or worst case, assumption regarding the value of P. Given the values of Z and E, what value of P will require the largest possible sample? A value of .50 will make the value of the expression $P(1 - P)$ larger than any possible value of P. There is no corresponding most pessimistic assumption that the researcher can make regarding the value of σ in problems that involve determining the sample size necessary to estimate a mean with given levels of Z and E.

Determining Sample Size for Stratified and Cluster Samples

The formulas for sample size determination presented in this chapter apply only to simple random samples. There also are formulas for determining required sample size and sampling error for other types of probability samples such as stratified and cluster samples. Although many of the general concepts presented in this chapter apply to these other types of probability samples, the specific formulas are much more complicated.[8] In addition, these formulas require information that frequently is not available or is difficult to obtain. For these reasons, sample size determination for other types of probability samples is beyond the scope of this introductory text. Those interested in pursuing the question of sample size determination for stratified and cluster samples are referred to advanced texts on the topic of sampling.

Population Size and Sample Size

You may have noticed that none of the formulas for determining sample size take into account the size of the population in any way. Students (and managers) frequently find this troubling. It seems to make sense that one should take a larger sample from a larger population. But this is not the case. Normally, there is no direct relationship between the size of the population and the size of the sample required to estimate a particular population parameter with a particular level of error and a particular level of confidence. In fact, the size of the population may have an effect only in those situations where the size of the sample is large in relation to the size of the population. One rule of thumb is that an adjustment should be made in the sample size if the sample size is more than 5 percent of the size of the total population. The normal presumption is that sample elements are drawn independently of one another (*independence assumption*). This assumption is justified when the sample is small relative to the population. However, it is not appropriate when the sample is a relatively large (5 percent or more) proportion of the population. As a result, the researcher must adjust the results obtained with the standard formulas. For example, the formula for the standard error of the mean, presented earlier, is as follows:

$$\sigma_{\bar{x}} = \frac{\sigma}{\sqrt{n}}$$

For a sample that is 5 percent or more of the population, the independence assumption is dropped, producing the following formula:

$$\sigma_{\bar{x}} = \frac{\sigma}{\sqrt{n}} \sqrt{\frac{N-n}{N-1}}$$

The factor $(N - n)/(N - 1)$ is referred to as the **finite population correction factor (FPC)**.

In those situations in which the sample is large (5 percent or more) in relation to the population, the researcher can appropriately reduce the required sample size using the FPC. This calculation is made using the following formula:

finite population correction factor (FPC)
An adjustment to the required sample size that is made in cases where the sample is expected to be equal to 5 percent or more of the total population.

$$n' = \frac{nN}{N + n - 1}$$

where n' = revised sample size
n = original sample size
N = population size

If the population has 2,000 elements and the original sample size is 400, then

$$n' = \frac{400(2,000)}{2,000 + 400 - 1} = \frac{800,000}{2,399}$$

$$n' = 333$$

With the FPC adjustment, a sample of only 333 is needed, rather than the original 400.

The key is not the size of the sample in relation to the size of the population, but whether the sample selected is truly representative of the population. Empirical evidence shows that relatively small but carefully chosen samples can quite accurately reflect characteristics of the population. Many well-known national surveys and opinion polls, such as the Gallup Poll and the Harris Poll, are based on samples of fewer than 2,000. These polls have shown that the behavior of tens of millions of people can be predicted quite accurately using samples that are minuscule in relation to the size of the population.

Determining How Many Sample Units Are Needed

Regardless of how the target sample size is determined, the researcher is confronted with the practical problem of figuring out how many sampling units (telephone numbers, addresses, etc.) will be required to complete the assignment. For example, if the target final sample size is 400, then obviously more than 400 telephone numbers will be needed to complete a telephone survey.

Some of the numbers on the list will be disconnected, some people will not qualify for the survey because they do not meet the requirements for inclusion in the population, and some will refuse to complete the survey. These factors affect the final estimate of the number of phone numbers, which may be used to place an order with a sample provider, such as Survey Sampling, Incorporated, or to ask the client for customer names and phone numbers for a satisfaction survey. This estimate must be reasonably accurate because the researcher wants to avoid paying for more numbers than are needed; on the other hand, the researcher doesn't want to run out of numbers during the survey and have to wait for more.

The In Practice feature provides a practical approach to developing these important estimates.

If you wish to complete 300 interviews in the United Kingdom, you need to determine the contact/completion rate in order to figure out how many calls will actually have to be made to complete the survey.

Estimating with Precision How Many Phone Numbers Are Needed

In **PRACTICE**

CALCULATING HOW MANY PHONE NUMBERS ARE NEEDED FOR A PROJect may seem like a difficult task, but following a few basic rules can make it simple. The formula used by SSI to calculate sample size involves four factors: (1) the number of completed interviews needed, (2) the working phone (or "reachable") rate, (3) the incidence rate, and (4) the contact/completion rate.

Completed Interviews

The number of completed interviews is based on the sample size calculation formula for simple random samples. It is the final sample size you want to achieve.

Working Phone Rate

The working phone rate varies with the sampling methodology used. An SSI RDD sample yields a 60 percent working phone rate. That is a good number to use in the formula for estimation purposes.

Incidence Rate

The incidence rate is the percentage of contacts that will qualify for the interview. Or put another way, what percentage of people who answer the phone (or reply to your mail questionnaire) will pass your screening questions? Accurate incidence data are critical to determining proper sample size. An incidence figure that is too high will leave you short of sample once your study is in the field.

Contact/Completion Rate

The last factor is the contact/completion rate. SSI defines this rate as the percentage of people who, once they qualify for your study, will agree to cooperate by completing the interview. There are several important elements you should consider when trying to reasonably estimate the completion rate:

- Contact rate
- Length of interview
- Sensitivity of topic
- Time of year
- Number of attempts/callbacks
- Length of time in the field

Provided that the interview is short (less than 10 minutes) and nonsensitive in nature, sufficient callbacks are scheduled, and the study will be in the field for an adequate period of time, SSI estimates a 30 percent completion rate. The completion rate should be adjusted according to the specifications of each study. If the subject matter is sensitive or the interview is long, the completion rate should be reduced. If the length of time in the field is less than one week, SSI recommends increasing the sample size by at least 20 percent.

An Example

Suppose you wish to complete 300 interviews in the United Kingdom. Using a random digit sample, you can expect a working phone rate of 60 percent. Start by dividing the number of completed interviews you need (300) by the working phone rate (.60), to yield 500. You need to reach heavy soft drink users (17 percent of adults), and you estimate that 30 percent of the people contacted will complete the interview. Divide 500 by the incidence rate for the group under study (.17) and then by the completion rate (.30). This calculation shows you need 9,804 phone numbers to complete this survey.[9] ■

Statistical Power

statistical power
The probability of not making a Type II error.

Although it is standard practice in marketing research to use the formulas presented in this chapter to calculate sample size, these formulas all focus on *Type I error*, or the error of concluding that there is a difference when there is not a difference. They do not explicitly deal with *Type II error*, or the error of saying that there is no difference when there is a difference. The probability of not making a Type II error is called **statistical power.**[10] The standard formulas for calculating sample size implicitly assume a power of 50 percent. For example, suppose a researcher is trying to determine which of two product concepts has stronger appeal to target customers and wants to be able to detect a 5 percent difference in the percentages of target customers who say that they are very likely to buy the products. The standard sample size formulas indicate that a sample size of approximately 400 is needed for each product test. By using this calculation, the researcher implicitly accepts the fact that there is a 50 percent chance of incorrectly concluding that the two products have equal appeal.

Table 13.4 shows the sample sizes required, at an Alpha of .05, for specific levels of power and specific levels of differences between two independent proportions. Formulas are available to permit power calculations for any level of confidence; however, they are somewhat complex and will not help you understand the basic concept of power. Programs available on the Internet can be used to make these calculations. To reproduce the numbers in Table 13.4, go to http://www.dssresearch.com/SampleSize/default.asp and do the following:

Table 13.4

Sample Size Required to Detect Differences between Proportions from Independent Samples at Different Levels of Power and an Alpha of .05

Difference to Detect	Power					
	50%	60%	70%	75%	80%	90%
0.01	19,205	24,491	30,857	34,697	39,239	52,530
0.05	766	977	1,231	1,384	1,568	2,094
0.10	190	242	305	343	389	518
0.15	83	106	133	150	169	226

- Click on the Two-Sample Using Percentage Values option under Sample Size.
- Enter the Sample 1 Percentage and the Sample 2 Percentage in the boxes so that the figures entered reflect the differences you want to be able to detect and the values are in the expected range. These figures are set at the 50 percent level (value of p in the standard sample size formula).
- Below those boxes, enter the Alpha and Beta Error Levels. Alpha is the value you would use for E in the standard sample size formula, and Beta is the probability of incorrectly failing to reject the null hypothesis of no difference when a real difference exists. Power is equal to $1 - $ Beta.
- Click on the Calculate Sample Size button at the bottom of the screen for the answer.

Summary

Determining sample size for probability samples involves financial, statistical, and managerial considerations. Other things being equal, the larger the sample is, the smaller the sampling error. In turn, the cost of the research grows with the size of the sample.

There are several methods for determining sample size. One is to base the decision on the funds available. In essence, sample size is determined by the budget. Although seemingly unscientific, this approach is often a very realistic one in the world of corporate marketing research. The second technique is the so-called rule of thumb approach, which essentially involves determining the sample size based on a gut feeling or common practice. Samples of 300, 400, or 500 are often listed by the client in a request for proposal. A third technique for determining sample size is based on the number of subgroups to be analyzed. Generally speaking, the more subgroups that need to be analyzed, the larger is the required total sample size.

In addition to these methods, there are a number of traditional statistical techniques for determining sample size. Three pieces of data are required to make sample size calculations: an estimate of the population standard deviation, the level of sampling error that the researcher or client is willing to accept, and the desired level of confidence that the sample result will fall within a certain range of the true population value.

Crucial to statistical sampling theory is the concept of the normal distribution. The normal distribution is bell-shaped and has only one mode. It also is symmetric about its mean. The standard normal distribution has the features of a normal distribution; however, the mean of the standard normal distribution is always equal to zero, and the standard deviation is always equal to one. The transformation formula is used to transform any value X from any normal distribution to its equivalent value Z from a standard normal distribution. The central limit theorem states that the distribution of the means of a large number of random samples taken from virtually any population approaches a normal distribution with a mean equal to μ and a standard deviation equal to $S_{\bar{x}}$, where

$$S_{\bar{x}} = \frac{\sigma}{\sqrt{n}}$$

The standard deviation of a distribution of sample means is called the standard error of the mean.

When the results of a sample are used to estimate a population mean, two kinds of estimates can be generated: point and interval estimates. The sample mean is the best point estimate of the population mean. An interval estimate is a certain interval or range of values within which the true population value is estimated to fall. Along with the magnitude of the interval, the researcher usually states the probability that the interval will include the true value of the population mean—that is, the confidence level. The interval is called the confidence interval.

The researcher who is interested in estimating proportions or percentages rather than or in addition to means uses the sampling distribution of the proportion. The sampling distribution of the proportion is a relative frequency distribution of the sample proportions of a large number of random samples of a given size drawn from a particular population. The standard error of a sampling distribution of proportion is computed as follows:

$$S_p = \sqrt{\frac{P(1 - P)}{n}}$$

The following are required to calculate sample size: the acceptable level of sampling error E, the acceptable level of confidence Z, and an estimate of the population standard deviation σ. The formula for calculating the required sample size for situations that involve the estimation of a mean is as follows:

$$n = \frac{Z^2 \, \sigma^2}{E^2}$$

The following formula is used to calculate the required sample size for problems involving proportions:

$$n = \frac{Z^2[P(1 - P)]}{E^2}$$

Finally, statistical power is the probability of not making a Type II error. A Type II error is the mistake of saying that there is not a difference when there is a difference. The standard sample size formula implicitly assumes a power of 50 percent. It may be important to use different levels of power depending on the nature of the decision in question.

Key Terms & Definitions

central limit theorem   The idea that a distribution of a large number of sample means or sample proportions will approximate a normal distribution, regardless of the distribution of the population from which they were drawn.

normal distribution   A continuous distribution that is bell-shaped and symmetric about the mean; the mean, median, and mode are equal.

proportional property of the normal distribution   The feature that the area between the mean and a given number of standard deviations from the mean is the same for all normal distributions.

standard normal distribution   A normal distribution with a mean of zero and a standard deviation of one.

standard deviation   A measure of dispersion calculated by subtracting the mean of the series from each value in a series, squaring each result, summing the results, dividing the sum by the number of items minus 1, and taking the square root of this value.

population distribution   A frequency distribution of all the elements of a population.

sample distribution   A frequency distribution of all the elements of an individual sample.

sampling distribution of the mean   A theoretical frequency distribution of the means of all possible samples of a given size drawn from a particular population; it is normally distributed.

standard error of the mean   The standard deviation of a distribution of sample means.

point estimate   A particular estimate of a population value.

interval estimate   An interval or range of values within which the true population value is estimated to fall.

confidence level   The probability that a particular interval will include the true population value; also called *confidence coefficient.*

confidence interval   The interval that, in all probability, includes the true population value.

sampling distribution of the proportion   A relative frequency distribution of the sample proportions of many random samples of a given size drawn from a particular population; it is normally distributed.

allowable sampling error   The amount of sampling error the researcher is willing to accept.

population standard deviation   The standard deviation of a variable for the entire population.

finite population correction factor (FPC)   An adjustment to the required sample size that is made in cases where the sample is expected to be equal to 5 percent or more of the total population.

statistical power   The probability of not making a Type II error.

Questions for Review & Critical Thinking

1. Explain how the determination of sample size is a financial, statistical, and managerial issue.
2. Discuss and give examples of three methods that are used in marketing research for determining sample size.
3. A marketing researcher analyzing the fast food industry noticed the following: The average amount spent at a fast food restaurant in California was $3.30, with a standard deviation of $.40. Yet in Georgia, the average amount spent at a fast food restaurant was $3.25, with a standard deviation of $.10.

What do these statistics tell you about fast food consumption patterns in these two states?

4. Distinguish among population, sample, and sampling distributions. Why is it important to distinguish among these concepts?

5. What is the finite population correction factor? Why is it used? When should it be used?

6. Assume that previous fast food research has shown that 80 percent of the consumers like curly french fries. The researcher wishes to have a standard error of 6 percent or less and be 95 percent confident of an estimate to be made about curly french fry consumption from a survey. What sample size should be used for a simple random sample?

7. You are in charge of planning a chili cook-off. You must make sure that there are plenty of samples for the patrons of the cook-off. The following standards have been set: a confidence level of 99 percent and an error of less than 4 ounces per cooking team. Last year's cook-off had a standard deviation in amount of chili cooked of 3 ounces. What is the necessary sample size?

8. Based on a client's requirements of a confidence interval of 99.74 percent and acceptable sampling error of 2 percent, a sample size of 500 is calculated. The cost to the client is estimated at $20,000. The client replies that the budget for this project is $17,000. What are the alternatives?

9. A marketing researcher must determine how many telephone numbers she needs to order from a sample provider to complete a survey of ATM users. The goal is to complete 400 interviews with ATM users. From past experience, she estimates that 60 percent of the phone numbers provided will be working phone numbers. The estimated incidence rate (percentage of people contacted who are ATM users) is 43 percent. Finally, she estimates from previous surveys that 35 percent of the people contacted will agree to complete the survey. How many telephone numbers should she order?

Working the Net

What size samples are needed for a statistical power of 70 percent in detecting a difference of 5 percent between the estimated percentages of recent CD buyers in two independent samples? Assume an expected percentage in the range of 50 percent and an Alpha error of 5 percent. Use the sample size calculator at http:/www.dssresearch.com/SampleSize/default.asp to get your answer. Instructions for using this calculator are provided in the Statistical Power section of this text.

Using WebSurveyor

Use the list of names provided on the CD-ROM included with this textbook ([cddrive]:Exercises\Chapter13\names.txt). Assume that the list includes all the members of a particular population.

Exercises

1. Use the formula from the chapter for calculating sampling error when estimating a proportion. Because the proposed sample sizes are relatively large percentages of the population (i.e., greater than 5 percent), use the finite population correction factor in your calculations. What is the sampling error at 95 percent confidence for random samples from this population of 100? of 200? of 400?
2. What would the sampling errors have been if you had not used the finite population correction factor for each of the sample sizes?
3. What is the basic logic behind the finite population correction factor?

Real-Life Research • 13.1

Millennium Telecom

Millennium Telecom is an emerging provider of bundled communications services for residential users. It offers local telephone service, long distance telephone service, digital cable, Internet service, and monitored home security service. Millennium is in the process of building awareness of its brand in selected areas of Texas, New Mexico, and Colorado. Now in its second year, the company plans to spend $4.2 million to promote awareness and brand image of its bundled communications services in the target area. Brand image and awareness are important to Millennium because it is competing with a number of much larger and better financed competitors, including AT&T, Southwestern Bell, and TCI Cable.

In the first year of the brand image campaign, Millennium spent $3 million pursuing the same goals of increasing awareness and brand image. In order to see if the campaign was successful, the company conducted tracking research by telephone. It conducted a pretest before the campaign began and a posttest at

PART 3:
Data Acquisition

the end of the year. The surveys were designed to measure awareness and image of Millennium. Changes in either measure from the pretest to the posttest were to be attributed to the effects of the ad campaign. No other elements of the marketing strategy were changed during the course of the campaign.

Unaided, or top-of-mind, awareness ("What companies come to mind when you think of companies that provide residential communication services?") increased from 21 percent in the pretest to 25 percent in the posttest. In the pretest, 42 percent reported having a positive image of Millennium. This figure increased to 44 percent in the posttest. Though both key measures increased, the sample sizes for the two tests were relatively small. Random samples of 100 consumers were used for both tests. Sampling error for the measure of awareness at 95.44 percent confidence is $\pm$ 8.7 percent. The comparable figure for the image measure is $\pm$ 9.9 percent. The value used for P in the formula is the posttest result. With these relatively large sampling errors and the relatively small changes in awareness and image, Millennium could only say with 95.44 percent confidence that awareness in the posttest was 25 percent $\pm$ 8.7 percent, or in the range of 16.3 percent to 33.7 percent. In regard to the image measure, it could only say with 95.44 percent confidence that the percentage of consumers with a positive image of Millennium in the posttest was 44 percent $\pm$ 9.9 percent, or in the range of 34.1 percent to 53.9 percent. Based on the relatively small changes in awareness and image and the relatively large errors associated with these measures, Millennium could not conclude with any confidence that either measure had actually changed.

The CEO of Millennium is concerned about the amount of money being spent on advertising and wants to know whether the advertising is actually achieving what it is supposed to achieve. She wants a more sensitive test so that a definitive conclusion can be reached regarding the effect of the advertising.

Questions

1. Show how the sampling errors for the posttest measures were calculated.
2. If the CEO wants to have 95.44 percent confidence that the estimates of awareness and positive image are within $\pm$ 2 percent of the true value, what is the required sample size?
3. What is the required sample size if the CEO wants to be 99.74 percent confident?
4. If the current budget for conducting the telephone interviews is $20,000 and the cost per interview is $19, can Millennium reach the goal specified in question 3? With the $20,000 budget, what error levels can it reach for both measures? What is the budget required to reach the goal set in question 3?

Real-Life Research • 13.2

Sky Kitchens

Sky Kitchens is the second largest airline caterer in the United States, providing nearly all the meals for passengers of three major airlines and several smaller commuter airlines. As part of a total quality management (TQM) program, its largest airline client, Continental Airlines, has recently met with representatives of Sky Kitchens to discuss a customer satisfaction program that it is planning to implement.

Continental plans to interview a sample of its customers four times a year. In the survey, it intends to ask customers to rate the quality of meals provided on a 1-to-10 scale, where 1 means poor and 10 means excellent. It has just completed a benchmark study of 1,000 customers. In that study, meals received an average rating of 8.7 on the 10-point scale, with a standard deviation of 1.65. Continental has indicated that it wants Sky Kitchens to guarantee a level of satisfaction of 8.5 in the first quarterly survey, to be conducted in three months. For its quarterly surveys, Continental plans to use a sample size of 500. In the new contract with Sky Kitchens, Continental wants to include a clause that will penalize Sky Kitchens $50,000 for each one-tenth of a point it falls below an average of 8.5 on the next survey's satisfaction scale.

Questions

1. What is the 95.44 percent confidence interval for the estimated satisfaction level in the benchmark survey? What is the 99.74 percent confidence interval?
2. Assume that the upcoming first-quarter satisfaction survey shows an average rating of 8.4 on satisfaction with meals. Compute the 95.44 percent confidence interval and the 99.74 confidence interval.
3. If you were negotiating for Sky Kitchens, how would you respond to Continental regarding the penalty clause?

Marketing Research across the Organization

1. You are a marketing researcher from Ford Motor Company at a time when Ford is gearing up to sell its popular Explorer sport utility vehicle in developed and developing nations throughout the world. Your audience consists of plant managers and engineers from factories in Belgium, Brazil, China, and South Africa who will be responsible for assembling the international version of the Ford Explorer. Purchase intent research shows that the percentage of persons who will "definitely purchase" or "probably purchase" the vehicle ranges from 78 percent in South America to 44 percent in Western Europe. Your audience has accepted these figures as absolute truths. How will you temper their understanding of purchase intent scores?
2. Why is it often important to get feedback from production and engineering departments in creating questionnaires for new product development? How should the researcher go about getting the feedback? How can the researcher make certain that the questionnaire is going to provide the information needed by the decision maker?
3. The vice president of finance has just informed the CEO that sales are expected to decline 5 percent next year and that the advertising and marketing research budgets will be cut at least 75 percent since those departments don't really produce anything anyway. How might you defend the current research budget and even argue for an increase next year?

Ethical Dilemma

Liberty Financial Companies

THE FEDERAL TRADE COMMISSION SAYS IT CAUGHT BIG BOSTON money manager Liberty Financial Companies failing to protect the anonymity of children on its kids' Web site and skimping on the prizes advertised there. The case is significant for the fast-growing world of Internet advertising and "data mining," because it suggests that advertisers won't be allowed to promote a Web survey as "anonymous" if they really keep track of who says what.

Without admitting or denying wrongdoing, Liberty reached a consent agreement with the FTC over the agency's complaint challenging its Web site http://www.younginvestor.com. The site still asks lots of personal questions, such as whether or not the children earn money from odd jobs. But from now on, Liberty promises it won't keep track of the name of, say, that 12-year-old in Cincinnati who earned $500 from babysitting last year.

A Liberty spokesman, L. Harrison Thayer, notes that the site has been changed to comply with new Internet privacy rules for children that were proposed by the FTC earlier this year. "We've changed the site to meet the emerging standards," he says. "At no time did our company ever compromise a child's privacy. We've never used [the survey information] for our purposes or shared it [with another entity]."

On the Web site, Liberty sought to persuade young Web surfers to fill out a survey by dangling a chance to win prizes and a free newsletter. Problem is, the FTC says, the free newsletter never came and the company didn't select as many prize winners as it represented on the site. What's more, the site falsely represented that personal information would be maintained anonymously. In fact, Liberty retained the names, addresses and e-mails of the people who participated in the cyberspace survey, the FTC complaint alleges.

According to the complaint, the younginvestor site asked survey questions about weekly allowances, spending habits, part-time work history, plans for college, and family finances, including ownership of any mutual funds. The company says it did nothing to breach privacy and was merely trying to raise awareness about investing. The site is "an opportunity to educate parents and children about investments and savings," says Liberty's Mr. Thayer. "There's a tremendous absence of useful education about family finances, and we saw this as a way to fill that gap."[11]

Questions

1. Were Liberty's actions unethical? Why or why not?
2. Do you accept Mr. Thayer's explanation of what happened?
3. Is Internet privacy an important issue to you? Why?
4. How does the privacy issue affect the marketing research industry?

Part Four

Data Analysis

14

Data Processing and Fundamental Data Analysis

15

Statistical Testing of Differences

16

Bivariate Correlation and Regression

17

Multivariate Data Analysis

Check it out!

Use the WebSurveyor CD-ROM that accompanies your text to help you work through the exercises and quantitative material in Part Four.

Chapter Fourteen

Learning Objectives

To get an overview of the data analysis procedure.

To develop an understanding of the importance and nature of quality control checks.

To understand the data entry process and data entry alternatives.

To learn how surveys are tabulated.

To learn how to set up and interpret crosstabulations.

To comprehend the basic techniques of statistical analysis.

MELANIE COLE, OF TECHNOLOGY DECISIONS, IS THE FIRM'S ACCOUNT executive for Texas Instruments (TI). She recently submitted a proposal to TI for a project involving the processing of 20,000 to 25,000 questionnaires to be collected by TI personnel from attendees at a series of high-tech trade shows over the next six months. On this project, she will be working directly with the manager from the sales group responsible for TI's trade show activities, Bill Reber. Cole did not take this into account when she wrote her proposal. Normally, she worked with marketing research department staff, who would interface between her and the managers for whom the research was being done. Knowing that these marketing researchers were well acquainted with editing, coding, data entry, and tabulation procedures, she did not cover those topics in any depth in her proposal.

SHE HAS JUST RECEIVED A LENGTHY EMAIL from Reber, who says that he likes the price quoted and the sample report included in the proposal. However, Cole can see that Reber is a process-oriented guy who wants lots of details regarding the accomplishment of various tasks. His questions, taken from the email, follow:

- Will the questionnaires be checked for logical consistency, accuracy, and completeness before they are entered into electronic files? How will this be done? What quality checks are built into this process?

- I'm assuming that no data entry will be done until questionnaires have been checked as suggested above. Is that correct?

- As you know from the sample questionnaire, the survey has seven open-ended questions. This information is very important to us. We intend to use feedback from trade show attendees—they are either customers or people we would like to have as customers—to guide us in the development of a number of sales and marketing initiatives. Therefore, it is important that we have an accurate and complete summarization of these comments. Obviously, there are way too many questionnaires for us to read and somehow summarize ourselves. In your proposal, you refer to the "coding" of open-ended questions. I have only the vaguest idea of what that means. What does it mean to "code" open-ended questions? How do you go about it? What does the process look like? What quality control checks are built into the process? Finally, can we [management] have some input in shaping the process?

Data processing and data analysis form the basis for many of the questions asked by the sales manager responsible for trade shows at Texas Instruments.

Find out more about Texas Instruments at

http://www.
ti.com

- In your proposal, you say you will enter data from the paper questionnaires after completion of the coding process. I'm assuming that you're talking about transferring the data from the paper questionnaire to an electronic file. How will this be done? What quality control procedures are built in so that I can be assured that the data in the electronic file accurately reflect the original responses on the paper questionnaires?

- You refer to crosstabulations in your proposal. What are crosstabulations and how are they produced? I know they are tables of some sort. Can we have input into the design of those tables?

- Finally, is there some way that we could have access to our data over the Internet? Having access to the tables would be okay, but we really would like to be able to have access to the data and a tool that would permit us to generate any tables that we might want to produce. Is this possible? ∎

This chapter will offer answers to Reber's questions by providing all of the background and tools needed to perform these important tasks. The seemingly mechanical data processing activities are a critical bridge between the data collection and data analysis phases of a project.

An Overview of the Data Analysis Procedure

Once data collection has been completed and questionnaires have been returned, the researcher may be facing anywhere from a few hundred to several thousand interviews, each ranging from a few pages to 20 or more pages. We recently completed a study involving 1,300 questionnaires of 10 pages each. The 13,000 pages amounted to a stack of paper nearly three feet high. How should a researcher transform all the information contained on 13,000 pages of completed questionnaires into a format that will permit the summarization necessary for detailed analysis? At one extreme, the researcher could read all the interviews, make notes while reading them, and draw some conclusions from this review of the questionnaires. The folly of this approach is fairly obvious. Instead of this haphazard and inefficient approach, professional researchers follow a five-step procedure for data analysis:

Step One.	Validation and editing (quality control)
Step Two.	Coding
Step Three.	Data entry
Step Four.	Machine cleaning of data
Step Five.	Tabulation and statistical analysis

Each of these five steps is discussed in detail in this chapter.

Step One: Validation and Editing

The purpose of the first step is twofold. The researcher wants to make sure that all the interviews actually were conducted as specified (validation) and that the questionnaires have been filled out properly and completely (editing).

Validation

First, the researcher must determine, to the extent possible, that each of the questionnaires to be processed represents a valid interview. Here, we are using the term *valid* in a different sense than in Chapter 9. In Chapter 9, *validity* was defined as the extent to which what was being measured was actually measured. In this chapter, **validation** is defined as the process of ascertaining that interviews were conducted as specified. In this context, no assessment is made regarding the validity of the measurement. The goal of validation is solely to detect interviewer fraud or failure to follow key instructions. Certain types of interviewing (e.g., door-to-door interviewing) offer no opportunity to observe or monitor the interviewing process while it is taking place. You may have noticed that the various questionnaires presented throughout the text almost always have a place to record the respondent's name, address, and telephone number. This information is seldom used in any way in the analysis of the data; it is collected only to provide a basis for validation.

> **validation**
> The process of ascertaining that interviews actually were conducted as specified.

Professional researchers know that interviewer cheating is not uncommon. Various studies have documented the existence and prevalence of interviewer falsification of several types. For this reason, validation is an integral and necessary step in the data processing stage of a marketing research project.

After all the interviews in a door-to-door, mall-intercept, or telephone survey have been completed, the research firm recontacts a certain percentage of the respondents surveyed by each interviewer. Typically, this percentage ranges from 10 percent to 20 percent. If a particular interviewer surveyed 50 people and the research firm normally validates at a 10 percent rate, five respondents surveyed by that interviewer would be recontacted by telephone. Telephone validation typically answers four questions:

1. Was the person actually interviewed?
2. Did the person who was interviewed qualify to be interviewed according to the screening questions on the survey? For example, the interview may have required that the person being interviewed come from a family with an annual household income of $25,000 or more. On validation, the respondent would again be asked whether the annual household income for his or her family was $25,000 or more per year.
3. Was the interview conducted in the required manner? For example, a mall survey should have been conducted in the designated mall. Was this particular respondent interviewed in the mall, or was she or he interviewed at some other place, such as a restaurant or someone's home?
4. Did the interviewer cover the entire survey? Sometimes interviewers recognize that a potential respondent is in a hurry and may not have time to complete the entire survey. If respondents for that particular survey are difficult

A mall survey should be conducted in the designated mall. An important part of data analysis is validating that the data were gathered as specified.

editing
The process of ascertaining that questionnaires were filled out properly and completely.

to find, the interviewer may be motivated to ask the respondent a few questions at the beginning and a few questions at the end and then fill out the rest of the survey without the respondent's input. Validation for this particular problem would involve asking respondents whether they were asked various questions from different points in the interview.

Validation also usually involves checking for other problems. For example: Was the interviewer courteous? Did the interviewer speculate about the client's identity or the purpose of the survey? Was the interviewer neat in appearance? Does the respondent have any other comments about the interviewer or the interview experience?

The purpose of the validation process, as noted earlier, is to ensure that interviews were administered properly and completely. Researchers must be sure that the research results on which they are basing their recommendations reflect the legitimate responses of target individuals.

Editing

Whereas validation involves checking for interviewer cheating and failure to follow instructions, **editing** involves checking for interviewer and respondent mistakes. Paper questionnaires usually are edited at least twice before being submitted for data entry. First, they are edited by the field service firm that conducted the interviews, and then they are edited by the marketing research firm that hired the field service firm to do the interviewing. CATI, Internet, and other software-driven surveys have built in logical checking. The editing process for paper surveys involves manual checking for a number of problems, including the following:

1. *Whether the interviewer failed to ask certain questions or record answers for certain questions.* In the questionnaire shown in Figure 14.1, no answer was recorded for question 19. According to the structure of the questionnaire, this question should have been asked of all respondents. Also, the respondent's name does not give a clear indication of gender. The purpose of the first edit—the field edit—is to identify these types of problems when there is still time to recontact the respondent and determine the appropriate answer to questions that were not asked. This may also be done at the second edit (by the

marketing research firm), but in many instances there is not time to recontact the respondent and the interview has to be discarded.

2. *Whether skip patterns were followed.* According to the **skip pattern** in question 2 in Figure 14.1, if the answer to this question is "Very unlikely" or "Don't know," the interviewer should skip to question 16. The editor needs to make sure that the interviewer followed instructions. Sometimes, particularly during the first few interviews in a particular study, interviewers get mixed up and skip when they should not or fail to skip when they should.

3. *Whether the interviewer paraphrased respondents' answers to open-ended questions.* Marketing researchers and their clients usually are very interested in the responses to open-ended questions. The quality of the responses, or at least what was recorded, is an excellent indicator of the competence of the interviewer who recorded them. Interviewers are trained to record responses verbatim and not to paraphrase or insert their own language. They also are usually instructed to probe the initial response. The first part of Figure 14.2 shows an example of an interviewer's paraphrasing and interpretation of a response to an open-ended question. The second part of Figure 14.2 shows the result of interviewer failure to probe a response. The response is useless from a decision-making perspective. It comes as no surprise that the respondent goes to Burger King most often because he likes it. The third part of Figure 14.2 shows how an initial meaningless response can be expanded to something useful by means of proper probing. A proper probe to the answer "Because I like it" would be "Why do you like it?" or "What do you like about it?" The respondent then indicates that he goes there most often because it is the fast food restaurant most convenient to his place of work.

skip pattern
Sequence in which later questions are asked, based on a respondent's answer to an earlier question.

The person doing the editing must make judgment calls in regard to substandard responses to open-ended questions. She or he must decide at what point particular answers are so limited as to be useless and whether respondents should be recontacted.

The editing process is extremely tedious and time-consuming. (Imagine for a moment reading through 13,000 pages of interviews!) However, it is a very important step in the processing of survey responses.

Step Two: Coding

As discussed in Chapter 11, **coding** refers to the process of grouping and assigning numeric codes to the various responses to a particular question. Most questions on surveys are closed-ended and precoded, meaning that numeric codes have been assigned to the various responses on the questionnaire itself. All answers to closed-ended questions should be precoded, as they are in question 1 on the questionnaire in Figure 14.1. Note that each answer has a numeric code to its right; the answer "0–2" has the code 1, the answer "3–5" has the code 2, and

coding
The process of grouping and assigning numeric codes to the various responses to a question.

Figure 14.1

Sample Questionnaire

Consumer Survey
Cellular Telephone Survey Questionnaire

Long Branch—Asbury, N.J.
(01–03) _001_

Date ___1–05–01___

Respondent Telephone Number___201-555-2322___

Hello. My name is ___Sally___ with POST Research. May I please speak with the male or female head of the household?

(IF INDIVIDUAL NOT AVAILABLE, RECORD NAME AND CALLBACK INFORMATION ON SAMPLING FORM.)

(WHEN MALE/FEMALE HEAD OF HOUSEHOLD COMES TO PHONE): Hello, my name is_____ ,
with POST Research. Your number was randomly selected, and I am not trying to sell you anything. I simply want to ask you a few questions about a new type of telephone service.

1. First, how many telephone calls do you make during a typical day?

(04)
0–2	1
3–5	2
6–10	. . . . .③
11–15	4
16–20	5
More than 20	6
Don't know	7

Now, let me tell you about a new service called cellular mobile telephone service, which is completely wireless. You can get either a portable model that may be carried in your coat pocket or a model mounted in any vehicle. You will be able to receive calls and make calls, no matter where you are. Although cellular phones are wireless, the voice quality is similar to your present phone service. This is expected to be a time-saving convenience for household use.

This new cellular mobile phone service may soon be widely available in your area.

2. Now, let me explain to you the cost of this wireless service. Calls will cost 26 cents a minute plus normal toll charges. In addition, the monthly minimum charge for using the service will be $7.50 and rental of a cellular phone will be about $40. Of course, you can buy the equipment instead of leasing it. At this price, do you think you would be very likely, somewhat likely, somewhat unlikely, or very unlikely to subscribe to the new phone service?

(05)
Very likely	1
Somewhat likely	. . . . .②
Somewhat unlikely	3
Very unlikely	. . . .(GO TO QUESTION 16) 4
Don't know	. . . .(GO TO QUESTION 16) 5

INTERVIEWER—IF "VERY UNLIKELY" OR "DON'T KNOW," GO TO QUESTION 16.

3. Do you think it is likely that your employer would furnish you with one of these phones for your job?

(06)
No	. . . .(GO TO QUESTION 5) 1
Don't know	. . . .(GO TO QUESTION 5) 2
Yes	. . . .(CONTINUE) . . . . ③

INTERVIEWER—IF "NO" OR "DON'T KNOW," GO TO QUESTION 5; OTHERWISE CONTINUE.

4. If your employer did furnish you with a wireless phone, would you also purchase one for household use?

(07)
Yes	. . . .(CONTINUE) . . . . .①
No	. . . .(GO TO QUESTION 16) 2
Don't know	. . . .(GO TO QUESTION 16) 3

PART 4:
Data Analysis

5. Please give me your best estimate of the number of mobile phones your household would use (write in "DK" for "Don't know").

Number of Units _____01_____ (08–09)

6. Given that cellular calls made or received will cost 26 cents a minute plus normal toll charges during weekdays, how many calls on the average would you expect to make in a typical weekday?

RECORD NUMBER _____06_____ (10–11)

7. About how many minutes would your average cellular call last during the week?

RECORD NUMBER _____05_____ (12–13)

8. Weekend cellular calls made or received will cost 8 cents per minute plus normal toll charges. Given this, about how many cellular calls on the average would you expect to make in a typical Saturday or Sunday?

RECORD NUMBER _____00_____ (14–15)

9. About how many minutes would your average cellular call last on Saturday or Sunday?

RECORD NUMBER _____ (16–17)

10. You may recall from my previous description that two types of cellular phone units will be available. The vehicle phone may be installed in any vehicle. The portable phone will be totally portable—it can be carried in a briefcase, purse, or coat pocket. The totally portable phones may cost about 25 percent more and may have a more limited transmitting range in some areas than the vehicle phone. Do you think you would prefer portable or vehicle phones if you were able to subscribe to this service?

(18)

Portable 1
Vehicle . . . . ②
Both 3
Don't know 4

11. Would you please tell me whether you, on the average, would use a mobile phone about once a week, less than once a week, or more than once a week from the following geographic locations.

	Less Than Once a Week	Once a Week	More Than Once a Week	Never	More Than
Monmouth County (IF "NEVER," SKIP TO QUESTION 12)	1	2	③	4	(19)
Sandy Hook	1	2	3	④	(20)
Kearsburg	1	2	3	④	(21)
Atlantic Highlands	1	2	③	4	(22)
Matawan–Middletown	①	2	3	4	(23)
Red Bank	①	2	3	4	(24)
Holmdel	1	2	③	4	(25)
Eatontown	1	②	3	4	(26)
Long Branch	1	2	3	④	(27)
Freehold	1	2	3	④	(28)
Manalapan	1	2	3	④	(29)
Cream Ridge	1	2	3	④	(30)
Belmar	1	2	3	④	(31)
Point Pleasant	1	2	③	4	(32)

I'm going to describe to you a list of possible extra features of the proposed cellular service. Each option I'm going to describe will cost not more than $3.00 a month per phone. Would you please tell me if you would be very interested, interested, or uninterested in each feature:

(continued)

	Very Interested	Interested	Uninterested	
12. Call forwarding (the ability to transfer any call coming in to your mobile phone to any other phone).	①	2	3	(33)
13. No answer transfer (service that redirects calls to another number if your phone is unanswered).	1	2	③	(34)
14. Call waiting (a signal that another person is trying to call you while you are using your phone).	1	②	3	(35)
15. Voice mailbox (a recording machine that will take the caller's message and relay it to you at a later time. This service will be provided at $5.00 per month).	1	2	③	(36)

16. What is your age group? (READ BELOW)

(37)

Under 25 1
25–44 . . . . ②
45–64 3
65 and over 4
Refused, no answer, or don't know 5

17. What is your occupation?

(38)

Manager, official, or proprietor . . . . ①
Professional (doctors, lawyers, etc.) 2
Technical (engineers, computer programmers, draftsmen, etc.) 3
Office worker/clerical 4
Sales 5
Skilled worker or foreman 6
Unskilled worker 7
Teacher 8
Homemaker, student, retired 9
Not now employed X
Refused . . . . Y

18. Into which category did your total family income fall in 1998? (READ BELOW)

(39)

Under $15,000 1
$15,000–$24,999 2
$25,000–$49,999 3
$50,000–$74,999 4
$75,000 and over . . . . ⑤
Refused, no answer, don't know 6

19. (INTERVIEWER—RECORD SEX OF RESPONDENT):

(40)

Male 1
Female 2

20. May I have your name? My office calls about 10 percent of the people I talk with to verify that I have conducted the interview.

Gave name . . . . ①
Refused 2

_____Jordan Beasley_____
Name

Thank you for your time. Have a good day.

PART 4:
Data Analysis

A. Example of Improper Interviewer Recording of Response to an Open-Ended Question

Question: Why do you go to Burger King most often among fast food/quick service restaurants? (PROBE)

Response recorded:

The consumer seemed to think Burger King had better tasting food and better quality ingredients.

B. Example of Interviewer Failure to Probe a Response

Question: Same as Part A.

Only response recorded:

Because I like it.

C. Example of Proper Recording and Probing

Question: Same as Part A.

Response recorded:

Because I like it. (P)* I like it, and I go there most often because it is the closet place to where I work. (AE)** No.

*(P) is an interviewer mark indicating he or she has probed a response.

**(AE) is interviewer shorthand for "Anything else?" This gives the respondent an opportunity to expand on the original answer.

Figure 14.2

Recording of Open-Ended Questions

so on. The interviewer can record the response by circling the numeric code next to the answer given by the respondent. In this case, the respondent's answer was seven calls per day. The code 3 next to the category "6–10" (calls per day) is circled.

Open-ended questions create a coding dilemma. They were phrased in an open-ended manner because the researcher either had no idea what answers to expect or wanted a richer response than is possible with a closed-ended question. Like editing, the process of coding responses to open-ended questions is tedious and time-consuming. In addition, the procedure is to some degree subjective.[1] For these reasons, researchers tend to avoid open-ended questions.

The Coding Process

The process of coding responses to open-ended questions is as follows:

1. *List responses.* Coders at the research firm prepare lists of the actual responses given to each open-ended question on a particular survey. In studies of a few hundred respondents, all responses may be listed. With larger samples, responses given by a sample of respondents are listed. The listing of responses may be done as part of the editing process or as a separate step, often by the same individuals who edited the questionnaires.

2. *Consolidate responses.* A sample list of responses to an open-ended question is provided in Table 14.1. Examination of this list indicates that a number of the responses can be interpreted to mean essentially the same thing; therefore, they can be appropriately consolidated into a single category. This process of consolidation might yield the list shown in Table 14.2.

Consolidating requires a number of subjective decisions—for example, does response number 4 belong in category 1, or should it have its own category? These decisions typically are made by a qualified research analyst and may involve client input.

3. *Set codes.* A numeric code is assigned to each of the categories on the final consolidated list of responses. Code assignments for the sample beer study question are shown in Table 14.2.

4. *Enter codes.* After responses have been listed and consolidated and codes set, the last step is the actual entry of codes. This involves several substeps:

   a. Read responses to individual open-ended questions on questionnaires.

   b. Match individual responses with the consolidated list of response categories, and determine the appropriate numeric code for each response.

   c. Write the numeric code in the appropriate place on the questionnaire for the response to the particular question (see Table 14.3).[2]

Here's an example of the process, using the listing of responses shown in Table 14.1 and the consolidation and setting of codes shown in Table 14.2.

- You turn to the first questionnaire and read this response to the question "Why do you drink that brand of beer?": "Because it's cheaper."
- You compare this response with the consolidated response categories and decide that it best fits into the "Low/lower price" category. The numeric code associated with this category is 2 (see Table 14.2).
- You enter the code in the appropriate place on the questionnaire (see Table 14.3).

Table 14.1

Sample of Responses to Open-Ended Question

Question: Why do you drink that brand of beer? (BRAND MENTIONED IN ANSWER TO PREVIOUS QUESTION)

Sample responses:

1. Because it tastes better.
2. It has the best taste.
3. I like the way it tastes.
4. I don't like the heavy taste of other beers.
5. It is the cheapest.
6. I buy whatever beer is on sale. It is on sale most of the time.
7. It doesn't upset my stomach the way other brands do.
8. Other brands give me headaches. This one doesn't.
9. It has always been my brand.
10. I have been drinking it for over 20 years.
11. It is the brand that most of the guys at work drink.
12. All my friends drink it.
13. It is the brand my wife buys at the grocery store.
14. It is my wife's/husband's favorite brand.
15. I have no idea.
16. Don't know.
17. No particular reason.

Table 14.2

Consolidated Response Categories and Codes for Open-Ended Responses from Beer Study

Response Category Descriptor	Response Items from Table 14.1 Included	Assigned Numeric Code
Tastes better/like taste/tastes better than others	1, 2, 3, 4	1
Low/lower price	5, 6	2
Does not cause headache, stomach problems	7, 8	3
Long-term use, habit	9, 10	4
Friends drink it/influence of friends	11, 12	5
Wife/husband drinks/buys it	13, 14	6

Automated Coding Systems

With such interviewing technologies as CATI and Internet surveys, data entry and coding are completely eliminated for closed-ended questions. However, when the text of open-ended questions is electronically captured, a coding process is still required. A number of developments are making it likely that the tedious coding process for open-ended questions will soon be replaced with computer-based systems requiring limited high-level human intervention and decision making.

The TextSmart™ module of SPSS is one example of the new breed of automated coding systems. Algorithms based on semiotics[3] are at the heart of these systems and show great promise for speeding up the coding process, reducing its cost, and increasing its objectivity. Basically, these algorithms use the power of computers to search for patterns in open-ended responses and in group responses, based on certain key words and phrases.

Table 14.3

Example Questionnaire Setup for Open-Ended Questions

37. Why do you drink that brand of beer? (BRAND MENTIONED IN PREVIOUS QUESTION)?

(48) _____2_____

Because it's cheaper. (P) Nothing. (AE) Nothing.

Step Three: Data Entry

Once the questionnaires have been validated, edited, and coded, it's time for the next step in the process—data entry. We use the term **data entry** here to refer to the process of converting information to a form that can be read by a computer. This process requires a data entry device, such as a computer terminal or a personal computer, and a storage medium, such as magnetic tape, a floppy disk, or a hard (magnetic) disk.

Intelligent Entry Systems

Most data entry is done by means of an intelligent entry system. With **intelligent data entry,** the information being entered into the data entry device is checked for internal logic, either by that device or by another device connected to it. The intelligent entry system can be programmed to avoid certain types of errors at the point of data entry, such as entry of invalid or wild codes and violation of skip patterns.

Consider question 2 on the questionnaire in Figure 14.1. The five valid answers have the associated numeric codes 1 through 5. An intelligent data entry system programmed for valid codes would permit the data entry operator to enter only one of these codes in the field reserved for the response to this question. If the operator attempts to enter a code other than those defined as valid, the device will inform the data entry operator in some manner that there is a problem. The data entry device, for example, might beep and display a message on the screen that the entered code is invalid. It will not advance to the next appropriate field until the code has been corrected. Of course, it is still possible to incorrectly enter a 3 rather than the correct answer 2. Referring again to question 2, note that if the answer to the question is "Very unlikely" or "Don't know," then the data entry operator should skip to question 16. An intelligent data entry device will make this skip automatically.

The Data Entry Process

The validated, edited, and coded questionnaires have been given to a data entry operator seated in front of a personal computer or computer terminal. The data entry software system has been programmed for intelligent entry. The actual data entry process is ready to begin. Usually, the data are entered directly from the questionnaires, because experience has shown that a large number of errors are introduced when questionnaire data are transposed manually to coding sheets. Going directly from the questionnaire to the data entry device and associated storage medium is much more accurate and efficient. To better understand the mechanics of the process, look again at Figure 14.1.

- In the upper right-hand corner of the questionnaire, the number 001 is written. This number uniquely identifies the particular questionnaire, which should be the first questionnaire in the stack that the data entry operator is preparing to enter. This number is an important point of reference because it permits the data entry staff to refer back to the original document if any errors are identified in connection with the data input.

- To the left of the handwritten number 001 is (01–03). This tells the data entry operator that 001 should be entered into fields 01–03 of the data record. Throughout the questionnaire, the numbers in parentheses indicate the proper location on the data record for the circled code for the answer to each question. Question 1 has (04) associated with the codes for the answers to the question. Thus, the answer to this question would be entered in field 04 of the data record. Now, take a look at the open-ended question in Table 14.3. As with closed-ended questions, the number in parentheses refers to the field on the data record where the code or codes for the response to this question should be entered. Note the number 2 written in to the right of (48); a 2 should be entered in field 48 of the data record associated with this questionnaire.

Figure 14.1 clearly illustrates the relationship between the layout of the questionnaire, in terms of codes (numbers associated with different answers to questions) and fields (places on the data record where the code is entered), and the layout of the data record.

Scanning

As all students know, the scanning of documents (test scoring sheets) has been around for decades. It has been widely used in schools and universities as an efficient way to capture and score responses to multiple-choice questions. However, until recently, its use in marketing research has been limited. This limited use can be attributed to two factors: setup costs and the need to record all responses with a No. 2 pencil. Setup costs include the cost of special paper, special ink in the printing process, and very precise placement of the bubbles for recording responses. The break-even point, at which the savings in data entry costs exceeded the setup costs, was in the 10,000 to 12,000 survey range. Therefore, for most surveys, scanning was not feasible.

However, changes in **optical scanning** and the advent of personal computers have changed this equation. Today, questionnaires prepared with any one of a number of Windows word-processing software packages and printed on a laser printer or by a standard printing process can be readily scanned, using the appropriate software and a scanner attached to a personal computer. In addition, the latest technology permits respondents to fill out the survey using almost any type of writing implement (any type of pencil, ballpoint pen, or ink pen). This eliminates the need to provide respondents with a No. 2 pencil and greatly simplifies the process of mailing surveys. Finally, the latest technology does not require respondents to carefully shade the entire circle or square next to their response choices; they can put shading, a check mark, an X, or any other type of mark in the circle or square provided for the response choice.[4]

As a result of these developments, the use of scannable surveys is growing dramatically. An analyst who expects more than 400 to 500 surveys to be completed will find scannable surveys to be cost-effective.

Though no reliable volume figures are available, it is an accepted fact that the amount of survey data being captured electronically is increasing. For example, electronic data capture is used in computer-assisted telephone interviewing, Internet surveys, disks-by-mail surveys, and TouchScreen kiosk surveys.

optical scanning
A form of data entry in which responses on questionnaires are read in automatically by the data entry device.

Data Entry at SDR, Incorporated

FOR MORE THAN 20 YEARS, ANN MORRELL HAS DIRECTED THE data entry effort at SDR, Incorporated, a data analysis research agency in Atlanta, Georgia. After obtaining a bachelor's degree in statistics from Hollins College in Virginia, Morrell joined SDR in order to contribute to an innovative firm that was a leader in the marketing research field, with its own proprietary software for tabulating survey results electronically.

Decades later, Morrell has acquired a wise perspective on managing data entry demands of projects. According to Morrell, one of the crucial steps in fielding a survey that can be processed within a client's budget is avoiding too many open-ended responses on the questionnaire. Problems typically arise (1) when a question offers both the response of "Other" and space to give details about the "Other" answer and (2) when respondents are asked, "Please share with us other comments or suggestions you might have" at the end of a questionnaire. Instead of numerical entries, such questions require manual coding of the responses according to a classification scheme and/or electronic recording of a verbatim transcription of the text response.

"Coding is the most expensive and most subjective part of the data entry process," Morrell said. "You and I could read the same text and code differently. As a result of this, the client and the research agency's project manager must weigh the level of detail in questions' structured responses with the number of responses likely to require open-ended coding and verbatim recording. If you have too many responses to code, the analysis can be cumbersome and understanding detailed responses can be very expensive.

"The key factor in having the right level of structured and unstructured responses to questions is the incidence rate of open-ended entries on the questionnaire," Morrell said. "On employee satisfaction surveys, the labor required for coding or verbatim recording is likely to be enormous. Loads and loads of codes will be recorded. Some respondents even attach additional pages to the survey form to convey all of their comments. On the other hand, projects with a lower degree of involvement for the respondents will have a lower demand for coding and verbatim work. Some clients may choose to not code or to not enter these few responses."

The rate of incidence for response coding is highly variable, according to Morrell. When estimating the costs for the data entry part of the project, the research agency's project manager must document the rate of incidence for response coding estimated by the client. "If you estimate a 30 percent incidence rate for open-ended responses, and it turns out to be 60 percent, then you need to go back to the client and apprise them of this," Morrell said. "We have only encountered troubles with clients when we haven't adequately documented the estimate of the rate of incidence for response coding before the study was fielded." ∎

Step Four: Machine Cleaning of Data

At this point, the data from all questionnaires have been entered and stored in the computer that will be used to process them. It is time to do final error checking before proceeding to the tabulation and statistical analysis of the survey results. Many colleges have one or more statistical software packages available for the tabulation and statistical analysis of data, including SAS (Statistical Analysis System) and SPSS (Statistical Package for the Social Sciences), which have proven to be the most popular mainframe computer statistical packages. Colleges may also have personal computer versions of SPSS and SAS; in addition to other PC statistical packages. The number of these other PC packages is large and growing.

Regardless of which computer package is used, it is important to do a final computerized error check of the data, or what is sometimes referred to as **machine cleaning of data.** This may be done through error checking routines and/or marginal reports.

Some computer programs permit the user to write **error checking routines.** These routines include a number of statements to check for various conditions. For example, if a particular field on the data records for a study should be coded with only a 1 or a 2, a logical statement can be written to check for the presence of any other code in that field. Some of the more sophisticated packages generate reports indicating how many times a particular condition was violated and the data records on which it was violated. With this list, the user can refer to the original questionnaires and determine the appropriate values.

Table 14.4 illustrates the **marginal report,** another approach to machine cleaning often used for error checking. The first row of this report lists the fields of the data record. The columns show the frequency with which each possible value was encountered in each field. For example, the second row in Table 14.4 shows that in field 111 of the data records for this study there are 100 "1" punches, 100 "2" punches, 1 "3" punch, and 99 "10" punches. This report permits the user to determine whether inappropriate codes were entered and whether skip patterns were properly followed. If all the numbers are consistent, there is no need for further cleaning. However, if logical errors (violated skip patterns and impossible codes) are detected, then the appropriate original questionnaires must be located and the corrections made in the computer data file. Note that these procedures cannot identify situations in which an interviewer or data entry operator incorrectly entered a 2 for a "no" response instead of a 1 for a "yes" response.

This is the final error check in the process. When this step is completed, the computer data file should be ready for tabulation and statistical analysis. Table 14.5 shows the data for the first 50 respondents (out of a total of 400) for the study associated with the questionnaire shown in Figure 14.1. Note that the apparent gaps in the data are a result of the skip called for in question 4. Also note that the gender data for respondent 001 has been filled in with a 2 for female.

machine cleaning of data
A final computerized error check of data.

error checking routines
Computer programs that accept instructions from the user to check for logical errors in the data.

marginal report
A computer-generated table of the frequencies of the responses to each question, used to monitor entry of valid codes and correct use of skip patterns.

Table 14.4

Sample Marginal Report (Marginal Counts of 300 Records)

FIELD	1	2	3	4	5	6	7	8	9	10	11	12	BL	TOT
111	100	100	1	0	0	0	0	0	0	99	0	0	0	300
112	30	30	30	30	30	30	30	30	30	0	0	0	0	300
113	30	30	30	30	30	30	30	30	30	30	0	0	0	300
114	67	233	0	0	0	0	0	0	0	0	0	0	0	300
115	192	108	0	0	0	0	0	0	0	0	0	0	0	300
116	108	190	0	0	0	0	0	0	0	0	0	2	0	300
117	13	35	8	0	2	136	95	7	2	0	0	0	2	298
118	0	0	0	0	0	0	0	0	0	0	0	2	298	2
119	29	43	12	1	2	48	50	6	4	1	0	0	104	196
1111	6	16	6	1	1	10	18	4	2	0	0	0	236	64
1113	3	4	1	1	0	1	2	0	1	0	0	0	288	12
1115	0	0	0	1	1	0	0	2	0	0	0	0	296	4
1117	24	2	22	0	1	239	9	2	0	0	0	0	1	299
1118	0	0	0	0	0	0	0	0	0	0	0	0	299	1
1119	4	49	6	0	0	81	117	5	2	0	0	0	36	264
1120	0	0	0	0	0	0	0	0	0	0	0	36	264	36
1121	5	60	6	0	0	84	116	4	3	1	0	0	21	279
1122	0	0	0	0	0	0	0	0	0	0	0	21	279	21
1123	118	182	0	0	0	0	0	0	0	0	0	0	0	300
1124	112	187	0	0	0	0	0	0	0	0	0	0	1	299
1125	47	252	0	0	0	0	0	0	0	0	0	1	0	300
1126	102	198	0	0	0	0	0	0	0	0	0	0	0	300
1127	5	31	5	1	0	33	31	9	1	0	0	0	184	116
1128	0	0	0	0	0	0	0	0	0	0	0	2	298	2
1129	0	3	1	0	0	4	8	2	1	0	0	0	281	19
1131	7	16	3	0	2	60	21	3	0	0	0	0	188	112
1133	1	3	1	0	0	2	3	1	0	0	0	0	289	11

Step Five: Tabulation and Statistical Analysis

The survey results have been stored in a computer file and are free of logical data entry and interviewer recording errors. The next step is to tabulate the survey results.

One-Way Frequency Tables

one-way frequency table
A table showing the number of respondents choosing each answer to a survey question.

The most basic tabulation is the **one-way frequency table,** which shows the number of respondents who gave each possible answer to each question. An example of this type of table appears in Table 14.6. This table shows that 144 consumers (48 percent) said they would choose a hospital in Saint Paul, 146 (48.7 percent) said they would choose a hospital in Minneapolis, and 10 (3.3 percent) said they didn't know which location they would choose. A printout is generated with a one-way frequency table for every question on the survey. In most instances, a one-way frequency table is the first summary of survey results seen by the research

PART 4:
Data Analysis

Table 14.5

Printout of Data for the First 50 Respondents for Cellular Telephone Survey

```
001323101060500    23443113244444313232 1521
00224                                  23412
00334                                  49622
00414                                  36221
00524                                  33312
00634                                  22612
00714                                  21321
008221  020405031033423244443444 4222229321
00925                                  36311
01044                                  23311
011613102400503301342344444344433 22330321
012622  0140072007334444444444444 132330511
013221  010603060323131233332332212 3216211
01424                                  29321
01514                                  40121
01624                                  22612
01774                                  20622
01854                                  34621
01924                                  25212
02024                                  23622
02114                                  16611
02214                                  36211
02314                                  15611
024131    0010100410221334444444444 2229611
02524                                  26621
026131  010103020312422142224441 4223222611
02724                                  10122
02814                                  59622
02924                                  39622
03024                                  49611
03134                                  53621
03234                                  32622
03321    01            124444444444 4211220211
03424                                  32622
035311  04103004301331311311131312 11220121
036232303010502013344144333442442 32320622
03724                                  37622
03814                                  40121
03934                                  30121
04024                                  16121
04124                                  26311
04264                                  26411
04324                                  20321
04414                                  26311
04524                                  19321
04634                                  19222
04724                                  29621
04824                                  31422
04924                                  33121
05014                                  21311
```

Table 14.6

One-Way Frequency Table

Q.30 If you or a member of your family were to require hospitalization in the future, and the procedure could be performed in Minneapolis or St. Paul, where would you choose to go?

	Total
Total	300
	100%
To a hospital in St. Paul	144
	48.0%
To a hospital in Minneapolis	146
	48.7%
Don't know/no response	10
	3.3%

analyst. In addition to frequencies, these tables typically indicate the percentage of those responding who gave each possible response to a question.

An issue that must be dealt with when one-way frequency tables are generated is what base to use for the percentages for each table. There are three options for a base:

1. *Total respondents.* If 300 people are interviewed in a particular study and the decision is to use total respondents as the base for calculating percentages, then the percentages in each one-way frequency table will be based on 300 respondents.

2. *Number of people asked the particular question.* Because most questionnaires have skip patterns, not all respondents are asked all questions. For example, suppose question 4 on a particular survey asked whether the person owned any dogs and 200 respondents indicated they were dog owners. Since questions 5 and 6 on the same survey were to be asked only of those individuals who owned a dog, questions 5 and 6 should have been asked of only 200 respondents. In most instances, it would be appropriate to use 200 as the base for percentages associated with the one-way frequency tables for questions 5 and 6.

3. *Number of people answering the question.* Another alternative base for computing percentages in one-way frequency tables is the number of people who actually answered a particular question. Under this approach, if 300 people were asked a particular question but 28 indicated "Don't know" or gave no response, then the base for the percentages would be 272.

Ordinarily, the number of people who were asked a particular question is used as the base for all percentages throughout the tabulations, but there may be special cases in which other bases are judged appropriate. Table 14.7 is a one-way frequency table in which three different bases are used for calculating percentages.

Some questions, by their nature, solicit more than one response from respondents. For example, consumers might be asked to name all brands of vacuum cleaners that come to mind. Most people will be able to name more than one brand. Therefore, when these answers are tabulated, there will be more responses than respondents. If 200 consumers are surveyed and the average consumer names three brands, then there will be 200 respondents and 600 answers. The question is, should percentages in frequency tables showing the results for these questions be based on the number of respondents or the number of responses? Table 14.8 shows percentages calculated using both bases. Most commonly, marketing researchers compute percentages for multiple-response questions on the basis of the number of respondents, reasoning that the client is primarily interested in the proportion of people who gave a particular answer.

Crosstabulations

Crosstabulations are likely to be the next step in analysis. They represent a simple-to-understand, yet powerful, analytical tool. Many marketing research studies go no further than crosstabulations in terms of analysis. The idea is to look at the responses to one question in relation to the responses to one or more other questions. Table 14.9 shows a simple crosstabulation that examines the relationship between cities consumers are willing to consider for hospitalization and their age. This crosstabulation includes frequencies and percentages, with the percentages based on column totals. This table shows an interesting relationship between age and likelihood of choosing Minneapolis or St. Paul for hospitalization. Consumers in successively older age groups are increasingly likely to choose St. Paul and increasingly less likely to choose Minneapolis.

Following are a number of considerations regarding the setup of crosstabulation tables and the determination of percentages within them:

- The previous discussion regarding the selection of the appropriate base for percentages applies to crosstabulation tables as well.
- Three different percentages may be calculated for each cell in a crosstabulation table: column, row, and total percentages. Column percentages are based on the column total, row percentages are based on the row total, and total percentages are based on the table total. Table 14.10 shows a crosstabulation table in which the frequency and all three of the percentages are shown for each cell in the table.
- A common way of setting up crosstabulation tables is to use columns to represent factors such as demographics and lifestyle characteristics, which are expected to be predictors of the state of mind, behavior, or intentions data

The base for each percentage must be determined before one-way frequency tables are run. If a survey question asks whether the person has a dog and 200 respondents indicate that they do, further questions designated for dog owners should have only 200 respondents.

crosstabulation
Examination of the responses to one question relative to the responses to one or more other questions.

Table 14.7

One-Way Frequency Table Using Three Different Bases for Calculating Percentages

Q.35 Why would you not consider going to St. Paul for hospitalization?

	Total* Respondents	Total Asked	Total Answering
Total	300 100%	64 100%	56 100%
They aren't good/service poor	18 6%	18 28%	18 32%
St. Paul doesn't have the services/equipment that Minneapolis does	17 6%	17 27%	17 30%
St. Paul is too small	6 2%	6 9%	6 11%
Bad publicity	4 1%	4 6%	4 7%
Other	11 4%	11 17%	11 20%
Don't know/no response	8 3%	8 13%	

*A total of 300 respondents were surveyed. Only 64 were asked this question because in the previous question those respondents said they would not consider going to St. Paul for hospitalization. Only 56 respondents gave an answer other than "Don't know."

Table 14.8

Percentages for a Multiple-Response Question Calculated on the Bases of Total Respondents and Total Responses

Q.34 To which of the following towns and cities would you consider going for hospitalization?

	Total Respondents	Total Responses
Total	300 100%	818 100%
Minneapolis	265 88.3%	265 32.4%
St. Paul	240 80.0%	240 29.3%
Bloomington	112 37.3%	112 13.7%
Rochester	92 30.7%	92 11.2%
Minnetonka	63 21.0%	63 7.7%
Eagan	46 15.3%	46 5.6%

PART 4:
Data Analysis

Table 14.9

Sample Crosstabulation

Q.30 If you or a member of your family were to require hospitalization in the future, and the procedure could be performed in Minneapolis or St. Paul, where would you choose to go?

		Age			
	Total	**18–34**	**35–54**	**55–64**	**65 or Over**
Total	300	65	83	51	100
	100%	100%	100%	100%	100%
To a hospital in St. Paul	144	21	40	25	57
	48.0%	32.3%	48.2%	49.0%	57.0%
To a hospital in Minneapolis	146	43	40	23	40
	48.7%	66.2%	48.2%	45.1%	40.0%
Don't know/no response	10	1	3	3	3
	3.3%	1.5%	3.6%	5.9%	3.0%

shown as rows of the table. In such tables, percentages usually are calculated on the basis of column totals. This approach permits easy comparisons of the relationship between, say, lifestyle characteristics and expected predictors such as sex or age. For example, in Table 14.9, this approach facilitates examination of how people in different age groups differ in regard to the particular factor under examination.

Table 14.10

Crosstabulation Table with Column, Row, and Total Percentages*

Q.34 To which of the following towns and cities would you consider going for hospitalization?

	Total	**Male**	**Female**
Total	300	67	233
	100.0%	100.0%	100.0%
	100.0%	22.3%	77.7%
	100.0%	22.3%	77.7%
St. Paul	265	63	202
	88.3%	94.0%	86.7%
	100.0%	23.6%	76.2%
	88.3%	21.0%	67.3%
Minneapolis	240	53	187
	80.0%	79.1%	80.3%
	100.0%	22.1%	77.9%
	80.0%	17.7%	62.3%
Bloomington	112	22	90
	37.3%	32.8%	38.6%
	100.0%	19.6%	80.4%
	37.3%	7.3%	30.0%

*Percentages listed are column, row, and total percentages, respectively.

Crosstabulations provide a powerful and easily understood approach to the summarization and analysis of survey research results. However, it is easy to become swamped by the sheer volume of computer printouts if a careful tabulation plan has not been developed. The crosstabulation plan should be created with the research objectives and hypotheses in mind. Because the results of a particular survey might be crosstabulated in an almost endless number of ways, it is important for the analyst to exercise judgment and select from all the possibilities only those crosstabulations truly responsive to the research objectives of the project. Spreadsheet programs such as Excel and nearly all statistics packages (SAS, SPSS, SYSTAT, STATISTICA) can generate crosstabulations. Chapter 15 discusses the chi-square test, which can be used to determine whether the results in a particular crosstabulation table are significantly different from what would be expected based on chance. In other words, confronted with the question of whether the response patterns of men significantly differ from those of women, the analyst can use this statistical procedure to determine whether the differences between the two groups likely occurred because of chance or likely reflect real differences.

A complex crosstabulation, generated using the UNCLE software package, is shown in Table 14.11. UNCLE was designed with the special needs of marketing researchers in mind and is widely used in the marketing research industry. As indicated, this more complex table is sometimes referred to as a *stub and banner table*. The column headings are the banner and the row titles are the stub. In this single table, the relationship between marital status and each of seven other variables is explored.

Table 14.11

A Stub and Banner Table

North Community College—Anywhere, U.S.A.
Q.1c. Are you single, married, or formerly married?

	Total	Zones			Gender		Age		
		1	2	3	M	F	18–34	35–54	55 and Over
Total	300	142	103	55	169	131	48	122	130
	100%	100%	100%	100%	100%	100%	100%	100%	100%
Married	228	105	87	36	131	97	36	97	95
	76%	74%	84%	65%	78%	74%	75%	80%	73%
Single	5	1	2	2	4	1	2	1	2
	2%	1%	2%	4%	2%	1%	4%	1%	2%
Formerly married	24	11	10	3	12	12	3	9	12
	8%	8%	10%	5%	7%	9%	6%	7%	9%
Refused to answer	43	25	4	14	22	21	7	15	21
	14%	18%	4%	25%	13%	16%	15%	12%	16%

PART 4:
Data Analysis

Graphic Representations of Data

You have probably heard the saying "One picture is worth a thousand words." Graphic representations of data use pictures rather than tables to present research results. Results—particularly key results—can be presented most powerfully and efficiently through graphs.

Marketing researchers have always known that important findings identified by crosstabulation and statistical analysis could be best presented graphically. However, in the early years of marketing research, the preparation of graphs was tedious, difficult, and time-consuming. The advent of personal computers, coupled with graphics software and laser printers, has changed all of this. Spreadsheet programs such as Excel have extensive graphics capabilities, particularly in their Windows versions. In addition, programs designed for creating presentations, such as PowerPoint, permit the user to generate a wide variety of high-quality graphics with ease. With these programs, it is possible to do the following:

- Quickly produce graphs.
- Display those graphs on the computer screen.
- Make desired changes and redisplay.
- Print final copies on a laser, inkjet, or dot matrix printer.

All of the graphs shown in this section were produced using a personal computer, a laser printer, and a graphics software package.

Race			Family Profile		Vote History		Registered Voter	
White	Black	Other	Child <18 years	Child >18 years	2–3 Times	4 Times or More	Yes	No
268	28	4	101	53	104	196	72	228
100%	100%	100%	100%	100%	100%	100%	100%	100%
207	18	3	82	39	80	148	58	170
77%	64%	75%	81%	74%	77%	76%	81%	75%
5	—	—	—	—	2	3	1	4
2%	—	—	—	—	2%	2%	1%	2%
8	6	—	5	6	10	14	3	21
7%	21%	—	5%	11%	10%	7%	4%	9%
38	4	1	14	8	12	31	10	33
14%	14%	25%	14%	15%	12%	16%	14%	14%

Doing Frequency and Crosstabulation Tables in Excel

IF YOU HAVE YOUR DATA IN AN EXCEL SPREADSHEET OR IF YOU CAN IMPORT THEM into an Excel spreadsheet, then you can use the Pivot Table feature in Excel to produce one-way frequency tables and crosstabulations. The spreadsheet should be prepared so that the columns represent numeric codes for responses to various survey questions and the rows represent responses given by each person surveyed.

To create a one-way frequency table, do the following:

- Select the Data sheet in the Pivot Table template and click on a cell containing data.
- Select the command Pivot Table Report under the Data menu.
- A dialog box will appear. Make sure the Excel list or database is selected. Click the Next button.
- In the Range box, enter the range that contains the database. Click the Next button.

- Another dialog box will appear. It is fairly detailed, with a number of different options. On the right side of the dialog box, you will see a list of all the fields in the database. In this case, they should be survey questions. The different answers to a question should appear as rows in the table. If, for example, you had the label Q1 at the top of the column that includes the responses to Q1 for all respondents, then you would drag the Q1 button into the area labeled ROW and drop it there.
- The button should read Sum of Q1. However, we want a count or frequency for Q1. Double-click on the Sum of Q1 button. In the dialog box that appears, select Count in the list and press the OK button. Count of Q1 should now appear in the DATA area.
- Click the Finish button. The tabulation you requested will appear on a separate sheet.[5]

Line Charts

Line charts are perhaps the simplest form of graphs. They are particularly useful for presenting a given measurement taken at several points over time. Figure 14.3 shows monthly sales data for Just Add Water, a retailer of women's swimwear. The results reveal similar sales patterns for 1997 and 1998, with peaks in June and generally low sales in January through March and September through December. Just Add Water is evaluating the sales data to identify product lines that it might add to improve sales during those periods.

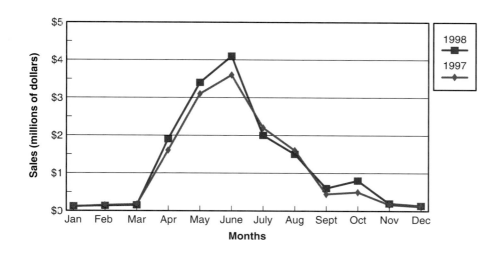

Figure 14.3

Line Chart for Sales of Women's Swimwear

Pie Charts

Pie charts are another type of graph that is frequently used. They are appropriate for displaying marketing research results in a wide range of situations. Figure 14.4 shows radio music preferences gleaned from a survey of residents of several Gulf Coast metropolitan areas in Louisiana, Mississippi, and Alabama. Note the three-dimensional effect produced by the software.

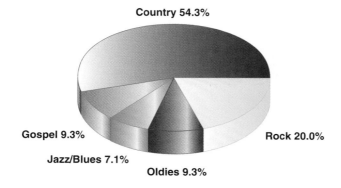

Bar Charts

Bar charts are the most flexible of the three types of graphs discussed in this section. Anything that can be shown in a line graph or a pie chart also can be shown in a bar chart. In addition, many things that cannot be shown—or effectively shown—in other types of graphs can be readily illustrated in bar charts. Four types of bar charts are discussed here.

1. *Plain bar chart.* As the name suggests, plain bar charts are the simplest form of bar chart. The same information displayed in the pie chart in Figure 14.4 is shown in the bar chart in Figure 14.5. Draw your own conclusions regarding

Figure 14.5

**Simple Two-Dimensional
Bar Chart for Types of
Music Listened to
Most Often**

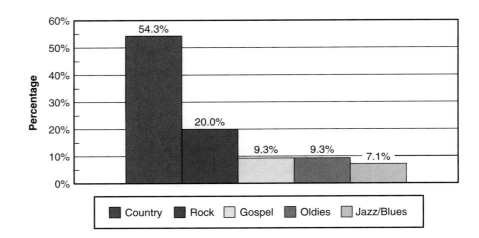

whether the pie chart or the bar chart is the more effective way to present this information. Figure 14.5 is a traditional two-dimensional chart. Many of the software packages available today can take the same information and present it with a three-dimensional effect, as shown in Figure 14.6. Again, decide for yourself which approach is visually more appealing and interesting.

Figure 14.6

**Simple Three-Dimensional
Bar Chart for Types of
Music Listened to
Most Often**

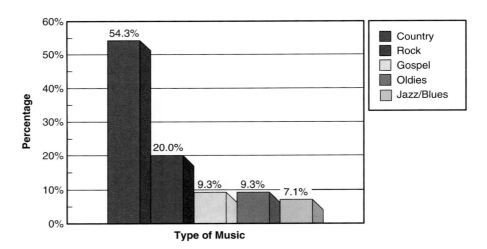

2. *Clustered bar chart.* The clustered bar chart is one of three type of bar charts useful for showing the results of crosstabulations. The radio music preference results are crosstabulated by age in Figure 14.7. The graph shows that country music is mentioned most often as the preferred format by those over 35 and those 35 or under. The graph also shows that rock music is a close second for those 35 or under and is least frequently mentioned by those over 35. The results suggest that if the target audience is those in the 35 or under age group, then a mix of country and rock music is appropriate. A focus on country music probably would be the most efficient approach for those over 35.

PART 4:
Data Analysis

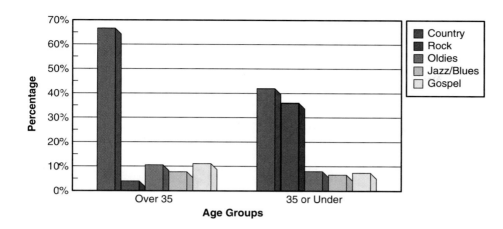

3. *Stacked bar chart.* Like clustered bar charts, stacked bar charts are helpful in graphically representing crosstabulation results. The same music preference data shown in Figure 14.7 are presented as a stacked bar chart in Figure 14.8.

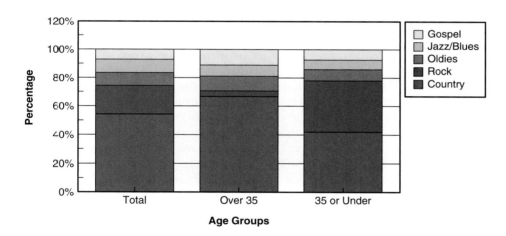

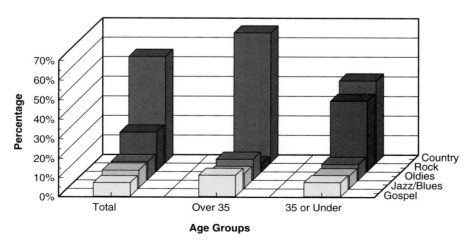

4. *Multiple-row, three-dimensional bar chart.* This type of bar chart provides what we believe to be the most visually appealing way of presenting crosstabulation information. The same music preference data displayed in Figures 14.7 and 14.8 are presented in a multiple-row, three-dimensional bar chart in Figure 14.9.

Descriptive Statistics

Descriptive statistics are the most efficient means of summarizing the characteristics of large sets of data. In a statistical analysis, the analyst calculates one number or a few numbers that reveal something about the characteristics of large sets of data.

Measures of Central Tendency

Before beginning this section, you should review the types of data scales presented in Chapter 9. Recall that there are four basic types of measurement scales: nominal, ordinal, interval, and ratio. Nominal and ordinal scales are sometimes referred to as nonmetric scales, whereas interval and ratio scales are referred to as metric scales. Many of the statistical procedures discussed in this section and in following sections require metric scales, while others are designed for nonmetric scales.

    The three measures of central tendency are the arithmetic mean, median, and mode. The **mean** is properly computed only from interval or ratio (metric) data. It is computed by adding the values for all observations for a particular variable, such as age, and dividing the resulting sum by the number of observations. With survey data, the exact value of the variable may not be known; it may be known only that a particular case falls in a particular category. For example, an age category on a survey might be 18–34 years of age. If a person falls into this category, the person's exact age is known to be somewhere between 18 and 34. With grouped data, the midpoint of each category is multiplied by the number of observations in that category, the resulting totals are summed, and the total is then divided by the total number of observations. This process is summarized in the following formula:

mean
The sum of the values for all observations of a variable divided by the number of observations.

$$\overline{X} = \frac{\displaystyle\sum_{i=1}^{h} f_i X_i}{n}$$

where f_i = frequency of the ith class
            X_i = midpoint of that class
            h = number of classes
            n = total number of observations

median
The value below which 50 percent of the observations fall.

The **median** can be computed for all types of data except nominal data. It is calculated by finding the value below which 50 percent of the observations fall. If all the values for a particular variable were put in an array in either ascending or descending order, the median would be the middle value in that array. The median is often used to summarize variables such as income when the researcher is concerned that the arithmetic mean will be affected by a small number of extreme values and, therefore, will not accurately reflect the predominant central tendency of that variable for that group.

The **mode** can be computed for any type of data (nominal, ordinal, interval, or ratio). It is determined by finding the value that occurs most frequently. In a frequency distribution, the mode is the value that has the highest frequency. One problem with using the mode is that a particular data set may have more than one mode. If three different values occur with the same level of frequency and that frequency is higher than the frequency for any other value, then the data set has three modes. The mean, median, and mode for sample data on beer consumption are shown in Table 14.12.

mode
The value that occurs most frequently.

Measures of Dispersion

Frequently used measures of dispersion include standard deviation, variance, and range. Whereas measures of central tendency indicate typical values for a particular variable, measures of dispersion indicate how spread out the data are. The dangers associated with relying only on measures of central tendency are suggested by the example shown in Table 14.13. Note that average beer consumption is the same in both markets—3 cans/bottles/glasses. However, the standard deviation is greater in market two, indicating more dispersion in the data. Whereas the mean suggests that the two markets are the same, the added information provided by the standard deviation indicates that they are different.

Table 14.12

Mean, Median, and Mode for Beer Consumption Data

A total of 10 beer drinkers (drink one or more cans, bottles, or glasses of beer per day on the average) were interviewed in a mall-intercept study. They were asked how many cans, bottles, or glasses of beer they drink in an average day.

Respondent	Number of Cans/ Bottles/Glasses Per Day
1	2
2	2
3	3
4	2
5	5
6	1
7	2
8	2
9	10
10	1

Mode = 2 cans/bottles/glasses
Median = 2 cans/bottles/glasses
Mean = 3 cans/bottles/glasses

Table 14.13

Measures of Dispersion and Measures of Central Tendency

Consider the beer consumption data presented in Table 14.12. Assume that interviewing was conducted in two markets. The results for both markets are shown.

Respondent	Number of Cans/Bottles/Glasses Market One	Number of Cans/Bottles/Glasses Market Two
1	2	1
2	2	1
3	3	1
4	2	1
5	5	1
6	1	1
7	2	1
8	2	3
9	10	10
10	1	10
Mean	3	3
Standard deviation	2.7	3.7

AcuPOLL Finds New Ways to Conduct Concept Tests

ELECTRONIC MEANS OF COLLECTING DATA HAVE BEGUN TO REVOlutionize many types of marketing research projects, such as concept testing. Prior to the introduction of computer-assisted interviewing software, data entry was labor-intensive and prone to nagging errors. Through a technological innovation, AcuPOLL® Precision Research of Cincinnati, Ohio, has brought data entry and data analysis into a system which renders almost instantaneous results for samples of up to 200 in size. This breakthrough has special value in concept-testing projects of new product development programs.

"Prior to AcuPOLL, researchers were limited to three or four ideas in a concept test," AcuPOLL CEO Jack Gordon said. "It was believed that beyond this number an order effect would occur (where respondents would compare additional objects to the first three or four presented). We have found no basis for this order effect using the AcuPOLL system. We can now test 40 ideas with the same set of consumers."[6] ■

The formula for computing the standard deviation for a sample of observations is as follows:

$$S = \sqrt{\frac{\sum_{i=1}^{n}(X_i - \bar{X})^2}{n-1}}$$

where
S = sample standard deviation
X_i = value of the ith observation
$\bar{X}$ = sample mean
n = sample size

The variance is calculated by using the formula for standard deviation with the square root sign removed. That is, the sum of the squared deviations from the mean is divided by the number of observations minus 1. Finally, the range is equal to the maximum value for a particular variable minus the minimum value for that variable.

Percentages and Statistical Tests

In performing basic data analysis, the research analyst is faced with the decision of whether to use measures of central tendency (mean, median, mode) or percentages (one-way frequency tables, crosstabulations). Responses to questions either are categorical or take the form of continuous variables. Categorical variables such as "Occupation" (coded 1 for professional/managerial, 2 for clerical, etc.) limit the analyst to reporting the frequency and relative percentage with which each category was encountered. Variables such as age can be continuous or categorical, depending on how the information was obtained. For example, an interviewer can ask people their actual age or ask them which category (under 35, 35 or older) includes their age. If actual age data are available, mean age can be readily computed. If categories are used, one-way frequency tables and crosstabulations are the most obvious choices for analysis. However, continuous data can be put into categories, and means can be estimated for categorical data by using the formula for computing a mean for grouped data (presented earlier).

Finally, statistical tests are available that can indicate whether two means—for example, average expenditures by men and average expenditures by women at fast food restaurants—or two percentages differ to a greater extent than would be expected by chance (sampling error) or whether there is a significant relationship between two variables in a crosstabulation table. These tests are discussed in Chapter 15.

Occupation is an example of a categorical variable. The only results that can be reported for a variable of this type are the frequency and the relative percentage with which each category was encountered.

Summary

Once the questionnaires have been returned from the field, a five-step process takes place. These steps are (1) validation and editing, which are quality control checks, (2) coding, (3) data entry, (4) machine cleaning of data, and (5) tabulation and statistical analysis. The first step in the process, making sure that the data have integrity, is critical. Otherwise, the age-old adage is true: "Garbage in, garbage out." Validation involves determining with as much certainty as possible that each questionnaire is, in fact, a valid interview. A valid interview in this sense is one that was conducted in an appropriate manner. The objective of validation is to detect interviewer fraud or failure to follow key instructions. Validation is accomplished by recontacting a certain percentage of the respondents surveyed by each interviewer. Any surveys found to be fraudulent are eliminated from the database. After the validation process is completed, editing begins. Editing involves checking for interviewer and respondent mistakes—making certain that all required questions were answered, that skip patterns were followed properly, and that responses to open-ended questions were accurately recorded.

Upon completion of the editing, the next step is to code the data. Most questions on surveys are closed-ended and precoded, which means that numeric codes already have been assigned to the various responses on the questionnaire. With open-ended questions, the researcher has no idea in advance what the responses will be. Therefore, the coder must establish numeric codes for response categories by listing actual responses to open-ended questions and then consolidating those responses and assigning numeric codes to the consolidated categories. Once a coding sheet has been created, all questionnaires are coded using the coding sheet categories.

The next step is data entry. Today, most data entry is done by means of intelligent entry systems that check the internal logic of the data. The data typically are entered directly from the questionnaires. New developments in optical scanning have made a more automated approach to data entry cost-effective for smaller projects.

Machine cleaning of data is a final, computerized error check of the data, performed through the use of error checking routines and/or marginal reports. Error checking routines indicate whether or not certain conditions have been met. A marginal report is a type of frequency table that helps the user determine whether inappropriate codes were entered and whether skip patterns were properly followed.

The final step in the data analysis process is tabulation of the data. The most basic tabulation involves a one-way frequency table, which indicates the number of respondents who gave each possible answer to each question. Generating one-way frequency tables requires the analyst to determine a basis for percentages. For example, are the percentages to be calculated based on total respondents, number of people asked a particular question, or number answering a particular question? Tabulation of data is often followed by crosstabulation—examination of the responses to one question in relation to the responses to one or more other questions. Crosstabulation is a powerful and easily understood approach to the analysis of survey research results.

Statistical measures provide an even more powerful way to analyze data sets. The most commonly used statistical measures are those of central tendency: the arithmetic mean, median, and mode. The arithmetic mean is computed only from interval or ratio data by adding the values for all observations of a particular variable and dividing the resulting sum by the number of observations. The median can be computed for all types of data except nominal data by finding the value below which 50 percent of the observations fall. The mode can be computed for any type of data by simply finding the value that occurs most frequently. The arithmetic mean is, by far, the most commonly used measure of central tendency.

In addition to central tendency, researchers often want to have an indication of the dispersion of the data. Measures of dispersion include standard deviation, variance, and range.

Key Terms & Definitions

validation   The process of ascertaining that interviews actually were conducted as specified.

editing   The process of ascertaining that questionnaires were filled out properly and completely.

skip pattern   Sequence in which later questions are asked, based on a respondent's answer to an earlier question.

coding   The process of grouping and assigning numeric codes to the various responses to a question.

data entry   The process of converting information to an electronic form.

intelligent data entry   A form of data entry in which the information being entered into the data entry device is checked for internal logic, either by that device or by another device connected to it.

optical scanning   A form of data entry in which responses on questionnaires are read in automatically by the data entry device.

machine cleaning of data   A final computerized error check of data.

error checking routines   Computer programs that accept instructions from the user to check for logical errors in the data.

marginal report   A computer-generated table of the frequencies of the responses to each question, used to monitor entry of valid codes and correct use of skip patterns.

one-way frequency table   A table showing the number of respondents choosing each answer to a survey question.

crosstabulation   Examination of the responses to one question relative to the responses to one or more other questions.

mean   The sum of the values for all observations of a variable divided by the number of observations.

median   The value below which 50 percent of the observations fall.

mode   The value that occurs most frequently.

Questions for Review & Critical Thinking

1. What is the difference between measurement validity and interview validation?

2. Assume that Sally Smith, an interviewer, completed 50 questionnaires. Ten of the questionnaires were validated by calling the respondents and asking them one opinion question and two demographic questions over again. One respondent claimed that his age category was 30–40, when the age category marked on the questionnaire was 20–30. On another questionnaire, in response to the question "What is the most important problem facing our city government?" the interviewer had written, "The city council is too eager to raise taxes." When the interview was validated, the respondent said, "The city tax rate is too high." As a validator, would you assume that these were honest mistakes and accept the entire lot of 50 interviews as valid? If not, what would you do?

3. What is meant by the editing process? Should editors be allowed to fill in what they think a respondent meant in response to open-ended questions if the information seems incomplete? Why or why not?

4. Give an example of a skip pattern on a questionnaire. Why is it important to always follow the skip patterns correctly?

5. It has been said that, to some degree, coding of open-ended questions is an art. Would you agree or disagree? Why? Suppose that, after coding a large number of questionnaires, the researcher notices that many responses have ended up in the "Other" category. What might this imply? What could be done to correct this problem?

6. Describe an intelligent data entry system. Why are data typically entered directly from the questionnaire into the data entry device?

7. What is the purpose of machine cleaning data? Give some examples of how data can be machine cleaned. Do you think that machine cleaning is an expensive and unnecessary step in the data tabulation process? Why or why not?

8. It has been said that a crosstabulation of two variables offers the researcher more insightful information than does a one-way frequency table. Why might this be true? Give an example.

9. Illustrate the various alternatives for using percentages in one-way frequency tables. Explain the logic of choosing one alternative method over another.

10. Explain the differences among the mean, median, and mode. Give an example in which the researcher might be interested in each of these measures of central tendency.

11. Calculate the mean, median, mode, and standard deviation for the following data set:

PART 4:
Data Analysis

Respondent	Times Visited Whitehall Mall in Past Six Months	Times Visited Northpark Mall in Past Six Months	Times Visited Sampson Mall in Past Six Months
A	4	7	2
B	5	11	16
C	13	21	3
D	6	0	1
E	9	18	14
F	3	6	8
G	2	0	1
H	21	3	7
I	4	11	9
J	14	13	5
K	7	7	12
L	8	3	25
M	8	3	9

12. Enter the following data into an Excel spreadsheet. Include the column headings (Q1, Q2, and Q3), as well as the numeric values. The definitions of the numeric values are provided at the bottom of the table. Use the Pivot Table feature in Excel (found under the Data option) to crosstabulate the likelihood of purchase (row) by gender (column) and income level (column). What conclusions can you draw about the relationship between gender and likelihood of purchase and that between income and likelihood of purchase?

Respondent	Likelihood of Purchse	Gender	Income
A	5	2	3
B	4	2	3
C	4	2	2
D	3	1	2
E	1	1	2
F	5	2	3
G	5	2	3
H	4	1	3
I	1	1	2
J	1	1	2
K	2	1	1
L	5	2	3
M	5	2	3
N	4	1	3
O	3	1	2
P	3	1	2
Q	4	2	3
R	5	2	3
S	2	1	1
T	2	1	1

Likelihood of purchase: very likely = 5, likely = 4, undecided = 3, unlikely = 2, very unlikely = 1

Gender: male = 1, female = 2

Income: under $30,000 = 1, $30,000 to $75,000 = 2, over $75,000 = 3

13. Using data from a newspaper or magazine article, create the following types of graphs:
   a. Line graph
   b. Pie chart
   c. Bar chart

Working the Net

What is statistics? To find out, go to the Web site of the American Statistical Association at http://www.amstat.org/education/whatis.html to explore (1) careers in statistics, (2) minorities in statistics, and (3) women in statistics.

Using WebSurveyor

YourPayments.com, a popular Internet transaction processing company, hired XYZ Marketing Research to help the company profile its customer base and identify new business opportunities. XYZ sent survey invitations to all of the customers listed in the YourPayments.com database. Over 1,000 people responded representing about 15 percent of the company's customers.

Using the WebSurveyor Desktop software, open the CHAPTER14 survey by selecting File and then Open from the main menu and navigating to the SURVEYS subdirectory under the directory where you installed the WebSurveyor Desktop software (usually c:\program files\websurveyor desktop 3).

Next, navigate to the Analysis page, click the Update Results button at the bottom of the page, and follow the prompts to load the survey results from the CD-ROM included with this textbook.

Exercises

Use the WebSurveyor analysis tools to prepare a presentation that answers the following questions:

1. What are the key characteristics of the current customers?
2. How should the company define its target market?
3. What services should the company offer?
4. How should the company promote its services?

PART 4:
Data Analysis

Real-Life Research • 14.1

Taco Bueno

Taco Bueno has recently opened its 15th store in Utah. Currently, the chain offers tacos, enchiladas, and burritos. Management is considering offering a super taco that would be approximately two and a half times as large as a regular taco and would contain 5 ounces of ground beef. The basic taco simply has spiced ground beef, lettuce, and cheese. Management feels that the super taco ought to have more toppings. Therefore, a marketing research study was undertaken to determine what those toppings should be. A key question on the survey was, "What, if anything, do you normally add to a taco that you have prepared at home besides meat?" The question is open-ended, and the coding categories that have been established for the question are shown in the table.

Responses	Code
Avocado	1
Cheese (Monterey Jack/cheddar)	2
Guacamole	3
Lettuce	4
Mexican hot sauce	5
Olive (black/green)	6
Onion (red/white)	7
Peppers (red/green)	8
Pimiento	9
Sour cream	0
Other	X

Questions

1. How would you code the following responses?
   a. I usually add a green, avocado-tasting hot sauce.
   b. I cut up a mixture of lettuce and spinach.
   c. I'm a vegetarian; I don't use meat at all. My taco is filled only with guacamole.
   d. Every now and then, I use a little lettuce, but normally I like cilantro.
2. Is there anything wrong with having a great number of responses in the "Other" category? What problems does this present for the researcher?

Real-Life Research • 14.2

Sunrise Mall

Sunrise Mall is an enclosed mall with more than 100 stores in Fort Lauderdale. Recently, management decided that it needed to know more about its target market and its competitors. A decision was made to conduct marketing research among both patrons and nonpatrons of Sunrise Mall. Management was interested in finding out why people did or did not shop at the mall, which stores were patronized most often, which ones were preferred, which ones were disliked, and how the image of Sunrise Mall compared with those of competing malls. In addition, it wanted to know what promotions would be most effective in attracting both patrons and nonpatrons to Sunrise Mall. The questionnaire developed for the study follows.

Good _____, I'm _____ of Americana Research, Inc. We are talking with people today about the shopping centers where they shop.

1. Are you 18 years of age or older?
Yes _____ −1   No _____ −2 (TERMINATE)

2. What shopping center is most convenient for you to shop?

Sunrise	−1	Galleria	−5
Northwest Mall	−2	Other (SPECIFY)	
Park Plaza	−3	_____	−6
Oak City	−4	_____	−7
		Refused/DK	−0

3. In which shopping center do you do most of your shopping?

Sunrise	−1	Galleria	−5
Northwest Mall	−2	Other (SPECIFY)	
Park Plaza	−3	_____	−6
Oak City	−4	_____	−7
		Refused/DK	−0

4a. Do you presently shop at Sunrise Mall?
Yes _____ −1   No _____ −2
(IF *YES*, GO TO Q.5) (IF *NO*, ASK Q.4b)

4b. Why do you not shop at Sunrise Mall? (PROBE) _____

_____

5. How often do you shop at Sunrise Mall?

More than once a week	−1
Once a week	−2
Twice a month	−3
Once a month	−4
Several times a year	−5
Refused	−0

PART 4:
Data Analysis

6a. In Sunrise, which one store do you shop in most often? (MARK "1" FOR MOST)

6b. Which second most often? (MARK "2" FOR SECOND)

Stores/Places	6a	6b	7a
Adrien's	_____	_____	_____
Bond's	_____	_____	_____
Britt's	_____	_____	_____
Craig's	_____	_____	_____
Firestone	_____	_____	_____
Graves	_____	_____	_____
Joske's	_____	_____	_____
Kresge's	_____	_____	_____
Lerner's	_____	_____	_____
Montgomery Ward	_____	_____	_____
Oshman's	_____	_____	_____
Piccadilly Cafeteria	_____	_____	_____
The Woman's Shop	_____	_____	_____
Thom McAn	_____	_____	_____
Walgreen's	_____	_____	_____
Weingarten's	_____	_____	_____
Other: (SPECIFY)	_____	_____	_____
_____	_____	_____	_____
_____	_____	_____	_____
_____	_____	_____	_____
_____	_____	_____	_____

7a. Which store in the entire center do you like least? (MARK "L" FOR LEAST) NONE ( ) (GO TO Q.8)

7b. Why do you like _____ the least? (PROBE) _____
_____
_____

8. What changes or improvements could be made at Sunrise Mall? (PROBE)
_____
_____
_____
_____

9. What other type of store or other business (not in the center) would you like to see in Sunrise Mall? (PROBE)
_____
_____
_____

10. Here is a list of various attributes of shopping centers. As I read each one, please tell me how you would rate Sunrise Mall in comparison with other shopping centers in Fort Lauderdale.

Would you say Sunrise Mall is *better than, the same as,* or *not as good as* other centers in regard to ⎯⎯⎯⎯ ? (START WITH STARRED ATTRIBUTE AND ASK FOR ALL)

Attributes	Better Than	Same As	Not As Good
Selection of merchandise	⎯⎯⎯⎯	⎯⎯⎯⎯	⎯⎯⎯⎯
Parking at center	⎯⎯⎯⎯	⎯⎯⎯⎯	⎯⎯⎯⎯
Appearance/atmosphere of center	⎯⎯⎯⎯	⎯⎯⎯⎯	⎯⎯⎯⎯
Appearance/atmosphere of stores*	⎯⎯⎯⎯	⎯⎯⎯⎯	⎯⎯⎯⎯
Special prices	⎯⎯⎯⎯	⎯⎯⎯⎯	⎯⎯⎯⎯
Center with stores I prefer	⎯⎯⎯⎯	⎯⎯⎯⎯	⎯⎯⎯⎯
Variety of eating places	⎯⎯⎯⎯	⎯⎯⎯⎯	⎯⎯⎯⎯
Housekeeping of grounds	⎯⎯⎯⎯	⎯⎯⎯⎯	⎯⎯⎯⎯
Housekeeping of stores	⎯⎯⎯⎯	⎯⎯⎯⎯	⎯⎯⎯⎯
Safe place to shop	⎯⎯⎯⎯	⎯⎯⎯⎯	⎯⎯⎯⎯
Helpfulness of salespeople	⎯⎯⎯⎯	⎯⎯⎯⎯	⎯⎯⎯⎯
Good eating places	⎯⎯⎯⎯	⎯⎯⎯⎯	⎯⎯⎯⎯
Special promotions	⎯⎯⎯⎯	⎯⎯⎯⎯	⎯⎯⎯⎯
Wide range of shopping facilities	⎯⎯⎯⎯	⎯⎯⎯⎯	⎯⎯⎯⎯
Hours open to shop	⎯⎯⎯⎯	⎯⎯⎯⎯	⎯⎯⎯⎯
Convenience to work	⎯⎯⎯⎯	⎯⎯⎯⎯	⎯⎯⎯⎯
Convenience to home	⎯⎯⎯⎯	⎯⎯⎯⎯	⎯⎯⎯⎯

11. What special events or promotions have you attended in Fort Lauderdale shopping centers in the past 12 months?

_____

_____

_____

NONE (   ) (GO TO Q.13)

12. What special event or promotion was your favorite?

_____

_____

13. What special event or promotion would you like to see sponsored by Sunrise Mall?

_____

_____

_____

And now, a few questions for statistical classification.

14. Are you:

Single	−1	Divorced	−4
Married	−2	Separated	−5
Widowed	−3	Refused	−0

15. In your home:
How many are adults age 18 and older? _____
How many are children under 18? _____
Total _____

16. In which of these brackets does your age fall?

18–24	−1	45–54	−4
25–34	−2	55–64	−5
35–44	−3	65 or over	−6

17. What is the last grade of school you completed?

None	−1	1–3 Years of college	−5
Some grade school	−2	College graduate	−6
Some high school	−3	Post graduate	−7
Completed high school	−4		

18. Are you employed?
Yes −1 (ASK Q.19)
No −2

18a. (IF MARRIED, ASK) is your (husband/wife) employed?
Yes −1 (ASK Q.20)
No −2

19. What type of work do you do? (INDICATE IN GRID BELOW)

20. What type of work does your (husband/wife) do? (INDICATE IN GRID BELOW)

	Q.19	Q.20
Professional/technical	−1	−1
Manager/officials/self-employed	−2	−2
Clerical or sales	−3	−3
Skilled worker	−4	−4
Service worker	−5	−5
Unskilled laborer	−6	−6
Farm operator or rancher	−7	−7
Unemployed or student	−8	−8
Retired	−9	−9
Refused	−0	−0

21. Which Fort Lauderdale papers do you read? (DO NOT READ LIST)

Globe	−1
Democrat	−2
Both	−3
Other (SPECIFY)	−4

22. What radio stations do you listen to?

Morning	Afternoon	Evening
_____	_____	_____
_____	_____	_____
_____	_____	_____

23. Which TV station do you prefer for news?
    Channel 2   −1   Channel 13   −4
    Channel 8   −2   Channel 26   −5
    Channel 11   −3   Channel 39   −6

24. Do you own or rent your home?
    Own   −1
    Rent   −2
    Other   −3
    Refused   −4

25. (IF LIVES IN SUNRISE MALL AREA, ASK) How long have you lived in this area?

    Less than 1 year   −1   8 years to 10 years   −5
    1 year to 3 years   −2   Over 10 years   −6
    3 years to 6 years   −3   Refused   −7
    6 years to 8 years   −4

26. I'm going to read several income categories. Please tell me in which group your total family income falls.

    Under $25,000   −1
    $25,000−50,000   −2
    Over $50,000   −3

Questions

1. Suppose you were in charge of specifying the crosstabulations for the study. Which questions would you crosstabulate?
2. Assume that you could only specify a total of 30 crosstabulations. Which 30 would you choose? (Crosstabbing one question with another question constitutes one crosstab. For example, crosstabbing "What shopping center is more convenient for you to shop?" with "Income of the Respondent" would count as one crosstab.)

Real-Life Research • 14.3

FirstCare

FirstCare is a group of twelve emergency medical treatment clinics in Seattle and Tacoma, Washington. The management group for FirstCare is considering using a communications campaign relying mainly on radio ads to boost its profile in Seattle and Tacoma. The ad agency of Brimble and McCarthy has been chosen to develop the campaign. Currently, the prospective campaign will focus on FirstCare's front-line health professionals. Two themes for the ad campaign are now being weighed. One theme ("We are ready!") focuses primarily on the special training given to FirstCare's staff, while another theme ("All the experts—all the time") focuses primarily on FirstCare's commitment to having trained professionals available at each FirstCare facility 24 hours each day. Brimble and McCarthy researchers have conducted a survey of consumers to gauge the appeal of the two campaigns. Overall results and results disaggregated by gender and by location are shown in the table.

| | Total | Gender | | Location | |
		Male	Female	Seattle	Tacoma
Total	400	198	202	256	144
	100.0%	100.0%	100.0%	100.0%	100.0%
Prefer "Ready" campaign	150	93	57	124	26
	37.5%	47.0%	28.2%	48.4%	18.1%
Prefer "All the time" campaign	250	105	145	132	118
	62.5%	53.0%	71.8%	51.6%	81.9%

Questions

1. Which theme appears to have more appeal overall?
2. What is the pattern of preference for the two campaigns between men and women?
3. Are the campaign themes equally attractive to residents of Seattle and Tacoma?

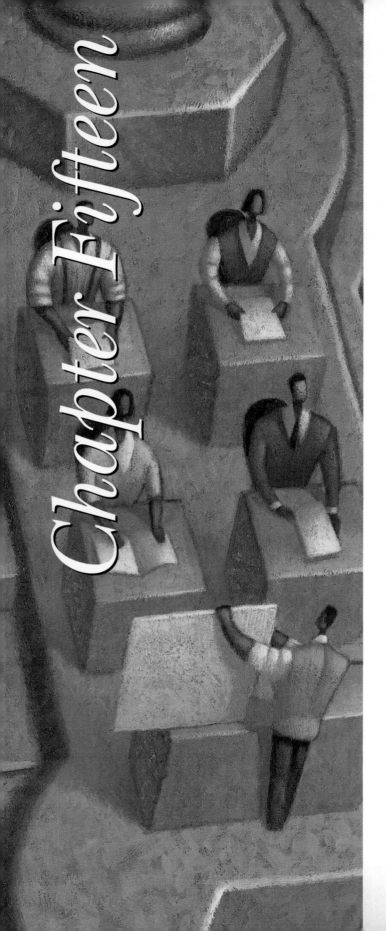

Chapter Fifteen

Statistical Testing
of Differences

Learning Objectives

*To become aware 1 of the nature of
statistical significance.*

*To understand the concept of hypothesis
development and how to test hypotheses.*

*To understand the difference between Type I
and Type II errors.*

*To be familiar with several of the more
common statistical tests of goodness of fit,
hypotheses about one mean, hypotheses about
two means, and hypotheses about proportions.*

To learn about analysis of variance.

B ILL STONE, OF WEED EATER, IS REVIEWING THE RESULTS OF A PRODUCT concept test just completed with Marketing and Product Counselors (MAPC). The test involved evaluation of three alternative enhancements to the company's best-selling product, the X1200. This product currently has 21.2 percent of the market.

THE TEST WAS DONE BY MALL-INTERCEPT INTERVIEWING IN FOUR cities—Atlanta, Dallas, Chicago, and Philadelphia. A total of 1,200 qualified consumers were surveyed—300 in each market. To qualify, consumers had to be homeowners, take care of their yards themselves, and own a power lawn edger.

THE SURVEY COVERED CURRENT BRAND OF LAWN EDGER USED, RATINGS of competitive brands, demographic and psychographic characteristics, and reactions to the new product concepts. The new concepts were three different approaches to improving the plastic line that does the trimming. The same people were asked about all three new versions of the system. The order of presentation of the new versions was randomly rotated from survey to survey to avoid any order bias.

AS NOTED ABOVE, THE SURVEY COVERED MANY ISSUES, BUT THE KEY questions for Stone were the purchase intent questions. Specifically, the basic approach used for all the purchase intent questions on the survey was "If an edger with this new system was available at stores where you normally shop and sold for $39.95, how likely would you be to buy it?" The response options were "very likely," "somewhat likely," "undecided," "somewhat unlikely," and "very unlikely." By Stone's calculations, the new product would need a "Top 2 box score" (sum of the "very likely" and "somewhat likely" responses) of 38 percent to reach the necessary sales volume.

THE TOP 2 BOX SCORES FOR THE THREE CONCEPTS WERE AS FOLLOWS: CONCEPT A, 27.3 percent; concept B, 35.3 percent; and concept C, 39.8 percent. Stone has framed the issues that must be addressed as follows:

- Concept C scored the best, but is it possible that the true result for concept C could be less than the 38 percent target level when sampling error is taken into account?

- Concept B scored just under the 38 percent target level, but is it possible that the true result could be 38 percent or higher after sampling error is taken into account? ■

Statistical testing of differences played a role in the analysis of the results of this study about future marketing of alternative enhancements to Weed Eater's best-selling product.

Find out more about the Weed Eater product at

  http://www. poulan.com

After reading this chapter, you will be able to answer the questions faced by Stone.

Evaluating Differences and Changes

The issue of whether certain measurements are different from one another is central to many questions of critical interest to marketing managers. Some specific examples of managers' questions follow:

- Our posttest measure of top-of-mind awareness is slightly higher than the level recorded in the pretest. Did top-of-mind awareness really increase or is there some other explanation for the increase? Should we fire or commend our agency?
- Our overall customer satisfaction score increased from 92 percent three months ago to 93.5 percent today. Did customer satisfaction really increase? Should we celebrate?
- Satisfaction with the customer service provided by our cable TV system in Dallas is, on average, 1.2 points higher on a 10-point scale than is satisfaction with the customer service provided by our cable TV system in Cincinnati. Are customers in Dallas really more satisfied? Should the customer service manager in Cincinnati be replaced? Should the Dallas manager be rewarded?
- In a recent product concept test, 19.8 percent of those surveyed said they were very likely to buy the new product they evaluated. Is this good? Is it better than the results we got last year for a similar product? What do these results suggest in terms of whether to introduce the new product?
- A segmentation study shows that those with incomes of more than $30,000 per year frequent fast food restaurants 6.2 times per month on average. Those with incomes of $30,000 or less go an average of 6.7 times. Is this difference real—is it meaningful?
- In an awareness test, 28.3 percent of those surveyed have heard of our product on an unaided basis. Is this a good result?

These are the eternal questions in marketing and marketing research. Although considered boring by some, statistical hypothesis testing is important because it helps researchers get closer to the ultimate answers to these questions. We say "closer" because certainty is never achieved in answering these questions in marketing research.

Statistical Significance

The basic motive for making statistical inferences is to generalize from sample results to population characteristics. A fundamental tenet of statistical inference is that it is possible for numbers to be different in a mathematical sense but not significantly different in a statistical sense. For example, suppose cola drinkers are asked to try two cola drinks in a blind taste test and indicate which they prefer; the results show that 51 percent prefer one test product and 49 percent prefer the other. There is a mathematical difference in the results, but the difference would appear to be minor and unimportant. The difference probably is well within the range of accuracy of researchers' ability to measure taste preference and thus probably is not significant in a statistical sense. Three different concepts can be applied to the notion of differences:

- *Mathematical differences.* By definition, if numbers are not exactly the same, they are different. This does not, however, mean that the difference is either important or statistically significant.
- *Statistical significance.* If a particular difference is large enough to be unlikely to have occurred because of chance or sampling error, then the difference is statistically significant.
- *Managerially important differences.* One can argue that a difference is important from a managerial perspective only if results or numbers are sufficiently different. For example, the difference in consumer responses to two different packages in a test market might be statistically significant but yet so small as to have little practical or managerial significance.[1]

This chapter covers different approaches to testing whether results are statistically significant.

Hypothesis Testing

A **hypothesis** is an assumption or guess that a researcher or manager makes about some characteristic of the population being investigated. The marketing researcher is often faced with the question of whether research results are different enough from the norm that some element of the firm's marketing strategy should be changed. Consider the following situations.

- The results of a tracking survey show that awareness of a product is lower than it was in a similar survey conducted six months ago. Are the results significantly lower? Are the results sufficiently lower to call for a change in advertising strategy?
- A product manager believes that the average purchaser of his product is 35 years of age. A survey is conducted to test this hypothesis, and the survey shows that the average purchaser of the product is 38.5 years of age. Is the survey result different enough from the product manager's belief to cause him to conclude that his belief is incorrect?
- The marketing director of a fast food chain believes that 60 percent of her customers are female and 40 percent are male. She does a survey to test this hypothesis and finds that, according to the survey, 55 percent are female and 45 percent are male. Is this result sufficiently different from her original theory to permit her to conclude that her original theory was incorrect?

All of these questions can be evaluated with some kind of statistical test. In hypothesis testing, the researcher determines whether a hypothesis concerning some characteristic of the population is likely to be true, given the evidence. A statistical hypothesis test allows us to calculate the probability of observing a particular result if the stated hypothesis is actually true.

hypothesis
Assumption or theory that a researcher or manager makes about some characteristic of the population under study.

There are two basic explanations for an observed difference between a hypothesized value and a particular research result. Either the hypothesis is true and the observed difference is likely due to sampling error, or the hypothesis is false and the true value is some other value.

Steps in Hypothesis Testing

Five basic steps are involved in testing a hypothesis. First, the hypothesis is specified. Second, an appropriate statistical technique is selected to test the hypothesis. Third, a decision rule is specified as the basis for determining whether to reject or fail to reject (FTR) the null hypothesis H_0. Please note that we did not say "reject H_0 or accept H_0." Although a seemingly small distinction, it is an important one. The distinction will be discussed in greater detail later on. Fourth, the value of the test statistic is calculated and the test is performed. Fifth, the conclusion is stated from the perspective of the original research problem or question.

Step One: Stating the Hypothesis   Hypotheses are stated using two basic forms: the null hypothesis H_0 and the alternative hypothesis H_a. The null hypothesis H_0 (sometimes called the *hypothesis of the status quo*) is the hypothesis that is tested against its complement, the alternative hypothesis H_a (sometimes called the *research hypothesis of interest*). Suppose the manager of Burger City believes that his operational procedures will guarantee that the average customer will wait two minutes in the drive-in window line. He conducts research, based on the observation of 1,000 customers at randomly selected stores at randomly selected times. The average customer observed in this study spends 2.4 minutes in the drive-in window line. The null hypothesis and the alternative hypothesis might be stated as follows:

- Null hypothesis H_0: Mean waiting time = 2 minutes
- Alternative hypothesis H_a: Mean waiting time $\neq$ 2 minutes

It should be noted that the null hypothesis and the alternative hypothesis must be stated in such a way that both cannot be true. The idea is to use the available evidence to ascertain which hypothesis is more likely to be true.

Step Two: Choosing the Appropriate Test Statistic   As you will see in the following sections of this chapter, the analyst must choose the appropriate statistical test, given the characteristics of the situation under investigation. A number of different statistical tests, along with the situations where they are appropriate, are discussed in this chapter. Table 15.1 provides a guide to selecting the appropriate test for various situations. All the tests in this table are covered in detail later in this chapter.

Step Three: Developing a Decision Rule   Based on our previous discussions of distributions of sample means, you may recognize that one is very unlikely to get a sample result that is exactly equal to the value of the population parameter. The problem is determining whether the difference, or deviation, between the actual value of the sample mean and its expected value based on the

Statistical Tests and Their Uses

Table 15.1

Area of Application	Subgroups or Samples	Level Scaling	Test	Special Requirements	Example
Hypotheses about frequency distribution	One	Nominal	χ²	Random sample	Are observed differences in the numbers of people responding to three different promotions likely/not likely due to chance?
	Two or more	Nominal	χ²	Random sample, independent samples	Are differences in the numbers of men and women responding to a promotion likely/not likely due to chance?
	One	Ordinal	K-S	Random sample, natural order in data	Is the observed distribution of women preferring an ordered set of make-up colors (light to dark) likely/not likely due to chance?
Hypotheses about means	One (large sample)	Metric (interval or ratio)	Z-test for one mean	Random sample, $n \geqslant 30$	Is the observed difference between a sample estimate of the mean and some set standard or expected value of the mean likely/not likely due to chance?
	One (small sample)	Metric (interval or ratio)	t-test for one mean	Random sample, $n < 30$	Same as for small sample above
	Two (large sample)	Metric (interval or ratio)	Z-test for one mean	Random sample, $n \geqslant 30$	Is the observed difference between the means for two subgroups (mean income for men and women) likely/not likely due to chance?
	Three or more	Metric (interval or ratio)	One-way ANOVA	Random sample	Is the observed variation between means for three or more subgroups (mean expenditures on entertainment for high, moderate, and low-income people) likely/not likely due to chance?
Hypotheses about proportions	One (large sample)	Metric (interval or ratio)	Z-test for one proportion	Random sample, $n \geqslant 30$	Is the observed difference between a sample estimate of proportion (percentage who say they will buy) and some set standard or expected value likely/not likely due to chance?
	Two (large sample)	Metric (interval or ratio)	Z-test for two proportions	Random sample, $n \geqslant 30$	Is the observed difference between estimated percentages for two subgroups (percentage of men and women who have college degrees) likely/not likely due to chance?

hypothesis could have occurred by chance (5 times out of 100, for example) if the statistical hypothesis is true. A decision rule, or standard, is needed to determine whether to reject or fail to reject the null hypothesis. Statisticians state such decision rules in terms of significance levels.

The significance level (α) is critical in the process of choosing between the null and alternative hypotheses. The level of significance—.10, .05, or .01, for example—is the probability that is considered too low to justify acceptance of the null hypothesis.

Consider a situation in which the researcher has decided that she wants to test a hypothesis at the .05 level of significance. This means that she will reject the null hypothesis if the test indicates that the probability of occurrence of the observed result (e.g., the difference between the sample mean and its expected value) because of chance or sampling error is less than 5 percent. Rejection of the null hypothesis is equivalent to supporting the alternative hypothesis.

Step Four: Calculating the Value of the Test Statistic   In this step, the researcher does the following:

- Uses the appropriate formula to calculate the value of the statistic for the test chosen.
- Compares the value just calculated to the critical value of the statistic (from the appropriate table), based on the decision rule chosen.
- Based on the comparison, determines to either reject or fail to reject the null hypothesis H_0.

Step Five: Stating the Conclusion   The conclusion summarizes the results of the test. It should be stated from the perspective of the original research question.

Types of Errors in Hypothesis Testing

Type I error (α error)
Rejection of the null hypothesis when, in fact, it is true.

Hypothesis tests are subject to two general types of errors, typically referred to as Type I error and Type II error. A **Type I error** involves rejecting the null hypothesis when it is, in fact, true. The researcher may reach this incorrect conclusion because the observed difference between the sample and population values is due to sampling error. The researcher must decide how willing she or he is to commit a Type I error. The probability of committing a Type I error is referred to as the *alpha (α) level*. Conversely, $1 - \alpha$ is the probability of making a correct decision by not rejecting the null hypothesis when, in fact, it is true.

Type II error (β error)
Acceptance of the null hypothesis when, in fact, it is false.

A **Type II error** involves failing to reject the null hypothesis when it actually is false. A Type II error is referred to as a *beta (ß) error*. The value $1 - $ ß reflects the probability of making a correct decision in rejecting the null hypothesis when, in fact, it is false. The four possibilities are summarized in Table 15.2.

As we consider the various types of hypothesis tests, keep in mind that when a researcher rejects or fails to reject the null hypothesis, this decision is never made with 100 percent certainty. There is a probability that the decision is correct and there is a probability that the decision is not correct. The level of α is set by the researcher, after consulting with his or her client, considering the

Table 15.2	**Type I and Type II Errors**		
Actual State of the Null Hypothesis		**Fail to Reject H_0**	**Reject H_0**
	H_0 is true	Correct $(1 - \alpha)$	Type I error (α)
	H_0 is false	Type II error (β)	Correct $(1 - \beta)$

resources available for the project, and considering the implications of making Type I and Type II errors. However, the estimation of ß is more complicated and is beyond the scope of our discussion. Note that Type I and Type II errors are not complementary; that is, $\alpha + ß \neq 1$.

It would be ideal to have control over n (the sample size), α (the probability of a Type I error), and ß (the probability of a Type II error) for any hypothesis test. Unfortunately, only two of the three can be controlled. For a given problem with a fixed sample size, n is fixed, or controlled. Therefore, only one of α and ß can be controlled.

Assume that for a given problem you have decided to set $\alpha = .05$. As a result, the procedure you use to test H_0 versus H_a will reject H_0 when it is true (Type I error) 5 percent of the time. You could set $\alpha = 0$ so that you would never have a Type I error. The idea of never rejecting a correct H_0 sounds good. However, the downside is that ß (the probability of a Type II error) is equal to 1 in this situation. As a result, you will always fail to reject H_0 when it is false. For example, if $\alpha = 0$ in the fast food service time example, where H_0 is mean waiting time = 2 minutes, then the resulting test of H_0 versus H_a will automatically fail to reject H_0 (mean waiting time = 2 minutes) whenever the estimated waiting time is any value other than 2 minutes. If, for example, we did a survey and determined that the mean waiting time for the people surveyed was 8.5 minutes, we would still fail to reject (FTR) H_0. As you can see, this is not a good compromise. We need a value of α that offers a more reasonable compromise between the probabilities of the two types of errors. Note that in the situation in which $\alpha = 0$ and ß = 1, $\alpha + ß = 1$. As you will see later on, this is not true as a general rule.

The value of α selected should be a function of the relative importance of the two types of errors. Suppose you have just been subjected to a diagnostic test. The purpose of the test is to determine whether you have a particular medical condition that is fatal in most cases. If you have the disease, a treatment that is painless, inexpensive, and totally without risk will cure the condition 100 percent of the time. Here are the hypotheses to be tested:

H_0: Test indicates that you do not have the disease.

H_a: Test indicates that you do have the disease.

Thus,

$$\alpha = P(\text{rejecting } H_0 \text{ when it is true})$$
$$= P(\text{test indicates that you have the disease when you do not have it})$$

$$\beta = P(\text{FTR } H_0 \text{ when in fact it is false})$$
$$= P(\text{test indicates that you do not have the disease when you do have it})$$

Clearly, a Type I error (measured by α) is not nearly as serious as a Type II error (measured by ß). A Type I error is not serious because the test will not harm you if you are well. However, a Type II error means that you will not receive the treatment you need even though you are ill.

The value of ß is never set in advance. When α is made smaller, ß becomes larger. If you want to minimize Type II error, then you choose a larger value for α in order to make ß smaller. In most situations, the range of acceptable values for α is .01 to .1.

In the case of the diagnostic test situation, you might choose a value of α at or near .1 because of the seriousness of a Type II error. Conversely, if you are more concerned about Type I errors in a given situation, then a small value of α is appropriate. For example, suppose you are testing commercials that were very expensive to produce, and you are concerned about the possibility of rejecting a commercial that is really effective. If there is no real difference between the effects of Type I and Type II errors, as is often the case, an α value of .05 is commonly used.

Accepting H_0 versus Failing to Reject (FTR) H_0

Researchers often fail to make a distinction between accepting H_0 and failing to reject (FTR) H_0. However, as noted earlier, there is an important distinction between these two decisions. When a hypothesis is tested, H_0 is presumed to be true until it is demonstrated to be likely to be false. In any hypothesis testing situation, the only other hypothesis that can be accepted is the alternative hypothesis H_a. Either there is sufficient evidence to support H_a (reject H_0) or there is not (fail to reject H_0). The real question is whether there is enough evidence in the data to conclude that H_a is correct. If we fail to reject H_0, we are saying that the data do not provide sufficient support of the claim made in H_a—not that we accept the statement made in H_0.

One-Tailed versus Two-Tailed Test

Tests are either one-tailed or two-tailed. The decision as to which to use depends on the nature of the situation and what the researcher is trying to demonstrate. For example, when the quality control department of a fast food organization receives a shipment of ground beef from one of its vendors and needs to determine whether the product meets specifications in regard to fat content, a one-tailed test is appropriate. The ground beef shipment will be rejected if it does not meet minimum specifications. On the other hand, the managers of the meat company that supplies the product should run two-tailed tests to determine two factors. First, they must make sure that the product meets the minimum specifications of their customer before they ship it. Second, they want to determine whether the product exceeds specifications because this can be costly to them. If they are consistently providing a product that exceeds the level of quality they have contracted to provide, their costs will be unnecessarily high.

The classic example of a situation requiring a two-tailed test is the testing of electric fuses. A fuse must trip, or break contact, when it reaches a preset temperature or else a fire may result. On the other hand, you do not want the fuse to break contact before it reaches the specified temperature or else it will shut off the electricity unnecessarily. The test used in the quality control process for testing fuses must, therefore, be two-tailed.

The quality control department of a fast food organization would probably do a one-tailed test to determine whether a shipment of ground beef met product specifications. However, a two-tailed test would probably be done by the managers of the meat company that supplied the ground beef.

Example of Performing a Statistical Test

Income is an important determinant of the sales of hot tubs. Tubs R Us (TRU) is a hot tub manufacturer in the process of developing sales estimates for one of its major markets in Southern California. According to the U.S. Census, the average annual family income in the market is $55,347. TRU has just completed a survey of 250 randomly selected households in the market to collect other data needed for its sales forecasting model, and its survey indicates that average annual family income in the market is $54,323. The actual value of the population mean (μ) is unknown. We have two estimates of μ: the census result and the survey result. The difference between these two estimates makes a substantial difference in the estimates of hot tub sales produced by TRU's forecasting model. In the calculations, the U.S. Census Bureau estimate is treated as the best estimate of μ.

To evaluate the census estimate, TRU decides to statistically compare it with its survey result. The statistics for the sample are

$$\overline{X} = \$54,323$$
$$S = \$4,323$$
$$n = 250$$

The following hypotheses are produced:

$$H_0: \mu = \$55{,}347$$
$$H_a: \mu \neq \$55{,}347$$

The decision makers at TRU are willing to use a test that will reject H_0 when it is correct only 5 percent of the time ($\alpha = .05$). This is the significance level of the test. TRU will reject H_0 if $|\overline{X} - \$55{,}347|$ is larger than can be explained by sampling error at $\alpha = .05$.

Standardizing the data so that the result can be directly related to Z-values in Table 2 in Appendix 2, we have the following criterion:

Reject H_0 if $\left| \dfrac{\overline{X} - \$55{,}347}{S/\sqrt{n}} \right|$ is larger than can be explained

by sampling error at $\alpha = .05$.

This expression can be rewritten as

$$\left| \frac{\overline{X} - \$55{,}347}{S/\sqrt{n}} \right| > k$$

What is the value of k? If H_0 is true and the sample size is large (≥ 30), then (based on the central limit theorem) X approximates a normal random variable with

$$\text{Mean} = \mu = \$55{,}347$$
$$\text{Standard deviation} = \frac{S}{\sqrt{n}}$$

That is, if H_0 is true, $(\overline{X} - \$55{,}347)/(S/\sqrt{n})$ approximates a standard normal variable Z for samples of 30 or larger with a mean equal to 0 and a standard deviation equal to 1.

We will reject H_0 if $|Z| > k$. When $|Z| > k$, either $Z > k$ or $Z < -k$, as shown in Figure 15.1. Given that

$$P(|Z| > k) = .05$$

the total shaded area is .05, with .025 in each tail (two-tailed test). The area between 0 and k is .475. Referring to Table 2 in Appendix 2, we find that $k = 1.96$. Therefore, the test is

$$\text{Reject } H_0 \text{ if } \left| \frac{\overline{X} - \$55{,}347}{S/\sqrt{n}} \right| > 1.96$$

and FTR H$_0$ otherwise. In other words,

$$\text{Reject H}_0 \text{ if } \frac{\overline{X} - \$55,347}{S/\sqrt{n}} > 1.96 \text{ or if } \frac{\overline{X}\ \$55,347}{S/\sqrt{n}} < 1.96$$

The question is, is $\overline{X} = \$54,323$ far enough away from $55,347 for TRU to reject H$_0$? The results show that

$$Z = \frac{\overline{X} - \$55,347}{S/\sqrt{n}}$$

$$= \frac{\$54,323 - \$55,347}{\$4,322/\sqrt{250}} = -3.75$$

Because $-3.75 < -1.96$, we reject H$_0$. On the basis of the sample results and $\alpha = .05$, the conclusion is that the average household income in the market is not equal to $55,347. If H$_0$ is true ($\mu = \$55,347$), then the value of $\overline{X}$ obtained from the sample ($54,323) is 3.75 standard deviations to the left of the mean on the normal curve for $\overline{X}$. A value of $\overline{X}$ this far away from the mean is very unlikely (probability is less than .05). As a result, we conclude that H$_0$ is not likely to be true, and we reject it.

Commonly Used Statistical Hypothesis Tests

A number of commonly used statistical hypothesis tests of differences are presented in the following sections. Many other statistical tests have been developed and are used, but a full discussion of all of them is beyond the scope of this text.

The distributions used in the following sections for comparing the computed and tabular values of the statistics are the Z-distribution, the t-distribution, the F-distribution, and the chi-square (χ^2) distribution. The tabular values for these distributions appear in Tables 2, 3, 4, and 5 of Appendix 2.

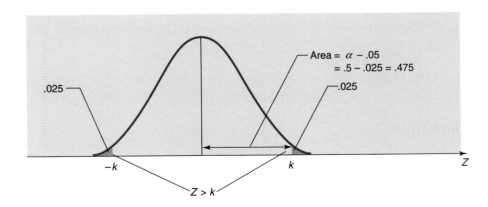

Figure 15.1

Shaded Area Is Significance Level α

Independent versus Related Samples

In some cases, one needs to test the hypothesis that the value of a variable in one population is equal to the value of that same variable in another population. Selection of the appropriate test statistic requires the researcher to consider whether the samples are independent or related. **Independent samples** are those in which measurement of the variable of interest in one sample has no effect on measurement of the variable in the other sample. It is not necessary that there be two different surveys, only that the measurement of the variable in one population have no effect on the measurement of the variable in the other population. In the case of **related samples,** measurement of the variable of interest in one sample may influence measurement of the variable in another sample.

If, for example, men and women were interviewed in a particular survey regarding their frequency of eating out, there is no way that a man's response could affect or change the way a woman would respond to a question in the survey. Thus, this would be an example of independent samples. On the other hand, consider a situation in which the researcher needed to determine the effect of a new advertising campaign on consumer awareness of a particular brand. To do this, the researcher might survey a random sample of consumers before introducing the new campaign and then survey the same sample of consumers 90 days after the new campaign was introduced. These samples are not independent. The measurement of awareness 90 days after the start of the campaign may be affected by the first measurement.

Degrees of Freedom

Many of the statistical tests discussed in this chapter require the researcher to specify degrees of freedom in order to find the critical value of the test statistic from the table for that statistic. The number of degrees of freedom is the number of observations in a statistical problem that are not restricted (that is, are free to vary).

The number of degrees of freedom (d.f.) is equal to the number of observations minus the number of assumptions or constraints necessary to calculate a statistic. Consider the problem of adding five numbers when the mean of the five numbers is known to be 20. In this situation, only four of the five numbers are free to vary. Once four of the numbers are known, the last value is also known (can be calculated) because the mean value must be 20. If four of the five numbers were 14, 23, 24, and 18, then the fifth number would have to be 21 to produce a mean of 20. We would say that the sample has $n - 1$ degrees of freedom. It is as if the sample had one less observation—the inclusion of degrees of freedom in the calculation adjusts for this fact.

Goodness of Fit

Chi-Square

As noted earlier in the text, data collected in surveys are often analyzed by means of one-way frequency counts and crosstabulations.[2] The purpose of a crosstabulation is to study relationships among variables. The question is, do the numbers

PART 4:
Data Analysis

of responses that fall into the various categories differ from what one would expect? For example, a study might involve partitioning users into groups by gender (male, female), age (under 18, 18–35, over 35), or income level (low, middle, high) and crosstabulating on the basis of answers to questions about preferred brand or level of use. The **chi-square** (χ^2) **test** enables the research analyst to determine whether an observed pattern of frequencies corresponds to, or fits, an "expected" pattern.[3] It tests the "goodness of fit" of the observed distribution to an expected distribution. We will look at the application of this technique to test distributions of crosstabulated categorical data for a single sample and for two independent samples.

Chi-Square Test of a Single Sample   Suppose the marketing manager of a retail electronics chain needs to test the effectiveness of three special deals (deal 1, deal 2, and deal 3). Each deal will be offered for a month. The manager wants to measure the effect of each deal on the number of customers visiting a test store during the time the deal is on. The number of customers visiting the store under each deal is as follows:

Deal	Month	Customers per Month
1	April	11,700
2	May	12,100
3	June	11,780
Total		35,580

The marketing manager needs to know whether there is a significant difference between the numbers of customers visiting the store during the time periods covered by the three deals. The chi-square (χ^2) one-sample test is the appropriate test to use to answer this question. This test is applied as follows:

1. Specify the null and alternative hypotheses.

   ■ Null hypothesis H_0: The numbers of customers visiting the store under the various deals are equal.
   ■ Alternative hypothesis H_a: There is a significant difference in the numbers of customers visiting the store under the various deals.

2. Determine the number of visitors who would be expected in each category if the null hypothesis were correct (E_i). In this example, the null hypothesis is that there is no difference in the numbers of customers attracted by the different deals. Therefore, an equal number of customers would be expected under each deal. Of course, this assumes that no other factors influenced the number of visits to the store. Under the null (no difference) hypothesis, the expected number of customers visiting the store in each deal period would be computed as follows:

$$E_i = \frac{\text{TV}}{N}$$

where   TV = total number of visits
        N = number of months

Thus,

$$E_i = \frac{35,580}{3} = 11,860$$

The researcher should always check for cells in which small expected frequencies occur because they can distort χ^2 results. No more than 20 percent of the categories should have an expected frequency of less than 5, and none should have an expected frequency of less than 1. This is not a problem in this case.

3. Calculate the χ^2 value, using the formula

$$\chi^2 = \sum_{i=1}^{k} \frac{(O_i - E_i)^2}{E_i}$$

where O_i = observed number in ith category
E_i = expected number in ith category
k = number of categories

For this example,

$$\chi^2 = \frac{(11,700 - 11,860)^2}{11,860} + \frac{(12,100 - 11,860)^2}{11,860}$$
$$+ \frac{(11,780 - 11,860)^2}{11,860}$$
$$= 7.55$$

4. Select the level of significance α. If the .05 level of significance (α) is selected, the tabular χ^2 value with 2 degrees of freedom ($k - 1$) is 5.99. (See Table 4 in Appendix 2 for $k - 1 = 2$ d.f., $\alpha = .05$.)

5. State the result. Because the calculated χ^2 value (7.55) is higher than the table value (5.99), we *reject the null hypothesis*. Therefore, we conclude with 95 percent confidence that customer response to the deals was significantly different. Unfortunately, this test tells us only that the overall variation among the cell frequencies is greater than would be expected by chance. It does not tell us whether any individual cell is significantly different from the others.

Chi-Square Test of Two Independent Samples Marketing researchers often need to determine whether there is any association between two or more variables. Before formulation of a marketing strategy, questions such as the following may need to be answered: Are men and women equally divided into heavy-, medium-, and light-user categories? Are purchasers and nonpurchasers equally divided into low-, middle-, and high-income groups? The chi-square (χ^2) test for two independent samples is the appropriate test in such situations.

The technique will be illustrated using the data from Table 15.3. A convenience store chain wants to determine the nature of the relationship, if any, between gender of customer and frequency of visits to stores in the chain. Frequency of visits has been divided into three categories: 1–5 visits per month (light user), 6–14 visits per month (medium user), and 15 and above visits per month (heavy user). The steps in conducting this test follow.

1. State the null and alternative hypotheses.

   ■ Null hypothesis H_0: There is no relationship between gender and frequency of visits.
   ■ Alternative hypothesis H_a: There is a significant relationship between gender and frequency of visits.

2. Place the observed (sample) frequencies in a $k \times r$ table (crosstabulation or contingency table), using the k columns for the sample groups and the r rows for the conditions or treatments. Calculate the sum of each row and each column. Record those totals at the margins of the table (they are called *marginal totals*). Also, calculate the total for the entire table (N).

Table 15.3

Data for X² Test of Two Independent Samples

Visits to Convenience Store by Males				Visits to Convenience Stores by Females			
Number X_m	Frequency f_m	Percent	Cumulative Percent	Number X_f	Frequency f_f	Percent	Cumulative Percent
2	2	4.4	4.4	2	5	7.0	7.0
3	5	11.1	15.6	3	4	5.6	12.7
5	7	15.6	31.1	4	7	9.9	22.5
6	2	4.4	35.6	5	10	14.1	36.6
7	1	2.2	37.8	6	6	8.5	45.1
8	2	4.4	42.2	7	3	4.2	49.3
9	1	2.2	44.4	8	6	8.5	57.7
10	7	15.6	60.0	9	2	2.8	60.6
12	3	6.7	66.7	10	13	18.3	78.9
15	5	11.1	77.8	12	4	5.6	84.5
20	6	13.3	91.1	15	3	4.2	88.7
23	1	2.2	93.3	16	2	2.8	91.5
25	1	2.2	95.6	20	4	5.6	97.2
30	1	2.2	97.8	21	1	1.4	98.6
40	1	2.2	100.0	25	1	1.4	100.0

$n_m = 45$ $\qquad\qquad\qquad\qquad\qquad$ $n_f = 71$

Mean number of visits by males, $\bar{X}_m = \dfrac{\sum X_m f_m}{45} = 11.49$ $\qquad$ Mean number of visits by females, $\bar{X}_f = \dfrac{\sum X_f f_f}{71} = 8.51$

	Male	Female	Totals
1–5 visits	14	26	40
6–14 visits	16	34	50
15 and above visits	15	11	26
Totals	45	71	116

3. Determine the expected frequency for each cell in the contingency table by calculating the product of the two marginal totals common to that cell and dividing that value by N.

	Male	Female
1–5 visits	$\dfrac{45 \times 40}{116} = 15.52$	$\dfrac{71 \times 40}{116} = 24.48$
6–14 visits	$\dfrac{45 \times 50}{116} = 19.40$	$\dfrac{71 \times 50}{116} = 30.60$
15 and above visits	$\dfrac{45 \times 26}{116} = 10.09$	$\dfrac{71 \times 26}{116} = 15.91$

The χ^2 value will be distorted if more than 20 percent of the cells have an expected frequency of less than 5 or if any cell has an expected frequency of less than 1. The test should not be used under these conditions.

4. Calculate the value of χ^2 using

$$\chi^2 = \sum_{i=1}^{r} \sum_{j=1}^{k} \frac{(O_{ij} - E_{ij})^2}{E_{ij}}$$

where O_{ij} = observed number in the ith row of the jth column
E_{ij} = expected number in the ith row of the jth column

For this example,

$$\chi^2 = \frac{(14 - 15.52)^2}{15.52} + \frac{(26 - 24.48)^2}{24.48} + \frac{(16 - 19.4)^2}{19.4}$$
$$+ \frac{(34 - 30.6)^2}{30.6} + \frac{(15 - 10.09)^2}{10.09} + \frac{(11 - 15.91)^2}{15.91}$$
$$= 5.12$$

5. State the result. The tabular χ^2 value at a .05 level of significance and $(r - 1) \times (k - 1) = 2$ degrees of freedom is 5.99 (see Table 4 of Appendix 2). Because the calculated $\chi^2 = 5.12$ is less than the tabular value, we *fail to reject (FTR) the null hypothesis* and conclude that there is no significant difference between males and females in terms of frequency of visits.

Kolmogorov-Smirnov (K-S) test

Test of the goodness of fit between the observed distribution and the expected distribution, using ordinal data.

Kolmogorov-Smirnov Test

The **Kolmogorov-Smirnov (K-S) test** is similar to the chi-square test of goodness of fit. It is concerned with the degree of agreement between the distribution of

PART 4:
Data Analysis

observed values and some theoretical or expected distribution. However, the K-S test is appropriate if the researcher is dealing with ordinal data.

Compaq Computers is preparing to introduce a new line of computers designed for the home market. Focus group research indicated that many potential new computer buyers in the home market are turned off by the colors traditionally used for computers in an office environment. Focus group participants were shown a wide range of colors, in addition to the traditional tans and grays used in an office environment, and expressed a preference for a brown color. Compaq then surveyed 500 individuals who do not currently own a computer but who indicated that they plan to buy a computer in the next six months. They were shown several shades of brown and asked to indicate their preference (see Figure 15.2). The survey results, in regard to color preference, are summarized in the following chart.

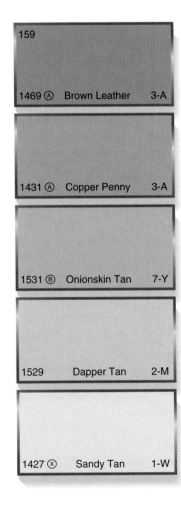

Figure 15.2

A Survey on Color Preference, to Which the Kolmogorov-Smirnov Test Can Be Applied

Shades	Number of Consumers Preferring a Particular Shade
Very light	150
Light	170
Medium	80
Dark	45
Very dark	55
Total	500

The manufacturer is interested in knowing whether these results might have occurred by chance or indicate a significant preference.

Because shade of color represents a natural ordering (ordinal data), the K-S test can be applied to test the preference hypothesis. The test involves specifying the cumulative frequency distribution that would be expected under the null hypothesis (theoretical distribution) and comparing it with the observed frequency distribution. The point at which the two distributions show the maximum deviation is determined, and the value of this deviation is used as the test statistic. The magnitude of the test statistic (D) indicates whether the divergence between the two distributions is likely to be due to chance or is indicative of a true preference.

The steps involved in the K-S test are as follows.

1. Specify the null and alternative hypotheses.

   ■ Null hypothesis H_0: There is no preference between the shades.
   ■ Alternative hypothesis H_a: There is a significant preference among the shades.

2. Establish the cumulative frequency distribution expected under the null hypothesis. The null hypothesis is that there is no difference in preference for the various shades of the new color. If this were true, the proportion of consumers preferring each shade would be equal to one-fifth, or .20.
3. Calculate the observed cumulative frequency distribution from the sample.
4. Select the level of significance α. If the .05 level of significance (α) is selected, the critical value of D for large samples is given by $1.36/\sqrt{n}$, where n is the sample size. In this case, the critical value is $1.36/\sqrt{500}$.

Table 15.4

Data for Kolmogorov-Smirnov Test

Color Shade	Observed Number	Observed Proportion	Observed Cumulative Proportion	Null Hypothesis Proportion	Null Cumulative Proportion	Absolute Difference (Observed and Null)
Very light	150	0.30	0.30	0.20	0.20	0.10
Light	170	0.34	0.64	0.20	0.40	0.24
Medium	80	0.16	0.80	0.20	0.60	0.20
Dark	45	0.09	0.89	0.20	0.80	0.09
Very dark	55	0.11	1.00	0.20	1.00	0.00

5. Determine the K-S *D* statistic. *D* is equal to the largest deviation in absolute terms between the observed cumulative frequency proportions and the expected cumulative frequency proportions. Table 15.4 provides the data in tabular form. The largest absolute difference is .24, which is the Kolmogorov-Smirnov *D* value.

6. State the result. Because the calculated *D* (.24) exceeds the critical value (.06), *the null hypothesis of no preference among shades is rejected.*

Hypotheses about One Mean

Z-Test

One of the most common goals of marketing research studies is to make some inference about the population mean. If the sample size is large enough ($n \geqslant 30$), the appropriate test statistic for testing a hypothesis about a single mean is the **Z-test.** For small samples ($n < 30$), the *t*-test with $n - 1$ degrees of freedom (where n = sample size) should be used.

Z-test
Hypothesis test used for a single mean if the sample is large enough and drawn from a normal population.

Video Connection, a Dallas video store chain, recently completed a survey of 200 consumers in its market area. One of the questions was "Compared to other video stores in the area, would you say Video Connection is much better than average, somewhat better than average, average, somewhat worse than average, or much worse than average?" Responses were coded as follows:

Response	Code
Much better	5
Somewhat better	4
Average	3
Somewhat worse	2
Much worse	1

The mean rating of Video Connection is 3.4. The sample standard deviation is 1.9. How can the management of Video Connection be confident that its video stores' mean rating is significantly higher than 3 (average in the rating scale)? The Z-test for hypotheses about one mean is the appropriate test in this situation. The steps in the procedure follow.

1. Specify the null and alternative hypotheses.

   ■ Null hypothesis H_0: $M \leqslant 3$ (M = response on rating scale)
   ■ Alternative hypothesis H_a: $M > 3$

2. Specify the level of sampling error (α) allowed. For $\alpha = .05$, the table value of Z(critical) = 1.64. (See Table 3 in Appendix 2 for d.f. = ∞, .05 significance, one-tail. The table for *t* is used because $t = Z$ for samples greater than 30.) Management's need to be very confident that the mean rating is significantly higher than 3 is interpreted to mean that the chance of being wrong because of sampling error should be no more than .05 (an α of .05).

3. Determine the sample standard deviation (S), which is given as $S = 1.90$.

4. Calculate the estimated standard error of the mean, using the formula

$$S_{\bar{X}} = \frac{S}{\sqrt{n}}$$

where $\quad S_{\bar{X}}$ = estimated standard error of the mean

In this case,

$$S_{\bar{X}} = \frac{1.9}{\sqrt{200}} = 0.13$$

5. Calculate the test statistic:

$$Z = \frac{(\text{Sample mean}) - \left(\begin{array}{c}\text{Population mean specified}\\ \text{under the null hypothesis}\end{array}\right)}{\text{Estimated standard error of the mean}}$$
$$= \frac{3.4 - 3}{0.13} = 3.07$$

6. State the result. *The null hypothesis can be rejected* because the calculated Z-value (3.07) is larger than the critical Z-value (1.64). Management of Video Connection can infer with 95 percent confidence that its video stores' mean rating is significantly higher than 3.

t-Test

t-test

Hypothesis test used for a single mean if the sample is too small to use the Z-test.

As noted earlier, for small samples ($n < 30$), the **t-test** with $n - 1$ degrees of freedom is the appropriate test for making statistical inferences. The *t*-distribution also is theoretically correct for large samples ($n \geqslant 30$). However, it approaches and becomes indistinguishable from the normal distribution for samples of 30 or more observations. Although the Z-test is generally used for large samples, some statistical packages (SAS, for example) use the *t*-test for all samples sizes.

To see the application of the *t*-test, consider a soft drink manufacturer that test markets a new soft drink in Denver. Twelve supermarkets in that city are selected at random, and the new soft drink is offered for sale in these stores for a limited period. The company estimates that it must sell 1,000 cases per week in each store for the brand to be profitable enough to warrant large-scale introduction. Actual average sales per store per week for the test are shown on page 525.

Here is the procedure for testing whether sales per store per week are more than 1,000 cases:

1. Specify the null and alternative hypotheses.

■ Null hypothesis H_0: $M \leqslant 1,000$ cases per store per week (M = average sales per store per week)

PART 4:
Data Analysis

■ Alternative hypothesis H_a: $M > 1,000$ cases per store per week

Store	Average Sales per Week (X_i)
1	870
2	910
3	1,050
4	1,200
5	860
6	1,400
7	1,305
8	890
9	1,250
10	1,100
11	950
12	1,260

$$\text{Mean sales per week, } \overline{X} = \frac{\sum_{i=1}^{n} X_i}{n} = 1087.1$$

2. Specify the level of sampling error (α) allowed. For $\alpha = .05$, the table value of t(critical) = 1.796. (See Table 3 in Appendix 2 for $12 - 1 = 11$ d.f., $\alpha = .05$, one-tail test. A one-tailed t-test is appropriate because the new soft drink will be introduced on a large scale only if sales per week are more than 1,000 cases.)

3. Determine the sample standard deviation (S) as follows:

$$S = \sqrt{\frac{\sum_{i=1}^{n} (X_i - \overline{X})^2}{n - 1}}$$

where X_i = observed sales per week in ith store
$\overline{X}$ = average sales per week
n = number of stores

For the sample data,

$$S = \sqrt{\frac{403,822.9}{(12 - 1)}} = 191.6$$

4. Calculate the estimated standard error of the mean ($S_{\overline{X}}$), using the following formula:

$$S_{\overline{X}} = \frac{S}{\sqrt{n}}$$

$$= \frac{191.6}{\sqrt{12}} = 55.31$$

5. Calculate the *t*-test statistic:

$$t = \frac{(\text{Sample mean}) - \left(\begin{array}{c}\text{Population mean}\\\text{under the null hypothesis}\end{array}\right)}{\text{Estimated standard error of the mean}}$$

$$= \frac{1,087.1 - 1,000}{55.31} = 1.57$$

6. State the result. *The null hypothesis cannot be rejected* because the calculated value of *t* is less than the critical value of *t*. Although mean sales per store per week ($\overline{X} = 1087.1$) are higher than 1,000 units, the difference is not statistically significant, based on the 12 stores sampled. On the basis of this test and the decision criterion specified, the large-scale introduction of the new soft drink is not warranted.

Hypotheses about Two Means

Marketers are frequently interested in testing differences between groups. In the following example of testing the differences between two means, the samples are independent.

The management of a convenience store chain is interested in differences between the store visit rates of men and women. Believing that men visit convenience stores more often than women, management collected data on convenience store visits from 1,000 randomly selected consumers. Testing this hypothesis involves the following steps:

1. Specify the null and alternative hypotheses.
- Null hypothesis H_0: $M_m - M_f \leq 0$; the mean visit rate of men (M_m) is the same as or less than the mean visit rate of women (M_f).
- Alternative hypothesis H_a: $M_m - M_f > 0$; the mean visit rate of men (M_m) is higher than the mean visit rate of women (M_f).

The observed difference in the two means (Table 15.3) is $11.49 - 8.51 = 2.98$.

2. Set the level of sampling error (α). The managers decided that the acceptable level of sampling error for this test is $\alpha = .05$. For $\alpha = .05$, the table value of $Z(\text{critical}) = 1.64$. (See Table 3 in Appendix 2 for d.f. $= \infty$, .05 significance, one-tail. The table for *t* is used because $t = Z$ for samples greater than 30.)

3. Calculate the estimated standard error of the differences between the two means as follows:

$$S_{X_{m-f}} = \sqrt{\frac{S_m^2}{n_m} + \frac{S_f^2}{n_f}}$$

where

S_m = estimated standard deviation of population *m* (men)
S_f = estimated standard deviation of population *f* (women)
n_m = sample size for sample *m*
n_f = sample size for sample *f*

Therefore,

$$S_{X_{m-f}} = \sqrt{\frac{(8.16)^2}{45} + \frac{(5.23)^2}{71}} = 1.37$$

Note that this formula is for those cases in which the two samples have unequal variances. A separate formula is used when the two samples have equal variances. When this test is run in SAS and many other statistical packages, two *t*-values are provided—one for each variance assumption.

4. Calculate the test statistic Z as follows:

$$Z = \frac{\left(\begin{array}{c}\text{Difference between means} \\ \text{of first and second sample}\end{array}\right) - \left(\begin{array}{c}\text{Difference between means} \\ \text{under the null hypothesis}\end{array}\right)}{\text{Standard error of the differences between the two means}}$$

$$= \frac{(11.49 - 8.51) - (0)}{1.37} = 2.18$$

Before launching new services designed for families with an annual income of more than $50,000, the bank needs to be certain about the percentage of its customers who meet or exceed this threshold income.

5. State the result. The calculated value of Z (2.18) is larger than the critical value (1.64), so *the null hypothesis is rejected.* Management can conclude with 95 percent confidence $(1 - \alpha = .95)$ that, on average, men visit convenience stores more often than do women.

Hypotheses about Proportions

In many situations, researchers are concerned with phenomena that are expressed in terms of percentages.[4] For example, marketers might be interested in testing for the proportion of respondents who prefer brand A versus those who prefer brand B or those who are brand loyal versus those who are not.

A Proportion in One Sample

A survey of 500 customers conducted by a major bank indicated that slightly more than 74 percent had family incomes of more than $50,000 per year. If this is true, the firm will develop a special package of services for this group. Before developing and introducing the new package of services, management wants to determine whether the true percentage is greater than 60 percent. The survey results show that 74.29 percent of the bank's customers surveyed reported family incomes of $50,000 or more per year. The procedure for the **hypothesis test of proportions** follows:

1. Specify the null and alternative hypotheses.

hypothesis test of proportions
Test to determine whether the difference between proportions is greater than would be expected because of sampling error.

- Null hypothesis H_0: $P \leq .60$
- Alternative hypothesis H_a: $P > .60$ (P = proportion of customers with family incomes of \$50,000 or more per year)

2. Specify the level of sampling error (α) allowed. For $\alpha = .05$, the table value of Z(critical) = 1.64. (See Table 3 in Appendix 2 for d.f. = ∞, .05 significance, one-tail. The table for t is used because $t = Z$ for samples greater than 30.)

3. Calculate the estimated standard error, using the value of P specified in the null hypothesis:

$$S_p = \sqrt{\frac{P(1 - P)}{n - 1}}$$

where P = proportion specified in the null hypothesis
n = sample size

Therefore,

$$S_p = \sqrt{\frac{.6(1 - .6)}{35 - 1}} = .084$$

4. Calculate the test statistic as follows:

$$Z = \frac{(\text{Observed proportion} - \text{Proportion under null hypothesis})}{\text{Estimated standard error } (S_p)}$$

$$= \frac{(0.7429 - 0.60)}{.084} = 1.7$$

The *null hypothesis is rejected* because the calculated Z-value is larger than the critical Z-value. The bank can conclude with 95 percent confidence ($1 - \alpha = .95$) that more than 60 percent of its customers have family incomes of \$50,000 or more. Management can introduce the new package of services targeted at this group.

Two Proportions in Independent Samples

In many instances, management is interested in the difference between the proportions of people in two different groups who engage in a certain activity or have a certain characteristic. For example, management of a convenience store chain had reason to believe, on the basis of a research study, that the percentage of men who visit convenience stores nine or more times per month (heavy users) was larger than the percentage of women who do so. The specifications required and the procedure for testing this hypothesis are as follows.

1. Specify the null and alternative hypotheses:

- Null hypothesis H_0: $P_m - P_f \leq 0$; the proportion of men (P_m) reporting nine or more visits per month is the same as or less than the proportion of women (P_f) reporting nine or more visits per month.

- Alternative hypothesis H_a: $P_m - P_f > 0$; the proportion of men (P_m) reporting nine or more visits per month is greater than the proportion of women (P_f) reporting nine or more visits per month.

The sample proportions and the difference can be calculated from Table 15.3 as follows:

$$P_m = \frac{26}{45} = .58$$

$$P_f = \frac{30}{71} = .42$$

$$P_m - P_f = .58 - .42 = .16$$

2. Set the level of sampling error α at .10 (management decision). For $\alpha = .10$, the table value of Z(critical) $= 1.28$. (See Table 3 in Appendix 2 for d.f. $= \infty$, .10 significance, one-tail. The table for t is used because $t = Z$ for samples greater than 30.)

3. Calculate the estimated standard error of the differences between the two proportions as follows:

$$S_{P_{m-f}} = \sqrt{P(1 - P)\left(\frac{1}{n_m} + \frac{1}{n_f}\right)}$$

where $P = \dfrac{n_m P_m + n_f P_f}{n_m + n_f}$

P_m = proportion in sample m (men)
P_f = proportion in sample f (women)
n_m = size of sample m
n_f = size of sample f

Therefore,

$$P = \frac{45(.58) + 71(.41)}{45 + 71} = .48$$

and $\quad S_{P_{m-f}} = \sqrt{.48(1 - .48)\left(\frac{1}{45} + \frac{1}{71}\right)} = .10$

4. Calculate the test statistic.

$$Z = \frac{\left(\begin{array}{c}\text{Difference between}\\\text{observed proportions}\end{array}\right) - \left(\begin{array}{c}\text{Difference between proportions}\\\text{under the null hypothesis}\end{array}\right)}{\begin{array}{c}\text{Estimated standard error of the differences}\\\text{between the two means}\end{array}}$$

$$= \frac{(.58 - .42) - 0}{.10} = 1.60$$

5. State the result. *The null hypothesis is rejected* because the calculated *Z*-value (1.60) is larger than the critical *Z*-value (1.28 for $\alpha = .10$). Management can conclude with 90 percent confidence ($1 - \alpha = .90$) that the proportion of men who visit convenience stores nine or more times per month is larger than the proportion of women who do so.

It should be noted that if the level of sampling error α had been set at .05, the critical *Z*-value would equal 1.64. In this case, we would fail to reject (FTR) the null hypothesis because *Z*(calculated) would be smaller than *Z*(critical).

Statistics on the Internet

The number of statistical resources available on the Internet is growing exponentially. A variety of special-purpose statistical programs and general information sites can now be accessed online. As we have consistently recommended, it is best to learn one of the popular statistical packages such as SPSS or STATISTICA or to use the excellent statistical features in a popular program such as Excel.

An expanded list of statistics sites is provided in Table 15.5. It should be noted that special-purpose programs found on the Internet may not offer the comprehensiveness, integration, data management, and manipulation features—or widespread use and familiarity—of the better known packages. All of this will probably change, and Web-accessible statistical software offering all the important features will be available on a per-usage basis.

There is a tremendous amount of statistical information and advice available over the Internet. The Web is becoming a very useful source of information on the selection of appropriate statistical techniques for a particular problem, the proper use of different statistical techniques, and emerging statistical techniques that have not yet found their way into mainstream statistical packages. Shown in Figure 15.3 is the opening page of the *Electronic Statistics Textbook* offered by StatSoft. You will find it to be an excellent source of advice and information on a wide range of statistical topics, from basic to advanced. In addition, news and special-interest groups can be a valuable source of information and advice regarding the proper use of statistical procedures. Your Web browser can be used to access new groups if you have set up this feature with your Internet service provider. New groups are typically accessed through the email menu.

Analysis of Variance (ANOVA)

analysis of variance (ANOVA)
Test for the differences among the means of two or more variables.

When the goal is to test the differences among the means of two or more independent samples, **analysis of variance (ANOVA)** is an appropriate statistical tool. Although it can be used to test differences between two means, ANOVA is more commonly used for hypothesis tests regarding the differences among the means of several (*C*) independent groups (where $C \geq 3$). It is a statistical technique that permits the researcher to determine whether the variability among or across the *C* sample means is greater than expected because of sampling error.

PART 4:
Data Analysis

Table 15.5

Statistical Software Sites on the Internet

ActivStats
http://www.datadesk.com/ActivStats

This site provides an excellent online statistics tutorial. You can find the usual info about the software, examples showing how it works, and various teacher support materials.

Autobox
http://www.autobox.com

Autobox is a tool for forecasting/time series analysis. The Web site includes links to the software as well as documentation. Home page layout is a little strange, but you can find some very useful and helpful information on this site.

Easystat
http://www.uni-koeln.de/themen/Statistik/easystat/index.e.html

This is a simple package which specializes in ANOVA models. Information is also provided in German.

Guide to Available Math Software
http://gams.nist.gov

This statistics site is maintained by the National Institute of Standards and Technology. It provides an index and cross-index of just about all the statistics software available.

Minitab
http://www.minitab.com

This is the home page for Minitab statistical software. It provides the standard product information, technical support, and other information.

NCSS Home Page
http://amsquare.com/ncss

This is the home page for the NCSS statistical software package. It includes links to a freeware probability calculator for Windows and a freeware version of NCSS.

The SAS Institute
http://www.sas.com

This site provides information on the SAS Institute and its products and services.

SPSS Inc.
http://www.spss.com

This site provides detailed product information and other statistics resources. SPSS is the general statistics package most popular among marketing researchers.

Stata Home Page
http://www.stata.com

This site provides in-depth information on the Stata statistics package. It also provides a list of other statistical software companies and NetCourses on how to use their software.

STATGRAPHICS
http://www.statgraphics.com

This site supports the STATGRAPHICS package for Windows. The site includes the standard product and contact information, tech support, and an excellent Graphics Gallery.

Statsoft, Inc.
http://www.statsoftinc.com

This is the site for the very powerful STATISTICA package. It also provides a wide range of resources, including some very helpful information on statistical issues.

SYSTAT
http://www.spssscience.com/systat

This package is now owned by SPSS. Some believe that it is oriented toward scientific research. It has some excellent graphics capabilities.

Unistat
http://www.unistat.com

This is a comprehensive statistics package that is integrated with Microsoft Office. A demo is available from the site.

Viz!on
http://www.datadesk.com/Viz!on

This is another Excel add-on that offers some very good graphics tools for Excel users.

xlSTAT Home Page
http://www.xlstat.com

This is yet another Microsoft Office add-on.

Figure 15.3

Opening Page of the _Electronic Statistics Textbook_

Source: © Copyright StatSoft, Inc., 1984–2000 _STATISTICA_ is a trademark of StatSoft, Inc.

ELECTRONIC TEXTBOOK StatSoft

To search the Electronic Statistics Textbook for terms and general statistical concepts, enter keywords/phrases below:

[Search] [Clear]

Search Tips

CLICK HERE to recommend this site to a friend!

| Britannica Internet Guide Award | StatSoft web site praised for Quality, Accuracy, Presentation and Usability. |

The complete Electronic Statistics Textbook can be downloaded for quick access from your local hard drive. Directions for correctly installing the textbook are also available.

This Electronic Statistics Textbook offers training in the understanding and application of statistics. The material was developed at the StatSoft R&D department based on many years of teaching undergraduate and graduate statistics courses and covers a wide variety of applications, including laboratory research (biomedical, agricultural, etc.), business statistics and forecasting, social science statistics and survey research, data mining, engineering and quality control applications, and many others.

The Electronic Textbook begins with an overview of the relevant elementary (pivotal) concepts and continues with a more in depth exploration of specific areas of statistics, organized by "modules," accessible by buttons, representing classes of analytic techniques. A glossary of statistical terms and a list of references for further study are included.

Proper citation: StatSoft, Inc. (1999). Electronic Statistics Textbook. Tulsa, OK: StatSoft. WEB: http://www.statsoft.com/textbook/stathome.html.

If your browser does not support the advanced features of the Electronic Textbook, click here.

Elementary Concepts in Statistics

Overview of Elementary Concepts in Statistics. In this introduction, we will briefly discuss those elementary statistical concepts that provide the necessary foundations for more specialized expertise in any area of statistical data analysis. The selected topics illustrate the basic assumptions of most statistical methods and/or have been demonstrated in research to be necessary components of one's general understanding of the "quantitative nature" of reality (Nisbett, et al., 1987). Because of space limitations, we will focus mostly on the functional aspects of the concepts discussed and the presentation will be very short. Further information on each of those concepts can be found in the Introductory Overview and Examples sections of this manual and in statistical textbooks. Recommended introductory textbooks are: Kachigan (1986), and Runyon and Haber (1976); for a more advanced discussion of elementary theory and assumptions of statistics, see the classic books by Hays (1988), and Kendall and Stuart (1979).

- What are variables?
- Correlational vs. experimental research
- Dependent vs. independent variables
- Measurement scales
- Relations between variables
- Why relations between variables are important
- Two basic features of every relation between variables
- What is "statistical significance" (p-value)
- How to determine that a result is "really" significant
- Statistical significance and the number of analyses performed
- Strength vs. reliability of a relation between variables
- Why stronger relations between variables are more significant

- Why significance of a relation between variables depends on the size of the sample
- Example: "Baby boys to baby girls ratio"
- Why small relations can be proven significant only in large samples
- Can "no relation" be a significant result?
- How to measure the magnitude (strength) of relations between variables
- Common "general format" of most statistical tests
- How the "level of statistical significance" is calculated
- Why the "Normal distribution" is important
- Illustration of how the normal distribution is used in statistical reasoning (induction)
- Are all test statistics normally distributed?
- How do we know the consequences of violating the normality assumption?

ELECTRONIC TEXTBOOK StatSoft

The Z- and t-tests described earlier normally are used to test the null hypothesis when only two sample means are involved. However, in situations in which there are three or more samples, it would be inefficient to test differences between the means two at a time. With five samples and associated means, 10 t-tests would be required to test all pairs of means. More important, the use of Z- or t-tests in situations involving three or more means increases the probability of a Type 1 error. Because these tests must be performed for all possible pairs of means, the more pairs, the more tests that must be performed. And the more tests performed, the more likely it is that one or more tests will show significant differences that are really due to sampling error. At an α of .05, this could be expected to occur in 1 of 20 tests on average.

One-way ANOVA is often used to analyze experimental results. Suppose the marketing manager for a chain of brake shops was considering three different services for a possible in-store promotion: wheel alignment, oil change, and tune-up. She was interested in knowing whether there were significant differences in potential sales of the three services.

Sixty similar stores (20 in each of three cities) were selected at random from among those operated by the chain. One of the services was introduced in each of three cities. Other variables under the firm's direct control, such as price and advertising, were kept at the same level during the course of the experiment. The experiment was conducted for a 30-day period, and sales of the new services were recorded for the period.

A brake shop might use analysis of variance to analyze experimental results with respect to several new services before deciding on a particular new service to offer.

Average sales for each shop are shown below. The question is, are the differences among the means larger than would be expected due to chance?

Chicago (Wheel Alignment)		Cleveland (Oil Change)		Detroit (Tune-Up)	
310	318	314	321	337	310
315	322	315	340	325	312
305	333	350	318	330	340
310	315	305	315	345	318
315	385	299	322	320	322
345	310	309	295	325	335
340	312	299	302	328	341
330	308	312	316	330	340
320	312	331	294	342	320
315	340	335	308	330	310
$\overline{X} = 323$		$\overline{X} = 315$		$\overline{X} = 328$	

1. Specify the null and alternative hypotheses.

■ Null hypothesis H_0: $M_1 = M_2 = M_3$; mean sales of the three items are equal.

■ Alternative hypothesis H_a: The variability in group means is greater than would be expected because of sampling error.

2. Sum the squared differences between each subsample mean $(\overline{X}_j)$ and the overall sample mean $(\overline{X}_t)$, weighted by sample size (n_j). This is called the *sum of squares among groups* or among group variation (SSA). SSA is calculated as follows:

$$SSA = \sum_{j=1}^{C} n_j(\overline{X}_j - \overline{X}_t)^2$$

In this example, the overall sample mean is

$$\overline{X}_t = \frac{20(323) + 20(315) + 20(328)}{60} = 322$$

Thus,

$$SSA = 20(323 - 322)^2 + 20(315 - 322)^2 + 20(328 - 322)^2$$
$$= 1{,}720$$

The greater the differences among the sample means, the larger the SSA will be.

3. Calculate the variation among group means as measured by the *mean sum of squares among groups* (MSA). The MSA is calculated as follows:

$$MSA = \frac{\text{Sum of squares among groups (SSA)}}{\text{Degrees of freedom (d.f.)}}$$

where   Degrees of freedom = number of groups $(C) - 1$

In this example,

$$\text{d.f.} = 3 - 1 = 2$$

Thus,

$$MSA = \frac{1{,}720}{2} = 860$$

4. Sum the squared differences between each observation (X_{ij}) and its associated sample mean $(\overline{X}_j)$, accumulated over all C levels (groups). Also called the *sum of squares within groups* or *within group variation*, it is generally referred to as the *sum of squared error* (SSE). For this example, the SSE is calculated as follows:

$$SSE = \sum_{j=1}^{C} \sum_{i=1}^{n_j} (X_{ij} - \overline{X}_j)^2$$
$$= (6{,}644) + (4{,}318) + (2{,}270) = 13{,}232$$

5. Calculate the variation within the sample groups as measured by the mean sum of squares within groups. Referred to as *mean square error* (MSE), it represents an estimate of the random error in the data. The MSE is calculated as follows:

$$\text{MSE} = \frac{\text{Sum of squares within groups (SSE)}}{\text{Degrees of freedom (d.f.)}}$$

The number of degrees of freedom is equal to the sum of the sample sizes for all groups minus the number of groups (C):

$$\text{d.f.} = \left(\sum_{j=1}^{K} n_j \right) - C$$
$$= (20 + 20 + 20) - 3 = 57$$

Thus,

$$\text{MSE} = \frac{13{,}232}{57} = 232.14$$

As with the Z-distribution and t-distribution, a sampling distribution known as the *F-distribution* permits the researcher to determine the probability that a particular calculated value of F could have occurred by chance rather than as a result of the treatment effect. The F-distribution, like the t-distribution, is really a set of distributions whose shape changes slightly depending on the number and size of the samples involved. To use the **F-test,** it is necessary to calculate the degrees of freedom for the numerator and the denominator.

6. Calculate the F-statistic as follows:

$$F = \frac{\text{MSA}}{\text{MSE}}$$
$$= \frac{860}{232.14} = 3.70$$

The numerator is the MSA, and the number of degrees of freedom associated with it is 2 (step 3). The denominator is the MSE, and the number of degrees of freedom associated with it is 57 (step 5).

7. State the results. For an alpha of .05, the table value of F(critical) with 2 (numerator) and 57 (denominator) degrees of freedom is approximately 3.15. (See Table 5 in Appendix 2 for d.f. for denominator = 5, d.f. for numerator = 2, .05 significance.) The calculated F-value (3.70) is greater than the table value (3.15), and so *the null hypothesis is rejected.* By rejecting the null hypothesis, we conclude that the variability observed in the three means is greater than expected due to chance.

F-test

Test of the probability that a particular calculated value could have been due to chance.

The results of an ANOVA generally are displayed as follows:

Source of Variation	Sum of Squares	Degrees of Freedom	Mean Square	F-Statistic
Treatments	1,720 (SSA)	2 (C − 1)	860 (MSA)	3.70 calculated
Error	13,232 (SSE)	57 (n − C)	232.14 (MSE)	
Total	14,592 (SST)	59 (n − 1)		

p-Values and Significance Testing

For the various tests discussed in this chapter, a standard—a level of significance and associated critical value of the statistics—is established and then the value of the statistic is calculated to see whether it beats that standard. If the calculated

What Is Meant by Statistically Significant?

In PRACTICE

PSYCHOLOGY PROFESSOR ROBERT ABELSON OF YALE UNIVERSITY GIVES some valuable perspective to researchers using significance testing in their work. Unbending insistence on the .05 level for p-values is misguided, in Abelson's view.[5]

We act foolishly when we celebrate results with $p = .05$, but wallow in self-pity when $p = .07$. It is more subtly misguided when we lay a "significant" outcome alongside a "nonsignificant" one and make a comparative claim. For example, we might say, "The experimental effect is significant for wombats but not for dingbats, confirming the hypothesized importance of the bats factor." The error here is easy to understand when results for the wombats reach $p = .05$, and for the dingbats only .07, but the error still applies in less obvious cases.

In *Statistics as Principled Argument,* I advanced five criteria for judging the quality of a research claim.[6] Corresponding to the acronym MAGIC, these criteria are magnitude of effect, articulation of effect, generality of effect, interestingness, and credibility. Of these five criteria, p-values have relevance only to credibility (for a novel finding) and generality (for a replication). Associated with credibility are several factors, such as theoretical coherence, plausibility of postulated psychological processes, and last and perhaps least, the p-value for the null-hypothesis test. Literal insistence on the .05 level is as silly as would be other arbitrarily rigid quality standards for research results, like 30 percent generality, or a higher level of interest than three quarters of the existing literature.

Null-hypothesis tests are cogent in scrutinizing surprising results that critics doubt. They address the alternative argument that some familiar chance mechanism could have produced the results. ∎

value of the statistic exceeds the critical value, then the result being tested is said to be statistically significant at that level.

However, this approach does not give the exact probability of getting a computed test statistic that is largely due to chance. The calculations to compute this probability, commonly referred to as the **p-value,** are tedious to perform by hand. Fortunately, they are easy for computers. The p-value is the most demanding level of statistical (not managerial) significance that can be met, based on the calculated value of the statistic. Computer statistical packages usually use one of the following labels to identify the probability that the distance between the hypothesized population parameter and the observed test statistic could have occurred due to chance:

- p-value
- ≤ PROB
- PROB =

The smaller the p-value, the smaller is the probability that the observed result occurred by chance (sampling error).

An example of computer output showing a p-value calculation appears in Table 15.6. This analysis shows the results of a t-test of the differences between means for two independent samples. In this case, the null hypothesis H_0 is that there is no difference between what men and women would be willing to pay for a new communications service. (The variable name is GENDER, with the numeric codes of 0 for males and 1 for females. Subjects were asked how much they would be willing to pay per month for a new wireless communications service that was described to them via a videotape. Variable ADDEDPAY is their response to the question.) The results show that women are willing to pay an average of $16.82 for the new service and men are willing to pay $20.04. Is this a significant difference? The calculated value for t of -1.328 indicates, via the associated p-value of .185, that there is an 18.5 percent chance that the difference is due to sampling error. If, for example, the standard for the test were set at .10 (willing to accept a 10 percent chance of incorrectly rejecting H_0), then the analyst would *fail to reject* H_0 in this case.

p-value
The exact probability of getting a computed test statistic that was largely due to chance. The smaller the p-value, the smaller the probability that the observed result occurred by chance.

Table 15.6

Sample STATISTICA t-Test Output

Stat. Basic Stats	Grouping: GENDER (pcs. sta) Group 1: G_1:1 Group 2: G_2:0						
Variable	Mean G_1:1	Mean G_2:0	t-value	df	P	Valid N G_1:1	Valid N G_2:0
ADDED PAY	16.82292	20.04717	-1.32878	200	.185434	96	106

What Is True?

SANDRA SCARR IS THE CHAIRPERSON AND CEO OF KINDERCARE LEARNING Centers, Incorporated, based in Montgomery, Alabama. She recently participated in a radio call-in show on National Public Radio (NPR), where the topic was whether mothers' employment adversely affects infants and toddlers.[7] While Scarr represented the view that mothers' employment does not adversely affect infants and toddlers in families where the mother works outside the home, a psychologist-author of a new book advocating that mothers remain at home took the contending position. During the broadcast, Scarr cited eight recent research studies involving thousands of families in four countries with psychometrically credible measures and appropriate analysis that supported her position. The advocate for mothers staying at home cited her own psychotherapeutic clients as evidence for pain associated with nonmaternal care in childhood. Scarr reports that both the NPR host and callers to the show seemed to weigh the evidence from both sides equally. Scarr cites this phenomenon of weighing intuitive evidence from a small and exceptional sample (the pool of clients for the psychotherapist) as equal to evidence from large and representative samples in multiple studies as indicative of a lack of agreed-upon rules about what constitutes evidence in public discussions and in the media.

In discussions in the scientific community, a realm of discourse is defined about what is "true." Among scientists and professional marketing researchers, there is common acceptance of probability and sampling theory and the relevance of these to understanding what constitutes evidence. Unfortunately, many laypersons in the public regularly use exceptions to disprove rules, and are at least as impressed by case histories and anecdotes as they are by scientific research results. Scarr believes such faulty use of evidence is a result of failing to educate the public to think of all knowledge as probabilistic and needing evaluation for reliability.

Scarr blames public health and government regulatory agencies for blemishing the use of statistical evidence. Epidemiological studies have become notorious for their abuse of statistical significance testing. With a sample size of 25,000, even minute associations between consuming one type of food and brain cancer may be found at a level of statistical significance of $p = .05$. But with the rise in use of electronic customer databases and scanner data, marketing researchers have also been more prone to confusing statistical significance with practical importance. Scarr believes that a better word for statistical significance would be reliability, because most English speakers link significance with importance. The intended meaning of statistical significance is the reproducibility of a result.

Conversely, some marketing research studies (along with studies in other social science fields) have abused the statistical significance test by having too few respondents (especially in subgroups of the sample to be compared). In such a situation, power to detect an association (or a difference in means) is weak. Consequently, the error rate is much higher than the 5 percent error researchers believe they are using. John Hunter of Michigan State University has estimated the average error rate (considering both Type I error and Type 2 error in studies) in the field of psychology is 60 percent.[8] This would suggest that someone flipping a coin would have a lower error rate than someone conducting a study with too few respondents. All of this is presented to stress the importance of a well-designed study with an appropriate sampling plan to permit a scientific appraisal of evidence. ■

Summary

The purpose of making statistical inferences is to generalize from sample results to population characteristics. Three important concepts applied to the notion of differences are mathematical differences, managerially important differences, and statistical significance.

A hypothesis is an assumption or theory that a researcher or manager makes about some characteristic of the population being investigated. By testing, the researcher determines whether a hypothesis concerning some characteristic of the population is valid. A statistical hypothesis test permits the researcher to calculate the probability of observing the particular result if the stated hypothesis actually were true. In hypothesis testing, the first step is to specify the hypothesis. Next, an appropriate statistical technique should be selected to test the hypothesis. Then, a decision rule must be specified as the basis for determining whether to reject or fail to reject the hypothesis. Hypothesis tests are subject to two types of errors called Type I (α error) and Type II (β error). A Type I error involves rejecting the null hypothesis when it is, in fact, true. A Type II error involves failing to reject the null hypothesis when the alternative hypothesis actually is true. Finally, the value of the test statistic is calculated, and a conclusion is stated that summarizes the results of the test.

Marketing researchers often develop crosstabulations, whose purpose usually is to uncover interrelationships among the variables. Usually the researcher needs to determine whether the numbers of subjects, objects, or responses that fall into some set of categories differ from those expected by chance. Thus, a test of goodness of fit of the observed distribution in relation to an expected distribution is appropriate. Two common tests of goodness of fit are chi-square and Kolmogorov-Smirnov.

Often marketing researchers need to make inferences about a population mean. If the sample size is equal to or greater than 30 and the sample comes from a normal population, the appropriate test statistic for testing hypotheses about means is the Z-test. For small samples, researchers use the t-test with $n - 1$ degrees of freedom when making inferences (n is the size of the sample).

When researchers are interested in testing differences between responses to the same variable, such as advertising, by groups with different characteristics, they test for differences between two means. A Z-value is calculated and compared to the critical value of Z. Based on the result of the comparison, they either reject or fail to reject the null hypothesis. The Z-test also can be used to examine hypotheses about proportions from one sample or independent samples.

When researchers need to test for differences among the means of three or more independent samples, analysis of variance is an appropriate statistical tool. It is often used for hypothesis tests regarding the differences among the means of several independent groups. It permits the researcher to test the null hypothesis that there are no significant differences among the population group means.

Key Terms & Definitions

hypothesis Assumption or theory that a researcher or manager makes about some characteristic of the population under study.

Type I error (α error) Rejection of the null hypothesis when, in fact, it is true.

Type II error (ß error) Acceptance of the null hypothesis when, in fact, it is false.

independent samples Samples in which measurement of a variable in one population has no effect on measurement of the variable in the other.

related samples Samples in which measurement of a variable in one population may influence measurement of the variable in the other.

chi-square test Test of the goodness of fit between the observed distribution and the expected distribution of a variable.

Kolmogorov-Smirnov (K-S) test Test of the goodness of fit between the observed distribution and the expected distribution, using ordinal data.

Z-test Hypothesis test used for a single mean if the sample is large enough and drawn from a normal population.

t-test Hypothesis test used for a single mean if the sample is too small to use the Z-test.

hypothesis test of proportions Test to determine whether the difference between proportions is greater than would be expected because of sampling error.

analysis of variance (ANOVA) Test for the differences among the means of two or more variables.

F-test Test of the probability that a particular calculated value could have been due to chance.

p-value The exact probability of getting a computed test statistic that was largely due to chance. The smaller the p-value, the smaller the probability that the observed result occurred by chance.

PART 4:
Data Analysis

Questions for Review & Critical Thinking

1. Explain the notions of mathematical differences, managerially important differences, and statistical significance. Can results be statistically significant and yet lack managerial importance? Explain your answer.
2. Describe the steps in the procedure for testing hypotheses. Discuss the difference between a null hypothesis and an alternative hypothesis.
3. Distinguish between a Type I error and a Type II error. What is the relationship between the two?
4. What is meant by the terms *independent samples* and *related samples*? Why is it important for a researcher to determine whether a sample is independent?
5. Your university library is concerned about student desires for library hours on Sunday morning (9:00 A.M.–12:00 P.M.). It has undertaken to survey a random sample of 1,600 undergraduate students (one-half men, one-half women) in each of four status levels (i.e., 400 freshmen, 400 sophomores, 400 juniors, 400 seniors). If the percentages of students preferring Sunday morning hours are those shown below, what conclusions can the library reach?

	Seniors	Juniors	Sophomores	Freshmen
Women	70	53	39	26
Men	30	48	31	27

6. A local car dealer was attempting to determine which premium would draw the most visitors to its showroom. An individual who visits the showroom and takes a test ride is given a premium with no obligation. The dealer chose four premiums and offered each for one week. The results are as follows.

Week	Premium	Total Given Out
1	Four-foot metal stepladder	425
2	$50 savings bond	610
3	Dinner for four at a local steak house	510
4	Six pink flamingos plus an outdoor thermometer	705

Using a chi-square test, what conclusions can you draw regarding the premiums?

7. A market researcher has completed a study of pain relievers. The following table depicts the brands purchased most often, broken down by men versus women. Perform a chi-square test on the data and determine what can be said regarding the crosstabulation.

Pain Relievers	Men	Women
Anacin	40	55
Bayer	60	28
Bufferin	70	97
Cope	14	21
Empirin	82	107
Excedrin	72	84
Excedrin PM	15	11
Vanquish	20	26

8. Five hundred women who use a particular type of makeup were interviewed regarding their preferences for six shades of the makeup. The results, showing the number who preferred each shade, follow. The results are listed in order from darkest to lightest.

	Number Preferring
Shade 1 (darkest)	52
Shade 2	57
Shade 3	83
Shade 4	187
Shade 5	61
Shade 6 (lightest)	60

Using the Kolmogorov-Smirnov test, test the null hypothesis of no preference between shades. Based on the results of the test, do you think it makes any difference which shade is used? Explain.

9. A child psychologist observed eight-year-old children behind a one-way mirror to determine how long they would play with a toy medical kit. The company that designed the toy was attempting to determine whether to give the kit a masculine or a feminine orientation. The lengths of time (in minutes) the children played with the kits are shown below. Calculate the value of Z and recommend to management whether the kit should have a male or a female orientation.

Boys	Girls	Boys	Girls
31	26	67	9
12	38	67	9
41	20	25	16
34	32	73	26
63	16	36	81
7	45	41	20
		15	5

10. American Airlines is trying to determine which baggage handling system to put in its new hub terminal in San Juan, Puerto Rico. One system is made by Jano Systems, and the second is manufactured by Dynamic Enterprises. American has installed a small Jano system and a small Dynamic Enterprises system in two of its low-volume terminals. Both terminals handle approximately the same quantity of baggage each month. American has decided to select the system that provides the minimum number of instances in which passengers disembarking must wait 20 minutes or longer for baggage. Analyze the data that follow and determine whether there is a significant difference at the .95 level of confidence between the two systems. If there is a difference, which system should American select?

Minutes of Waiting	Jano Systems (Frequency)	Dynamic Enterprises (Frequency)
10–11	4	10
12–13	10	8
14–15	14	14
16–17	4	20
18–19	2	12
20–21	4	6
22–23	2	12
24–25	14	4
26–27	6	13
28–29	10	8
30–31	12	6
32–33	2	8
34–35	2	8
36 or more	2	2

11. Menu space is always limited in fast food restaurants. However, McDonalds has decided that it needs to add one more salad dressing to its menu for its garden salad and chef salad. It has decided to test market four flavors: Caesar, Ranch-Style, Green Goddess, and Russian. Fifty restaurants were selected in the North-Central region to sell each new dressing. Thus, a total of 200 stores were used in the research project. The study was conducted for two weeks; the units of each dressing sold are shown below. As a researcher, you want to know if the differences among the average daily sales of the dressings are larger than can be reasonably expected by chance. If so, which dressing would you recommend be added to the inventory throughout the United States?

Day	Caesar	Ranch-Style	Green Goddess	Russian
1	155	143	149	135
2	157	146	152	136
3	151	141	146	131
4	146	136	141	126
5	181	180	173	115
6	160	152	170	150
7	168	157	174	147
8	157	167	141	130
9	139	159	129	119
10	144	154	167	134
11	158	169	145	144
13	184	195	178	177
14	161	177	201	151

Working the Net

1. Which conference in the National Football League is more fun to watch? To compare the average total offense yardage for teams from the NFC with that for teams from the AFC, go to http://www.nfl.com. Select "Stats" and then "Total Offense." Conduct a *t*-test comparing the two means to determine if the difference is statistically significant.

2. What kinds of publications can you obtain to assist your marketing research efforts? To find out, go to http://www.marketingtools.com.

Real-Life Research • 15.1

I Can't Believe It's Yogurt

Phil Jackson, research manager for I Can't Believe It's Yogurt (ICBIY), is trying to develop a more rational basis for evaluating alternative store locations. ICBIY has been growing rapidly, and historically the issue of store location has not been critical. It didn't seem to matter where stores were located—all were successful. However, the yogurt craze has faded, and some of its new stores and a few of its old ones are experiencing difficulties in the form of declining sales.

ICBIY wants to continue expanding, but recognizes that it must be much more careful in selecting locations than it was in the past. It has determined that the percentage of individuals in an area who have visited a frozen yogurt store in the past 30 days is the best predictor of the potential for one of its stores—the higher that percentage, the better.

ICBIY wants to locate a store in Denver and has identified two locations that, on the basis of the other criteria, look good. It has conducted a survey of households in the areas that would be served from each location. The results of that survey are shown below.

Yogurt Store Patronage	Both Areas	Area A	Area B
Have patronized in past 30 days	465	220	245
Have not patronized	535	280	255

Questions

1. Determine whether there is a significant difference at the .05 level between the two areas.
2. Based on this analysis, what would you recommend to ICBIY regarding which of the two areas it should choose for the new store? Explain your recommendation.

Real-Life Research • 15.2

Regina Vacuum Cleaners

Regina Vacuum Cleaners has embarked on an image enhancement program for its product line, which has been in a state of decline. Focus group research identified the use of color as something that would capture consumer interest and, possibly, significantly improve sales. Based on mall-intercept testing of six different colors for the bag of the company's main product, an upright vacuum, researchers have chosen yellow as the preferred color. They have just completed a survey of 1,000 consumers with demographic profiles that fit the target market. This research also was conducted using a mall-intercept format. The results, showing the number of consumers who prefer each shade of yellow, appear in the table.

Color	Number of Consumers Who Preferred It
Shade 1 (darkest)	70
Shade 2	85
Shade 3	140
Shade 4	160
Shade 5	150
Shade 6	135
Shade 7	85
Shade 8	75
Shade 9	40
Shade 10 (lightest)	60

Questions

1. Use the Kolmogorov-Smirnov test to determine whether the observed distribution of preferences is likely due to chance or indicates a significant preference for a particular shade or shades of the color.
2. Based on the results of the statistical test, what recommendation would you make to Regina Vacuum Cleaners regarding customer preference?

PART 4:
Data Analysis

Real-Life Research • 15.3

Silverado Power

Dave LaFrance is the new marketing research director for Silverado Power, an investor-owned, vertically integrated electric utility involved in the generation, transmission, distribution, and energy service domains of the electricity industry. Dave was hired to help Silverado transition to a competitive environment for energy services, which will occur in one year. In this environment, customers will be allowed to select their provider of electricity, much as customers now select long-distance telecommunications service from providers such as Sprint, MCI, and AT&T.

One of the crucial questions for Silverado is that of current customer retention. How many current customers will switch to another provider of electric services during the first six months of competition? To address this question, Dave and his team designed and fielded a survey in the current service territory of Silverado. They had 500 customers give complete answers to all questions. Initial results indicate that 30 percent of customers would switch. The margin of error is 4 percent, which means that (at the 95 percent confidence level) the actual percentage of customers switching could be a low as 26 percent or as high as 34 percent. Silverado senior management is concerned about this error range of 4 percent, which means that error spans a total of 8 percentage points. Future customer retention efforts must be budgeted now, and Silverado senior management wants firmer numbers on which to base strategies and budgets.

Questions

1. How could the error range be reduced without collecting more data?
2. Do you think Silverado senior management would find this approach to reducing the error range satisfactory?
3. If 500 more respondents were surveyed and 30 percent of them indicated that they would switch, what would the error range become?

Chapter Sixteen

Bivariate Correlation and Regression

Learning Objectives

To comprehend the nature of correlation analysis.

1

To understand bivariate regression analysis.

2

To become aware of the coefficient of determination R^2.

3

To understand Spearman rank-order correlation.

4

J OE CHAN AND HIS BOSS, TONYA BOYD, manage the sales force for TexArka Commercial Leasing in Dallas, Texas. They are in the process of doing a careful evaluation of the performance of individual salespersons in their organization. After examining the results for the past two years, Chan believes that *years of experience in the industry* is the best indicator of the volume of sales a salesperson will produce. On the other hand, Boyd believes that *number of calls made* by a salesperson is the best predictor of the sales volume. They have discussed the issue with Adam Davidson, the analyst who works in their department. He suggested that correlation analysis be used to resolve their debate.

DAVIDSON TOOK THE DATA FOR SALESPEOPLE WHO HAVE WORKED FOR THE company for the last two years and ran two separate correlations. First, for each salesperson, he correlated sales with number of years in the industry. Second, he ran correlations between sales and number of calls made. The correlation coefficient between sales and years in the industry was .27. The correlation coefficient between sales and number of calls made was .54. His conclusion is that number of calls made is more closely associated with sales volume produced. ∎

Correlation analysis provides a means of evaluating salesperson performance for this Dallas, Texas company.

Find out more about correlation analysis at

http://www.statsoft. com/textbook/ stbasic. html#correlations

This chapter addresses correlation analysis and related techniques. After you read the chapter, you will be prepared to decide whether Davidson's conclusion is correct. If it is, what are the implications for Chan and Boyd?

Bivariate Analysis of Association

In many marketing research studies, the interests of the researcher and manager go beyond issues that can be addressed by the statistical testing of differences discussed in Chapter 15. They may be interested in the degree of association between two variables. Statistical techniques appropriate for this type of analysis are referred to as **bivariate techniques.** When more than two variables are involved, the techniques employed are known as *multivariate techniques.* Multivariate techniques are discussed in Chapter 17.

bivariate techniques
Statistical methods of analyzing the relationship between two variables.

independent variable
The symbol or concept that the researcher has some control over or can manipulate to some extent and that is hypothesized to cause or influence the dependent variable.

dependent variable
A symbol or concept expected to be explained or caused by the independent variable.

When the degree of association between two variables is analyzed, the variables are classified as the **independent** (predictor) **variable** and the **dependent** (criterion) **variable.** Independent variables are those that are believed to affect the value of the dependent variable. Independent variables such as price, advertising expenditures, or number of retail outlets may be used to predict and explain sales or market share of a brand—the dependent variable. Bivariate analysis can help provide answers to questions such as the following: How does the price of our product affect its sales? What is the relationship between household income and expenditures on entertainment?

It must be noted that none of the techniques presented in this chapter can be used to prove that one variable caused some change in another variable. They can be used only to describe the nature of statistical relationships between variables.

The analyst has a large number of bivariate techniques from which to choose. This chapter discusses two procedures that are appropriate for metric (ratio or internal) data—bivariate regression and Pearson's product moment correlation—and one that is appropriate for ordinal (ranking) data—Spearman rank-order correlation. Other statistical procedures that can be used for analyzing the statistical relationship between two variables include two-group t-test, chi-square analysis of crosstab or contingency tables, and ANOVA (analysis of variance) for two groups. All of these procedures were introduced and discussed in Chapter 15.

Bivariate Regression

bivariate regression analysis
Analysis of the strength of the linear relationship between two variables when one is considered the independent variable and the other the dependent variable.

Bivariate regression analysis is a statistical procedure appropriate for analyzing the relationship between two variables when one is considered the dependent variable and the other the independent variable. For example, a researcher might be interested in analyzing the relationship between sales (dependent variable) and advertising (independent variable). If the relationship between advertising expenditures and sales can be accurately captured by regression analysis, the researcher can predict sales for different levels of advertising. When the problem involves using two or more independent variables (e.g., advertising and price) to predict the dependent variable of interest, multiple regression analysis (discussed in Chapter 17) is appropriate.

Nature of the Relationship

One way to study the nature of the relationship between the dependent and the independent variable is to plot the data in a scatter diagram. The dependent variable Y is plotted on the vertical axis, while the independent variable X is plotted on the horizontal axis. By examining the scatter diagram, one can determine whether the relationship between the two variables, if any, is linear or curvilinear. If the relationship appears to be linear or close to linear, linear regression is appropriate. If a nonlinear relationship is shown in the scatter diagram, curve-fitting nonlinear regression techniques are appropriate. These techniques are beyond the scope of this discussion.

PART 4:
Data Analysis

Figure 16.1 depicts several kinds of underlying relationships between the X (independent) and Y (dependent) variables. Scatter diagrams (a) and (b) suggest a positive linear relationship between X and Y. However, the linear relationship shown in (b) is not as strong as that portrayed in (a); there is more scatter in the data shown in (b). Diagram (c) shows a perfect negative, or inverse, relationship between variables X and Y. An example might be the relationship between price and sales. As price goes up, sales go down. As price goes down, sales go up. Diagrams (d) and (e) show nonlinear relationships between the variables; appropriate curve-fitting techniques should be used to mathematically describe these relationships. The scatter diagram in (f) shows no relationship between X and Y.

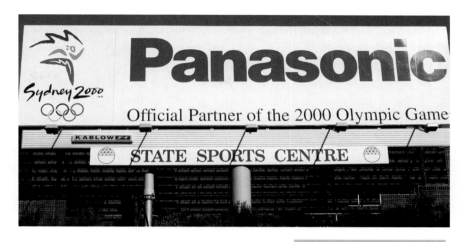

Bivariate regression analysis can help answer such questions as "How does advertising affect sales?"

Example of Bivariate Regression

Stop 'N Go recently conducted a research effort designed to measure the effect of vehicular traffic past a particular store location on annual sales at that location. To control for other factors, researchers identified 20 stores that were virtually identical on all other variables known to have a significant effect on store sales (e.g., square footage, amount of parking, demographics of the surrounding neighborhood). This particular analysis is part of an overall effort by Stop 'N Go to identify and quantify the effects of various factors that affect store sales. The ultimate goal is to develop a model that can be used to screen potential sites for store locations and select, for actual purchase and store construction, the ones that will produce the highest level of sales.

After identifying the 20 sites, Stop 'N Go took a daily traffic count for each site over a 30-day period. In addition, from internal records, the company obtained total sales data for each of the 20 test stores for the preceding 12 months (see Table 16.1).

A scatterplot of the resulting data is shown in Figure 16.2. Visual inspection of the scatterplot suggests that total sales increase as average daily vehicular traffic increases. The question now is how to characterize this relationship in a more explicit, quantitative manner.

Least Squares Estimation Procedure   The least squares procedure is a fairly simple mathematical technique that can be used to fit data for X and Y to a line that best represents the relationship between the two variables. No straight line will perfectly represent every observation in the scatterplot. This is reflected

Figure 16.1

**Types of Relationships
Found in Scatter Diagrams**

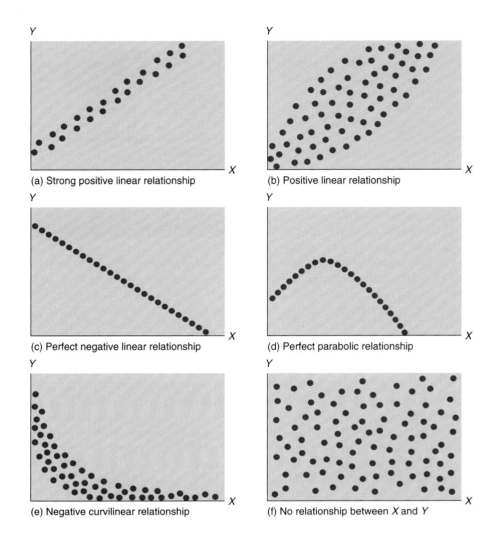

(a) Strong positive linear relationship

(b) Positive linear relationship

(c) Perfect negative linear relationship

(d) Perfect parabolic relationship

(e) Negative curvilinear relationship

(f) No relationship between X and Y

in discrepancies between the actual values (dots on the scatter diagram) and predicted values (values indicated by the line). Any straight line fitted to the data in a scatterplot is subject to error. A number of lines could be drawn that would seem to fit the observations in Figure 16.2.

The least squares procedure results in the straight line that fits the actual observations (dots) better than any other line that could be fitted to the observations. Put another way, the sum of the squared deviations from the line (squared differences between dots and the line) will be lower for this line than for any other line that can be fitted to the observations.

PART 4:
Data Analysis

Table 16.1

Annual Sales and Average Daily Vehicular Traffic

Store Number (i)	Average Daily Vehicular Count in Thousands (X_i)	Annual Sales in Thousands of Dollars (Y_i)
1	62	1,121
2	35	766
3	36	701
4	72	1,304
5	41	832
6	39	782
7	49	977
8	25	503
9	41	773
10	39	839
11	35	893
12	27	588
13	55	957
14	38	703
15	24	497
16	28	657
17	53	1,209
18	55	997
19	33	844
20	29	883

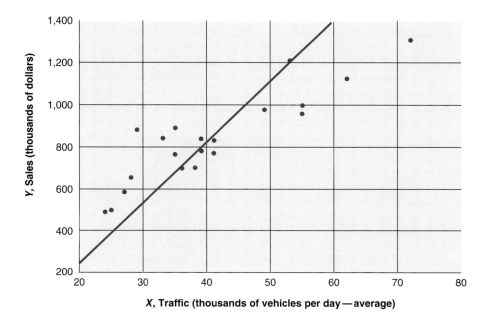

Figure 16.2

Scatterplot of Annual Sales by Traffic

The general equation for the line is $Y = a + bX$. The estimating equation for regression analysis is

$$Y = \hat{a} + \hat{b}X + e$$
where Y = dependent variable, annual sales in thousands of dollars
$\hat{a}$ = estimated Y intercept for regression line
$\hat{b}$ = estimated slope of regression line, regression coefficient
X = independent variable, average daily vehicular traffic in thousands of vehicles
e = error, difference between actual value and value predicted by regression line

Values for $\hat{a}$ and $\hat{b}$ can be calculated from the following equations:

$$\hat{b} = \frac{\sum X_i Y_i - n\overline{X}\,\overline{Y}}{\sum X_i^2 - n(\overline{X})^2}$$
$$\hat{a} = \overline{Y} - \hat{b}\overline{X}$$
where $\overline{X}$ = mean value of X
$\overline{Y}$ = mean value of Y
n = sample size (number of units in the sample)

With the data from Table 16.2, $\hat{b}$ is calculated as follows:

$$\hat{b} = \frac{734{,}083 - 20(40.8)(841.3)}{36{,}526 - 20(40.8)^2} = 14.72$$

The value of $\hat{a}$ is calculated as follows:

$$\hat{a} = \overline{Y} - \hat{b}\,\overline{X}$$
$$= 841.3 - 14.72(40.8) = 240.86$$

Thus, the estimated regression function is given by

$$\hat{Y} = \hat{a} + \hat{b}X$$
$$= 240.86 + 14.72(X)$$

where $\hat{Y}$ (Y hat) is the value of the estimated regression function for a given value of X.

According to the estimated regression function, for every additional 1,000 vehicles per day in traffic (X), total annual sales will increase by \$14,720 (estimated value of b). The value of $\hat{a}$ is 240.86. Technically, $\hat{a}$ is the estimated value of the dependent variable (Y, or annual sales) when the value of the independent variable (X, or average daily vehicular traffic) is zero.

PART 4:
Data Analysis

Table 16.2

Least Squares Computation

Store	X	Y	X²	Y²	XY
1	62	1,121	3,844	1,256,641	69,502
2	35	766	1,225	586,756	26,810
3	36	701	1,296	491,401	25,236
4	72	1,304	5,184	1,700,416	93,888
5	41	832	1,681	692,224	34,112
6	39	782	1,521	611,524	30,498
7	49	977	2,401	954,529	47,873
8	25	503	625	253,009	12,575
9	41	773	1,681	597,529	31,693
10	39	839	1,521	703,921	32,721
11	35	893	1,225	797,449	31,255
12	27	588	729	345,744	15,876
13	55	957	3,025	915,849	52,635
14	38	703	1,444	494,209	26,714
15	24	497	576	247,009	11,928
16	28	657	784	431,649	18,396
17	53	1,209	2,809	1,461,681	64,077
18	55	997	3,025	994,009	54,835
19	33	844	1,089	712,336	27,852
20	29	883	841	779,689	25,607
Sum	816	16,826	36,526	15,027,574	734,083
Mean	40.8	841.3			

The Regression Line   Predicted values for Y, based on calculated values for $\hat{a}$ and $\hat{b}$, are shown in Table 16.3. In addition, errors for each observation $(Y - \hat{Y})$ are shown. The regression line resulting from the $\hat{Y}$ values is plotted in Figure 16.3.

The Strength of Association: R^2   The estimated regression function describes the nature of the relationship between X and Y. Another important factor is the strength of the relationship between the variables. How widely do the actual values of Y differ from the values predicted by the model?

The **coefficient of determination,** denoted by R^2, is the measure of the strength of the linear relationship between X and Y. The coefficient of determination measures the percentage of the total variation in Y that is "explained" by the variation in X. The R^2 statistic ranges from 0 to 1. If there is a perfect linear relationship between X and Y (all the variation in Y is explained by the variation in X), then R^2 equals 1. At the other extreme, if there is no relationship between X and Y, then none of the variation in Y is explained by the variation in X and R^2 equals 0.

coefficient of determination
The percentage of the total variation in the dependent variable explained by the independent variable.

$$R^2 = \frac{\text{Explained variation}}{\text{Total variation}}$$

where
explained variation = total variation − unexplained variation

Table 16.3

Predicted Values and Errors for Each Observation

Store	X	Y	$\hat{Y}$	$Y - \hat{Y}$	$(Y - \hat{Y})^2$	$(Y - \bar{Y})^2$
1	62	1,121	1,153.3	-32.2951	1,043	78,232
2	35	766	755.9	10.05716	101	5,670
3	36	701	770.7	-69.6596	4,852	19,684
4	72	1,304	1,300.5	3.537362	13	214,091
5	41	832	844.2	-12.2434	150	86
6	39	782	814.8	-32.8098	1,076	3,516
7	49	977	962.0	15.02264	226	18,414
8	25	503	608.8	-105.775	11,188	114,447
9	41	773	844.2	-71.2434	5,076	4,665
10	39	839	814.8	24.19015	585	5
11	35	893	755.9	137.0572	18,785	2,673
12	27	588	638.2	-50.2088	2,521	64,161
13	55	957	1,050.3	-93.2779	8,701	13,386
14	38	703	800.1	-97.0931	9,427	19,127
15	24	497	594.1	-97.0586	9,420	118,542
16	28	657	652.9	4.074415	17	33,966
17	53	1,209	1,020.8	188.1556	35,403	135,203
18	55	997	1,050.3	-53.2779	2,839	24,242
19	33	844	726.5	117.4907	13,804	7
20	29	883	667.6	215.3577	46,379	1,739
Sum	816	16,826	16,826.0		171,604.8	871,860.2
Mean	40.8	841.3				

The coefficient of determination for the Stop 'N Go data example is computed as follows. (See Table 16.3 for calculation of $(Y - \hat{Y})^2$ and $(Y - \bar{Y})^2$.)

$$R^2 = \frac{\text{Total variation} - \text{Unexplained variation}}{\text{Total variation}}$$

$$= 1 - \frac{\text{Unexplained variation}}{\text{Total variation}}$$

$$= 1 - \frac{\sum_{i=1}^{n} (Y_i - \hat{Y}_i)^2}{\sum_{i=1}^{n} (Y_i - \bar{Y})^2}$$

$$= 1 - \frac{171,604.8}{871,860.2} = .803$$

Of the variation in Y (annual sales), 80 percent is explained by the variation in X (average daily vehicular traffic). There is a very strong linear relationship between X and Y.

Statistical Significance of Regression Results   In computing R^2, the total variation in Y was partitioned into two component sums of squares:

PART 4:
Data Analysis

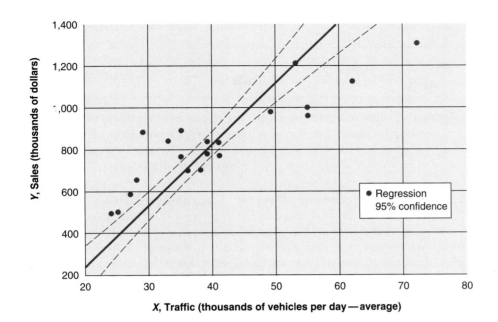

Figure 16.3

**Least Squares Regression
Line Fitted to Sample Data**

Total variation = Explained variation + Unexplained variation

The total variation is a measure of variation of the observed Y values around their mean $\bar{Y}$. It measures the variation of the Y values without any consideration of the X values.

Total variation, known as the *total sum of squares* (SST), is given by

$$\text{SST} = \sum_{i=1}^{n}(Y_i - \bar{Y})^2 = \sum_{i=1}^{n}Y_i^2 - \left(\frac{\sum_{i=1}^{n}Y_i^2}{n}\right)$$

The explained variation, or the **sum of squares due to regression** (SSR), is given by

sum of squares due to regression
The variation explained by the regression.

$$\text{SSR} = \sum_{i=1}^{n}(\hat{Y}_i - \bar{Y})^2 = a\sum_{i=1}^{n}Y_i + b\sum_{i=1}^{n}X_iY_i - \left(\frac{\sum_{i=1}^{n}Y_i}{n}\right)^2$$

Figure 16.4 depicts the various measures of variation (i.e., sum of squares) in a regression. SSR represents the differences between Y_i (the values of Y predicted by the estimated regression equation) and $\bar{Y}$ (the average value of Y). In a well-fitting regression equation, the variation explained by regression (SSR) will represent a large portion of the total variation (SST). If $Y_i = \hat{Y}_i$ at each value of X, then a perfect fit has been achieved. All the observed values of Y are then on the computed regression line. Of course, in that case, SSR $\neq$ SST.

CHAPTER 16:
Bivariate Correlation and Regression

error sum of squares
The variation not explained by the regression.

The unexplained variation, or **error sum of squares** (SSE), is obtained from

$$\text{SSE} = \sum_{i=1}^{n}(Y_i - \hat{Y}_i)^2 = \sum_{i=1}^{n}Y_i^2 - a\sum_{i=1}^{n}Y_i - b\sum_{i=1}^{n}X_iY_i$$

In Figure 16.4, note that SSE represents the residual differences (error) between the observed and predicted Y values. Therefore, the unexplained variation is a measure of scatter around the regression line. If the fit were perfect, there would be no scatter around the regression line and SSE would be zero.

Hypotheses Concerning Overall Regression Here we, as the researchers, are interested in hypotheses regarding the computed R^2 value for the problem. Is the amount of variance explained in the result (by our model) significantly greater than we would expect due to chance? Or, as with the various statistical tests discussed in Chapter 15, to what extent can we rule out sampling error as an explanation of the results? Analysis of variance (an F-test) is used to test the significance of the results.

In studying the relationship between vehicular traffic and sales, the coefficient of determination may be used to measure the percent of the total variation.

An analysis of variance table is be set up as shown in Table 16.4. The computer output for our example appears in Table 16.5. The breakdowns of the total sum of squares and associated degrees of freedom are displayed in the form of an analysis of variance (ANOVA) table. We use the information in this table to test the significance of the linear relationship between Y and X. As noted previously, an F-test will be used for this purpose. Our hypotheses are as follows:

■ Null hypothesis H_0: There is no linear relationship between X (average daily vehicular traffic) and Y (annual sales).

■ Alternative hypothesis H_a: There is a linear relationship between X and Y.

As in other statistical tests, we must choose α. This is the likelihood that the observed result occurred by chance, or the probability of incorrectly rejecting the null hypothesis. In this case, we decide on a standard level of significance: $\alpha = .05$. In other words, if the calculated value of F exceeds the tabular value, we are willing to accept a 5 percent chance of incorrectly rejecting the null hypothesis. The value of F, or the F-ratio, is computed as follows (see Table 16.5 on p. 560):

PART 4:
Data Analysis

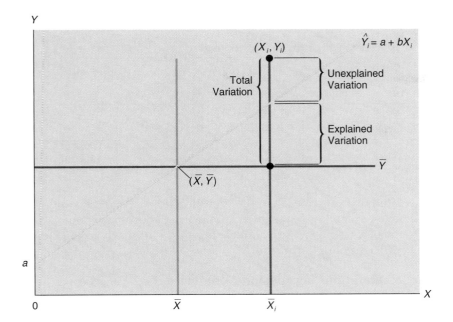

Figure 16.4

Measures of Variation in a Regression

$$F = \frac{MSR}{MSE}$$
$$= \frac{700,255.4}{9,533.6} = 73.45$$

We will reject the null hypothesis if the calculated F-statistic is greater than or equal to the table, or critical, F-value. The numerator and denominator degrees of freedom for this F-ratio are 1 and 18, respectively. As noted earlier, it was decided that an alpha level of .05 ($\alpha = .05$) should be used.

The table, or critical, value of F with 1 (numerator) and 18 (denominator) degrees of freedom at $\alpha = .05$ is 4.49 (see Table 5 in Appendix 2). Because the

Table 16.4

Analysis of Variance

Source of Variation	Degrees of Freedom	Sum of Squares	Mean Square	F-Statistic
Regression (explained)	1	SSR	$MSR = \dfrac{SSR}{1}$	$F = \dfrac{MSR}{MSE}$
Residual (unexplained)	$n-2$	SSE	$MSE = \dfrac{SSE}{n-2}$	
Total	$n-1$	SST		

Table 16.5

Regression Analysis Output

STAT. MULTIPLE REGRESS.	Regression Summary for Dependent Variable: Y R=.89619973 R^2 =.80317395 Adjusted R^2=.79223917 F(1,18)=73.451 p<.00000 Std. Error of estimate: 97.640					
N=20	BETA	St. Err. of BETA	B	St. Err. of B	t(18)	p-level
Intercpt			240.8566	73.38347	3.282164	.004141
X	.896200	.104570	14.7168	1.71717	8.570374	.000000

calculated value of F is greater than the critical value, we reject the null hypothesis and conclude that there is a significant linear relationship between the average daily vehicular traffic (X) and annual sales (Y). This result is consistent with the high coefficient of determination R^2 discussed earlier.

Hypotheses about the Regression Coefficient b   Finally, we may be interested in making hypotheses about b, the regression coefficient. As you may recall, b is the estimate of the effect of a one-unit change in X on Y. The hypotheses are as follows:

■ Null hypothesis H$_0$: $b = 0$
■ Alternative hypothesis H$_a$: $b \neq 0$

The appropriate test is a t-test, and, as you can see from the last line of Table 16.5, the computer program calculates the t-value (8.57) and the p-value (probability of incorrectly rejecting the null hypothesis of .0000). See Chapter 15 for a more detailed discussion of p-values. Given the α criterion of .05, we would reject the null hypothesis in this case.

Correlation Analysis

Correlation for Metric Data: Pearson's Product Moment Correlation

correlation analysis
Analysis of the degree to which changes in one variable are associated with changes in another.
Pearson's product moment correlation
Correlation analysis technique for use with metric data.

Correlation is the degree to which changes in one variable (the dependent variable) are associated with changes in another. When the relationship is between two variables, the analysis is called simple, or bivariate, **correlation analysis.** With metric data, **Pearson's product moment correlation** may be used.

In our example of bivariate regression, we used the coefficient of determination R^2 as a measure of the strength of the linear relationship between X and Y. Another descriptive measure, called the *coefficient of correlation R*, describes the degree of association between X and Y. It is the square root of the coefficient of determination with the appropriate sign (+ or –):

$$R = \pm \sqrt{R^2}$$

PART 4:
Data Analysis

The value of R can range from -1 (perfect negative correlation) to $+1$ (perfect positive correlation). The closer R is to ± 1, the stronger the degree of association between X and Y. If R is equal to zero, then there is no association between X and Y.

If we had not been interested in estimating the regression function, we could have computed R directly from the data for the convenience store example, using this formula:

$$
\begin{aligned}
R &= \frac{n \sum XY - (\sum X)(\sum Y)}{\sqrt{[n \sum X^2 - (\sum X)^2][n \sum Y^2 - (\sum Y)^2]}} \\
&= \frac{20(734,083) - (816)(16,826)}{\sqrt{[20(36,526) - (816)^2][20(15,027,574) - (16,826)^2]}} \\
&= .896
\end{aligned}
$$

In this case, the value of R indicates a positive correlation between the average daily vehicular traffic and annual sales. In other words, successively higher levels of sales are associated with successively higher levels of traffic.

Correlation for Ordinal Data: Spearman Rank-Order Correlation

Researchers often need to analyze the degree of association between two ordinally scaled variables. The authors recently worked with an ad agency that wanted to determine whether there was a correlation between a company's ranking on product quality and its market share rank. The agency did a small pilot study with users of the product category to obtain quality ranks for the 12 companies in the industry. Market share estimates for the 12 companies were developed, and because the agency did not believe they were very accurate, the companies were ranked based on relative market share. Note that in the case of both quality rank and market share rank, a smaller number (higher rank) indicates a higher result. The resulting data are provided in Table 16.6. Three different conclusions are possible regarding the rankings:

1. They are positively correlated.
2. They are negatively correlated.
3. They are independent.

The **Spearman rank-order correlation** coefficient R_s is the appropriate measure for analyzing these data. The Spearman rank-order correlation coefficient is defined by

$$
R_s = 1 - \left(\frac{6 \sum_{i=1}^{n} d_i^2}{n^3 - n} \right)
$$

where d_i = difference in ranks of the two variables

       n = number of items ranked

Spearman rank-order correlation
Correlation analysis technique for use with ordinal data.

Beware of False Relationships!

BEWARE OF SPURIOUS RELATIONSHIPS WHEN DOING CORRELATION and regression analyses. Two or more variables may move together but have nothing to do with each other. If a causal relationship is proposed, then the cause must precede—or at least occur simultaneously with—the effect. A classic case of spuriousness is the relationship between number of fire trucks at a fire and size of the fire. More trucks implies, but does not cause, a larger fire.

A more subtle example involves performance on the Scholastic Aptitude Test (SAT). It has been shown that music students outperform other students on the SAT. This leads people to conclude that if you want your children to get higher scores on the SAT, then you should make sure they take music lessons. Statistics have been offered to bolster this argument. According to the College Board, students who studied the arts for more than four years scored 59 points higher on the verbal portion of the SAT and 44 points higher on the math portion than students with no experience in the arts. Does this prove that experience in the arts causes or contributes to higher test scores? Possibly, but more information is needed. It may be that students in the arts are different in other important ways. They may have more support from their parents at home. They may go to "better" schools. They may be smarter to begin with, or they may be different in any number of other ways. The point is that the evidence does not prove the existence of a causal relationship.[1] ■

With the data from Table 16.6, R_s is calculated as follows:

$$R_s = 1 - \left(\frac{6(44)}{(12)^3 - 12} \right) = .85$$

Based on this analysis, the two rankings are positively correlated. Higher rankings on one are associated with higher rankings on the other.

The value of the coefficient of rank correlation ($R_s = .85$) can be tested against the null hypothesis using a *t*-distribution for a given sample size ($n = 12$) as follows:

$$t = R_s \sqrt{\frac{n - 2}{1 - R_s^2}}$$

$$= .85 \sqrt{\frac{12 - 2}{1 - .85^2}} = 5.1$$

Table 16.6

Quality Image Rank versus Market Share Rank

| Company | Ranks | | d_i | d |
	Quality Image Rank X	Market Share Rank Y		
A	4	3	1	1
B	6	7	−1	1
C	9	5	4	16
D	7	6	1	1
E	1	2	−1	1
F	3	4	−1	1
G	11	12	−1	1
H	5	9	−4	16
I	8	8	0	0
J	12	10	2	4
K	10	11	−1	1
L	2	1	1	1

$$\sum_{i=1}^{n} d_i^2 = 44$$

The extent of the relationship between a company's quality image and its market share can be analyzed using the Spearman rank-order correlation coefficient.

The agency believes that there is a positive relationship between a company's quality image and its market share. The null and alternative hypotheses were formulated as follows:

- Null hypothesis H_0: $R_s = 0$
- Alternative hypothesis H_a: $R_s > 0$

The table value for t with 10 $(n − 2)$ degrees of freedom is 2.23 (at $\alpha = .05$). Because the calculated t-value (5.1) is higher than the table, or critical, value (2.23), we reject the null hypothesis and conclude that there is a positive association between a company's quality image and its market share rank.

CHAPTER 16:
Bivariate Correlation and Regression

Using the Right Measure of Correlation

THE SPEARMAN RANK-ORDER CORRELATION COEFFICIENT IS THE correct procedure for estimating the degree of association between ranked objects. But what would the difference be if Pearson's product moment correlation were inappropriately used for gauging the association between ranked objects? Such a case might occur if a marketing researcher mistook the rankings for metric ratings.

In order to examine this question, a data set of twelve ranked objects was analyzed first with the correct Spearman rank-order correlation and then subsequently with the incorrect Pearson's product moment correlation. The rankings were made by 436 patrons of the Georgia Shakespeare Festival during the summer season in Atlanta, Georgia. The ranked objects were twelve live-entertainment events that were then competing in the local market. Some of these events were the Shakespeare Festival's presentation of *Cyrano de Bergerac* and *Henry V;* a touring Broadway musical, *42nd St.,* a folk music concert featuring Peter, Paul, and Mary; a pop music concert featuring Kenny Loggins; and a professional baseball game between the Atlanta Braves and the San Francisco Giants. The two tables of 66 unique coefficients were then compared.[2]

The comparison revealed that the inappropriately applied Pearson product moment correlations were sometimes inflated and at other times deflated. In all, decisions on about 8 out of 66 coefficients would have been made incorrectly at $p = .05$. This is 12 percent of the decisions. In summary, this comparison of correct and incorrect correlation coefficients suggests that using the appropriate rank-order correlation does indeed matter. With this data set, the error was three times the 5 percent error a mistaken marketing researcher would have expected. ■

The Spearman rank-order correlation coefficient (R_s), like the coefficient of correlation R, has a lower limit of −1 and an upper limit of +1; that is, $-1 \leq R_s \leq 1$.

Summary

The techniques used to analyze the relationship between variables taken two at a time are called bivariate analyses. Bivariate regression analysis allows a single dependent variable to be predicted from knowledge about a single independent variable. One way to examine the underlying relationship between a dependent and an independent variable is to plot them on a scatter diagram. If the relationship appears to be linear, then linear regression analysis may be used. If it is curvilinear, then curve-fitting techniques should be applied. The general equation for a straight line fitted to two variables is given by

$$Y = a + bX$$

where
Y = dependent variable
X = independent variable
a = Y intercept
b = amount Y increases with each unit increase in X

Both a and b are unknown and must be estimated. This process is known as simple linear regression analysis. Bivariate least squares regression analysis is a mathematical technique for fitting a line to measurements of the two variables X and Y. The line is fitted so that the algebraic sum of deviations of the actual observations from the line is zero and the sum of the squared deviations is less than it would be for any other line that might be fitted to the data.

The estimated regression function describes the nature of the relationship between X and Y. In addition, researchers want to know the strength of the relationship between the variables. This is measured by the coefficient of determination, denoted by R^2. The coefficient of determination measures the percent of the total variation in Y that is "explained" by the variation in X. The R^2 statistic ranges from 0 to 1. An analysis of variance (ANOVA) approach also can be used for regression analysis. The total variation is known as the total sum of squares (SST). The explained variation, or the sum of squares due to regression (SSR), represents the variability explained by the regression. The unexplained variation is called the error sum of squares (SSE).

Correlation analysis is the measurement of the degree to which changes in one variable are associated with changes in another. If the researcher is using ordinal data, then the appropriate technique is Spearman rank-order correlation. Correlation analysis will tell the researcher whether the variables are positively correlated, negatively correlated, or independent.

Key Terms & Definitions

bivariate techniques Statistical methods of analyzing the relationship between two variables.

independent variable The symbol or concept that the researcher has some control over or can manipulate to some extent and that is hypothesized to cause or influence the dependent variable.

dependent variable   A symbol or concept expected to be explained or caused by the independent variable.

bivariate regression analysis   Analysis of the strength of the linear relationship between two variables when one is considered the independent variable and the other the dependent variable.

coefficient of determination   The percentage of the total variation in the dependent variable explained by the independent variable.

sum of squares due to regression   The variation explained by the regression.

error sum of squares   The variation not explained by the regression.

correlation analysis   Analysis of the degree to which changes in one variable are associated with changes in another.

Pearson's product moment correlation   Correlation analysis technique for use with metric data.

Spearman rank-order correlation   Correlation analysis technique for use with ordinal data.

Questions for Review & Critical Thinking

1. What are the major differences among the following bivariate statistical procedures: Pearson's product moment correlation, Spearman rank-order correlation, and regression analysis?
2. Give an example of a marketing problem for which use of each of the three procedures listed in Question 1 would be appropriate.
3. A sales manager of a life insurance firm administered a standard multiple-item job satisfaction scale to all the members of the firm's sales force. The manager then correlated (Pearson's product moment correlation) job satisfaction score with years of school completed for each salesperson. The resulting correlation was .11. On the basis of this analysis, the sales manager concluded: "A salesperson's level of education has little to do with his or her job satisfaction." Would you agree or disagree with this conclusion? Explain the basis for your position.
4. What purpose does a scatter diagram serve?
5. Explain the meaning of the coefficient of determination. What does this coefficient tell the researcher about the nature of the relationship between the dependent and independent variables?
6. How does Pearson's product moment correlation differ from Spearman rank-order correlation?
7. It has been observed in the past that when an AFC team wins the Super Bowl, the stock market rises in the first quarter of the year in almost every case. When an NFC team wins the Super Bowl, the stock market falls in the first quarter in most cases. Does this mean that the direction of movement of the stock market is caused by which conference wins the Super Bowl? What does this example illustrate?

PART 4:
Data Analysis

8. The following table gives data collected by a convenience store chain for 20 of its stores.

Column 1: ID number for each store

Column 2: Annual sales for the store for the previous year in thousands of dollars

Column 3: Average number of vehicles that pass the store each day, based on actual traffic counts for one month

Column 4: Total population that lives within a two-mile radius of the store, based on 1990 census data

Column 5: Median family income for households within a two-mile radius of the store, based on 1990 census data

Store ID No.	Annual Sales (thousands of dollars)	Average Daily Traffic	Population in Two-Mile Radius	Average Income in Area
1	$1,121	61,655	17,880	$28,991
2	$ 766	35,236	13,742	$14,731
3	$ 595	35,403	19,741	$ 8,114
4	$ 899	52,832	23,246	$15,324
5	$ 915	40,809	24,485	$11,438
6	$ 782	40,820	20,410	$11,730
7	$ 833	49,147	28,997	$10,589
8	$ 571	24,953	9,981	$10,706
9	$ 692	40,828	8,982	$23,591
10	$1,005	39,195	18,814	$15,703
11	$ 589	34,574	16,941	$ 9,015
12	$ 671	26,639	13,319	$10,065
13	$ 903	55,083	21,482	$17,365
14	$ 703	37,892	26,524	$ 7,532
15	$ 556	24,019	14,412	$ 6,950
16	$ 657	27,791	13,896	$ 9,855
17	$1,209	53,438	22,444	$21,589
18	$ 997	54,835	18,096	$22,659
19	$ 844	32,916	16,458	$12,660
20	$ 883	29,139	16,609	$11,618

Answer the following:
a. Which of the other three variables is the best predictor of sales? Compute correlation coefficients to answer the question.
b. Do the following regressions:
   1. Sales as a function of average daily traffic
   2. Sales as a function of population in a two-mile radius
c. Interpret the results of the two regressions.

9. Interpret the following:
   a. $Y = .11 + .009X$, where Y is the likelihood of sending children to college and X is family income in thousands of dollars. Remember: It is family income in *thousands*.
      1. According to our model, how likely is a family with an income of $30,000 to send their children to college?
      2. What is the likelihood for a family with an income of $50,000?
      3. What is the likelihood for a family with an income of $17,500?
      4. Is there some logic to the estimates? Explain.
   b. $Y = .25 - .0039X$, where Y is the likelihood of going to a skateboard park and X is age.
      1. According to our model, how likely is a 10-year-old to go to a skateboard park?
      2. What is the likelihood for a 60-year-old?
      3. What is the likelihood for a 40-year-old?
      4. Is there some logic to the estimates? Explain.
10. The following ANOVA summary data are the result of a regression with sales per year (dependent variable) as a function of promotion expenditures per year (independent variable) for a toy company.

$$F = \frac{MSR}{MSE} = \frac{34,276}{4,721}$$

The degrees of freedom are 1 for the numerator and 19 for the denominator. Is the relationship statistically significant at $\alpha = .05$? Comment.

Working the Net

1. What is the correlation between the U.S. unemployment rate and import prices for 1995–1997? Go to the Bureau of Labor Statistics at http://stats.bls.gov:80/cgi-bin/surveymost?bls and select "U.S. Economy." Locate the data for "Unemployment Rate" and "U.S. Import Price Index" for 1995–1997. Load both series of data into a spreadsheet or statistical analysis program and compute the correlation.
2. How can an individual become more familiar with statistical software program capabilities?

   For STATISTICA, go to http://www.statsoft.com

   For SPSS, go to http://www.spss.com

   For SAS, go to http://www.sas.com

   For Minitab, go to http://www.minitab.com

Real-Life Research • 16.1

Burger Street Image Analysis

Burger Street is a regional fast food chain serving central and northern New Mexico. The chain's sales have become stagnant, and researchers recently conducted focus groups in Albuquerque and Santa Fe to try to find out why. Two groups were conducted in each market. The groups were conducted by a professional moderator in special facilities equipped with viewing booths, one-way mirrors, and audio- and videotaping equipment. Participants were selected so that they were reasonably representative of fast food users in the two markets. Each group had three to four Burger Street users and six to seven users of competitive chains.

A major objective of the research was to determine the overall image of each fast food chain. Based on the focus groups, four factors were identified as most important in determining overall image: *perceived food quality, food taste, value* (what you got versus what you paid), and *speed of service.*

Based on these results, Burger Street decided to conduct a quantitative study to determine the relative importance of each of these factors in determining overall image of a fast food restaurant. Key questions on the survey included an overall rating of each of the major chains with which the respondent was familiar and ratings of each of those chains in the four key areas.

Burger Street plans to use the survey results to decide how to position the chain (*great-tasting food, highest-quality fast food, outstanding value,* or *fastest service*) and where to focus its efforts to produce the biggest improvement in its image and, presumably, its sales.

Ratings of Burger Street from 20 randomly selected respondents are provided in the table below. All ratings are on a 10-point scale, where 10 was defined as *excellent* and 1 was defined as *poor.*

Overall Rating	Rating of			
	Food Quality	Food Taste	Value	Speed of Service
10	10	9	8	9
9	8	8	9	8
9	8	8	8	9
9	7	8	8	8
10	9	9	8	9
8	8	8	7	7
8	7	7	7	7
10	9	9	8	9
7	7	6	6	7
7	7	6	7	8
8	9	7	7	9
9	9	8	8	9
10	10	9	9	9
7	7	6	8	7
7	8	7	8	7
7	8	6	9	6
7	8	6	6	5
9	10	8	7	8
9	9	8	8	8
9	8	8	6	9

Questions

1. Use Excel or a statistical package to run correlations between the overall rating and each of the four individual attribute ratings. Which of the individual items is most highly correlated with the overall rating? What are the correlations between the other items and the overall rating? Would you draw any conclusions based on these results? If so, what conclusions would you draw?

2. Run bivariate regression analyses, using each of the individual ratings as the predictor (or independent) variable and the overall rating as the dependent variable. What does this analysis suggest regarding the relative importance of each of the four items in determining the overall rating of Burger Street?

3. How do the correlation results differ from the regression results? Which results provide better insights into what Burger Street should do to improve its position? Why?

4. Based on the statistical results, what would you advise Burger Street to do to improve its image? How should it position itself and what elements should it focus on?

Real-Life Research • 16.2

Selling Chevrolets to Female Car Buyers

Women are becoming increasingly important in America's car lots. Today they buy about 45 percent of all new cars sold in the United States, up from 23 percent in 1970. In addition, they influence 80 percent of all new car purchases. Most important for American manufacturers, 76 percent of female car buyers bought domestic cars. If they choose an import, women are more likely to buy Japanese cars than are men; men are more likely to buy European models. The domestic line of cars most popular among women is the Chevrolet; in the late 1980s, about 14 percent of female new car buyers purchased Chevrolets.

Chevrolet has been targeting the women's market since about 1985, making it the leader in this area among divisions of General Motors. Recently, Chevrolet launched an extensive direct mail and print campaign aimed exclusively at women. Secondary research by Chevrolet's marketing researchers noted that women accounted for 60 percent of new car purchases in 2000. Additional secondary research has uncovered some interesting facets of the female automobile purchaser. Women are less comfortable than men are in dealing with the financial aspects of purchasing their car. Thus, it is likely that manufacturers and car dealerships that make women feel more comfortable with financial aspects can build a dominant market share among female purchasers. Also, women tend to be more brand loyal in car buying than men are. Women pick up on showroom details that men usually ignore. For example, they notice whether a showroom or service area is dirty or noisy. They are more aware of smells, decorative details, and overall environment.

The company decided to test these theories by means of empirical research:

- It randomly selected 25 dealerships from the population of all Chevrolet dealerships.
- During a one-week period, 100 randomly selected women were interviewed at each dealership.

Results of that study are summarized in the following table.

Column 1: ID number assigned to each dealership

Column 2: Percent of women who purchased a car from the particular dealership (they were tracked for 30 days after the interview)

Column 3: Average rating assigned to overall decor of dealership on a 10-point scale (10 = excellent and 1 = poor)

Column 4: Average rating assigned to cleanliness of dealership (10 = extremely clean and 1 = extremely dirty)

Column 5: Average age of the women interviewed, in years

Dealer ID#	Percent Who Purchased	Average Decor Rating	Average Cleanliness Rating	Average Size
1	11	6.2	8.7	39
2	30	9.2	9.4	44
3	20	8.4	7.3	22
4	9	5.9	6.9	29
5	5	5.2	5.5	34
6	6	6.0	8.8	45
7	5	6.6	6.8	53
8	14	7.1	8.2	21
9	12	6.8	6.9	26
10	7	5.9	4.9	35
11	3	5.1	6.6	27
12	4	8.3	6.3	72
13	5	6.3	7.3	44
14	14	7.8	7.1	39
15	12	7.0	9.1	47
16	4	4.9	7.0	44
17	3	5.2	5.4	34
18	9	6.7	7.3	44
19	8	6.5	8.2	58
20	4	5.9	6.2	62
21	6	6.1	6.3	37
22	11	7.0	7.9	48
23	19	8.8	8.9	41
24	21	9.1	9.4	22
25	22	8.8	8.3	55

Questions

1. Which of the other three variables is the best predictor of the percent who purchased? Use correlation analysis.
2. Do the following regressions:
   a. Percent who purchased as a function of decor rating
   b. Percent who purchased as a function of cleanliness rating
3. Interpret the results of the two regressions. Which rating has the larger effect on purchasing? Explain.
4. What do your results suggest that the effect of a one-unit increase in decor rating on percent purchasing would be?
5. If you were a marketing manager for Chevrolet, what would you be inclined to do based on the statistical results? Explain.

Real-Life Research • 16.3

Find Any Error?

Bloomberg Personal is a monthly investment magazine published for upscale U.S. retail investors. Each issue of *Bloomberg Personal* now includes a section entitled "Global Reach," which gives a brief description of activity in the national stock and bond markets of foreign countries. The performance of foreign financial markets can be useful in gauging current economic conditions for consumers in these foreign countries.

In the December 1997 issue, nine countries were featured, including Japan, Australia, Russia, and China.[3] In addition, an inset box included the following information:

Here's how closely some markets have mirrored the S & P 500 (a stock index of 500 leading firms in the U.S.) since 1992. The closer the figure is to 1.0, the higher the correlation.

Canada	.62
UK	.41
France	.39
Germany	.37
Italy	.22
Singapore	.19
Chile	.15
Brazil	.14
Philippines	.08
Turkey	−.02

Source: "A Mirror to the World," *Bloomberg Personal,* December 1997. Reprinted by permission.

Questions

1. What other information would be essential to have before you could use these secondary data in a marketing research report?
2. If you had this other information and the precision of measurement was acceptable to you, what is the story these numbers would begin to tell about the linkages between the U.S. stock market and the stock markets of some other nations in the world?

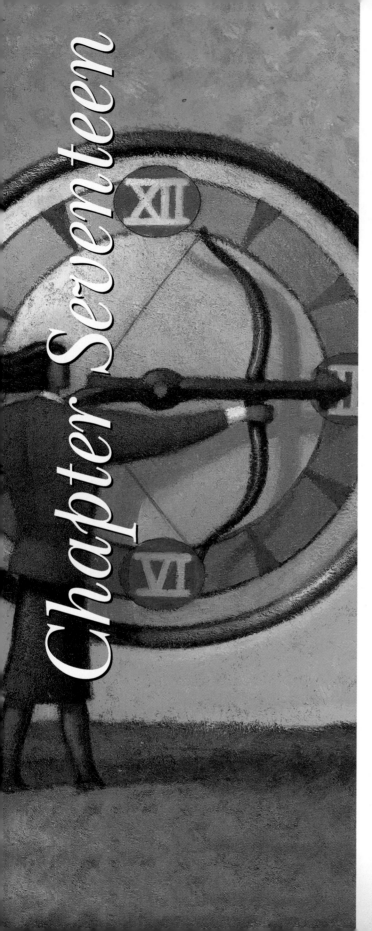

Chapter Seventeen

Multivariate Data Analysis

Learning Objectives

To define multivariate data analysis.

To describe multiple regression analysis and multiple discriminant analysis.

To learn about cluster analysis and factor analysis.

To gain an appreciation of perceptual mapping.

To develop an understanding of conjoint analysis.

E D ENGLISH IS DIRECTOR OF MARKETING FOR UNITED WIRELESS Communications. United was recently created by the merger of three smaller wireless companies, which gave United national coverage. English is in the process of developing market segmentation and product strategies as well as marketing strategies to build the United brand, which is currently unknown to consumers.

UNITED HAS JUST COMPLETED A LARGE national survey that was designed to provide information for the development of the product and market segmentation strategies. English has just reviewed the crosstabulations from the research firm and is concerned about a number of issues addressed by the study. He is not satisfied with the analysis. The crosstabulations suggest answers to some of his questions but lead to no clear conclusions. He has four general concerns:

This wireless company is doing research to increase brand awareness. Multivariate procedures are powerful tools for analyzing various types of marketing research data.

■ First, he has certain theories regarding the importance of various product/ service attributes and their relative importance. For example, he believes that the range of geographic coverage offered in an area should be the best predictor of how much consumers in the market will be willing to pay per month for wireless service. This theory is based on previous research conducted by United. English has heard from some of his colleagues that multiple regression analysis provides a way to test this theory. However, the research firm that conducted the study is not experienced in the use of this multivariate analysis technique.

■ Second, English is interested in developing a better understanding of the factors that predict whether someone has or does not have wireless telephone service. Half of those surveyed in the recent study have wireless service and half do not. He wants to know how those who have wireless service differ from those who do not have it in regard to the importance they attach to various features of wireless service. He has heard that multiple discriminant analysis can be used to test these differences.

■ Third, he believes that the market can be segmented on the basis of the importance that consumers attach to different features of wireless communications service. If this is true, identifying those "important" features would be very useful in helping him decide how the new service should be positioned and what features to target in his market communications.

Find out more about segmentation models by checking out the case studies at

 http://www. appliedmetrix.com

> Finally, English believes that the way consumers feel about some of the attributes of wireless service may be strongly correlated with the way they feel about other attributes. If this is true, then he may be able to build his positioning and communication strategy around clusters of product attributes or features that resonate most strongly with target consumers. ■

These issues and questions are addressed in this chapter. Multivariate analysis procedures are powerful tools for analyzing various types of marketing research data, and they provide a basis for testing all of the issues of concern to English.

Multivariate Analysis Procedures

Advances in computer hardware and software have provided the basis for remarkable developments in the use of powerful statistical procedures for the analysis of marketing research data. These developments have made it possible to analyze large amounts of complex data with relative ease. In particular, multivariate analysis procedures have been extremely significant in this data analysis revolution.

multivariate analysis
A general term for statistical procedures that simultaneously analyze multiple measurements on each individual or object under study.

The term **multivariate analysis** is used to refer to the simultaneous analysis of multiple measurements on each individual or object being studied.[1] Some experts consider any simultaneous statistical analysis of more than two variables to be multivariate analysis. Multivariate analysis procedures are extensions of the univariate and bivariate statistical procedures discussed in Chapters 15 and 16.

A number of techniques fall under the heading of multivariate analysis procedures. In this chapter, we will consider six of these techniques:

- Multiple regression analysis
- Multiple discriminant analysis
- Cluster analysis
- Factor analysis
- Perceptual mapping
- Conjoint analysis

You may have been exposed to multiple regression analysis in introductory statistics courses. The remaining procedures are newer, less widely studied, or both. Summary descriptions of the techniques are provided in Table 17.1.

Although awareness of multivariate techniques is still low, they have been around for decades and have been widely used for a variety of commercial purposes. Fair Isaac & Co. has built a $70-million business around the commercial use of multivariate techniques.[2] The firm and its clients have found that they can predict with surprising accuracy who will pay their bills on time, who will pay late, and who will not pay at all. The federal government uses secret formulas, based on the firm's analyses, to identify tax evaders. Fair Isaac has also shown that results from its multivariate analyses help in identifying the best sales prospects.

Table 17.1

Brief Descriptions of Multivariate Analysis Procedures

Multiple regression analysis	Enables the researcher to predict the level of magnitude of a dependent variable based on the levels of more than one independent variable.
Multiple discriminant analysis	Enables the researcher to predict group membership on the basis of two or more independent variables.
Cluster analysis	Is a procedure for identifying subgroups of individuals or items that are homogeneous within subgroups and different from other subgroups.
Factor analysis	Permits the analyst to reduce a set of variables to a smaller set of factors or composite variables by identifying underlying dimensions in the data.
Perceptual mapping	Is appropriate when the goal is to analyze consumer perception of companies, products, brands, and the like.
Conjoint analysis	Provides a basis for estimating the utility that consumers associate with different product features or attributes.

Multivariate Software

The computational requirements for the various multivariate procedures discussed in this chapter are substantial. As a practical matter, running the various types of analyses presented requires a computer and appropriate software. Just over a decade ago, most types of multivariate analysis discussed in this chapter were done on mainframes or minicomputers, as personal computers were limited in power, memory, storage capacity, and range of software available. Those limitations are in the past. Personal computers today have the power to handle just about any problem that a marketing researcher might encounter. Most problems can be solved in a matter of seconds, and there is a wide variety of outstanding Windows software available for multivariate analysis. Two of the best packages are SPSS for Windows and STATISTICA for Windows.

Both packages include a full range of software modules for integrated database creation and management, data transformation and manipulation, graphing, descriptive statistics, and multivariate procedures. Both have easy-to-use graphical interfaces. Additional information on the SPSS product line can be found at http://www.spss.com; information on STATISTICA can be found at http://www.StatSoft.com. A number of other useful resources are available at these two sites:

■ Technical support, product information, FAQs (frequently asked questions), various downloads, and product reviews

- Examples of successful applications of multivariate analysis to solve real business problems
- Discussions of data mining and data warehousing applications

STATISTICA provides a particularly useful *Electronic Statistics Textbook*. This book can be downloaded or reviewed online. There is no charge, and we strongly encourage you to use this outstanding, concise resource. SPSS, STATISTICA, or any of a number of other programs will serve you well when solving the problems at the end of this chapter.

Multiple Regression Analysis

multiple regression analysis
A procedure for predicting the level or magnitude of a (metric) dependent variable based on the levels of multiple independent variables.

Researchers use multiple regression analysis when their goal is to examine the relationship between two or more metric predictor (independent) variables and one metric dependent (criterion) variable.[3] Under certain circumstances, described later in this section, nominal predictor variables can be used if they are recoded as binary variables.

Multiple regression analysis is an extension of bivariate regression, discussed in Chapter 16. Instead of fitting a straight line to observations in a two-dimensional space, multiple regression analysis fits a plane to observations in a multidimensional space. The output obtained and the interpretation are essentially the same as for bivariate regression. The general equation for multiple regression is as follows:

$$Y = a + b_1X_1 + b_2X_2 + b_3X_3 + \cdots + b_nX_n$$

where Y = dependent or criterion variable
a = estimated constant
b_1-b_n = coefficients associated with the predictor variables so that a change of one unit in X will cause a change of b_1 units in Y; values for the coefficients are estimated from the regression analysis
X_1-X_n = predictor (independent) variables that influence the dependent variable

For example, consider the following regression equation (in which values for a, b_1, and b_2 have been estimated by means of regression analysis):

$$\hat{Y} = 200 + 17X_1 + 22X_2$$

where $\hat{Y}$ = estimated sales in units
X_1 = advertising expenditures
X_2 = number of salespersons

This equation indicates that sales increase by 17 units for every $1 increase in advertising and 22 units for every one-unit increase in number of salespersons.

Applications of Multiple Regression Analysis

There are many possible applications of multiple regression analysis in marketing research:

- Estimating the effects various marketing mix variables have on sales or market share
- Estimating the relationship between various demographic or psychographic factors and the frequency with which certain service businesses are visited
- Determining the relative influence of individual satisfaction elements on overall satisfaction
- Quantifying the relationship between various classification variables, such as age and income, and overall attitude toward a product or service
- Determining which variables are predictive of sales of a particular product or service

Multiple regression analysis can be used to estimate the relationship between various demographic or psychographic factors and the frequency with which a service business is hired.

Multiple regression analysis can serve one or a combination of two basic purposes: (1) predicting the level of the dependent variable, based on given levels of the independent variables, and (2) understanding the relationship between the independent variables and the dependent variable.

Measures of Multiple Regression Analysis

In the discussion of bivariate regression in Chapter 16, a statistic referred to as the **coefficient of determination,** or R^2, was identified as one of the outputs of regression analysis. This statistic can assume values from 0 to 1 and provides a measure of the percentage of the variation in the dependent variable that is explained by variation in the independent variables. For example, if R^2 in a given regression analysis is calculated to be .75, this means that 75 percent of the variation in the dependent variable is explained by variation in the independent variables. The analyst prefers to have a calculated R^2 close to 1. Frequently, variables are added to a regression model to see what effect they have on the R^2 value.

The *b* values, or **regression coefficients,** are estimates of the effect of individual independent variables on the dependent variable. It is appropriate to determine the likelihood that each individual *b* value is the result of chance. This calculation is part of the output provided by virtually all statistical software packages. Typically, these packages compute the probability of incorrectly rejecting the null hypothesis of $b_n = 0$.

coefficient of determination
A measure of the percentage of the variation in the dependent variable explained by variations in the independent variables.

regression coefficients
Estimates of the effect of individual independent variables on the dependent variable.

Dummy Variables

In some situations, the analyst needs to include nominally scaled independent variables such as gender, marital status, occupation, and race in a multiple regression analysis. *Dummy variables* can be created for this purpose. Dichotomous nominally scaled independent variables can be transformed into dummy variables by coding one value (e.g., female) as 0 and the other (e.g., male) as 1. For nominally scaled independent variables that can assume more than two values, a slightly different approach is required. Consider a question regarding racial group with three possible answers: African American, Hispanic, or Caucasian. Binary or dummy variable coding of responses requires the use of two dummy variables, X_1 and X_2, which might be coded as follows:

	X_1	X_2
If person is African American	1	0
If person is Hispanic	0	1
If person is Caucasian	0	0

Potential Use and Interpretation Problems

The analyst must be sensitive to certain problems that may be encountered in the use and interpretation of multiple regression analysis results. These problems are summarized in the following sections.

Collinearity   One of the key assumptions of multiple regression analysis is that the independent variables are not correlated with each other.[4] If they are correlated, then the estimated b values (regression coefficients) will be biased and unstable. Conventional wisdom says that this is not a problem if the regression model is intended strictly for purposes of prediction. However, if the goal of the analysis is to determine how each of the predictor variables influences the dependent variable, the possibility that the b values are biased because of **collinearity** becomes a serious problem.

> **collinearity**
> The correlation of independent variables with each other, which can bias estimates of regression coefficients.

The simplest way to check for collinearity is to examine the matrix showing the correlations between each variable in the analysis. One rule of thumb is to look for correlations between independent variables of .30 or greater. If correlations of this magnitude exist, then the analyst should check for distortions of the b values. One way to do this is to run regressions with the two or more collinear variables included and then run regressions again with the individual variables. The b values in the regression with all variables in the equation should be similar to the b values computed for the variables run separately.

There are a number of strategies for dealing with collinearity. Two of the most commonly used strategies are (1) to drop one of the variables from the analysis if two variables are heavily correlated with each other and (2) to combine the correlated variables in some fashion (e.g., an index) to form a new composite independent variable, which can be used in subsequent regression analyses.

> **causation**
> The inference that a change in one variable is responsible for (caused) an observed change in another variation.

Causation   Although regression analysis can show that variables are associated or correlated with each other, it cannot prove **causation.** Causal relationships can be confirmed only by other means (see Chapter 8). A strong logical or theoretical basis must be developed to support the idea that there is a causal relationship between the independent variables and the dependent variable. However, even a strong logical base supported by statistical results demonstrating correlation can be considered only an *indicator* of causation.

Scaling of Coefficients   The magnitudes of the regression coefficients associated with the various independent variables can be compared directly only if they are scaled in the same units or if the data have been standardized. Consider the following example:

$$\hat{Y} = 50 + 20X_1 + 20X_2$$

where $\hat{Y}$ = estimated sales volume
   X_1 = advertising expenditures in thousands of dollars
   X_2 = number of salespersons

At first glance, it appears that an additional dollar spent on advertising and an additional salesperson added to the sales force have equal effects on sales. However, this is not true, because X_1 and X_2 are measured in different kinds of units. Direct comparison of regression coefficients requires that all independent variables be measured in the same units (e.g., dollars or thousands of dollars) or that the data be standardized. *Standardization* is achieved by taking each number in a series, subtracting the mean of the series from the number, and dividing the result by the standard deviation of the series. The formula for the standardization process is as follows:

$$\frac{X_i - \bar{X}}{\sigma}$$

where X_i = individual number from a series of numbers
   $\bar{X}$ = mean of the series
   σ = standard deviation of the series

Sample Size   The value of R^2 is influenced by the number of predictor variables relative to sample size.[5] Several different rules of thumb have been proposed; they suggest that the number of observations should be equal to at least 10 to 15 times the number of predictor variables. For the preceding example (sales volume as a function of advertising expenditures and number of salespersons) with two predictor variables, a minimum of 20 to 30 observations would be required.

Example of Multiple Regression Analysis

This sample problem and others in this chapter use data from the research described in the appendix to this chapter. Ed English, the marketing director for United Wireless Communications (see opening vignette), believes that five variables are important in determining how much target customers are willing to pay each month to have wireless service. The five items are consumer importance ratings of the following service features: range of coverage, mobility, sound quality, ability to place and receive calls when away from home, and average monthly bill. This hypothesis is based on the results of focus groups and other research conducted by United. All six variables (the dependent variable and five predictor variables) were measured in the survey. The five predictor variables were all measured on a nine-point scale, where 9 means the attribute is "very important" and 1 means the attribute is "very unimportant." The five predictors can be found under question 3 in the survey.

To test English's hypothesis, the following model was estimated, using multiple regression analysis:

$$\hat{Y} = a + b_1 X_1 + b_2 X_2 + b_3 X_3 + b_4 X_4 + b_5 X_5$$

where
$\hat{Y}$ = dependent variable, amount willing to pay each month to have wireless service (ADDED)
a = constant term, or Y-axis intercept
$b_1 - b_5$ = regression coefficients to be estimated
X_1 = first independent variable, importance rating of range of coverage (RANGE)
X_2 = second independent variable, importance rating of mobility (MOBILITY)
X_3 = third independent variable, importance rating of sound quality (SOUND)
X_4 = fourth independent variable, importance rating of ability to place and receive calls when away from home (PRECEIV)
X_5 = fifth independent variable, importance rating of average monthly bill (AVGBILL)

The estimated regression equation is

$$\hat{Y} = .82 + .44 X_1 + .69 X_2 + .21 X_3 + .45 X_4 + 1.44 X_5$$

Complete regression results generated with the STATISTICA software package are shown in Table 17.2. These results provide the following information:

■ All the regression coefficients (b_1, b_2, and so on) have positive signs. This indicates that higher importance ratings on each of the five independent variables are associated with the willingness to pay more for wireless service, as expected.

■ The regression coefficient (b) shows the estimated effect of a one-unit increase in each of the associated independent variables on the dependent variable. The estimated unstandardized coefficients are shown under the column labeled "B." The results show, for example, that a one-unit increase in the importance rating of RANGE is associated with a $.44 increase in the

Table 17.2

Regression Summary for Dependent Variable: ADDED

$R = .86573182$ $R^2 = .74949158$ Adjusted $R^2 = .74303518$
$F(95,194) = 116.09$ $p < 0.0000$ Std. error of estimate: 1.4863

	BETA	ST. ERR OF BETA	B	ST. ERR OF B	t(194)	p-LEVEL
Intercept			0.82	1.67	0.49	0.62
RANGE	0.21	0.05	0.44	0.10	4.25	0.00
MOBILITY	0.52	0.05	0.69	0.07	10.54	0.00
SOUND	0.07	0.04	0.21	0.13	1.67	0.10
PRECEIV	0.21	0.06	0.45	0.12	3.65	0.00
AVGBILL	0.32	0.04	1.44	0.17	8.33	0.00

amount an individual is willing to pay per month for wireless service. The column labeled "BETA" shows the regression coefficient computed with standardized data. According to these estimates, MOBILITY has a greater effect on the amount prospective customers are willing to pay for the service than does any of the other four independent variables. AVGBILL is second in importance, and RANGE and PRECEIV are tied for third place. Interestingly, according to the model, SOUND has the smallest relative effect on the amount prospective customers are willing to pay.

- The adjusted R^2 value is .743, indicating that 74.3 percent of the variation in the amount consumers are willing to pay for wireless service is explained by the variation in the five independent, or predictor, variables.

Multiple Discriminant Analysis

Although **multiple discriminant analysis** is similar to multiple regression analysis,[6] there are important differences. In the case of multiple regression analysis, the dependent variable must be metric; in multiple discriminant analysis, the dependent variable is nominal or categorical in nature. For example, the dependent variable might be usage status for a particular product or service. A particular respondent who uses the product or service might be assigned a code of 1 for the dependent variable, and a respondent who does not use it might be assigned a code of 2. Independent variables might include various metric measures, such as age, income, and number of years of education. The goals of multiple discriminant analysis are as follows:

- Determine if there are statistically significant differences between the average discriminant score profiles of two (or more) groups (in this case, users and nonusers).
- Establish a model for classifying individuals or objects into groups on the basis of their values on the independent variables.

multiple discriminant analysis
A procedure for predicting group membership for a (nominal or categorical) dependent variable on the basis of two or more independent variables.

- Determine how much of the difference in the average score profiles of the groups is accounted for by each independent variable.

The general discriminant analysis equation follows:

$$Z = b_1 X_1 + b_2 X_2 + \cdots + b_3 X_n$$

where
Z = discriminant score
$b_1 - b_n$ = discriminant weights
$X_1 - X_n$ = independent variables

discriminant score

A score that is the basis for predicting to which group a particular object or individual belongs; also called *Z-score.*

discriminant coefficient

Estimate of the discriminatory power of a particular independent variable; also called *discriminant weight.*

The **discriminant score,** usually referred to as the *Z-score,* is the score derived for each individual or object by means of the equation. This score is the basis for predicting the group to which the particular object or individual belongs. *Discriminant weights,* often referred to as **discriminant coefficients,** are computed by means of the discriminant analysis program. The size of the discriminant weight (or coefficient) associated with a particular independent variable is determined by the variance structure of the variables in the equation. Independent variables with large discriminatory power (large differences between groups) have large weights, and those with little discriminatory power have small weights.

The goal of discriminant analysis is the prediction of a categorical variable. The analyst must decide which variables would be expected to be associated with the probability of a person or object falling into one of two or more groups or categories. In a statistical sense, the problem of analyzing the nature of group differences involves finding a linear combination of independent variables (the discriminant function) that shows large differences in group means.

Applications of Multiple Discriminant Analysis

Discriminant analysis can be used to answer many questions in marketing research:

- How are consumers who purchase various brands different from those who do not purchase those brands?
- How do consumers who show high purchase probabilities for a new product differ in demographic and lifestyle characteristics from those with low purchase probabilities?
- How do consumers who frequent one fast food restaurant differ in demographic and lifestyle characteristics from consumers who frequent another fast food restaurant?
- How do consumers who have chosen either indemnity insurance, HMO coverage, or PPO coverage differ from one another in regard to health care use, perceptions, and attitudes?

Example of Multiple Discriminant Analysis

United's marketing director wants to know if the five importance ratings used in the regression analysis predict whether an individual currently has a wireless telephone. Wireless telephone ownership is captured by question 7 on the survey in the Appendix. Those who currently have wireless telephones were assigned the code of 1, and those who do not currently have wireless telephones were assigned the code of 0. Previous research conducted by United suggested that the five independent variables (RANGE, MOBILITY, SOUND, PRECEIV, and AVGBILL) should be good predictors of wireless telephone ownership. The following discriminant model was designed to test this hypothesis:

$$Z = b_1 X_1 + b_2 X_2 + b_3 X_3 + b_4 X_4 + b_5 X_5$$

where
Z = discriminant score
$b_1 - b_5$ = discriminant coefficients or weights
X_1 = first independent variable, importance rating of range of coverage (RANGE)
X_2 = second independent variable, importance rating of mobility (MOBILITY)
X_3 = third independent variable, importance rating of sound quality (SOUND)
X_4 = fourth independent variable, importance rating of ability to place and receive calls when away from home (PRECEIV)
X_5 = fifth independent variable, importance rating of average monthly bill (AVGBILL)

The discriminant analysis results are

$$Z = -.02X_1 + .22X_2 - .36X_3 + .55X_4 - .07X_5$$

These results show that the ability to place and receive calls when away from home (PRECEIV) is the most important variable in discriminating between current users and nonusers of wireless telephone service, and range of coverage (RANGE) is the least important variable.

Another important role of discriminant analysis is to classify objects or people. In this example, the goal was to correctly classify consumers into two groups—those that currently have wireless telephone service and those that do not have wireless telephone service. To determine whether the estimated discriminant model is a good predictor, a *classification matrix* (sometimes called a *confusion matrix*) is used. The classification matrix produced for this problem is shown in Table 17.3. This table shows that the model correctly predicted 73.8 percent of current wireless nonusers as nonusers. However, it incorrectly predicted that 33, or 26.2 percent, of the nonusers were users. The model also predicted that 71.6 percent of current wireless users were users but that 28.4 percent were nonusers. Overall, the model correctly classified 73 percent of all respondents as wireless users or nonusers. This is far better than an analyst would expect to do on a chance basis. Thus, the conclusion is that the five independent variables are significant predictors of whether or not a particular individual is a current wireless user.

Table 17.3

Classification Matrix (pcstext.sta)

Rows: Observed classifications
Columns: Predicted classifications

	Percent Correct	G_1:0 p=.63000	G_2:1 p=.37000
G_1:0	73.8	93	33
G_2:1	71.6	21	53
Total	73.0	114	86

Statistical tests are available to indicate whether the resulting classification is better than could be expected by chance. When group sizes are unequal and the goal is to correctly predict membership in the two groups, one simple approach is to use the proportional chance criterion. The formula is as follows:

$$C_{\text{PRO}} = p^2 - (1 - p)^2$$

where p = proportion of individuals in group 1
$1 - p$ = proportion of individuals in group 2

In this case, group 1 (nonusers) includes 126 people, or 63 percent of the total (126/200). Calculation of the proportional chance criterion follows:

$$
\begin{aligned}
C_{\text{PRO}} &= .63^2 - (1 - .63)^2 \\
&= 5.397 - .137 \\
&= 5.534, \text{ or } 53.4\%
\end{aligned}
$$

The classification matrix model correctly classified 93 of the nonusers and 53 of the users, for a total of 146 out of 200, or 73 percent, correctly classified. This exceeds the proportional chance criterion of 53.4 percent by a wide margin and shows that the model did a better job than could be expected by chance.

Cluster Analysis

cluster analysis
A general term for statistical procedures that classify objects or people into some number of mutually exclusive and exhaustive groups on the basis of two or more classification variables.

The term **cluster analysis** generally refers to statistical procedures used to identify objects or people that are similar in regard to certain variables or measurements. The purpose of cluster analysis is to classify objects or people into some number of mutually exclusive and exhaustive groups so that those within a group are as similar as possible to one another.[7] In other words, clusters should be homogeneous internally (within cluster) and heterogeneous externally (between clusters).

Procedures for Clustering

A number of different procedures (based on somewhat different mathematical and computer routines) are available for clustering people or objects. However, the general approach underlying all of these procedures involves measuring the similarities among people or objects in regard to their values on the variables used for clustering. Often, similarities among the people or objects being clustered are determined on the basis of some type of distance measure. This approach is best illustrated graphically. Suppose an analyst wants to group, or cluster, consumers on the basis of two variables: monthly frequency of eating out and monthly frequency of eating at fast food restaurants. Observations on the two variables are plotted in a two-dimensional graph in Figure 17.1. Each dot indicates the position of one consumer in regard to the two variables. The distance between any pair of points is positively related to how similar the corresponding individuals are when the two variables are considered together (the closer the dots, the more similar the individuals). In Figure 17.1, consumer X is more like consumer Y than like either Z or W.

Inspection of Figure 17.1 suggests that three distinct clusters emerge on the basis of simultaneously considering frequency of eating out and frequency of eating at fast food restaurants:

- Cluster 1 includes those people who do not frequently eat out or frequently eat at fast food restaurants.
- Cluster 2 includes consumers who frequently eat out but seldom eat at fast food restaurants.
- Cluster 3 includes people who frequently eat out and also frequently eat at fast food restaurants.

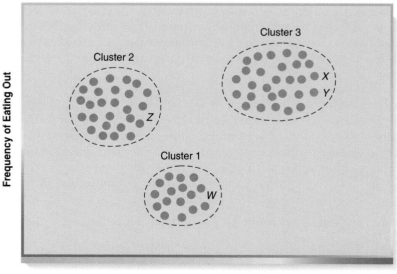

Figure 17.1

Cluster Analysis Based on Two Variables

The fast food company can see that its customers are to be found among those who, in general, eat out frequently. To provide more insight for the client, the analyst should develop demographic, psychographic, and behavioral profiles of consumers in cluster 3.

As shown in Figure 17.1, clusters can be developed from scatterplots. However, this time-consuming, trial-and-error procedure becomes more tedious as the number of variables used to develop the clusters or the number of objects or persons being

Clustering people according to how frequently and where they eat out is a way of identifying a particular consumer base. An upscale restaurant can see that its customers fall into Cluster 2 and possibly Cluster 3 in Figure 17.1.

clustered increases. You can readily visualize a problem with two variables and fewer than 100 objects. Once the number of variables increases to three and the number of observations increases to 500 or more, visualization becomes virtually impossible. Fortunately, computer algorithms are available to perform this more complex type of cluster analysis. The mechanics of these algorithms are complicated and beyond the scope of this discussion. The basic idea behind most of them is to start with some arbitrary cluster boundaries and modify the boundaries until a point is reached where the average interpoint distances within clusters are as small as possible relative to average distances between clusters.

Example of Cluster Analysis

United Wireless Communications wants to explore the issue of market segmentation using the data from the consumer survey. It believes that the market can be segmented on the basis of the eight attribute importance responses (question 3) and that the resulting clusters might be further described on the basis of demographic and usage data.

In order to address this issue, cluster analysis was performed using the K-means procedure. Because cluster analysis does not produce a "best" solution, United experimented with a number of different solutions before choosing a three-cluster solution on the basis of the distinctness of the clusters. The sizes of the three clusters and their average ratings on the eight attribute importance questions are summarized in Table 17.4. Average attribute ratings are also summarized in a line graph in Figure 17.2. This solution has the following characteristics:

- Cluster 3 is the largest, with 83 respondents, and cluster 2 is the smallest, with 55 respondents.
- In regard to attribute importance ratings, clusters 2 and 3 are the most similar. They have almost identical average importance ratings on six of the eight attributes. They do differ significantly in regard to price sensitivity (TELEPHON and INSTALL). Members of cluster 3 assign a much higher

PART 4:
Data Analysis

Table 17.4	Cluster Sizes and Average Ratings on Attribute Importance Variables		
Variable	**Cluster 1** ($n = 62$)	**Cluster 2** ($n = 55$)	**Cluster 3** ($n = 83$)
RANGE	6.8	8.1	8.2
MOBILITY	4.5	8.1	8.2
SOUND	8.1	8.5	8.5
PLACE	6.7	8.3	8.7
PRECEIV	6.8	8.5	8.6
AVGBILL	8.6	8.4	8.8
TELEPHON	8.1	6.3	8.7
INSTALL	7.2	5.1	8.5

importance to the price of the required equipment and installation/activation charges.

■ Cluster 1 differs markedly from clusters 2 and 3. In particular, members of this cluster view RANGE, MOBILITY, PLACE, and PRECEIV to be significantly less important than do the members of the other two clusters.

■ Members of clusters 2 and 3 are the best targets for the new wireless service, based on the importance they place on the RANGE, MOBILITY, PRECEIV, and PLACE variables. In the early stages of product introduction, cluster 3 members represent the most attractive target because of their relative insensitivity to price. Cluster 2 members might be targeted later, assuming that prices fall over time, which is the projected scenario.

The clusters also differ in regard to demographic and usage data. This issue was addressed by crosstabulating cluster membership with the various demographic and usage measures available in the survey.

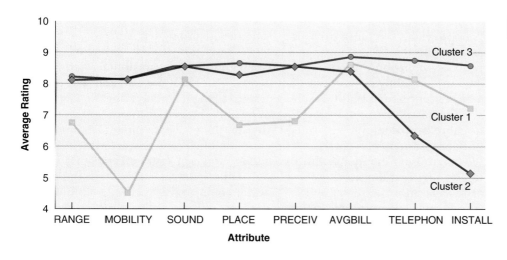

Figure 17.2

Average Attribute Importance Ratings for Three Clusters

- Cluster 1 individuals are the lightest users of all telephone services. They are about equally likely to be male or female, are least likely (by a narrow margin) to be married, are younger than members of the other groups, and come from households with the largest number of adults.
- Cluster 2 individuals are the heaviest users of most telephone services. They are much more likely to be female and are very similar to the members of cluster 3 on most other demographic measures.
- Cluster 3 members are between the other two groups in regard to usage of most telephone services. They are more likely to be male than female, are most likely to be married, are older than members of the other groups, and are willing to pay the highest amount, on average, for wireless service.

United's management is, as always, left with the question of what to do based on these findings. Preliminary analysis suggests that the company's initial target should be members of cluster 3, for the reasons just mentioned. Later, as prices fall, an appropriate strategy might be to expand the target to include the members of cluster 2. Members of cluster 1 should be targeted only after United has achieved saturation penetration levels among members of clusters 2 and 3. This plan can be operationalized by more careful analysis of the demographic characteristics of the members of the three clusters and the implementation of a sales and media plan to maximize communication with the most likely prospects.

Factor Analysis

factor analysis
A procedure for simplifying data by reducing a large set of variables to a smaller set of factors or composite variables by identifying underlying dimensions of the data.

The purpose of **factor analysis** is data simplification.[8] The objective is to summarize the information contained in a large number of metric measures (e.g., rating scales) with a smaller number of summary measures, called *factors*. As with cluster analysis, there is no dependent variable.

Many phenomena of interest to marketing researchers are actually composites, or combinations, of a number of measures. These concepts are often measured by means of rating questions. For instance, in assessing consumer response to a new automobile, a general concept such as "luxury" might be measured by asking respondents to rate different cars on attributes such as "quiet ride," "smooth ride," or "plush carpeting." The product designer wants to produce an automobile that is perceived as luxurious but knows that a variety of features probably contribute to this general perception. Each attribute rated should measure a slightly different facet of luxury. The set of measures should provide a better representation of the concept than a single global rating of "luxury."

Several measures of a concept can be added together to develop a composite score or to compute an average score on the concept. Table 17.5 shows data on six consumers who each rated an automobile on four characteristics. You can see that those respondents who gave higher ratings on "smooth ride" also tended to give higher ratings on "quiet ride." A similar pattern is evident in the ratings of "acceleration" and "handling." These four measures can be combined into two summary measures by averaging the pairs of ratings. The resulting summary measures might be called "luxury" and "performance" (see Table 17.6).

PART 4:
Data Analysis

Table 17.5	Importance Ratings of Luxury Automobile Features				
	Respondent	**Smooth Ride**	**Quiet Ride**	**Acceleration**	**Handling**
	Bob	5	4	2	1
	Roy	4	3	2	1
	Hank	4	3	3	2
	Janet	5	5	2	2
	Jane	4	3	2	1
	Ann	5	5	3	2
	Average	4.50	3.83	2.33	1.50

Factor Scores

Factor analysis produces one or more factors, or composite variables, when applied to a number of variables. A *factor*, technically defined, is a linear combination of variables. It is a weighted summary score of a set of related variables, similar to the composite derived by averaging the measures. However, in factor analysis, each measure is first weighted according to how much it contributes to the variation of each factor.

In factor analysis, a factor score is calculated on each factor for each subject in the data set. For example, in a factor analysis with two factors, the following equations might be used to determine factor scores:

$$F_1 = .40A_1 + .30A_2 + .02A_3 + .05A_4$$
$$F_2 = .01A_1 + .04A_2 + .45A_3 + .37A_4$$

where $F_1 - F_n$ = factor scores
$A_1 - A_n$ = attribute ratings

With these formulas, two factor scores can be calculated for each respondent by substituting the ratings she or he gave on variables A_1 through A_4 into each equation. The coefficients in the equations are the factor scoring coefficients to

Table 17.6	Average Ratings of Two Factors		
	Respondent	**Luxury**	**Performance**
	Bob	4.5	1.5
	Roy	3.5	1.5
	Hank	3.5	2.5
	Janet	5.0	2.0
	Jane	3.5	1.5
	Ann	5.0	2.5
	Average	4.25	1.92

be applied to each respondent's ratings. For example, Bob's factor scores are computed as follows:

$$F_1 = .40(5) + .30(4) + .02(2) + .05(1) = 3.29$$
$$F_2 = .01(5) + .04(4) + .45(2) + .37(1) = 2.38$$

In the first equation, the factor scoring coefficients, or weights, for A_1 and A_2 (.40 and .30) are large, whereas the weights for A_3 and A_4 are small. The small weights on A_3 and A_4 indicate that these variables contribute little to score variations on factor 1 (F_1). Regardless of the ratings a respondent gives to A_3 and A_4, they have little effect on his or her score on F_1. However, variables A_3 and A_4 make a large contribution to the second factor score (F_2), whereas A_1 and A_2 have little effect. These two equations show that variables A_1 and A_2 are relatively independent of A_3 and A_4 because each variable takes on large values in only one scoring equation.

The relative sizes of the scoring coefficients are also of interest. Variable A_1 (with a weight of .40) is a more important contributor to factor 1 variation than is A_2 (with a smaller weight of .30). This finding may be very important to the product designer when evaluating the implications of various design changes. For example, the product manager might want to improve the perceived luxury of the car through product redesign or advertising. The product manager may know, based on other research, that a certain expenditure on redesign will result in an improvement of the average rating on "smooth ride" from 4.3 to 4.8. This research may also show that the same expenditure will produce a half-point improvement in ratings on "quiet ride." The factor analysis shows that perceived luxury will be enhanced to a greater extent by increasing ratings on "smooth ride" than by increasing ratings on "quiet ride" by the same amount.

Factor Loadings

factor loading
The correlation between each factor score and each of the original variables.

The nature of the factors derived can be determined by examining the **factor loadings.** Using the scoring equations presented earlier, a pair of factors scores (F_1 and F_2) are calculated for each respondent. Factor loadings are determined by calculating the correlation (from +1 to −1) between each factor (F_1 and F_2) score and each of the original ratings variables. Each correlation coefficient represents the loading of the associated variable on the particular factor. If A_1 is closely associated with factor 1, the loading or correlation will be high, as shown for the sample problem in Table 17.7. Because the loadings are correlation coefficients, values near +1 or −1 indicate a close positive or negative association. Variables A_1 and A_2 are closely associated (highly correlated) with scores on factor 1, and variables A_3 and A_4 are closely associated with scores on factor 2. Stated another way, variables A_1 and A_2 have high loadings on factor 1 and serve to define the factor; variables A_3 and A_4 have high loadings on and define factor 2.

Naming Factors

Once each factor's defining variables have been identified, the next step is to name the factors. This is a somewhat subjective step, combining intuition and knowledge of the variables with an inspection of the variables that have high

PART 4:
Data Analysis

Table 17.7

Factor Loadings for Two Factors

Variable	Correlation with	
	Factor 1	Factor 2
A_1	.85	.10
A_2	.76	.06
A_3	.06	.89
A_4	.04	.79

loadings on each factor. Usually, a certain consistency exists among the variables that load highly on a given factor. For instance, it is not surprising to see that the ratings on "smooth ride" and "quiet ride" both load on the same factor. Although we have chosen to name this factor "luxury," another analyst, looking at the same result, might decide to name the factor "prestige."

Number of Factors to Retain

In factor analysis, the analyst is confronted with a decision regarding how many factors to retain. The final result can include from one factor to as many factors as there are variables. The decision is often made by looking at the percentage of the variation in the original data that is explained by each factor. In this case, the first and second factors explain a total of 92.5 percent of the variability in the four measures (see Table 17.8). The last two factors explain only 7.5 percent of the variation and contribute little to the objective of data simplification.

There are many different decision rules for choosing the number of factors to retain. Probably the most appropriate decision rule is to stop factoring when additional factors no longer make sense. The first factors extracted are likely to exhibit logical consistency; later factors are usually harder to interpret, as they are more likely to contain a large amount of random variation.

Example of Factor Analysis

Once again, we refer to the United survey results for an example of factor analysis. In this instance, United is interested in determining or identifying attributes that go together. As suggested earlier, this will permit United to identify clusters

Table 17.8

Percentage of Variation in Original Data Explained by Each Factor

Factor	Percent of Variation Explained
1	55.0
2	37.5
3	4.8
4	2.7

of benefits that are associated in the minds of target customers and to design market communications that speak to these related benefits. As you may recall, factors identified via factor analysis represent underlying supervariables constructed from pieces of the original input variables.

After experimenting with several different solutions, we settled on the three-factor solution as the "best" solution, based on statistical and interpretability criteria. Factor analysis procedures produce a number of different types of output. One key type of output is the matrix of factor loadings. Factor loadings, as noted earlier, are the simple correlations between each of the original input variables and each factor, or supervariable, identified in the analysis. The factor loadings for the three-factor solution to this problem are shown in Table 17.9. Information on the proportion of the total variance in the original eight input variables explained by each factor is provided at the bottom of the table. These data show that the three factors explain 72 percent of the variance in the eight original input variables. An interpretation of the factors follows:

- Factor 1 loads heavily or correlates on the following input variables: RANGE, MOBILITY, PLACE, and PRECEIV. We conclude that "staying in touch" is an appropriate name for this factor; different analysts might look at these results and come up with somewhat different names for the factor. However, given the four variables on which this factor loads, it clearly has something to do with the ability to reach and be reached by other people at all times.
- Factor 2 correlates or loads on the variables AVGBILL, TELEPHON, and INSTALL. A quick review indicates that all of these variables have something to do with cost; therefore, we simply call this the "cost" factor.
- Factor 3 correlates strongly with only one of the original input variables—SOUND. Therefore, we call it the "sound quality" factor.

This analysis suggests, for example, that it would be logical to send consumers information about RANGE, MOBILITY, PLACE, and PRECEIV issues in the same mailing. The analysis might also provide useful direction for the design of initial market communications.

Table 17.9

Factor Loadings (Varimax raw) (pcstext.sta)
Extraction: Principal Components

	Factor 1	Factor 2	Factor 3
RANGE	0.70	−0.10	0.39
MOBILITY	0.83	−0.09	0.07
SOUND	0.03	0.03	0.96
PLACE	0.85	0.19	−0.12
PRECEIV	0.91	−0.02	0.02
AVGBILL	−0.04	0.69	0.29
TELEPHON	−0.01	0.83	−0.11
INSTALL	0.06	0.77	0.02
Proportion of total variance	0.34	0.23	0.15

Perceptual Mapping

Perceptual mapping, as the name suggests, involves the production of perceptual maps. Perceptual maps are visual representations of consumer perceptions of a product, brand, company, or any other object in two or more dimensions. Ordinarily, such maps show the extremes of the dimensions on the ends of the X and Y axes. Figure 17.3 shows a sample perceptual map. Assuming that "good value" and "fast service" are features that target customers want in restaurants of this type, the analyst can clearly see that restaurant B is in the best position (high on good value and fast service), and restaurant D is in the worst position (high on poor value and slow service).

A number of different approaches are used to develop perceptual maps, including factor analysis, multidimensional scaling, discriminant analysis, and correspondence analysis. One approach, built around factor analysis, is discussed in the following section.[9]

Example of Perceptual Mapping

The results in the factor analysis example discussed earlier were based on a survey in which respondents rated only one automobile on a number of characteristics of interest. In many situations, management needs ratings data on a competitive set of products. For example, each respondent might be asked to rate several different automobiles on a number of different attributes or characteristics.

The basic format for any factor analysis is a correlation matrix, which shows the correlation for each pair of variables. In the case of the problem presented in the previous section, the format is a 4-by-4 matrix of correlations.

perceptual mapping
A procedure that produces visual representations of consumer perceptions of products, brands, companies, or other objects.

Figure 17.3

Sample Perceptual Map

Table 17.10	Factor Scores for Four Automobile Concepts				
Attribute	**Cadillac Seville**	**Lincoln Continental**	**BMW 540**	**Chrysler 300**	
Smooth ride	4.50	4.17	2.00	1.67	
Quiet ride	3.83	3.50	1.83	1.83	
Acceleration	2.33	4.00	4.17	2.17	
Handling	1.50	3.83	4.00	1.83	
Score 1	3.07	2.87	1.53	1.22	
Score 2	1.71	3.17	3.57	1.66	

If ratings data were obtained for several automobiles, a separate set of factor scores could be calculated for each model. Factor scores could be calculated for each factor, for each individual, and for each automobile rated. Averaging these factor scores across all individuals or groups of individuals would produce an average score for each product. These average factor scores would represent the coordinate positions of the automobiles in a perceptual map.

Table 17.10 shows the average attribute ratings for four automobiles. Factor scores for each automobile, calculated with the scoring equations introduced earlier, are also shown in this table. These factor scores are plotted in the perceptual map shown in Figure 17.4. This perceptual map is based on the average factor scores taken across all subjects. It shows that the Lincoln Continental and the Cadillac Seville are seen as being more luxurious than the BMW 540 and the Chrysler 300, and the Lincoln Continental and the BMW 540 are seen as offering a higher level of performance than the Chrysler 300 and the Cadillac Seville.

Conjoint Analysis

conjoint analysis
A procedure used to quantify the value that consumers associate with different levels of product/service attributes.

Conjoint analysis is a popular multivariate procedure used by marketers to help determine what features a new product or service should have and how it should be priced. It can be argued that conjoint analysis has become popular because it is a more powerful, more flexible, and often less expensive way to address these important issues than is the traditional concept testing approach.[10]

Conjoint analysis is not a completely standardized procedure.[11] A typical conjoint analysis application involves a series of steps covering a variety of procedures; it is not a single procedure as is, for example, regression analysis. Fortunately, conjoint analysis is not difficult to understand, as we demonstrate in the following example concerning the attributes of golf balls.

Example of Conjoint Analysis

Put yourself in the position of a product manager for Titleist, a major manufacturer of golf balls. From focus groups recently conducted, past research studies of various types, and your own personal experience as a golfer, you know that

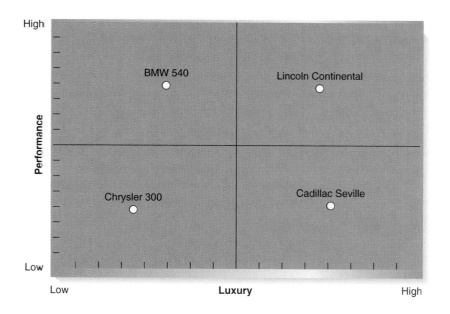

Figure 17.4

Perceptual Map of Average Factor Scores for Four Automobile Concepts

Conjoint analysis could be used by a manufacturer of golf balls to determine the three most important features of a golf ball and which ball meets the most needs of both consumer and manufacturer.

golfers tend to evaluate golf balls in terms of three important features or attributes: average driving distance, average ball life, and price.

You also recognize a range of feasible possibilities for each of these features or attributes, as follows:

1. Average driving distance
   - 10 yards more than the golfer's average
   - Same as the golfer's average
   - 10 yards less than the golfer's average
2. Average ball life
   - 54 holes
   - 36 holes
   - 18 holes
3. Price per ball
   - $2.00
   - $2.50
   - $3.00

From the perspective of potential purchasers, the ideal golf ball would have the following characteristics:

- Average driving distance—10 yards above average
- Average ball life—54 holes
- Price—$2.00

From the manufacturer's perspective, which is based on manufacturing cost, the ideal golf ball would probably have these characteristics.

CHAPTER 17:
Multivariate Data Analysis

597

- Average driving distance—10 yards below average
- Average ball life—18 holes
- Price—$3.00

This golf ball profile is based on the fact that it costs less to produce a ball that travels a shorter distance and has a shorter life. The company confronts the eternal marketing dilemma: The company would sell a lot of golf balls but would go broke if it produced and sold the ideal ball from the golfer's perspective. However, the company would sell very few balls if it produced and sold the ideal ball from the manufacturer's perspective. As always, the "best" golf ball from a business perspective lies somewhere between the two extremes.

A traditional approach to this problem might produce information of the type displayed in Table 17.11. As you can see, this information does not provide new insights regarding which ball should be produced. The preferred driving distance is 10 yards above average, and the preferred average ball life is 54 holes. These results are obvious without any additional research.

Table 17.11

Traditional Nonconjoint Rankings of Distance and Ball Life Attributes

Average Driving Distance		Average Ball Life	
Rank	Level	Rank	Level
1	275 yards	1	54 holes
2	250 yards	2	36 holes
3	225 yards	3	18 holes

Considering Features Conjointly   In conjoint analysis, rather than having respondents evaluate features individually, the analyst asks them to evaluate features conjointly or in combination. The results of asking two different golfers to rank different combinations of "average driving distance" and "average ball life" conjointly are shown in Tables 17.12 and 17.13.

As expected, both golfers agree on the most and least preferred balls. However, analysis of their second through eighth rankings makes it clear that the first golfer is willing to trade off ball life for distance (accept a shorter ball life for longer distance), while the second golfer is willing to trade off distance for longer ball life (accept shorter distance for a longer ball life).

Table 17.12

Conjoint Rankings of Combinations of Distance and Ball Life for Golfer 1

Distance	Ball Life		
	54 holes	36 holes	18 holes
275 yards	1	2	4
250 yards	3	5	7
225 yards	6	8	9

Table 17.13

Conjoint Rankings of Combinations of Distance and Ball Life for Golfer 2

	Ball Life		
Distance	54 holes	36 holes	18 holes
275 yards	1	3	6
250 yards	2	5	8
225 yards	4	7	9

This type of information is the essence of the special insight offered by conjoint analysis. The technique permits marketers to see which product attribute or feature potential customers are willing to trade off (accept less of) to obtain more of another attribute or feature. People make these kinds of purchasing decisions every day (e.g., they may choose to pay a higher price for a product at a local market for the convenience of shopping there).

Estimating Utilities The next step is to calculate a set of values, or *utilities,* for the three levels of price, the three levels of driving distance, and the three levels of ball life in such a way that, when they are combined in a particular mix of price, ball life, and driving distance, they predict a particular golfer's rank order for that particular combination. Estimated utilities for golfer 1 are shown in Table 17.14. As you can readily see, this set of numbers perfectly predicts the original rankings. The relationship among these numbers or utilities is fixed, though there is some arbitrariness in their magnitude. In other words, the utilities shown in Table 17.14 can be multiplied or divided by any constant and the same relative results will be obtained. The exact procedures for the estimation of these utilities are beyond the scope of this discussion. They are normally calculated by using procedures related to regression, analysis of variance, or linear programming.

Table 17.14

Ranks (in parentheses) and Combined Metric Utilities for Golfer 1—Distance and Ball Life

	Ball Life		
	54 holes	36 holes	18 holes
Distance	50	25	0
275 yards	(1)	(2)	(4)
	150	125	100
250 yards	(3)	(5)	(7)
	110	85	60
225 yards	(6)	(8)	(9)
	50	25	0

The tradeoffs that golfer 1 is willing to make between "ball life" and "price" are shown in Table 17.15. This information can be used to estimate a set of utilities for "price" that can be added to those for "ball life" to predict the rankings for golfer 1, as shown in Table 17.16.

This step produces a complete set of utilities for all levels of the three features or attributes that successfully capture golfer 1's tradeoffs. These utilities are shown in Table 17.17.

Simulating Buyer Choice   For various reasons, the firm might be in a position to produce only two of the 27 golf balls that are possible with each of the three levels of the three attributes. The possibilities are shown in Table 17.18. If the calculated utilities for golfer 1 are applied to the two golf balls the firm is able to make, then the results are the total utilities shown in Table 17.19. These results indicate that golfer 1 will prefer the ball with the longer life over the one

Table 17.15

Conjoint Rankings of Combinations of Price and Ball Life for Golfer 1

| Price | Ball Life | | |
	54 holes	36 holes	18 holes
$2.00	1	2	4
$2.50	3	5	7
$3.00	6	8	9

Table 17.16

Ranks (in parentheses) and Combined Metric Utilities for Golfer 1—Price and Ball Life

| Price | Ball Life | | |
	54 holes 50	36 holes 25	18 holes 0
$2.00	(1)	(2)	(4)
	70	45	20
$2.50	(3)	(5)	(7)
	55	30	5
$3.00	(6)	(8)	(9)
	50	25	0

Table 17.17

Complete Set of Estimated Utilities for Golfer 1

| Distance | | Ball Life | | Price | |
Level	Utility	Level	Utility	Level	Utility
275 yards	100	54 holes	50	$1.25	20
250 yards	60	36 holes	25	$1.50	5
225 yards	0	18 holes	0	$1.75	0

Table 17.18

Ball Profiles for Simulation

Attribute	Distance Ball	Long-Life Ball
Distance	275	250
Life	18	54
Price	$2.50	$3.00

Table 17.19

Estimated Total Utilities for the Two Sample Profiles

Attribute	Distance Ball		Price	
	Level	Utility	Level	Utility
Distance	275	100	250	60
Life	18	0	54	50
Price	$2.50	5	$3.00	0
Total utility	105	110		

with the greater distance because it has a higher total utility. The analyst need only repeat this process for a representative sample of golfers to estimate potential market shares for the two balls. In addition, the analysis can be extended to cover other golf ball combinations.

The three steps discussed here—collecting tradeoff data, using the data to estimate buyer preference structures, and predicting choice—are the basis of any conjoint analysis application. Though the tradeoff matrix approach is simple, useful for explaining conjoint analysis, and effective for problems with small numbers of attributes, it is currently not widely used. An easier and less time-consuming way to collect conjoint data is to have respondents rank or rate product descriptions on a paper questionnaire or to use PC-based interviewing software that applies certain rules to determine what questions and product profiles to present to each respondent based on his or her previous answers.

As suggested earlier, there is much more to conjoint analysis than has been discussed in this section. However, if you understand this simple example, then you understand the basic concepts that underlie conjoint analysis.

Limitations of Conjoint Analysis

Like many research techniques, conjoint analysis suffers from a certain degree of artificiality. Respondents may be more deliberate in their choice processes in this context than in a real situation. The survey may provide more product information than respondents would get in a real market situation. Finally, it is important to remember that the advertising and promotion of any new product or service can lead to consumer perceptions that are very different from those created via descriptions used in a survey.

Modeling of Modern Mailings

MULTIVARIATE TECHNIQUES ARE OFTEN USED BY DIRECT mail firms to "score" lists and eliminate people with a very low probability of responding. Multivariate modeling has become an integral part of the marketing strategy of most direct mail and telemarketing firms. There are a number of reasons for this. First, the budget available may not cover the cost of mailing or phoning every person in a database. Second, the budget may be big enough, but contacting every person in the database will not be profitable. Third, perhaps some customers in a database are so profitable that they should be contacted many times in a given time period while others should be contacted only once or twice. The bottom line is that some customers and prospects in a database are less likely to respond to direct mail or telemarketing offers than others.

Multivariate modeling allows the marketer to "score" the customer or prospect in terms of their probability of responding. Models predicting probability of response are built on results of past mailing campaigns. Of course, we need certain information about each person in the database used for the past campaign or campaigns to do the necessary analysis. Some of the information that we might have is date the person first entered the database, source of the customer (direct mail, print, broadcast, etc.), date of their most recent purchase, total dollar purchases to date, total number of purchases to date, number of times they were mailed to, products or services purchased in the past and various demographic characteristics.

With data like those indicated above, a statistician could build a model in the following steps:

- Obtain the names and records of all persons who responded to the mailing.
- Divide responders into two groups.
- Draw a random sample of non-responders and divide that sample into two groups.
- Create a "calibration sample" that consists of half of the responders and half of the non-responders.
- Create a "validation sample" that includes the other half of the responders and the other half of the sample of non-responders.
- Use the calibration file to build the predictive model or scoring equation. A regression model might be used to estimate a scoring equation that would look something like this:

$$Y = a + b_1 X_1 + b_2 X_2 + b_3 X_3 + b_n X_n$$

"Y" = the probability of response. The "X"s represent the importance of each variable selected to be included in the model in predicting likelihood to respond. The "b"s are the weights assigned to each variable in the modeling process.

- Apply the scoring equation to all of the records in the validation file. This means that every record

602

PART 4:
Data Analysis

in the validation file will now have a "predicted or expected" likelihood of responding (purchasing) that ranges from zero to one. The average of all the predicted probabilities should equal the average response rate for the mailing.

- Sort all of the records in the validation file in descending order of their estimated probability of response.
- Divide the sorted file into 10 equal groups or deciles and calculate the actual response rate for each decile. If the model is poor then the actual response rate for each decile will be similar to the average overall response rate for the mailing. In other words, the modeling process wasn't able to find segments, measured in deciles, that did better or worse than average. If the model did well, the top decile will show a response rate greater than the response rate of the second decile, which will be greater than the response rate of the third decile, and so on. The greater the spread between the top (best) and the bottom (worst) decile, the better the model.

If the results are good then we can, for example, decide to eliminate deciles with estimated response rates below some threshold level that we choose. In this manner, we can use multivariate analysis to help us save resources and focus on the people in our list with a higher probability of responding.[12] ■

Summary

Multivariate analysis refers to the simultaneous analysis of multiple measurements on each individual or object being studied. Some of the more popular multivariate techniques include multiple regression analysis, multiple discriminant analysis, cluster analysis, factor analysis, perceptual mapping, and conjoint analysis.

Multiple regression analysis enables the researcher to predict the magnitude of a dependent variable based on the levels of more than one independent variable. Multiple regression fits a plane to observations in a multidimensional space. One statistic that results from multiple regression analysis is called the coefficient of determination, or R^2. The value of this statistic ranges from 0 to 1. It provides a measure of the percentage of the variation in the dependent variable that is explained by variation in the independent variables. The b values, or regression coefficients, indicate the effect of the individual independent variables on the dependent variable.

Whereas multiple regression analysis requires that the dependent variable be metric, multiple discriminant analysis uses a dependent variable that is nominal or categorical in nature. Discriminant analysis can be used to determine if statistically significant differences exist between the average discriminant score profiles of two (or more) groups. The technique can also be used to establish a model for classifying individuals or objects into groups on the basis of their scores on the independent variables. Finally, discriminant analysis can be used to determine how much of the difference in the average score profiles of the groups are accounted for by each independent variable. The discriminant score, called a *Z*-score, is derived for each individual or object by means of the discriminant equation.

Cluster analysis enables a researcher to identify subgroups of individuals or objects that are homogeneous within the subgroup yet different from other subgroups. Cluster analysis requires that all independent variables be metric, but there is no specification of a dependent variable. Cluster analysis is an excellent means for operationalizing the concept of market segmentation.

The purpose of factor analysis is to simplify massive amounts of data. The objective is to summarize the information contained in a large number of metric measures such as rating scales with a smaller number of summary measures called factors. As in cluster analysis, there is no dependent variable in factor analysis. Factor analysis produces factors, each of which is a weighted composite of a set of related variables. Each measure is weighted according to how much it contributes to the variation of each factor. Factor loadings are determined by calculating the correlation coefficient between factor scores and the original input variables. By examining which variables load heavily on a given factor, the researcher can subjectively name that factor.

Perceptual maps can be produced by means of factor analysis, multidimensional scaling, discriminant analysis, or correspondence analysis. The maps provide a visual representation of how brands, products, companies, and other objects are perceived relative to each other on key features such as quality and value. All the approaches require, as input, consumer evaluations or ratings of the objects in question on some set of key characteristics.

Conjoint analysis is a technique that can be used to measure the tradeoffs potential buyers make on the basis of the features of each product or service available to them. The technique permits the researcher to determine the relative value of each level of each feature. These estimated values are called utilities and can be used as a basis for simulating consumer choice.

Key Terms & Definitions

multivariate analysis   A general term for statistical procedures that simultaneously analyze multiple measurements on each individual or object under study.

multiple regression analysis   A procedure for predicting the level or magnitude of a (metric) dependent variable based on the levels of multiple independent variables.

coefficient of determination   A measure of the percentage of the variation in the dependent variable explained by variations in the independent variables.

regression coefficients   Estimates of the effect of individual independent variables on the dependent variable.

collinearity   The correlation of independent variables with each other, which can bias estimates of regression coefficients.

causation   The inference that a change in one variable is responsible for (caused) an observed change in another variable.

multiple discriminant analysis   A procedure for predicting group membership for a (nominal or categorical) dependent variable on the basis of two or more independent variables.

discriminant score   A score that is the basis for predicting to which group a particular object or individual belongs; also called *Z-score*.

discriminant coefficient   An estimate of the discriminatory power of a particular independent variable; also called *discriminant weight*.

cluster analysis   A general term for statistical procedures that classify objects or people into some number of mutually exclusive and exhaustive groups on the basis of two or more classification variables.

factor analysis   A procedure for simplifying data by reducing a large set of variables to a smaller set of factors or composite variables by identifying underlying dimensions of the data.

factor loading   The correlation between each factor score and each of the original variables.

perceptual mapping   A procedure that produces visual representations of consumer perceptions of products, brands, companies, or other objects.

conjoint analysis   A procedure used to quantify the value that consumers associate with different levels of product/service attributes.

Questions for Review & Critical Thinking

1. Distinguish between multiple discriminant analysis and cluster analysis. Give several examples of situations in which each might be used.
2. What purpose does multiple regression analysis serve? Give an example of how it might be used in marketing research. How is the strength of multiple regression measures of association determined?
3. What is a dummy variable? Give an example using a dummy variable.
4. Describe the potential problem of collinearity in multiple regression. How might a researcher test for collinearity? If collinearity is a problem, what should the researcher do?
5. A sales manager examined age data, education level, a personality factor that indicated level of introvertedness/extrovertedness, and level of sales attained by the company's 120-person sales force. The technique used was multiple regression analysis. After analyzing the data, the sales manager said, "It is apparent to me that the higher the level of education and the greater the degree of extrovertedness a salesperson has, the higher will be an individual's level of sales. In other words, a good education and being extroverted cause a person to sell more." Would you agree or disagree with the sales manager's conclusions? Why?
6. The factors produced and the results of the factor loadings from factor analysis are mathematical constructs. It is the task of the researcher to make sense out of these factors. The following table lists four factors produced from a study of cable TV viewers. What label would you put on each of these four factors? Why?

		Factor Loading
Factor 1	I don't like the way cable TV movie channels repeat the movies over and over.	.79
	The movie channels on cable need to spread their movies out (longer times between repeats).	.75
	I think the cable movie channels just run the same things over and over and over.	.73
	After a while, you've seen all the pay movies, so why keep cable service.	.53
Factor 2	I love to watch love stories.	.76
	I like a TV show that is sensitive and emotional.	.73
	Sometimes I cry when I watch movies on TV.	.65
	I like to watch "made for TV" movies.	.54
Factor 3	I like the religious programs on TV (negative correlation).	−.76
	I don't think TV evangelism is good.	.75
	I do not like religious programs.	.61
Factor 4	I would rather watch movies at home than go to the movies.	.63
	I like cable because you don't have to go out to see the movies.	.55
	I prefer cable TV movies because movie theaters are too expensive.	.46

PART 4:
Data Analysis

7. The following table is a discriminant analysis that examines responses to various attitudinal questions from cable TV users, former cable TV users, and people who have never used cable TV. Looking at the various discriminant weights, what can you say about each of the three groups?

		Users	Formers	Nevers
			Discriminant Weights	
Users				
A19	Easygoing on repairs	−.40		
A18	No repair service	−.34		
A7	Breakdown complainers	+.30		
A5	Too many choices	−.27		
A13	Antisports	−.24		
A10	Antireligious	+.17		
Formers				
A4	Burned out on repeats		+.22	
A18	No repair service		+.19	
H12	Card/board game player		+.18	
H1	High-brow		−.18	
H3	Party hog		+.15	
A9	VCR preference		+.16	
Nevers				
A7	Breakdown complainer			−.29
A19	Easygoing on repairs			+.26
A5	Too many choices			+.23
A13	Antisports			+.21
A10	Antireligious			−.19

8. The following table shows regression coefficients for two dependent variables. The first dependent variable is willingness to spend money for cable TV. The independent variables are responses to attitudinal statements. The second dependent variable is stated desire never to allow cable TV in their homes. By examining the regression coefficients, what can you say about persons willing to spend money for cable TV and those who will not allow cable TV in their homes?

	Regression Coefficients
Willing to Spend Money for Cable TV	
Easygoing on cable repairs	−3.04
Cable movie watcher	2.81
Comedy watcher	2.73
Early to bed	−2.62
Breakdown complainer	2.25
Lovelorn	2.18
Burned out on repeats	−2.06
Never Allow Cable TV in Home	
Antisports	+0.37
Object to sex	+0.47
Too many choices	+0.88

1. Does Nestlé have an interest in conjoint analysis? To find out, go to http://www.nestle.com/all%5Fabout/environment/index.html and look at the presentation on Nestlé and the environment.
2. Can conjoint analysis be used to determine the type of new house a person may choose? Go to http://www.sawtooth.com/news/sawtoothnews/newsarch/basics.htm to answer this question.

Real-Life Research • 17.1

Burger Street Image Analysis II

Burger Street, the restaurant chain discussed in Real-Life Research 16.1, has completed its analysis. Management is now wondering whether the analysis was done correctly. The consultant whom Burger Street hired to help with strategy development suggested that, instead of doing a series of bivariate regressions and correlations, the analyst should have estimated a model that considered all the predictor variables simultaneously.

Specifically, the consultant says that multiple regression analysis should have been used, with "overall image rating" as the dependent variable and ratings on "perceived food quality," "food taste," "value" (what you got versus what you paid), and "speed of service" as the independent variables. In particular, the consultant believes that the bivariate results may be misleading and should not be used as a basis for the strategy development he is working on. Furthermore, he says that the multivariate results will provide better estimates of the relative importance of each predictor in determining Burger Street's overall image (regression coefficients). And he believes that the multivariate approach will provide a better overall estimate of the percentage of variation in the dependent variable that is explained by variation in the predictor variables (R^2). Some managers at Burger Street wonder if the consultant is just trying to impress them and increase the size of his bill.

Review the background information for Real-Life Research 16.1. For that case, you were asked to run a number of bivariate correlations and regressions. If you have not done so already, run the analyses requested.

Questions

1. Do you agree with the consultant? Why or why not?
2. Run a multivariate regression analysis using "overall rating" as the dependent variable and the four other ratings items as predictors. Discuss the results and compare them to those obtained with bivariate regression analysis. What does multivariate regression analysis show that the bivariate regres-

sion did not show? Are any of the regression assumptions violated in the multivariate regression you ran? If so, which ones? How can you address those violations?

3. Run factor analysis on the four predictor variables. How many factors are there in the solution that you chose? Do the factors make sense? What would you call the factors you identified? Explain why you named them as you did.

Real-Life Research • 17.2

The Oklahoma Power Company

The Oklahoma Power Company recently experienced difficulties in getting rate increases from the state's public utility commission. Accordingly, management was concerned about the image of the organization among Oklahoma residents. A decision was made to conduct a marketing research study that would examine the image of Oklahoma Power. The following table shows a factor analysis of the variables used to analyze the company's image.

Q#	Descriptor	Factor 1	Factor 2	Factor 3	Factor 4
Q18	Service and information—safety	0.82			
Q19	Service and information—efficiency	0.79			
Q16	Information from Oklahoma Power—safety	0.77			
Q15	Involvement of personnel	0.74			
Q17	Information from Oklahoma Power—efficiency	0.74			
Q13	Speakers	0.74			
Q14	Safety demonstrations	0.73			
Q12	Information about classes	0.69			
Q8	Courtesy of personnel		0.87		
Q7	Helpfulness of personnel		0.87		
Q9	Responsiveness		0.75		
Q1	Oklahoma Power Company		0.62		
Q6	Continuity of service		0.57		
Q2	Overall job		0.56		
Q3	Rates			0.81	
Q4	Rate calculation			0.79	
Q5	Sources of electricity			0.58	
Q11	Information on bill				0.75
Q10	Way of presenting bill				0.78

Questions

1. How would you identify the four factors in the table?
2. How might this information help management in understanding and evaluating a semantic differential from which these variables were derived?

Real-Life Research • 17.3

Custom Car Wash Systems

Custom Car Wash Systems offers car wash franchises throughout the United States. Currently, 872 car washes franchised by Custom are in operation. As part of its service to franchisees, Custom runs a national marketing and advertising program.

Carl Bahn is the senior vice president in charge of marketing for Custom. He is currently in the process of designing the marketing and advertising campaigns for the upcoming year. Bahn believes that it is time for Custom to take a more careful look at user segments in the market. Based on other analyses, he and his associates at Custom have decided that the upcoming campaign should target the heavy user market. Through other research, Custom has defined "heavy car wash users" as those individuals who have their cars washed at a car wash facility three or more times per month on average. "Light users" are defined as those who use such a facility less than three times a month but at least four times a year. "Nonusers" are defined as those who use such a facility less than four times per year. Bahn and his associates are currently in the process of attempting to identify those factors that discriminate between heavy and light users. In the first stage of this analysis, they conducted interviews with 50 customers at 100 of their locations for a total of 5,000 interviews. Crosstabulation of the classification variables with frequency of use suggests that four variables may be predictive of usage heaviness: vehicle owner age, annual income of vehicle owner, age of vehicle, and socioeconomic status of vehicle owner (based on an index of socioeconomic variables).

Custom retained a marketing research firm called Marketing Metrics to do further analysis for the company. Marketing Metrics evaluated the situation and decided to use multiple discriminant analysis to further analyze the survey results and identify the relative importance of each of the four variables in determining whether a particular individual is a heavy or light user. The firm obtained the following results:

$$Z = .18X_1 + .53X_2 - .49X_3 + .93X_4$$

where X_1 = age of vehicle owner
X_2 = annual income of vehicle owner
X_3 = age of vehicle
X_4 = socioeconomic status of owner (as measured by an index in which a higher score means higher status)

Questions

1. What would you tell Bahn about the importance of each of the predictor variables?
2. What recommendations would you make to him about the type of people Custom should target, based on its interest in communicating with heavy users?

Appendix: Wireless Communications Data Set

This appendix includes a description of a data set obtained from an actual survey done for a client in the wireless communications business. The client is referred to as United Wireless. Here, you will also find descriptions of the research objectives, the methodology used, and the physical layout of the data set.

Research Objectives

The objectives of the research were as follows:

- To determine the likelihood of purchasing the new wireless communications service at various monthly service charges and equipment costs.
- To measure the importance of various wireless communications service attributes.
- To determine expected usage patterns and usage heaviness for the new wireless service.
- To determine usage heaviness of existing residential and long-distance telephone services.
- To measure current expenditures on local and long-distance services.
- To determine, for purposes of market segmentation, the demographic characteristics of likely purchasers and nonpurchasers.

Methodology

A summary description of the methodology employed for this research follows:

- *Sample size.* 200 consumers
- *Qualified respondents.* Individuals 18 years of age or older from households with annual incomes of $30,000 or more
- *Sample area.* National probability sample
- *Sample type.* Random sample based on random digit dialing
- *Sampling error.* ±7.1 percent with 95 percent confidence
- *Data collection method.* All surveying was done by means of central-location telephone interviewing, using a computer-assisted approach. Interviewing was supervised and unobtrusively monitored. All interviewing was conducted from a central-location telephone interviewing facility.
- *Interview length.* Surveys averaged 10 minutes in length.
- *Survey timing.* All interviewing was conducted during February 2000.
- *Questionnaire.* A copy of the questionnaire employed for the study follows this methodology summary.

Description of the Data Set

The description of the data set is keyed to the questionnaire. The data are available on the CD-ROM in the back of this textbook in two formats: ASCII and .dbf. The ASCII file has the name unitedwireless.TXT, and the other file has the name unitedwireless.dbf. The unitedwireless.dbf file can be directly imported into most statistical packages by using the import feature.

The locations of the numerical representations of the responses to each question for the ASCII file are shown in parentheses throughout the questionnaire. The variable names for the .dbf file are shown in the left margin in capital letters. If you employ the import feature of the statistical package you are using, these names should be correctly imported with the data and will appear at the top of the column containing the data for the particular question.

Wireless Survey

ADDED

1. Before we begin the next exercise, how much more would you be willing to pay each month to receive wireless service? This is in addition to what you are currently paying for basic telephone service to your home. **ENTER THE AMOUNT. TYPE "O" FOR NOTHING, "5" FOR $5, ETC.**

_____ Additional amount willing to pay to receive wireless service (4–6)

2. Considering the phone service that you currently have, please indicate the probability that you will purchase one of the new wireless services presented as an **addition** to your existing service.

Indicate your likelihood to purchase each wireless service on a 0 to 100 scale, where 0 means you are not at all likely to purchase that telephone service and 100 means you are extremely likely to purchase that telephone service for your home.

W25100

a. How likely would you be to purchase the new wireless service if your monthly service charge was $25 and the cost of the telephone was $100?

_____ Likelihood to purchase (7–9)

W500

b. How likely would you be to purchase the new wireless service if your monthly service charge was $50 and the cost of the telephone was $0?

_____ Likelihood to purchase (10–12)

3. Now I would like for you to rate several attributes on their level of importance to you when selecting telephone service. For each factor, use a 9-point scale, where 9 means the attribute is **"very important"** and 1 means the attribute is **"very unimportant"** to you when selecting local telephone service. How important is . . . **READ LIST AND ROTATE**

	Attributes	VI								VU	
RANGE	Range of coverage	9	8	7	6	5	4	3	2	1	(13)
MOBILITY	Mobility	9	8	7	6	5	4	3	2	1	(14)
SOUND	Sound quality (sound and static)	9	8	7	6	5	4	3	2	1	(15)
PLACE	Ability to place calls when away from home	9	8	7	6	5	4	3	2	1	(16)
PRECEIV	Ability to place and receive calls when away from home	9	8	7	6	5	4	3	2	1	(17)
AVGBILL	Average monthly telephone bill	9	8	7	6	5	4	3	2	1	(18)
TELEPHON	Price of telephone equipment	9	8	7	6	5	4	3	2	1	(19)
INSTALL	Installation /activation charges	9	8	7	6	5	4	3	2	1	(20)

CAR

4. If you purchased wireless service, what percentage of your calls (made and received) on the wireless service would be from your car? **ENTER A PERCENTAGE FROM 0 TO 100**

_____ Percentage of wireless calls from your car (21–23)

MET

5. What percentage of calls using wireless service would be within the Orlando metropolitan area?

_____ Percentage of wireless calls within metropolitan area (24–26)

HOME **6.** And what percentage of your wireless calls would be made in and around your home or neighborhood?

_____ Percentage of wireless calls in and around the home (27–29)

And now, I have just a few questions concerning telephone usage in your household.

CELL **7.** Do you own or use a wireless phone?

(30)
1 YES
2 NO

MAKES **8.** Considering the local telephone calls of all members of your household for a **typical day,** how many calls would you say your household MAKES in a typical day?

_____ Number of calls MADE by household per day (31–32)

RECV **9.** How many calls would you say your household receives in a typical day?

_____ Number of calls RECEIVED by household per day (33–34)

LMAKE **10.** Now considering the number of long-distance calls of all members of your household for a **typical week,** how many long-distance calls would you say your household MAKES in a typical week?

_____ Number of long-distance calls MADE by household per week (35–36)

LRECV **11.** How many long-distance calls would you say your household receives in a typical week?

_____ Number of long-distance calls RECEIVED by household per week (37–38)

MONTHLY **12.** How much is your average monthly telephone bill, including **local and long-distance charges?**

_____ Average monthly telephone bill (39–41)

PAYCALL **13.** How often do you use a pay telephone for personal calls in a typical month?

_____ Number of pay telephone calls per mo. (42–43)

GENDER **14.** INDICATE GENDER BY OBSERVATION

(44)
1 MALE
2 FEMALE

MARRIED **15.** Are you married?

(45)
1 YES
2 NO
3 RF

AGE **16.** Which of the following categories includes your age?

(46)
1 18–24
2 25–34
3 35–44
4 45–54
5 55–64
6 65 and older
7 RF

ADULTS **17.** How many adults age 18 and over are currently living in your household including yourself?

_____ Number of adults (47)

CHILDREN   **18.** Do you have any children age 18 and under currently living in your household?

        (48)
        1   YES
        2   NO
        3   RF

INCOME   **19.** Which of the following categories includes the total annual income of all members of your household before taxes?

        (49)
        1   Less than $35,000
        2        $35,000 to $49,999
        3        $50,000 to $74,999
        4        $75,000 or more
        5   DK/RF

Thanks for participating.

Name _____   Telephone _____

Address _____

Interviewer # _____   Length of interview _____

Source: Courtesy of DSS Research.

Marketing Research across the Organization

1. The question of data interpretation is not fully resolved in business today. Someone must still look at the data and decide what they really mean. Often this is done by the people in marketing research. Defend the proposition that persons in engineering, finance, and production should interpret all marketing research data when the survey results affect their operations. What are the arguments against this position?

2. Marketing research data analysis for a large electric utility found that confidence in the abilities of the repairperson is customers' primary determinant of their satisfaction or dissatisfaction with the electric utility. Armed with these findings, the utility embarked on a major advertising campaign extolling the heroic characteristics of the electric utility repairperson. The repairpeople hated the campaign. They knew that they couldn't live up to the customer expectations created by the advertising. What should have been done differently?

3. When marketing research is used in strategic planning, it often plays a role in determining long-term opportunities and threats in the external environment. Threats, for example, may come from competitors' perceived future actions, new competitors, governmental policies, changing consumer tastes, or a variety of other sources. Management's strategic decisions will determine the long-term profitability, and perhaps even the survival, of the firm. Most top managers are not marketing researchers or statisticians; therefore, they need to know how much confidence they can put into the data. Stated differently, when marketing researchers present statistical results, conclusions, and recommendations, they must understand top management's tolerance for ambiguity and imprecision. Why? How might this understanding affect what marketing researchers present to management? Under what circumstances might the level of top management's tolerance for ambiguity and imprecision shift?

The Johnson Poll

WHEN THE JOHNSON ORGANIZATION* TRAINS ITS INTERVIEWers, it explains a rather unusual pay plan. Several pages of the interviewer training manual are shown below.

Expectations

1. Our clients are our number one priority.
2. Schedule yourself at least 15 hours a week (and more)!
3. Maintain consistent productivity. If you are working 15/20 hours a week, you should be making $6–$8 per hour. If you are working 25/34 hours a week, you should be making $8–$10 per hour. If you are working 35+ hours a week, you should be making $10–$12 per hour.
4. Maintain an enthusiastic and positive attitude.
5. Keep your work environment clean.
6. Respondents can hear background noise, so if someone is being too noisy and it is interfering with your work, let them know, through motions or verbally, to be quiet.
7. Dress in a presentable manner. (Dressing comfortably is important but most tend to take pride and do better work if not in "sweats.")
8. As long as you are hitting and exceeding nightly quotas, you should be making BIG BUCKS!

Compensation

Compensation is based on productivity! (Our pay system rewards those who work hard!) For each survey you complete, you will be paid a certain amount based on "quota." Quota is set on a per hour basis.

Anticipating Quota   Guidelines for setting quota:

1. Length of survey
2. Incidence
3. Area

Pay Days   Pay days are every other Friday. Each pay period ends on the Friday night before pay day. See a manager to have your check direct deposited.

First Month   Take at quota pay even if you are under quota. We will bump you to minimum wage nightly, if necessary.

*Disguised name of one of America's most well-known research organizations.

Second Month Take at quota pay even if you are under quota. However, you will not be bumped to minimum wage nightly.

Quota per Hour	35-Hour Team Regular Pay		
	Under Quota	At Quota	Above Quota
0.5	6.00	20.00	22.00(+1)
0.75	4.00	13.33	14.67(+1)
1.0	3.00	10.00	11.00(+1)
1.5	2.00	6.67	7.33(+1)
2.0	1.50	5.00	5.50(+1)
2.5	1.20	4.00	4.40(+1)
3.0	1.00	3.33	3.67(+1)
3.5	0.86	2.86	3.14(+2)
4.0	0.75	2.50	2.75(+2)
4.5	0.67	2.22	2.44(+2)
5.0	0.60	2.00	2.20(+2)
5.5	0.55	1.82	2.00(+2)
6.0	0.50	1.67	1.83(+3)
6.5	0.47	1.54	1.69(+3)
7.0	0.43	1.43	1.57(+3)
7.5	0.40	1.33	1.47(+3)
8.0	0.25	1.25	1.38(+4)
8.5	0.25	1.18	1.29(+4)
9.0	0.25	1.11	1.22(+4)
9.5	0.25	1.05	1.16(+4)
10.0	0.25	1.00	1.10(+5)
12.0	0.25	0.83	0.92(+6)

The basic pay plan for a 35-hour interviewer who is making quota is $10 per hour. For example, if the quota is 5 per hour, and the interviewer makes the quota, the pay is $2 × 5 = $10. If the interviewer only completes three interviews with the same quota, the pay is $.60 × 3 = $1.80. However, if the interviewer completes eight interviews with the five-unit quota, then the pay is $2.20 × 8 = $2 bonus = $19.60. Thus, there is a strong incentive to exceed quota.

Questions

1. Are there any ethical issues associated with this pay plan?
2. What sorts of problems are created when there is a strong incentive to beat the quota?
3. Can this system inject bias into the data? If so, what type?
4. Does this pay scheme help create a positive image for the marketing research industry? Explain.

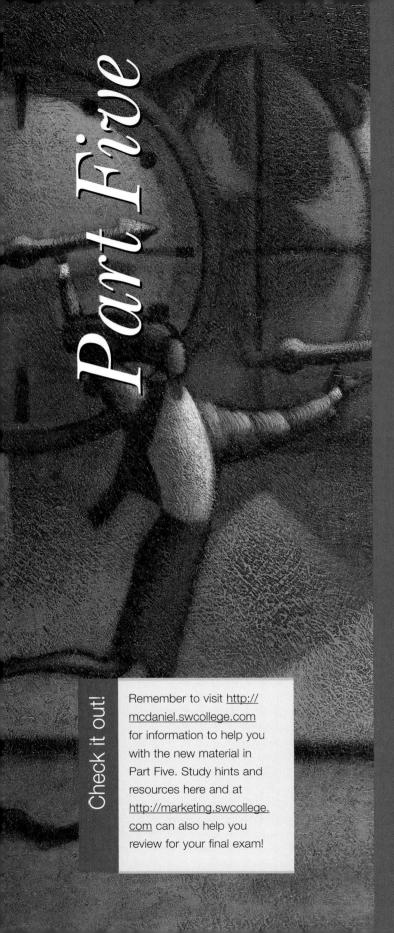

Part Five

Marketing Research in Action

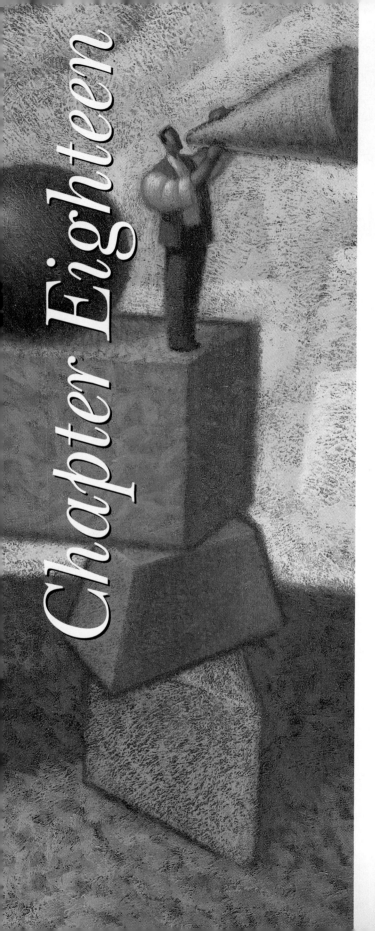

Chapter Eighteen

Communicating the Research Results

Learning Objectives

To become aware of the primary purposes of a research report.

To learn how to organize and prepare a research report.

To learn how to make a personal presentation.

To understand the effective use and communication of marketing research information.

To appreciate the role of trust in a researcher–client relationship.

J OHN SPEILBERG, A NEW YORK–BASED RESEARCHER, LIKES TO TELL OF HIS
carefully prepared 250-page report (including tables and statistical analyses) prepared for one of America's largest candy manufacturers. The report and presentation to three top executives culminated approximately six months of difficult research. Speilberg felt that he had several significant findings to report, including new market segments to explore and several new product concept ideas.

AFTER LISTENING TO A LABORIOUS HOUR-long presentation with many facts, figures, and tables, the president of the candy company suddenly rose and said, "Damn it, John, I've been listening to this mumbo-jumbo for over an hour, and I'm thoroughly confused. I know I won't be much better off trying to read through a report that's thicker than most dictionaries. I want a five-page summary on my desk tomorrow by 8:00." With that pronouncement, he left the room.

SPEILBERG LEARNED A LESSON THAT HAS HELPED HIM THROUGHOUT HIS career: No matter how appropriate the research design, how proper the statistical analyses, how representative the sample, how carefully worded the questionnaire, how stringent the quality-control checks for field collection of the data, or how well matched the research was to the original research objectives, everything will be for naught if the researcher cannot communicate with the decision makers. ■

In presenting research results to one of America's largest candy manufacturers, John Speilberg, a New York–based researcher, learned an important lesson about communicating research results. Without clear communication of results, decision makers will not be able to act effectively.

Find out more about effective business communication at

http://www. westwords.com/ guffey/ students.html

What is the role of the research report? How can marketing researchers communicate more effectively? What constitutes a "good" report? What pitfalls should be avoided in writing a research report? What are the key factors in deciding whether or not to use a research report? These questions will be addressed in this chapter.

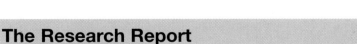

The Research Report

Once all the data have been collected and analyzed, it is time for the researcher to package the information in a report to the research users. The marketing research report should satisfy the following objectives.

- *Explain why the research was done.* A brief statement of the motivations for doing the research often helps users to put the information in context. This is particularly true when a decision maker is reviewing a report done some time ago or may not be familiar with the reasons for doing the original research.
- *State the specific research objectives.* Every marketing research report should have a detailed list of research objectives that guided the design and execution of the research and the analysis of the results.
- *Explain how the research was done.* Users need to know how the research was conducted so that they can determine how much weight to put on the results in arriving at the decisions they need to make. How the data were collected, the sampling and analytical procedures used, and other details regarding the methodology should be clearly specified.
- *Present the findings of the research.* The basic findings of the research should be clearly enumerated. This section of the report provides the basis for the conclusions and recommendations that the researcher will draw from those findings.
- *Provide conclusions and recommendations.* The report, to be actionable, must provide clear statements of the conclusions and recommendations that flow from the research findings. In preparing the report, the researcher must be sure that there is a clear linkage between the research findings and the conclusions and recommendations. The users of the information need to understand that the conclusions and recommendations made are supported by data and are not merely the opinions of the researcher.

Organizing the Report

In some cases, corporate policy may dictate the exact format of the research report. The most common organization for marketing research reports today is outlined below:

1. *Table of contents:* A list of the major sections
2. *Background and objectives:* Approximately one page of background information and one page listing the objectives, both of which usually come from the request for proposal and discussions with the client
3. *Executive summary:* A two- to four-page summary of findings, conclusions, and recommendations
4. *Methodology:* A two- to five-page description of how the research was conducted, which may be supported by more detailed and technical material in appendices
5. *Findings:* The largest section of most reports, providing a detailed presentation of the research results
6. *Appendices:* The last section of the report, containing (a) a *copy of the questionnaire,* which enables users to see exactly how questions were asked so that they can properly interpret key findings; (b) *crosstabulations* for every question in the survey, which enable users to look at specific issues not addressed in the findings; and (c) *other supporting material,* such as detailed technical discussions of research procedures and techniques

Make Your Point

IN EARLY 2000, GENERAL HUGH SHELTON, CHAIRMAN OF THE JOINT CHIEFS of Staff, sent out an unusual order to U.S. military bases across the world. Basically his message was—get to the point, forget the bells and whistles. PowerPoint presentations emailed around the world by military personnel were using so much of the defense department's classified bandwidth that they were actually slowing down more critical communications between headquarters and field units. General Shelton was telling all military personnel that all the snazzy effects are not needed and that they should just stick to the information. This is the most recent assault on a growing electronic menace: The PowerPoint Briefing. Yes, business executives complain about the endless PowerPoint presentations put on by eager middle managers in meeting rooms across the country. However, in the military, PowerPoint has become one of the most dreaded facts of daily life.

"The idea behind most of these briefings is for us to sit through 100 slides with our eyes glazed over and then to do what all military organizations hope for . . . to surrender to an overwhelming mass," says Navy Secretary Richard Danzek. Instead of carefully developing 10 or 12 slides on a legal pad and taking them to the graphics department for production, officers can now create hundreds of slides in a few hours without ever leaving their desks.[1] ■

Formatting the Report

The preparation of marketing research reports has changed dramatically in recent years. In the quest to find more efficient and effective ways to convey research results, marketing researchers have gravitated to **presentation software.** Although a number of presentation software packages are available, Microsoft's PowerPoint dominates the market.

As discussed in Chapter 15, information often can be presented in a more efficient and compelling manner in graphs than in words or tables. However, until recently, tools for the efficient and speedy creation of graphs were lacking. The marketing research report of today is filled with graphics. In their requests for proposals, clients typically specify that they want graphics-based reports. Research reports that might have included 50 or more pages of text in the past are now presented in 10 to 12 pages of text and 20 to 30 pages of graphs. This permits busy executives to quickly grasp key findings and move ahead to conclusions and recommendations. The use of color in graphs has further enhanced communication and made reports more exciting to read. Current software presentation packages make it easy for the analyst to do the following:

■ Create bulleted charts using various font styles and sizes with bold, italicized, and underlined text.

presentation software
Personal computer software that provides easy-to-use platforms for creating effective reports and presentations.

Today, research reports that in the past might have included 50 or more pages of text are presented in 10 to 12 pages of text and 20 to 30 pages of graphics.

- Design various styles of graphs and, with a few mouse clicks, experiment with different types of graphs (pie, bar, line, etc.) that might be used to display a particular research finding.
- Apply various special effects, full-motion video, and sound when moving from page to page in an electronic presentation. It is becoming increasingly common to use a personal computer attached to a color projection panel or a large multisync monitor. The presenter controls the presentation using a mouse, and the software can be programmed to use various fades between slides and to include video (such as focus group comments) and sound clips at various points.

In summary, the predominant reporting style in marketing research today has the following characteristics:

- It minimizes the use of words.
- It feeds information to clients in what might be termed "minibites."
- It makes extensive use of bulleted charts and graphic presentations of results.

Examples of pages from reports prepared using presentation software are provided in Figures 18.1 through 18.9.

Interpreting the Findings

The most difficult task for individuals who are writing a research report for the first time is interpreting the findings to arrive at conclusions and then using these conclusions to formulate recommendations. The **executive summary** is the portion of the report that explains why the research was done, what the research found, what the data mean, and what action, if any, should be taken, based on the research. The difficulties of this process are completely understandable, given that the marketing researcher is often inundated with piles of computer printouts, stacks of questionnaires, bundles of respondent contact and recontact sheets, and a scratch pad full of notes on the project. There is, however, a systematic method that the researcher can follow to draw conclusions.

The research objectives stated early in the marketing research process should serve as the primary guide for interpreting findings and drawing conclusions. These objectives should have been stated as specifically as possible, perhaps even with an explicit priority rank for each objective. Although the questionnaire should have been designed to touch on facets of the objectives,

executive summary

The portion of a research report that explains why the research was done, what was found, what those findings mean, and what action, if any, management should undertake.

Figure 18.1

Bulleted Chart

Executive Summary

Visit Information:

- **Overall.** 45.9% say they have visited a casino in the last 6 months.

- **By market.** Visit rate is highest from Tampa (23.2%) and lowest from Panama City (4.1%).

- **By demographics.** Those 54 and younger are more likely to have visited than those 55+. Positive relationship with income. Those in $71K+ bracket most likely to have visited.

- **Number of visits.** The average is just over 1.1 times across markets. Frequency highest for Miami (6.1) and lowest for Saint Petersburg (.39).

specific bits of information about any one objective may be spread across the questionnaire. Computer printouts often contain information in statistical order rather than in the order in which managers will use the data. Consequently, the researcher's first task is to pull together all the printouts and results that pertain to each of the various objectives. A system will evolve as the researcher focuses attention on the objectives one at a time.

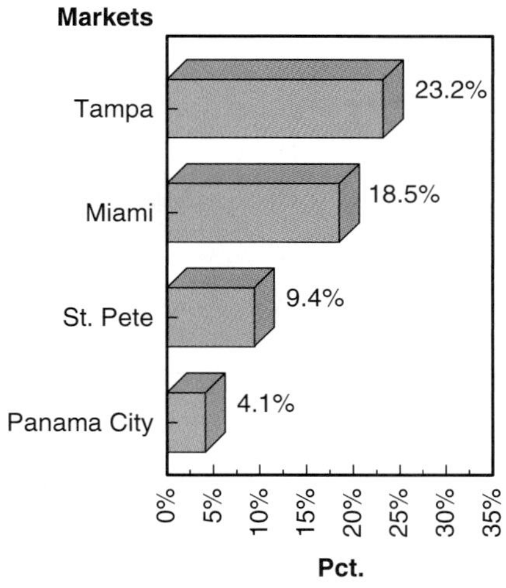

Figure 18.2

Text and 3-D Horizontal Bar Chart

Visited Casino Past 6 Months

- **Overall.** For visited a casino in the past 6 months, the average for all markets is 13.8%.
- **Tampa leads.** 23.2% of those surveyed said they had visited an area casino.
- **Panama City.** Only 4.1% have visited a casino.

Markets

Market	Pct.
Tampa	23.2%
Miami	18.5%
St. Pete	9.4%
Panama City	4.1%

0% 5% 10% 15% 20% 25% 30% 35%

Pct.

Figure 18.3

Multiple 3-D Bar Charts

Note: Each bar chart has its own page in the research report.

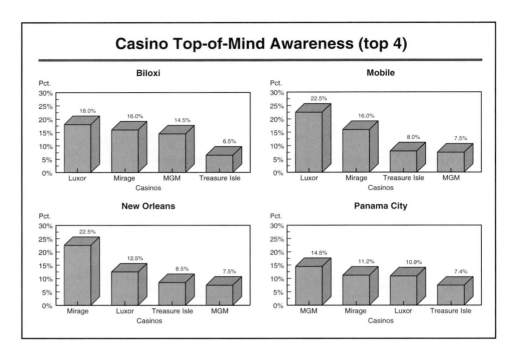

For example, assume that Burger King is reconsidering its breakfast menu. An objective of its breakfast research study is "to determine the feasibility of adding (1) bagels and cream cheese, (2) a western omelette, or (3) French toast." All crosstabulations and one-dimensional tables referring to these food items should be brought together. Generally, the researcher first examines the

Figure 18.4

Area Chart for Summary Measures

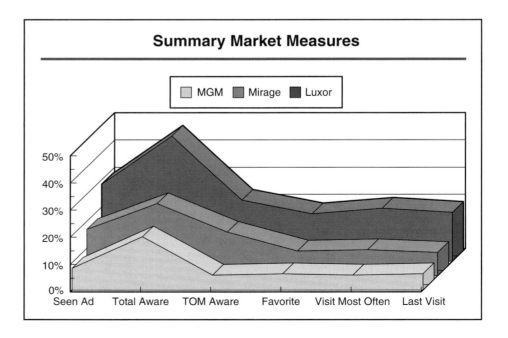

PART 5:
Marketing Research in Action

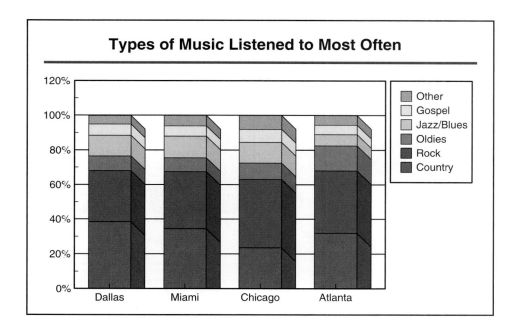

Types of Music Listened to Most Often

Figure 18.5

Stacked Bar Chart with 3-D Effect

one-dimensional tables to get the overall picture—that is, understand which of the three breakfast items was most preferred. Next, crosstabulations are analyzed to obtain a better understanding of the overall data—that is, to get a clear view of which age group is most likely to prefer French toast.

Conclusions are generalizations that answer the questions raised by the research objectives or otherwise satisfy the objectives. These conclusions are

conclusions
Generalizations that answer the questions raised by the research objectives or otherwise satisfy the objectives.

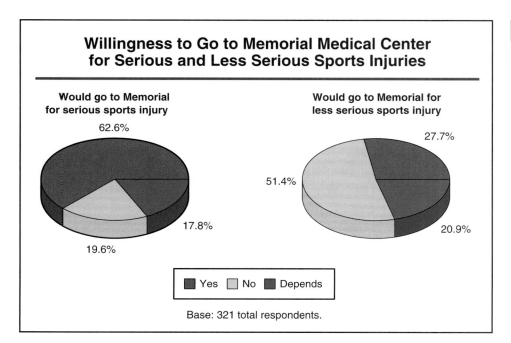

Figure 18.6

Pie Charts with 3-D Effect

Figure 18.7

Mixing Pie and Bar Charts

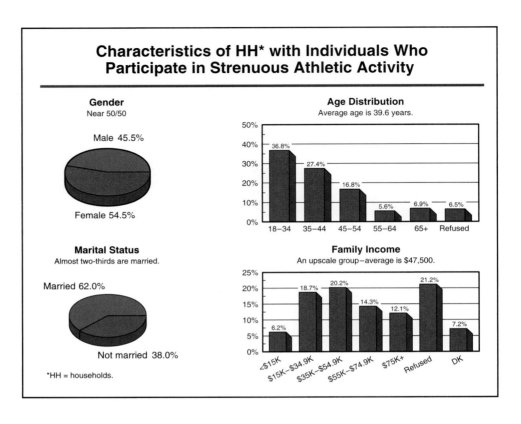

Characteristics of HH* with Individuals Who Participate in Strenuous Athletic Activity

Gender
Near 50/50

Male 45.5%

Female 54.5%

Marital Status
Almost two-thirds are married.

Married 62.0%

Not married 38.0%

*HH = households.

Age Distribution
Average age is 39.6 years.

18–34	35–44	45–54	55–64	65+	Refused
36.8%	27.4%	16.8%	5.6%	6.9%	6.5%

Family Income
An upscale group—average is $47,500.

<$15K	$15K–$34.9K	$35K–$54.9K	$55K–$74.9K	$75K+	Refused	DK
6.2%	18.7%	20.2%	14.3%	12.1%	21.2%	7.2%

Figure 18.8

Line Chart with Table

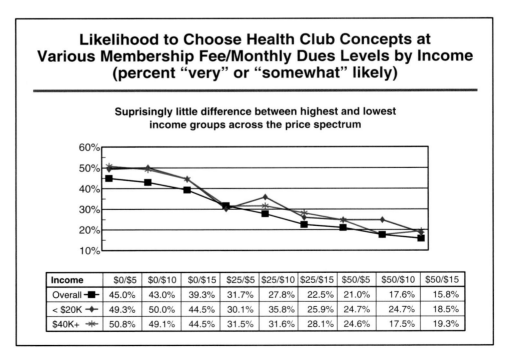

Likelihood to Choose Health Club Concepts at Various Membership Fee/Monthly Dues Levels by Income (percent "very" or "somewhat" likely)

Suprisingly little difference between highest and lowest income groups across the price spectrum

Income	$0/$5	$0/$10	$0/$15	$25/$5	$25/$10	$25/$15	$50/$5	$50/$10	$50/$15
Overall ■	45.0%	43.0%	39.3%	31.7%	27.8%	22.5%	21.0%	17.6%	15.8%
< $20K ◆	49.3%	50.0%	44.5%	30.1%	35.8%	25.9%	24.7%	24.7%	18.5%
$40K+ ✳	50.8%	49.1%	44.5%	31.5%	31.6%	28.1%	24.6%	17.5%	19.3%

PART 5:
Marketing Research in Action

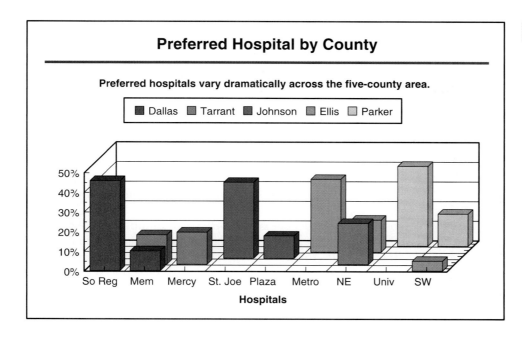

Figure 18.9

XYZ Bar Chart with 3-D Effect

derived through the process of *induction,* or generalizing from small pieces of information. The researcher should try to merge the information and then paraphrase it in a few descriptive statements that generalize the results. In short, the conclusion of a research report should be a statement or series of statements that communicate the results of the study to the reader but would not necessarily include any of the data derived from the statistical analysis.

Formulating Recommendations

Recommendations are gained from the process of deduction. The marketing researcher applies the conclusions to specific areas in order to make suggestions for marketing strategies or tactics. A recommendation usually focuses on how the client can gain a differential advantage. A *differential advantage* is a true benefit offered by a potential marketing mix that the target market cannot obtain anywhere else (e.g., United Airlines having exclusive U.S. carrier landing rights at a foreign airport).

In some cases, a marketing researcher must refrain from making specific recommendations and instead fall back on more general ones. For example, the marketing researcher might not have sufficient information about the resources and experience base of the company or about the decision maker to whom the report is being directed. Or the researcher may have been notified that the recommendations will be determined by the decision maker. Under these circumstances, the researcher offers conclusions and stops at that point.

The final report, whether written or personal or both, represents the culmination of the research effort. The quality of the report and its recommendations often determine whether a research user will return to a supplier. Within a cor-

recommendations
Conclusions applied to marketing strategies or tactics that focus on a client's achievement of differential advantage.

An analysis of the likelihood of joining a health club based on income may yield a recommendation that focuses on how the client can gain a differential advantage over its competitors.

poration, an internal report prepared by a research department may have less impact, but a history of preparing excellent reports may lead to merit salary increases and, ultimately, promotion for a research staff member.

The Personal Presentation

Clients may expect a personal presentation of the research results. A personal presentation serves many purposes. It requires that the interested parties assemble and become reacquainted with the research objectives and methodology. It also brings to light any unexpected events or findings and highlights the research conclusions. In fact, for some decision makers in the company, the personal presentation will be their *only* exposure to the findings; they will never read the report. Other managers may only skim the written report, using it as a memory-recall trigger for points made in the personal presentation. In short, effective communication in the personal presentation is absolutely critical.

Presentation Materials

We recommend the use of four material aids in a personal presentation:

1. *Presentation outline.* Every audience member should be supplied a presentation outline that briefly details the presentation flow (major parts) and significant findings. The outline should not contain statistics or tables, but it should have ample white space for the person to jot down notes or comments.
2. *Visuals.* In the not-too-distant past, the most commonly used visual devices were a slide projector and an overhead projector. Today, more researchers use laptop personal computers, presentation software, and a projector that permits them to display their presentation on a screen of almost any size. Not only can traditional charts be shown, but spreadsheets as well. The researcher can display "what if?" situations as questions arise from the audience. Summaries, conclusions, and recommendations should be highlighted with visuals.
3. *Executive summary.* Each audience member should have a copy of the executive summary (preferably several days in advance). Enabling managers to contemplate questions in advance of the presentation allows for a more fruitful discussion.
4. *Copies of the final report.* The report serves as physical evidence of the research. Its comprehensive nature should make clear that it includes much detail that was omitted in the personal presentation. It should be made available to interested parties at the end of the presentation.

Presenting More Confidently

Seize the opportunity. A key building block for developing confidence as a speaker is to speak, and speak often. Seize every opportunity you can, personally and professionally, to speak in public.

Use the "as if" principle. If your goal is to be a persuasive presenter, then start acting "as if" you are. Dress, speak and behave like a confident speaker.

Realize you are an expert. If you have been asked to give a presentation, then there is probably a reason. Namely, people perceive you to be an expert or an authority on a subject and they want to hear what you have to say. Trust yourself as a presenter and you'll project confidence.

Meet your audience before you present. A good way to build confidence is to arrive early and, as guests enter the room, introduce yourself, shake hands and look them in the eye. This will help you get rid of your nervousness and it sets the stage for a relaxed, natural delivery.

Visualize your success. Before you present, mentally walk yourself and your emotions through your presentation.

See yourself speaking with confidence and poise; hear yourself speaking with eloquence; feel your energy as you stand before an enthusiastic audience.

Make anxiety your ally. Anxiety is natural for most people before a presentation. This is nature's way of preparing you for action. You need to learn to use it effectively. Those jittery feelings provide the basis for a dynamic presentation—they increase your energy, heighten your awareness and sharpen your intellect.

Rehearse, rehearse, rehearse. Rehearsal helps you to get the point where you can make a presentation without thinking about doing it. It familiarizes your mind and body with the mechanics of presenting and frees you to focus on the message, not the way you deliver it.

Remember that your audience wants you to succeed. Remember that you and your audience are on the same team, moving together toward a solution. When you give a winning presentation, they win too.[2] ■

Making a Personal Presentation

An effective personal presentation is tailored to the audience. It takes into account the receivers' frame of reference, attitudes, prejudices, educational background, and time constraints. The speaker must select words, concepts, and illustrative figures to which the audience can relate. A good presentation allows time for questions and discussion.

One reason personal presentations are sometimes inadequate is that the speaker lacks an understanding of the barriers to effective communication. A second factor is that the speaker fails to recognize or admit that the purpose of many research reports is persuasion. *Persuasion* does not imply stretching or bending the truth, but rather using research findings to reinforce conclusions and recommendations. In preparing a personal presentation, the researcher should keep the following questions in mind:

- What do the data really mean?
- What impact do they have?
- What have we learned from the data?
- What do we need to do, given the information we now have?
- How can future studies of this nature be enhanced?
- What could make this information more useful?

Presentations on the Internet

With PowerPoint 2000, publishing presentations to the Web is easier than ever. Publication to the Web enables individuals to access the presentation, regardless of where they are or when they need to access it. In addition, researchers can present results at multiple locations on the Internet. The steps are very simple:

1. Open your presentation in PowerPoint. To see what your slides will look like on the Web, choose "Web Page Preview" from the "File" menu. After you have made any edits, choose "Save as Web Page" from the same menu.
2. The "Save As" dialog box allows you to change the title of your presentation to whatever you want displayed in the title bar of your visitor's browser.
3. The "Publish" button takes you to the "Publish as Web Page" dialog box, where you can customize your presentation.
4. The "Web Options" dialog box lets you specify the way your published file will be stored on the Web server and whether to update internal links to these files automatically.
5. You can choose to make your presentation viewable in Netscape Navigator. However, it won't be as user-friendly as it is in Internet Explorer 5.0.[3]

Effective Use of Research Information

Marketing managers today are faced with the significant task of making more effective use of marketing research information. Effective use of research information can enhance productivity and reduce the time it takes to get a new product to market. All companies could make more effective use of marketing research information. Even firms that currently use research information very effectively, such as AMOCO, Citicorp, Kraft General Foods, and Eastman Kodak, still feel they could do a better job. The task is complicated by the fact that different marketing managers use and value research information differently.

A research study surveyed Fortune 500 companies in the chemical, consumer packaged goods, and telecommunications industries, along with 40 executives of large- and medium-sized companies, all of whom were members of The

Strategic Planning Institute, an international business think tank. The purpose of the research was to identify the key factors in the effective use of marketing research. Those factors were identified as follows:

1. *The perceived credibility and usefulness of the report to the users.* A good study "has data of recommendations that can be used to formulate a strategy." It "redirects activities, accentuates the positive, and corrects weaknesses." A good study also has a clearly defined scope, shows how the quantitative analysis meshes with the qualitative information, and contains no "big surprises" or radical recommendations. At the least, a good study "provides an understanding that wasn't there before."

2. *The degree of client/researcher interaction.* Managers often assess a study's credibility or value even before the final presentation of findings. And this assessment often is based on their involvement (or lack thereof) with the study design and its conduct. "If involvement is low . . . then the lack of communication can cause surprises and the quality of the study becomes a moot point . . . because the study is likely to be shelved."

3. *The organizational climate for research.* Managers have to receive top management's approval for the use of research studies and consultants. One manager noted, "It's crucial to have signals from the top that encourage the use of outside help and openness to new ideas."

4. *The personalities and job tenure of key users.* Some managers have a pro-innovation bias and are willing to try almost anything. Other managers view outside information as threatening to their decision-making authority. Also, other research has shown that senior managers (those with longer tenure) value more sources of marketing research information and tend to use more "soft information" than do younger managers. Senior managers also tend to make more conservative decisions. When managers have been in the same business for a long time, they naturally believe they "know the markets and customers in depth" and that marketing researchers are unlikely to offer any new information.[4]

Jeannine Bergers Everett is director of marketing research for the Boston Consulting Group's worldwide Consumer and Retail Practice Group. In the In Practice feature, she discusses the importance of creating value-added research to increase usage of marketing research information.

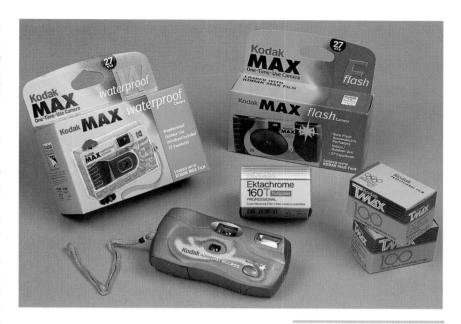

Even firms that currently use research information very effectively, such as Eastman Kodak, AMOCO, Citicorp, and Kraft, still feel that they could do a better job.

Managers Require Value-Added Strategic Information

MOST MARKETING MANAGERS TRULY BELIEVE THAT MARketing research can be valuable. But they also claim that most of what they see isn't delivering the kind of information they need in order to make business decisions.

Transforming a traditional marketing research organization into a value-added strategic research team takes time, commitment, and something researchers are particularly good at: research. The first question to explore is what the company really needs from its research team. Finding the answer begins with a decision audit.

Before they can change the status quo, researchers need to understand the impact of their past projects on the business. What business decision was being considered with each report and what costs were involved? Which recommendations were made, which ones taken? Answers to these questions will clarify how the organization operates and the importance it assigns to research.

Action statements. Every research proposal should state why the research is being done, beyond such vague terms as "to explore," "to understand," or "to determine." In customer-advocate organizations, the research objective is to "decide." Researchers also delineate the standards for the decision, and every item in the study directly relates to those measures. This brings the research department and management to-gether to discuss the range of possible actions and the decision criteria for each action.

Recommendations for action. Every report should include recommendations. In exploratory organizations, there's lots of data but few recommendations. In fact, the first section of exploratory reports usually deals with methodology, the least relevant topic to the client. Silent-advisor and order-taker organizations tend to bury researchers' recommendations. The report might say what customers think and feel, but shies away from the bottom line—what needs to be done.

The recommendation is the first sentence of the report, followed by a clear rationale that relates to the action statement and criteria set forth in the proposal. Not surprisingly, the recommendations leave less room for debate regarding the value of the research investment, or the implications of the results.

Study debriefs. Executive summaries on top of 40-page reports are a poor way to influence decision makers. Instead of sending a bulky report through interoffice mail, gather the key players together and give management a bullet-point run-down of the results. This presents the opportunity for asking questions, as well as for discussing next steps.

Full backroom principle. Involve senior management in the research. Too often, the closest they get to the customers is a written report or a formal presentation. Having managers meet customers face-to-face creates the opportunity for real-time idea building and strategy discussion.[5] ∎

The Role of Trust

In a survey of 779 researchers and research users on the importance of trust between the researcher and the decision makers, it was found that trust was more a function of interpersonal factors than individual factors. Trust was defined as relying on one another. The most important interpersonal factor was the perceived integrity of the researcher. This was followed by the perceived willingness of the researcher to reduce research uncertainty for the users—to use fewer data analysis skills and more data interpretation skills. In other words, the researcher is expected to use a broad understanding of the marketplace and research insights to construct clear explanations about research findings. Researchers need to think: "Yes, the relationship is significant at the .05 level, but what does this mean in the marketplace?"[6] Other important determinants of trust identified in the study are researcher confidentiality, level of expertise, and congeniality.

Perhaps one of the most practical ways to build trust and thus get managers to use research information is to employ customer satisfaction surveys. AT&T's marketing research department, for example, uses a customer satisfaction tracking system to monitor its internal clients' perceptions on an ongoing basis. The system consists of two separate questionnaires. One is a very general, short survey and is completed periodically by marketing directors and other high-level executives. The executives rate the research department on five separate attributes, as well as overall support. The questionnaire is deliberately short because of the respondents' limited exposure to research and the tremendous demands on their time. The second questionnaire is more detailed and directed to the specific client who requested the study. The surveys provide AT&T researchers with a good way to monitor how they are doing, build trust and confidence in the department, and provide useful decision-making information for the corporation.[7]

Doing "good" research per se does not guarantee that the findings will be used. The researcher must understand how managers think and must work with them to remove potential bias against using the research findings. Remember, marketing research has value only when it is considered and acted on by management.

Summary

The six primary sections of a contemporary marketing research report are, in order, the table of contents, background and objectives, executive summary, methodology, findings, and appendices with supporting information.

The primary objectives of the marketing research report are to state the specific research objectives, explain why and how the research was done, present the findings of the research, and provide conclusions and recommendations. Most of these elements are contained in the executive summary. The conclusions do not necessarily contain statistical numbers derived from the research but rather generalize the results in relation to the stated objectives. Nor do conclusions suggest a course of action. This is left to the recommendations, which direct the conclusions to specific marketing strategies or tactics that would place the client in the most positive position in the market.

The marketing research report of today makes heavy use of graphics to present key findings. For most researchers, PowerPoint is the software of choice for creating research reports. In terms of mechanics, reports minimize the use of words, feed information to clients in "minibites," and make extensive use of bulleted charts and graphics. In addition to the written report, a personal presentation of research results is often required. For this, the researcher needs four material aids: the presentation outline, visuals, an executive summary, and copies of the final report to give to the audience after completion of the presentation. It is common for research reports to be published on the Internet by the client or by the researcher at the client's request. This has the advantage of making the results available to individuals worldwide in the client's organization. The Internet can also be used to support simultaneous presentation of the research results in multiple locations.

Marketing researchers obviously want marketing managers to use the information they provide and to use it appropriately. The marketing researcher needs to understand how managers think and the potential barriers to the use of research information. This task is complicated by the fact that different marketing managers use research information differently and put varying levels of value on marketing research results. The key determinants of whether marketing research data are used are the perceived credibility and usefulness of the information to users, the degree of client/researcher interaction, the organizational climate for research, and the personalities and job tenure of key users. Trust between client and researcher also plays an important role in determining whether or not research managers use marketing research information. Trust is derived from the perceived integrity of the researcher and her or his willingness to help reduce uncertainty for users. Other determinants of trust are researcher confidentiality, level of expertise, and congeniality.

Key Terms & Definitions

presentation software   Personal computer software that provides easy-to-use platforms for creating effective reports and presentations.

executive summary   The portion of a research report that explains why the research was done, what was found, what those findings mean, and what action, if any, management should undertake.

conclusions   Generalizations that answer the questions raised by the research objectives or otherwise satisfy the objectives.

recommendations   Conclusions applied to marketing strategies or tactics that focus on a client's achievement of differential advantage.

Questions for Review & Critical Thinking

1. What are the roles of the research report? Give examples.
2. Distinguish among findings, conclusions, and recommendations in a research report.
3. Why should research reports contain executive summaries? What should be contained in an executive summary?
4. Discuss the basic components of the research report. List several criteria that may be used to evaluate a research report and give examples of each.
5. How does presentation software affect the quality and content of presentations and reports?
6. What should be done to ensure the success of a personal presentation? Critique the following paragraphs from a research report:

   The trouble began when the Department of Agriculture published the hot dog ingredients—everything that may legally qualify—because it was asked by the poultry industry to relax the conditions under which the ingredients might also include chicken. In other words, can a chickenfurter find happiness in the land of the frank?

   Judging by the 1,066 mainly hostile answers that the department got when it sent out a questionnaire on this point, the very thought is unthinkable. The public mood was most felicitously caught by the woman who replied, "I don't eat feather meat of no kind."

7. What are the advantages of publishing reports on the Internet?
8. Develop one or more visual aids to present the following data. Indicate why you chose each particular form of visual aid.

Candidate	No. of Local Employees	Revenue (in millions of dollars)	Target as Charter or Affiliate Member	Potential Membership Fee
Mary Kay Cosmetics	958	$360	Charter	$50,000
Arrow Industries	950	50	Charter	20,000
NCH Corp.	800	427	Charter	50,000
Stratoflex, Inc.	622	81	Charter	25,000
BEI Defense Sys.	150	47	Affiliate	7,500
Atlas Match Corp.	150	82	Affiliate	7,500
Mangren R&D	143	20	Affiliate	7,500
Jet Research Ctr.	157	350	Affiliate	7,500

Working the Net

1. Go to http://www.gallup.com and examine some of the special reports on American opinions, such as those found under "Social Issues and Policy." Do these reports meet the criteria discussed in the text for good marketing research reports? Why or why not?
2. Go to http://www.presentersuniversity.com. Describe the different ways this organization can help an individual become a more effective speaker.

Using WebSurveyor

One of the benefits of using the Internet in connection with research projects is the ability to easily share results with others via the Internet. Using the WebSurveyor Desktop software, open the CHAPTER18 survey by selecting File and then Open from the main menu and navigating to the SURVEYS subdirectory under the directory where you installed the Websurveyor Desktop software (usually c:\program files\websurveyor desktop 3).

Next navigate to the analysis page, click the Update Results button at the bottom of the page, and follow the prompts to load the survey results from the CD-ROM incuded with this textbook.

Exercises

1. Use the WebSurveyor analysis tools to build a report that can be shared via a Web site.
2. If you have a personal Web site or a class Web site, post the report that you generate on that site.
3. Have at least one other student or student team in your class review the results you posted and comment on them via email.

web**SURVEYOR**™
When you need to know. Now.

Real-Life Research • 18.1

The United Way

The United Way was concerned about nondonors' attitudes toward the organization. Specifically, management was interested in why certain people do not give to the United Way. It also was interested in determining what factors might convert nondonors to donors. The executive summary from the research report is presented here. Each heading and the text that follows it appear on a slide.

Executive Summary Objectives and Methodology

- The general purposes of this study were to determine the attitudes of non-contributors toward the United Way, to assess the reasons for not contributing, and to ascertain factors that may influence nonparticipants to contribute.
- The study used primary data gathered through a self-administered questionnaire.
- Descriptive research design methods were used to examine the survey results for numerical comparison.
- The study employed nonprobability samples (e.g., convenience samples and judgment samples).
- Primary data were collected through a newly developed self-administered questionnaire administered to 134 respondents consisting of co-workers, friends, and students.

Findings

- The percentage of the respondents having positive perceptions of the United Way was greater than those having negative perceptions; however, the majority of the respondents had no opinions concerning the United Way.
- Only 5.2 percent rated the United Way fair or poor in providing benefits to those in need.
- The United Way actually spends 9 percent to 10 percent of contributions on administrative costs, although 80.6 percent believed that the United Way used more than 10 percent of its contributions on administrative costs.
- Primary reasons for not contributing were contribution to other charities or religious organizations, personal financial circumstances, lack of knowledge of how donated funds are used, personal beliefs, absence of favorite charities, pressure to contribute, and preference to donate time rather than money.
- Of those who were asked to contribute, pressure seemed somewhat important in influencing their decision not to contribute.
- Of those respondents who indicated that personal financial reasons influenced their decision not to give, 35.6 percent indicated they would give to the United Way if asked.

- Other charities and religious denominations appear to be in competition with the United Way for donated dollars.
- Many respondents indicated that they would contribute if they could specify the charity to receive their contribution, had more knowledge about the United Way and the charities it supports, were asked to give, had less pressure to give, had availability of payroll deduction, and had the option of spreading contributions over time.
- Of the respondents whose place of employment participated in the United Way campaign, 79.6 percent had been asked to give but did not.
- Workplace campaigns reach a large number of executives and professional and administrative personnel in the higher-income brackets but do not reach a significant number of service personnel or lower-income households.

Conclusions

- Negative perceptions do not appear to be a major factor affecting reasons for not contributing; however, a positive perception does not necessarily translate into a contribution.
- Noncontributors lack sufficient information regarding the United Way to form a perception of the organization.
- There is a lack of knowledge concerning the United Way and the organizations to which it allocates contributions.
- Respondents believe that the United Way uses more for administrative costs than it actually does.
- The United Way is in competition for a limited number of charity dollars.

Recommendations

- Conduct additional research to determine noncontributor's level of knowledge of the United Way and the purpose that the United Way serves.
- Increase education for potential contributors regarding the United Way's purpose, the organizations it supports, and the United Way's reasonable administrative costs.
- Expand the frequency of campaigns in the workplace and develop ways to increase awareness of the methods of contributing.
- Develop appropriate competitive marketing strategy to address the United Way's competitors.

Questions

1. Do you think that the executive summary provides guidance for decision-making information?
2. Are all of the elements present that should be included in an executive summary as discussed in this chapter?
3. Do the findings, conclusions, and recommendations logically follow from the objectives? Why or why not?

Real-Life Research • 18.2

TouchWell Tracking Research

TouchWell is a large health plan in a major metropolitan area in the western United States. TouchWell has been buffeted by all of the problems experienced by managed care organizations, including the following:

- Fierce competition from other plans
- Financial concerns associated with rising medical costs on the one hand and pressure to keep premiums low on the other hand
- The stream of negative publicity about HMOs and managed care plans

However, TouchWell has managed to continue to grow during this period through aggressive marketing to both business decision makers, who make choices among group health insurance plans for their employees, and consumers. Its marketing programs have been guided by an equally aggressive marketing research program. Senior managers at TouchWell are convinced that they could make better decisions if they had the information necessary to make those decisions. Their research program has included a mix of qualitative and quantitative research covering market segmentation, product testing, communications testing, and tracking research (sometimes referred to as attitude, awareness, and usage—AA&U—research).

A high-level presentation to TouchWell's senior management by Alpha Research, covering four waves of tracking research, follows. The presentation includes key measurements from the tracking research, such as unaided plan awareness, general impressions of HMOs, reasons for negative impressions, and impressions of TouchWell and key competitors.

TouchWell believes that maintaining high plan awareness is an important part of the process of selling to both business decision makers and consumers. Impressions of HMOs in general provide management with some idea of the context in which they are selling their product, and specific impressions of TouchWell and its major competitors provide measures of image.

TouchWell Tracking Research

Summary of Findings from 1997 and 2000

prepared by Alpha Research

Background

- The information summarized in this report is based on telephone surveys conducted by Alpha Research in 1997 and 2000
- Two waves of research were conducted in each year:
  - ➤ 1997—April and October.
  - ➤ 2000—January and November.
- In all the waves of research, separate samples and survey instruments were used for:
  - ➤ Consumers with group health coverage through an employer who were the decision makers for group health coverage for the household.
  - ➤ Individuals from companies that offer group health coverage to their employees who make decisions regarding coverage for their companies.
- Random samples were used for all surveys. Sample sizes were as follows:
  - ➤ 1997 Pretest—Business (400), Consumer (500).
  - ➤ 1997 Posttest—Business (400), Consumer (400).
  - ➤ 2000 Pretest—Business (400), Consumer (400).
  - ➤ 2000 Posttest—Business (400), Consumer (400).

Consumers: Unaided Plan Awareness

- Important measure of consumer franchise.
- Awareness helps establish legitimacy throughout the sales process.
- Has value in making both the first and the second sale.
- TouchWell has led all carriers since the 1997 posttest.
- Among the leaders, Kaiser and NYL Care trail.

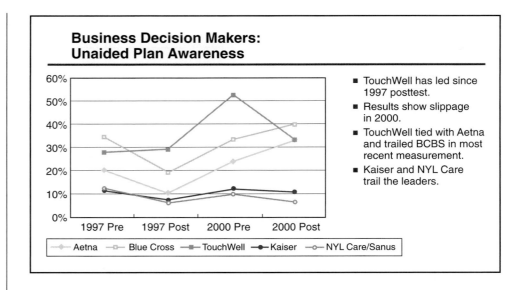

Business Decision Makers: Unaided Plan Awareness

- TouchWell has led since 1997 posttest.
- Results show slippage in 2000.
- TouchWell tied with Aetna and trailed BCBS in most recent measurement.
- Kaiser and NYL Care trail the leaders.

Legend: Aetna — Blue Cross — TouchWell — Kaiser — NYL Care/Sanus

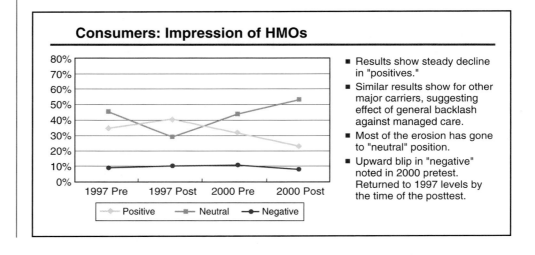

Consumers: Impression of HMOs

- Results show steady decline in "positives."
- Similar results show for other major carriers, suggesting effect of general backlash against managed care.
- Most of the erosion has gone to "neutral" position.
- Upward blip in "negative" noted in 2000 pretest. Returned to 1997 levels by the time of the posttest.

Legend: Positive — Neutral — Negative

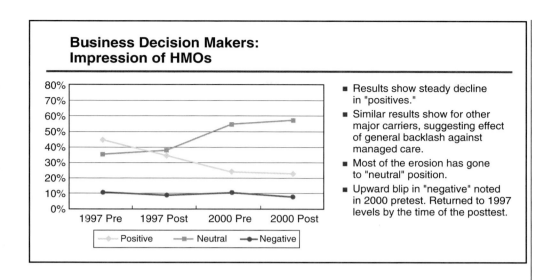

Business Decision Makers: Impression of HMOs

- Results show steady decline in "positives."
- Similar results show for other major carriers, suggesting effect of general backlash against managed care.
- Most of the erosion has gone to "neutral" position.
- Upward blip in "negative" noted in 2000 pretest. Returned to 1997 levels by the time of the posttest.

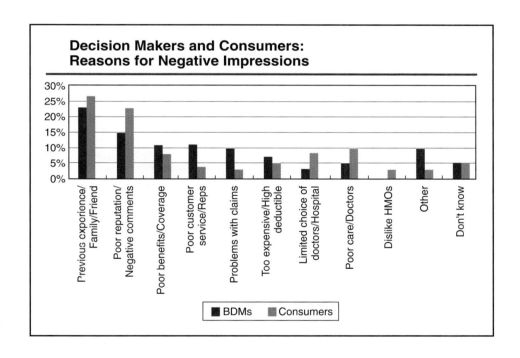

Decision Makers and Consumers: Reasons for Negative Impressions

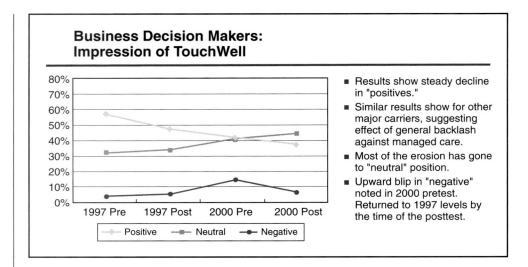

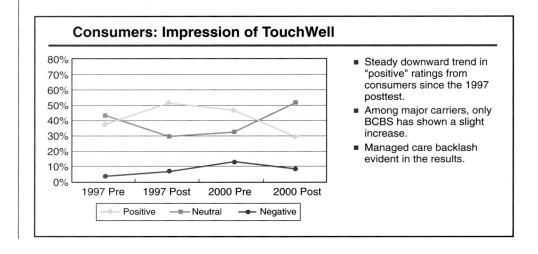

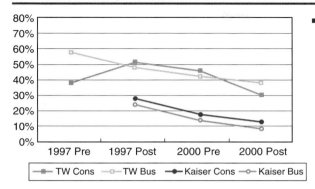

Consumers and Business Decision Makers: Positive Impressions of TouchWell and Kaiser

- Though both show a declining trend, TouchWell leads Kaiser by a wide margin among both consumers and business decision makers.

Questions

1. Comment on the general quality of the presentation. Are the slides easy to understand? Do they effectively convey key information? What suggestions would you have for improving this presentation?
2. Comment on the content of the slides regarding unaided plan awareness for both consumers and business decision makers. What are the implications for TouchWell?
3. What do the slides show with respect to the image or impressions that consumers and business decision makers have regarding HMOs? How have these impressions changed over time? What are the major reasons for negative impressions of HMOs among business decision makers and consumers?
4. What has happened to TouchWell's image over the four waves of research? How do these changes differ for business decision makers and consumers?

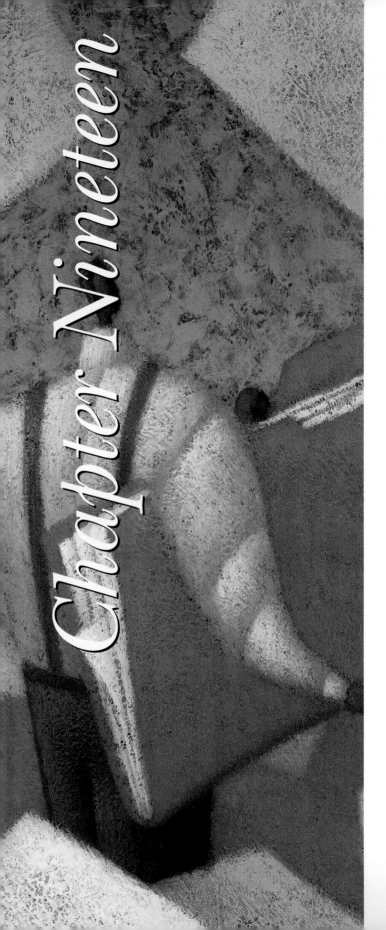

Chapter Nineteen

Managing Marketing Research and Research Ethics

Learning Objectives

To understand what clients want from a marketing research supplier or department.

To appreciate the role of communication in managing marketing research.

To learn about the research management goals of assurance of data quality, adherence to time schedules, cost control, maintenance of client profitability, and staff development.

To examine unethical practices among marketing research suppliers, clients, and marketing research field services.

To become familiar with respondents' rights.

To discover methods by which the level of professionalism in marketing research can be raised.

RICHMOND, VA.–BASED PLEASANTS HARDWARE HAS SERVED THE GREATER Richmond area since 1915. While Pleasants is local, with 175 employees, it is not a small "mom and pop" hardware store. In 1996, the company opened a second, 110,000-square-foot store in the affluent and burgeoning west end of Richmond.

RESULTS AFTER THE FIRST YEAR WERE NOT good. The new store had not taken root: sales fell well short of company goals. Moreover, it was announced that not only was Home Depot (the largest home improvement chain) moving into the Richmond market, it was building a store within ¼ mile of the struggling Pleasants store. Lowes—the number two home improvement chain—already had a very strong presence in Richmond.

PLEASANTS MANAGEMENT DECIDED TO work with Edelmann Scott, Incorporated, a Richmond marketing research and advertising firm, to determine what might be done to effectively compete against the huge chains. To determine this, Pleasants agreed to a strategic process which included four essential steps:

1. a visioning session involving the entire management team and other stakeholders within the organization;

2. qualitative research;

3. quantitative validation of the direction; and

4. implementation.

THE PLEASANTS VISIONING SESSION INCLUDED THE TOP 15 PEOPLE IN THE COMpany including store managers, purchasing agents, finance officers, and, of course, marketing staff. The session ended with 11 key benefit statements which ranged from being the "power tool headquarters" to a "satisfaction guarantee," from "only trusted quality products carried" to "free delivery on anything."

THE FOCUS GROUPS WERE USED TO BETTER UNDERSTAND THE COMPETITIVE landscape and to reduce the number of benefit statements. Focus groups results pointed to Pleasants' quality service, but also being more expensive than the national chains. The quantitative research revealed the following:

■ Who is Pleasants? The consumer said they are knowledgeable and willing to help with good selection and quality items. But, it costs more to shop there.

Understanding what clients are looking for and working with clients to come to successful conclusions are important elements of managing the marketing research process. Knowing that those who care most about its pledge of quality are busy, upscale homeowners who are likely to be female helped Pleasants Hardware determine its marketing branding campaign.

Find out how Pleasants Hardware has positioned itself in the Internet marketplace at

http://www.
pleasants-inc.com

- Why does the customer care? They can get what they need to get it right the first time, saving time, money, and frustration.

- Who cares the most? The busy, more upscale homeowner, who is more likely to be female.

A BRANDING LINE WAS DEVELOPED FOR ALL OF PLEASANTS' EXTERNAL COMMUnications, "Get It Right the First Time." This theme was a very natural and consumer-friendly way to bring the positioning to life.

EDELMANN SCOTT CREATED AN OVERALL PLAN OF BRAND TELEVISION ADVERtising where they illustrated familiar and humorous situations of folks not getting it right the first time; periodic instructional events (how to refinish furniture, power wash decks, etc.) to build traffic and reinforce the positioning; cooperative product advertising which tied into the branding advertising; instore signage and promotions to bring the message into the store; and public relations such as a Pleasants "Get It Right" speakers bureau and newspaper howto articles to help people get it right the first time.

AFTER THE FIRST SEVEN MONTHS OF THE CAMPAIGN LAUNCH, PLEASANTS MAY be the only local hardware store in the nation that actually experienced a gain in overall sales upon a Home Depot opening. Importantly, it did so without discounting heavily: margins actually increased vs. the same period a year ago.[1] ■

The Pleasants story illustrates how a marketing research firm can work with a client to be successful in the marketplace. What do clients want from a marketing research department or research firm? What is involved in managing the research function? Why is there a trend toward strategic partnerships? What role does ethics play in marketing research management? These questions will be addressed in this chapter.

What Do Clients Want?

Market Directions, a marketing research firm in Kansas City, Missouri, asked marketing research clients across the United States to rate the importance of several statements about research companies and research departments. Replies from a wide range of industries are summarized in the following top-10 list:

1. Maintains client confidentiality.
2. Is honest.
3. Is punctual.
4. Is flexible.
5. Delivers against project specifications.
6. Provides high-quality output.

7. Is responsive to the client's needs.

8. Has high quality-control standards.

9. Is customer-oriented in interactions with client.

10. Keeps the client informed throughout a project.[2]

The two most important factors, confidentiality and honesty, are ethical issues, which are covered later in this chapter. The remaining issues relate to managing the research function and maintaining good communication.

Communication

The key to good supplier–client relations is excellent communication. Every project should have a liaison who serves as a communication link between the supplier and the client. In large firms, this individual may be an account executive or project manager, while in small firms, he or she may be an owner or partner. But, whatever the job title, the liaison must communicate accurately, honestly, and frequently with the client.

Before a project begins, the communication liaison should go over the project objectives, methodology, and timing with the client to make certain that there are no misunderstandings. The client should then sign off on the questionnaire, thereby agreeing that the questionnaire is sufficient to gather the raw data needed to accomplish the research objectives.

The liaison must ascertain how often the client wants progress reports. At a minimum, these reports should be issued weekly. The report should cover the status of the project, unusual problems encountered, and, if it is a cost-plus project, expenses incurred to date. *Cost-plus* refers to actual costs plus an additional markup to cover overhead. Cost-plus projects are typically found in situations where a research department of a large corporation, such as Ford Motors, conducts a project for another department.

Chapter 18 covered the importance of good communication in preparing the research report. Good communication is also important when a research supplier is vying for new business. Ron Sellers, research director for Bank One, describes the importance of making a good first impression in the In Practice feature.

Managing the Research Process

Research management has five important goals beyond excellent communication: assurance of data quality, adherence to time schedules, cost control, client profitability management, and staff management and development.

Data Quality Management

Perhaps the most important objective of research management is to ensure the quality or integrity of the data produced by the research process. You have probably heard announcers on television say, "The poll had a margin of error of 3

research management
Overseeing the development of excellent communication systems, data quality, time schedules, cost controls, client profitability, and staff development.

In PRACTICE

Making a Good First Impression Is Critical

TAKE IT FROM SOMEONE WHO HAS MADE FIRST CONTACT WITH ALL too many companies: there are ways that vendors communicate very clearly the quality of the work they are likely to do, even in this first contact. As a client or as a vendor, here are some things to look for.

Knowledge of the client's expectations and needs. Vendors sometimes assume that all clients want the same thing, whether that is low price, in-house RDD sample, or great food during focus groups. While you spend your time conveying how low your costs are, your potential client may be wondering about the level of service she'll receive or your company's experience in her industry. I've been insulted by vendors who want to sell me on their focus group facility solely because they cater gourmet meals and are within 20 minutes of three championship golf courses. I'm there to do serious research, not to eat eggplant Parmesan and play 18 holes!

The quality of the communications. What you say is important, but how you say it and how it looks are also vital. I once rejected a bid from a potential vendor because it had a typographical error . . . in the letterhead! If the company could let something that major get through without noticing (or could notice it and just not care), what are the chances that the work they do will show any attention to detail? Using poor grammar in a cover letter, spelling the client's name wrong, providing brochures that are yellowed, worn, or written on, or sending out something that just looks like poor quality clearly communicates the kind of work the client can expect.

The amount of information available. Some vendors seem to have a thoughtful answer to almost any question. Others apparently can't believe they're being asked questions. Clients will often want details. What tab package or statistical software is being used? What are the demographics of the area from which a focus group facility can recruit? What respondent incentives are necessary in this market? How many clients can fit comfortably in a viewing area? What is the interviewer-to-supervisor ratio at the field center? What are the focus group room sizes? If the firm can't or won't easily answer questions such as these, a client is likely to go to another vendor that knows its business more completely.

The level of service the client can expect. One of the most important things research vendors are paid for is service, service in recruiting or interviewing, service in confirming respondents or validating interviews, service the night of the groups or the day of the presentation. Vendors that don't return calls, don't meet bid deadlines, are rude or indifferent on the phone, provide only partial information, are unwilling to follow the parameters of the request for proposal, or make sure to tell the client everything they can't do rather than what they can—all are supplying very strong hints of what the service will be like during the project.[3] ■

percent." Some problems and implicit assumptions are associated with this statement. First, you learned in the discussion of sampling error in Chapter 12 that this statement is missing an associated level of confidence. In other words, how confident are the pollsters that the poll has a margin of error of 3 percent? Are they 68.26 percent confident, 95.44 percent confident, 99.74 percent confident, or confident at some other level? Second, this statement does not make clear that the margin of error applies only to *random sampling error.* The implicit, or unstated, assumption is that there are no other sources of error, that all other sources of error have been effectively dealt with by the research design and procedures, or that all other sources of error have been effectively randomized by taking summary measures across the entire sample. By definition, error is random when there are just as many errors in one direction as in the other direction, leaving overall measures, such as averages, unaffected. Marketing research managers can help assure high-quality data by having policies and procedures in place to minimize sources of error (see Chapter 6).

Managers must also have in place procedures to ensure the careful proofing of all text, charts, and graphs in written reports and other communications provided to the client. Mistakes may mislead a client into making the wrong decision. Suppose the data suggest purchase intent at 25 percent but the report shows 52 percent; this typographical mistake could easily lead to an incorrect decision. If the client finds even small mistakes, the credibility of the researcher and all of the research findings may be brought into serious question. The rule of thumb is to never provide information to the client that has not been very carefully checked.

Effective time management is becoming increasingly important in all aspects of professional life. One requirement of research management is to keep a project on the schedule specified by the client.

Time Management

A second goal of research management is to keep the project on schedule. Time management is important in marketing research because clients often have a specified time schedule that they must meet. For example, it may be absolutely imperative that the research results be available on March 1 so that they can be presented at the quarterly meeting of the new product committee. The findings will affect whether the test product will receive additional funding for development.

Two problems that can play havoc with time schedules are inaccuracies in estimates of the incidence rate and the interview length. A lower-than-expected incidence rate will require more interviewing resources than originally planned to get the job done on time. If the research manager does not have idle resources to devote to the project, then it will take longer to complete. The same is true for a longer-than-anticipated interview.

Recall that the *incidence rate* is the percentage of persons or households out of the general population that fit the qualifications to be interviewed in a particular study. Often, estimates of incidence rate are based not on hard-and-fast data, but on data that are incomplete, known to be relatively inaccurate, or dated. Incidence rate problems can not only increase the amount of time required to complete the sample for the project but also negatively affect the costs of the data collection phase of the research.

The project manager must have early information regarding whether or not a project can be completed on time. If a problem exists, the manager must first determine whether anything can be done to speed up the process. Perhaps training additional interviewers would help expedite completion of the survey. Second, the researcher must inform the client that the project is going to take longer than expected. The researcher can then explore with the client whether a time extension is possible or what changes the client might be willing to make to get the project completed on the original time schedule. For example, the client might be willing to reduce the total sample size or shorten the length of the interview by eliminating questions that are judged to be less critical. Thus, it is very important that the system be structured so that both the researcher and the client are alerted to potential problems within the first few days of the project.

Time management, like cost control, requires that systems be put in place to inform management as to whether or not the project is on schedule. Policies and procedures must be established to efficiently and quickly solve schedule problems and promptly notify the client about the problem and potential solutions. In the In Practice feature, Joshua Libresco, executive vice president of OSR Group, a marketing research firm in San Rafael, California, offers several tips on how overworked marketing research project directors can better manage their time and still provide high-quality work.

Doing High-Quality Work— On Time

HERE ARE SEVEN TIPS ON TIME MANAGEMENT FOR MARKETing management project research directors.

Manage expectations. Most job descriptions for project directors mention writing skills, facility with mathematics, organizational ability and experience with presentations, but managing expectations may be the most critical skill to master. If you're pretty sure that the work will be done by Thursday, don't say you're "shooting for Wednesday." You're better off promising Friday and giving yourself a chance to be a hero.

Think about priorities. When the client has a crisis, sometimes you just have to drop everything and help out. Clients are, after all, the ones paying our salaries. Even without a crisis, however, it doesn't hurt to think about your priorities. The time-management books suggest concentrating on the most important tasks only, and ignoring the others until they too join the "most important" list. If you don't mind a messy desk, this is pretty good advice.

Think about leverage. What if the client is not in crisis mode, but you still have 10 things to do? Concentrate first on the tasks that require contributions from others. If the interviewers are waiting for your briefing or the data processing people are waiting for your codes, then everyone's work is backing up.

Provide regular updates. It is amazing how many games of voice-mail tag can be avoided by filling out a simple form. Set up a form that you can fax or e-mail every day explaining how many interviews have been finished, where the incidence is coming out, how you are doing on interview length and whatever other facts your client requires. If you are working with 10 field services on a study, get them to fill out update forms too—this saves you another 10 calls a day.

Be on the lookout for problems. A statistician I worked with used to say, "All lists are bad"—actually, he used a stronger term—"the trick is to find out why this particular list is bad." Project directing is problem solving. Incidence estimates will be off, questionnaires will be too long, respondents will be uncooperative, and lists will be, uh, bad. Spending a little extra time on instructions, briefings and safety checks today will save a lot of extra work tomorrow.

When you discover a problem, let the client know quickly. You can stick a problem in a folder for a day or two, but it's not likely to solve itself. The sooner the client hears about the problem, the sooner he or she can adjust schedules or budgets. In my experience, you can almost always go back to a client—once—to discuss changes in specifications, schedules and budgets. But you need to bring these issues up early, when your client still has some flexibility. Surprises at the 11th hour are both painful and time-consuming for everyone.

If you need to bring up a problem, don't be afraid to suggest some solutions as well. Suggesting solutions will help to solve the issue quickly and efficiently. As a general rule, the range of possible solutions is not hard to come up with. The following should cover about 80% of all of the possible problems:

- Order more sample.
- Change the screening criteria.
- Raise the incentives.
- Rebrief the interviewers.
- Reschedule the focus groups.
- Reduce the number of interviews.
- Lengthen the interviewing schedule.
- Increase the budget.

The challenge is in getting beyond the issue of who is to blame and determining which solution will work best this time.[4] ∎

Cost Management

In comparison to data quality and time management, cost management is straightforward. All it requires is adherence to good business practices, such as procedures for cost tracking and control. In particular, good procedures for cost control include the following elements:

- Systems that accurately capture data collection and other costs associated with the project on a daily basis
- Daily reporting of costs to the communication liaison. Ideally, reports should show actual costs in relation to budget.

- Policies and practices in the research organization that require the liaison to communicate the budget picture to clients and to senior managers at the research company
- Policies and practices that quickly identify over-budget situations and then find causes and seek solutions

If the project is over budget because the client provided information that proved to be erroneous (e.g., incidence rate, interview length), then it is imperative that the client be offered options early in the process: a higher cost, smaller sample size, shorter interview, or some combination of these. If the firm waits until the project is complete to communicate this problem to the client, the client is likely to say, "You should have told me sooner—there is nothing I can do now." In this situation, the firm will probably have to swallow the cost overrun.

Client Profitability Management

While marketing research departments may be able to focus on doing "on demand" projects for internal clients, marketing research suppliers have to think about profitability. The old adage that 20 percent of the clients generate 80 percent of the profits is often true.

Custom Research Incorporated (CRI), of Minneapolis, realized a few years back that it had too many clients—or too few good ones.[5] The company divided its clients into four categories based on the client's perceived value to CRI's bottom line (see Figure 19.1). Only 10 of CRI's 157 customers fell into the most desirable category (generating a high dollar volume and a high profit margin). Another 101 customers contributed very little to the top or bottom line. In short,

Figure 19.1

CRI's Client Profitability Analysis

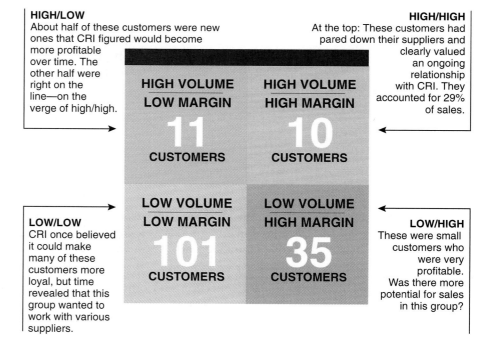

HIGH/LOW
About half of these customers were new ones that CRI figured would become more profitable over time. The other half were right on the line—on the verge of high/high.

HIGH VOLUME
LOW MARGIN
11
CUSTOMERS

HIGH VOLUME
HIGH MARGIN
10
CUSTOMERS

HIGH/HIGH
At the top: These customers had pared down their suppliers and clearly valued an ongoing relationship with CRI. They accounted for 29% of sales.

LOW/LOW
CRI once believed it could make many of these customers more loyal, but time revealed that this group wanted to work with various suppliers.

LOW VOLUME
LOW MARGIN
101
CUSTOMERS

LOW VOLUME
HIGH MARGIN
35
CUSTOMERS

LOW/HIGH
These were small customers who were very profitable. Was there more potential for sales in this group?

PART 5:
Marketing Research in Action

CRI was spending too much time and too many valuable employee resources on too many unprofitable customers.

In assessing which customers to keep, CRI calculated the profit for each one by subtracting all direct costs and selling expenses from the total revenues brought into CRI by that customer for the year. That is, CRI asked, "What costs would we not incur if this customer went away?" The cut-off points for high and low scores were purely subjective; they corresponded to CRI's goals for profit volume and profit margin. CRI management decided that it had to systematically drop a large number of old customers and carefully screen potential new customers. CRI's screening questions for new customers are shown in Table 19.1.

Using the new customers analysis, CRI went from 157 customers and $11 million in revenue to 78 customers and $30 million in revenue. Most importantly, profits more than doubled. Managers had calculated they'd need to reap about 20 to 30 percent more business from some two dozen companies to help make up for the roughly 100 customers they planned to "let go" within two years. This was accomplished by building a close personal relationship with the clients that remained. The process involved CRI's researching the industry, the client company, and its research personnel to fully understand the client's needs. For each

Table 19.1

Screening Questions Used by CRI and the Rationale for Each Question

Question	Rationale
How did you hear about us?	A bad answer: "I found you in the Yellow Pages." Unlike many companies, CRI doesn't ask this question so that it can decide how to divvy up the marketing dollars. "If someone finds us in the Yellow Pages, they have no reason to use us over anyone else," CRI cofounder Judy Corson explains. A good answer: "A colleague of mine worked with you at another company."
What kind of work is it (in terms of industry or scope)?	More than anything, the answer reveals whether the caller is trying to price a quick, one-time project or one that's totally outside CRI's realm. If so, the caller is referred to an indirect competitor.
What's your budget?	That's akin to asking someone how much money he or she makes, but the prospect's response to a ballpark guess on the cost of the project helps CRI ascertain what the client has in mind.
What are your decision criteria?	CRI knows that it doesn't fare well in blind bidding or in drawn-out, committee-style decisions, so it's interested in dealing with callers who have some level of decision-making power—and assiduously avoids getting involved in anything that smells like a bidding war.
Whom are we competing against for your business?	CRI likes to hear the names of its chief rivals, a half-dozen large companies, including the M/A/R/C Group, Market Facts, and Burke Marketing Research.
Why are you thinking of switching?	"There's a two-edged sword here," explains cofounder Jeff Pope. "Clients that are hard to break into are better because they don't switch too easily. But you need a way to get in—so a legitimate need for a new supplier is OK." Each month only 2 or 3 of 20 to 30 callers answer enough questions correctly to warrant more attention. So why spend time with the rest? "Do unto others. . . . You never know where people will go."

Source: Susan Greco, "Choose or Lose," *INC.* (December 1998), pp. 57–59, 62–66.

client, CRI created a "Surprise and Delight" plan to deliver a "value-added" bonus to the client. For example, Dow Brands received some complimentary software that CRI knew the company needed. This one-on-one relationship marketing has been the key to CRI's success.

Staff Management and Development

The primary asset of any marketing research firm is its people. Proprietary techniques and models can help differentiate a marketing research company, but eventually its success depends on the professional nature of its staff and their determination to deliver a quality product. Consequently, recruiting and retaining a competent, enthusiastic staff are crucial and constant management challenges.

Kathleen Knight is president and CEO of BAIGlobal, Incorporated, a Tarrytown, New York marketing research firm. She offers several suggestions for staff development in a research firm:

1. *Create an environment that encourages risk taking, experimentation, and responsibility.* The benefits to the research firm, such as new service development, new techniques, and business growth, outweigh any potential risks. However, employees need to feel support in taking risks. New ideas and different business approaches need to be treated with respect and given room to develop.
2. *Foster recognition and accountability.* Recognize good effort and reward it. One of the best forms of reward is visibility within the company. Make sure that everyone knows when an outstanding job was done and that excellence matters.
3. *Provide job autonomy within a certain structure.* Marketing research is a technical science, and the numbers have to add up. But it also is a business, and projects have to generate money to pay the bills. Within these boundaries, there are many different ways to get the job done. Let employees put their personal stamp on a project and they will feel like true partners in their work.
4. *Attract and support people with entrepreneurial attitudes.* Set business goals and management parameters; then let the staff determine the path to take to get the job done. This allows each person to leverage his or her own abilities and achieve the highest level of success.
5. *Connect rewards to a business result.* Providing open financial data to researchers seems to create a business consciousness that is exciting for all. Often, very talented researchers know little about the financial dynamics of the industry. They welcome the chance to learn and thus become more accountable for bottom-line results.
6. *Open your financial books.* Research firms can provide senior employees with full financial information to let them know how well they are doing across the months and years. The bottom line is the best aggregate measure of performance—individually, as a group, and as a firm. Opening the books establishes a common mission and goal across the organization.
7. *Offer diversity within your organization.* It's fun and exciting to learn new products, serve new clients, and work with a new research team. A chance at a new position is often the spark someone needs to really do well within a firm. And the possibility of this kind of job change seems to add to the satisfaction that employees feel. If you pay attention to individuals and create a career

Global versus U.S. Research Management

PLANNING IS WHAT IS MOST DIFFERENT IN GLOBAL MARKETING research from research done in the United States. In the planning stages, global research requires formalizing a number of components frequently handled as a matter of course in domestic research. Of course, the objective must be identified and agreed upon. But, in addition, other issues to identify and agree on include:

- Who is the key client(s)?
- Who has input on what?
- Who has sign-off on what?
- Who will get/interpret/use the findings (and in what order)?
- An "angel" should be identified.
- Whose budget?

One misconception about global research centers on cost. The fact is that many kinds of research in the United States are a relative bargain. The reasons for this include that in the United States, we have an infrastructure that allows us to use interviewing techniques that turn out to be more economical (mall intercept and telephone). The cost of local and long-distance telephone service is lower in the United States than in much of the world. While door-to-door interviewing now is rare in the United States, it's common in many countries.

Other costs that are not usually a part of our domestic research projects include multiple translations, international coordination, multiple client coordination, and long-distance proj-

ect management. The relative strength of the U.S. dollar is also a factor.

The best way to address these issues is, at the planning stages, find a high-level "angel" at headquarters, if possible. This "angel" need not be involved in the day-to-day issues of the research—ideally it is the chairman, CEO, or president. He or she should be an individual whose interest alone in the project requires others to act and provide the needed support.

Also, clearly identify the project leader. One person should have the responsibility of the day-to-day issues related to the study. While this individual does not have decision-making authority on all topics, he or she should have ready access to those who do.

Although good project managers confirm project specifications in writing, it's very important that the planning stages of global projects be documented in writing as well. Given the scope of the decisions frequently made from global research and the associated costs, good documentation is more than prudent.

Stick to schedules and budgets as much as possible.

Establish communications processes that will be used to coordinate with local research firms, regional offices or global subsidiaries, and so forth. Check versions of software and opportunities for e-mail communications.

Prepare your clients for budget shock. A joke that was told in the '90s is still not far from the truth: "Global research is twice as expensive and takes twice as long as research in the United States. Unless one is talking about Japan—then it's three times as expensive and takes twice as long."[6] ■

Global ISSUES

path across disciplines within your organization, it's more likely that talented researchers will stay.

8. *Provide clear promotional paths.* Employees like to know how they can advance and want to feel some control over their careers. Clear criteria and expectations go a long way toward helping researchers feel comfortable. In the marketing research business, the best training is as an apprentice, working with other senior researchers doing interesting work. Talented people will grow and prosper where the expectations are that senior managers will be mentors, that junior staff will learn, and that excellent work produced together will lead to everyone's career advancement.[7]

Marketing Research Ethics

ethics

Moral principles or values, generally governing the conduct of an individual or group.

According to the survey cited at the beginning of the chapter, the two most important factors for research clients in their relationships with research departments/suppliers are client confidentiality and honesty. Each is a question of ethics. **Ethics** are moral principles or values generally governing the conduct of an individual or group. Ethical behavior is not, however, a one-way relationship. Clients, as well as field services, must also act in an ethical manner. Table 19.2 details some of the unethical practices most common among the various groups involved in marketing research.

Supplier Ethics

Unethical research supplier practices range from low-ball pricing to violating client confidentiality.

Low-Ball Pricing   A research supplier should quote a firm price based on a specific incidence rate and questionnaire length. If either of the latter two items changes, then the client should expect a change in the contract price. Low-ball

Table 19.2	Unethical Practices in Marketing Research		
	Research Suppliers	**Research Clients**	**Field Services**
	Low-ball pricing	Issuing bid requests when a supplier has been predetermined	Overreporting hours worked
	Underpaying field services	Soliciting free advice and methodology via bid requests	Falsifying data
	Allowing subjectivity into the research		Using professional respondents
	Abusing respondents	Making false promises	Not validating data
	Selling unnecessary research	Issuing unauthorized requests for proposal	
	Violating client confidentiality		

PART 5:
Marketing Research in Action

pricing in any form is unethical. In essence, **low-ball pricing** is quoting an unrealistically low price to secure a firm's business and then using some means to substantially raise the price. For example, quoting a price based on an unrealistically high incidence rate (percentage of people in the sampling universe who qualify to participate in the survey) is a form of low-ball pricing. Offering to conduct a focus group at $5,000 a group and, after the client commits, saying, "The respondents' fees for participating in the group discussion are, of course, extra" is a form of low-balling.

Underpaying Field Services A number of large research organizations have acquired a reputation for "grinding down" field service fees. After a field service has completed the work and returned it to the supplier, it has almost no leverage to exact payment. Not only are field service bills cut, but payment periods of three to six months are not uncommon. These practices are patently unethical.

Allowing Subjectivity into the Research Using biased samples, misusing statistics, ignoring relevant data, and creating a research design with the goal of supporting a predetermined objective must be avoided by research suppliers. One of the fastest-growing areas of research today is so-called *advocacy studies*. These studies are commissioned by companies or industries for public relations purposes or to advocate or prove a position. For example, Burger King once used positive responses to the following question in an advocacy study in an attempt to justify the claim that its method of cooking hamburgers was preferred over that of McDonald's: "Do you prefer your hamburgers flame-broiled or fried?" When another researcher rephrased the question—"Do you prefer a hamburger that is grilled on a hot stainless-steel grill or cooked by passing the meat through an open gas flame?"—the results were reversed: McDonald's was preferred to Burger King.

Kiwi Brands, a shoe polish company, commissioned a study on the correlation between ambition and shiny shoes. The study found that 97 percent of self-described ambitious young men believe polished shoes are important. In many cases, advocacy studies simply use samples that are not representative of the population. For example, a news release for a diet products company trumpeted: "There's good news for the 65 million Americans currently on a diet." A company study had shown that people who lose weight can keep it off—the sample consisted of 20 graduates of the company's program, who also endorsed its products in commercials.

When studies are released to the news media, the methodology should be readily available to news reporters. Typically, this information is withheld, often on the ground that the material is proprietary. A survey done for Carolina Manufacturer's Service, a coupon redemption company, found that "a broad cross-section of Americans find coupons to be true incentives for purchasing products." The description of the methodology was available only at a price: $2,000.

Abusing Respondents Respondent abuse can take several forms. Perhaps the most common is lengthy interviews. This problem stems in part from the "as

low-ball pricing
Quoting an unrealistically low price to secure a firm's business and then using some means to substantially raise the price.

long as you're in the field" mentality of many product managers. It is not uncommon for clients to request additional "nice to know" questions, or even exploratory questions on an entirely separate project. This leads to lengthy questionnaires, 30-minute telephone interviews, and 40-minute mall-intercept interviews. As a result of long interviews and telephone sales pitches, more and more Americans are refusing to participate in survey research. The refusal rate for telephone surveys now averages 60 percent, an increase of 10 percent over 10 years. Forty-nine percent of the people who do participate say the surveys are "too personal." Eighty-four percent of U.S. households received a telemarketing call in the past year, and 31 percent claim to have been approached by a telemarketer who was selling under the guise of research, adding to the confusion between legitimate research and telemarketing.[8]

Interest in a product or service is often discerned during the interviewing process, and the researcher knows the interviewees' potential purchasing power from their answers to income and other pertinent financial questions. Although the introduction phase of the questionnaire usually promises confidentiality, some researchers have sold names and addresses of potential customers to firms seeking sales leads. Individuals willing to participate in the survey research process have a right to have their privacy protected.

Dick Whittington, vice president of marketing research at American Express, recently wrote an open letter to his colleagues in the research industry regarding respondent satisfaction. A summary of his position is presented in the In Practice feature.

Selling Unnecessary Research   A research supplier dealing with a client who has little or no familiarity with marketing research often has the opportunity to "trade the client up." For example, if a project called for four focus groups and a telephone survey of approximately 350 consumers, the research supplier might sell eight groups and 500 door-to-door interviews, with a 400-interview telephone follow-up in six months.

It is perfectly acceptable to offer a prospective client several research designs with several alternative prices when and if the situation warrants alternative designs. The supplier should point out the pros and cons of each method, along with sample confidence intervals. The client, in consultation with the supplier, then can decide objectively which design best suits the company's needs.

The Marketing Research Industry Must Improve Respondent Satisfaction

In PRACTICE

IN EVER-INCREASING NUMBERS, RESEARCH RESPONDENTS ARE TELLING US how dissatisfied they are with the interview process. We clearly have not met their expectations . . . and most of them blame the perceived client sponsor for these shortcomings. It is clearly time for a change. If you doubt me, look at your latest completion incidences—which can range from 9 percent to 40 percent on the low end—talk to your favorite provider partners throughout the interview chain, and then spend some time with your own respondents. Stand back and listen. I have, and I'm convinced.

Remember, respondents are people just like us. Their most valuable and precious commodity is time. Everyone has too much to do and too little time to do it. And knowing the pressures this puts on me, I'm very disturbed when large numbers of respondents volunteer that:

- Interviews are intrusive, inconvenient, and way too long.
- They are boring and repetitive.
- Many just plain don't make sense.
- Interviewers mislead and manipulate . . . just to get completions and/or to get the specific responses they desire.
- Many respondents are not even thanked and few feel adequately compensated for their time and efforts.

The attitude of the research community seems to be, "The respondent doesn't know who I am so if I abuse them a bit, who cares?" And this attitude, together with its accompanying behavior, could very well kill the research business as we know it today.

Thinking about these issues, my priorities seem to coalesce on four main points:

1. It's time to quit pointing fingers at others and time to get our own house in order. If we eliminated all fraudulent telemarketing, successfully identified ourselves as an industry, got everyone educated and certified as professional researchers, and quieted all the privacy advocates, we would definitely have less to complain about, but we would still have a broken product and one that irritated and alienated respondents.

2. Respondents are our industry's only unique resource, and it's about time we started treating them as such. The respondent feedback I've summarized above says we face a serious customer satisfaction problem. And if we don't solve it, then the resultant defections will put us in a resource management crisis.

3. According to respondents, the interview experience can and does affect brand and company perceptions. And most respondents feel that they know exactly who to blame for nearly every bad interview experience—the client, not the research provider. Maybe it's about time we started treating all respondents as if they knew

exactly who sponsored every study.

4. Respondents are people like you and me, with similar time pressures and responsibilities. It's time we started recognizing this and showing that we respect and value them and their time as much as we respect and value the information they provide. Actually, this is just another form of the golden rule, and I don't believe we treat respondents as we would want to be treated.

These four reengineering priorities suggest a host of potential actions or solutions. I have compiled the following list; it's not exhaustive, but it's a great start.

- **Limit interview length** by staying single-minded and avoiding the nice-to-know.
- **Prerecruit** more often.
- **Confine use of the more intrusive methods,** days, and times to when they're really necessary.
- **Tell respondents how long it will really take,** even before they agree to participate.
- **Adequately compensate** them for their time and value.

- **Be honest,** no matter what.
- **Always say thanks.**
- **Require that interviewers look and act professional** at all times.
- **Train interviewers** in customer service and satisfaction.
- **Measure respondent satisfaction** and tie it to performance assessments and compensation for everyone in the research chain: interviewer, field service provider, and client manager.
- **Control recontact frequency.**
- **Represent respondent needs and rights** to your company and client. Learn to say "no" and make it stick.
- **Make interviews easier** and more convenient for the respondent.
- **Make them involving,** interesting, and yes, even fun.

Minimally, I expect this effort to result in a code of "Survey Research Standards and Practices" and a "Respondent Bill of Rights." We at American Express are already working on our own versions of these documents, and we will be happy to share them with anyone considering respondent satisfaction improvements.[9] ■

Violating Client Confidentiality   Information about a client's general business activities or the results of a client's project should not be disclosed to a third party. The supplier should not even disclose the name of a client unless permission is received in advance.

The thorniest issue in confidentiality is determining where "background knowledge" stops and conflict arises as a result of work with a previous client. One researcher put it this way:

I get involved in a number of proprietary studies. The problem that often arises is that some studies end up covering similar subject matter as previous studies. Our code of ethics states that you cannot use data from one project in a related project for a competitor. However, since I often know some information about an area, I end up compromising my original client. Even though upper management formally states that it should not be done, they also expect it to be done to cut down on expenses. This conflict of interest situation is difficult to deal with. At least in my firm, I don't see a resolution to the issue. It is not a onetime situation, but rather a process that perpetuates itself. To make individuals redo portions of studies which have recently been done is ludicrous, and to forgo potential new business is almost impossible from a financial perspective.[10]

Client Ethics

Like research suppliers, clients (or users) also have a number of ethical dos and don'ts. Some of the more common client problems are requesting bids when a supplier has been predetermined, requesting bids to obtain free advice and methodology, making false promises, and issuing unauthorized RFPs.

Requesting Bids When a Supplier Has Been Predetermined It is not uncommon for a client to prefer one research supplier over another. Such a preference may be due to a good working relationship, cost considerations, ability to make deadlines, friendship, or quality of the research staff. Having a preference per se is not unethical. It is unethical, however, to predetermine which supplier will receive a contract and yet ask for proposals from other suppliers to satisfy corporate requirements. Requiring time, effort, and money from firms that have no opportunity to win the contract is very unfair.

Requesting Bids to Obtain Free Advice and Methodology Client companies seeking bargain basement prices have been known to solicit detailed proposals, including complete methodology and a sample questionnaire, from a number of suppliers. After "picking the brains" of the suppliers, the client assembles a questionnaire and then contracts directly with field services to gather the data. A variation of this tactic is to go to the cheapest supplier with the client's own proposal, derived by taking the best ideas from the other proposals. The client then attempts to get the supplier to conduct the more elaborate study at the lower price.

Making False Promises Another technique used by unethical clients to lower their research costs is to hold out a nonexistent carrot. For example, a client might say, "I don't want to promise anything, but we are planning a major stream of research in this area, and if you will give us a good price on this first study, we will make it up to you on the next one." Unfortunately, the next one never comes—or if it does, the same line is used on another unsuspecting supplier.

Requesting Proposals without Authorization In each of the following situations, a client representative sought proposals without first receiving the authority to allocate the funds to implement them:

1. A client representative decided to ask for proposals and *then* go to management to find out whether she could get the funds to carry them out.
2. A highly regarded employee made a proposal to management on the need for marketing research in a given area. Although managers were not too enthused about the idea, they told the researcher to seek bids so as not to dampen his interest or miss a potentially (but, in their view, highly unlikely) good idea.

3. A client representative and her management had different ideas on what the problem was and how it should be solved. The research supplier was not informed of the management view, and even though the proposal met the representative's requirements, it was rejected out of hand by management.
4. Without consulting with the sales department, a client representative asked for a proposal on analyzing present sales performance. Through fear of negative feedback, corporate politics, or lack of understanding of marketing research, the sales department blocked implementation of the proposal.

Field Service Ethics

Marketing research field services are the production arm of the research industry. They are the critical link between the respondent and the research supplier. It is imperative that they properly record information and carefully follow sampling plans. Otherwise, even the best research design will produce invalid information (garbage in; garbage out). Maintaining high ethical standards will aid a field service in procuring good raw data for the research firm.

Overreporting Hours Worked   Because field services are located hundreds, if not thousands, of miles away from the research suppliers, there is rarely any person-to-person contact between the two organizations. Lacking personal supervision by the research supplier, some field service managers pad the number of hours worked by the interviewers. Field services usually receive a commission based on the number of interviewing hours. Thus, there is an implicit incentive to overreport hours worked or to use slow, inefficient interviews. Because of the widespread tendency to overreport interviewing hours, some research suppliers cut virtually every bill submitted by field services. Other suppliers simply avoid field services that submit above-average bills on a consistent basis.

Falsifying Data   Because field services pay interviewers minimum wage or only slightly above it, they do not always attract the highest-caliber worker. Historically, field service managers have experienced problems with interviewer cheating, which ranges from sitting down at the kitchen table and filling out questionnaires to using telephone numbers of friends and pay phones to bypass the validation process. When the field service calls a pay phone number to validate an interview, the phone rings but no one answers. The unsuspecting validator assumes that no one is home and goes to the next questionnaire.

Good field service managers can weed out dishonest interviewers. In a few cases, field service managers have worked with dishonest interviewers to provide phony interviews. A common ploy is to report that the work was properly validated when, in fact, the field service manager knows that the interviews are fake. Only further validation by the research supplier will uncover the ruse.

In other cases, dishonest field services have been identified by the research client. Big users of marketing research, such as Kraft General Foods, maintain a data bank of respondents' names, addresses, and phone numbers. Kraft also uses a number of different research suppliers and has its own in-house research department. When a field service receives an interviewing assignment from a

PART 5:
Marketing Research in Action

research supplier, the field service rarely knows for whom the supplier is working. An unscrupulous field service manager or interviewer who uses the same pay phone number on projects for two different suppliers may actually be working for the same client. By pulling together phone numbers of interviewees from several research suppliers, Kraft General Foods has been able to identify both dishonest interviewers and dishonest field services.

Using Professional Respondents The problem of professional respondents arises most often in the recruitment of focus group participants. Virtually all field services maintain a database of people willing to participate in qualitative discussion groups, along with a list of their demographic characteristics. Maintaining such a list is good business and quite ethical. When qualifications for group participants are easy (e.g., pet owners, persons who drive SUVs), there is little temptation to use professional respondents. However, when a supplier wants, for example, persons who are heavy users of Oxydol detergent or who own a Russian Blue cat, it is not unheard of for a group recruiter to call a professional respondent and say, "I can get you into a group tomorrow with a $40 respondent fee and all you need to say is that you own a Russian Blue cat."

In an attempt to weed out professional respondents, a research supplier may specify that the participant must not have been a member of a qualitative discussion group within the past six months. However, dishonest field services will simply tell the professional respondent to deny having participated in a group within the past six months.

Data Collection Code of Ethics

The Marketing Research Association is an association to which primarily field services belong. The organization is dedicated to promoting excellence in data collection. To this end, it recently enacted a new code of ethics, which addresses the following issues:

- The accuracy of statements given to respondents to secure cooperation
- The protection of respondent anonymity and the need to obtain consent when anonymity cannot be assured
- Respect for the respondent's right to refuse cooperation
- The need for parental consent before interviewing children
- Treating respondents with respect and not attempting to influence responses

The code also offers rules regarding field services responsibilities to research firms:

- Research should be conducted per client specifications.
- The confidentiality of techniques, information, clients, and respondents will be protected.
- Multiple surveys are not administered sequentially during one interview without express permission of the research firm to do so.
- Research results are reported accurately and promptly.

- No misrepresentations are made with regard to qualifications, experience, skills, or facilities.
- Membership in the MRA is not to be used as proof of competency.

The rules regarding clients' responsibilities to data collectors state the following:

- Clients will provide safe products/services and disclose all product contents.
- Clients will provide instructions.
- Clients will not request activities that violate the code or are prohibited by law.[11]

Violation of the new ethics code can result in suspension from the Marketing Research Association.

Respondents' Rights

Respondents in a marketing research project typically give their time and opinions and receive little or nothing in return. These individuals, however, do have certain rights that should be upheld by all marketing researchers (see Figure 19.2). All potential participants in a research project have the right to choose, the right to safety, the right to be informed, and the right to privacy.

The Right to Choose Everyone has the right to determine whether or not to participate in a marketing research project. Some people, such as poorly educated individuals or children may not fully appreciate this privilege. A person who would like to terminate an interview or experiment may give short, incomplete answers or even false data.

The fact that a person has consented to be part of an experiment or to answer a questionnaire does not give the researcher carte blanche to do whatever she or he wants. The researcher still has an obligation to the respondent. For example, if a person participating in a taste test involving a test product and several existing products prefers the test product, the researcher does not have the right to use the respondent's name and address in a promotion piece, saying that "Ms. Jones prefers new Sudsies to Brand X."

The Right to Safety Research participants have the right to safety from physical or psychological harm. While it is unusual for a respondent to be exposed to physical harm, there have been cases of persons becoming ill during food taste tests. Also, on a more subtle level, researchers rarely warn respondents that a test product contains, say, a high level of salt. An unwitting respondent with hypertension could be placed in physical danger if the test ran several weeks.

It is much more common for a respondent to be placed in a psychologically damaging situation. Individuals might experience stress when an interviewer presses them to participate in a study. Others might experience stress when they cannot answer questions or are given a time limit to complete a task (for exam-

Figure 19.2

Respondents' Rights

The Right to Choose

The Right to Safety

The Right to Be Informed

The Right to Privacy

ple, "You have five minutes to browse through this magazine, and then I will ask you a series of questions").

The Right to Be Informed　Research participants have the right to be informed of all aspects of a research task. Knowing what is involved, how long it will take, and what will be done with the data, a person can make an intelligent choice as to whether to participate in the project.

Often, it is necessary to disguise the name of the research sponsor to avoid biasing the respondent. For example, it is poor research practice to say, "We are conducting a survey for Pepsi; which brand of soft drink do you consume most often?" In cases in which disguising the sponsor is required, a debriefing should take place following the completion of the interview. The debriefing should cover the study's purpose, the sponsor, what happens next with the data, and any other pertinent information. A debriefing can reduce respondent stress and build goodwill for the research industry. Unfortunately, taking the time to debrief a respondent is a cost that most companies are unwilling to incur.

In some business and academic research, the researcher may offer to provide the respondent with a copy of the research results as an incentive to obtain his or her participation in the project. When a commitment has been made to disseminate the findings to survey respondents, it should be fulfilled. On more than one occasion, we have participated in academic surveys where the carrot of research results was offered but never delivered.

The Right to Privacy　All consumers have the right to privacy. Consumer privacy can be defined in terms of two dimensions of control. The first dimension includes control of unwanted telephone, mail, or personal intrusion in the consumer's environment, and the second concerns control of information about the consumer. Consumer privacy can be viewed in the context of any interaction, profit or nonprofit, between marketer and consumer, including (but not limited to) credit and cash sales, consumer inquiries, and marketer-initiated surveys. The very nature of the marketing research business requires interviewers to invade an individual's privacy. An interviewer calls or approaches strangers, requests a portion of their limited free time, and asks them to answer personal questions—sometimes *very* personal questions. Perhaps the greatest privacy issue for consumers today is the role of marketing databases (see Chapter 4).

Ethics and Professionalism

Today's business ethics are actually a subset of the values held by society as a whole. The values that underlie marketing decisions have been acquired through family, educational and religious institutions, and social movements (e.g., women's rights, environmental protection). A marketing researcher with a mature set of ethical values accepts personal responsibility for decisions that affect the community. Considerations include the following:

- Employees' needs and desires and the long-range best interests of the organization
- The long-range goodwill and best interests of people who are directly affected by company activities (a bonus: good publicity for the firm)
- The societal values and conditions that provide the basis for the social structure in which the company exists

High standards of ethics and professionalism go hand in hand. Good ethics provide a solid foundation for professionalism, and striving for a lofty level of professionalism requires ethical behavior on the part of researchers.

Challenges to Professionalism
Numerous signs indicate that professionalism has not reached the desired level in the marketing research industry. Examples include push polling and sales pitches disguised as research.

push polling
A style of research gatherng in which zealous political supporters deride one candidate to lead voters to support the other candidate.

Push Polls. A lack of professionalism is evident in **push polling,** in which zealous political supporters make derogatory and damaging statements about one candidate to lead voters to support the other candidate. In contrast to legitimate political polls, which may be 10 or more minutes long, include a range of questions, and have a statistical sample of 500 or so respondents, push polling calls usually are of short duration (often 30 seconds), include one or two "questions/statements," and target many thousands of people, with no statistical sampling involved.

The National Council on Public Polls (NCPP) and the American Association of Political Consultants (AAPC) have both issued statements to the public and the press, warning about push polling. A California law, passed in 1996, requires that calls "that advocate support of, or opposition to, a candidate, ballot measure, or both" must announce "during the course of the call that it has been paid for or furnished by the candidate, committee, or other organization." The interpretive language accompanying this bill specifically states that legitimate political polling is not meant to be affected by this legislation.[12]

PART 5:
Marketing Research in Action

Marketing Research Ethics Are a Worldwide Concern

CONCERNS ABOUT RE-STRICTIVE GOVERN-MENT POLICIES AND regulations for the marketing research industry extend beyond U.S. borders. For example, the European Commission, a pan-European governing body based in Brussels, issues directives that could come to prevail throughout its member countries. One such directive, aimed at data privacy, states that respondents cannot be asked questions about "sensitive subjects" without their written permission.

In Ireland, the marketing research community is banding together to try to thwart a government ruling that political poll results cannot be published during a specified time period (say, two weeks) immediately before an election. The polls can be conducted, but the findings can't be made known to the general public. Some other governments have toyed with the same restriction.

In the United Kingdom, the Data Protection Act is designed primarily to prevent abuse of household financial records and information stored by database marketers. But the act also covers marketing research databases and records of all individual survey respondents. It says a firm cannot gather data on individuals, coupled with their address, without written consent, and that individuals have the right to see their personal data.

British research firms must be licensed (registered) to collect data, but they can request an exemption to the written consent provision. Of course, there is always the possibility that a change in government policy might result in such exemptions being denied. ∎

Global ISSUES

Sales Pitches Disguised as Research.   Another serious problem for the industry is the use of sales pitches disguised as marketing research. Although this problem is caused by people outside the marketing research industry, it casts a negative light on legitimate researchers.

The Council of American Survey Research Organizations (CASRO), a trade association representing approximately 180 full-service marketing research firms, has long opposed using sales pitches disguised as marketing research. In 1992, the Council for Marketing and Opinion Research (CMOR) was created by the American Marketing Association, CASRO, the Marketing Research Association, and the Advertising Research Foundation. CMOR is an umbrella organization designed to serve as a unified voice for survey research companies in their dealings with respondents, legislators, and regulators. CMOR's objectives are to protect the research industry against unnecessarily restrictive legislation, deal with waning respondent cooperation, and fight sales pitches disguised as research. CMOR, for example, has asked *sugging marketers* (firms selling under the guise of research) to use more forthright and honest marketing techniques. Another problem is *frugging*, which is fund-raising under the guise of research.

At one time, the Sierra Club used frugging; after a call from CMOR, it agreed not to use the technique again.

The Better Business Bureau, in a memorandum describing legitimate marketing research, states that "real" marketing research does not sell. The U.S. Postal Service has issued cease-and-desist orders to several companies that conducted fraudulent operations under the guise of research.

Fostering Professionalism

Because of the specialized knowl-

edge and expertise they possess, members of a profession have influence and power over those for whom they provide a particular service. The tools of a doctor or lawyer cannot easily be obtained and sold in the marketplace; these professions guard their knowledge and control who has access to it. Although marketing researchers and marketers wield power and influence over their customers and even society, the marketing industry does not have a credentialing process or high entry barriers. The argument can be made that the marketers who most need to think, believe, and behave with professionalism are those in marketing research.

The distinction between a profession and professionalism is important: A **profession** and membership in it are objectively determined (e.g., by medical board exams), whereas **professionalism** is evaluated on more personal and subjective levels. A study designed to measure the level of professionalism in marketing research found that researchers had autonomy in their jobs, were permitted to exercise judgment, and were recognized for their level of expertise and ability to work independently.[13] These characteristics are marks of professionalism. However, most researchers did not readily identify the contribution that marketing makes to society, nor did most firms tend to reward researchers' participation in professional organizations. These characteristics do not indicate a high level of professionalism.

Several steps have been taken recently to improve the level of professionalism in the marketing research industry. For example, CASRO has sponsored symposia dealing with ethical issues in survey research. CASRO also has created a code of ethics that has been widely disseminated to research professionals. The CASRO board has worked with groups such as the Marketing Research Association to provide input to legislatures considering antimarketing research legislation. In the In Practice feature, Diane Bowers, executive director of CASRO, discusses CASRO's efforts to raise professionalism in the marketing research industry.

Researcher Certification Today, it is far too easy to begin practicing marketing research. We have seen several "fast talkers" convince unwary clients that

profession
An organization whose membership is determined by objective standards, such as an examination.

professionalism
A quality said to be possessed by a worker with a high level of expertise, the freedom to exercise judgment, and the ability to work independently.

PART 5:
Marketing Research in Action

Raising Professionalism in the Marketing Research Industry

THE PROFESSIONALISM OF RESEARCH REQUIRES THAT WE PROVIDE as scientifically sound a product as possible: our data must be reliable and defensibly so because our end user clients will demand that the survey results we provide are actionable. Yet, we must realize that projectable surveys are harder to come by, at least via our usual methods.

We must be thinking of new ways to gather useful data from representative samples. Our end user clients demand this.

We must demonstrate that we regulate ourselves. The public and the government demand this.

And we must strengthen our ethical codes and our business principles. Our profession and our industry demand this.

To accomplish these tasks the U.S. research industry is working with the FTC and the Federal Communications Commission (FCC) to address abuses by research pretenders and to document that we enforce our mandatory codes of standards and ethics.

CASRO has been working diligently toward benchmarking best practices in research, particularly in the area of measuring client satisfaction and cycle time and quality.

CASRO has reviewed its research quality standards for conformity to the proposed European quality standards. While we want to ensure that we are consistent with U.S. law and that we accommodate the economic and professional needs of both small and large research companies who comprise our CASRO membership, we are making progress toward a universal set of quality standards that will give us stronger credentials and credibility with clients, the public, and government regulators.[14] ■

they are qualified researchers. Unfortunately, relying on poor information to make major decisions has resulted in loss of market share, reduction in profits, and, in some cases, bankruptcy.

Certification has generated a great deal of debate among members of the marketing research industry. It should be noted that certification is not licensing. *Licensing* is a mandatory procedure administered by a governmental body that allows one to practice a profession. *Certification* is a voluntary program administered by a nongovernmental body that provides a credential for differentiation in the marketplace. The issue of certification is sensitive because it directly affects marketing researchers' ability to practice their profession freely. The pros and cons of certification are summed up in Table 19.3.[15]

The issues of certification are complex and emotionally driven. Not surprisingly, a great diversity of opinion regarding certification exists within the research industry.

Table 19.3

The Pros and Cons of Certification

Pro	Con
It is not necessary to test every competency for every type of research. Other diverse groups, such as the American Society of Interior Design, have a successful certification program.	There is no single criterion on which to judge a researcher. The profession is too diverse, so the exam would have to be very basic.
Organizations are composed of members; members use their collective voice to create a certification program. Researchers could be certified through continuing education programs and phased listing.	Politics would play a big part in the process, it would be expensive and time-consuming, and there isn't a viable organization to oversee the process.
Certification would help to establish marketing research as a true profession. It demonstrates to government regulators that the industry is concerned about competency. The certification process would provide a forum for discussing what is considered to be professional behavior.	Because certification is voluntary, there is no guarantee that poor researchers wouldn't continue to operate. Certification, therefore, would not legitimize the profession. Also, a certification program probably would require grandfathering in many current researchers. Thus some incompetent researchers probably would be certified.
Certification would help the public distinguish between legitimate surveys and those done with a built-in bias. (Certified researchers would not conduct biased polls.) Certified researchers would be held more accountable through such things as mandatory methodology disclosures.	There is no evidence that certification would create higher quality research.
Current organizational ethical codes have not been effective in preventing abuses. Self-regulation may forestall governmental regulation.	Because certification is voluntary, it never resolves ethical issues.
Certification would help protect consumers and clients because the research profession now suffers a multitude of poorly trained and inexperienced practitioners. Certification would at least provide research users with some assurance of knowledge, experience, and commitment to the profession.	Certification can't guarantee competence.

Source: Terri Rittenburg and Gene Murdock, "The Pros and Cons of Certifying Marketing Researchers," *Marketing Research* (Spring 1994), pp. 5–9.

Summary

Clients want high ethical standards from marketing research departments and marketing research suppliers. Other factors of importance to clients include punctuality, flexibility, and having their research specifications met.

Research management has five important goals beyond excellent communication: assurance of data quality, adherence to time schedules, cost control, client profitability management, and staff management and development. Marketing research managers can help assure high-quality data by attempting to minimize sources of error. Time management requires a system to notify management of potential problems and policies to efficiently and quickly solve behind-schedule problems. Cost management demands good cost-tracking procedures and cost-control processes. Client profitability management requires that the marketing research supplier determine how much each client contributes to the researcher's overall profitability. Unprofitable clients should be dropped; marginally profitable clients should be developed into high-profit clients or dropped. The supplier should use relationship marketing to build a solid, increasingly profitable long-term relationship with clients identified as high-profit contributors. Finally, staff management and development requires that employees be encouraged to take risks and assume responsibility, be recognized for a job well done, and be offered job autonomy, financial rewards tied to business results, new challenges, and a clear career path.

High ethical standards are required of all players in the marketing research industry. Unethical practices by some suppliers include low-ball pricing, underpaying field services, allowing subjectivity into the research, abusing respondents, selling unnecessary research, and violating client confidentiality. Unethical practices performed by some research clients include requesting bids when a supplier has been predetermined, requesting bids to gain free advice or methodology, making false promises, and issuing unauthorized requests for proposals. Unethical practices of marketing research field services include overreporting hours worked, falsifying data, using professional respondents, and not validating data.

Respondents have certain rights, including the right to choose whether to participate in a marketing research project, the right to safety from physical and psychological harm, and the right to be informed of all the aspects of the research task. They should know what is involved, how long it will take, and what will be done with the data. Respondents also have the right to privacy.

The level of professionalism in the marketing research industry can be raised through the efforts of organizations like CASRO and CMOR as well as socially concerned marketing research firms. Researcher certification continues to be a highly controversial and emotional issue within the research community.

Key Terms & Definitions

research management Overseeing the development of excellent communication systems, data quality, time schedules, cost controls, client profitability, and staff development.

ethics Moral principles or values, generally governing the conduct of an individual or group.

low-ball pricing Quoting an unrealistically low price to secure a firm's

business and then using some means to substantially raise the price.

push polling A style of research gathering in which zealous political supporters deride one candidate to lead voters to support the other candidate.

profession An organization whose membership is determined by objective standards, such as an examination.

professionalism   A quality said to be possessed by a worker with a high level of expertise, the freedom to exercise judgment, and the ability to work independently.

Questions for Review & Critical Thinking

1. Describe four different ways a manager can help ensure high data quality.
2. What policies need to be put in place to assure that research projects are handled in a timely manner? What steps should be taken if a project falls behind schedule?
3. How can a research supplier develop its employees?
4. Should every firm conduct a client profitability study? Why?
5. What do you see as the role of a code of ethics within an organization? What can be done to ensure that employees follow this code of ethics?
6. Who would you say has the greatest responsibility within the marketing research industry to raise the standards of ethics—marketing research suppliers, marketing research clients, or field services?
7. What role should the federal government play in establishing ethical standards for the marketing research industry? How might such standards be enforced?
8. If respondents consent to interviews after being told they will be paid $20 for their opinions, do they forfeit all respondent rights? If so, what rights have been forfeited?
9. What is the relationship between ethics and professionalism? What do you think can be done to raise the level of professionalism within the marketing research industry?

Working the Net

1. Elrick & Lavidge is an old-line marketing research firm. Go to its Web site at http://www.elavidge.com and evaluate its Web communications with potential new clients.
2. Go to CMOR's Web site at http://www.cmor.org for a discussion of the latest issue regarding respondent cooperation.

Real-Life Research • 19.1

Barker Research International

Barker Research International* is not one of America's largest marketing research firms, but it is one of the best known. Its national polls on a variety of subjects appear frequently in the national media.

Barker has its own interviewers working from four central-location telephone interviewing facilities in New Jersey, Utah, Oklahoma, and Florida. Management believes that the most efficient way to pay interviewers is on a quota basis. Quotas are set using three criteria: the area being called, average length of survey, and the incidence rate. The company recognizes that cooperation rates are higher in some cities and states than in others, so the final quota for a specific study is modified after considering time and incidence rate.

The charts used by Barker for time and incidence rate are shown below. No interviewer is allowed to work for more than 35 hours per week; therefore, none are full-time employees. Barker's quota system for pay is as follows:

Quota per Hour	Under Quota	At Quota	Above Quota
1	3.00	10.50	11.55
3	1.00	3.50	3.85

For the first month, an interviewer is paid minimum wage, even if she or he is always under quota. After that, the interviewer is paid strictly on production.

Average Time of Survey (minutes)	Quota
2	12–15
3	8–10
4	6–8
5	5–5.5
6	4.5–5
7	4.5
8	4
9–10	3–3.5
11–12	2.5–3
13–15	2.5
16	2–2.5
17–20	2
21–24	1.5
25	1

*This is an actual firm. The name, however, has been disguised.

Incidence of Survey	Quota
0–5%	.1–.4
6–10%	.5–.75
11–15%	.75–1
16–19%	1
20–30%	1–1.5
31–40%	1.5–2
41–50%	2–3
50+%	Regular based on time

Questions

1. Is this a good system for controlling interviewing costs?
2. Is this system ethical?
3. What problems do you see with paying an incentive for being over quota?

Real-Life Research • 19.2

XYZ Acura

After having his Acura repaired, a customer received in the mail the following letter, accompanied by the survey on the next page from XYZ* Acura.

Dear Al,

Thank you for selecting XYZ Acura as your servicing dealer.

As a consumer myself, I recognize the need for quality service. Today, it seems the trust, friendship, and genuine care of the local "five and dime" is long forgotten in corporate America. As a team at XYZ Acura, we meet weekly to discuss our clients. We want your experience here to be pleasant and enjoyable. As our client, you are the most important part of our team.

Attached, please find a sample of the survey you may soon receive from Acura. When you receive the actual survey, please complete the form and send it to Acura. If you feel you cannot respond in a "very satisfied" manner, call me. Together, we can solve virtually any problem.

Sincerely,

Joyce Franklin
Service Manager

Questions

1. Is Acura getting reliable data about the quality of the dealer's service? Are the data valid?
2. Are the actions of the dealership ethical? Why or why not?

*The survey and letter are real. The names of the dealership and people are fictitious.

ACURA

Please answer the following questions about your most recent Acura dealer service or repair visit:

1. Is the dealer listed at the top of the preceding page your most recent servicing Acura leader?
◯ Yes - (SKIP TO QUESTION 2)　　◯ No - Please write in the name and location of the dealer where you had your most recent service.

Dealer Name: _____

City and State: _____

2. How long has it been since your most recent service or repair visit?
◯ One month or less　　◯ Three months　　◯ More than six months
◯ Two months　　◯ Four to six months

SERVICE OR REPAIR EXPERIENCE

Please tell us about your most recent service or repair experience:

MAKING AN APPOINTMENT
3. (If you did not make an advanced appointment, please skip to Question 4.)
a. Was your appointment scheduled for the day you requested?
◯ Yes - (SKIP TO QUESTION 3c)　　◯ No - (CONTINUE)

On the scale provided, please rate your satisfaction with the appointment experience.

	Very DISsatisfied				Very Satisfied	No Opinion
b. (If No to Q. 3a) How soon your Acura could be brought in for servicing	①	②	③	④	⑤	◯
c. Courtesy of the person you spoke with when making your appointment	①	②	③	④	⑤	◯
d. Promptness in handling your request for an appointment	①	②	③	④	⑤	◯

Still thinking about your most recent service or repair experience:

BRINGING IN YOUR ACURA
4. Please rate your Service Advisor on the following:

	Very DISsatisfied				Very Satisfied	No Opinion
a. Promptness in greeting you and writing up your service order	①	②	③	④	⑤	◯
b. Helpfulness	①	②	③	④	⑤	◯
c. Courtesy	①	②	③	④	⑤	◯
d. Knowledge/expertise	①	②	③	④	⑤	◯
e. Spent sufficient time with you	①	②	③	④	⑤	◯
f. Understanding of your service/repair request	①	②	③	④	⑤	◯
g. Explanation of cost estimate	①	②	③	④	⑤	◯
h. Overall Service Advisor performance	①	②	③	④	⑤	◯

DURING SERVICE/REPAIRS
5. Please rate your servicing dealer:

	Very DISsatisfied				Very Satisfied	No Opinion
a. Length of time it took to complete the service or repair work	①	②	③	④	⑤	◯
b. Contacting you about changes in cost/time estimate	①	②	③	④	⑤	◯
c. Cleanliness and appearance of service area	①	②	③	④	⑤	◯
d. Courtesy extended to you	①	②	③	④	⑤	◯
e. Cleanliness and appearance of customer waiting area	①	②	③	④	⑤	◯
f. Availability of parts needed to service your car	①	②	③	④	⑤	◯

IMPORTANT
Do not return the survey to the dealer. Get more from life. . . buckle up!

Thank you for choosing XYZ ACURA for your service needs. We hope that your experience has been positive and that you will continue to allow us to offer you high quality Service and Parts.

You may soon receive a Service Survey like this from Acura.

If for any reason you feel you cannot fill in the "5's" on your survey, indicating you were **"Very Satisfied,"** please call one of us listed below.

Our Goal is 100% Customer Satisfaction, and we pledge all of our available talent and resources to the achievement of this goal.

Please call me

Joyce Franklin
Service Manager

Trip Boswell
Asst. Service Manager

(400) 423-0000

IMPORTANT
Do not return the survey to the dealer. Get more from life. . . buckle up!

1. The key to successful marketing research is providing decision-making information and then having management act on that information. Decision makers in such areas as finance, engineering, and production have very different backgrounds from those of marketing researchers. Whether such managers will use research results will depend on their trust in the validity of the findings, their levels of comfort with the marketing research function and with the marketing researcher, and how well the findings fit their preconceived notions. What can researchers do, in the short term, to get managers from different areas to use research findings? In the long term?

2. Today, the compensation package of top-level managers frequently is based in part on the results of customer satisfaction studies. Generally speaking, the higher the level of satisfaction is, the greater the compensation. What are the pros and cons of such a plan? If you were called into the office of the senior vice president of production and asked to justify basing 15 percent of her compensation on customer satisfaction research, what would you say? What would you say to the senior vice president of finance? Of engineering?

Ethical Dilemma

Recess Is Over: It's Time to Do Your Marketing Research

DURING MORNING CLASS TIME RECENTLY, 60 ELEMENTARY school children sat expectantly in the lunchroom of St. Mary's Star of the Sea School in Beverly, Mass., waiting for instructions about what to do with the cups of beverage in front of them. The kids had just completed 15 minutes of strenuous exercise in the gym and were now ready to dive into the serious business of tasting and evaluating sports drinks.

Following directions given by researchers from Education Market Resources, the children filled in questionnaires measuring how much they enjoyed each of the unnamed drinks. The youngsters loved the process, says their principal, Sister Danielle Sullivan. "I think they felt they were making decisions that mattered," she says. The beverage marketer loved it, too. That day, the company learned a valuable lesson: which of its flavors were deemed "yucky" and, more importantly, which varieties kids would push their parents to buy.

Opening Doors

Until seven years ago, when Education Market Resources opened, this kind of in-school product testing was almost unheard of. But in the cash-strapped, increasingly free-market world of education, more schools are opening their doors to companies that want to test which products kids will clamor for.

Researchers say the data obtained from kids during school are especially reliable. The kids "know that's where they are asked to interact," says Robert Reynolds, president of Education Market Resources, which conducts 90% of its research in classrooms. "So they're very open to interacting with us. We had a vice president of marketing with McDonald's at one of our sites out in Los Angeles and he couldn't believe the difference in how the kids were interacting."

Is it valuable information? Marketers think so. A leading cerealmaker halted the launch of a campaign to introduce alien figures in one of its brands after test marketing in schools showed kids were ho-hum over the product. "They were going to spend literally millions of dollars to try to increase market share with this whole new concept," Mr. Reynolds says, "and the kids didn't even like it."

Working for Peanuts

For all the money a marketer saves, rewards for participating schools are modest. Depending on the complexity of the activity and the number of kids involved, schools earn between $800 to a few thousand dollars for each encounter with Education Market Resources. Gwen Ater, a sixth-grade teacher at Heatherstone Elementary School in Kansas City, Kan., says she gets $5 a student for surveys such as the one she and her class recently completed for Toys 'R' Us. "We're in a district that has good resources, but for things like class trips it's great," Ms. Ater says.

And then there's the argument that kids are wasting valuable learning time "working for peanuts." Ginny Markell, president of the national PTA, says her group opposes product testing during school hours because kids can't afford to give up the instructional time. "School is not an appropriate place for children to be surveyed, to be questioned for any form of research," Ms. Markell says. "The time that they have in the classroom needs to be dedicated to quality education."

Source: Peggy Farber, "Marketing Researchers Turn Classrooms into Test Labs," *Advertising Age* (October 25, 1999), p. 24.

Questions

1. Do you think that conducting marketing research in elementary schools is unethical? Why or why not?
2. Should parental consent be required for all marketing research conducted in elementary schools?
3. Do you agree with the statements made by Ginny Markell? Why or why not?
4. What are the pros and cons of conducting marketing research in an extremely poor school district? Should it be allowed? Why or why not?

Photo Credits

Chapter 1: (p. 3) PNC Bank; (p. 5) The Goodyear Tire & Rubber Company; (p. 7) Courtesy of United Parcel Service; (p. 13) © 2001 PhotoDisc, Inc.

Chapter 2: (p. 29) © Duomo/CORBIS; (p. 35) © 2001 PhotoDisc, Inc.; (p. 39) Courtesy of Vividence Corporation; (p. 41) © 2001 PhotoDisc, Inc.; (p. 44) Foote, Cone & Belding Chicago/Gatorade.

Chapter 3: (p. 53) © 2001 PhotoDisc, Inc.; (p. 55) © David Young-Wolff/PhotoEdit; (p. 62) Photos courtesy of Magellan Corporation. © 2000 All Rights Reserved; (p. 66) © 2001 PhotoDisc, Inc.

Chapter 4: (p. 87) Wal-Mart.

Chapter 5: (p. 123) Volvo Car Corporation; (p. 128) © Spencer Grant/PhotoEdit; (p. 146) © Spencer Grant/PhotoEdit.

Chapter 6: (p. 166) © 2001 PhotoDisc, Inc.; (p. 178) © Jeff Greenberg/PhotoEdit; (p. 195) © James L. Amos/CORBIS.

Chapter 7: (p. 207) Bose Corporation; (p. 216) Sonic Corp.; (p. 221) The PreTesting Co., Tenafly, NJ.

Chapter 8: (p. 241) Sony Electronics, Inc.; (p. 259) © 2001 PhotoDisc, Inc.; (p. 264) © 2001 PhotoDisc, Inc.

Chapter 9: (p. 285) © 2001 PhotoDisc, Inc; (p. 303) © Mark Richards/PhotoEdit.

Chapter 10: (p. 313) © Spencer Grant/PhotoEdit; (p. 315) American Cancer Society; (p. 317) Location courtesy of Bob Williams Jaguar, 9620 Montgomery Road, Cincinnati, OH 45242; (p. 328) © 2001 PhotoDisc, Inc.; (p. 334) YMCA of Greater Cincinnati.

Chapter 11: (p. 351) © 2001 PhotoDisc, Inc.; (p. 360) © 2001 PhotoDisc, Inc.; (p. 379) Marketing Masters; (p. 380) © 2001 PhotoDisc, Inc.

Chapter 12: (p. 395) © 2001 PhotoDisc, Inc.; (p. 401) © 2001 PhotoDisc, Inc.; (p. 411) © 2001 PhotoDisc, Inc.; (p. 413) © 2001 PhotoDisc, Inc.

Chapter 13: (p. 429) © 2001 PhotoDisc, Inc.; (p. 436) © 2001 PhotoDisc, Inc.; (p. 439) © 2001 PhotoDisc, Inc.; (p. 446) © 2001 PhotoDisc, Inc.

Chapter 14: (p. 464) © Wolfgang Kaehler/CORBIS; (p. 479) © 2001 PhotoDisc, Inc.; (p. 491) © 2001 PhotoDisc, Inc.

Chapter 15: (p. 505) © 2001 PhotoDisc, Inc.; (p. 513) © 2001 PhotoDisc, Inc.; (p. 527) © 2001 PhotoDisc, Inc.; (p. 533) © 2001 PhotoDisc, Inc.

Chapter 16: (p. 549) © 2001 PhotoDisc, Inc.; (p. 551) Dallas and John Heaton/CORBIS; (p. 558) © 2001 PhotoDisc, Inc.

Chapter 17: (p. 575) © 2001 PhotoDisc, Inc.; (p. 579) © 2001 PhotoDisc, Inc.; (p. 588) © 2001 PhotoDisc, Inc.; (p. 597) © 2001 PhotoDisc, Inc.

Chapter 18: (p. 621) © 2001 PhotoDisc, Inc.; (p. 624) R. W. Jones/CORBIS; (p. 630) © 2001 PhotoDisc, Inc.

Chapter 19: (p. 653) © 2001 PhotoDisc, Inc.; (p. 662) © 2001 PhotoDisc, Inc.; (p. 672) © 2001 PhotoDisc, Inc.

Comprehensive Cases

A
Lufthansa Business
Travel Survey

B
Discover Card
Satisfaction Survey

C
Rockingham National
Bank Visa Card Survey

Appendix One

Comprehensive Case A

Lufthansa Business Travel Survey

Company Background   Lufthansa, founded in Cologne, Germany in 1953, is one of the world's leading and most successful airlines: number 2 in scheduled passenger traffic (43.8 million passengers in 1999) and the world's top cargo carrier. Total revenue for 1999 reached $8.9 billion. Following its privatization in 1997, it gained more than 400,000 shareholders and now ranks among Germany's biggest public companies. With major hubs in Frankfurt and Munich, Lufthansa flies to 323 destinations in 88 countries. High-quality service to business air travelers is important to the continued growth of Lufthansa within the new economy of the European Union.

Purpose of the Study   Brava Research has been engaged to conduct survey research on the topic of business air traveler satisfaction, so that the facets of satisfaction for these customers can be better understood. Lufthansa management hopes to be able to prioritize customer needs and match company resources to those needs, so that revenues will grow 5 percent in the next fiscal year.

Research Approach   From a variety of sources, such as travel agents, travel associations, hotels, and subscribers to *The Wall Street Journal—Europe,* Brava assembled a list of those making frequent air travel arrangements in Europe. Its team of interviewers then completed telephone interviews with 338 qualified respondents in the United Kingdom. The data were collected during October 2000.

Analysis note: In the data set on the CD-ROM, missing responses are denoted by the following two characters: −9.

LUFTHANSA BUSINESS AIR TRAVEL SURVEY
Fall Quarter
FINAL
Revised 10/9/00

Air Travel Decisions Intro

1. **a.** Hello, may I please speak to (READ NAME FROM TOP OF SCREEN)? (IF PERSON NO LONGER WITH COMPANY, SAY, "May I speak to the person who replaced (him/her)?)

Respondent available	1
Respondent unavailable	2
No such person	3
No name at top of screen	4

    b. Hello, I'm _____ from Brava Research. I'm looking for the person at this location who is most responsible for making decisions about booking air travel in Europe through companies like British Airways, Sabena, Lufthansa, Air France, or other airlines.

Respondent available	1
Respondent unavailable	2
No such person	3
No air travel used	4

(REINTRODUCE YOURSELF IF NEW RESPONDENT COMES ON THE LINE)

   c. We are talking to people like yourself about business air travel. Brava Research regularly monitors business air travel worldwide and would like to include your opinions. In the past year, have you made any decisions about using [LUFTHANSA] for air travel arrangements for your company's employees traveling in Europe?

Yes	1
No	2

Importance Ratings

2&3. First, we'd like to understand the importance of the price you pay versus the quality of service you receive with regard to business air travel when flying within Europe. To do this, I'd like you to divide 100 percent between price and quality of service. The higher the percentage you assign to one over the other, the more important it is to your choice of carrier. Please keep in mind the total must equal 100 percent. (RESPONSES MUST SUM TO 100. ROTATE PRICE AND QUALITY)

Out of 100%, what percent would you give to price? [_____]

Out of 100%, what percent would you give to quality of service? [_____]

                                (ENTER WHOLE NUMBER. RESPONSES MUST SUM TO 100)

Key Measures

4. Now I would like you to rate [LUFTHANSA] on several items. Overall, how satisfied are you with [LUFTHANSA]? Would you say you are . . . (READ LIST)

Completely satisfied?	4
Somewhat satisfied?	3
Somewhat dissatisfied?	2
Completely dissatisfied?	1

5. How likely are you to continue to use [LUFTHANSA] as an airline for business travel? Would you say you would be . . . (READ LIST)

Extremely likely?	5
Very likely?	4
Somewhat likely?	3
Not very likely?	2
Not at all likely?	1

6. How likely would you be to recommend [LUFTHANSA] to a friend or colleague for business air travel? Would you say you would be . . . (READ LIST)

Extremely likely?	5
Very likely?	4
Somewhat likely?	3
Not very likely?	2
Not at all likely?	1

(ASK IF ANY RESPONSE IS 4 OR BELOW FOR QUESTION 5 OR 6)

Why do you say you are not completely satisfied with [LUFTHANSA]'s service?

[_____

_____

_____

CODING USE ONLY _____]

7. Now consider *only the price you pay for business air travel,* and using any number on a 10-point scale, where 1 is a poor price and 10 is an excellent price, how would you rate [LUFTHANSA]?

One—poor price	1
Two	2
Three	3
Four	4
Five	5
Six	6
Seven	7
Eight	8
Nine	9
Ten—excellent price	10

8. Considering *only the quality of business air travel,* and using any number on a 10-point scale, where 1 is poor quality and 10 is excellent quality, how would you rate [LUFTHANSA]?

One—poor quality	1
Two	2
Three	3
Four	4
Five	5
Six	6
Seven	7
Eight	8
Nine	9
Ten—excellent quality	10

Performance

For this next section, I'd like you to rate [LUFTHANSA] on a variety of characteristics, and I would like for you to think ONLY about business air travel.

We'll be using a 10-point scale, where 1 means poor and 10 means excellent. Please feel free to use any number between 1 and 10. From time to time, I may remind you that we are ONLY talking about your business air travel needs. If you have no experience with a characteristic, simply reply "No experience."

[EXAMPLE OF ON-SCREEN DISPLAY]

One—poor	1
Two	2
Three	3
Four	4
Five	5
Six	6
Seven	7
Eight	8
Nine	9
Ten—excellent	10
No experience/Not applicable	11

Considering only [LUFTHANSA], what would your rating be for [INSERT CHARACTERISTIC]? (REPEAT SCALE AS NECESSARY) (ROTATE CHARACTERISTICS)

	Rating
9. Is competitively priced	_____
10. Is a first-rate company	_____
11. Gives customized service	_____
12. Understands your business travel needs	_____

A P P E N D I X   1 :
Comprehensive Cases

13. Works as part of your team   _____
14. Treats you as an important customer   _____
15. Provides the service it promises   _____
16. Helps you solve your business travel problems   _____
17. Knows where your luggage is at all times   _____
18. Delivers your luggage in good condition   _____
19. Gets your luggage there when it should   _____
20. Gives you confidence your luggage will get there   _____
21. Communicates with you regularly   _____

22. Now consider the price you pay relative to the quality of the products and services you receive. Using a 10-point scale, where 1 means poor value and 10 means excellent value, how would you rate overall value provided by [LUFTHANSA]?

One—poor	1
Two	2
Three	3
Four	4
Five	5
Six	6
Seven	7
Eight	8
Nine	9
Ten—excellent	10

Overall value   [_____]

Classification Data

I have just a few more questions for classification purposes only.

23. Considering ALL of your business air travel with ALL airlines, in dollars per month what is the average amount your location spends on business air travel in Europe? (IF NECESSARY, SAY, "Your best estimate will do.")

[_____]
(ENTER WHOLE NUMBER; DO NOT ACCEPT RANGE)

24. For classification purposes only, may I please have your title? (DO NOT READ LIST)

Owner/partner/proprietor	1
Sr. management/CEO/President/Vice President/CFO	2
Manager/supervisor—travel arrangements	3
Nonmanagerial personnel—travel arrangements	4
Analyst/planner/technician/designer/other professional	5
Security/receptionist/admin.	6
Other (SPECIFY)	7
Refused/Don't know	8

(IF RESPONDENT SAYS, "I handle travel arrangements," VERIFY MANAGEMENT OR NON-MANAGEMENT)

25. How many employees work for your company at your location?

(ENTER NUMBER) [_____]

Verification Data

26. a. May I please have your first and last name? (ENTER RESPONDENT'S NAME, AND VERIFY SPELLING)

First name [———————————————————————————————————]
Last name [———————————————————————————————————]

b. I would also like to verify that the number I dialed is your correct telephone number. Your area code and telephone number is [AREA CODE AND TELEPHONE NUMBER]. Is this correct?

Yes   1
No   2
Refused/Don't know   3

(IF NO) What is the correct area code and telephone number?

[———————————————————————]
(INTERVIEWER NOTE: ENTER 10-DIGIT NUMBER WITHOUT DASHES, SPACES, COMMAS, OR PARENTHESES)

c. Thank you for your cooperation, and remember, your opinion counts! Have a nice day!

Questions

1. What is the mean rating for overall satisfaction?
2. How do attribute ratings of business air travel correlate with the likelihood of recommending Lufthansa to a friend or colleague?
3. In terms of overall satisfaction, how do respondents giving at least 50 points to price differ from those giving at least 50 points to quality?
4. In terms of baggage handling, how do respondents giving at least 50 points to price differ from those giving at least 50 points to quality?

Comprehensive Case B

Discover Card Satisfaction Survey

Company Background   Discover Financial Services recently introduced its Discover Platinum Card. This credit card offers the following highlighted features: (1) no annual fee, (2) 0% APR on purchases for 5 months, (3) low introductory 5.9% APR on balance transfers, (4) 2% cash back program, and (5) 100% fraud protection. Managers at Discover Financial Services are expecting revenues to increase by 10% in the 12 months following the introduction of the Discover Platinum Card.

Purpose of the Study   Far Horizons Research has been hired to help Discover Financial Services conduct survey research on the topic of consumer loyalty. Specifically, Discover's management wants researchers to explain the possible influence of customers' interactions with Discover's call-center service representatives on their loyalty to the Discover card. Management will then be better able to decide whether to initiate a $250,000 effort to upgrade training for call-center representatives.

Research Approach   Using a Discover list of those calling into the Discover customer service call center in the last three months, Far Horizons Research completed telephone interviews with 244 respondents in the United States in September 2000.

Analysis note: In the data set on the CD-ROM, missing responses are denoted by the following two characters: −9.

DISCOVER CARD SATISFACTION

1. Hello, I'm _____ with Far Horizons Research, calling on behalf of [DISCOVER] credit card.
   May I please speak with (INSERT CUSTOMER NAME)?
   (IF NECESSARY, ASK TO SPEAK WITH THE PERSON WHO HAS SPOKEN WITH CUSTOMER SERVICE **RECENTLY** REGARDING A [DISCOVER] CREDIT CARD)
   (IF NEW RESPONDENT COMES TO PHONE, REPEAT INTRODUCTION BEFORE CONTINUING)

Respondent available	1
Respondent not available (SCHEDULE CALLBACK)	2
NO SUCH PERSON (TALLY & TERMINATE: WRONG NUMBER)	3

2. We are conducting a customer satisfaction study for [DISCOVER] credit card. They are interested in obtaining your opinions regarding your recent interaction with their credit card customer service department.
   (NOTE: IF RESPONDENT ASKS HOW LONG THE SURVEY WILL TAKE, SAY, "This survey will take just a few minutes of your time.")
   (NOTE: IF FURTHER INFORMATION IS REQUIRED, SAY, "We are not selling anything; we are only interested in your opinions today.")
   (NOTE: IF RESPONDENT HAS CANCELLED CARD, SAY, "Even though you no longer have the card/account, [DISCOVER] is interested in your opinions.")

Yes	1
No, not now (SCHEDULE CALLBACK)	2
Customer not available (SCHEDULE CALLBACK)	3
No one has called (TALLY & TERMINATE: NER USAGE)	4

3. During your most recent call to the credit card service department, what was the purpose of your call? (DO NOT READ LIST. RECORD ALL THAT APPLY) (IF RESPONDENT UNSPECIFIC, PROBE: "Could you be more specific?")

Ask about a disputed charge	1
Cancel the card/Close the account	2
Increase your credit line	3
Lower your annual fee	4
Lower your interest rate	5
Question about late fees	6
Request an emergency authorization to exceed your credit limit	7
Waive the annual fee	8
Waive the late fee	9
Some other reason (SPECIFY)	10
Inquire about my account balance	11
Transfer funds to another Discover account	12
Request a new card	13
Report a lost/stolen card	14
Transfer funds out of my Discover account	15
Refusal (TALLY & TERMINATE: REFUSAL)	16

[END OF SCREENER]

a. (ASK IF Q.3 = 2. OTHERWISE, SKIP TO Q.4) And is your account currently closed?

Yes	1
No	2

4. Overall how satisfied (are/were) you with your [DISCOVER] credit card? Would you say you are . . . (READ LIST)

Very satisfied?	5
Satisfied?	4
Neither satisfied or dissatisfied?	3
Dissatisfied?	2
Very dissatisfied?	1

a. (IF ANY CODE AT Q.3 EXCEPT 2 OR IF Q.3a = 2 OR DK, ASK. OTHERWISE, SKIP TO Q.4b) How likely are you to KEEP your [DISCOVER] credit card in the future? Would you say you . . . (READ LIST)

Would definitely keep and use it?	5
Would probably keep and use it?	4
Might or might not keep and use it?	3
Would probably not keep and use it?	2
Would definitely not keep and use it?	1

b. How likely would you be to recommend the card to a friend or family member? Would you say you would be . . . (READ LIST)

Extremely likely to recommend?	5
Very likely?	4
Somewhat likely?	3
Not very likely?	2
Not at all likely to recommend?	1

c. Considering the price charged and the overall quality of service, please rate the VALUE of the credit card. Would you say it (is/was) . . . (READ LIST)

Excellent?	5
Very good?	4
Good?	3
Fair?	2
Poor?	1

5. Now I would like to know how you felt about the Customer Service Representative during the last contact you had regarding the [DISCOVER] credit card. I am going to read you a list of statements and for each one, please tell me whether you agree completely, agree somewhat, neither agree nor disagree, disagree somewhat, or disagree completely.

    [EXAMPLE OF ON-SCREEN DISPLAY]

Agree completely	5
Agree somewhat	4
Neither agree nor disagree	3
Disagree somewhat	2
Disagree completely	1

Would you say the Customer Service Representative . . . (READ LIST) (REPEAT SCALE IF NECESSARY) (ROTATE STATEMENTS)
(INTERVIEWER NOTE: ENSURE THAT RESPONDENT IS RATING THE CUSTOMER SERVICE REPRESENTATIVE SPOKEN TO DURING HIS/HER MOST RECENT CALL)

	AC	**AS**	**NAD**	**DS**	**DC**
a. Was someone who could take care of you?	5	4	3	2	1
b. Handled your call efficiently?	5	4	3	2	1
c. Was courteous?	5	4	3	2	1
d. Was concerned about your needs?	5	4	3	2	1
e. Was competent?	5	4	3	2	1
f. Had the authority to take action?	5	4	3	2	1
g. Told you what you could expect to occur in the handling of your request?	5	4	3	2	1
h. Was friendly?	5	4	3	2	1
i. Was professional?	5	4	3	2	1
j. Listened to you?	5	4	3	2	1
k. Made you feel important?	5	4	3	2	1
l. Trusted you?	5	4	3	2	1
m. Demonstrated that he or she valued you?	5	4	3	2	1

[POINT OF COMPLETION]

6. (RECORD SEX)

Male	1
Female	2

These last few questions are for classification purposes only. You may refuse to answer any of these questions.
(IF RESPONDENT APPEARS TO BE AT ALL IRRITATED DURING THE DEMOGRAPHIC SECTION, THANK AND TERMINATE IMMEDIATELY)

7. What is your age? (IF NECESSARY, READ LIST)

Under 18	1
18 to 24 years	2
25 to 34 years	3
35 to 44 years	4
45 to 54 years	5
55 to 64 years	6
65 years to 74 years	7
75 years or older	8
(DO NOT READ) Refused	9

8. What is the last grade of school you completed? (IF NECESSARY, READ LIST)

Some high school or less	1
Completed high school	2
Technical school	3
Some college	4
Completed college	5
Post-graduate school	6
(DO NOT READ) Refused	7

9. What is your marital status? (READ LIST)

Married/Living with someone	1
Single (never married)	2
Widowed/Divorced/Separated	3
(DO NOT READ) Refused	4

10. Which of the following groups best represent your household income before taxes? (READ LIST)

Under $15,000	1
$15,000 but less than $20,000	2
$20,000 but less than $30,000	3
$30,000 but less than $40,000	4
$40,000 but less than $50,000	5
$50,000 but less than $75,000	6
$75,000 but less than $100,000	7
$100,000 but less than $150,000	8
$150,000 or more	9
(DO NOT READ) Refused	10

11. May I verify that I have reached you at (READ AREA CODE AND PHONE NUMBER FROM TOP OF SCREEN)?

Yes [SKIP TO LAST SCREEN]	1
No, incorrect number	2
Refused [SKIP TO LAST SCREEN]	3

12. May I please have your correct phone number? [ENTER AREA CODE AND PHONE NUMBER. DO NOT ENTER SPACES, COMMAS, COLONS, DASHES, OR PARENTHESES)

[————————————]

Thank you for taking time to complete our survey [today/tonight]. Your answers will be very useful to [DISCOVER] credit card. Have a nice [day/evening].

Questions

1. What is the most frequently cited reason for calling into the Discover customer service call center? What is the least frequently cited reason?
2. How do ratings of overall satisfaction correlate with consumers' likelihood of keeping the card? With their likelihood of recommending the Discover card to a friend?
3. Compare the mean satisfaction ratings across all of the age groups. Which age group reports the highest overall satisfaction?
4. In a regression model with ratings of representative friendliness and competence as independent variables and the likelihood of keeping the card as the dependent variable, is a linear relationship discernible? Which appears to have more influence on the dependent variable, friendliness or competence?

APPENDIX 1:
Comprehensive Cases

Comprehensive Case C

Rockingham National Bank Visa Card Survey

Company Background   Rockingham National Bank, located in Chicago, Illinois, is attempting to expand the market for its Visa card. It is examining certain target groups to determine its ability to penetrate the credit card market with special offers.

Purpose of the Study   The purpose of this research study is to evaluate how teachers in Illinois will respond to specific credit card promotional offers. Specifically, the questionnaire was designed to achieve the following objectives:

- Develop a demographic, psychographic, credit card ownership, and credit card usage profile of teachers.
- Determine the likelihood of teachers to respond to several different concepts for a credit card offer.
- Determine which demographic, psychographic, attitudinal, credit card ownership, and credit card usage variables are the best predictors of likelihood to respond to the concept credit card offers.
- Make predictions regarding the likely level of response to a credit card offer to the teacher market.
- Identify those features most likely to induce teachers to respond to a credit card offer.

Research Approach   All data were collected by means of central location telephone interviewing from the Ameridata facility in Arlington, Texas by experienced Ameridata interviewers.

The interviews were conducted with software-driven interfaces to virtually eliminate tabulation errors. All interviewing was supervised and monitored by Ameridata personnel.

The geographic area covered was the state of Illinois. The sample was selected following the criteria for a simple random sample; qualified respondents were individuals licensed to teach in Illinois. A total of 400 interviews were completed.

ROCKINGHAM BANK CREDIT CARD SURVEY OF TEACHERS

(ASK TO SPEAK TO RESPONDENT LISTED ON THE SAMPLE SHEET. IF ANOTHER MEMBER OF THE HOUSEHOLD IS WILLING TO DO THE SURVEY, THANK THE PERSON FOR HIS OR HER WILLINGNESS, BUT EXPLAIN THAT YOU NEED TO COMPLETE THE INTERVIEW WITH THE LISTED RESPONDENT.)

Hello, my name is _____ with Ameridata Research, an independent marketing research firm. I would like to ask you a few questions about credit card usage. First, let me assure you this is not a sales call, you will not be contacted again, and my questions will only take a few minutes of your time.

(READ ONLY IF NEEDED) Let me assure you that this is not a sales call; we are only conducting research on credit card usage and are interested in your opinions about credit cards.

1. First of all, please tell me whether you strongly agree, agree, neither agree nor disagree, disagree, or strongly disagree with each of the following statements (READ LIST; ROTATE):

		SA	A	NAD	D	SD	DK
a.	Money may not be everything, but it's got a big lead over whatever is second.	5	4	3	2	1	6
b.	Money can't buy happiness.	5	4	3	2	1	6
c.	It is important for me to be fashionable and chic.	5	4	3	2	1	6
d.	I buy things even though I can't afford them.	5	4	3	2	1	6
e.	I make only the minimum payments on my credit cards.	5	4	3	2	1	6
f.	I sometimes buy things to make myself feel better.	5	4	3	2	1	6
g.	Shopping is fun.	5	4	3	2	1	6
h.	During the last three years, my financial situation has gotten worse.	5	4	3	2	1	6
i.	I am satisfied with my present financial situation.	5	4	3	2	1	6
j.	Buying things gives me a lot of pleasure.	5	4	3	2	1	6
k.	You can tell a lot about people by the credit cards they use.	5	4	3	2	1	6
l.	I attach great importance to money.	5	4	3	2	1	6
m.	I attach great importance to credit cards.	5	4	3	2	1	6
n.	I attach great importance to material possessions.	5	4	3	2	1	6
o.	I generally read all offers that I receive through the mail just to know what they are about.	5	4	3	2	1	6

2. Please tell me which of the following credit cards you carry with you. Do you carry . . . (PROBE FOR VISA OR MASTERCARD)
   1   Visa? (ASK FOR NUMBER OF VISA CARDS) _____
   2   MasterCard? (ASK FOR NUMBER OF MASTERCARDS) _____
   3   Discover?
   4   American Express?
   5   Optima?
   6   AT&T Universal?
   7   GM?
   8   Ford?
   9   None   (SKIP TO Q.11)

3. Which card do you use the most often? (PROBE FOR ONE ANSWER ONLY; IF RESPONDENT IS UNABLE TO GIVE ONLY ONE RESPONSE, TAKE THE FIRST RESPONSE GIVEN)
   1   Visa
   2   MasterCard
   3   Discover
   4   American Express
   5   Optima
   6   AT&T Universal
   7   GM
   8   Ford
   9   DON'T KNOW   (SKIP TO Q.11)

APPENDIX 1:

Comprehensive Cases

(IF "VISA" OR "MASTERCARD" IS MENTIONED IN Q.3, ASK Q.4. OTHERWISE, SKIP TO Q.11)

4. Which bank issued this Visa/MasterCard?
[MASTERCARD ISSUERS]
1   Associates National Bank
2   Chase Manhattan
3   Citibank
4   Credit union issued
5   First Bank
6   Household
7   MBNA
8   Other
9   DK
[VISA ISSUERS]
1   Associates National Bank
2   Bank of America
3   Citibank
4   Credit union issued
5   First Bank
6   Household
7   MBNA
8   Other
9   DK

5. Why do you use [ANSWER FROM Q.3] most often?
1   Convenience
2   Only card owned/carried
3   Interest rate
4   Wide acceptance
5   Cash back
6   Cash rebate
7   Billing cycle/grace period
8   No annual fee
9   Issued by a local bank
10   Corporate/business card
11   Credit limit
12   Itemized bill
13   It's a Gold Card.
14   Rebate toward automobile purchase
15   Relationship with organization sponsoring card (IF YES, "Which organization?")
16   Other

6. What is the interest rate on the balances that you carry on the card you use most often?
1   Less than 8 percent
2   8–8.9 percent
3   9–9.9 percent
4   10–10.9 percent
5   11–11.9 percent
6   12–12.9 percent
7   13–13.9 percent
8   14–14.9 percent
9   15–15.9 percent
10   16–16.9 percent
11   17–17.9 percent
12   18–18.9 percent
13   19–19.9 percent
14   20 percent or more

7. What is your credit limit on the card you can use the most?

_____ Credit limit

8. Is the card you use most often a Gold Card?

1 Yes

2 No

3 DK

9. Does the card you use most often . . . (READ LIST)

	Yes	No	DK
Charge an annual fee?	1	2	3
Offer cash rebates/cash back on purchases?	1	2	3
Offer extended warranties on products you buy?	1	2	3
Offer buyer protection policies on products you buy (to replace the product if damaged, lost or stolen)?	1	2	3
Offer a photo credit card?	1	2	3

10. Besides a lower interest rate, what feature or features would a new card need to have to convince you to obtain it?

1 No annual fee

2 Preapproved

3 Rebate/cash back/free offers

4 Business/corporate card

5 Gold Card

6 High credit limit

7 Wide acceptance

8 Other

11. Have you received any credit card offers in the past year?

1 Yes (CONTINUE)

2 No (SKIP TO Q.17)

3 DK (SKIP TO Q.17)

12. Approximately how many credit offers have you received in the past year?

_____ Number of offers received

13. Have you responded to any of these offers?

1 Yes (CONTINUE)

2 No (SKIP TO Q.16)

3 DK (SKIP TO Q.17)

14. To which offer or offers did you respond?

1 Visa

2 MasterCard

3 Discover

4 American Express

5 Optima

6 AT&T Universal

7 GM

8 Ford

9 Other

APPENDIX 1:

Comprehensive Cases

15. Why did you respond [to this offer/these offers]? (ASK FOR EACH RESPONSE IN Q.12)
    1   No annual fee
    2   Preapproved
    3   Interest rate
    4   Build credit rating
    5   Convenience/emergencies
    6   Rebate/cash back/free offers
    7   Business/corporate card
    8   Gold Card
    9   Credit limit
   10 Travel
   11 Grocery shopping
   12 Wide acceptance
   13 Other
   (SKIP TO Q.17)

16. Why didn't you respond to any of the offers? (PROBE)
    1   Interest rate too high
    2   Have too many credit cards
    3   Credit card balances too high
    4   Credit limit
    5   Interest rate confusing
    6   Do not use credit cards
    7   Do not need any more credit cards
    8   Not preapproved/fear of being turned down
    9   Other
   10 DK

17. Have you closed or stopped using any credit cards in the past year?
    1   Yes   (CONTINUE)
    2   No   (SKIP TO Q.20)
    3   DK   (SKIP TO Q.20)

18. Which card or cards have you stopped using?
    1   Visa
    2   MasterCard
    3   Discover
    4   American Express
    5   Optima
    6   AT&T Universal
    7   Other

19. Why have you stopped using this card? (ASK FOR EACH RESPONSE IN Q.18)
    1   Interest rate
    2   Annual fee
    3   Own too many credit cards
    4   Balance too high
    5   Billing problems
    6   Never used it
    7   Limited acceptance
    8   Consolidation of debt
    9   Other

20. Would you say that your attitudes toward the use of credit cards have changed in the past year?
1 Yes (CONTINUE)
2 No (SKIP TO Q.22)
3 DK (SKIP TO Q.22)

21. (IF "YES" IN RESPONSE TO Q.20, ASK) How have your attitudes changed? (PROBE)

22. In comparison with a year ago, would you say you are using your credit cards . . . (READ LIST)
1 Less often?
2 About the same?
3 More often?
4 DK

23. In comparison with a year ago, which of the following statements is true in regard to your total credit card balances? (READ LIST)
1 They are less.
2 They are about the same.
3 They are greater.
4 DK

24. Now, I would like to find out how you feel about a particular credit card offer. We are not making this offer to you today—we are only interested in how you feel about the offer. (READ LIST OF OFFER FEATURES. RESPONDENTS WILL BE ASKED ABOUT ONE OF THE FOLLOWING SCENARIOS—100 FOR EACH SCENARIO)

	Preapproved	Application
6.0% Intro APR		
9.9% Intro APR		

- You receive [an application/a preapproved application] for a Limited Edition Visa card.
- There is no annual fee.
- It has a [9.9 /6.0] percent initial APR through March 2002.
- After that, the APR will be 16.9 percent.
- You can immediately transfer balances from other cards up to your credit limit—you can do this through March 2002 with no cash advance fees.
- It has a credit limit of up to $5,000.

25. On a scale of 0 to 100, where 0 is not at all likely and 100 is extremely likely, how likely would you be to respond to this offer?
_____ Likelihood

26. What, if anything, do you particularly LIKE about this offer? (PROBE: "Anything else?")
1 No annual fee
2 Good interest rate
3 Good offer in general
4 Features/benefits
5 Ability to transfer balances
6 Credit limit
7 Appealing offer in general
8 Advantages over other offers
9 Mastercard/Visa brand
10 Identifies you as a professional
11 Prestige of Limited Edition's name
12 Other

27. What, if anything, do you particularly DISLIKE about this offer? (PROBE: "Anything else?")
- 1   Interest rate too high
- 2   Don't use credit cards
- 3   Interest rate confusing
- 4   Not competitive with current card
- 5   Interest rate change after March
- 6   No reason
- 7   Other
- 8   DK

28. Is the interest rate in the Visa credit card offer clear and understandable?
- 1   Yes
- 2   No
- 3   DK/NS

29. Using a scale of 1 to 10, where 1 is poor and 10 is excellent, please tell me how you would rate the following product features in the Visa credit card offer that was just described. (ROTATE TO REFLECT INTRODUCTORY PERCENTAGE RATE AND BEING PREAPPROVED/HAVING TO APPLY)
- _____ No annual fee
- _____ 9.9/6.0 percent introductory rate through March 2002
- _____ 16.9 percent APR after March 2002
- _____ Being preapproved/receiving an application
- _____ Ability to transfer balances from other cards
- _____ Credit limit of up to $5,000

30. Do you consider this Visa credit card offer to be better than, about the same as, or worse than . . .

	Better	Same	Worse	DK
Discover Card?	1	2	3	4
American Express Optima Card?	1	2	3	4
AT&T Universal Card?	1	2	3	4
GM or Ford Card?	1	2	3	4
Other MasterCard/Visa for teaching professionals?	1	2	3	4
Credit card you use most often?	1	2	3	4

31. (IF BETTER OR WORSE IN Q.30, ASK) Why do you feel that way? (PROBE)

32. In evaluating a credit card offer, how important are the following things to you? Please use a 1 to 10 scale, where 1 is very unimportant and 10 is very important. How important is . . .? (READ LIST AND ROTATE)
- _____ Being preapproved?
- _____ Interest rate?
- _____ Annual fee?
- _____ Credit limit?
- _____ Billing cycle/grace period?
- _____ Reputation of issuer?
- _____ Extended warranty/buyer protection?
- _____ No charges if monthly balance is paid?
- _____ Cash advance?
- _____ Financing payment plan?
- _____ 24-hour service for lost or stolen cards?
- _____ Ability to transfer balances from other cards?
- _____ Rebates?

Finally, just a few questions to help us classify your responses.

33. (INDICATE SEX OF RESPONDENT)
- 1   Male
- 2   Female

34. Are you currently married or not married?
1 Married
2 Not married
3 RF

35. Which of the following categories includes your age? Are you . . .
1 18–24?
2 25–34?
3 35–44?
4 45–54?
5 55–64?
6 65 or over?
7 RF

36. What is the highest level of education completed by the primary wage earner in your household?
1 Less than high school graduate
2 High school graduate
3 Some college
4 College graduate
5 Any postgraduate work
6 RF

37. What is your occupation? (PROBE FOR TYPE OF BUSINESS, ETC.)

_____

38. (IF MARRIED) What is your spouse's occupation? (PROBE FOR TYPE OF BUSINESS, ETC.)

_____

39. Which of the following categories includes the total annual income of all the working members of your household before taxes?
1 Under $15,000
2 $15,000–$24,999
3 $25,000–$39,999
4 $40,000–$54,999
5 $55,000–$69,999
6 $70,000 or more
7 DK
8 RF

That concludes our survey, and I would like to thank you for taking the time to assist us.
NAME _____
TELEPHONE (_____) _____
INTERVIEWER NUMBER _____

Questions

1. Use the survey results to respond to each of the research objectives specified at the beginning of the case.
2. How are those who use Visa or MasterCard most often different from those who use American Express most often?
3. Describe respondents' attitudes toward credit limits.
4. Discuss credit card offers and the teachers' responses. Also, discuss credit card closings.
5. How did respondents react to the new credit card proposals?
6. Use multivariate statistics to determine the strongest predictors of response to the new credit card offers.

APPENDIX 1:
Comprehensive Cases

Statistical Tables

Appendix Two

Table 1

Random Digits

63271	59986	71744	51102	15141	80714	58683	93108	13554	79945
88547	09896	95436	79115	08303	01041	20030	63754	08459	28364
55957	57243	83865	09911	19761	66535	40102	26646	60147	15702
46276	87453	44790	64122	45573	84358	21625	16999	13385	22782
55363	07449	34835	15290	76616	67191	12777	21861	68689	03263
69393	92785	49902	58447	42048	30378	87618	26933	40640	16281
13186	29431	88190	04588	38733	81290	89541	70290	40113	08243
17726	28652	56836	78351	47327	18518	92222	55201	27340	10493
36520	64465	05550	30157	82242	29520	69753	72602	23756	54935
81628	36100	39254	56835	37636	02421	98063	89641	64953	99337
84649	48968	75215	75498	49539	74240	03466	49292	36401	45525
63291	11618	12613	75055	43915	26488	41116	64531	56827	30825
70502	53225	03655	05915	37140	57051	48393	91322	25653	06543
06426	24771	59935	49801	11082	66762	94477	02494	88215	27191
20711	55609	29430	70165	45406	78484	31639	52009	18873	96927
41990	70538	77191	25860	55204	73417	83920	69468	74972	38712
72452	36618	76298	26678	89334	33938	95567	29380	75906	91807
37042	40318	57099	10528	09925	89773	41335	96244	29002	46453
53766	52875	15987	46962	67342	77592	57651	95508	80033	69828
90585	58955	53122	16025	84299	53310	67380	84249	25348	04332
32001	96293	37203	64516	51530	37069	40261	61374	05815	06714
62606	64324	46354	72157	67248	20135	49804	09226	64419	29457
10078	28073	85389	50324	14500	15562	64165	06125	71353	77669
91561	46145	24177	15294	10061	98124	75732	00815	83452	97355
13091	98112	53959	79607	52244	63303	10413	63839	74762	50289
73864	83014	72457	22682	03033	61714	88173	90835	00634	85169
66668	25467	48894	51043	02365	91726	09365	63167	95264	45643
84745	41042	29493	01836	09044	51926	43630	63470	76508	14194
48068	26805	94595	47907	13357	38412	33318	26098	82782	42851
54310	96175	97594	88616	42035	38093	36745	56702	40644	83514
14877	33095	10924	58013	61439	21882	42059	24177	58739	60170
78295	23179	02771	43464	59061	71411	05697	67194	30495	21157
67524	02865	39593	54278	04237	92441	26602	63835	38032	94770
58268	57219	68124	73455	83236	08710	04284	55005	84171	42596
97158	28672	50685	01181	24262	19427	52106	34308	73685	74246
04230	16831	69085	30802	65559	09205	71829	06489	85650	38707
94879	56606	30401	02602	57658	70091	54986	41394	60437	03195
71446	15232	66715	26385	91518	70566	02888	79941	39684	54315
32886	05644	79316	09819	00813	88407	17461	73925	53037	91904
62048	33711	25290	21526	02223	75947	66466	06332	10913	75336
84534	42351	21628	53669	81352	95152	08107	98814	72743	12849
84707	15885	84710	35866	06446	86311	32648	88141	73902	69981
19409	40868	64220	80861	13860	68493	52908	26374	63297	45052
57978	48015	25973	66777	45924	56144	24742	96702	88200	66162
57295	98298	11199	96510	75228	41600	47192	43267	35973	23152
94044	83785	93388	07833	38216	31413	70555	03023	54147	06647
30014	25879	71763	96679	90603	99396	74557	74224	18211	91637
07265	69563	64268	88802	72264	66540	01782	08396	19251	83613
84404	88642	30263	80310	11522	57810	27627	78376	36240	48952
21778	02085	27762	46097	43324	34354	09369	14966	10158	76089

APPENDIX 2:

Statistical Tables

Table 2

Standard Normal Distribution: *Z*-values

Entries in the table give the area under the curve between the mean and *Z* standard deviations above the mean. For example, for *Z* = 1.25, the area under the curve between the mean and *Z* is .3944.

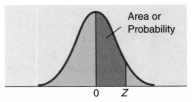

Area or Probability

Z	.00	.01	.02	.03	.04	.05	.06	.07	.08	.09
.0	.0000	.0040	.0080	.0120	.0160	.0199	.0239	.0279	.0319	.0359
.1	.0398	.0438	.0478	.0517	.0557	.0596	.0636	.0675	.0714	.0753
.2	.0793	.0832	.0871	.0910	.0948	.0987	.1026	.1064	.1103	.1141
.3	.1179	.1217	.1255	.1293	.1331	.1368	.1406	.1443	.1480	.1517
.4	.1554	.1591	.1628	.1664	.1700	.1736	.1772	.1808	.1844	.1879
.5	.1915	.1950	.1985	.2019	.2054	.2088	.2123	.2157	.2190	.2224
.6	.2257	.2291	.2324	.2357	.2389	.2422	.2454	.2486	.2518	.2549
.7	.2580	.2612	.2642	.2673	.2704	.2734	.2764	.2794	.2823	.2852
.8	.2881	.2910	.2939	.2967	.2995	.3023	.3051	.3078	.3106	.3133
.9	.3159	.3186	.3212	.3238	.3264	.3289	.3315	.3340	.3365	.3389
1.0	.3413	.3438	.3461	.3485	.3508	.3531	.3554	.3577	.3599	.3621
1.1	.3643	.3665	.3686	.3708	.3729	.3749	.3770	.3790	.3810	.3830
1.2	.3849	.3869	.3888	.3907	.3925	.3944	.3962	.3980	.3997	.4015
1.3	.4032	.4049	.4066	.4082	.4099	.4115	.4131	.4147	.4162	.4177
1.4	.4192	.4207	.4222	.4236	.4251	.4265	.4279	.4292	.4306	.4319
1.5	.4332	.4345	.4357	.4370	.4382	.4394	.4406	.4418	.4429	.4441
1.6	.4452	.4463	.4474	.4484	.4495	.4505	.4515	.4525	.4535	.4545
1.7	.4554	.4564	.4573	.4582	.4591	.4599	.4608	.4616	.4625	.4633
1.8	.4641	.4649	.4656	.4664	.4671	.4678	.4686	.4693	.4699	.4706
1.9	.4713	.4719	.4726	.4732	.4738	.4744	.4750	.4756	.4761	.4767
2.0	.4772	.4778	.4783	.4788	.4793	.4798	.4803	.4808	.4812	.4817
2.1	.4821	.4826	.4830	.4834	.4838	.4842	.4846	.4850	.4854	.4857
2.2	.4861	.4864	.4868	.4871	.4875	.4878	.4881	.4884	.4887	.4890
2.3	.4893	.4896	.4898	.4901	.4904	.4906	.4909	.4911	.4913	.4916
2.4	.4918	.4920	.4922	.4925	.4927	.4929	.4931	.4932	.4934	.4936
2.5	.4938	.4940	.4941	.4943	.4945	.4946	.4948	.4949	.4951	.4952
2.6	.4953	.4955	.4956	.4957	.4959	.4960	.4961	.4962	.4963	.4964
2.7	.4965	.4966	.4967	.4968	.4969	.4970	.4971	.4972	.4973	.4974
2.8	.4974	.4975	.4976	.4977	.4977	.4978	.4979	.4979	.4980	.4981
2.9	.4981	.4982	.4982	.4983	.4984	.4984	.4985	.4985	.4986	.4986
3.0	.4986	.4987	.4987	.4988	.4988	.4989	.4989	.4989	.4990	.4990

APPENDIX 2:

Statistical Tables

A-21

Table 3

t-Distribution

Entries in the table give *t*-values for an area or probability in the upper tail of the *t*-distribution. For example, with 10 degrees of freedom and a .05 area in the upper tail, $t_{.05}=1.812$.

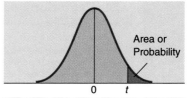

Area or Probability

Degrees of Freedom	Area in Upper Tail				
	.10	.05	.025	.01	.005
1	3.078	6.314	12.706	31.821	63.657
2	1.886	2.920	4.303	6.965	9.925
3	1.638	2.353	3.182	4.541	5.841
4	1.533	2.132	2.776	3.747	4.604
5	1.476	2.015	2.571	3.365	4.032
6	1.440	1.943	2.447	3.143	3.707
7	1.415	1.895	2.365	2.998	3.499
8	1.397	1.860	2.306	2.896	3.355
9	1.383	1.833	2.262	2.821	3.250
10	1.372	1.812	2.228	2.764	3.169
11	1.363	1.796	2.201	2.718	3.106
12	1.356	1.782	2.179	2.681	3.055
13	1.350	1.771	2.160	2.650	3.012
14	1.345	1.761	2.145	2.624	2.977
15	1.341	1.753	2.131	2.602	2.947
16	1.337	1.746	2.120	2.583	2.921
17	1.333	1.740	2.110	2.567	2.898
18	1.330	1.734	2.101	2.552	2.878
19	1.328	1.729	2.093	2.539	2.861
20	1.325	1.725	2.086	2.528	2.845
21	1.323	1.721	2.080	2.518	2.831
22	1.321	1.717	2.074	2.508	2.819
23	1.319	1.714	2.069	2.500	2.807
24	1.318	1.711	2.064	2.492	2.797
25	1.316	1.708	2.060	2.485	2.787
26	1.315	1.706	2.056	2.479	2.779
27	1.314	1.703	2.052	2.473	2.771
28	1.313	1.701	2.048	2.467	2.763
29	1.311	1.699	2.045	2.462	2.756
30	1.310	1.697	2.042	2.457	2.750
40	1.303	1.684	2.021	2.423	2.704
60	1.296	1.671	2.000	2.390	2.660
120	1.289	1.658	1.980	2.358	2.617
∞	1.282	1.645	1.960	2.326	2.576

APPENDIX 2:
Statistical Tables

Table 4

Chi-Square Distribution

Entries in the table give χ^2_α values, where α is the area or probability in the upper tail of the chi-square distribution. For example, with 10 degrees of freedom and a .01 area in the upper tail, $\chi^2_\alpha = 23.2093$.

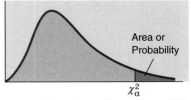

Area or Probability

χ^2_α

Degrees of Freedom	Area in Upper Tail									
	.995	.99	.975	.95	.90	.10	.05	.025	.01	.005
1	.0000393	.000157	.000982	.000393	.015709	2.70554	3.84146	5.02389	6.63490	7.87944
2	.0100251	.0201007	.0506356	.102587	.210720	4.60517	5.99147	7.37776	9.21034	10.5966
3	.0717212	.114832	2.15795	.351846	.584375	6.25139	7.81473	9.34840	11.3449	12.8381
4	.206990	.297110	.484419	.710721	1.063623	7.77944	9.48773	11.1433	13.2767	14.8602
5	.411740	.554300	.831211	1.145476	1.61031	9.23635	11.0705	12.8325	15.0863	16.7496
6	.675727	.872085	1.237347	1.63539	2.20413	10.6446	12.5916	14.4494	16.8119	18.5476
7	.989265	1.239043	1.68987	2.16735	2.83311	12.0170	14.0671	16.0128	18.4753	20.2777
8	1.344419	1.646482	2.17973	2.73264	3.48954	13.3616	15.5073	17.5346	20.0902	21.9550
9	1.734926	2.087912	2.70039	3.32511	4.16816	14.6837	16.9190	19.0228	21.6660	23.5893
10	2.15585	2.55821	3.24697	3.94030	4.86518	15.9871	18.3070	20.4831	23.2093	25.1882
11	2.60321	3.05347	3.81575	4.57481	5.57779	17.2750	19.6751	21.9200	24.7250	26.7569
12	3.07382	3.57056	4.40379	5.22603	6.30380	18.5494	21.0261	23.3367	26.2170	28.2995
13	3.56503	4.10691	5.00874	5.89186	7.04150	19.8119	22.3621	24.7356	27.6883	29.8194
14	4.07468	4.66043	5.62872	6.57063	7.78953	21.0642	23.6848	26.1190	29.1413	31.3193
15	4.60094	5.22935	6.26214	7.26094	8.54675	22.3072	24.9958	27.4884	30.5779	32.8013
16	5.14224	5.81221	6.90766	7.96164	9.31223	23.5418	26.2962	28.8454	31.9999	34.2672
17	5.69724	6.40776	7.56418	8.67176	10.0852	24.7690	27.5871	30.1910	33.4087	35.7185
18	6.26481	7.01491	8.23075	9.39046	10.8649	25.9894	28.8693	31.5264	34.8053	37.1564
19	6.84398	7.63273	8.90655	10.1170	11.6509	27.2036	30.1435	32.8523	36.1908	38.5822
20	7.43386	8.26040	9.59083	10.8508	12.4426	28.4120	31.4104	34.1696	37.5662	39.9968
21	8.03366	8.89720	10.28293	11.5913	13.2396	29.6151	32.6705	35.4789	38.9321	41.4010
22	8.64272	9.54249	10.9823	12.3380	14.0415	30.8133	33.9244	36.7807	40.2894	42.7958
23	9.26042	10.19567	11.6885	13.0905	14.8479	32.0069	35.1725	38.0757	41.6384	44.1813
24	9.88623	10.8564	12.4011	13.8484	15.6587	33.1963	36.4151	39.3641	42.9798	45.5585
25	10.5197	11.5240	13.1197	14.6114	16.4734	34.3816	37.6525	40.6465	44.3141	46.9278
26	11.1603	12.1981	13.8439	15.3791	17.2919	35.5631	38.8852	41.9232	45.6417	48.2899
27	11.8076	12.8786	14.5733	16.1513	18.1138	36.7412	40.1133	43.1944	46.9630	49.6449
28	12.4613	13.5648	15.3079	16.9279	18.9392	37.9159	41.3372	44.4607	48.2782	50.9933
29	13.1211	14.2565	16.0471	17.7083	19.7677	39.0875	42.5569	45.7222	49.5879	52.3356
30	13.7867	14.9535	16.7908	18.4926	20.5992	40.2560	43.7729	46.9792	50.8922	53.6720
40	20.765	22.1643	24.4331	26.5093	29.0505	51.8050	55.7585	59.3417	63.6907	66.7659
50	27.9907	29.7067	32.3574	34.7642	37.6886	63.1671	67.5048	71.4202	76.1539	79.4900
60	35.5346	37.4848	40.4817	43.1879	46.4589	74.3970	79.0819	83.2976	88.3794	91.9517
70	43.2752	45.4418	48.7576	51.7393	55.3290	85.5271	90.5312	95.0231	100.425	104.215
80	51.1720	53.5400	57.1532	60.3915	64.2778	96.5782	101.879	106.629	112.329	116.321
90	59.1963	61.7541	65.6466	69.1260	73.2912	107.565	113.145	118.136	124.116	128.299
100	67.3276	70.0648	74.2219	77.9295	82.3581	118.498	124.342	129.561	135.807	140.169

Table 5

F-Distribution

Entries in the table give F_α values, where α is the area or probability in the upper tail of the *F*-distribution. For example, with 12 numerator degrees of freedom, 15 denominator degrees of freedom, and a .05 area in the upper tail, $F_{.05} = 2.48$.

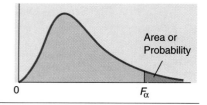

Area or Probability

0 F_α

Table of $F_{.05}$ Values

Denominator Degrees of Freedom	Numerator Degrees of Freedom																		
	1	2	3	4	5	6	7	8	9	10	12	15	20	24	30	40	60	120	∞
1	161.4	199.5	215.7	224.6	230.2	234.0	236.8	238.9	240.5	241.9	243.9	245.9	248.0	249.1	250.1	251.1	252.2	253.3	254.3
2	18.51	19.00	19.16	19.25	19.30	19.33	19.35	19.37	19.38	19.40	19.41	19.43	19.45	19.45	19.46	19.47	19.48	19.49	19.50
3	10.13	9.55	9.28	9.12	9.01	8.94	8.89	8.85	8.81	8.79	8.74	8.70	8.66	8.64	8.62	8.59	8.57	8.55	8.53
4	7.71	6.94	6.59	6.39	6.26	6.16	6.09	6.04	6.00	5.96	5.91	5.86	5.80	5.77	5.75	5.72	5.69	5.66	5.63
5	6.61	5.79	5.41	5.19	5.05	4.95	4.88	4.82	4.77	4.74	4.68	4.62	4.56	4.53	4.50	4.46	4.43	4.40	4.36
6	5.99	5.14	4.76	4.53	4.39	4.28	4.21	4.15	4.10	4.06	4.00	3.94	3.87	3.84	3.81	3.77	3.74	3.70	3.67
7	5.59	4.74	4.35	4.12	3.97	3.87	3.79	3.73	3.68	3.64	3.57	3.51	3.44	3.41	3.38	3.34	3.30	3.27	3.23
8	5.32	4.46	4.07	3.84	3.69	3.58	3.50	3.44	3.39	3.35	3.28	3.22	3.15	3.12	3.08	3.04	3.01	2.97	2.93
9	5.12	4.26	3.86	3.63	3.48	3.37	3.29	3.23	3.18	3.14	3.07	3.01	2.94	2.90	2.86	2.83	2.79	2.75	2.71
10	4.96	4.10	3.71	3.48	3.33	3.22	3.14	3.07	3.02	2.98	2.91	2.85	2.77	2.74	2.70	2.66	2.62	2.58	2.54
11	4.84	3.98	3.59	3.36	3.20	3.09	3.01	2.95	2.90	2.85	2.79	2.72	2.65	2.61	2.57	2.53	2.49	2.45	2.40
12	4.75	3.89	3.49	3.26	3.11	3.00	2.91	2.85	2.80	2.75	2.69	2.62	2.54	2.51	2.47	2.43	2.38	2.34	2.30
13	4.67	3.81	3.41	3.18	3.03	2.92	2.83	2.77	2.71	2.67	2.60	2.53	2.46	2.42	2.38	2.34	2.30	2.25	2.21
14	4.60	3.74	3.34	3.11	2.96	2.85	2.76	2.70	2.65	2.60	2.53	2.46	2.39	2.35	2.31	2.27	2.22	2.18	2.13
15	4.54	3.68	3.29	3.06	2.90	2.79	2.71	2.64	2.59	2.54	2.48	2.40	2.33	2.29	2.25	2.20	2.16	2.11	2.07
16	4.49	3.63	3.24	3.01	2.85	2.74	2.66	2.59	2.54	2.49	2.42	2.35	2.28	2.24	2.19	2.15	2.11	2.06	2.01
17	4.45	3.59	3.20	2.96	2.81	2.70	2.61	2.55	2.49	2.45	2.38	2.31	2.23	2.19	2.15	2.10	2.06	2.01	1.96
18	4.41	3.55	3.16	2.93	2.77	2.66	2.58	2.51	2.46	2.41	2.34	2.27	2.19	2.15	2.11	2.06	2.02	1.97	1.92
19	4.38	3.52	3.13	2.90	2.74	2.63	2.54	2.48	2.42	2.38	2.31	2.23	2.16	2.11	2.07	2.03	1.98	1.93	1.88
20	4.35	3.49	3.10	2.87	2.71	2.60	2.51	2.45	2.39	2.35	2.28	2.20	2.12	2.08	2.04	1.99	1.95	1.90	1.84
21	4.32	3.47	3.07	2.84	2.68	2.57	2.49	2.42	2.37	2.32	2.25	2.18	2.10	2.05	2.01	1.96	1.92	1.87	1.81
22	4.30	3.44	3.05	2.82	2.66	2.55	2.46	2.40	2.34	2.30	2.23	2.15	2.07	2.03	1.98	1.94	1.89	1.84	1.78
23	4.28	3.42	3.03	2.80	2.64	2.53	2.44	2.37	2.32	2.27	2.20	2.13	2.05	2.01	1.96	1.91	1.86	1.81	1.76
24	4.26	3.40	3.01	2.78	2.62	2.51	2.42	2.36	2.30	2.25	2.18	2.11	2.03	1.98	1.94	1.89	1.84	1.79	1.73
25	4.24	3.39	2.99	2.76	2.60	2.49	2.40	2.34	2.28	2.24	2.16	2.09	2.01	1.96	1.92	1.87	1.82	1.77	1.71
26	4.23	3.37	2.98	2.74	2.59	2.47	2.39	2.32	2.27	2.22	2.15	2.07	1.99	1.95	1.90	1.85	1.80	1.75	1.69
27	4.21	3.35	2.96	2.73	2.57	2.46	2.37	2.31	2.25	2.20	2.13	2.06	1.97	1.93	1.88	1.84	1.79	1.73	1.67
28	4.20	3.34	2.95	2.71	2.56	2.45	2.36	2.29	2.24	2.19	2.12	2.04	1.96	1.91	1.87	1.82	1.77	1.71	1.65
29	4.18	3.33	2.93	2.70	2.55	2.43	2.35	2.28	2.22	2.18	2.10	2.03	1.94	1.90	1.85	1.81	1.75	1.70	1.64
30	4.17	3.32	2.92	2.69	2.53	2.42	2.33	2.27	2.21	2.16	2.09	2.01	1.93	1.89	1.84	1.79	1.74	1.68	1.62
40	4.08	3.23	2.84	2.61	2.45	2.34	2.25	2.18	2.12	2.08	2.00	1.92	1.84	1.79	1.74	1.69	1.64	1.58	1.51
60	4.00	3.15	2.76	2.53	2.37	2.25	2.17	2.10	2.04	1.99	1.92	1.84	1.75	1.70	1.65	1.59	1.53	1.47	1.39
120	3.92	3.07	2.68	2.45	2.29	2.17	2.09	2.02	1.96	1.91	1.83	1.75	1.66	1.61	1.55	1.50	1.43	1.35	1.25
∞	3.84	3.00	2.60	2.37	2.21	2.10	2.01	1.94	1.88	1.83	1.75	1.67	1.57	1.52	1.46	1.39	1.32	1.22	1.00

Table of $F_{.01}$ Values

Denominator Degrees of Freedom	Numerator Degrees of Freedom																		
	1	2	3	4	5	6	7	8	9	10	12	15	20	24	30	40	60	120	∞
1	4052	4999.5	5403	5625	5764	5859	5928	5982	6022	6056	6106	6157	6209	6235	6261	6287	6313	6339	6366
2	98.50	99.00	99.17	99.25	99.30	99.33	99.36	99.37	99.39	99.40	99.42	99.43	99.45	99.46	99.47	99.47	99.48	99.49	99.50
3	34.12	30.82	29.46	28.71	28.24	27.91	27.67	27.49	27.35	27.23	27.05	26.87	26.69	26.60	26.50	26.41	26.32	26.22	26.13
4	21.20	18.00	16.69	15.98	15.52	51.21	14.98	14.80	14.66	14.55	14.37	14.20	14.02	13.93	13.84	13.75	13.65	13.56	13.46
5	16.26	13.27	12.06	11.39	10.97	10.67	10.46	10.29	10.16	10.05	9.89	9.72	9.55	9.47	9.38	9.29	9.20	9.11	9.06
6	13.75	10.92	9.78	9.15	8.75	8.47	8.26	8.10	7.98	7.87	7.72	7.56	7.40	7.31	7.23	7.14	7.06	6.97	6.88
7	12.25	9.55	8.45	7.85	7.46	7.19	6.99	6.84	6.72	6.62	6.47	6.31	6.16	6.07	5.99	5.91	5.82	5.74	5.65
8	11.26	8.65	7.59	7.01	6.63	6.37	6.18	6.03	5.91	5.81	5.67	5.52	5.36	5.28	5.20	5.12	5.03	4.95	4.86
9	10.56	8.02	6.99	6.42	6.06	5.80	5.61	5.47	5.35	5.26	5.11	4.96	4.81	4.73	4.65	4.57	4.48	4.40	4.31
10	10.04	7.56	6.55	5.99	5.64	5.39	5.20	5.06	4.94	4.85	4.71	4.56	4.41	4.33	4.25	4.17	4.08	4.00	3.91
11	9.65	7.21	6.22	5.67	5.32	5.07	4.89	4.74	4.63	4.54	4.40	4.25	4.10	4.02	3.94	3.86	3.78	3.69	3.60
12	9.33	6.93	5.95	5.41	5.06	4.82	4.64	4.50	4.39	4.30	4.16	4.01	3.86	3.78	3.70	3.62	3.54	3.45	3.36
13	9.07	6.70	5.74	5.21	4.86	4.62	4.44	4.30	4.19	4.10	3.96	3.82	3.66	3.59	3.51	3.43	3.34	3.25	3.17
14	8.86	6.51	5.56	5.04	4.69	4.46	4.28	4.14	4.03	3.94	3.80	3.66	3.51	3.43	3.35	3.27	3.18	3.09	3.00
15	8.68	6.36	5.42	4.89	4.56	4.32	4.14	4.00	3.89	3.80	3.67	3.52	3.37	3.29	3.21	3.13	3.05	2.96	2.87
16	8.53	6.23	5.29	4.77	4.44	4.20	4.03	3.89	3.78	3.69	3.55	3.41	3.26	3.18	3.10	3.02	2.93	2.84	2.75
17	8.40	6.11	5.18	4.67	4.34	4.10	3.93	3.79	3.68	3.59	3.46	3.31	3.16	3.08	3.00	2.92	2.83	2.75	2.65
18	8.29	6.01	5.09	4.58	4.25	4.01	3.84	3.71	3.60	3.51	3.37	3.23	3.08	3.00	2.92	2.84	2.75	2.66	2.57
19	8.18	5.93	5.01	4.50	4.17	3.94	3.77	3.63	3.52	3.43	3.30	3.15	3.00	2.92	2.84	2.76	2.67	2.58	2.49
20	8.10	5.85	4.94	4.43	4.10	3.87	3.70	3.56	3.46	3.37	3.23	3.09	2.94	2.86	2.78	2.69	2.61	2.52	2.42
21	8.02	5.78	4.87	4.37	4.04	3.81	3.64	3.51	3.40	3.31	3.17	3.03	2.88	2.80	2.72	2.64	2.55	2.46	2.36
22	7.95	5.72	4.82	4.31	3.99	3.76	3.59	3.45	3.35	3.26	3.12	2.98	2.83	2.75	2.67	2.58	2.50	2.40	2.31
23	7.88	5.66	4.76	4.26	3.94	3.71	3.54	3.41	3.30	3.21	3.07	2.93	2.78	2.70	2.62	2.54	2.45	2.35	2.26
24	7.82	5.61	4.72	4.22	3.90	3.67	3.50	3.36	3.26	3.17	3.03	2.89	2.74	2.66	2.58	2.49	2.40	2.31	2.21
25	7.77	5.57	4.68	4.18	3.85	3.63	3.46	3.32	3.22	3.13	2.99	2.85	2.70	2.62	2.54	2.45	2.36	2.27	2.17
26	7.72	5.53	4.64	4.14	3.82	3.59	3.42	3.29	3.18	3.09	2.96	2.81	2.66	2.58	2.50	2.42	2.33	2.23	2.13
27	7.68	5.49	4.60	4.11	3.78	3.56	3.39	3.26	3.15	3.06	2.93	2.78	2.63	2.55	2.47	2.38	2.29	2.20	2.10
28	7.64	5.45	4.57	4.07	3.75	3.53	3.36	3.23	3.12	3.03	2.90	2.75	2.60	2.52	2.44	2.35	2.26	2.17	2.06
29	7.60	5.42	4.54	4.04	3.73	3.50	3.33	3.20	3.09	3.00	2.87	2.73	2.57	2.49	2.41	2.33	2.23	2.14	2.03
30	7.56	5.39	4.51	4.02	3.70	3.47	3.30	3.17	3.07	2.98	2.84	2.70	2.55	2.47	2.39	2.30	2.21	2.11	2.01
40	7.31	5.18	4.31	3.83	3.51	3.29	3.12	2.99	2.89	2.80	2.66	2.52	2.37	2.29	2.20	2.11	2.02	1.92	1.80
60	7.08	4.98	4.13	3.65	3.34	3.12	2.95	2.82	2.72	2.63	2.50	2.35	2.20	2.12	2.03	1.94	1.84	1.73	1.60
120	6.85	4.79	3.95	3.48	3.17	2.96	2.79	2.66	2.56	2.47	2.34	2.19	2.03	1.95	1.86	1.76	1.66	1.53	1.38
∞	6.63	4.61	3.78	3.32	3.02	2.80	2.64	2.51	2.41	2.32	2.18	2.04	1.88	1.79	1.70	1.59	1.47	1.32	1.00

Reprinted by permission of the Biometrika Trustees from Table 18, Percentage Points of the F-Distribution, by E. S. Pearson and H. O. Hartley, *Biometrika Tables for Statisticians*, Vol. 1, 3rd Edition, 1966.

APPENDIX 2:
Statistical Tables

Endnotes

Chapter 1

1. Kendra Parker, "Got Questions? All You Have to Do Is Ask." Reprinted from *American Demographics* magazine (November 1999), pp. 36–39. Copyright © 1999. Courtesy of Intertec Publishing Corp., Stamford, Connecticut. All rights reserved.
2. "Three Firms Show That Good Research Makes Good Ads," *Marketing News* (March 13, 1995), p. 18.
3. American Marketing Association, "New Marketing Research Definition Approved," *Marketing News* (January 2, 1987), pp. 1, 14.
4. "Quality: How to Make It Pay," *Business Week* (August 8, 1994), pp. 54–59.
5. Ibid.
6. "Why Some Customers Are More Equal Than Others," *Fortune* (September 19, 1994), pp. 215–224.
7. Ibid.
8. Parker, "Got Questions?" p. 37.
9. Norihiko Shirouzu, republished with permission of *The Wall Street Journal*, from "Japan's High-School Girls Excel in Art of Setting Trends," *The Wall Street Journal* (April 24, 1998), pp. B1, B7; permission conveyed through Copyright Clearance Center, Inc.
10. "At Ford, E-Commerce Is Job 1," *Business Week* (February 22, 2000), pp. 74–78.
11. Dana James, "The Future of Online Research," *Marketing News* (January 3, 2000), pp. 1, 11.
12. Chris Yalonis, "The Revolution in E-research," *1999 CASRO Journal*, pp. 131–134. Reprinted with permission from the Council of American Survey Research Organizations.
13. Ibid.
14. Dana James, "Precision Decision," *Marketing News* (September 27, 1999), pp. 23–24.
15. Christine Wright-Isak and David Prensky, "Early Marketing Research: Science and Application," *Marketing Research* (Fall 1993), pp. 16–23.
16. Percival White, *Market Analysis: Its Principles and Methods,* 2nd ed. (New York: McGraw-Hill Book Co., 1921, 1925).
17. Much of this section is taken from David W. Steward, "From Methods and Projects to Systems and Process: The Evolution of Marketing Research Techniques," *Marketing Research* (September 1991), pp. 25–34.
18. "Why Go Out? To Get Away," *Roper Reports 98-8, Executive Summary* (January 2000), p. 3.
19. Gail Gaboda, "For Business Travelers, There's No Place Like Home," *Marketing News* (September 15, 1997), pp. 19–20. Reprinted by permission of the American Marketing Association.
20. Adapted from Yumiko Ono, republished with permission of *The Wall Street Journal,* from "Marketers Seek the Naked Truth in Consumers' Psyches," *The Wall Street Journal* (May 30, 1997), pp. B1, B13; permission conveyed through Copyright Clearance Center, Inc.

Chapter 2

1. Rachel X. Weissman, "The Green Flag Is Up." Reprinted from *American Demographics* magazine (April 1999), pp. 33–36. Copyright © 1999. Courtesy of Intertec Publishing Corp., Stamford, Connecticut. All rights reserved.
2. Philip Barnard, CEO of the Kantar Group, in a speech given at The University of Texas at Arlington on April 9, 1999.
3. "Acquisitions No Hindrance to Growth," *Marketing News* (June 7, 1999), p. H6.
4. Jack Honomichl, "Firms Play Name Game as Acquisitions Ruled '98," *Marketing News* (June 7, 1999), p. H2.
5. Jay Roth, "The Marketing Research Industry Monitor," *CASRO Journal* (1993), pp. 21–27.
6. William Cook and Theodore Dunn, "The Changing Face of Advertising Research in the Information Age: An ARF Copy Research Council Survey," *Journal of Advertising Research* (January 1996), pp. 55–71.
7. "Kraft's Miracle Whip Targets Core Consumers with '97 Ads," *Advertising Age* (February 3, 1997), p. 12.
8. Richard Gibson, "A Cereal Maker's Quest for the Next Grapenuts," *Wall Street Journal* (January 23, 1997), pp. B1, B7.
9. Data provided by Mary Klupp, Futures Research Manager, Ford Motor Company.
10. "Strategy Planning," *Business Week* (August 26, 1996), pp. 46–51.
11. "Kendall-Jackson Loses Suit Against Gallo over Turning Leaf Wines," *Wine Spectator* (May 31, 1997), p. 10.
12. Scott Hume, "Research Partnerships Here to Stay," *Advertising Age* (October 14, 1991), p. 33.
13. Philip Barnard, "The Expanding Universe of Marketing Research, *1999 CASRO Journal*, pp. 39–45. Reprinted with permission of the Council of American Survey Research Organizations.
14. Ibid.
15. Paul Boughton, "Marketing Research Partnerships: A Strategy for the '90s," *Marketing Research* (December 1992), pp. 8–12; also see "Maximizing the Client-Researcher Partnership," *Marketing News* (September 13, 1993), p.

38; and "Partnering with Clients: The External Researcher as Internal Resource," *Marketing Research* (Spring 1997), pp. 49–50.

16. "ACNielsen, in the 'Honomichl Global 25,'" *Marketing News* (August 16, 1999), pp. H2, H4.

17. Cyndee Miller, "Research Firms Go Global to Make Revenue Grow," *Marketing News* (January 6, 1997), pp. 1, 22. Reprinted by permission of the American Marketing Association.

Chapter 3

1. "Vegetarianism Can Wait: Meat Is Back," from *Roper Reports* (March 1999), p. 7. Reprinted by permission of Roper Starch Worldwide.

2. "Hey Kid, Buy This," *Business Week* (June 30, 1997), pp. 63–66.

3. Paul Conner, "Defining the Decision Purpose of Research," *Marketing News* (June 9, 1997), p. H15. Reprinted by permission of the American Marketing Association.

4. "Hey Kid," p. 67.

5. Diane Schmalensee and Dawn Lesh, reprinted with permission from *Marketing Research,* published by the American Marketing Association. "How to Make Research More Actionable," *Marketing Research* (Winter 1998/Spring 1999), pp. 23–26.

6. Joseph Rydholm, "What Do Clients Want from a Research Firm?" *Quirk's Marketing Research Review* (October 1995), p. 82.

7. Fred Luthans and Janet K. Larsen, "How Managers Really Communicate," *Human Relations 39* (1986), pp. 161–178; and Harry E. Penley and Brian Hawkins, "Studying Interpersonal Communication in Organizations: A Leadership Application," *Academy of Management Journal 28* (1985), pp. 309–326.

8. Rohit Deshpande and Scott Jeffries, "Attitude Affecting the Use of Marketing Research in Decision Making: An Empirical Investigation," in *Educators' Conference Proceedings,* Series 47, edited by Kenneth L. Bernhardt et al. (Chicago: American Marketing Association, 1981), pp. 1–4.

9. Rohit Deshpande and Gerald Zaltman, "Factors Affecting the Use of Market Research Information: A Path Analysis," *Journal of Marketing Research 19* (February 1982), pp. 14–31; Rohit Deshpande [1984], "A Comparison of Factors Affecting Researcher and Manager Perceptions of Market Research Use," *Journal of Marketing Research 21* (February 1989), pp. 32–38; Hanjoon Lee, Frank Acito, and Ralph Day, "Evaluation and Use of Marketing Research by Decision Makers: A Behavioral Simulation," *Journal of Marketing Research 24* (May 1987), pp. 187–196; and Michael Hu, "An Experimental Study of Managers' and Researchers' Use of Consumer Market Research," *Journal of the Academy of Marketing Science 14* (Fall 1986), pp. 44–51.

10. Rohit Deshpande and Gerald Zaltman, "A Comparison of Factors Affecting Use of Marketing Information in Consumer and Industrial Firms," *Journal of Marketing Research 24* (February 1987), pp. 114–118.

11. "The High-Paced Pursuit of Happiness," *Roper Reports 99-8; Executive Summary* (January 2000), pp. 1, 2.

Chapter 4

1. Emily Nelson, "Why Wal-Mart Sings, 'Yes, We Have Bananas!'" *Wall Street Journal* (October 6, 1998), pp. B1, B4; and Emily Nelson, "Logistics Whiz Rises at Wal-Mart," *Wall Street Journal* (March 11, 1999), pp. B1, B8.

2. For a rebuttal to some of the limitations of secondary data, see Tim Powell, "Despite Myths, Secondary Research Is a Valuable Tool," *Marketing News* (September 21, 1991), pp. 28, 33.

3. "The Information Gold Mine," *Business Week E.Biz* (July 26, 1999), p. EB18.

4. Stacy Small, "Fly Me to the Moon." Reprinted from *American Demographics* magazine (March 2000), pp. 50–52. Copyright © 2000. Courtesy of Intertec Publishing Corp., Stamford, Connecticut. All rights reserved.

5. "A Potent New Tool for Selling Database Marketing," *Business Week* (September 5, 1994), pp. 56–62.

6. "Coupon Clippers, Save Your Scissors," *Business Week* (June 20, 1994), pp. 164–166.

7. "Nuggets of Data from Taped Phone Calls," *Business Week* (March 8, 1999), p. 113.

8. "Interview with Mike Foytik, DSS Research," conducted by Roger Gates (November 29, 2000). Reprinted by permission.

9. This section is adapted from Nick Wingfield, "A Marketer's Dream," *Wall Street Journal* (December 7, 1998), p. R20.

10. Ibid.

11. "Data Warehouse Generates Surprises, Leads for Camelot," *Advertising Age* (January 4, 1999), p. 20.

12. "What've You Done for Us Lately?" *Business Week* (April 23, 1999), pp. 29–34.

13. The four applications are from Peter Peacock, "Data Mining in Marketing: Part I," *Marketing Management* (Winter 1998), pp. 9–18; also see "Data Mining Digs In," *American Demographics* (July 1999), pp. 38–45.

14. "Looking for Patterns," *Wall Street Journal* (June 21, 1999), pp. R16, R20.

15. "Control of Private Data Belongs in the Hands of Consumers, Not Vendors," *Los Angeles Times* (March 20, 2000), p. C-3.

16. This section is from Daniel Melmik, "Federal Statistics at Your Fingertips." *American Demographics* (September 1998), pp. 25–30.

17. "How to Get Wired," *Business Week* (October 17, 1994), pp. 242–244.

18. Max Hopper, "Rattling SABRE—New Ways to Compete on Information," *Harvard Business Review* (May–June 1990), p. 125.

19. Ibid.

20. "Avon Malling," *American Demographics* (April 1999), pp. 38–40.

21. This application is from Shelly Reese, "Bad Mufflers Make Good Data." Reprinted from *American Demographics* magazine (November 1998), pp. 42–44. Copyright © 1998. Courtesy of Intertec Publishing Corp., Stamford, Connecticut. All rights reserved.

22. The hotel survey data are from "What's Most Important in a Hotel?" *Roper Reports 99-6* (November 1999), p. 7.

Chapter 5

1. Joseph Rydholm, "Preserving the Preservationists," *Quirk's Marketing Research Review* (March 2000), pp. 18–19, 74–75. Reprinted by permission.
2. "Focus Groups Illuminate Quantitative Research," *Marketing News* (September 23, 1996), p. 41.
3. For an article on blending qualitative and quantitative research, see Rebecca Quarles, "Blurring the Traditional Boundaries Between Qualitative and Quantitative Research," *CASRO Journal* (1999), pp. 47–50.
4. "10 Trends in Qualitative Research," *Quirk's Marketing Research Review* (December 1999), pp. 30–33.
5. "Motives Are as Important as Words When Group Describes a Product," *Marketing News* (August 28, 1987), p. 49.
6. Peter Tuckel, Elaine Leppo, and Barbara Kaplan, "Focus Groups under Scrutiny," *Marketing Research* (June 1992), pp. 12–17; see also "Break These Three Focus Group Rules," *Quirk's Marketing Research Review* (December 1999), pp. 50–53.
7. Marilyn Rausch, "Qualities of a Beginning Moderator," *Quirk's Marketing Research Review* (December 1996), p. 24. Reprinted by permission of *Quirk's Marketing Research Review.*
8. Yvonne Martin Kidd, "A Look at Focus Group Moderators Through the Client's Eyes," *Quirk's Marketing Research Review* (May 1997), pp. 22–26. Reprinted by permission of *Quirk's Marketing Research Review.*
9. Dona Vitale, reprinted with permission from *Marketing News,* published by the American Marketing Association, "Get More Out of Groups by Putting More In" (March 1, 1999), p. 18.
10. For insights on qualitative report writing, see Lynn Greenberg, "The Challenge of Qualitative Report Writing," *Quirk's Marketing Research Review* (December 1999), pp. 36–41.
11. Judith Langer, reprinted with permission from *Marketing News,* published by the American Marketing Association, "15 Myths of Qualitative Research: It's Conventional but Is It Wisdom?" (March 1, 1999), pp. 13–14.
12. B. G. Yovoich, "Focusing on Consumers' Needs and Motivations." Reprinted with permission from the March 1991 issue, pp. 13–14 of *Business Marketing.* Copyright Crain Communications Inc., 1991.
13. Ibid.
14. Ibid.
15. Walter S. Brown, "Toto, I Don't Think We're in Kansas Anymore," *Quirk's Marketing Research Review* (December 1995), pp. 12–13, 58. Reprinted by permission of *Quirk's Marketing Research Review.*
16. Kate Maddox, "Virtual Panels Add Real Insight for Marketers," *Advertising Age* (June 29, 1998), pp. 34, 40; and "Turning the Focus Online," *Marketing News* (February 28, 2000), p. 15; see also "The Hows, Whys, Whens and Wheres of Online Focus Groups," *MRA Alert* (December 1999), p. 21.
17. Ibid.; see also "Anatomy of an Online Focus Group," *Quirk's Marketing Research Review* (December 1999), pp. 57–60.
18. "On-Line Focus Groups: Mainstream in the Millennium," *Quirk's Marketing Research Review* (December 1999), pp. 54–56.
19. Mary Beth Solomon, "Is 'Internet Focus Group' an Oxymoron?" *Quirk's Marketing Research Review* (December 1998), pp. 35–38. Reprinted by permission.
20. Ibid.
21. Ibid.
22. "Virtual Research Room Ads Banner Rates," *Advertising Age* (May 3, 1999), p. S26.
23. Tom Greenbaum, "Internet Focus Groups Are Not Focus Groups—So Don't Call Them That," *Quirk's Marketing Research Review* (July 1998), pp. 62–63. Reprinted by permission.
24. "More Better Faster," *Quirk's Marketing Research Review* (March 1996), pp. 10–11, 50–52.
25. "The Next Best Thing to Being There," *Quirk's Marketing Research Review* (December 1995), pp. 10–11, 15; and "Videoconference Focus Groups Gaining Airtime," *Marketing News* (November 9, 1999), pp. 2, 16.
26. Ibid.
27. The material on viewing focus groups on the Internet is from David Nelems, "Advantage Internet: Add On-Line Focus Group Viewing to the List of Benefits the Web Offers Researchers," *Quirk's Marketing Research Review* (March 2000), pp. 54–57.
28. Naomi Henderson, "Art and Science of Effective In-Depth Qualitative Interviews," *Quirk's Marketing Research Review* (December 1998), pp. 24–31. Reprinted by permission; "Dangerous Intersections," *Marketing News* (February 28, 2000), p. 18; and "Go In-Depth with Depth Interviews," *Quirk's Marketing Research Review* (April 2000), pp. 36–40.
29. "The Art and Science . . . ," p. 26.
30. "Projective Profiting Helps Reveal Buying Habits of Power Segments," *Marketing News* (August 28, 1987), p. 10.
31. Rebecca Piirto, "Measuring Minds in the 1990s," *American Demographics* (October 1990), pp. 31–35; see also Doreen Mole, "Projective Technique to Uncover Consumers' Attitudes," *Quirk's Marketing Research Review* (March 1992), pp. 26–28; and "Take a Quality Approach to Qualitative Research," *Marketing News* (June 7, 1999), p. H35.
32. "Putting a Face on the Big Brands," *Fortune* (September 19, 1994), p. 80.
33. Rebecca Piirto, "Beyond Mind Games," p. 52.
34. Ronald Lieber, "Storytelling: A New Way to Get Closer to Your Customer," *Fortune* (February 3, 1997), pp. 102–110; see also "Marketers Seek the Naked Truth in Consumers' Psyches," *The Wall Street Journal* (May 30, 1997), pp. B1, B13.
35. Jeffrey Ball, republished with permission of *The Wall Street Journal,* from "But How Does It Make You Feel?" *The Wall Street Journal* (May 3, 1999), pp. B1, B4; permission conveyed through Copyright Clearance Center, Inc.

Chapter 6

1. "*Fast Company*–Roper Starch Surveys," *Roper Starch Worldwide 1999*

ENDNOTES

Year in Review (January 2000), p. 16. Reprinted by permission.

2. Patricia E. Moberg, "Biases in Unlisted Phone Numbers," *Journal of Advertising Research* 22 (August–September 1982), p. 55.

3. Thomas S. Gruca and Charles D. Schewe, "Researching Older Consumers," *Marketing Research* (September 1992), pp. 18–23.

4. Thomas Danbury, "Current Issues in Survey Sampling," *CASRO Journal* (1991), p. 37.

5. Reprinted with permission from the Council for Marketing and Opinion Research, *Respondent Cooperation and Industry Image Survey*, (1999), p. 4.

6. Ibid., pp. 5–7.

7. Jerry Rosenkranz, "Don't Knock Door-to-Door Interviewing," *CASRO Journal* (1991), p. 45.

8. A. B. Blankenship and George Edward Breen, "Format Follows Function," *Marketing Tools* (June 1997), pp. 18–20.

9. Ibid.

10. Jennifer Lach, "Meet You in Aisle Three," *American Demographics* (April 1999), pp. 41–42.

11. David Whitlark and Michael Gearts, "Phone Surveys: How Well Do Respondents Represent Average Americans?" *Marketing Research* (Fall 1998), pp. 13–17; see also "This Is Not a Sales Call," *Quirk's Marketing Research Review* (May 2000), pp. 32–34.

12. Ibid.

13. Leif Gjestland, "Net? Not Yet," *Marketing Research* (Spring 1996), pp. 26–29. Reprinted by permission of the American Marketing Association.

14. For a discussion of voice mail and related technologies, see Peter J. DePaulo and Rick Weitzer, "Interactive Phone Technology Delivers Survey Data Quickly," *Marketing News* (January 3, 1994), p. 15; John R. Dickinson, A. J. Faria, and Dan Friesen, "Live vs. Automated Telephone Interviewing," *Marketing Research* (Winter 1994), pp. 28–34; Tim Triplett, "Survey System Has Human Touch without the Human," *Marketing News* (October 24, 1994), p. 16; and "IVR: How Is It Different from Telephone Interviewing?" *Quirk's Marketing Research*

Review (May 1999), pp. 28–30.

15. Charles D. Parker and Kevin F. McCrohan, "Increasing Mail Survey Response Rates: A Discussion of Methods and Induced Bias," in John Summey, R. Viswanathan, Ronald Taylor, and Karen Glynn, eds., *Marketing: Theories and Concepts for Era of Change* (Atlanta: Southern Marketing Association, 1983), pp. 254–256.

16. Douglas Berdie, "Reassessing the Value of High Response Rates to Mail Surveys," *Marketing Research* (September 1989), pp. 52–65; Jean Charles Chebat and Ayala Cohen, "Response Speed in Mail Surveys: Beware of Shortcuts," *Marketing Research* (Spring 1993), pp. 20–25; and Robert J. Sutton and Linda L. Zeits, "Multiple Prior Notifications, Personalization, and Reminder Surveys," *Marketing Research* (December 1992), pp. 14–21.

17. "The Future of Online Research," *Marketing News* (January 3, 2000), pp. 1, 11.

18. This list is partially derived from Chris Yalonis, "The Revolution in e-Research," *CASRO Marketing Research Journal* (1999), pp. 131–133; see also "The Power of On-Line Research," *Quirk's Marketing Research Review* (April 2000), pp. 46–48.

19. "Marketing Research on the Internet Has Its Drawbacks," *The Wall Street Journal* (March 21, 2000), p. B4.

20. Dennis Gonier, "The Research Emperor Gets New Clothes," *CASRO Marketing Research Journal* (1999), pp. 109–114.

21. Douglas Rivers, "Fulfilling the Promise of the Web," *Quirk's Marketing Research Review* (February 2000), pp. 34–41.

22. Duane Bachmann, John Elfrink, and Gary Vazzara, "E-mail and Snail Mail Face Off in Rematch," *Marketing Research* (Winter 1999/Spring 2000), pp. 11–15.

23. James Watt, "Using the Internet for Quantitative Survey Research," *Quirk's Marketing Research Review* (June/July 1997), pp. 18–19, 67–71.

24. Ibid.

25. Bill MacElroy, "Comparing Seven Forms of Online Surveying," *Quirk's Marketing Research Review* (July

1999), pp. 40–45.

26. Ibid.

27. Watt, "Using the Internet . . ."

28. Information specific recruiting sources is from David Bradford, "Recruiting Sources for On-Line Studies," *Quirk's Marketing Research Review* (July 1999), pp. 36–39.

29. Tracy Tuten, Michael Bosnjak, and Wolfgang Bandilla, "Banner-Advertised Web Surveys," *Marketing Research* (Winter 1999/Spring 2000), pp. 17–21.

30. Bill Ahlhauser, "Introductory Notes on Web Interviewing," *Quirk's Marketing Research Review* (July 1999), pp. 20–26.

31. "Industry Split over Net Research Group," *Marketing News* (June 5, 2000), pp. 5, 8.

32. Ibid.

33. Kay Parker, "Old-Line Toes Online," *Business 2.0* (June 13, 2000), pp. 176–181.

Chapter 7

1. Joseph Rydholm, "Extending Excellence—Mystery Shops Help Bose Make Sure Its Customer Service Matches Its Reputation for Quality," *Quirk's Marketing Research Review* (January 1998), pp. 10–11, 51–52. Reprinted by permission.

2. E. W. Webb, D. T. Campbell, K. D. Schwarts, and L. Sechrest, *Unobtrusive Measures: Nonreaction Research in the Social Sciences* (Chicago: Rand McNally, 1966), pp. 113–114.

3. For an excellent review article on ethnographic research methods, see Eric Arnould and Melanie Wallendorf, "Market-Oriented Ethnography: Interpretation Building and Marketing Strategy Formulation," *Journal of Marketing Research* (November 1994), pp. 484–504; see also "Breaking Tradition: Untraditional Marketing Research Techniques from the Social Sciences Are Gaining Ground," *Marketing Research* (Fall 1999), pp. 21–24.

4. Kendra Parker, "How Do You Like Your Beef?" Reprinted from *American Demographics* magazine (January 1999), pp. 35–37. Copyright 1999. Courtesy of Intertec Publishing Corp., Stamford, Connecticut. All

5. Ibid.

6. Al Goldsmith, "Mystery Shopping 101," *Quirk's Marketing Research Review* (January 1997), pp. 33–34. Reprinted by permission of *Quirk's Marketing Research Review.*

7. Karen Gomes Moore, "The Many Uses of Mystery Shopping," *Quirk's Marketing Research Review* (January 1999), pp. 22–23, 56.

8. Dan Prince, "How to Ensure an Objective Mystery Shop," *Quirk's Marketing Research Review* (January 1996), pp. 22, 32–34; and "Patterns Revealed: The Evolution of a Mystery Shopping Program," *Quirk's Marketing Research Review* (January 1997), pp. 12–13, 42.

9. Moore, "The Many Uses . . .," p. 23; see also "Are Quality and Timeliness Competing Priorities," *Quirk's Marketing Research Review* (January 2000), pp. 32–33.

10. "Going for the Gold," *Quirk's Marketing Research Review* (January 1999), 20–21, 55; and personal communication, Celina Abernathy, Sonic Drive-In, December 15, 2000.

11. Neal Templin, republished with permission of *The Wall Street Journal* "Undercover with a Hotel Spy," *The Wall Street Journal* (May 12, 1999), pp. B1, B12; permission conveyed through Copyright Clearance Center, Inc.

12. Calvin Woodward, "Watch and Learn," *The Fort Worth Star Telegram* (June 21, 1997), pp. C1–C2. Reprinted by permission of The Associated Press.

13. Donal Dinoon and Thomas Garavan, "Ireland: The Emerald Isle," *International Studies of Management and Organization* (Spring/Summer 1995), pp. 137–164. Reprinted by permission from M. E. Sharp, Inc., Armonk, NY 10504.

14. "Attention Shoppers: This Man Is Watching You," *Fortune* (July 19, 1999), pp. 131–133.

15. Werner Kroeber-Riel, "Activation Research: Psychological Approaches in Consumer Research," *Journal of Consumer Research* 6 (March 1979), pp. 240–250.

16. Rebecca Gardyn, "What's on Your Mind?" *American Demographics* (April 2000), pp. 31–33.

17. Ibid.

18. John Cacioppo and Richard Petty, "Physiological Responses and Advertising Effects," *Psychology and Marketing* (Summer 1985), pp. 115–126.

19. Michael Eysenek, "Arousal, Learning, and Memory," *Psychological Bulletin 83* (1976), pp, 389–404.

20. James Grant and Dean Allman, "Voice Stress Analyzer Is a Marketing Research Tool," *Marketing News* (January 4, 1988), p. 22.

21. Glen Brickman, "Uses of Voice-Pitch Analysis," *Journal of Advertising Research 20* (April 1980), pp. 69–73; Ronald Nelson and David Schwartz, "Voice-Pitch Analysis," *Journal of Advertising Research 19* (October 1979), pp. 55–59; and Nancy Nighswonger and Claude Martin, Jr., "On Using Voice Analysis in Marketing Research," *Journal of Marketing Research 18* (August 1981), pp. 350–355.

22. "Device Tracks What Drivers Listen To on Radio," *Fort Worth Star Telegram* (January 13, 2000), p. 5A.

23. "Real-World Device Sheds New Light on Ad Readership Tests," *Marketing News* (June 5, 1987), pp. 1, 18.

24. "RAMS Helps Best Western Tout Worldwide Positioning," *Marketing News* (January 6, 1997), p. 25.

25. "Nielsen Ready to Wire for People Meter Service," *The Seattle Times* (December 13, 1999), p. E3.

26. J. Walker Smith, "The Promise of Single Source—When, Where, and How," *Marketing Research* (December 1990), pp. 3–5. Reprinted by permission of the American Marketing Association. Another good article on the future of scanning is by Laurence Gold, "High Technology Data Collection for Measurement and Testing," *Marketing Research* (March 1992), pp. 29–38.

27. "They Didn't Get SMART," *American Demographics* (August 1999), pp. 33–35.

28. Laurence Gold, "The Coming of Age of Scanner Data," *Marketing Research* (Winter 1993), pp. 20–23.

29. The material on Information Resources Incorporated is from their public relations department, March 16, 2000.

30. Based on an undated speech entitled "New Technology Contributions to New Product and Advertising Strategy Testing: The ERIM Testsight System," by Laurence Gold, vice president, Marketing, ACNielsen Company.

31. "A Plan to Track Web Use Stirs Privacy Concern," *Wall Street Journal* (May 1, 2000), pp. B1, B18.

32. Vividence Web site: www.vividence. com, May 15, 2000.

33. "New Gizmos Alert Marketers When Ads Pique a Consumer's Interest," *Wall Street Journal* (April 26, 2000), pp. B1, B4.

Chapter 8

1. Thomas D. Cook and Donald T. Campbell, *Experimentation: Design Analysis Issues for Field Settings* (Chicago: Rand McNally, 1979).

2. See Claire Selltiz et al., *Research in Social Relations*, rev. ed. (New York: Holt, Rinehart and Winston, 1959), pp. 80–82.

3. A good example of a laboratory experiment is described in Caroll Mohn, "Simulated-Purchase 'Chip' Testing vs. Trade-Off Conjoint Analysis—Coca-Cola's Experience." *Marketing Research* (March 1990), pp. 49–54.

4. A. G. Sawyer, "Demand Artifacts in Laboratory Experiments in Consumer Research," *Journal of Consumer Research 2* (March 1975), pp. 181–201; and N. Giges, "No Miracle in Small Miracle: Story Behind Failure," *Advertising Age* (August 1989), p. 76.

5. John G. Lynch, "On the External Validity of Experiments in Consumer Research," *Journal of Consumer Research 9* (December 1982), pp. 225–239.

6. Jerome Williams, William Qualls, and Sonya Grier, "Racially Exclusive Real Estate Advertising, Public Policy Implications for Fair Housing Practices," *Journal of Public Policy in Marketing* (Fall 1995), pp. 225–244. Reprinted by permission of the American Marketing Association.

7. For a more detailed discussion of this and other experimental issues, see Thomas D. Cook and Donald T.

Campbell, "The Design and Conduct of Quasi-Experiments and True Experiments in Field Settings," in M. Dunnette, ed., *Handbook of Industrial and Organizational Psychology* (Skokie, IL: Rand McNally, 1978).

8. Ibid.

9. For further discussion of the characteristics of various types of experimental designs, see Donald T. Campbell and Julian C. Stanley, *Experimental and Quasi-Experimental Design for Research* (Chicago: Rand McNally, 1966); see also Richard Bagozzi and Youjar Ti, "On the Use of Structural Equation Models in Experimental Design," *Journal of Marketing Research 26* (August 1989), pp. 225–270.

10. Thomas D. Cook and Donald T. Campbell, *Quasi-Experimentation: Design and Analysis Issues for Field Settings* (Boston: Houghton Mifflin, 1979), p. 56.

11. Alvin Achenbaum, "Market Testing: Using the Marketplace as a Laboratory," in Robert Ferber, ed., *Handbook of Marketing Research* (New York: McGraw-Hill, 1974), pp. 4–32; T. Karger, "Test Marketing as Dress Rehearsals," *Journal of Consumer Marketing 2* (Fall 1985), pp. 49–55; Tim Harris, "Marketing Research Passes Toy Marketer Test," *Advertising Age* (August 24, 1987), pp. 1, 8; and John L. Carefoot, "Marketing and Experimental Designs in Marketing Research: Uses and Misuses," *Marketing News* (June 7, 1993), p. 21.

12. Christopher Power, "Will It Sell in Podunk? Hard to Say," *Business Week* (August 10, 1992), pp. 46–47.

13. Jay Klompmaker, G. David Hughes, and Russell I. Haley, "Test Marketing in New Product Development," *Harvard Business Review* (May-June 1976), p. 129; and N. D. Cadbury, "When, Where and How to Test Market," *Harvard Business Review* (May-June 1985), pp. 97–98.

14. Ibid.

15. Joseph Rydholm, "To Test or Not to Test," *Quirk's Marketing Research Review* (February 1992), pp. 61–62.

16. "Test Marketing Is Valuable, but It's Often Abused," *Marketing News* (January 2, 1987), p. 40.

17. Rydholm, "To Test or Not to Test."

18. "Campbell Launches New Line of 'Supper Soups' in Test Markets," http://www.shareholder.com/campbell, January 17, 2001.

19. "Blockbuster Test Markets PC Games," *Radar.com* (April 5, 2000).

20. Stephanie Thompson, "Tropicana Tries Drenchers in Test Markets," *Advertising Age* (January 31, 2000), p. 14.

21. "Shell Test-Markets Robotic Gas Pump," *Robotics World* (May 1, 2000), p. 16.

22. Tsukasa Furukawa, "Japan Test Markets Recycled Batteries," *American Metal Market* (April 2000), p. 11.

23. "Procter & Gamble Company Canadian Test Market," *Market News Publishing* (July 14, 2000), p. 27.

24. "Miller's Plastic Bottle Still in 16 Test Markets," *Modern Brewery Age* (October 1999), p. 1.

25. Benjamin Lipstein, "The Design of Test Market Experiments," *Journal of Advertising* (December 1965), pp. 2–7; and Jeffery D. Zbar, "Blockbuster's CD-ROM Crash Course," *Advertising Age* (May 23, 1994), p. 18.

26. For a discussion of typical American cities and metropolitan areas, see Jane Rippeteau, "Where's Fort Wayne When You Need It?" *The Marketer* (July-August 1990), pp. 46–49; and Judith Waldrop, "All American Markets," *American Demographics* (January 1992), pp. 24–30.

27. Melvin Prince, "Choosing Simulated Test Marketing Systems," *Marketing Research* (September 1992), pp. 14–16.

28. G. L. Urban and G. M. Katz, "Pretest Market Models: Validation and Managerial Implications," *Journal of Marketing Research* (August 1983), pp. 221–234; Standford Odesky and Richard Kerger, "Using Focus Groups for a Simulated Trial Process," *Quirk's Marketing Research Review* (April 1994), pp. 38–40, 53; and Frank Toboloski, "Package Design Requires Research," *Marketing News* (June 6, 1994), p. 4.

29. Raymond R. Burke, "Virtual Shopping: Breakthrough in Marketing Research," *Harvard Business Review* (March-April 1996), pp. 120–131.

30. Power, "Will It Sell in Podunk? Hard to Say."

31. Alain Genestre and Paul Herbig, "What Does Marketing Really Mean to the Japanese?" *Marketing Intelligence and Planning* 13 (September 1995), pp. 16–27.

Chapter 9

1. From "Going Global," from *Roper Starch Worldwide 1999 Year in Review* (January 2000), p. 10. Reprinted by permission of Roper Starch Worldwide, Inc.

2. Adapted from Brian Toyne and Peter G. P. Walters, *Global Marketing Management: A Strategic Perspective* (Boston: Allyn & Bacon, 1989), p. 201. Used with permission of Allyn & Bacon.

3. F. N. Kerlinger, *Foundations of Behavioral Research,* 3rd ed. (New York: Holt, Rinehart and Winston, 1986), p. 403; see also Mel Crask and R. J. Fox, "An Exploration of the Internal Properties of Three Commonly Used Research Scales," *Journal of the Marketing Research Society* (October 1987), pp. 317–319.

4. Adapted from Claire Selltiz, Laurence Wrightsman, and Stuart Cook, *Research Methods in Social Relations,* 3rd ed. (New York: Holt, Rinehart and Winston, 1976), pp. 164–168.

5. Martin Weinberger, "Seven Perspectives on Consumer Research," *Marketing Research* (December 1989), pp. 9–17. Reprinted by permission of the American Marketing Association.

6. Bill MacElroy, "The Anonymity Gradient," *Quirk's Marketing Research Review* (October 1997), pp. 34–35. Reprinted by permission.

7. From "Aspirations—The Great Life?" *Roper Reports 00–1 Executive Summary* (February 2000), p. 4. Reprinted by permission of Roper Starch Worldwide.

Chapter 10

1. Joseph Rydholm, "Something Old,

Something New," *Quirk's Marketing Research Review* (October 1999), pp. 16–17, 73. Reprinted by permission.

2. See Brian Sternthal and C. Samuel Craig, *Consumer Behavior: An Information Processing Perspective* (Englewood Cliffs, N.J.: Prentice Hall, 1982), pp. 157–162; see also Barbara Loken and Ronald Hoverstad, "Relationships between Information Recall and Subsequent Attitudes: Some Exploratory Findings," *Journal of Consumer Research 12* (September 1985), pp. 155–168.

3. Robert E. Smith and William Swinyard, "Attitude Behavior Consistency: The Impact of Product Trial versus Advertising," *Journal of Marketing Research 20* (August 1983), pp. 257–267.

4. See Richard Lutz, "The Rise of Attitude Theory in Marketing," in Harold Kassarjian and Thomas Robertson, eds., *Perspectives in Consumer Behavior*, 4th ed. (Upper Saddle River, N.J.: Prentice Hall, 1991), pp. 317–339.

5. The first five factors are taken from John Mowen and Michael Minor, *Consumer Behavior*, 5th ed. (Upper Saddle River, N.J.: Prentice Hall, 1998), p. 263.

6. Linda F. Alwitt and Ida E. Berger, "Understanding the Link Between Environmental Attitudes and Consumer Product Usage: Measuring the Moderating Role of Attitude Strength," in Leigh McAlister and Michael Rothschild, eds., *Advances in Consumer Research*, vol. 20 (Provo, UT: Association for Consumer Research, 1992), pp. 194–198.

7. Kevin Bokeno, "Gimme What You've Got Now," *Quirk's Marketing Research Review* (February 1999), pp. 36, 38–39. Reprinted by permission.

8. For an excellent discussion of the semantic differential, see Charles E. Osgood, George Suci, and Percy Tannenbaum, *The Measurement of Meaning* (Urbana: University of Illinois Press, 1957).

9. Ibid., pp. 140–153, 192, 193; see also William D. Barclay, "The Semantic Differential As an Index of Brand Attitude," *Journal of Advertising Research 4* (March 1964), pp. 30–33.

10. Theodore Clevenger, Jr., and Gilbert A. Lazier, "Measurement of Corporate Images by the Semantic Differential," *Journal of Marketing Research 2* (February 1965), pp. 80–82.

11. Sabra Brock, "Marketing Research in Asia: Problems, Opportunities, and Lessons," *Marketing Research* (September 1989), pp. 44–51. Reprinted by permission of the American Marketing Association.

12. Michael J. Etzel, Terrell G. Williams, John C. Rogers, and Douglas J. Lincoln, "The Comparability of Three Stapel Forms in a Marketing Setting," in Ronald F. Bush and Shelby D. Hunt, eds., *Marketing Theory: Philosophy of Science Perspectives* (Chicago: American Marketing Association, 1982), pp. 303–306.

13. E. B. Feltser, "The Numbers Game: Refining Multi-Point Scales," *Quirk's Marketing Research Review* (March 1997), pp. 22–24. Copyright © by E. B. Feltser. Reprinted by permission of the author.

14. M. V. Kalwani and A. J. Silk, "On the Reliability and Prediction Validity of Purchase Intension Measures," *Marketing Science I* (Summer 1982), pp. 243–287.

15. Glen Urban, John Hauser, and Nikhilesh Dholakia, *Essentials of New Product Management* (Englewood Cliffs, N.J.: Prentice Hall, 1987), p. 145; see also Tony Siciliano, "Purchase Intent: Separating Fat from Fiction," *Marketing Research 21* (Spring 1993), p. 56.

16. M. M. Givon and Z. Shapira, "Response to Rating Scalings," *Journal of Marketing Research* (November 1984), pp. 410–419; and D. E. Stem, Jr., and S. Noazin, "The Effects of Number of Objects and Scale Positions on Graphic Position Scale Reliability," in R. F. Lusch et al., *1985 AMA Educators' Proceedings* (Chicago: American Marketing Association, 1985), pp. 370–372.

17. Thomas Semon, reprinted with permission from *Marketing News*, published by the American Marketing Association, from "Scale Ratings Always Betrayed by Arithmetic," (August 30, 1999), p. 7.

18; This section is based on James H. Myers and Mark I. Alpert, "Determinant Buying Attitudes: Meaning and Management," *Marketing Management* (Summer 1997), pp. 50–56.

19. William Wells and Leonard Lo Scruto, "Direct Observation of Purchasing Behavior," *Journal of Marketing Research* (August 1996), pp. 42–51.

20. These scales are taken from *Roper Reports 00-3 Executive Summary* (May 2000), pp. 1–3.

Chapter 11

1. Jennifer Lach, "Intelligence Agents—Upper Crust," Reprinted from *American Demographics* magazine (March 1999), p. 58. Copyright 1999. Courtesy of Intertec Publishing Corp., Stamford, Connecticut. All rights reserved.

2. Andrew Bean and Michael Roezkowski, "The Long and Short of It," *Marketing Research* (Winter 1995), pp. 21–26.

3. Lewis Winters, "Innovations in Open-Ended Questions," *Marketing Research* (June 1991), pp. 69–70. Reprinted by permission of the American Marketing Association.

4. Nanci Glassman, reprinted with permission from *Marketing Research*, published by the American Marketing Association, from "Screening Questions," by Nanci Glassman and Myron Glassman, (Fall 1998), pp. 27–30.

5. Lynn Newman, "That's a Good Question," *American Demographics* (June 1995), pp. 10–15. Reprinted from *American Demographics* magazine with permission. Copyright © 1995, Cowles Business Media, Ithaca, New York.

6. This section on questionnaire software is from Steven Struhl and Chris Kuever, "High Tech Surveys Have Arrived," *Quirk's Marketing Research Review* (July 1998), pp. 16, 72–83.

7. Joseph Marinelli and Anastasia Schleck, "Collecting, Processing Data for Marketing Research Worldwide," *Marketing News* (August 18, 1997), pp. 12, 14.

8. Internal company documents supplied to the authors by MARC, Incorporated.

9. Ibid.

Chapter 12

1. For excellent discussions of sampling, see Seymour Sudman, *Applied Sampling* (New York: Academic Press, 1976); and L. J. Kish, *Survey Sampling* (New York: John Wiley and Sons, 1965).

2. For discussions of the debate surrounding the 1990 census, see Eugene Carlson, "Backers of an Adjusted Census Won't Take No for an Answer," *Wall Street Journal* (November 3, 1987), p. 35; and Steven A. Holmes, "Two Communities, Poles Apart, Illustrate Debate on Census," *Wall Street Journal* August 30, 1997), p. 2.

3. J. A. Brunner and G. A. Brunner, "Are Voluntarily Unlisted Telephone Subscribers Really Different?" *Journal of Marketing Research 8* (February 1971), pp. 121–124, 395–399.

4. G. J. Glasser and G. D. Metzger, "Random-Digit Dialing as a Method of Telephone Sampling," *Journal of Marketing Research 9* (February 1972), pp. 59–64; and S. Roslow and L. Roslow, "Unlisted Phone Subscribers Are Different," *Journal of Advertising 12* (August 1972), pp. 59–64.

5. Charles D. Cowan, "Using Multiple Sample Frames to Improve Survey Coverage, Quality, and Costs," *Marketing Research* (December 1991), pp. 66–69.

6. James McClove and P. George Benson, *Statistics for Business and Economics* (San Francisco: Dellen Publishing Co., 1988), pp. 184–185; and "Probability Sampling in the Real World," *CATI NEWS* (Summer 1993), pp. 1, 4–6.

7. "George Gallup's Nation of Numbers," *Esquire* (December 1983), pp. 91–92.

8. Kelley E. Fish, James H. Barnes, and Benjamin F. Banahan III, "Convenience or Calamity: Pharmaceutical Study Explores the Effects of Sample Frame Error on Research Results," *Journal of Health Care Marketing* (Spring 1994), pp. 45–49.

9. R. J. Jaeger, *Sampling in Education and the Social Sciences* (New York: Longman, 1984), pp. 28–35.

10. Ibid.

11. Newton Frank, "The Uses and Abuses of Self-Selection Polls," *1991 CASRO Journal*, pp. 113–115.

12. Lewis C. Winters, "What's New in Telephone Sampling Technology?" *Marketing Research* (March 1990), pp. 80–82; and *A Survey Researcher's Handbook of Industry Terminology and Definitions* (Fairfield, CT: Survey Sampling, Inc. 1992), pp. 3–20.

13. For discussions of related issues, see John E. Swan, Stephen J. O'Connor, and Seug Doug Lee, "A Framework for Testing Sampling Bias and Methods of Bias Reduction in a Telephone Survey," *Marketing Research* (December 1991), pp. 23–34; and Charles D. Cowan, "Coverage Issues in Sample Surveys: A Component of Measurement Error," *Marketing Research* (June 1991), pp. 65–68.

14. For an excellent discussion of stratified sampling, see William G. Cochran, *Sampling Techniques*, 2nd ed. (New York: John Wiley and Sons, 1963).

15. Sudman, *Applied Sampling*, pp. 110–121.

16. Ibid.

17. Earl R. Babbie, *The Practice of Social Research*, 2nd ed. (Belmont, CA: Wadsworth Publishing, 1979), p. 167.

18. Adapted from "Probability Sampling: A Simplified Explanation," a brochure published by Opinion Research Corporation, Princeton, New Jersey, 1992.

19. "Convenience Sampling Outpacing Probability Sampling" (Fairfield, CT: Survey Sampling, Inc., March 1994), p. 4.

20. Leo A. Goodman, "Snowball Sampling," *Annuals of Mathematical Statistics 32* (1961), pp. 148–170.

21. Erin White, "Marketing Research on the Internet Has Its Drawbacks," *Wall Street Journal* (March 2, 2000).

22. Douglas Rivers, "Fulfilling the Promise of the Web," *Quirk's Marketing Research Review* (February 2000), pp. 34–41.

23. Roger Gates and Michael Foytik, "Implementing an HRA on the Internet: Lessons Learned," Society of Prospective Medicine (October 1998).

24. Beth Clarkson, "Research and the Internet: A Winning Combination," *Quirk's Marketing Research Review* (July 1999), pp. 46–51.

25. Gates and Foytik, "Implementing an HRA on the Internet."

26. "*BYTE* Learns a Lesson on Web Surveys," *BYTE* (September 1996), p. 32.

Chapter 13

1. Tom McGoldrick, David Hyatt, and Lori Laffin, "How Big Is Big Enough?" *Marketing Tools* (May 1998), pp. 54–58.

2. Thomas T. Semon, "Save a Few Bucks on Sample Size, Risk Millions in Opportunity Loss," *Marketing News* (January 3, 1994), p. 19. Reprinted by permission of the American Marketing Association.

3. McGoldrick et al., "How Big Is Big Enough?" pp. 54–58.

4. Ibid.

5. Ibid.

6. Gang Xu, "Estimating Sample Size for a Descriptive Study in Quantitative Research," *Quirk's Marketing Research Review* (June 1999), pp. 14, 52–53.

7. Ibid.

8. For discussions of these techniques, see Bill Williams, *A Sampler on Sampling* (New York: John Wiley and Sons, 1978); and Richard Jaeger, *Sampling in Education and the Social Sciences* (New York: Longman, 1984).

9. Survey Sampling, Incorporated, "Estimate Sample Size with Precision," *The Frame* (January 1999), p. 1.

10. David Anderson, Dennis Sweeney, and Thomas Williams, *Statistics for Business and Economics*, 4th ed. (St. Paul, MN: West Publishing, 1990),

pp. 355–357.

11. Aaron Lucchitti, republished with permission of *The Wall Street Journal*, "FTC Tackles an 'Anonymous' Web Survey," from *The Wall Street Journal* (May 7, 1999), p. B2; permission conveyed through Copyright Clearance Center, Inc.

Chapter 14

1. Joseph Rydholm, "Dealing with Those Pesky Open-Ended Responses," *Quirk's Marketing Research Review* (February 1994), pp. 70–79.

2. Raymond Raud and Michael A. Fallig, "Automating the Coding Process with Neural Networks," *Quirk's Marketing Research Review* (May 1993), pp. 14–16, 40–47; and Eric DeRosia, "Data Processing Made Easy," *Quirk's Marketing Research Review* (February 1993), pp. 18, 34.

3. For information on semiotics see Paul Cobley, Litza Jansz, and Richard Appignanesi, *Introducing Semiotics* (Melbourne, Australia: Totem Books, 1997); Marcel Danesi, *Of Cigarettes, High Heels and Other Interesting Things: An Introduction to Semiotics* (New York: St. Martin's Press, 1998); and Umberto Eco, *Semiotics and the Philosophy of Languages* (Bloomington, IN: Indiana University Press, 1986).

4. Joseph Rydholm, "Scanning the Seas: Scannable Questionnaires Give Princess Cruises Accuracy and Quick Turnaround," *Quirk's Marketing Research Review* (May 1993), pp. 6–7, 26–27; and Norma Frendberg, "Scanning Questionnaires Efficiently," *Marketing Research* (Spring 1993), pp. 38–42.

5. Jayavel Sounderpandian, *Market Research and Using Microsoft® Excel* (Cincinnati, OH: South-Western College Publishing, 1999).

6. AcuPOLL Precision Research, http://www.acupoll.com/faq, January 22, 2001.

Chapter 15

1. Hank Zucker, "What Is Significance?" *Quirk's Marketing Research Review* (March 1994), pp. 12, 14; Gorden A. Wyner, "How High Is Up?" *Marketing Research* (Fall 1993), pp. 42–43; Gordon A. Wyner, "The 'Significance' of Marketing Research," *Marketing Research* (Winter 1993), pp. 43–45; and Patrick M. Baldasare and Vikas Mittel, "The Use, Misuse and Abuse of Significance," *Quirk's Marketing Research Review* (November 1994), pp. 16, 32.

2. Thomas Exter, "What's Behind the Numbers," *Quirk's Marketing Research Review* (March 1997), pp. 53–59.

3. Tony Babinec, "How to Think About Your Tables," *Quirk's Marketing Research Review* (January 1991), pp. 10–12. For a discussion of these issues, see Gopal K. Kanji, *100 Statistical Tests* (London: Sage Publications, 1993), p. 75.

4. Gary M. Mullet, "Correctly Estimating the Variances of Proportions," *Marketing Research* (June 1991), pp. 47–51,

5. Robert P. Abelson, "On the Surprising Longevity of Flogged Horses: Why There Is a Case for the Significance Test," *Psychological Science*, Vol. 8 (January 1, 1997), pp. 12–15. Reprinted by permission of Cambridge University Press.

6. Robert P. Abelson, *"Statistics as Principled Argument"* (Mahwah, NJ: Erlbaum, 1997).

7. Sandra Scarr, "Rules of Evidence: A Larger Context for the Statistical Debate," *Psychological Science*, Vol. 8 (January 1, 1997), pp. 16–17.

8. John E. Hunter, "Needed: A Ban on the Significance Test," *Psychological Science*, Vol. 8 (January 1, 1997), pp. 3–7.

Chapter 16

1. Thomas Exter, "What's Behind the Numbers," *Market Tools* (March 1997), pp. 58–59.

2. Mark Peterson, "The Motivation-Emotion-Matching (MEM) Model of Television Advertising Effects," dissertation at Georgia Institute of Technology, 1994. Reprinted by permission.

3. "A Mirror to the World," *Bloomberg Personal* (December 1997), p. 49.

Chapter 17

1. For an excellent and highly understandable presentation of all of the multivariate techniques presented in this chapter, see Joseph Hair, Rolph Anderson, Ron Tatham, and William Black, *Multivariate Data Analysis*, 5th ed. (New York: Prentice Hall, 1998); see also Charles J. Schwartz, "A Marketing Researcher's Guide to Multivariate Analysis," *Quirk's Marketing Research Review* (November 1994), pp. 12–14.

2. Joseph R. Garber, "Deadbeat Repellant," *Forbes* (February 14, 1994), p. 164.

3. For a thorough discussion of regression analysis, see Norman Draper and Harry Smith, *Applied Regression Analysis* (New York: Wiley and Sons, 1966).

4. Charlotte H. Mason and William D. Perreault, Jr., "Collinear Power and Interpretation of Multiple Regression Analysis," *Journal of Marketing Research* (August 1991), pp. 268–280; Doug Grisaffe, "Appropriate Use of Regression in Customer Satisfaction Analyses: A Response to William McLauchlan," *Quirk's Marketing Research Review* (February 1993), pp. 10–17; and Terry Clark, "Managing Outliers: Qualitative Issues in the Handling of Extreme Observations in Market Research," *Marketing Research* (June 1989), pp. 31–45.

5. See Hair et al., *Multivariate Data Analysis*, p. 46.

6. William D. Neal, "Using Discriminant Analysis in Marketing Research: Part 1," *Marketing Research* (September 1989), pp. 79–81; William D. Neal, "Using Discriminant Analysis in Marketing Research: Part 2," *Marketing Research* (December 1989), pp. 55–60; and Steven Struhl, "Multivariate and Perceptual Mapping with Discriminant Analysis," *Quirk's Marketing Research Review* (March 1993), pp. 10–15, 43.

7. See Girish Punj and David Stewart, "Cluster Analysis in Marketing Research: Review and Suggestions for Application," *Journal of Marketing Research 20* (May 1983), pp. 134–148; and G. Ray Funkhouser,

Anindya Chatterjee, and Richard Parker, "Segmenting Samples," *Marketing Research* (Winter 1994), pp. 40–46.

8. This section is based on material prepared by Glen Jarboe, University of Texas at Arlington; see also Paul Green, Donald Tull, and Gerald Albaum, *Research for Marketing Decision,* 5th ed. (Englewood Cliffs, NJ: Prentice Hall, 1988), pp. 553–573.

9. For a complete discussion of the production of perceptual maps using factor analysis, see Glen Urban and John Hauser, *Design and Marketing of New Products,* 2nd ed. (Englewood Cliffs, NJ: Prentice Hall, 1993), pp. 233–241; for a more concisely formatted discussion, see Glen Urban, John Hauser, and Mikhilesh Dholakia, *Essentials of New Product Management* (Englewood Cliffs, NJ: Prentice Hall, 1987), pp. 57–58, 105–119; and for a humorous look at perceptual mapping, see "Company Brief: House of Windsor," *The Economist* (August 29, 1992), p. 53.

10. Dick Wittink and Phillipe Cattin, "Commercial Use of Conjoint Analysis: An Update," *Journal of Marketing* (July 1989), pp. 91–96; see also Rajeev Kohli, "Assessing Attribute Significance in Conjoint Analysis: Nonparametric Tests and Empirical Validation," *Journal of Marketing Research* (May 1988), pp. 123–133.

11. Examples of current issues and applications are provided in Richard Smallwood, "Using Conjoint Analysis for Price Optimization," *Quirk's Marketing Research Review* (October 1991), pp. 10–13; Paul E. Green, Abba M. Krieger, and Manoj K. Agarwal, "Adaptive Conjoint Analysis: Some Caveats and Suggestions," *Journal of Marketing Research* (May 1991), pp. 215–222; Paul E. Green and V. Srinivasan, "Conjoint Analysis in Marketing: New Developments with Implications for Research and Practice," *Journal of Marketing* (October 1990), pp. 3–19; Joseph Curry, "Determining Product Feature Price Sensitivities," *Quirk's Marketing Research Review* (November 1990), pp. 14–17; Gordon A.

Wyner, "Customer-Based Pricing Research," *Marketing Research* (Spring 1993), pp. 50–52; Steven Struhl, "Discrete Choice Modeling Comes to the PC," *Quirk's Marketing Research Review* (May 1993), pp. 12–15, 36–41; Steven Struhl, "Discrete Choice: Understanding a Better Conjoint . . .," *Quirk's Marketing Research Review* (June/July 1994), pp. 12–15, 36–39; Bashir A. Datoo, "Measuring Price Elasticity," *Marketing Research* (Spring 1994), pp. 30–34; Gordon A. Wyner, "Uses and Limitations of Conjoint Analysis—Part 1," *Marketing Research* (June 1992), pp. 42–44; and Gordon A. Wyner, "Uses and Limitations of Conjoint Analysis—Part II," *Marketing Research* (September 1992), pp. 46–47.

12. David Shepard, "Modeling a Modern Mailing," *Marketing Tools* (November/December 1994), pp. 4–9. Reprinted by permission.

Chapter 18

1. Greg Jaffe, "What's Your Point, Lieutenant? Just Cut to the Pie Charts," *The Wall Street Journal* (April 26, 2000), p. A1.

2. Darlene Price and John Messerschmitt, "Try These Eight Power Points for Presenting More Confidently," *Presentations,* August 1999, p. 84.

3. Neil Randall, "Presentations on the Web," *PC Magazine* (May 23, 2000), pp. 104–106.

4. Amil Menon, "Are We Squandering Our Intellectual Capital?" *Marketing Research* (Summer 1994), pp. 18–22. Excerpted with permission from *Marketing Research,* published by the American Marketing Association.

5. Jeannine Bergers Everett, "The Missing Link," *Marketing Research* (Spring 1997), pp. 33–36. Reprinted with permission from *Marketing Research,* published by the American Marketing Association.

6. Christine Moorman, Rohit Deshpande, and Gerald Zaltman, "Factors Affecting Trust in Market Research Relationships," *Journal of Marketing 57* (January 1993), pp. 81–101.

7. Richard Kitaeff, "How Am I Doing?" *Marketing Research* (June 1992), pp. 38–39.

Chapter 19

1. Terry Fink, adapted from "A Pleasants Surprise," *Quirk's Marketing Research Review* (May 1999), pp. 18–19, 71–73. Reprinted by permission.

2. Joseph Rydholm, "What Do Clients Want from a Research Firm?" *Quirk's Marketing Research Review* (October 1996), p. 80.

3. Ron Sellers, "Message to Research Firms: Your First Impression Might Be Your Last," *Quirk's Marketing Research Review* (November 1995), pp. 22, 39–40. Reprinted by permission of *Quirk's Marketing Research Review.*

4. Joshua Libresco, reprinted with permission from *Marketing News,* published by the American Marketing Association, from "Advice for the Juggler," (January 4, 1999), pp. 13, 23.

5. Susan Greco, "Choose or Lose." Reprinted with permission *Inc.* magazine, February 2001. Copyright 1998 by Gruner & Jahr USA Publishing, publisher of *Inc.* magazine, 38 Commercial Wharf; Boston, MA 02110.

6. Brad Frevert, reprinted with permission from *Marketing News,* published by the American Marketing Association, from "Is Global Research Different?" (Spring 2000), pp. 49–51.

7. Kathleen Knight, "Finding and Retaining Research Staff: A Perspective," *Quirk's Marketing Research Review* (February 1998), pp. 18, 54. Reprinted by permission.

8. The Council for Marketing and Opinion Research, *Respondent Cooperation and Industry Image Survey* (Port Jefferson, New York: Author, 1999), p. 4, 5, 30, 46; see also Barbara Bickart and David Schmittlein, "The Distribution of Survey Contact and Participation in the United States: Constructing a Survey-Based Estimate," *Journal of Marketing Research* (May 1999), pp. 286–294.

9. Dick Whittington, "A Plea for Improving Respondent Satisfaction

with the Interview Process: An Open Letter to My Research Colleagues," *CASRO Journal* (1993), pp. 122–124; reprinted by permission of the author; and Richard Whittington, "It's Time to Apply Customer Satisfaction to Interviews," *Marketing News* (August 16, 1993), p. A14; reprinted by permission of the American Marketing Association.

10. Shelby Hunt, Lawrence Chonko, and James Wilcox, "Ethical Problems of Marketing Researchers," *Journal of Marketing Research* (August 1984), p. 314. Reprinted by permission of the American Marketing Association.

11. Betsy Peterson, "Ethics Revisited," *Marketing Research* (Winter 1996), pp. 47–48.

12. Diane Bowers, "Tackling a Tacky Technique," *Marketing Research* (Fall 1996), p. 56.

13. Robert Lusch and Mathew O'Brien, "Fostering Professionalism," *Marketing Research* (Spring 1997), pp. 25–31.

14. Diane Bowers, "A 1999 Snapshot of the U.S. Survey Research Industry," *CASRO Journal* (1999), pp. 23–25. Reprinted with permission from the Council of American Survey Research Organizations.

15. See also Stephen McDaniel and Roberto Solano-Mendez, "Should Marketing Researchers Be Certified?" *Journal of Advertising Research 33* (July/August 1993), pp. 20–31.

Glossary

ad hoc mail surveys Questionnaires sent to selected names and addresses without prior contact by the researcher; sometimes called *one-shot mail surveys*.

after-only with control group design True experimental design that involves random assignment of subjects or test units to experimental and control groups, but no premeasurement of the dependent variable.

allowable sampling error The amount of sampling error the researcher is willing to accept.

analysis of variance (ANOVA) Test for the differences among the means of two or more variables.

applied research Research aimed at solving a specific, pragmatic problem—better understanding of the marketplace, determination of why a strategy or tactic failed, or reduction of uncertainty in management decision making.

appropriate time order of occurrence The occurrence of a change in an independent variable before an observed change in the dependent variable.

attitude An enduring organization of motivational, emotional, perceptual, and cognitive processes with respect to some aspect of a person's environment.

audit The examination and verification of the sales of a product.

balanced scales Measurement scales that have the same number of positive and negative categories.

basic, or pure, research Research aimed at expanding the frontiers of knowledge rather than solving a specific, pragmatic problem.

before and after with control group design True experimental design that involves random assignment of subjects or test units to experimental and control groups and pre- and postmeasurements of both groups.

BehaviorScan A scanner-based research system that can manipulate the marketing mix for household panels in geographically dispersed markets and then electronically track consumer purchases.

bivariate regression analysis Analysis of the strength of the linear relationship between two variables when one is considered the independent variable and the other the dependent variable.

bivariate techniques Statistical methods of analyzing the relationship between two variables.

call record sheets Interviewers' logs, listing the number of contacts and the results of each contact.

cartoon test A projective test in which the respondent fills in the dialogue of one of two characters in a cartoon.

case analysis Reviewing information from situations that are similar to the current one.

causal research Research designed to determine whether a change in one variable likely caused an observed change in another.

causation The inference that a change in one variable is responsible for (caused) an observed change in another variable.

census A collection of data obtained from or about every member of the population of interest.

central limit theorem The idea that a distribution of a large number of sample means or sample proportions will approximate a normal distribution, regardless of the distribution of the population from which they were drawn.

central-location telephone interviews Interviews conducted by calling respondents from a centrally located marketing research facility.

chance variation The difference between the sample value and the true value of the population mean.

chi-square test Test of the goodness of fit between the observed distribution and the expected distribution of a variable.

closed-ended questions Questions that require the respondent to choose from a list of answers.

cluster analysis A general term for statistical procedures that classify objects or people into some number of mutually exclusive and exhaustive groups on the basis of two or more classification variables.

cluster sample Probability sample in which the sampling units are selected in groups to reduce data collection costs.

coding The process of grouping and assigning numeric codes to the various responses to a question.

coefficient of determination A measure of the percentage of the variation in the dependent variable explained by variations in the independent variables.

collinearity The correlation of independent variables with each other, which can bias estimates of regression coefficients.

comparative scales Measurement scales in which one object, concept, or person is compared with another on a scale.

completely automated telephone surveys (CATS) Interviews that use interactive voice response (IVR) technology to ask the questions.

computer-assisted telephone interviews (CATI) Central-location telephone interviews in which interviewers enter respondents' answers directly into a computer.

conclusions Generalizations that answer the questions raised by the research objectives or otherwise satisfy the objectives.

concomitant variation The degree to which a presumed cause and a presumed effect occur or vary together.

concurrent validity The degree to which another variable, measured at the same point in time as the variable of interest, can be predicted by the measurement instrument.

confidence interval The interval that, in all probability, includes the true population value.

confidence level The probability that, a particular interval will include the true population value; also called *confidence coefficient*.

conjoint analysis A procedure used to quantify the value that consumers associate with different levels of product/service attributes.

constant sum scales Measurement scales that ask the respondent to divide a given number of points, typically 100, among two or more attributes, based on their importance to him or her.

constitutive definition A statement of the meaning of the central idea or concept under study, establishing its boundaries; also known as *theoretical*, or *conceptual, definition*.

construct Specific type of concept that exists at a higher level of abstraction.

construct validity The degree to which a measurement instrument represents and logically connects, via the underlying theory, the observed phenomenon to the construct.

consumer drawings A projective technique in which respondents draw what they are feeling or how they perceive an object.

consumer orientation The identification of and focus on the people or firms most likely to buy a product and the production of a good or service that will meet their needs most effectively.

contamination The inclusion in a test of a group of respondents who are not normally there—for example, outside buyers who see an advertisement intended only for those in the test area and enter the area to purchase the product being tested.

content validity The representativeness, or sampling adequacy, of the content of the measurement instrument.

convenience samples Nonprobability samples used primarily for reasons of convenience.

convergent validity The degree of correlation among different measurement instruments that purport to measure the same construct.

cookie A text file placed on a user's computer in order to identify the user when she or he revisits the Web site.

correlation analysis Analysis of the degree to which changes in one variable are associated with changes in another.

criterion-related validity The degree to which a measurement instrument can predict a variable that is designated a criterion.

crosstabulation Examination of the responses to one question relative to the responses to one or more other questions.

custom, or ad hoc, research firms Companies that carry out customized marketing research to address specific projects for corporate clients.

data entry The process of converting information to an electronic form.

data mining The use of statistical and other advanced software to discover nonobvious patterns hidden in a database.

database marketing Marketing that relies on the creation of a large computerized file of customers' and potential customers' profiles and purchase patterns.

decision support system (DSS) An interactive, personalized information management system, designed to be initiated and controlled by individual decision makers.

dependent variable A symbol or concept expected to be explained or caused by the independent variable.

depth interviews One-on-one interviews that probe and elicit detailed answers to questions, often using nondirective techniques to uncover hidden motivations.

descriptive function The gathering and presentation of statements of fact.

descriptive studies Research studies that answer the questions who, what, when, where, and how.

design control Use of the experimental design to control extraneous causal factors.

determinant attitudes Those consumer attitudes most closely related to preferences or to actual purchase decisions.

diagnostic function The explanation of data or actions.

dichotomous questions Closed-ended questions that ask the respondents to choose between two answers.

discriminant coefficient An estimate of the discriminatory power of a particular independent variable; also called *discriminant weight*.

discriminant score A score that is the basis for predicting to which group a particular object or individual belongs; also called *Z-score*.

discriminant validity A measure of the lack of association among constructs that are supposed to be different.

discussion guide A written outline of topics to be covered during a focus group discussion.

disguised observation The process of monitoring people who do not know they are being watched.

disproportional, or **optimal, allocation** Sampling in which the number of elements taken from a given stratum is proportional to the relative size of the stratum and the standard deviation of the characteristic under consideration.

door-to-door interviews Interviews conducted face to face with consumers in their homes.

editing The process of ascertaining that questionnaires were filled out properly and completely.

electroencephalograph (EEG) A machine that measures electrical pulses on the scalp and generates a record of electrical activity in the brain.

equivalent form reliability The ability of two very similar forms of an instrument to produce closely correlated results.

error checking routines Computer programs that accept instructions from the user to check for logical errors in the data.

error sum of squares The variation not explained by the regression.

ethics Moral principles or values, generally governing the conduct of an individual or group.

ethnographic research The study of human behavior in its natural context, involving observation of behavior and physical setting coupled with depth interviews to obtain participants' perspectives.

evaluative research Research done to assess program performance.

executive interviews The industrial equivalent of door-to-door interviewing.

executive summary The portion of a research report that explains why the research was done, what was found, what those findings mean, and what action, if any, management should undertake.

experience surveys Discussions with knowledgeable individuals, both inside and outside the organization, who may provide insights into the problem.

experiment Research approach in which one variable is manipulated and the effect on another variable is observed.

experimental design A test in which the researcher has control over and manipulates one or more independent variables.

experimental effect The effect of the treatment variable on the dependent variable.

exploratory research Preliminary research conducted to increase understanding of a concept, to clarify the exact nature of the problem to be solved, or to identify important variables to be studied.

external validity The extent to which causal relationships measured in an experiment can be generalized to outside persons, settings, and times.

F-test Test of the probability that a particular calculated value could have been due to chance.

face validity The degree to which a measurement seems to measure what it is supposed to measure.

factor analysis A procedure for simplifying data by reducing a large set of variables to a smaller set of factors or composite variables by identifying underlying dimensions of the data.

factor loading The correlation between each factor score and each of the original variables.

field experiments Tests conducted outside the laboratory in an actual environment, such as a market.

field management companies Firms that provide such support services as questionnaire formatting, screener writing, and coordination of data collection.

field service firms Companies that only collect survey data for corporate clients or research firms.

finite population correction factor (FPC) An adjustment to the required sample size that is made in cases where the sample is expected to be equal to 5 percent or more of the total population.

focus group A group of 8 to 12 participants who are led by a moderator in an in-depth discussion on one particular topic or concept.

focus group facility Research facility consisting of a conference room or living room setting and a separate observation room with a one-way mirror or live audiovisual feed.

focus group moderator A person hired by the client to lead the focus group; this person should have a background in psychology or sociology or, at least, marketing.

frame error Error resulting from an inaccurate or incomplete sampling frame.

galvanic skin response (GSR) A change in the electric resistance of the skin associated with activation responses; also called *electrodermal response.*

garbologists Researchers who sort through people's garbage to analyze household consumption patterns.

geographic information system (GIS) Computer-based system that uses secondary and/or primary data to generate maps that visually display various types of data geographically.

goal orientation A focus on the accomplishment of corporate goals; a limit set on consumer orientation.

graphic rating scales Measurement scales that include a graphic continuum, anchored by two extremes.

group dynamics The interaction among people in a group.

history The intervention, between the beginning and end of an experiment, of outside variables or events that might change the dependent variable.

hypothesis A conjectural statement about a relationship between two or more variables that can be tested with empirical data.

hypothesis test of proportions Test to determine whether the difference between proportions is greater than would be expected because of sampling error.

incidence rate Percentage of people or households in the general population that fit the qualifications to be sampled.

independent samples Samples in which measurement of a variable in one population has no effect on measurement of the variable in the other.

independent variable A symbol or concept over which the researcher has some control and that is hypothesized to cause or influence the dependent variable.

information management The development of a system for capturing, processing, and storing data so that they can be readily retrieved when needed for management decision making.

InfoScan tracking service A scanner-based data system that collects information on consumer packaged goods.

instant analysis Moderator debriefing, offering a forum for brainstorming by the moderator and client observers.

instrument variation Changes in measurement instruments (e.g., interviews or observers) that might explain differences in measurements.

intelligent data entry A form of data entry in which the information being entered into the data entry device is checked for internal logic, either by that device or by another device connected to it.

Interactive Marketing Research Organization (IMRO) An organization dedicated to the development, dissemination, and implementation of interactive marketing research concepts, practice, and information.

internal consistency reliability The ability of an instrument to produce similar results when used on different samples during the same time period to measure a phenomenon.

internal database A collection of related information developed from data within the organization.

internal validity The extent to which competing explanations for the experimental results observed can be ruled out.

interrupted time-series design Research in which repeated measurement of an effect "interrupts" previous data patterns.

interval estimates An interval or range of values within which the true population value is estimated to fall.

interval scales Scales that have the characteristics of ordinal scales, plus equal intervals between points to show relative amounts; they may include an arbitrary zero point.

interviewer error, or **interviewer bias** Error that results from the interviewer's influencing—consciously or unconsciously—the respondent.

itemized rating scales Measurement scales in which the respondent selects an answer from a limited number of ordered categories.

judgment samples Nonprobability samples in which the selection criteria are based on the researcher's personal judgment about representativeness of the population under study.

Kolmogorov-Smirnov (K-S) test Test of the goodness of fit between the observed distribution and the expected distribution, using ordinal data.

laboratory experiments Experiments conducted in a controlled setting.

laser scanners Devices that read the UPC codes on products and produce instantaneous information on sales.

Likert scales Measurement scales in which the respondent specifies a level of agreement or disagreement with statements expressing either a favorable or an unfavorable attitude toward the concept under study.

longitudinal study Study in which the same respondents are resampled over time.

low-ball pricing Quoting an unrealistically low price to secure a firm's business and then using some means to substantially raise the price.

machine cleaning of data A final computerized error check of data.

mail panels Precontacted and prescreened participants who are periodically sent questionnaires.

mall-intercept interviews Interviews conducted by intercepting mall shoppers (or shoppers in other high-traffic locations) and interviewing them face to face.

management decision problem A statement specifying the type of managerial action required to solve the problem.

marginal report A computer-generated table of the frequencies of the responses to each question, used to monitor entry of valid codes and correct use of skip patterns.

marketing The process of planning and executing the conception, pricing, promotion, and distribution of ideas, goods, and services to create exchanges that satisfy individual and organizational objectives.

marketing concept A business philosophy based on consumer orientation, goal orientation, and systems orientation.

marketing mix The unique blend of product/service, pricing, promotion, and distribution strategies designed to meet the needs of a specific group of consumers.

marketing research The planning, collection, and analysis of data relevant to marketing decision making and the communication of the results of this analysis to management.

marketing research objective A goal statement, defining the specific information needed to solve the marketing research problem.

marketing research problem A statement specifying the type of information needed by the decision maker to help solve the management decision problem and how that information can be obtained efficiently and effectively.

marketing strategy A plan to guide the long-term use of a firm's resources based on its existing and projected internal capabilities and on projected changes in the external environment.

maturation Changes in subjects occurring during the experiment that are not related to the experiment but may affect subjects' response to the treatment factor.

mean The sum of the values for all observations of a variable divided by the number of observations.

measurement The process of assigning numbers or labels to persons, objects, or events in accordance with specific rules for representing quantities or qualities of attributes.

measurement error Systematic error that results from a variation between the information being sought and what is actually obtained by the measurement process.

measurement instrument bias Error that results from the design of the questionnaire or measurement instrument; also known as *questionnaire bias*.

median The value below which 50 percent of the observations fall.

MOBILTRAK A device that picks up radio signals to determine which FM radio stations people are listening to in their cars.

mode The value that occurs most frequently.

mortality Loss of test units or subjects during the course of an experiment, which may result in a nonrepresentative experimental group.

multidimensional scales Scales designed to measure several dimensions of a concept, respondent, or object.

multiple-choice questions Closed-ended questions that ask the respondent to choose among several answers; also called *multichotomous questions*.

multiple discriminant analysis A procedure for predicting group membership for a (nominal or categorical) dependent variable on the basis of two or more independent variables.

multiple regression analysis A procedure for predicting the level or magnitude of a (metric) dependent variable based on the levels of multiple independent variables.

multiple time-series design An interrupted time-series design with a control group.

multivariate analysis A general term for statistical procedures that simultaneously analyze multiple measurements on each individual or object under study.

mystery shoppers People who pose as consumers and shop at a company's own stores or those of its competitors to collect data about customer–employee interactions and to gather observational data; they may also compare prices, displays, and the like.

neural network A computer program that mimics the processes of the human brain and thus is capable of learning from examples to find patterns in data.

newsgroup An internet site where people can read and post messages devoted to a specific topic.

nominal scales Scales that partition data into mutually exclusive and collectively exhaustive categories.

nonbalanced scales Measurement scales that are weighted toward one end or the other of the scale.

noncomparative scales Measurement scales in which judgment is made without reference to another object, concept, or person.

nonprobability sample A subset of a population in which the chances of selection for the various elements in the population are unknown.

nonresponse bias Error that results from a systematic difference between those who do and those who do not respond to a measurement instrument.

nonsampling error All error other than sampling error; also called *measurement error*.

normal distribution A continuous distribution that is bell-shaped and symmetric about the mean; the mean, median, and mode are equal.

observation research The systematic process of recording patterns of occurrences or behaviors without normally communicating with the people involved.

one-group pretest–posttest design Pre-experimental design with pre- and postmeasurements but no control group.

one-shot case study design Pre-experimental design with no pretest observations, no control group, and an after-measurement only.

one-way frequency table A table showing the number of respondents choosing each answer to a survey question.

one-way mirror observation The practice of watching behaviors or activities from behind a one-way mirror.

online focus groups Focus groups conducted via the Internet.

open-ended questions Questions to which the respondent replies in her or his own words.

open observation The process of monitoring people who know they are being watched.

operational definition A statement of precisely which observable characteristics will be measured and the process for assigning a value to the concept.

opportunity identification Using marketing research to find and evaluate new opportunities.

optical scanning A form of data entry in which responses on questionnaires are read in automatically by the data entry device.

ordinal scales Scales that maintain the labeling characteristics of nominal scales and have the ability to order data.

p-value The exact probability of getting a computed test statistic that was largely due to chance. The smaller the *p*-value, the smaller the probability that the observed result occurred by chance.

paired comparison scales Measurement scales that ask the respondent to pick one of two objects in a set, based on some stated criteria.

Pearson's product moment correlation Correlation analysis technique for use with metric data.

people meters Components of a microwave computerized rating system, used to measure national TV audiences, that transmits demographic information overnight.

People Reader A machine that simultaneously records the respondent's reading material and eye reactions.

perceptual mapping A procedure that produces visual representations of consumer perceptions of products, brands, companies, or other objects.

photo sort A projective technique in which a respondent sorts photos of different types of people, identifying those people who she or he feels would use the specified product or service.

physical control Holding constant the value or level of extraneous variables throughout the course of an experiment.

pilot studies Surveys using a limited number of respondents and often employing rigorous sampling techniques than are employed in large, quantitative studies.

point estimates A particular estimate of a population value.

population The entire group of people about whom information is

needed; also called *universe* or *population of interest*.

population distribution A frequency distribution of all the elements of a population.

population specification error Error that results from incorrectly defining the population or universe from which a sample is chosen.

population standard deviation The standard deviation of a variable for the entire population.

predictive function Specification of how to use descriptive and diagnostic research to predict the results of a planned marketing decision.

predictive validity The degree to which a future level of a criterion variable can be forecast by a current measurement scale.

pre-experimental designs Designs that offer little or no control over extraneous factors.

presentation software Personal computer software that provides easy-to-use platforms for creating effective reports and presentations.

pretest A trial run of a questionnaire.

primary data New data gathered to help solve the problem under investigation.

probability sample A subset of a population that can be assumed to be a representative cross-section because every element in the population has a known nonzero chance of being selected.

processing error Error that results from the incorrect transfer of information from a survey document to a computer.

profession An organization whose membership is determined by objective standards, such as an examination.

professionalism A quality said to be possessed by a worker with a high level of expertise, freedom to exercise judgment, and the ability to work independently.

programmatic research Research conducted to develop marketing

options through market segmentation, market opportunity analyses, or consumer attitude and product usage studies.

projective test A technique for tapping respondents' deepest feelings by having them project those feelings into an unstructured situation.

proportional allocation Sampling in which the number of elements selected from a stratum is directly proportional to the size of the stratum relative to the size of the population.

proportional property of the normal distribution The feature that the area between the mean and a given number of standard deviations from the mean is the same for all normal distributions.

pupilometer A machine that measures changes in pupil dilation.

purchase intent scales Scales used to measure a respondent's intention to buy or not buy a product.

push polling A style of research gathering in which zealous political supporters deride one candidate to lead voters to support the other candidate.

Q-sorting A measurement scale employing a sophisticated form of rank ordering using card sorts.

qualitative research Research whose findings are not subject to quantification or quantitative analysis.

quantitative research Research that uses mathematical analysis.

quasi-experiments Studies in which the researcher lacks complete control over the scheduling of treatment or must assign respondents to treatments in a nonrandom manner.

questionnaire A set of questions designed to generate the data necessary to accomplish the objectives of the research project; also called an *interview schedule* or *survey instrument*.

quota samples Nonprobability samples in which quotas, based on demographic or classification factors selected by the researcher, are established for population subgroups.

random-digit dialing A method of generating lists of telephone numbers at random.

random error, or **random sampling error** Error that results from chance variation.

randomization The random assignment of subjects to treatment conditions to ensure equal representation of subject characteristics.

rank-order scales Measurement scales in which the respondent compares two or more items and ranks them.

Rapid Analysis Measurement System (RAMS) A hand-held device that allows respondents to record how they are feeling by turning a dial.

ratio scales Scales that have the characteristics of interval scales, plus a meaningful zero point so that magnitudes can be compared arithmetically.

recommendations Conclusions applied to marketing strategies or tactics that focus on a client's achievement of differential advantage.

recruited Internet sample A sample group recruited to ensure representativeness of a target population.

refusal rate The percentage of persons contacted who refused to participate in a survey.

regression coefficients Estimates of the effect of individual independent variables on the dependent variable.

regression to the mean Tendency of subjects with extreme behavior to move toward the average for that behavior during the course of an experiment.

related samples Samples in which measurement of a variable in one population may influence measurement of the variable in the other.

reliability The degree to which measures are free from random error and, therefore, provide consistent data.

request for proposal (RFP) A solicitation sent to marketing research suppliers inviting them to submit a formal proposal, including a bid.

research design The plan to be followed to answer the marketing research objectives.

research management Overseeing the development of excellent communication systems, data quality, time schedules, cost controls, client profitability, and staff development.

research panel A group of individuals who agree to participate in a series of research studies over time.

research request An internal document used by large organizations that describes a potential research project, its benefits to the organization, and estimated costs; it must be formally approved before a research project can begin.

response bias Error that results from the tendency of people to answer a question incorrectly through either deliberate falsification or unconscious misrepresentation.

return on quality Management objective based on the principles that (1) the quality being delivered is at a level desired by the target market and (2) that level of quality must have a positive impact on profitability.

rule A guide, a method, or a command that tells a researcher what to do.

sample A subset of all the members of a population of interest.

sample design error Systematic error that results from an error in the sample design or sampling procedures.

sample distribution A frequency distribution of all the elements of an individual sample.

sampling The process of obtaining information from a subset of a larger group.

sampling distribution of the mean A theoretical frequency distribution of the means of all possible samples of a given size drawn from a particular population; it is normally distributed.

sampling distribution of the proportion A relative frequency distribution of the sample proportions of many random samples of a given size drawn from a particular population; it is normally distributed.

sampling error Error that occurs because the sample selected is not perfectly representative of the population.

sampling frame A list of population elements from which units to be sampled can be selected or a specified procedure for generating such a list.

scale A set of symbols or numbers so constructed that the symbols or numbers can be assigned by a rule to the individuals (or their behaviors or attitudes) to whom the scale is applied.

scaled-response questions Closed-ended questions in which the response choices are designed to capture the intensity of the respondent's feeling.

scaling Procedures for assigning numbers (or other symbols) to properties of an object in order to impart some numerical characteristics to the properties in question.

screened Internet sample A self-selected sample group in which quotas are imposed, based on some desired sample characteristics.

screeners Questions used to identify appropriate respondents.

secondary data Data that have been previously gathered.

selection bias Systematic differences between the test group and the control group due to a biased selection process.

selection error Error that results from following incomplete or improper sampling procedures or not following appropriate procedures.

selective research Research used to test decision alternatives.

self-administered questionnaires Questionnaires filled out by respondents with no interviewer present.

semantic differential scales Measurement scales that examine the strengths and weaknesses of a concept by having the respondent rank it between dichotomous pairs of words or phrases that could be used to describe it; the means of the responses are then plotted as a profile, or image.

sentence and story completion tests Projective tests in which respondents complete sentences or stories in their own words.

shopper behavior research Observation of consumers, either in person or on videotape, in a variety of shopping settings.

shopper pattern studies Drawings that record the footsteps of a shopper through a store's aisles.

Shoppers' Hotline A scanner-based research system that comprises 55,000 households, which use an in-home scanner to record purchase information on an ongoing basis.

simple random sample Probability sample selected by assigning a number to every element of the population and then using a table of random numbers to select specific elements for inclusion in the sample.

simulated test market (STM) Use of survey data and mathematical models to simulate test market results at a much lower cost; also called *pretest market.*

situation analysis Studying the decision-making environment within which the marketing research will take place.

skip pattern Sequence in which questions are asked, based on a respondent's answer.

snowball samples Nonprobability samples in which additional respondents are selected based on referrals from initial respondents.

Solomon four-group design Research in which two experimental groups and two control groups are used to control for all extraneous variable threats.

Spearman rank-order correlation Correlation analysis technique for use with ordinal data.

split-half technique A method of assessing the reliability of a scale by dividing the total set of measurement items in half and correlating the results.

spurious association A relationship between a presumed cause and a presumed effect that occurs as a result of an unexamined variable or set of variables.

SSL (secure socket layer) technology A computer encryption system that secures sensitive information.

stability Lack of change in results from test to retest.

standard deviation A measure of dispersion calculated by subtracting the mean of the series from each value in a series, squaring each result, summing the results, dividing the sum by the number of items minus 1, and taking the square root of this value.

standard error of the mean The standard deviation of a distribution of sample means.

standard normal distribution A normal distribution with a mean of zero and a standard deviation of one.

Stapel scales Measurement scales that require the respondent to rate, on a scale ranging from 15 to 25, how closely and in what direction a descriptor adjective fits a given concept.

static-group comparison design Pre-experimental design that utilizes an experimental and a control group, but subjects or test units are not randomly assigned to the two groups and no premeasurements are taken.

statistical control Adjusting for the effects of confounded variables by statistically adjusting the value of the dependent variable for each treatment condition.

statistical power The probability of not making a Type II error.

storytelling A projective technique in which respondents are required to tell stories about their experiences, with a company or product, for example; also known as the *metaphor technique.*

strategic partnership An alliance formed by two or more firms with unique skills and resources to offer a new service for clients, provide strategic support for each firm, or in some other manner create mutual benefits.

stratified sample Probability sample that is forced to be more representative though simple random sampling of mutually exclusive and exhaustive subsets.

structured observation A study in which the observer fills out a questionnaire-like form on each person or event observed or counts the number of times a behavior or activity occurs.

sum of squares due to regression The variation explained by the regression.

supervisor's instructions Written directions to the field service firm on how to conduct the survey.

surrogate information error Error that results from a discrepancy between the information needed to solve a problem and that sought by the researcher.

survey objectives An outline of the decision-making information sought through the questionnaire.

survey research Research in which an interviewer interacts with respondents to obtain facts, opinions, and attitudes.

syndicated service research firms Companies that collect, package, and sell the same general market research data to many firms.

systematic error, or **systematic bias** Error that results from problems or flaws in the execution of the research design; sometimes called *nonsampling error.*

systematic sampling Probability sampling in which the entire population is numbered and elements are selected using a skip interval.

systems orientation The creation of systems to monitor the external environment and deliver the marketing mix to the target market.

***t*-test** Hypothesis test used for a single mean if the sample is too small to use the *Z*-test.

temporal sequence An appropriate causal order of events.

test market Testing of a new product or some element of the marketing mix using an experimental or quasi-experimental design.

test-retest reliability The ability of the same instrument to produce consistent results when used a second time under conditions as similar as possible to the original conditions.

testing effect An effect that is a byproduct of the research process itself.

third-person technique A projective technique in which the interviewer learns about respondents' feelings by asking them to answer for a third party, such as "your neighbor" or "most people."

traffic counters Machines used to measure vehicular flow over a particular stretch of roadway.

treatment variable The independent variable that is manipulated in an experiment.

true experimental design Research using an experimental group and a control group, to which test units are randomly assigned.

Type I error (α error) Rejection of the null hypothesis when, in fact, it is true.

Type II error (ß error) Acceptance of the null hypothesis when, in fact, it is false.

unidimensional scales Scales designed to measure only one attribute of a concept, respondent, or object.

unrestricted Internet sample A self-selected sample group consisting of anyone who wishes to complete an Internet survey.

unstructured observation A study in which the observer simply makes notes on the behavior or activity being observed.

validation The process of ascertaining that interviews actually were conducted as specified.

validity The degree to which what was being measured was actually measured.

variable A symbol or concept that can assume any one of a set of values.

videoconferencing Televising a focus group session at a focus group facility or company site so that more staff can view customer opinions.

voice pitch analysis Studying changes in the relative vibration frequency of the human voice to measure emotion.

word association test A projective test in which the interviewer says a word and the respondent must mention the first thing that comes to mind.

***Z*-test** Hypothesis test used for a single mean if the sample is large enough and drawn from a normal population.

Index